Group Portrait
Internationalizing the Disciplines

edited by

Sven Groennings
and
David S. Wiley

The American Forum
45 John Street, Suite 1200, New York, New York 10038

The American Forum for Global Education
International Education Series

Kurt E. Müller, series editor

J. David Edwards and Maria J. Sayers, *Federal Funding for Foreign Language and International Education in Elementary and Secondary Schools*

Robert E. Freeman, ed., *Promising Practices in Global Education: A Handbook with Case Studies*

Rosemarie Benya, comp., and Kurt E. Müller, ed., *Children and Languages: Research, Practice, and Rationale for the Early Grades*

Kurt E. Müller, ed., *Languages in Elementary Schools*

Sven Groennings and David S. Wiley, ed., *Group Portrait: Internationalizing the Disciplines*

ISBN 0-944675-42-5

Contents

Preface

Rose L. Hayden and Kurt E. Müller

It is not often that a diverse set of organizations can rightfully claim parentage of a publication with a gestation period of a decade and a half. But such is the situation with this book. As officers of the National Council on Foreign Language and International Studies, we were pleased to preside over the project that produced these essays. Following a key tenet in our activities, the National Council always worked in concert with other organizations to promote the internationalization of American education. In separate overview chapters, editors Sven Groennings and David Wiley note the contributions of the Council on Learning and the President's Commission on Foreign Language and International Studies toward setting the stage on which the disciplinary associations were able to commission the essays that follow. The editors elucidate as well the curricular debates that occurred on campuses and in associations, in which the advocates of international education saw two alternatives: the addition of courses within each discipline to specifically address international dimensions of the discipline or the infusion of international content in key courses.

The journals of the disciplinary associations reflect their members' corporate sense of important issues. If articles in these journals focus on domestic phenomena, the association sanctions such a limited inquiry as sufficient. Applying market terms to academic inquiry, we could identify a domestic set of phenomena and a set of research consumers for whom American issues have been clearly sufficient. With an expansive period of American academic research coupled to increasing economic and diplomatic influence abroad, however, we ran the risk of, and fell prey to, a tendency to assume that American experience was replicable in other societies. In such circumstances, the few likely critics are those who will warn against cultural imperialism and those accepting

Rose L. Hayden is Vice President of Eagle Multimedia Services, Inc. She was President of the National Council on Foreign Language and International Studies. Formerly Executive Vice President of the National Council, Kurt E. Müller is a consultant in foreign languages and international education.

Benjamin Lee Whorf's hypothesis that people the world over do not reach the same conclusions from the same evidence. This argument was often advanced by Global Perspectives in Education (GPE), one of the partners in forming the American Forum.

In seeking to convince American society it should learn about others, both in the industrial and in the developing world, and that it should reach others through the medium of their own language, not always through ours, both GPE and the National Council on Foreign Language and International Studies engaged in an uphill struggle. Arguments that American competitiveness abroad requires familiarity with other languages and cultures fell on deaf ears during an expansion of American economic and cultural influence. During the mid-1980s, the continuing slide of the U.S. balance of trade directed attention to international competition, but converts to international education as a contributing factor were few. Many of the early reports on American competitiveness looked at tax policies, labor relations, industrial plants, and so forth and compared these with our competitors' situations. Absent from these inquiries was concern that American education was failing to direct attention to the world beyond our borders. In 1988, the American Forum invited participants to examine education as a component of international competence. By the close of the decade, political, industrial, and commercial leaders began to include education as part of the solution to America's balance-of-trade problem. Thus, in examining international competitiveness, the National Governors Association created a task force on international education as one of four task forces examining state responses to foreign economic challenges. Placing international education on their agenda, the nation's governors applied to education a trend that was already underway in economic development. Competition and trade growth had thoroughly permeated state economies. Building on recommendations of the President's Commission on Foreign Language and International Studies, the governors recognized inadequate preparation for global competition as a national problem, but they declared that it was no longer simply a federal problem.

As educational competitiveness gains importance in this debate, concentration on the often lamented gaps between U.S. students' achievements in math and science and their counterparts elsewhere are being broadened to include knowledge of other languages and cultures. In summing up a governors' task force conference, Governor Thomas Kean of New Jersey advocated removing the specialty status of international education and placing it squarely on the agenda for education reform. "International literacy goes hand in hand with domestic political literacy," writes Kean, recognizing that international education had lost its identification as an elite preserve. The governors' association accepted its importance for all citizens.

The evidence is clear. If, prior to October 1987, skeptics had doubted the global interrelations of the financial markets, for example, the aftershock on the exchanges in Europe and Asia immediately following the red ink in New York should have convinced them of the global nature of manufacturing, marketing, trade, and finance. This realization is stated in the preamble to the Omnibus Trade and Competitiveness Act of 1988: "There has arisen a new global economy in which trade, technological development, investment and services form an integrated system." The majority of the following essays were written prior to the 1987 stock-market crash. As most of them were being written, 70% of American goods and services had to compete against foreign sources at home or abroad; the figure has since risen to 80%.

Market forces in manufacturing and trade do not interest most academics, who generally regard these concerns as unrelated to their pursuits. Indeed, although parallel, the development of these essays proceeded independently of the external events just cited. As Dr. Groennings shows, however, the two are clearly related. With our accelerating integration into a global economy, global communications systems, and a global community of knowledge, American higher education is adapting to the world-wide information revolution. The chief characteristic of this adaptation may be an increased willingness to look at our experiences from multiple perspectives. Some examples from our essays will be instructive.

Decrying the almost universal parochialism of American undergraduates, Ole Holsti asks whether the neglect of foreign perspectives on American political problems intensifies this parochialism and further contributes to incomplete analyses. If such neglect is widespread, the nation can hardly hope to produce industrial and political leaders who can understand others and effectively present our views to them. Across the contributing disciplines, authors recognize that this parochialism has extended to the practices in their own disciplines. The export of American political science exposed American political scientists to phenomena elsewhere that caused them to reformulate the problems for which they had developed explanations. In psychology, several authors note a tendency to generalize based on inadequately diverse observations. Harry Triandis and Richard Brislin note that researchers hypothesize a theory based on limited observations in their own countries but that a theory cannot be considered rigorous until it is tested in various parts of the world, recording variations among cultures. Piaget's work on cognitive development is cited as an example of such multinational testing. Virginia Sexton and Henryk Misiak write that in 1944 "the name, research, and theories of Jean Piaget were practically unknown to American psychologists and psychology students, except for a few developmental psychologists." Consequently, American psychologists were considerably behind their European colleagues in following developments in their field. Documenting the ethnocentricity of American sociology and accepting the title "queen of the provincial sciences" for his discipline, Michael Armer proceeds to outline its "deparochialization."

During the 1970s, humanists often complained that social scientists allied themselves with students on the elimination of general-education requirements. Several of these essays, in political science, psychology, and journalism, reverse the pendulum swing, using a humanistic argument in calling for language study as the necessary avenue into another culture.

In documenting developments that American academics have missed because of unfamiliarity with other languages and cultures, these essays call for academic practice in individual disciplines to face the 21st century with a global view.

R.L.H.
K.E.M.

Acknowledgements

In his remarks on the origin and conduct of the project that led to this publication, David Wiley notes the range of association responses to the invitation by the National Council on Foreign Language and International Studies to participate in a discipline-based review of the international dimensions of the participating disciplines. The ability of each association to take part within the period prescribed under terms of the grant received from the U.S. Department of Education also differed widely and is reflected in the varying dates of original publication of each of the essays contained in this volume. Because the picture that results from these individual portraits argues forcibly for an undergraduate curriculum that encourages students to consider the global dimensions of their subject matter, the project sponsors intended from the start to collect in one volume the papers of the various disciplines. All involved in this project are grateful to the American Forum for its support in realizing this project goal. The former National Council staff is particularly appreciative of David Wiley's efforts in commissioning and assembling the collection of papers, of Sven Groennings's articulate assessment of the implications of disciplinary developments for higher education in general, and of John Brademas's continuing advice and encouragement to both the National Council and the American Forum.

In collecting a set of papers from several disciplines that were published over a span of years, several issues arise that must be resolved editorially. While inclusiveness demands waiting for the last participant to submit its papers, the urgency with which the project staff approached their task dictated forging ahead with little delay. Since the articles met the standards of each association that published them, it seems reasonable to simply reproduce each contribution. The reader who approaches an essay in an alien discipline, however, discovers usage that is almost foreign. Consequently, we have endeavored to edit the enclosed texts with a view toward the non-specialist reader. In attempting to proceed with deliberate speed, I have not given the authors an opportunity to review these revisions, and, if I have misinterpreted any of their comments, I beg their indulgence.

Editors routinely impose a "house style" on their authors, and academic authors are accustomed to revising their documentation to conform to the dictates of a given journal or publisher. When examining publications across disciplines, the reader is struck by considerable variation in these styles. However one defines disciplinary boundaries, style varies within a discipline from one country to another as well as from one journal to the next. In producing this volume, we have retained the documentation style prevalent in each discipline although we have standardized abbreviations. The specialty reader will thereby recognize a familiar documentation system, and we shall facilitate additional research within the discipline. The dictates of my own disciplinary style would require extensive review of the cited items to resolve questions that are of interest to other editors but need hardly concern the reader. Anticipating the indulgence of other editors, therefore, we present a collection that should interest both the discipline-based scholar and the professional educator.

The associations were advised that the papers would be collected and published by the National Council after individual publication for the discipline. Their permission has also been solicited after this initial appearance. In recognizing the role of each association, we also wish to acknowledge the original publication. Of the contributions representing the discipline of geography, "Geography and International Knowledge," written by a committee of the Association of American Geographers, was published as a booklet by AAG in 1982, as the National Council approached the association to solicit its participation in the project. The article by Marvin W. Mikesell is taken from the revised booklet, edited by Salvatore J. Natoli and Andrew R. Bond, *Geography in Internationalizing the Undergraduate Curriculum*, Washington, D.C.: AAG, 1985, pages 67–80.

The history essays and the list of goals for world history courses appeared in *The History Teacher*, 18 (1985), pages 501–35. The journalism contributions were published in a monograph edited for the Association for Education in Journalism and Mass Communication by Christine L. Ogan and Bonnie J. Brownlee. The volume appeared as *From Parochialism to Globalism: International Perspectives in Journalism Education*, Bloomington, Ind.: AEJMC, 1986. The philosophy articles were published in *Teaching Philosophy* 8.2 (1985), pages 99–150, under the guest editorship of David Hoekema. The five essays on comparative politics were published in *PS*, the journal of the

American Political Science Association, 17.3 (1984), pages 545–63. The international relations essays appeared in *News for Teachers of Political Science*, 40 (1984), pages 10–23. The essays and bibliography commissioned by the American Psychological Association were published in APA's journal, *American Psychologist*, 39.9 (1984), pages 996–1042. Edward Tiryakian's essay appeared in *International Sociology* 1.2 (1986), pages 155–71. The remaining chapters appear here for the first time.

K.E.M.
Series Editor

Introduction

John Brademas

As we Americans look to our place in the world of the twenty-first century, we confront some disturbing realities. For example, the congressional hearings of 1987 into the Iran-Contra affair raised deeply troubling questions about the way we conduct our foreign policy. Certainly the hearings exposed an astonishing lack of knowledge on the part of our top decision makers about Iran, its society, religious traditions, and political system. The scandal surrounding the actions of the United States government in Iran is but the latest in a series of diplomatic and intelligence failures that have marred the past 40 years of American history, all lapses traceable in part to our ignorance of other countries and cultures.

The powerful dynamics of the new, globalized economy mean that the era of American economic hegemony is over. As we become increasingly dependent on international trade, we need people trained to work effectively with Japanese business councils, Arab oil ministries, Swiss banks, European agricultural officials, and Third World governments. The economies of the world's nations are now so interdependent that if we in the United States fail to follow developments elsewhere, we shall lose our competitive edge; in certain fields, we already have.

It must be obvious that none of the challenges of our time is more urgent or more difficult than building among the nations of the world a structure of relationships that will prevent war and encourage peace. Summit meetings only dramatize that challenge. Because, for better or for worse, history has thrust great power on us, the United States has great responsibility for helping build a peaceful and stable world. For that reason alone, Americans must learn much more about the people who populate the other parts of this planet.

On all these fronts—an effective foreign policy, a prosperous economy, the security of our borders—it is clearly in our national interest to study carefully and fully other languages, cultures, and countries. That we are not doing as well

John Brademas is President of New York University.

1

as we need to in this respect is evident. That our institutions of learning are partly to blame is equally clear.

Over the past few years, we have seen a tidal wave of reports on the performance of American schools, colleges, and universities. Nearly all these studies deplore our deficiencies in teaching modern foreign languages and about other countries and cultures, and the reports uniformly urge much greater attention to such instruction.

In recent years American colleges and universities have been helped in preparing students to become more knowledgeable about other areas and languages through funds provided by the federal government as well as by non-governmental programs that enable Americans to study abroad.

I was chief sponsor over twenty years ago of the International Education Act, which authorized grants to colleges and universities in the United States to support study and research about foreign countries and important issues in international affairs. The main purposes of that legislation are, in very modest fashion, now being pursued under Title VI of the Higher Education Act, which has survived repeated budget attacks by the Reagan Administration. In fact, in 1986 Congress passed and the President signed, a five-year reauthorization of this legislation. The new statute continues existing international programs and adds three new ones: summer institutes for intensive language training for college faculty and school teachers; help to colleges in buying foreign periodicals; and a study of the feasibility of establishing a National Endowment for International Studies.

Congress has also in recent years demonstrated strong support for international exchanges. For example, Congress voted nearly $250 million a year in both fiscal years 1986 and 1987 for educational and cultural exchanges, including the Fulbright program. For both years, these amounts represented substantial increases over 1981 levels. In that year, Republicans and Democrats on Capitol Hill joined in a successful fight to prevent the Administration from inflicting drastic cuts in the Fulbright exchange and several companion programs.

If foreign language, area studies, and international exchanges are essential to producing students and scholars knowledgeable about the rest of the world, these initiatives are also ones in which the federal government has a crucial role. But there is a responsibility here that goes beyond what the government does. Colleges and universities must themselves insist on building international perspectives into the courses they offer and the research they undertake.

Because at modern American Colleges and universities curricula are given shape and direction within the context of academic disciplines, it is to these disciplines and the courses of study they prescribe that we must turn if we are serious about preparing students to understand other nations, cultures, and peoples.

Herein lies the contribution of this significant book. In bringing together the observations of scholars spanning seven fields, editors Sven Groennings and David Wiley have produced the first comprehensive survey of international studies from the viewpoint of individual academic disciplines. These chapters demonstrate strikingly the growing effort of scholars to develop intercultural contexts within which the study of their particular fields can proceed—whether in geography, history, political science, sociology, psychology, journalism, or philosophy. A second finding, as Dr. Groennings observes, is that "the disciplines influence one another and find one another relevant as they seek a global perspective."

As if in a snapshot, *Group Portrait* captures a vital moment in the nation's intellectual development as the academy moves toward internationalizing the college and university curriculum. Prepared under the auspices of the National Council on Foreign Language and International Studies, this book is a valuable reference tool for scholars interested in the advances of their disciplines. To those of us who have long advocated the strengthening of international studies and research, this book also demonstrates that colleges and universities are indispensable in preparing Americans for work and life in a world that will never be narrow again.

3

Project Scope and History

David S. Wiley

This book presents the collected essays of authors in seven academic disciplines in the United States on the topic of international perspectives in those academic fields. The essays were developed during the period 1981–1986 in a Project of the National Council on Foreign Language and International Studies (NCFLIS) with the financial support of the United States Department of Education under the Undergraduate International Studies Program of Title VI of the Higher Education Act and of Michigan State University through provision of space and time of the Project Coordinator. The project was titled "International Studies in the Undergraduate Curriculum: The Role of the Disciplines and Professional Associations."

The National Council invited a range of scholarly associations to join this project. Eight accepted the invitation. Each association was to invite scholars respected in their discipline to write about what undergraduate students in their field should learn about the world and the international perspectives within that field.

The participating associations were the American Association of Geographers, American Historical Association (through the World History Association), American Philosophical Association, American Political Science Association, American Psychological Association, American Sociological Association, Association for Education in Journalism and Mass Communication, and the American Association of Colleges for Teacher Education. Because this book is limited to internationalizing the curriculum of the academic disciplines, the six papers produced for the American Association of Colleges of Teacher Education in 1984 have been omitted.

Collectively, the diverse essays in this volume represent a call to North American universities to reconsider the still relatively exclusive domestic focus

David S. Wiley is Director of the African Studies Center at MIchigan State University and was Co-Chairperson of the National Council's Task Force on Elementary, Secondary, and Undergraduate Education as well as Director of this project.

of mainstream courses in most disciplinary departments. This volume provides a cross-section of opinion within the North American academy on a question that normally is not at the center of debate within faculty associations or academic departments: namely, what ought undergraduate majors have learned about the world by the time they leave the university with a B.A. or B.S. majoring in "our department"?

Origins of the Project

This project had its inception in the meetings of the Task Force on Elementary, Secondary, and Undergraduate Education (TFESUE) of NCFLIS. Under the leadership of Dr. Allen Kassof, first executive director of the National Council, a major study of national targets for the training of advanced graduate scholars was conducted in 1981, followed by the creation of the Task Force to give concerted attention to K–12 and undergraduate education.

Under the leadership of Dr. Rose L. Hayden, a select group of specialists in undergraduate and K–12 education were assembled to constitute the TFESUE and subsequently met on several occasions in New York and Detroit. Members with direct concern for undergraduate education included:

- Barbara Burn, Dean, International Education, University of Massachusetts-Amherst (formerly of the President's Commission on Foreign Language and International Studies);

- John Carpenter, Dean, College of Education, Florida International University;

- Larry E. Condon, former president, Global Perspectives in Education;

- Marylee S. Crofts, TFESUE Co-Chair and, at that time, Outreach Coordinator, African Studies Center, Michigan State University;

- Gerard Ervin, Foreign Language Coordinator, College of Humanities, Ohio State University;

- Anna Ochoa, Associate Professor of Education, Indiana University;

- John Porter, President, Eastern Michigan University; and

- David Wiley, Director, African Studies Center, Michigan State University

Committed to developing a series of highly specific targets of action in K–12 and undergraduate education, the Task Force sought to achieve a significant improvement in the quantity and quality of international studies in the educational system. The Task Force completed several projects for K–12 education, including the National Council publication *Internationalizing Your School: A Handbook and Resource Guide for Teachers, Administrators, Parents and School Board Members* (1983). A similar concern simultaneously was being pursued by the Council on Learning which had raised the need for increased international higher education in its magazine, *Change*, and in its series of special publications on international education, "Education and the World View." One of these was *The Role of the Scholarly Disciplines* (1980), which reported on a 1979 conference of 28 representatives of social science, humanities, and professional field associations and foundation representatives. It identified the problem of the neglect of international subject matter.

Thus the focus on the disciplines originated in an emerging consensus that there was a problem across levels of education. International knowledge could not be taught well at the precollegiate level without being an integral part of higher education. Student exposure would have to occur beyond introductory general studies courses; it would require infusion throughout the curriculum; and it would have to occur in the student's major field. In this context, the role of the disciplines and knowledge about the status of disciplinary internationalization become crucial.

Therefore this project sought to initiate a series of cooperative activities within several of the major scholarly organizations. There were to be four specific goals.

Leadership for Internationalization from the Disciplines

First, we invited the disciplinary associations to call for increased attention by their member professionals and institutions to the urgent national need for international education for citizen understanding and American competence in a global era. Because of the national influence and prestige of these associations throughout colleges and universities, they have become "norm setters" which establish the criteria by which members are rewarded in their academic departments. They also define through role models the characteristics of a successful member in the field. Thus, we hoped their considerable influence might be harnessed to the aims of this project.

Change in the quality of undergraduate instruction in the academic disciplines is perhaps the most difficult target to achieve in higher education because the disciplines have strong mandates primarily for advanced training in theory, methods, and (frequently) statistical requirements. By and large, faculty are not tangibly rewarded for either their focus on undergraduate instruction or their inclusion of international perspectives in undergraduate courses. There is indeed some evidence that the number of specifically international and area studies courses in the major social science disciplines has decreased in recent years. Some faculty report that American sociology undergraduates have been surprised to find international content in, for instance, a presumably domestic course on "Marriage and the Family." Some students have even complained about course modules on international subjects which they felt detracted from domestic topics.

Recently, the disciplines have also felt the pressures of the competitive job market on their students and have responded with efforts to teach more advanced technical skills to the undergraduate student, as well as general "advancement" in the theory and methods of their discipline. As a result, many disciplinary departments have pressured universities to allot more credit hours *within* the discipline for student majors, thereby reducing the number of external electives and general education requirements where much international content may be found.

At the same time, faculty in these departments are generally committed to high quality teaching, and those with international interests and experience often comment on the lack of international content in the mainstream courses of their fields. Faculty in these disciplines also value global literacy in their undergraduates, knowing that major international trends and parameters have a significant impact on domestic systems. As a result, there is some new openness to considering international content in many departments across the nation.

Disseminating Model Course Syllabi

A second goal of the project was to increase the dissemination of model course syllabi which had innovatively incorporated international content within a traditionally domestic course. We felt no need to concentrate on the specifically international courses on international relations, world history, contemporary global issues, or area studies which usually achieve low enrollments. Rather, to reach the majors in a discipline, international content must be infused into the seven or eight standard or mainstream courses which undergraduate majors are expected to take. Thus, the syllabi were not to be drawn from the international relations or area studies course in disciplinary departments, but were sought in the introductory courses in which most freshmen and sophomores begin work in the field and core disciplinary courses (usually with large enrollments) essential for an undergraduate major. Thus we focused most of all on the "American Government" course in political science, the "Marriage and Family" or "Race and Ethnicity" course in sociology, or the "Abnormal Psychology" course in undergraduate psychology. Only if time permitted, did we seek syllabi in the avowedly international courses concerning global issues or international, comparative, and area studies.

However, infusing international and comparative content has been slow in most fields. We believed that instructors frequently will accept new curricular strategies, revisions of syllabi, and new texts and readings for their courses, especially if there is good evidence of the success of the new curriculum in

7

meeting undergraduates' needs. In recent years, some faculty have developed good courses with international content and have sought better collections of readings with material from outside the United States, but often these are unknown to colleagues in the field. This project, then, would encourage the associations to locate these innovative syllabi course by course, assemble them, and make them available within the discipline.

Two good examples of the results which were developed may be seen in J. Michael Armer, ed., *Syllabi and Resources for Internationalizing Courses in Sociology* (Washington, D.C.: American Sociological Association, Resource Materials for Teaching, 1983) and C. James Scheirer and Anne M. Rogers, comp., *The Undergraduate Psychology Curriculum from an Intercultural Perspective: Selected Courses*, (Washington, D.C.: American Psychological Association, 1983). Unfortunately, several associations found too few innovatively internationalized syllabi in their field to publish.

A Bibliography on Undergraduate International Studies

The third task of the project was to compile a current bibliography on international perspectives in the undergraduate curriculum. This could be especially useful for the hundreds of American institutions of higher education which are considering the locus and content of international perspectives in the requirements of entering the university, in the general studies or general education courses required of all undergraduates, and in the departments in which majors are taken. This work is continuing at Michigan State University. Because good bibliographical publications exist already on foreign language for the undergraduate, on the foreign student, and on study abroad, these topics were excluded.

Essays on International Perspectives in the Disciplines

The fourth major goal of the project resulted in the essays in this volume. We sought to encourage the disciplinary associations to specify the levels of international knowledge needed to achieve some minimal competence needed by undergraduates in two- and four-year colleges and universities for understanding the global realities of the late twentieth century. After surveying the field, we believed that too many appeals for increased "global knowledge" were utopian and that unrealistic goals or lack of clarity about goals should be avoided. It is easy to identify the abysmal ignorance of undergraduates in knowledge of world affairs and to call for "increased international understanding and global knowledge." It is far more difficult to specify the nature of the learning that should occur in each discipline and in the various courses. This project, we hoped, would specify realistic and particular changes in courses and curricula.

Each of the participating associations was given $6,000 to commission four to six essays and collect innovative international course syllabi. Specifically, the associations were requested to seek essays from

> among the most prestigious members of the professional association ... faculty at well-known research universities, for whom teaching undergraduates has been a secondary concern at best, but who are seen as opinion leaders in the field. Their articles would be given more attention, especially by members of the largest departments in the discipline, and the resultant impact would be more extensive.

Those papers were to concern either "What undergraduate student majors ought to learn about the outside world in our discipline," or "What is an attainable global perspective for undergraduates within our discipline," or "What is the minimum acceptable level of global education which our discipline should provide to its undergraduate majors."

Two associations, the American Economics Association and the American Anthropological Association, declined to participate because they felt their fields were international by definition and because of the short duration of the project. Others, such as the College Art Association and American Musicological Association, did not find the project attractive. A number of the associations had difficulty bringing their scholars to focus on the task, some writing essays not strictly addressing the issue of what should be taught to undergraduate majors. In some other associations, senior scholars in the field first accepted the commission to write on the topic, but then, several months or even a year later, declined on the grounds of other commitments. I judged that this frequently reflected the low career salience of spending the scarce resource of time on undergraduate teaching issues, despite the honoraria issued. In the final analysis, in the halls of academic prestige, and especially in the disciplinary associations, teaching and undergraduate education still do not rank very high.

Because of the scale of this project and the lack of staff with released time to operate it, the project gave exclusive attention to increasing international studies and not foreign language instruction, even though the Task Force realized the potential importance of incorporating international studies into foreign language classes. Increasing the international content in foreign language undergraduate courses remains an area of vast need of research and curricular planning.

In the end, more than 40 essays were produced by leading scholars in seven associations; almost all are presented here with little alteration. The volume is a "group portrait" of a number of disciplinary families, each addressing in their own unique way how they will incorporate the realities and the visions of the global and foreign horizons.

9

The Implementation of the Project: Planning and Procedures

The project was managed and organized at the Center for International Programs, Michigan State University. Office facilities, equipment, and various other support were provided by Michigan State University through the African Studies Center under the dean of international studies and programs. Funding was provided over three years by the U.S. Department of Education through the Undergraduate International Studies Program of Title VI (Ms. Susanna Easton, program officer).

Advisory oversight was provided in the earliest stages by the members of the Task Force on Elementary, Secondary, and Undergraduate Education of the National Council. General oversight throughout the project was provided by Dr. Rose L. Hayden, president of the National Council. Results of the study and action undertaken were shared directly with members of the NCFLIS Senior Advisors, a panel of 23 distinguished members of the national educational community.

This work owes much to the vision of Allen Kassof, the first executive director of NCFLIS, who established the Task Force on Elementary, Secondary and Undergraduate Education. The project and volume are greatly indebted to Dr. Hayden, who, with many years of experience in international and foreign language studies, has worked with the greatest of creativity, energy and vision toward a relevant global education for the coming generations of young Americans and for the development of international perspectives in the nation, the marketplace, the school, the media, and the academy.

Higher Education, International Education, and the Academic Disciplines

Sven Groennings

In colleges and universities, the academic disciplines are often the gatekeepers of educational change. Because it is in the disciplines that faculties, curricula, and research are based, basic changes in the curriculum do not occur until faculty in their disciplinary and departmental arenas are ready to implement them. The harbingers of changes in the curriculum are new perspectives in the disciplines.

As the general purpose of education is to prepare students for the world in which they are living, there is a growing expectation that the curriculum must enlarge our students' understanding of the new international circumstances and of peoples and cultures beyond our borders. Without exception, such missions devolve upon the faculties of the academic disciplines.

Colleges and universities across the United States are seeking to become increasingly international in their missions, program planning, faculty development, research, service, continuing education, technical assistance, student selection, and opportunities for student learning on campus and abroad. In search of internationally oriented intellectual frameworks, process models of programmatic development, and substantive concentrations appropriate to their particular institutions, they are investigating international connections within and among the disciplines.

Current research in New England shows that of 40 institutions examined, all 40 are experiencing lively change along the international dimension. Viewed as a whole, this change is profound, providing evidence that internationalization

Sven Groennings is Senior Vice President of the Center for Educational Competitiveness. He has served recently as Visiting Professor of Higher Education at the University of Georgia. Previously he was Director of the Fund for the Improvement of Postsecondary Education.

11

is becoming one of the most powerful substantive developments in the history of American higher education.

At issue in this development is the role of the academic disciplines, which are the bedrock of academic structure and thus shape academic substance. Does internationalization at colleges and universities have depth beyond planning at the top and the activities of a few campus entrepreneurs? Is activity within the disciplines contributing to the push toward internationalization? Alternatively, are interdisciplinary and multidisciplinary developments circumventions of the intellectual and professional directions of the faculty in their disciplines? Is internationalization faddish in nature, or does activity within the disciplines establish that it is a long-term trend? The following chapters suggest that internationalization is becoming a megatrend.

Primarily through faculty representatives, the disciplines present in these pages their own evolving global and international perspectives, showing the impact of the wider world upon the disciplines and the relevance of the disciplines to the international understanding of undergraduates.

The purposes of this introductory essay are to set the disciplines' self-portrait into the frameworks of change in higher education and change in international education; to review alternative ways to reach undergraduates; and to consider the implications of the chapters that follow. Context will frame this essay's focus on the disciplines and curricular strategies.

Impetus to Change in Higher Education

Along the path of change in higher education one finds patterns and processes, stimuli and barriers, and most saliently, the vision and priority that are always central to any new thrust. While some recent changes have originated within the academy—writing across the curriculum, the teaching of critical thinking, and the behavioral revolution in the social sciences—many of the most far-reaching changes have been in response to developments largely beyond our institutions, to changes in society, the economy, technology, and national needs. Historically this kind of change has loomed large, for example, as we responded to the industrial revolution, to returning veterans, to demands for access to higher education, and to the implications to Sputnik, or as postwar Europe adjusted its curricula toward greater emphasis on science.

Today one of the most powerful forces external to the campus is the globalization of nearly everything, most obviously the economy, communications, and national security. It is such a fundamental change that one is tempted to propose, by lighthearted analogy and borrowing from geophysics, a plate tectonics theory of curricular change: the earth moves, the curriculum responds. The tremors are not only national, but also local, with implications for local employment, leadership education, and general understanding. For today's undergraduates, who will be in their early thirties as we enter the next century, little seems more certain than the quickening impact on their lives of the rest of the world.

As we have pursued quality in education, we have tried to improve not only performance standards but also the relevance of what students learn. We have steadily undertaken new things, providing new substance, reaching new learners, teaching in new ways as we have enlarged our understanding of how pertinent learning can happen, adapting in order to be relevant to the broader environment, indeed expanding the very purposes of the university beyond teaching and research to service. The record shows that successful colleges and universities are not static but evolve in symbiotic relationship with their environment.

Society will need their graduates and their research to build its future, and those institutions will prosper that are most relevant to the future of society.

Because it is the learner-centered teaching activity that prepares society to respond to change, the curriculum is important. The educational sector may or may not be a cause of technological or other changes transforming our country and future, but it is the great explainer, familiarizing people with things to come, making change acceptable, preparing the nation for positive engagement. When education lags, the nation's ability to adapt, to progress, and to compete is impeded. The greater the rate of change in technology and the world around us, the more and the faster education needs to adapt.

The great majority of America's colleges and universities are currently reappraising their undergraduate curricula. They are doing so in the wake of a spate of significant reports which, although differing in approach and emphasis, all call for change in undergraduate education. A recurring theme, common to all, is the need for international education. In its chapter on "A Minimum Required Curriculum," the Association of American Colleges' report includes international and multicultural experiences, explaining that "At this moment in history colleges are not being asked to produce village squires but citizens of a shrinking world and a changing America."[1] A National Endowment for the Humanities report declares as essential to a college education an understating of the development of Western civilization, proficiency in a foreign language as an avenue into another culture, and familiarity with at least one non-Western culture or civilization.[2] A report by the National Institute of Education states, "the best preparation for the future is...an education that will enable students to adapt to a changing world" and that, among other abilities, "adaptation to change requires that one draw on history and on the experience of other cultures."[3] More forcible than any of these in its advocacy of international education is the report of the National Commission on the Role and Future of

State Colleges and Universities, which makes its case in the context of the need to meet international economic competition.[4] The most recent of the reports, from the Carnegie Foundation for the Advancement of Teaching, conveys the same message: "One of the most urgent challenges, we believe, is to extend the campus beyond the borders of our nation and make connections to the wider world community."[5]

A decade earlier, in *Educating for Survival*, Ernest Boyer and Martin Kaplan expressed a more wholesale view of change needed. Reviewing the philosophy and structure of the college curriculum across two centuries, they pointed out that every core curriculum of the past has evolved in relation to our national development and had been guided by a vision of commonality. They proposed restructuring the curriculum in accord with the new global interrelations and interdependence: "the future must be part of the curriculum to be studied. If consideration of the past and present emphasizes American society's internal connectedness, looking ahead will underscore complex global relations."[6]

Between 1983 and 1987 seventeen reports appeared on the international competitiveness of the American economy. In general, these have focused on tax and trade policies; on innovative productivity and its science and engineering requisites; and on human resource development in terms of worker retraining and overcoming illiteracy. The most recent of these reports, *An Action Agenda for American Competitiveness*, also highlights the linkage between international competitiveness and international knowledge: "Given the increased internationalization of the economy, college and universities are strongly encouraged to increase their teaching of international studies, including foreign languages and cultures"; "Given the growing interdependence of the American and world economies, it is crucial that U.S. students and workers become more knowledgeable about other countries and cultures"; "Colleges and universities must significantly strengthen their international studies courses—language, cultural, political, economic—and make them readily available to U.S. business executives as part of their own lifelong learning programs."[7]

The various reports on the international competitiveness of the American economy and on the undergraduate curriculum and its purposes followed several major examinations of the state of international education on the nation's campuses. In providing background on the exposure of undergraduate students to international perspectives, a report by the American Council on Education indicated that only 3% of the students were enrolled in any courses focusing specifically on international events or on foreign peoples and cultures.[8] Perhaps most widely cited for its conclusion that "Americans' incompetence in foreign languages is nothing short of scandalous,"[9] the report of the President's Commission of Foreign Language and International Studies was broad in scope, addressing learning needs at all levels of education as well as scholarly

14

exchanges and public policy. For undergraduates it recommended strengthened course offerings, 2–3 required courses in international studies, and the integration of international and comparative perspectives in the teaching of most undergraduate courses. It also recommended funding of 200 undergraduate international studies programs to help push institutions toward a commitment to undergraduate international studies. A background paper based in part on a survey of university and college presidents indicates that these leaders generally believe that there should be an international component in every course of study.[10]

Another massive report, by Richard Lambert for the Association of American Universities, focuses on needs in developing foreign language and area studies programs, which are essential to providing expertise for government service and for academic continuity.[11] Its concern is largely graduate education. His forthcoming sequel focuses on undergraduate education.

Never before has there been such a rush of reports on higher education. Overall, they have been constructive in stimulating discussion across the country about how to improve undergraduate education by focusing on the development of skills, the assessment of learning, and the relevance of the content. While the perspective of these reports is national and the objectives general, every report includes an international dimension.

One comprehensive and multifaceted work focusing entirely on the international dimension of the undergraduate curriculum was based on the assumption that the advancement of international learning must come from the academic institutions themselves. The accomplishments of the Council on Learning's Education and the World View project include an assessment of the knowledge of freshmen and seniors about the world, a review of programs and strategies for advancing international learning, and a handbook presenting exemplary international programs at all kinds of institutions.[12] Without closely examining what is going on within them, this work discusses the role of the scholarly disciplines. *Group Portrait* takes the next step, portraying evolving thought and directions within a group of disciplines and thereby illuminating segments of the empirical basis for internationalizing the curriculum.

Paradigm Shift in International Education

While these reports have called for more international education, this field itself has been undergoing a profound shift caused by the globalization of the economy. A university is naturally an international institution: theory and method transcend national boundaries. In fulfilling the university function of addressing the universe of phenomena, our scholars commonly engage in research in other countries. In reverse flow, our universities have attracted millions of foreign students and thousands of foreign intellectuals, who have given new directions to our disciplines. In the years ahead, the international role of universities will grow rapidly as this country's economic competitiveness will depend increasingly on the production of new knowledge and the provision of sophisticated services internationally. Thrusts into fields such as biotechnology will require complementary international focus, not only because of the implications of the work but also to achieve leadership.

Before World War II American higher education was not very international in either focus or clientele. Thereafter the institutions grew in size and number, benefitting from a rapid expansion in the numbers of students served: from two million students in 1945 to five and a half million in 1965 to more than twelve million in 1985. This extraordinary expansion made it possible to greatly diversify the course offerings. As the United States became a world superpower, the number of internationally focused courses increased. In 1946, not fully two years after it had passed the G.I. Bill entitling veterans to student financial assistance, the federal government utilized the gains from selling surplus military equipment overseas to initiate the Fulbright program, which across its forty years has enabled more than 60,000 Americans to study and teach abroad. In 1949 the government began technical and developmental assistance programs which have involved more than a hundred universities and many thousands of faculty members in work abroad. These programs built international expertise and relationships. However, it was not common that they built international studies.

One of the pressing national needs after World War II, in the wake of decolonization, the creation of new countries, and the beginning of global political competition, was language and area expertise. Various major foundations, especially the Ford Foundation, assisted in supporting the development of the needed capabilities. In parallel, beginning in 1958, first through Title VI of the National Defense Education Act, and since 1980 through Title VI of the Higher Education Act, the federal government has helped provide support for as many as a hundred campus-based centers, most of which focus on world areas. While the federal government has contributed much less of the wherewithal than the universities, it has been a catalyst and has provided prestige, the margin of excellence, and the drawing power for other funding. The Foreign Language and Area Studies Fellowship Program has supported the graduate eduction of more than 20,000 students, most of whom are teaching in colleges and universities and whose presence on our campuses is of crucial importance for the internationalization of curricula. Across the years there have been more than 200 awards to advance undergraduate international education at a variety of institutions. In all these ways, outside support totaling perhaps half a billion dollars enormously enhanced the international capabilities of American higher education.

Into the 1960s the emphasis was upon developing expertise in special programs at the graduate level in major universities. The driving rationale was national security. By the mid-1960s, when the area study programs were well established, the foundations largely left the field and moved their seed money elsewhere, especially in response to Lyndon Johnson's Great Society and War on Poverty. With Vietnam, the international field lost popularity, and by the beginning of the 1970s, the academic marketplace seemed largely saturated. Ironically, interest on the part of the academic and foreign-affairs communities in the languages of an area has in the past been inversely proportional to our involvement in hostilities in that area. In his book on the use of languages in the armed forces, Kurt Müller notes that immediately prior to World War II, the Department of State suspended its language program at the same time as the War and Navy Departments began theirs.[13] At no time during the Vietnam War did college enrollments in Vietnamese exceed 29 students; nor did more than six colleges and universities offer Vietnamese.[14]

In the meantime we began to experience the globalization of the economy, which was to have a profound effect on the rationale for international education and to change the nature of the support for and the developmental dynamics of international education.

The international dimension of American life became vivid in all parts of the country, becoming more of an immediate and everyday reality than issues of national security. Local stores stocked foreign goods, while doing American business increasingly meant doing business with the rest of the world. The new technologies brought the world into the living room and the stock market. One professional field after another developed an international dimension, from public health to agriculture to architecture. We learned painful lessons in international marketing, for example that the automobile name "Nova" in Spanish can be heard as "No va," meaning "It doesn't go." We read, in contrast, that when a Japanese businessman was asked in what language he did his business, he replied very simply: "The language of my customer."

Reflection on changed circumstances led to the conclusion that we needed new learning. In the 1980 reauthorization of the Higher Education Act, Congress moved NDEA VI to HEA VI to demonstrate that the international dimension is integral to higher education. The Congress understood that the area studies programs it had promoted had been shaped before the era of global economic competition and that their social science and humanities faculties, however positively significant in other regards, lacked connection to the new economic imperative. To Title VI it added Part B for international business, hoping in part that the juxtaposition with foreign language and area study programs would spark some creativity. It was at this point in the legislative history that corporate and local economic interests joined the national security and academic interests in supporting this legislation. However, the lack of connection between area studies centers and business programs has persisted.

Currently the international field is undergoing a paradigm shift along three fundamental dimensions. First, its rationale is moving beyond the predominant emphasis on national security toward a vigorous emphasis on economic change and international competitiveness. Second, the field is shifting its Washington focus toward additional centers whose interests are more heavily economic, such as Boston and Seattle, Philadelphia and Atlanta, i.e., toward nation-wide local interest alongside nation-state national interest.

The evidence that the economic and accompanying technological developments that today are the new dynamic in international education is to be found in all parts of the country. Economic concern and the relevance of higher education to international competitiveness led the Southern Governors Association to establish its Advisory Council on International Education, the Western Interstate Commission for Higher Education to work with the Western Governors Association in addressing issues of international trade and to survey international programs at academic institutions; the New England Board of Higher Education to undertake a project on the internationalization of the New England economy and its implications for higher education; and the National Governors Association to call for emphasis on international education, and specifically on foreign languages and geography in secondary and post-secondary education.

Third, international education is moving beyond the production of experts, whose supply will continue to be essential, toward general education for citizenship and all the professions. Whereas the Fulbright program focuses on experts, technical assistance programs provide expertise to other countries, and area study programs create expertise, the globalization of the American economy is moving educational concern beyond such professional levels into the general domain. Attention is shifting from graduate education to undergraduate education, and internationalization has become important not only at the institutions educating toward expertise but at higher education institutions generally. At issue now is the approach to international education within general education.

Ubiquitous Momentum

While the chapters in this book focus mainly on the social sciences, the internationalization of curricula and innovation in international learning are occurring much more broadly, for example, in business education, foreign language study, and teacher training.

Only recently has the business curriculum begun to incorporate international components and to do so across functional areas. Curricula were established when the United States was more insular than it is today and when international commerce was peripheral and it was not so important to understand worldwide business conditions and opportunities. Indeed, a decade ago, the American Council on Education found that 75 percent of students completing business doctorates, i.e., those who would constitute our future faculties, had never taken a course in the international aspects of their business studies.[15] It became generally understood that curriculum was lagging behind the development and promise of international business as the value of United States exports began to approach a quarter trillion dollars annually, our firms invested an equal amount abroad, foreign investment in this country became significant in numerous communities, we imported nearly half the oil we consumed, exported a third of our farm products, and found that one sixth of our manufacturing jobs were related to exporting. Our service industries became international, as overseas loans by American banks exceeded $300 billion, the insurance business became increasingly international, and domestic transportation systems became integral parts of the global market. The capital market, too, has demonstrated its global characteristic. In an era in which perhaps a third of our exporting and importing was being conducted within our multinational corporations, the management of major corporations was becoming inherently international. Moreover, the United States during the 1980s began to face growing trade deficits; the figure for 1986 exceeded $156 billion. As perhaps only 250 firms account for 80% of our exports, export participation has seemed very weak, suggesting lack of familiarity with exporting and a need for education to redress this deficiency.

The American Assembly of Collegiate Schools of Business (AACSB), which sets accreditation standards for business curricula, has become an engine of reform, illustrating the influence of external pressure in advancing curricular change. Through several phases, it developed an accreditation standard which made it very clear that every business student should be exposed to the international dimension through one or more elements of the curriculum.[16] Clearly, not all institutions will meet this standard in the same way, given differences in business school missions and capabilities. Some are meeting it by requiring students to take internationally focused courses outside the business schools, although AACSB's intent is to move toward internationalization within the business curriculum.

Within that course of study, there are three strategic choices. One is to put everyone through an introductory course in international business. A second possibility, perhaps suitable to a few institutions having a very specialized faculty, is to require each student to take an international course within the major, e.g., in marketing, finance, accounting, or in management, which might even be broadened to include consideration of political context, labor movements, and crosscultural communication. A third possibility, which surely is best for institutions that have a small faculty or that produce generalists and managers whose careers will be in small businesses, is to pursue a modular infusion strategy. The shortage of candidates for faculty positions who have concentrated academically in international business is another factor leading most institutions to undertake modular infusion.

Successful pursuit of the third option requires faculty development and the creation of model teaching. units. Such models are being developed and widely reviewed, and the AACSB has been responding to the latter need by providing a series of seminars across the country. In sum, faculty in numerous schools of business are considering the options and undertaking curricular internationalization.

Extraordinary, after a long period of declining enrollments, now reversed, is the revitalization of foreign language study. Among the causes of this reversal are the movement toward restoring or establishing more rigorous college entrance and general curriculum requirements and the evidence that foreign language study promotes increasingly important crosscultural understanding and effective English usage. Probably an equally powerful causal factor is the economic and technological development that is changing the international dimension more generally. Indeed, new directions in foreign language learning illustrate this thesis.

Despite their richness in the virtues of the humanities, language departments specializing in literature were losing enrollments at a time of very rapid expansion of both international communication and enrollments in colleges and universities. Interest grew in learning language for special purposes as well as for oral communication. Courses proliferated in business French, German, and Spanish, on some campuses in direct connection with business curricula. At the same time, in perhaps no other field has there developed such ubiquitous use of the new technologies: videocassettes, disks, narrowcast television, laboratories, interactive computer programs and satellitic communication are all being used to teach foreign languages, and generally in support of the thrust toward competence in communicating which is being stimulated by the global economy.

Increasingly, foreign languages will be taught toward the objective of achieving oral proficiency, among other proficiencies. Oral proficiency testing is coming nationally, radiating outward from projects undertaken by the Educational Testing Service, the American Council on the Teaching of Foreign Languages, and the Modern Language Association. Numerous colleges and universities have made inquiries to foundations about funding to move ahead. Proficiency testing will contribute to the renewal of the foreign language field, further signaling the importance of learning a language as a skill to be used.

Student motivation has already been affected by desire to present credentials to prospective employers. On the horizon are generally recognized national standards adapted from those developed by the federal government's Foreign Service Institute and Interagency Language Roundtable which will provide clear yardsticks of learning progress, moving the measurement of achievement from a semester-passed criterion to one based on the skill attained, with tracking and collaboration across levels of education and the opportunity to earn credentials however and whenever individuals choose. The use of tapes will ensure consistency in performance evaluation, and some academic language teachers are now qualifying as certifiers. We may anticipate benchmarks of account-ability for teachers and catalytic effects on curricular development and curricular evaluation, on the design of teaching materials, and on parallel testing in increasing numbers of languages. Another change is on a slightly more distant horizon. Much as language teaching developed toward teaching the 500 most used words, there will be development toward teaching the themes that are central to cross-cultural understanding and effective communication. In sum, fundamental change in the foreign language field is another sign of a changing academic era, responding to a changing environment, with the result, as philosopher Thomas Kuhn has memorably said about paradigm shifts, that "the pieces are sorting themselves out and coming together in a new way."

Global economic competitiveness is causing pressure to improve American education at all levels. Particularly stunning is the report by the Carnegie Forum Task Force on Teaching as a Profession,[17] wherein the introductory framework bears the subtitle "A Changing World Economy" and focuses mainly on meeting competition from Asia. Its basic message is that in a knowledge-based inter-national economy, the United States will have to lead through education in order to avoid suffering serious consequences.

Teacher education is becoming subject to pressures for internationalization. In cooperation with the American Association of Colleges for Teacher Educa-tion, the National Council for the Accreditation of Teacher Education has promulgated an accreditation standard, the thrust of which is that international education should be considered a fundamental part of basic education and that global perspectives should permeate all aspects of a teacher education program. The new standard is now in force for accreditation visits. Guidelines are being published for each set of curriculum components, including the liberal arts component. Seminars are being conducted across the country on how to implement the internationalization guidelines.

The development of an accreditation standard is a long process. In part because numerous surveys have indicated that citizen knowledge about the rest of the world is low in comparison with that of inhabitants of many other countries, the international content of teacher education has been an issue for

21

longer than a decade. Since the schools are the key institutions of American citizen education, professional teacher and administrator conferences, including meetings of the chief state school officers, increasingly have addressed international education. There have been curricular adaptations in high schools, among them world civilization courses. Several cities have established international magnet high schools; Oregon and New York, among other states, have adopted a global education requirement, albeit loosely defined, for high school graduation. Textbook writers have been preparing classroom materials, more than 6,000 teachers have been involved in internationally focused in-service training programs, and many schools of education permit the student teaching internship to occur outside the United states. Work on curricular materials for teacher education is underway at several universities. The project that was the impetus for nearly all the chapters in this book also included work at Ohio State University in preparing position papers on curricular programs in teacher education and the collection of syllabi of undergraduate courses in teacher education which include a significant amount of international content.

Thus we can view this volume's treatment of liberal arts and social science disciplines in the context of a ubiquitous momentum for internationalization.

The Academic Disciplines

It is ultimately in the disciplines that we see the extent to which colleges and universities adapt to their changing environments. As the disciplines have evolved toward narrow specialization and as their focus has been on the development of theory and method, on science qua science, rather than on geographic content arenas, one might assume that there are major barriers to internationalization. The enormous growth of American universities and the concentration of databases and research money in this country have to some extent predisposed many disciplines toward American substantive concentration. Moreover, research abroad tends to be costly.

Yet, to contrary effect, some disciplines are obviously international at the core, probably especially geography and anthropology. In general, the evolution of the disciplines has involved expansion of intellectual frameworks. Economics, for example, obviously has grown broader in perspective as the economic environment has developed from self-contained local units to national communities and now to a global economy. There is pervasive evidence in the following chapters of the impact of international and indeed global change upon the disciplines. The evidence includes new theoretical constructs, new ways of doing research, the use of foreign data to test hypotheses, the emergence of a global perspective, and the involvement of an increasing number of faculty members. As the disciplines become more international, international learning occurs as part of general learning, even in many courses whose titles do not convey such content. Textbooks provide signs of this change, and we can observe it in both business courses and social science courses.

Brief introductions to three of the disciplines included in this volume will illustrate patterns of change:

Communications/Journalism

In this field, change can affect the continuing education of adults. Journalism education increasingly reflects the era of global information and connectedness because it is necessary to prepare media personnel to convey world news when every community is affected by international trends and events and when world news often has a local connection or local news can only be explained in an international context.

Increasingly, courses treat differences between the work of U.S.-based and foreign-based reporters, transborder information flows, and comparisons of American and foreign broadcast and print media systems as they are influenced by economic and political circumstances, history, social structure, and local culture. Intended to enable future journalists to be sensitive to the contexts of the foreign news they will receive, edit, and present to American readers, listeners, and viewers, this approach has become essential to responsible journalism. The perceptions gained also provide insight into foreign receptivity to different kinds of advertising, which is another facet of communication.

Political Science

This discipline is significantly American in its origins, and its main focus has been on American government and politics. In the 1960s the behavioral revolution pushed it from the study of formal structure and process toward a search for data to test hypotheses. The data and the excitement in this discipline were overwhelmingly American.

Nonetheless, changing circumstances beyond the United States began to have an enormous effect on political science. Attention to the developing countries revealed that the focus on formal structures which had been characteristic of the study of European government would have little explanatory potential. There was a turn to sociological and economic analyses of the bases of politics, and a subfield of "comparative politics" replaced "foreign governments." Comparative began to include American. Foreigners tested behavioral theory with their own data so that the validity of hypotheses tested in the United States became viewed in wider context. Meanwhile, many political scientists became experts in various fields of public policy and, particularly as some public policies are transnational in their effects, there is growing concern with the comparative understanding of public policy. There is a rapidly growing subfield, for example, of comparative political economy. The impact of external factors on decision making within countries has become manifest even in very large countries. All these phenomena are having the effect of blurring lines of separation between domestic and comparative or international divisions within political science.

Often it is in courses in international relations or international politics that students acquire basic knowledge about this country's interests in other countries and their interests in the United States, as well as the purposes, instruments, and patterns of foreign policy, international problems and their resolution, alliances, international organizations and diplomacy, and concepts of nationalism, sovereignty, balance of power, and interdependence. On many campuses there are also topical courses, for example on national security, deterrence, or arms control. In the teaching of such courses there is increasingly a global rather than a between-nations perspective, as the economy, super-power rivalry, and communications systems have become global. While the nation-state remains the basic unit of action and analysis, the behavior of states is now commonly presented to students in the context of power, resources, motivation, and constraints in the global system. Also there is growing emphasis, beyond descriptions of interests and strategies, on explaining behavior and outcomes in the context of interactive world politics. These shifts signal the coming of a global perspective.

History

The field of history serves as a cornerstone of the general curriculum and of liberal education. If there is any one field in which a debate about relevance will be of general interest across a campus, that field will be history. At the cutting edge of change is a general debate about the appropriateness of the traditional freshman course in western civilization, which has a national enrollment of approximately 600,000 and has provided both a common intellectual experience for great numbers of students and an instructional arena for improving student skills in writing and discussion. This traditional course has been defended as being fundamental to our understanding of our intellectual roots and continuing national interest in Europe as well as of the democratic and other cultural values which undergird our institutions and behavior.

If there will be only one basic non-American history course in any curriculum, its choice depends on relevance. Leading historians are asking whether a course focused on Western civilization, which reflects what was overwhelmingly important in the world when such courses were created between the World Wars, is adequate in a post-colonial world in which more of our national trade is with Asia than with Europe and a large proportion of the political and strategic problems we face in the world are not European. The issue, some say, is not only what students need to know to make sense of the their world, but is also becoming a matter of ethnic roots: Western civilization courses reflected and integrated the cultural heritages of most immigrants to this country years ago, but today, as the number of blacks, Hispanics, and Asians in the United States increases, some parts of the country are on the verge of having majority populations of quite different roots. Given the globalization of both politics and the economy, say the advocates of change, it is time to develop the third phase of history's contribution to civic education: from American history to Western civilization to global history.

Increasingly at issue is how to reconcile the focus on Western civilization with a world view. Central to possibilities for reconciliation is the development of a new field of world history that is moving beyond the presentation of parallel continental histories and seeking organization around new conceptual constructs. Changes in scope are bringing changes in proportional treatment assigned to component topics and in the level of generalization. Changes in the focus of inquiry lead to changed methods of inquiry, to discovering new patterns and conveying a different understanding of history, with more comparison and probably more emphasis on long-term processes, groups of people and cross-cultural analysis. Within the discipline, such change would be a fundamental shift, as was the behavioral revolution in the social sciences. It can change expectations about what historians should know and teach and change the graduate education of historians. These things are starting to happen, while at the same time a wider circle of academics is becoming concerned about the objectives of the survey course in a global era.

Reaching Undergraduates

Within the last five years, nearly half the nation's colleges and universities have been considering ways to increase the international aspects of their curricula. It is now generally assumed that international education is an essential component of general education, that a true liberal arts education must be international in scope, and that all students not in the liberal arts should be exposed to international perspectives. Even if a university is distinguished in aspects of its international dimension, its average student may proceed through the undergraduate years without exposure to international content unless it occurs in entry level courses. The current issue is how to reach the students most appropriately. In addressing this issue, one commonly experiences any or all of the following overlapping tensions.

Core Courses or Distribution Requirements

The easiest way to ensure that students are exposed to international content is to require a suitable course and to define any number of courses as suitable. Many institutions have done this. Some have designed new courses, notably to enable students to meet an institutions's new requirements that they take a course introducing them to non-Western cultures. In this distribution requirements model, each discipline typically offers its own courses as it defines them. Some disciplines have a vested interest in the pattern of options, others seek inclusion. The selection of an options approach to meet a general purpose has the advantage of involving several disciplines. It is much more demanding and challenging to design a particular core course, on the global economy, for example. There are costs of faculty development and new teaching loads, and often one meets skepticism about the intellectual depth of survey courses as well as the intellectual challenge of creating them. The designation of a core course requires a general agreement that its content is so fundamentally important as to be part of general education; indeed, it must meet a general need more appropriately and powerfully than can be accomplished by optional courses representing a variety of perspectives. The classic core course is Western Civilization, whose appropriateness now is subject to re-evaluation.

Area Studies or Functionalist Approaches.

Especially since significant numbers of faculty members are area studies specialists, it has often been area studies that have tugged the disciplines in international directions. Several disciplines, notably geography, history, and political science, typically offer courses focusing on world areas, and there is a sharp increase in demand for courses focusing on China and Japan. Prestigious and large institutions tend to offer area study programs. While they usually are a form of professional education at the graduate level, there also are under-graduate area study programs. However, very few institutions have the critical mass of resources needed to offer a strong area studies program in any world region. For most institutions, other approaches to international education are more appropriate. Some have moved toward a globally focused curriculum based on world problems, issues, or topics such as economic development, national security, population trends, food and mineral resources, and environmental protection.

Disciplinarity or Interdisciplinarity

One school of thought holds that students need interdisciplinary approaches because understanding world problems requires multiple perspectives and because graduates will enter a working world characterized by interdisciplinary problem-solving in contexts of interrelated systems. Programs in area studies, global perspectives, and world issues are interdisciplinary, as are majors in international relations and some civilizational and intercultural approaches. There has been so much focus on international studies in the interdisciplinary sense that one often may look past the disciplinary. Most of the courses are within a discipline, and many faculty believe that it is fundamentally important for students to gain international understanding with the rigor and conceptual tools associated with the disciplines. Internationalization may be promoted by comparative analysis within the disciplines. Institutions which seek the infusion of international perspectives throughout the curriculum presume infusion within the disciplines. To internationalize a curriculum actually means to institutionalize that change within the disciplines; this achieved, the interdisciplinary and multidisciplinary acquire much greater strength.

Different institutions will address the approach to internationalization differently, in keeping with their mission and resources. Many approaches have merit, but one element is fundamental: the contribution of the academic disciplines. The disciplines are the bedrock, providing depth of knowledge, theoretical understanding, modes of analysis, and substantive building blocks for interdisciplinarity. The strength of any interdisciplinary approach is a function of the contributions of the disciplines. Faculty commitment and support for internationalization may reflect the structural, curricular, and inter-personal political reality of the department.

The Disciplines among the Causes of Internationalization

In the chapters that follow and on campuses across the country there is evidence of a pervasive and increasing internationalization of the disciplines. Occasionally it is nascent, yet it is also ubiquitous. It is an academic megatrend. Multifaceted internationalization is occurring rapidly on the campuses because the disciplines' practitioners are contributing to the processes. Departments are seeking faculty with international backgrounds, advocating international curricular content, and contributing to the building of international programs. Accordingly, the disciplines have become causal factors contributing to the internationalization of higher education. Indeed, without them there would be little internationalization beyond student exchange.

The internationalization of the disciplines is one of five causes of the internationalization of higher education. The most powerful cause is the global economic transformation. It is a second wave, following global political-military aspects of national security. The larger wave, felt in local communities in all parts of the country, it is the primary reason for increased student enrollment in international business courses and in international relations courses in the liberal arts as well as for the resurgence of foreign language learning. The global economy is bringing new and reinforced relevance to the international dimension of academic activity, and the impact is ubiquitous and profound. It is causing internationalization to be arguably the most powerful substantive redirection in the history of American higher education.

There used to be two ideological extremes of advocacy for international education, one driven by concerns about national security, the other by humanitarian considerations. Economic change, which has made the international local, has transcended these advocacies and broadened the scope of international studies and the constituency for international education.

A third cause of internationalization is the consciousness-raising provided by the numerous national reports, which have been widely read and mutually reinforcing.

A fourth factor is the coming of accreditation standards requiring international content in the curriculum, first in business education and newly in teacher education.

For the fifth factor, we turn to people. Internationalization is progressing because all three human elements—leaders, students, and faculties—are advancing it. There has been a rise to campus leadership of individuals with international experience who are committed to international education. These people are defining the vision, leading the planning, and directing the change. This phenomenon coincides with a rapid growth in the number of incoming and currently enrolled students who have traveled abroad, who envision internationally related careers, and who expect their education to have an international component.

Faculties also have become more international in their interests and increasingly are inclined toward a global perspective. Across the country they are offering a remarkable array of topically focused international courses. To some extent there is a status "pecking order" associated with international activity: international opportunities increase with the level of faculty achievement; the greater the activity of a department, the more internationally oriented its faculty becomes, with the major research universities having become pervasively international in perspective, activity, and professional contacts. State universities as well as many community colleges and private institutions have become involved increasingly in technical assistance programs involving faculty assignments abroad. It is a general phenomenon that the most acceptable and desired area of faculty development, in addition to the acquisition of computer skills, is in the international domain. Many colleges and universities are utilizing overseas centers and federal contractual relationships as means of advancing the internationalization of their faculties. The changing vision of the faculties is internationalizing the disciplines and shaping the curricular future.

Conclusions and Agenda

Because of the internationalization of nearly every aspect of American life, international education has become a centerpiece of discussion at campuses across the country. Numerous institutions are defining their educational mission to include international education and are developing an integrative planning framework for the advancement of international activities. In parallel, they have been considering afresh what kind of learning will be most important for the future and should be basic to the undergraduate experience. Perhaps everywhere this question has been asked, the answer has included an international focus. The chapters that follow confirm that at the same time the disciplines are undergoing a conspicuous internationalization.

Like the scientific revolution, internationalization is leading to a ubiquitous, pervasive and permanent redirection of the intellectual framework. Yet, like the early scientific revolution, it is a disorderly development, lacking clear definition, boundaries, and agreement. It is a many-splendored chaos with momentum, and it is crossdisciplinary.

These chapters establish very clearly that the disciplines influence one another and find one another relevant as they seek a global perspective. This finding is not consistent with the standard assumption that the disciplines are entities unto themselves, segmenting knowledge in such narrow ways as to make it difficult to gain a world view. To the contrary, they have been looking to one another for new frameworks, strategies of inquiry, and modes of explication. Shared commitment to behavioral science has brought them together, and shared commitment to international knowledge has brought people from different disciplines into such professional organizations as the International Studies Association. To the extent that international studies are inherently interdisciplinary, they are conducive to the integration of the disciplines. There is much creativity at the junctures of the disciplines as well as in response to external change. One may wonder whether the powerfully integrative force of technological and economic globalization will accelerate the fuzzing of disciplinary boundaries.

The chapters that follow could have catalytic effects. They are rich in perspectives and serve as a means by which the disciplines may inform one another about their internationalization. Although a few of the authors have addressed the questions of what a student should know and how that knowledge is related to the mission of his or her discipline, it is clear that overall consideration of this question within the disciplines remains weak. This is an important question at a time that national reports and academic institutions have provided formulations of the purposes of undergraduate education which include international education among those purposes at the same time that the disciplines are becoming more international. Faculty members typically regard themselves first as members of their disciplines and secondly as members of their employing institutions. The latter have made their objectives much clearer than have the former. As the disciplines today are expected to contribute to international education, it follows that a constructive next step for the disciplines to take would be to address their goals for international education and the learning outcomes they might provide. These chapters provide a collection of considerations toward meeting that challenge.

The agenda for undergraduate international education within the disciplines is otherwise mainly in the areas of program development and dissemination. There is a need to make known the exemplary programs that are being developed, to circulate syllabi, and to encourage and provide programs for faculty development. There also is a need for impact on the production of new Ph.D.'s who will become our next generation of professors and in this regard a need for the encouragement of research which incorporates international content. First of all, however, there is a need for dialogue, for a national conversation about the role of the academic disciplines in the development of international education. This volume is intended to contribute to that conversation.

This is a time for reflection and fresh creativity. There is a conceptual challenge ahead and an intellectual agenda to be shaped. There is also a leadership function in linking the visions of institutions, learning outcomes, and the role of the academic disciplines.

Notes

[1] Association of American Colleges, *Integrity in the College Curriculum: A Report to the Academic Community* (Washington, D.C.: AAC, 1985) 23.

[2] Study Group on the State of the Humanities in Higher Education, *To Reclaim a Legacy: A Report on the Humanities in Higher Education* (Washington, D.C: National Endowment for the Humanities, 1984).

[3] National Institute of Education Study Group on the Conditions of Excellence in American Higher Education, *Involvement in Learning: Realizing the Potential of American Higher Education* (Washington, D.C.: NIE, 1984) 43.

[4] American Association of State Colleges and Universities, *To Secure the Blessings of Liberty* (Washington, D.C.: AASCU, 1986).

[5] Ernest L. Boyer, *College: The Undergraduate Experience in America* (New York: Harper and Row, 1987) 228.

[6] Ernest L. Boyer and Martin Kaplan, *Educating for Survival* (New Rochelle, N.Y.: Change Magazine Press, 1977) 71.

[7] Business-Higher Education Forum, Northeast-Midwest Congressional Coalition, and Congressional Clearinghouse on the Future, *An Action Agenda for American Competitiveness* (Washington, D.C.: Business-Higher Education Forum, 1986) 8, 23, 26.

[8]American Council on Education, *Education for Global Interdependence, A Report from the International Education Project* (Washington, D.C.: ACE, 1975) 7. This report also lists the finding of the 1973 survey conducted by the American Association of Colleges of Teacher Education which showed that only 5% of those preparing to become teachers were exposed to any global content or perspectives in the coursework for teacher certification.

[9] *Strength through Wisdom: A Critique of U.S. Capability.* A report to the President from the President's Commission on Foreign Language and International Studies (Washington, D.C.: GPO, 1979) 5.

[10] James E. Harf, "Undergraduate International Studies: The State of the Art and Prescriptions for the Future," *President's Commission on Foreign Language and International Studies: Background Papers and Studies* (Washington, D.C.: GPO) 90–109.

[11] Richard D. Lambert et al., *Beyond Growth: The Next Stage in Language and Area Studies.* A Report by the Association of American Universities (Washington, D.C.: AAU, 1984).

[12] The Council on Learning's project publications include one book: Humphrey Tonkin and Jane Edwards, *The World in the Curriculum* (New Rochelle, N.Y.: Change, 1981) and several booklets: *The Role of the Scholarly Disciplines* (1980), *What College Students Know and Believe about Their World,* (1981), and *Education and the World View* (1980). For an overview, see Robert Black and George W. Bonham, "The Council on Learning Project on Undergraduate Education: Education and The World View," in *New Directions in International Education. The Annals of the American Academy of Political and Social Science,* 449 (1980) 102–13.

[13] Kurt E. Müller, *Language Competence: Implications for National Security* (New York: Praeger, 1986) 13.

[14] Müller, 110.

[15] International Education Project, *Business and International Education* (Washington, D.C.: ACE, 1977) 21. Occasional Paper 4. A 1984 follow-up study commissioned by the National Council on Foreign Language and International Studies found that the 75% figure had in the meantime risen to 83%. See Lee C. Nehrt, "The Internationalization of Doctoral Programs in Business," unpublished paper, (March 1985).

[16] For background, see Lee C. Nehrt, *Case Studies of the Internationalization of the Business School Curriculum* (Washington, D.C.: American Assembly of Collegiate Schools of Business, 1981).

[17] *A Nation Prepared: Teachers for the 21st Century.* Report of the Task Force on Teaching as a Profession (Washington, D.C.: Carnegie Forum on Education and the Economy, 1986).

31

GEOGRAPHY

Traditionally among the most international of the disciplines, geography is undergoing a revival stemming from the fundamental relevance of geographic knowledge in an era of global interdependencies and the widely expressed concern, based on numerous surveys, that the typical student's geographic knowledge is deficient.

This section on geography reflects the achievements of two projects undertaken by the Association of American Geographers. The Association was publishing a booklet, *Geography and International Knowledge* (1982), at the time that the NCFLIS Project on International Education in the Undergraduate Disciplines was beginning; this booklet was a product of the Association's Committee on Geography and International Studies. When it joined the NCFLIS project, the Association proceeded to a second stage of activity. It expanded on the themes it had addressed in the booklet, added a focus on culture and nationality, and published a book by a group of authors, *Geography in Internationalizing the Undergraduate Curriculum* (1985), edited by Salvatore J. Natoli and Andrew R. Bond. The Association's overall design was parallel to that of the other disciplinary associations working with NCFLIS; its book includes five chapters and a section on instructional strategies.

The following pages include the text of the original booklet, which focuses on the international characteristics of geography, the contributions of geographic curricula to international studies, and international applications of geography. One chapter from the Association's 1985 book, Marvin W. Mikesell's "Culture and Nationality," is also included.

Geography and International Knowledge

Association of American Geographers

In 1921 the geographer Isaiah Bowman, who advised President Woodrow Wilson on new boundaries after World War I, published a magisterial survey of the problems of his time and called it *The New World*. Today we also face a new world, as will each succeeding generation.

Now we can see the terrestrial globe as a unit and recall Archibald MacLeish's words describing the famous photograph taken by the Apollo VIII mission—the earth with the moon's cratered surface across the foreground: "To see the earth as we now see it, small and blue and beautiful in that eternal silence where it floats, is to see ourselves as riders on the earth together."[1]

We can now capture the unity and the limitations of our earthly home in such phrases as "One World," "Planet Earth," and "Spaceship Earth." But the surface of this earth, our home, our source of food and energy, and the site of our economic and social activities, is limited and fragile. The earth's resources are finite and the environment is easily degraded and polluted. Our activities upset ecological balances at peril to our future. At the same time science and technology enlarge the available resources. In many countries population is increasing at an alarming rate, is out-stripping the pace of economic growth, and can endanger the area itself and neighboring areas as well. The highly localized nature of the world's energy resources poses many international problems.

The world has shrunk for communication and travel. Most areas are accessible within minutes by telephone and television can capture a crisis anywhere for millions of viewers in many lands. Jet aircraft connect most cities on all continents within almost twenty-four hours.

Yet the world is also fragmented. More than 150 countries are now members of the United Nations and the number continues to grow. Race, religion, language, nationalism, ideologies, and rivalries separate people from one another.

Now more than ever, citizens of the United States and of other countries cannot be ignorant of the world, its nature, its divisions, its interrelations, and its problems. Nevertheless, American ignorance about the world persists and has been reported at great length in the press and in educational journals over the past several years. Several recent studies among Americans have documented their lack of foreign language proficiency, knowledge about other cultures, and understanding about important international relationships.[2]

We might ask why our nation's education system has failed to teach its citizens about other nations, their languages, and their cultures. In a 1980 survey by the Educational Testing Service, only twenty-eight percent of college seniors could correctly identify a curve representing the world's past and probable future consumption of fossil fuels, such as petroleum, natural gas, and coal. Although the standard of living of the United States depends upon the supply of these sources of energy, only twenty-nine percent could recognize the member nations of the Organization of Petroleum Exporting Countries (OPEC), the organization largely responsible for the recent dramatic increases in the price of gasoline. Only twenty-four percent could properly distinguish a basic cause of the great global problem of inadequate nutrition.[3] A study of eighth-grade students in the United States found that only thirty-five percent could correctly identify Egypt on a map and only thirty-one percent could identify the United Kingdom.[4]

Along with reports on the inadequacy of American education to deal with global problems at many levels—diplomatic, commercial, industrial, scientific, cultural, and educational—came a string of sobering documents on the urgency of many international problems.[5] Such reports as *North-South: A Program for Survival, Overcoming World Hunger,* and *Global 2000,* all published in 1980, point to increasing conflict among nations, the specter of future mass starvation, floods of refugees, greater food instability and dependency, monetary crises, and an intensifying struggle for control of renewable and non-renewable natural resources. Standing over it all, of course, is the apocalyptic threat of the incineration of humankind in the nuclear fireball.

People cannot resolve such problems without knowing the facts and understanding their meaning. Geography can contribute to an informed world view and thus to a favorable international climate for the peaceful settlement of disputes and for productive measures to ameliorate many world problems.

Perhaps no one has contributed more than novelist James A. Michener to helping us understand a number of foreign cultures and countries, and he has emphasized the role of geography in this understanding:

The more I work in the social studies field the more convinced I become that geography is the foundation of all... When I begin work on a new area ... I invariably start with the best geography I can find.... I need to ground myself in the fundamentals which have governed and in a sense limited human development.... The virtue of the geographical approach is that it forces the reader to relate man to his environment. It forestalls loose generalization founded mainly on good intentions or hope. It gives a solid footing to speculation and it reminds the reader that he is dealing with real human beings who are just as circumscribed as he.... With the growing emphasis on ecology and related problems of the environment, geography will undoubtedly grow in importance and relevance.... I suppose that my books on Hawaii, Israel and Spain have won a rather wide readership primarily because my work—carried on over periods of many years—has provided a solid tactile base for what I had to say. My characters were not drifting in space; they were rooted in the ground.[6]

International Characteristics of Geography

Geography illuminates many aspects of the world in which we live, and it can make strong and necessary contributions to international knowledge. Some particular contributions of the discipline follow

- Geography clarifies the interrelationships and associations in and among specific habitats on the face of the globe because it deals with the totality of human-land relations that require knowledge of natural resources and their physical and biological environments on one hand, and of societies, cultures, and economies on the other.

- Geography portrays location and its significance on thematic maps that show more accurately than any other portrayal the important relationships to other places. These powerful tools clarify many important and fundamental relationships.

- Geography focuses on how constituent parts of the world differ from one another in their associated resources, cultures, and economies. Through regional geography we can develop an appreciation of the rich diversity of the world and the reasons for differences among countries and regions.

- Geography studies how commodities, capital, ideas, and political influences move between and among nations. Geography thereby demonstrates how distances, routes, and transport modes influence the relations among countries of the world.

- Geography views the earth as a unit and puts individual countries, regions, and problems in a world context.

Environment and Society

Geography is unusual among social sciences, and among the sciences generally, in its concern with the interconnections between the environment and society, and between resources and the economy. Geographers regard the bio-physical realm as equal to the nation-state in the ways nations conduct their daily affairs. The anthropologist Robert H. Lowie saw clearly the importance of natural conditions for culture: "Everything that contributes to our insight into the conditions offered by nature deepens our insights into the character of culture."[7]

Because nations and their people gather, modify, and exchange resources within and among the world's patterns of human settlement, geographers use these patterns as a basic context for study. Locations of resources and other phenomena are matters of profound importance within the framework of human settlements. Significant also are the people's perceptions of resources they use to fashion a livelihood, and these resources include both natural features and the accumulated physical and cultural structures.

In studying the interrelationships of environment and society, geographers draw on their own field observations and on the findings of other physical and social scientists to create an integrated understanding of the environment used by human groups. Through field investigations and case studies geographers can both perceive and demonstrate how a place functions, whether it be a ranch, a coffee estate, a village, an urban "commuter field," or larger parts of the earth, such as provinces or nations.

Geographers are also alert to economic and social relationships that extend beyond the immediate area where environment and society interact. If sheep are overgrazing certain areas of Iran, it may be because there is a large market for karakul coats in Europe and prices for skins there are high, rather than because of an inherent local imbalance between stock-keeping and pasturage. Local circumstances alone can seldom explain the human use of environment and the environment-society interrelationships in a place. In studying the environment and society, geographers constantly discover and follow threads of connection that link people and places everywhere.

Maps and Location

The geographer is expert in constructing and using maps that depict locations and distributions. The map itself serves as a concrete example of how different the world looks from different angles. It is important to note that each country sees the world from the viewpoint of its own locations, history, economy, and culture.

A map is not scenery; it is not a decoration to be hung on the wall behind the news announcer or placed on book covers. The map is a tool that helps each of us gain a concrete understanding of relationships that places have with other places and the relationships that societies have with environment and resources.

Yet we receive constant reminders of how ignorance and wisdom coexist. The *North–South* (or Brandt Commission) report contains much that is perceptive, useful, and well reasoned. Nevertheless, the map chosen for its cover, land in bright red with a black boundary dividing countries of the "North" from those of the "South," leaves much to be desired. Inside the cover is the following statement: "The map on the front cover is based upon the Peters Projection rather than the more familiar Mercator Projection." It then claims that the "projection represents an important step away from the prevailing Eurocentric geographical and cultural concept of the world," but this projection is neither more nor less Eurocentric than Mercator's, nor is any other. Mapmakers can put any place at the center of the world.

Since the earth is a sphere, no flat map can depict at the same time true areas, true angles or direction, true distances, and true shapes. Only a globe can accurately show them all at once. In a flat map one must choose which quality is important for a specific purpose, either for the whole world or for parts of it. Once the purpose is clear, the geographer or cartographer can select or design the projection that best serves this purpose.

As a visual device, the map appeals to our mind's need to integrate and synthesize knowledge. Its value is that it says things to us in a different, non-verbal way. It tells us things we cannot know in other ways, and it does it all with amazing economy.

The marriage of computer technology with map generation has made it possible for maps to illustrate particular points and with minimal delay and cost.[8] For example, figure 1 was generated and posted in one geography department within one hour of the announcement of the release of the American hostages being held in Iran. In real time one could trace their path as they returned to the United States over several days in January 1981.

The azimuthal equidistant projection shows true direction, distance, and path from one place on the globe to other places and presents one picture of accessibility of the world to the given center. Figure 2 presents the world as seen from Moscow. The map shows the distance and shortest route over land and water surfaces one would follow in a direct flight from Moscow to other parts of the globe. North America lies on the other side of Scandinavia and Greenland. Figure 3 presents the world as seen from Beijing (Peking) with Japan and mainland Asia nearby, and the United States beyond Siberia, Alaska, and Canada. Figure 4 shows the world in relation to Washington, D.C. Leaders of the Soviet Union, China, and the United States see the world from very different angles, physically as well as politically.

37

Figure 1. Route of the hostages, 20 January 1981.
Computer-generated two-point equidistant projection aligned on Washington, D.C., and Tehran.

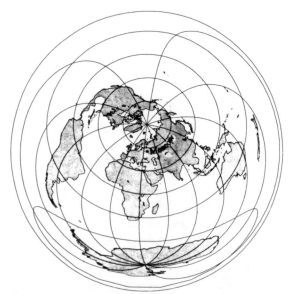

Figure 2.
Computer-generated azimuthal equidistant projection centered on Moscow.

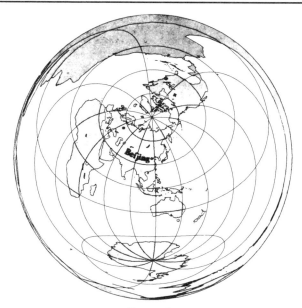

Figure 3.
Azimuthal equidistant projection centered on Beijing, Peoples' Republic of China.

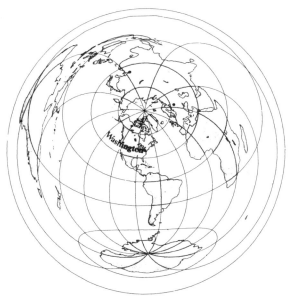

Figure 4.
Azimuthal equidistant projection centered on Washington, D.C.

Maps are major tools for understanding many types of relationships in specific places. Figure 5 portrays vividly the high degree of concentration of

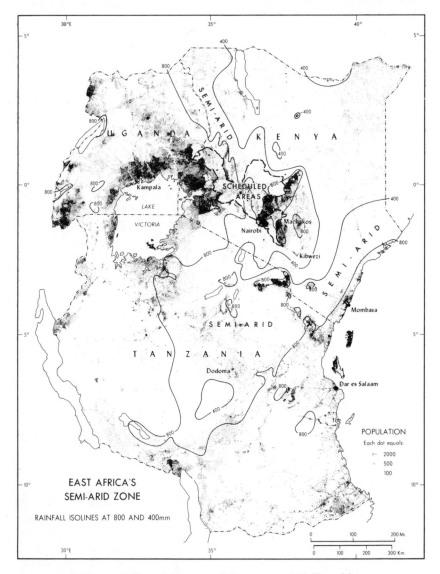

Figure 5. Population in relation to rainfall, East Africa

population in three countries of East Africa: Kenya, Tanzania, and Uganda. This map poses a major question: Why is the distribution of population so very irregular, with heavy concentrations in some areas separated by vast thinly populated stretches? Without the map we may not be sufficiently aware of the concentration or be inspired to study the relationship with other phenomena, such as the role of farm size and economic viability, land ownership, population pressure, agricultural productivity, and particularly the amount of rainfall.

The World Bank has introduced a new type of map based on LANDSAT images. These maps depict land cover or land use and serve as geo-data bases for regional planning. Compared with maps compiled in traditional ways, they are inexpensive and quick to produce and are especially valuable in providing cartographic information for many poorly-mapped overseas areas. The World Bank has produced such maps for the state of Orissa, in India, for Nepal, and for Bangladesh.[9]

Maps such as these pose serious questions about the relationships among peoples, among countries, and between environment and society. The essential point is that the map is a multi-faceted tool. A thorough knowledge of its versatility can help us gain a correspondingly thorough knowledge and understanding of our world.

Realms and Regions

From maps, which depict location, relative position, and associated phenom-ena, it is logical to consider another key concept in geography: the region, which integrates in a specific area the diverse physical and human phenomena that vary markedly in their distribution and expression on the surface of the earth.

Regional geography courses have long been a cornerstone of under-graduate geographic education, and the idea that one might become an "area specialist" often is born in classes of this kind. At the introductory level these tend to take the form of comprehensive "world regional" overviews, in which students gain a broad, highly generalized perspective on the great geographic realms. At upper levels such courses focus upon individual realms, such as Southeast Asia or Africa south of the Sahara, and their characteristics.

The regional tradition of geography contributes enormously to a better understanding of the world by students whose education otherwise includes only limited systematic study of foreign areas. Classical regional geography has among its merits the integration of information about environments as well as societies, so that students can begin to comprehend the ways that people with different cultures and in various environments organize themselves and their activities spatially. A sizeable and distinguished literature reflect this preoccupation.

41

Periods of intense intellectual ferment have often stirred geography. During the 1950s and 1960s, regional geography underwent intense examination and to some extent geographers diverted attention and energies to other subfields of geography.[10] Geographers questioned whether possible ethnocentrism colored their studies or whether long-held generalizations were still valid. As courses in regional geography were curtailed, thousands of students lost the opportunity to turn to it for a spatial orientation to the world realms in which they might be developing an interest.

The intense examination of regional geography's content and philosophy resulted in some positive changes: increasing the emphasis on field work, improving language competence, and establishing stronger affiliations with area programs. The reinvigorated regional geography emerged unmatched as a vehicle to convey world understanding. The fundamental world-regional framework that identifies major geographic realms continues to constitute a powerful pedagogic device. Regional studies confirm essential homogeneities and highlight internal diversities; they can be based effectively upon a prodigious array of both topical and sub-regional studies done by geographers in the field. Regional geography examines dominant as well as exceptional environments at various scales; it affords opportunities for comparative study (for example, of cultural adaptation to similar environments in widely separated areas of the world); it is surely the most relevant approach to problems of resource distribution and consumption; it provides insights into forces behind the location of economic activities; and it creates a substantive background for any understanding of spatial-political accommodation. Primarily, however, regional geography reveals that, in a world of change and interaction, traditions remain strong, retain their distinctions, and attitudes and values often differ sharply from those held in the United States.

Regional geography can also contribute to international studies in the abstract, by developing an appreciation and respectful understanding of the achievements and problems of societies and cultures other than one's own. Comprehending crucial aspects of the historic development, and, more importantly, of the spatial legacy of colonialism in Africa is fundamental to assessing the obstacles to future development faced by African states. The regional configurations defined by the federal map of India can be appreciated no better than through a geographical view of India's internal diversity.

Spatial Interaction

It is hardly necessary to underscore the interconnectedness of the modern world, but in the context of international education it is appropriate to emphasize geography's long-term concern with "spatial interaction."

The study of spatial interaction involves analyzing flows, interdependence, underlying structures, and actual and potential scarcity of resources. Resource location and movement is central to understanding even the broadest outlines of interactance networks. The geography of energy, in an international context, is the geography of highly localized resources, of vulnerable pipelines, narrow straits, and great distances between producing and consuming areas, of increasingly inaccessible reserves, of sharp differences in cultures, economies, and policies, as well as of the patterns of production and consumption.

An intricate structure of relationships exists among participants in international trade, a structure that is under stress from various directions. In the United States partial dependence upon imported oil is currently a primary concern: policy mistakes (made in ignorance of political and cultural realities in foreign areas) have especially serious consequences. The United States also imports large quantities of strategic minerals, some of them from areas undergoing major political-ideological change (Zimbabwe, Namibia). Again, the geographic perspective is crucial, relating economic matters to political, ideological, and spatial ones.

Geographic manifestations of world interaction include not only the movement of fuels, minerals, and manufactured products but also the production and distribution of food (like energy, a potential strategic weapon), the development of a variety of international alliances and blocs, the extension of national jurisdiction over maritime areas, the growing international competition in the Antarctic, and the changing functions of international political boundaries. The slogan, "a bushel for a barrel," widely voiced during the frustrations of the energy crisis of the early 1970s, oversimplifies a dangerous and one-sided (i.e., non-geographic) view of world production. The ideas behind such a slogan erroneously limit the alternatives available to OPEC countries not only for selling their petroleum but also for importing food. Above-average grain harvests in exporting countries such as Argentina and Australia can dramatically minimize the impact of food as an American political instrument. A geographic perspective is necessary to understand correctly the long-term global distribution systems.

The rising pressure on known and accessible natural resources has opened an era of seabed exploration and exploitation that is changing both the economic and political world map. The North Sea has become virtually occupied territory, studded by oil-drilling platforms and crossed by an expanding network of pipelines. In effect, the political map of Western Europe is being redrawn as Norway's boundary with the United Kingdom on the continental shelf takes on a significance comparable to its land boundary with Sweden. The seaward rush has extended maritime jurisdictions so that a worldwide, 200-mile Exclusive Economic Zone is about to make its appearance, possibly a forerunner of 200-mile maritime sovereignties. Already a further step—the mid-ocean median line—has been mooted. This comparatively quiet territorial transformation is now extending into the Antarctic, where national claims (in abeyance since the signing of the Antarctic Treaty) may soon renew their appearance on land as well as at sea. Unchecked exploitation of maritime fauna in Antarctic seas may disturb and endanger marine food webs throughout the world.

The formation of groups of states is transforming the world map. The concept of international associations for cooperative purposes is not new, but the number and types of blocs, unions, alliances, and other international organizations is unprecedented. The geography of supra-nationalism reveals changing realms of the world, resulting in large measure from interstate economic, political, cultural, and strategic associations. One significant result involves the changing functions of certain international boundaries. Thus political boundaries within international blocs tend to display functional decline, whereas boundaries between blocs become more divisive (and are often marked by barriers against movement). States acting in unison, such as the Association of South East Asian Nations (ASEAN), can have far-reaching effects on international affairs. A Nigeria-led Organization of African Unity (OAU) may yet pose a more powerful challenge to South Africa than might any individual or front-line group of states. International organizations extend the "reach" of strong states and augment the position of less influential countries; they constitute a growing element in global interaction.

World interaction affects everyone. A frost in Brazil raises coffee prices in the United States; a strike in Africa's Copperbelt affects American metal producers. A poor wheat harvest in the United States and Canada threatens the hungry of South Asia and may reduce the quality of the diet in the Soviet Union. A host of geographic studies of such relationships give proof of the discipline's usefulness in this aspect of international education.

Global Perspectives

Geographers are not only trained in working with a global scale, but are also comfortable in such work. According to the National Council for the Social Studies, "Global education refers to efforts to cultivate in young people a perspective of the world which emphasizes the interconnections among cultures, species, and the planet. The purpose of global education is to develop in youth the knowledge, skills, and attitudes needed to live effectively in a world possessing limited natural resources and characterized by ethnic diversity, cultural pluralism, and increasing interdependence."[11] Geographic learning is essential to global education.

Of all the social and natural sciences, geography has perhaps the strongest international, global tradition. This results in part from the early roles of geographers as explorers and cartographers, and it has been sustained through the discipline's twentieth-century modernizations. The relationships between human societies and natural environments were first studied at global scales, and from these speculative efforts there developed the clear need for greater objectivity through measurement and classification. World climatic, pedologic, and biotic schemata evolved from these early regionalizations, and these have been revised and refined numerous times. Students thus acquire a global functional-regional overview at the outset of their undergraduate education, because virtually every introductory sequence (whether physical or human geography) incorporates a world perspective.

Geography has benefitted from a number of long-continuing discussions arising from global assessments. Models and theories developed from localized data are tested in broader context.[12] These ideas were—and continue to be—studied not only as theoretical constructs but also for their illumination of the world at large.

Geography's global perspective continues in upper-level education as well as in introductory studies. The systematic subfields of geography (whether political, cultural, economic, medical, urban, or agricultural) place their subject matter in an international context, thus promoting global communication and understanding. Professional geographers working in international spheres have been trained in both regional and topical fields of specialization. A cadre of university and college faculty with experience in foreign areas exists with considerable international experience and with knowledge of one or more foreign languages. During the 1960s, when international studies centers and programs emerged in many institutions of higher learning, this international tradition of geography proved a valuable asset. It is an asset to be exploited again in a time when international understanding must be strengthened in both the pre-college and the college curricula.

Contributions of Geographic Curricula to International Studies

Developing a world citizenship perspective is a major goal of educational institutions in a global age.[13] The rest of the world increasingly affects the lives of Americans as the behaviors of Americans affect other nationalities. Decisions and behaviors of one group have both transnational and transgenerational consequences. A well-educated person needs to make judgments in managing cultural diversity and change; managing human-environment relations; managing population growth and the inequities in the distribution of well-being,

power, and safety; and managing conflict and violence.[14] Geographic education contributes heavily to the ability to make such judgments.

As part of its project on Education and the World View, the Council on
Learning commissioned the Educational Testing Service to conduct a Survey
of Global Understanding with a nationally representative random sample of
3,000 undergraduate students at 185 colleges and universities.[15] Although an
interdisciplinary committee developed the survey, it nevertheless contained a
large amount of what geographers teach in college courses.[16] Yet the survey
revealed that college seniors averaged only half a geography course per student
and that sixty percent of the students had taken no college geography courses.
The entire student sample (equally composed of two-year college students and
freshmen and seniors in four-year institutions) averaged only forty-three percent correct answers on a global understanding test and seniors alone scored
only fifty percent correct, not a particularly satisfying result.[17] A clear need
exists for a more substantial role for geography in the curriculum of American
schools and colleges.

As The Atlantic Council of the United States observed: "The work of the
President's Commission on Foreign Language and International Studies, and
surveys by the former Office of Education, the Educational Testing Service, the
Council on Learning, and others have all revealed a frightening degree of
ignorance, even on the parts of university and graduate students, of the
contemporary world around us. They have revealed grave deficiencies in
knowledge of geography, any foreign language, basic political science,
economics, and modern history, especially recent history which bears so heavily
upon the coming years."[18] And the report continues, "There is unnecessary
ignorance of geography."[19]

John W. Studebaker, former United States Commissioner of Education,
some years ago recommended that "throughout the secondary schools and in
the colleges and universities a real emphasis now be laid upon acquainting the
American citizens with the realities of the world through intensive courses in
world geography."[20]

Geographic education contributes toward preparing students for two overlapping roles: as world citizens in a democratic society and as professionals
trained for international work.[21]

World Citizens in a Democratic Society

A great number of societies compose the population of the world. The
societies differ from one another in attitudes, cultures, policies, economies, and
technologies, exist in a variety of bio-physical environments, and have varied
interconnections. These important differences have evolved as the products of
adaptation to physical, cultural, and social environments, of the diffusion of

ideas and artifacts, of the mingling of peoples, and of independent invention. The human environments created and occupied by these societies are the result of both historical experiences in place and past migrations. Recognizing the historical reasons for certain events can make these events both more intelligible[22] and less threatening. Much political extremism derives from ignorance of things foreign.

Courses in cultural, social, and historical geography provide the background for thinking comparatively and for understanding more deeply the processes that lead to regional differentiation. Regional courses that concentrate on a particular cultural realm, such as Latin America or the Mediterranean world, provide a substantive introduction to setting societies in their landscapes and to the cultural, physical, and social systems functioning there. Experience shows that even one good course can provide students with new perspectives and deep insights.

The world's nations have become increasingly interdependent because limited and unevenly distributed resources mandate trade among nations. When supplies of some resources diminish, societies must select alternate resources in order to maintain standards of living. Changes in resource supply require internal shifts in labor organization, work sites, and even the capacity to do certain types of work. As a consequence, trading patterns among nations may shift and political alliances may change. Thus, the overall phenomenon of interdependency remains, although individual dependencies may change.

Studies in physical geography cast light on the causes of interdependency and explain its occurrence by addressing the distribution of the earth's physical and biological phenomena. Economic geography, transportation geography, spatial analysis, studies of resource use and management, and urban geography contribute further to understanding interdependence among nations and can also develop a sense of stewardship in the human use of the earth.

As the geographic scale of observation changes, so do perspectives. Controls on phenomena operating at local scales fade into insignificance when examined at global scales, whereas other correlations and inter-dependencies become evident. The advancing desert of the southern Sahara can decimate an entire nation's pastoral economy because these small nations on the Saharan border are already precariously close to being entirely desert. In larger nations, such a condition could be offset by the productivity of other humid areas within the nation's boundaries. Students gain practical experience in scale-change in cartography and in field courses and develop map-reading skills in geographic-techniques courses as well as in work associated with regional study.

Field work heightens appreciation of concrete realities and of problems with data, cultivates the development of techniques for systematically acquiring otherwise unavailable data, makes the student aware of the magnitude of the problem of compiling data, especially in the underdeveloped world, and reveals the limitations of existing data bases. Field work also focuses attention on mistakes that inevitably result from arbitrary decisions in classification. Indeed, field training can develop a healthy skepticism toward all published data. Extended field work abroad gives advanced students experience as aliens in exotic cultural and physical environments. The sense of "otherness" can provide students with the background for tolerating diversity as they meet people who hold value systems different from their own and who behave with different motivations. Students can be comfortable in dealing with people in other cultures without feeling compelled to imitate them.

Professionals in International Work

Geography is a necessary ingredient for training professionals to work abroad or with foreign nationals, or in other words, for all those engaged in international work. The study of geography and other social sciences can help professionals develop an understanding of the perceptions, world views, and value systems of other peoples of the world.

Americans need to know how other peoples perceive us, and our behavior toward the rest of the world must include this knowledge. Other societies behave differently than we do and their behavior results from their value systems. Because a nation's foreign policy derives fundamentally from its value system, it must consider how geosystems, biosystems, and cultural systems relate to ecological constraints. Economic strategists must know about resources and must recognize that those resources are products of cultural definition. Skills in air photo interpretation, remote sensing, topographic and thematic mapping, and courses in physical and economic geography and resource management help develop the ability to assess the resource base. Behavioral and social geography courses provide the tools to understand how perceptions, world views, and value systems affect the human use of resources.

Some International Applications of Geography

Geography is integral to effective international affairs. The products of geographic research can improve international business negotiations, supply needed dimensions in planning for economic, urban, and regional development throughout the world, and prepare individuals for government service abroad.

International Applications of Geography in Business

As many of the devastated countries recovered after World War II, the premier position of the United States became increasingly sensitive to competition from the international business ventures of other highly industrialized nations. These nations have challenged the virtual American monopolies in the automobile, electronics, chemical, and other highly technological information industries. Foreign manufacturers have reduced American comparative advantage by aggressive marketing initiatives and by sending business representatives abroad who are well versed in the cultures and languages of the countries they visit.[23] It would be erroneous to attribute the decline in the United States market share of overseas business solely to our inadequate foreign language capabilities or our limited geographical knowledge of other regions. Yet many corporate executives see these inadequacies as important factors in weakening American business performance in other countries.

Business executives have called upon universities to develop programs in international trade and business that would include such subjects as location theory, transportation systems, regional geography, and spatial problems of multinational operations, as well as the requisite training for business managers in marketing, economic analysis, finance, and management. To illustrate, the department of geography of the State University of New York at Buffalo, in cooperation with the School of Management, has developed two programs that fill this need. One program provides for a concentration on the geography of world trade and international business within the M.A. program in geography. The degree recipient receives the M.A. in geography and a certificate in the international trade concentration. The other is a joint degree program of the department of geography and the School of Management. This program requires 75 hours of graduate study, six graduate-level hours of a foreign language, and many management courses. Graduates of the program receive an M.B.A. and an M.A. in geography with international trade certification. Both programs require an internship with a firm engaged in international trade.

According to James E. McConnell, professor of geography and coordinator of the international trade concentration at the State University of New York at Buffalo, the response to the program is encouraging, and local corporations request graduate interns to help them with a variety of problems. The international business community has offered regular fellowship monies to support the program and also supplies guest lecturers. McConnell gauges the success of the program by the positive response he has received: "We have evidence of people in jobs; we continue to receive financial and moral support from the Buffalo World Trade Association; and we are getting support from the Department and the Dean."[24] The department also has received many inquiries from other departments and institutions.

Geography in Planning for Economic, Urban, and Regional Development

Economic development, urbanization, and regional progress are closely interrelated and can be treated together.

> The competent geographer has the ideas, tools, and experience to make substantial contributions to the understanding of the *economic development* process wherever it may occur.... In a very substantial sense, studies of the *economic development process are studies of society as a whole, and to this study geography can be said to bring both a focus and a method*. Underlying geographic study is the basic assumption that the localized association of phenomena is significant to society, and one way of dealing with social problems in the broadest sense, whether economic, political, or more narrowly cultural, is to study these localized associations as they occur in reality and are related to each other. Geographers are more apt, and perhaps better trained, to deal with those associations which have a direct and manifest relationship with the occupance of the surface of the earth.[25]

Implicit in Norton Ginsburg's statement is the understanding that economic development is both continuing and geographically specific, that it has both temporal and ecological dimensions. Wealth and poverty, concomitants of development, tend to be highly localized. This is true not only at the local scale, where associations of people, resources, and activities meld into distinctive mini-systems, but also at regional, national, and supra-national scales. The world map of economic development, whether based upon a conventional measure such as gross national product per capita or upon some more complex synthesis of social and economic variables, displays a distinctive and variegated pattern, but that pattern is a far cry from the oversimplified thinking that partitions the globe into a so-called "North" and so-called "South." At the national scale, too, the developmental maps of India and China, for example, display similar variety, which reflects territorial differences in developmental process and attainment. Indeed, the distribution of wealth and poverty in the United States itself is geographically distinctive. Rather than "one nation indivisible," this country has marked regional differences in wealth; and Appalachia, the Indian reservation resource-poor areas with limited accessibility, and the slums of many northeastern cities stand out sharply as the backward areas of the most highly developed and wealthiest country on earth.

Such differences in development, wealth, poverty, and welfare require both description and explanation. Explanation in turn requires sophisticated conceptual and technical tools of spatial and non-spatial analysis. Both in their research and in their capacities as consultants and advisers, geographers have amply demonstrated their capacity for dealing with the complex issues that bear upon the wealth of nations and the internal variations within them, one of the great domestic and international problems of our time.

Invariably, economic development is associated with a world-wide process of societal transformation from rural to urban, a process involving shifts in occupational structure, greater areal specialization and interdependence, and higher income levels. Geographers have made many contributions studying the genesis and evolution of this process in the past and to planning for its future. Geographers have studied, for example, the development of areas of supply for the city, city-centered market areas, complex urban networks, interactions among cities, basic and non-basic components in the support of the city, land use, the city in relation to resources and location, problems such as pollution, congestion, housing, transportation, and growth poles in economic development and regional planning.

Careful geographical assessment of human and natural resources and the problems attendant on each of these is necessary for successful regional planning. Regional planning programs abound in both developed and underdeveloped nations, but it is among the latter that governments frequently call on foreign experts and aid to formulate and implement programs for development. In assessing planning needs in the developing countries, geographical expertise is almost a prerequisite for effectively appraising and analyzing human and natural resource systems and for providing locational parameters to guide the planning process.

Wolfram Drewes, a geographer and senior resource planner with the World Bank, has written that geographers must deal with basic questions about the location and quantification of natural resources. Geographers help in delimiting areas of need and in assessing the feasibility of developing small areas, larger functional regions, or river basins. Their knowledge of areas, societies, and languages helps them contribute effectively to regional planning.[26]

The contributions that a geographer can make to economic development and to urban and regional planning can be illustrated by the work in Indonesia of Brian J.L. Berry. Professor Berry has helped guide the South Sumatra Regional Development Project, evaluate urban public works proposed for a third five-year plan with increasing emphasis on equity goals, and develop guidelines for a national urban development strategy for the fourth five-year plan. He has written

> Whatever I provided that was creative and different in these ventures came from my background in geography: knowledge of regional systems, of the role of cartography in resource assessment and planning, of urban systems, and of urban geography. From geography, too, came an essential awareness of cultural differences.[27]

Government Service in International Fields

By virtue of their training in identifying patterns of human activities as they relate to natural and cultural environments, and their intensive knowledge of foreign areas, geographers are well prepared for government service in international fields. The best-trained among them are those who have specialized in specific regions of the world and have well-developed foreign language skills, along with systematic specialties. Geographers have distinguished themselves in government service in many countries and will continue to do so. Others may not serve abroad ordinarily, but are employed in a number of Federal agencies that deal with foreign area assessment, such as the Department of State, the Department of Commerce, the Agency for International Development, the Central and Defense Intelligence Agencies, and the Department of Agriculture.

Many geographers have served on missions to advise nations on their development strategies, on local and regional development problems, or on specific problems such as urban planning, industrial location, water supply and transfer, irrigation projects, afforestation and reforestation, population redistribution, transportation, and responses to natural hazards. Others work in a variety of supporting occupations as cartographers, educational consultants, survey consultants, or special library program advisers.

Geography in Liberal Education

In its summary statement, The Council on Learning's National Task Force on Education and the World View recommended a reemphasis in the secondary school curriculum on "social studies, history, geography, and foreign language arts," and for the college graduate "a deeper knowledge and understanding of another culture, as seen through its history, geography, language, literature, philosophy, economics, and politics."[28]

In today's highly interdependent world a liberal education should develop in each individual the realization that his or her own country, region, or ethnic, religious, social, or linguistic group is but one among many, each with differing characteristics, and that other countries, regions, or social groups are not necessarily odd, irrational, or inferior. We may argue that one cannot see one's own country and culture in perspective until one has studied other lands and peoples. Only then can one understand that one's own civilization is but one among a family of civilizations with common elements yet distinctive characteristics, evolving from common antecedents in different directions yet with much cultural borrowing, and facing similar problems yet with particular combinations of attitudes, policies, technologies, physical environments, and evolved economic systems.[29] Geography has a key role to play in developing such understanding.

Notes

[1] Archibald MacLeish, *Riders on the Earth* (Boston: Houghton Mifflin, 1978) p. xiv.

[2] *A Survey of Global Understanding* (Princeton, N.J.: Educational Testing Service, 1980); The Presidents Commission on Foreign Language and International Studies, *Strength through Wisdom: A Critique of U.S. Capability* (Washington, D.C.: GPO, 1979); *President's Commission on Foreign Language and International Studies; Background Papers and Studies* (Washington, D.C.: GPO, 1979); *New Directions in International Education, The Annals of the American Academy of Political and Social Science,* May 1980; Barbara B. Burn, *Expanding the International Dimension of Higher Education* (San Francisco: Jossey-Bass, 1980), a report prepared for the Carnegie Council on Policy Studies in Higher Education; and Paul Simon, *The Tongue-Tied American: Confronting the Foreign Language Crisis* (New York: Continuum, 1980).

[3] Thomas S. Barrows, Stephen F. Klein, and John L.D. Clark, *What College Students Know and Believe about Their World,* synopsis by Nathaniel Hartshorne (New Rochelle, N.Y.: Change, 1981), pp. 18–19, 22.

[4] Robert N. Saveland, ed., *Place Vocabulary Research Project, A Report to the Commission on Education of the International Geographical Union* (Athens, Georgia: U of Georgia, Geography Curriculum Project, 1980).

[5] *North-South: A Program for Survival,* The Report of the Independent Commission on International Development Issues under the Chairmanship of Willy Brandt (Cambridge, Mass.: MITP, 1980); Presidential Commission on World Hunger, *Overcoming World Hunger: The Challenge Ahead* (Washington, D.C.: GPO, 1980); The World Bank, *World Development Report* (Washington, D.C.: World Bank, 1980); and *The Global 2000 Report to the President: Entering the Twenty-First Century,* 3 vols. (Washington, D.C.: GPO, 1980).

[6] James A. Michener, "The Mature Social Studies Teacher,"*Social Education,* November 1970, pp. 764–65.

[7] Robert H. Lowie, *The History of Ethnological Theory* (New York: Farrar and Rinehart, 1937), pp. 261–62.

[8] The authors wish to express their appreciation to Philip M. Voxland, Director, Social Science Research Facilities Center, University of Minnesota, for compiling figures 1–4.

[9] International Bank for Reconstruction and Development, Agriculture and Rural Development Department, Economic and Resource Division, *Orissa, India, Land Cover—Land Use Association,* 1:1,000,000 (Washington D.C.: International Bank for Reconstruction and Development, 1977); idem, Resources Planning Unit, *Nepal,* 2 sheets, 1:500,000 (Washington, D.C.: World Bank, 1980); and Idem, *Bangladesh, Land Use Classification Related to Land Cover Reflections Obtained from Landsat Imagery,* map 2, 1:500,000 (Washington, D.C.: World Bank, 1981).

[10] Commission on College Geography, *Introductory Geography—Viewpoints and Themes,* CCG General Series 5 (Washington, D.C.: Association of American Geographers, 1967).

[11] *The Social Studies Professional* 59 (May 1981):5.

[12] J.H. von Thünen's nineteenth-century agricultural model, for example, was based on a single, market-oriented estate in Germany but proved applicable at regional

and even global levels. Among its leading merits is its provision of an organizational framework for learning. Certainly the wider applications of the von Thünen model are subject to discussion, and this discussion is itself instructive. Sir Halford Mackinder's "Heartland Theory," published in 1904, initiated a debate that has continued to this day. Ellsworth Huntington's environmentalism of the first half of the twentieth century produced counterarguments in a lengthy debate recently joined by sociobiologists. William Morris Davis's concept of a peneplanation process provided a universal for physical geography, and led to significant field research in many areas of the world. Walter Christaller's location theory sought spatial order in the relative position of central places in Germany but its regularities have been observed also in China.

[13] Lee Anderson and James Becker, "Global Perspectives in the Social Studies," *Journal of Research and Development in Education,* 13, no. 2 (1980):1.

[14] Charles W. Merrifield, "Development Ethics: A Functionalist View" (Paper delivered at the International Studies Association-West meeting, Portland, Oregon, March 1979).

[15] Thomas S. Barrows, et al., *College Students' Knowledge and Beliefs: A Survey of Global Understanding,* The Final Report of the Global Understanding Project, Educational Testing Service (New Rochelle, N.Y.: Change, 1981).

[16] A. David Hill, "A Survey of Global Understanding of American College Students: A Report to Geographers," *The Professional Geographer,* 33, no. 2 (1981):237–45.

[17] Ibid., p. 239.

[18] The Atlantic Council's Working Group on the Successor Generation, *The Successor Generation: Its Challenges and Responsibilities* (Washington, D.C.: The Atlantic Council of the United States, 1981), p. 13.

[19] Ibid., p. 17.

[20] "Dr. Studebaker Calls for Geography," *NCGE Perspective* (Newsletter of the National Council for Geographic Education)9, no. 5 (June 1981):6. The address was delivered at a National Conference of College and University Presidents, Baltimore, Maryland, 3–4 March 1942.

[21] International Geographical Union, Commission on Geographic Education, "Outline of Structure for the Handbook for Teachers on Implementing the Recommendation on Education for International Understanding, Cooperation, and Peace, and Education Relating to Human Rights and Fundamental Freedoms" (Mimeographed for the meeting for planning the Handbook, 8 December 1979), p. 3.

[22] Roger Scruton, "Humane Education," *American Scholar* 4 *(1980):498.*

[23] The President's Commission on Foreign Language and International Studies, *Strength through Wisdom,* p. 7.

[24] James E. McConnell to Salvatore J. Natoli, 11 February 1981.

[25] Norton S. Ginsburg, "Geographic Research Opportunities in the Field of Economic Development," *The Professional Geographer,* 5, no. 4 (July 1953):13, emphasis added. See also Norton Ginsburg, ed., *Essays on Geography and Economic Development,* Department of Geography, Research Paper 62 (Chicago: U of Chicago, 1969); and Norton Ginsburg, *Atlas of Economic Development* (Chicago: U of Chicago P, 1961).

[26] Wolfram U. Drewes, "Applied Geography in the Development of Latin America as Part of the Third World," in *Studying Latin America: Essays in Honor of Preston E.*

James, ed. David J. Robinson (Ann Arbor, Mich.: University Microfilms International for Department of Geography, Syracuse U, 1980), pp. 245–67.

[27] Brian J.L Berry to Harm J. de Blij, 2 March 1981. Professor Berry is dean of the school of urban and public affairs at Carnegie-Mellon U.

[28] Council on Learning, *Task Force Statement on Education and the World View* (New Rochelle, N.Y.: Council on Learning, 1981).

[29] Chauncy D. Harris, "The Geographic Study of Foreign Areas and Cultures in Liberal Education," in *Geography in Undergraduate Liberal Education,* A Report of the Geography in Liberal Education Project (Washington, D.C.: Association of American Geographers, 1965), p. 25.

Culture and Nationality

Marvin W. Mikesell

Whatever else may be said about the methods and objectives of geographical education, it is axiomatic that we should seek to make our perplexing world less perplexing.[1] Above all, we need to cultivate understandings that minimize the sense of bewilderment and dismay that Americans often experience when reading newspapers or listening to news broadcasts. To be sure, some categories of unwelcome news are so repetitive that they may be taken for granted. The Cold War, in spite of periodic phases of detente, has been a pervasive reality since 1945. Most Americans are also at least vaguely aware of the existence of a Third World, supposedly nonaligned, that is inspired by colonial grievances and unrealized (and maybe unrealizable) aspirations. Warfare fostered by territorial disputes, national anxiety generated by lack of access to vital resources, and revolutions led by "land reformers" seeking to oust "oligarchs" seem almost to be constants of the human condition. Although disquieting, such events and attitudes have a familiarity that breeds contempt. "So what else is new?"

Nationalism against the Nation State

Less well-known and hence more challenging to those who seek international understanding are problems created by the often discordant relationship between cultural identity and political jurisdiction. For example, of the many provocative maps in the *State of the World Atlas* (Kidron and Segal 1981) probably the most difficult for Americans to understand is the one devoted to "Nationalism against the Nation State." Very few of the 156 countries in our world are culturally homogeneous. In Europe only Denmark and Portugal lack significant minorities. In Africa, Tunisia is the only state blessed with such uniformity. And in Asia, Saudi Arabia and adjacent mini-states, Japan, and Korea are exceptions to a more general pattern of culturally complex states.

Marvin W. Mikesell is Professor of Geography at the University of Chicago.

North America has only one relatively homogeneous state (Costa Rica) and South America has only Uruguay and Chile that might be considered in this category. In fact, Iceland is the world's only clear case of "ethnic purity." These few examples are exceptions to a more general pattern of cultural complexity and current or potential cultural conflict. Americans accustomed to thinking of countries inhabited by specific peoples are ill-equipped to understand the pervasive importance of minority-group problems and so are likely to be shocked by news of language riots, religious persecution, and terrorist acts committed by previously unknown groups.

Confusion about who might be regarded as "good guys" or "bad guys" in Lebanon is a compelling current illustration of this dilemma. If Lebanon had only two contending groups we might attempt an extrapolation from the Cold War and speak of "right" or "left" (i.e., "wrong") Lebanese. In fact, Lebanon has six contending groups (Maronite, Greek Catholic and Greek Orthodox Christians, Sunni and Shia Muslims, and Druze) and none of them is inspired by attitudes or aspirations that fit our dichotomous view of the world. The sense in which Lebanese are in fact Lebanese is both the essence of their problem and the basis of our confusion.

As an unsuccessful experiment in pluralistic theocracy, Lebanon may be the extreme example of a non-nation state. Yet it is no more than an exaggerated illustration of the ethnic disparity found in many other countries. Why is this reality so difficult for Americans to comprehend? One reason has already been suggested: our instinctive tendency to associate countries with people: Belgium with Belgians, Italy with Italians, and so on. Recognition that countries may have more than one distinctive group (e.g., Flemings and Walloons in the case of Belgium) is seldom evident among Americans. Hence we may be surprised to learn that there is cultural tension in Belgium and are sure to be baffled when Italians claim to be Aostans, Friulans, Sards, and Tyroleans. An additional difficulty is created by the naive assumption that culturally complex countries must be comparable to the American "melting pot." In fact, the melting pot analogy does not fit even the American experience very well, because many of our ethnic groups are not immigrants in the process of assimilation (e.g., Puerto Ricans, French-speakers in Louisiana, Indians wherever they are found) and the blending process is never complete. Use of a "salad bowl"analogy would be more helpful, not only in our context but also in reference to other New World countries that have both immigrant and native "subcultures."

One might expect to find conceptual frameworks in our scholarly literature that enhance understanding of cultural complexity. In fact, the concepts most widely used are ill-suited to a world in which contending cultures threaten the cohesion of states. On close examination, images of harmonious "dual," "plural," or "mosaic" societies prove to be no more helpful than the melting-pot image of American society. It follows that the issue of cultural complexity should be confronted directly and not by use of misleading analogies designed to mask or minimize complexity. At the risk of violating the "eleventh commandment" of academic behavior I can also assert (reluctantly and with some personal embarrassment) that the understanding we should promote will require abandonment of a lot of professional baggage. Cultural geography must be devoted to cultures and not to landscapes created by robots. Regional geography must offer more than *a priori* wisdom. And theoretical human geography must be or at least try to be more than a surrogate for chess.

A Possible Program

Lists of States

For teachers who wish to deal directly with the cultural dimension of world geography, a program can be recommended that should serve as an antidote for the shock mentioned previously. It is best to begin by compiling a list of the world's many countries. At first thought this prospect may seem forbidding. In fact, 156 country names would not exceed the capacity of a typical blackboard or a few sheets of paper. Once compiled this list can be annotated by use of the *Statesman's Yearbook* and encylopedias so that knowledge is gained of the cultural groups found in particular states. This exercise will produce evidence that only about 10 states lack conspicuous minorites. Students who have done their homework well may argue about the "purity" of even these states. Chile has some Indians, Denmark has a small German minority, Japan has Korean immigrants and the Ainu, Portugal has refugees from its former African colonies, Saudi Arabia has many foreign laborers, and Tunisia has several communities of persistent Berber speech. Only Iceland is likely to survive critical scrutiny. In any event, the purpose of the exercise would be not to challenge the exceptions but rather to provide the rule: most of the world's countries have more than one linguistic or religious group.

Ethnic Groups

Having progressed this far it will be well to raise the question of how many linguistic or religious groups can be identified in the world. A return visit to encyclopedias and other sources of general information, such as Murdock's *Ethnographic Atlas* (1967), will produce estimates ranging from a few hundred to over a thousand. Comparison of Murdock's figure for well recognized societies with the countries described in the *Statesman's Yearbook* yields an arresting fraction: 156/862. Once recorded this fraction is sure to invite speculation on how the gap between numerator and denominator might be reduced. Attempts to adjust political jurisdiction to reflect cultural reality will generate new and more heated debates. One might start by eliminating Belgium or by breaking Yugoslavia into its several ethnic components. In either case, the problem seemingly solved would be balanced by new and perhaps unexpected problems. For example, annexation of the Flemish part of Belgium by the Netherlands would add several million Catholics to a predominantly Protestant country. And what would be the fate of an independent Slovenia? If thought is shifted to world scale most students will concede that substantial reduction of the cultural/political fraction could be accomplished only by a new era of imperialism or world war.

Cultural Conflict

Acceptance of the current world order should lead to serious study of the problems inherent in that order. The next stage in the program might be a compilation of current or recent cases of cultural conflict. Examples of "subordinate" groups that have, for various reasons, become "insubordinate" are easy to find: Basques in Spain, Croats in Yugoslavia, Arabs in Israel, Tamils in Sri Lanka, Magyars in Romania, Catholics in Ulster, Sikhs in India, Muslims in the Philippines, Kurds in Iran, French separatists in Canada, and so on. Indeed, some countries have several contending groups, e.g., Afghanistan, Burma, India, Lebanon, Yugoslavia. The situation in the USSR, where language is the basis of identity and religion is denied official recognition, is sure to inspire special comment. Contrary examples where religion rather than language is the basis of identity and a source of present or potential conflict can also be found, e.g., Cyprus before partition, India, Lebanon, Nigeria, and several other countries.

Group Reports

Sooner or later (and preferably sooner) students should be encouraged to read about and report on specific groups. Information will be easy to find on some often-studied groups: Basques, French Canadians, Flemings or Walloons, Kurds, North American Indians, Palestinians, and "Orange" and "Green" Irishmen. In each of these cases diligent research should produce data on the size and distribution of the group, evidence of contentment or discontent, and suggestions of either permissive or repressive government policies. Reports will tend to be anecdotal and repetitive and so provide a foundation for comparison. I have suggested elsewhere (Mikesell 1983) that dissidence usually reflects frustration, i.e., "wanting in" or "wanting out" of a larger society. In the former, publications often display a set of diagnostic terms: "recognition," "access," "participation." In the latter, the corresponding terms are "autonomy," "separation," "independence." Minority groups are often divided into two factions with one operating above ground and advocating the first set of goals and another operating below ground and devoted to the latter goals. Confusion of aspiration may also be evident, and some groups, like the Shi'ites of Lebanon, are just "Mad as Hell and Not Going to Take it Anymore!" Discontent may become so pronounced and frustration so persistent that terrorist acts may be undertaken, e.g., skyjacking, sabotage, assassination. Needless to say, terrorism is not on the agenda of most geography teachers. It is, alas, a legitimate topic in human and certainly cultural geography—and something Americans need to try to understand. That acts of desperation and vindictiveness are far from the norms of human behavior does not make them unpredictable or even rare.

The Ideal and Reality

Excursions into the realm of "cultural pathology" can and should be balanced by consideration of what constitutes relative health. Although most countries have minorities, not all have serious problems. In addition to Switzerland, that often cited and nearly ideal case of harmonious pluralism, many other specific examples of relative harmony can be discovered. In fact, since cultural complexity can be a threat to national cohesion, most states have policies designed to prevent or at least minimize cultural discord: separation of church and state, bilingual education, affirmative action, local or regional autonomy, and so on. Students should be encouraged to speculate on what might constitute an ideal or workable policy. The merits and difficulties of bilingual education would be a good focus for debate.

In any instructional program that requires student initiative, it is difficult to predict results. Nevertheless, the program described would have the advantage of logical progression from the general to the particular and back to the general. It could also entail movement from naive idealism to harsh realities and then to a more realistic idealism. An exercise that begins with a blackboard full of country names, moves by stages to reports on particular groups and problems, and concludes with attempts to describe a model situation should have inherent, demonstrable merit. Interest in this ultra-relevant topic is sure to be evident. And, as the attached bibliography demonstrates, literature is abundant.

Special Problems

In the discussion offered thus far it has been assumed that treatment of culture and nationality demands student initiative as well as professional "performance." It may be doubted that this topic can be handled effectively by lectures alone. Student research, oral reports, and even debate are essential requirements along with comparison designed to prevent the effort from becoming purely anecdotal. It should also be noted that students will tend to become champions of the groups they select for study. Balanced, two-sided reports are not likely to be offered and if the group "adopted" has major complaints, the impinging government will usually be denounced as "oppressive" or "insensitive." Nor are students reporting on secessionist movements likely to recall the attitude that prevailed north of the Mason-Dixon line on the eve of our Civil War.

More serious is the problem of dealing intelligently rather than piously with evidence of cultural prejudice. Majorities often really are "silent," and the literature that reflects their views is both hard to find and embarrassing to recommend. For example, it is doubtful that many teachers would feel comfortable leading a discussion keyed to the angry complaints presented in Wilmot Robertson's *The Dispossessed Majority* (1976). Conversely, works designed to expose prejudice as an unnecessary evil or a product of ignorance usually fail to appreciate the power of "cultural patriotism." The presence in any country of mavericks unwilling to accept the mores of the national culture is likely to provoke feelings of resentment. The liberal doctrine of inherent good will is at best a weak analytical tool. Nor is it realistic to expect that sub-national identity should be abandoned in the cause of some larger national identity. The tension found on most cultural frontiers may well be a constant of the human condition.

These pessimistic remarks do not mean that problem solving and search for conflict-avoidance strategies should be dismissed from the agenda of courses or seminars devoted to culture and nationality. The fact that *all* problems cannot be solved does not mean that *some* cannot be solved. It is essential in class discussions to press for specific recommendations even in cases, such as the Arab-Israeli conflict, that seem at present to be hopeless. A good device to encourage such recommendations is to ask students to direct their attention not to a present contentious generation but rather to a less handicapped and even hypothetical future generation. One can also assume, as an exercise in imagination, that governments might be more intelligent or judicious than they usually are and try to prevent rather than provoke conflicts.

We must also acknowledge that the literature on culture and nationality although abundant, as the attached list suggests, is still "immature" in many respects and sprawls over several disciplines. The immaturity of the literature is suggested by a plethora of edited compilations and a scarcity of coherent works by single authors. There is no textbook on this topic, and no discipline has mastered its inherent complexities. Maps are another perplexing program. The only comprehensive work, *Atlas Narodov Mira* (1964), is out of print and, for most teachers hopelessly Cyrillic. Yet, maps can be found and criticized, which is the fate one should expect of analytical tools. That balanced, two-sided accounts of cultural discord are hard to find can also be regarded as an asset, for awareness of this reality is in itself a valuable lesson.

Cultural Hierarchy

Geographers are accustomed, indeed programmed, to appreciate the importance of scale. They are also prone in their analytical efforts to see or construct hierarchies. The notion of a settlement or central-place hierarchy is well known. The notion of a hierarchy of cultural affiliation is less well known and is seldom suggested in our literature. The idea is easy for students to comprehend, because they have no difficulty identifying realms or levels of culture that influence their own lives. Language, religion, and community or professional attachments are usually announced without hesitation. The highest level, scale, or cultural affiliation that most students can recognize is nationality. Some may also have a vague awareness of their participation in Western civilization or the influence on their lives of Judeo-Christian doctrine. If so, they will be able to appreciate that they would feel more comfortable in a Sicilian or even Bulgarian village than in a comparable settlement in Maharashtra or Zimbabwe. Still, country affiliation is the scale or level that students are best able to understand.

Given this understanding, the problems implicit in the study of culture and nationality can be summarized in a single thought: not all people are comfortable in their country "box." Some indeed may be acutely uncomfortable and may refuse even to recognize the legitimacy of the box. To express the same thought differently, some people are unable to accept that their particular cultural identity should be superseded by a higher level of identity. In some cases this difficulty is easy to explain. For example, Kurds want to have their own country and dislike being identified as Turks, Syrians, Iraqis, or Iranians. Nor are Palestinians able or willing to think of themselves as Israelis. Some countries have the advantage of a neutral designation, which does not imply subordination. Thus Welsh freely admit that they are British but refuse to be identified as English. Similarly, Basques and Catalans can be and indeed are Iberians but refuse to be labeled as Spaniards.

For governments seeking to maintain an essential degree of national cohesion the difficulties created by subordinate groups who refuse to accept a large affiliation (and hence become insubordinate) can be acute. If such people are suppressed, their sense of sub-national or anti-national awareness is likely to increase rather than decrease. If the distinction between "we" and "they" is exacerbated by awareness of the distinction between "have not" and "have," such groups may turn to a-cultural and anti-cultural ideology, e.g., Marxism.

Models of such behavior are easy to construct. It is more difficult to predict the acceptance or rejection of the position assigned to a group in a cultural hierarchy. For example, Alsatians, who speak a dialect of German, not only accept but are proud of their participation in French culture, whereas Bretons, who seldom speak more than French, may be reluctant to accept this affiliation.

That French Canadians living outside Quebec feel more Canadian than those in Quebec presents fewer problems for research or imagination. In any case, the concept of a hierarchy of cultural affiliation offers numerous attractive opportunities in the study of the often uncomfortable relationship between political jurisdiction and linguistic or religious distributions. For governments, the challenge presented by minority groups is both simple and complicated: how to prevent minorities from challenging the integrative or suppressive authority of the state. As indicated earlier, only about 10 of the 156 countries in the world are totally free of this problem.

Perplexing Questions

In the courses or seminars devoted to problems of great inherent complexity, success can be measured by the quality of questions. The following questions posed recently by my students are especially perplexing:

1. With so few real nation states in the world, how can one explain the pervasive force of nationalism?

2. Is the force (and indeed the curse) of nationalism a manifestation of megalomania or of paranoia?

3. If, as Marxists believe, it is economic or class conflict that turns the wheels of modern history, how can one explain the frequency and currency of linguistic and religious conflict?

4. Is the liberal doctrine of inherent good will an operational concept or merely an illusion that is dispelled once we become aware of the tension that seems always to be evident on cultural frontiers?

5. Can successful minority-group policies be acclaimed as transferable models or must each state and each sub-state or multi-state group proceed on the basis of trial and error?

6. If the number of states is too small to provide comfortable accommodation for the much larger number of societies, how can the tension inherent in this discordant relationship be reduced?

7. Is it conceivable in some future time (i.e., AD 2084) that a more enlightened world will accept the prospect of "trial separation" or "no-fault divorce" for unhappy cultural unions, especially those accomplished with the aid of a "shotgun"?

To suggest that these questions are perplexing is not to deny the value of the partial wisdom that is implicit in their content and tone. The study of culture and nationality will never be a direct or easy route to international understanding. The subject is distressing in many ways and seldom inspires positive feelings about human nature. This somber thought can be muted by the realization that it is an imperfect "real world" that we are obliged to live in and should try to understand. The fact that most country boxes have "apples" and "oranges" in them (and some may have hand grenades) is a compelling reality that we and our students may hope to see with unusual clarity and analyze with appropriate skill.

Bibliography[1]

At first glance the appended bibliography may seem overwhelming, for the works cited reflect the perspectives of several disciplines, and their number would exceed the grasp of even unusually diligent students. In fact, the list only hints at the rich resources that are available. The most useful resource for class use is the series of pamphlets issued by the London-based Minority Rights Group (36 Craven Street, London WC2N 5NG, UK). These include accounts of specific groups (e.g., Armenians, Baha'is, Tibetans, and so on) and also more general or generic essays, such as "Teaching about Prejudice," "Constitutional Law and Minorities," and "Latin American Women." The Minority Rights Group has also published a three-volume inventory (Ashworth 1980) that includes a rich store of information and suggestions for further reading. The most important scholarly journal devoted to the topic of this essay is the *Canadian Review of Studies in Nationalism*, (University of Prince Edward Island, Charlottetown, PEI C1A 4P3, Canada).

No work can be adopted as a textbook. Crawford Young's *The Politics of Cultural Pluralism* (1976) and Philip Mason's *Patterns of Dominance* (1971) may be the most useful single-authored books. Eric Fischer's *Minorities and Minority Problems* (1980) is comprehensive in scope but does not offer appropriate guidance to the relevant literature. The issues of the *Journal of International Affairs* devoted to political integration in "multinational states" and "multi-state nations" (Connelly 1973) are useful for orientation and definition.

As indicated previously, the fact that the bibliography includes so many edited compilations is a sign of the "immaturity" of the literature. Most of the works listed consist of unconnected case studies. The most rewarding are those edited by Esman (1977) and Heisler (1977). The single most impressive work in the bibliography is probably Stephens' monumental volume on *Linguistic Minorities in Western Europe* (1976). A minimal reading list is appended to my essay on "The Myth of the Nation State" (1983). The documentation offered with Knight's "Identity and Territory" (1982) is more extensive and more clearly reflects the interests of political geographers. That geographers have a long commitment to combined cultural and political study is suggested by the references to Dominian's pioneer work on *The Frontiers of Language and Nationality in Europe* (1917) and Wilkinson's *Maps and Politics* (1951). The anthologies edited by Evenden and Cunningham (1973), Williams (1982), and Boal and Douglas (1983) may indicate revival of this interest. The Discussion Papers in Geolinguistics, published in Britain in the North Staffordshire Polytechnic and edited by Williams, are a welcome recent innovation. Raitz's essay, "Ethnic Maps of North America" (1978), is a useful introduction to the broader topic of the art and science of ethnographic cartography. The best technical article, not listed in the bibliography, is Wilfred Krallert's "Methodische Probleme der Völker- und Sprachenkarten," pp. 99–120 in *International Yearbook of Cartography* (Chicago: Rand McNally, 1961).

Note

[1] I am indebted to John Hedstrom for an initial version of the attached bibliography and have also profited from reports offered since 1980 by students in courses and seminars devoted to the broad topic of this essay.

General

Agar, M. 1974. *Ethnography and Cognition*. Minneapolis: Burgess.

Atlas Narodov Mira. 1964. Moscow: Main Administration of Geodesy and Cartography.

Bertelsen, J. 1976. *The Palestinian Arabs: A Non-State Nation Systems Analysis*. Beverly Hills: Sage.

Birch, A. 1978. *Political Integration and Disintegration in the British Isles*. London: Allen and Unwin.

———. 1978. "Minority Nationalist Movements and Theories of Political Integration," *World Politics* 2:325-344.

Burks, R.V. 1973. *East European History: An Ethnic Approach*, AHA pamphlet 425. Washington D.C.: American Historical Association.

Connor, W. 1972. "Nation-Building or Nation-Destroying?", *World Politics* 2:319-55.

———. 1978. "A Nation is a Nation, is a State, is an Ethnic Group, is a...," *Ethnic and Radical Studies* 4:377-400.

Crane, R. 1967. "The Role of Ethnic Nationalism in the Modernization and Stabilization of the Third World," discussion paper HI-936-DP, Hudson Institute.

Davis, S. 1977. *Victims of the Miracle: Development and the Indians of Brazil*. New York: Cambridge UP.

Drummond, R. 1977. "Nationalism and Ethnic Demands: Some Speculation on a Congenial Note," *Canadian Journal of Political Science* 2:375-89.

Enloe, C. 1973. *Ethnic Conflict and Political Development*. Boston: Little, Brown.

———. 1980. *Police, Military, and Ethnicity: Foundations of State Power*. New Brunswick, N.J.: Transaction.

———. 1980. *Ethnic Soldiers: State Security in Divided Societies*. Athens, Ga.: U of Georgia P.

Gabel, J. 1975. *False Consciousness: An Essay on Reification*. New York: Harper and Row.

Gordon, M. 1978. *Human Nature, Class, and Ethnicity.* New York: Oxford UP.

Gross, F. 1966. *World Politics and Tension Areas.* New York: New York UP.

———. 1978. *Ethnics in a Borderland.* Westport, Conn.: Greenwood.

Grove, J. 1974. "Differential Political and Economic Patterns of Ethnic and Race Relations: A Cross-National Analysis," *Race*, 1:302–28.

Grove, J. 1977. "A Cross-National Examination of Cross-Cutting and Reinforcing Cultural Cleavages," *International Journal of Comparative Sociology* 4:217–27.

Hourani, A.H. 1947. *Minorities in the Arab World.* London: Oxford UP.

Isaacs, H. 1975. *Idols of the Tribe: Group Identity and Political Change.* New York: Harper and Row.

Isaacs, H. 1979. *Power and Identity: Tribalism and World Politics*, Headline Series 246. New York: Foreign Policy Association.

Isajiw, W. 1974. "Definitions of Ethnicity," *Ethnicity*, 3:111–24.

Jolliffe, J. 1978. *East Timor: Nationalism and Colonialism.* Queensland, Australia: Queensland UP.

Kohn, H. 1967. "Minorities," *Encyclopedia Brittanica 15*.

LeVine, R., and D. Campbell. 1972. *Ethnocentrism: Theories of Conflict, Ethnic Attitudes, and Group Behavior.* New York: Wiley.

Lockwood, W. 1977. *Toward a Theory of Ethnicity: A Working Bibliography...* Exchange Bibliography 1296. Chicago: Council of Planning Librarians.

Mason, P. 1971. *Patterns of Dominance.* New York: Oxford UP

Murdock, G.P. 1967. *Ethnographic Atlas.* Pittsburgh: U of Pittsburgh P.

Noble, L.G. 1977. *Philippine Policy toward Sabah.* Tucson: U of Arizona P.

Nordlinger, E. 1972. *Conflict Regulation in Divided Societies*, Harvard Studies in International Affairs 29. Cambridge: Center for International Affairs, Harvard U.

Obler, J., J. Steiner, and G. Dierickx. 1977. *Decision-Making in Smaller Democracies: The Consociational "Burden."* Beverly Hills: Sage.

Robertson, W. 1976. *The Dispossessed Majority.* Cape Canaveral: Howard Allen.

Sharp, N. 1977. *The Rule of the Sword: The Story of West Irian.* Victoria, Australia: Kibble Books.

da Silva, M. 1975. "Modernization and Ethnic Conflict: The Case of the Basques," *Comparative Politics*, 1:227–51.

Southall, A. 1970. "The Illusion of Tribe," *Journal of Asian and African Studies* 1:28-50.

The Statesman's Yearbook: Statistical and Historical Annual of the States of the World. (annual). New York: St. Martin's.

Stephens, M. 1976. *Linguistic Minorities in Western Europe.* Llandysul Dyfed, Wales: Gomer.

Van Dyke, V. 1977. "The Individual, the State, and Ethnic Communities in Political Theory," *World Politics*, 2:343–69.

Young, C. 1975. "Nationalism and Separatism in Africa," pp. 57-74 in Martin Kilson (ed.), *New States in the Modern World.* Cambridge: Harvard UP.

Young, C. 1976. *The Politics of Cultural Pluralism.* Madison: U of Wisconsin P.

Zolberg, A. 1974. "The Making of Flemings and Walloons: Belgium: 1830–1914," *Journal of Interdisciplinary History 4:179–235*.

————. 1976. "Culture, Territory, Class: Ethnicity Demystified," paper at Edinburgh Congress of International Political Science Association, 1976.

Edited Compilations

Ashworth, G., ed. 1977–1980. *World Minorities*, Vol. 1–3. London: Minority Rights Group.

Barth, F., ed. 1969. *Ethnic Groups and Boundaries: The Social Organization of Culture Difference*. Boston: Little, Brown.

————, ed. 1978. *Scale and Social Organization*. Oslo: Universitetsforlaget.

Bell, W., and W. Freeman, ed. 1974. *Ethnicity and Nation-Building: Comparative, International, and Historical Perspectives*. Beverly Hills: Sage Publications.

Bertelsen, J., ed. 1977. *Nonstate Nations in International Politics: Comparative System Analyses*. New York: Praeger.

Clarke, S., and J. Obler, ed. 1976. *Urban Ethnic Conflict: A Comparative Perspective*. Chapel Hill: Institute for Research in Social Science, U of North Carolina.

Connelly, B., ed. 1973. *Political Integration in Multinational States*. *Journal of International Affairs* 1.

————, ed. 1973. *Political Integration of Multi-State Nations*. *Journal of International Affairs* 2.

Denitch, B., ed. 1979. *Legitimation of Regimes: International Frameworks for Analysis*. Beverly Hills: Sage Publications.

Depres, L., ed. 1975. *Ethnicity and Resource Competition in Plural Societies*. Chicago: Aldine.

Dofny, J., and A. Akiwowo, ed. 1980. *National and Ethnic Movements*. Beverly Hills: Sage Publications.

Durchacek, I., ed. 1977. *Federalism and Ethnicity*. *Publius*, Fall 1977.

Esman, M., ed. 1977. *Ethnic Conflict in the Western World*. Ithaca: Cornell UP.

Glazer, N., and D. Moynihan, ed. 1975. *Ethnicity: Theory and Experience*. Cambridge: Harvard UP.

Grant, R., and E.S. Welhofer, ed. 1979. *Ethno-Nationalism, Multinational Corporations, and the Modern State*. Denver: Graduate School of International Studies, U of Denver.

Hall, R., ed. 1979. *Ethnic Autonomy—Comparative Dynamics: The Americas, Europe, and the Developing World*. New York: Pergamon Press.

Halseth, J., and B. Glasrud, ed. 1977. *The Northwest Mosaic: Minorty Conflicts in Pacific Northwest History*. Boulder: Pruett Publishing.

Heisler, M., ed. 1977. *Ethnic Conflict in the World Today*, Annals of the American Academy of Political and Social Science 6.

Henderson, G., R.N. Lebow, and J. Stoessinger, ed. 1974. *Divided Nations in a Divided World*. New York: McKay.

Kang, T., ed. 1979. *Nationalism and the Crises of Ethnic Minorities in Asia*. Westport, Conn.: Greenwood Press.

Laquer, W., and G. Mosse, ed. 1971. "Nationalism and Separatism," *Journal of Contemporary History* 6, 1.

Mol, H., ed. 1978. *Identity and Religion: International, Cross-Cultural Approaches.* Beverly Hills: Sage Publications.

Neumann, S., ed. 1976. *Small States and Segmented Societies: National Political Integration in a Global Environment.* New York: Praeger.

Pi-Sunyer, O., ed. 1971. *The Limits of Integration: Ethnicity and Nationalism in Modern Europe.* Amherst: U of Massachusetts, Dept. of Anthropology Research Report 9.

Said, A., and L. Simmons, ed. 1976. *Ethnicity in an International Context.* New Brunswick, N.J.: Transaction Books.

Sinai, A., ed. 1975. "Ethnic and Religious Minorities in the Middle East," Parts 1 & 2, *Middle East Review*, Fall and Winter issues.

Suhrke, A., and L.G. Noble, ed. 1977. *Ethnic Conflict in International Relations.* New York: Praeger.

Whitaker, B., ed. 1972. *The Fourth World: Victims of Group Oppression.* New York: Schocken.

Wollenberg, C., ed. 1970. *Ethnic Conflict in California History.* Alhambra, Cal.: Borden Publishing.

Nationalism

Berlin, I. 1972. "The Bent Twig: A Note on Nationalism," *Foreign Affairs* 10.

Deutsch, K. 1979. *Tides Among Nations.* New York: Free Press.

Emerson, R. 1960. *From Empire to Nation.* Cambridge, Mass.: Harvard UP.

Hayes, C.J.H. 1931. *The Historical Evolution of Modern Nationalism.* New York: Macmillan.

Hertz, F.O. 1944. *Nationality in History and Politics.* London: Routledge and Kegan Paul.

Kohn, H. 1944. *The Idea of Nationalism.* New York: Macmillan.

Orwell, G. 1968. "Notes on Nationalism," in *Collected Essays, Journalism, and Letters*, Vol. 3. New York: Harcourt, Brace and World (written in 1945; see also *Animal Farm* and *1984*).

Seton-Watson, H. 1977. *Nations and States: An Enquiry into the Origins of Nations and the Politics of Nationalism.* Boulder, Colo.: Westview Press.

Shafer, B. 1972. *Faces of Nationalism: New Realities and Old Myths.* New York: Harvest.

Shafer, B. 1976. *Nationalism: Its Nature and Interpreters*, 4th ed., AHA pamphlet 701. Washington, DC: American Historical Association.

Snyder, L. 1976. *Varieties of Nationalism: A Comparative Study.* Hinsdale, Ill.: Dryden Press.

Human Rights

Capotorti, F. 1979. *Study on the Rights of Persons belonging to Ethnic, Religious, and Linguistic Minorities.* New York: United Nations.

Emerson, R. 1975. "The fate of human rights in the Third World," *World Politics* 1:201–26.

Gadgil, D.R. 1968. *Human Rights in a Multinational Society,* Gokhale Institute Studies 53. Bombay, India: Asia Publishing House.

Gastil, R., ed. 1979. *Freedom in the World: Political Rights and Civil Liberties.* New York: Freedom House.

Glaser, K. and S. Possony. 1979. *Victims of Politics: The State of Human Rights.* New York: Columbia UP.

Haksar, U. 1974. *Minority Protection and International Bill of Human Rights.* Bombay, India: Allied Publishers.

Horowitz, I.L. 1980. *Taking Lives: Genocide and State Power,* 3rd ed. New Brunswick, N.J.: Transaction Books.

U.S. House of Representatives. 1976. *Investigation into Certain Past Instances of Genocide and Exploration of Policy Options for the Future* (hearings). Washington, D.C.: GPO.

Self-Determination

Buchheit, L. 1978. *Secession: The Legitimacy of Self-Determination.* New Haven: Yale UP.

Cobban, A. 1969. *The Nation State and National Self-Determination.* London; Collins.

Connor, W. 1967. "Self-Determination: The New Phrase," *World Politics* 4:30–53.

Emerson, R. 1964. *Self-Determination Revisited in the Era of Decolonization,* Occasional Papers in International Affairs 9. Cambridge: Harvard U, Center for International Affairs.

Gros Espiel, H. 1980. *The Right to Self-Determination: Implementation of United Nations Resolutions.* New York: United Nations.

Gross, L. 1975. "The Right of Self-Determination in International Law," pp. 136–57 in M. Kilson, ed., *New States in the Modern World.* Cambridge: Harvard UP.

Lansing, R. 1921. *The Peace Negotiations: A Personal Narrative.* Cambridge: Houghton Mifflin.

Ronen, D. 1979. *The Quest for Self-Determination.* New Haven: Yale UP.

Marxist Perspectives

Dreyer, J.T. 1976. *China's Forty Millions: Minority Nationalities and National Integration in the People's Republic of China.* Cambridge: Harvard UP.

Grigulevich, I.R. and S.Y. Kozlov, ed. 1974. *Races and Peoples: Contemporary Ethnic and Racial Problems.* Moscow: Progress Publishers.

Katz, Z., R. Rogers, and F. Harned, ed. 1975. *Handbook of Major Soviet Nationalities.* New York: Free Press.

Institute of Marxism-Leninism. 1977. *Leninism and the National Question.* Moscow: Progress Publishers.

Laquer, W.Z., ed. 1962. "Nationalism, Communism, and the Uncommitted Nations." *Survey: A Journal of Soviet and East European Studies* 43.

Lenin, V.I. 1968. *National Liberation, Socialism, and Imperialism: Selected Writings.* New York: International Publishers.

Simmonds, G., ed. 1977. *Nationalism in the USSR and Eastern Europe in the Era of Brezhnev and Kosygin*. Detroit: U of Detroit P.

Stalin, J. 1975. *Marxism and the National-Colonial Question*. San Francisco: Proletarian Publishers.

Tillett, L. 1977. "The National Minorities Factor in the Sino-Soviet Dispute," *Orbis*, Summer 1977:241–60.

Works by Geographers

Ambrose, J. 1980. "Micro-Scale Language Mapping: An Experiment in Wales and Brittany," *Discussion Papers in Geolinguistics* 2.

Boal, F.W. and J.N.H Douglas, ed. 1982. *Integration and Division: Geographical Perspectives on the Northern Ireland Problem*. London: Academic Press.

Beauregard, L., ed. 1980. "La Problématique Géopolitique du Québec," *Cahiers de Géographie du Québec* 61.

Cartwright, D. 1980. "Bilingual Districts: The Elusive Territorial Component in Canada's Official Languages Act," *Discussion Papers in Geolinguistics* 1.

Clarke, C., D. Ley, and C. Peach, ed. 1984. *Geography and Ethnic Pluralism*. Winchester, Mass.: Allen and Unwin.

Dominian, L. 1917. *Frontiers of Language and Nationality in Europe*. New York: American Geographical Society.

Evenden, L.J., and F.F. Cunningham, ed. 1973. *Cultural Discord in the Modern World*. Vancouver, B.C.: Geographical Series 20.

Fischer, E. 1980. *Minorities and Minority Problems*. New York: Vantage.

Gottman, J., ed. 1980. *Centre and Periphery: Spatial Variation in Politics*. Beverly Hills: Sage Publications.

Heslinga, M.W. 1971. *The Irish Border as a Cultural Divide*, 2nd ed. Assen, Netherlands: Van Gorcum.

Hoffman, G. 1977. "Regional Policies and Regional Consciousness in Europe's Multinational Societies," *Geoforum* 8:121–29.

Kidron, M. and R. Segal. 1981. *The State of the World Atlas*. New York: Simon and Schuster.

Knight, D.B. 1982. "Identity and Territory: Geographical Perspectives on Nationalism and Regionalism," *Annals of the Association of American Geographers* 72:514-531.

Lowenthal, D. 1972. *West Indian Societies*. New York: Oxford UP.

Lunden, T. 1980. "Language, Geography, and Social Development in Norden," *Discussion Papers in Geolinguistics* 3.

Mikesell, M.W. 1983. "The Myth of the Nation State," *Journal of Geography* 82:257–69.

Miller, J. 1978. *Linguistic Regionalism and National Language Policy in the Philippines*. Syracuse University, Department of Geography, Discussion Paper 52.

Patrick, R.A. 1976. *Political Geography and the Cyprus Conflict, 1963–1971*. Waterloo, Ont.: U of Waterloo, Department of Geography Publication Series 4.

Raitz, K. 1978. "Ethnic Maps of North America," *Geographical Review* 68:335–50.

Sopher, D., ed. 1980. *An Exploration of India: Geographical Perspectives on Society and Culture*. Ithaca: Cornell UP.

Wilkinson, H.R. 1951. *Maps and Politics: A Review of the Ethnographic Cartography of Macedonia*. Liverpool: Liverpool UP.

Williams, C.H., ed. *National Separatism*. Vancouver: U of British Columbia P.

Wixman, R. 1980. *Language Aspects of Ethnic Patterns and Processes in the North Caucasus*. Chicago: U of Chicago, Department of Geography Research Paper 191.

HISTORY

As international in its roots as geography, history is facing the challenge of providing a global perspective in a global era. World history is emerging as a subdiscipline, transcending and integrating the established field of regional history. The challenges include reconciling the enduringly important focus on Western civilization with a world perspective. They also include difficult issues for historiography and reconsideration of the education of historians.

In participating in the NCFLIS project, the World History Association asked four of the most distinguished scholars of world history: "What is an attainable global perspective for undergraduates in history?" Complementing these essays by William H. McNeill, L.S. Stavrianos, Philip D. Curtin, and Immanuel Wallerstein is Kevin Reilly's list of commonly articulated pedagogical goals for world history courses. These articles are reprinted, with permission, from *The History Teacher* 18.4 (1985), pages 501–35.

As part of the NCFLIS project, Kevin Reilly edited *World History: Selected Reading Lists and Course Outlines from American Colleges and Universities* (New York: M. Wiener, 1985), which presents 45 syllabi. The first half of this volume outlines introductory and survey courses which in various ways introduce students to the entire globe. Suggesting ways in which history courses can be made more global, the second half of his book focuses on topical and comparative approaches.

The World Is So Full of a Number of Things

William H. McNeill

> The world is so full of a number of things
> I'm sure we should all be as happy as kings.
>
> —Robert Louis Stevenson

In 1885, when Stevenson wrote these lines, the world seemed rather more orderly and secure than it does today, at least for speakers of English, and the history that mattered and ought therefore to be taught in schools was far more precisely defined than it is now. In schools and colleges today the number of things in the world is so dauntingly large that there is almost no agreement (certainly no firm agreement) as to what, amidst such confusion, really matters. As long as such uncertainty prevails, teaching world history or global awareness remains all but impossible. A conscientious teacher can only convey confusion and, perhaps, despair at failing to master the complexity of it all.

Yet the need for clarifying order is impossible to exorcise. Since 1945, if not before, it has been obvious to educators and the general public alike that Americans needed a broader acquaintance with history than anything that traditional national history, supplemented by Western Civilization, could provide. The Chinese mattered for American politics and policy; so did Moslems and Indians, Africans and Amerindians; and treating these peoples merely as passive beings, brought into the modern world by European traders, missionaries, and colonial administrators, lost all plausibility after World War II, when European colonial empires began to break up. If Americans were to avoid the error of assuming that everyone everywhere shared the same outlook and aspirations and could be counted on to behave in the same way, e.g., by

William H. McNeill is Robert A. Millikan Distinguished Service Professor Emeritus of History at the University of Chicago.

organizing not more than two moderate political parties so as to hold elections and decide which party should govern for the next few years, a serious effort to understand the diverse cultural heritages of the principal branches of humanity would be necessary. The cost to the United Sates of misunderstanding other people's traditions could be serious, as evidenced in Vietnam, where armed American missionaries proved incapable of converting the inhabitants to our way of life despite a prolonged and serious effort to do so.

After World War II many persons recognized the importance of achieving a better understanding of the world beyond American borders, and at the graduate level American universities made a remarkably successful effort to initiate top-notch, scholarly study of all the principal parts of the earth. Funding from the Ford Foundation and others hastened this expansion. Ready availability of foreign scholars provided a vital resource for starting up new projects. NDEA fellowships brought the federal government into the act. And by the 1960s hundreds of highly trained and genuinely competent experts began to emerge from U.S. graduate schools.

They were expected to teach undergraduates as well as staff the CIA and fill other administrative roles in a country that found itself increasingly entangled with peoples of alien background and historical experience. But despite their competence—and even because of it—success in the undergraduate classroom was minimal. Young Ph.D.s, fired with enthusiasm for what they had learned in graduate school and aware of how very much more there was to learn about the particular portion of the globe they had chosen to study, set out to reproduce for undergraduates as much of the complexity they had savored in graduate school as seemed feasible. Most undergraduates responded with indifference. Why bother with so much confusing detail about a part of the world they did not expect to live in? Why indeed? Especially since mastery of what had happened in one small part of the globe dictated inattention to, and near total ignorance about, all the rest of the earth? Yet from the teachers' point of view, the ideal of graduate study and of ambitious professionalism, emphasizing the mastery of local languages needed for using local primary sources, made any effort at global perspective seem intellectually irresponsible. Who could master all the world's languages? And without such access, who could be a respectable historian?

The educational scene in the United States was beset by still another anomaly in the post-war decades because, in response to the decay of European hegemony, high school and junior college teachers were told by their administrative superiors to teach world history, even though four-year colleges and universities found it impossible to offer such a course. Textbook companies came to the rescue, providing teachers in high schools and junior colleges with what they needed to teach world history, that is, a textbook with that title, or its equivalent, on the cover.

Textbook writers took the task seriously, of course, but got little help from the rest of the history profession. Generally speaking, they took one of two courses: either dividing the earth up geographically so as to give each continent something like equal treatment, or else draping humanity's past on the familiar skeleton inherited from Western Civilization courses and interrupting the story from time to time with chapters on what was happening elsewhere. Neither structure resulted in genuine world history. The first pattern created a series of parallel continental histories; the second barely disguised a Eurocentric vision which everyone agreed had become inadequate. Nevertheless, the effort behind these texts, and the teaching that goes on in high schools and junior colleges today, is entirely admirable inasmuch as it attempts to cope with current requirements for intelligent citizenship. This is so even if the vision that teachers impart in their world history courses remains a confusing "number of things" that cohere, if at all, around the all-conquering Europeans of the modern era, who are the only obvious link among the different parts of the earth with which the course attempts to deal.

The tacit assumption behind most existing world history courses that world history truly begins only in modern times with the European discoveries overlooks earlier contact across the civilized world of Eurasia and into Africa—contacts that shaped the evolution of local high cultures from the very beginning of civilization. It has the even more serious defect of implying that European expansion in modern times was somehow a unique and world-making process, without precedent in earlier ages. But other cultures (including some in pre-Columbian America and in sub-Saharan Africa) in fact had eras of efflorescence and subsequent expansion, playing model-setting roles for neighbors and neighbors' neighbors in the deeper past. A just perspective recognizes the recent expansion of Europe as merely the latest in a series of similar processes, since different centers asserted primacy over the rest of the earth at different times in the past. Only by taking world relationships before 1500 into account and adjusting the scale of discussion to approximately global proportions can a really satisfactory world history emerge.

How to change the scale of our discourse and treat the history of the world in an intellectually rigorous and intelligible fashion is a hurdle that must be crossed if really good world history courses are ever going to be taught. It is a hurdle at which the history profession in the United States has hitherto balked. Only a handful of historians have even tried to think globally. The vast majority have remained content to cultivate their gardens as defined by the conventions and limits of their Ph.D. training.

There are reasons for such behavior of course. Rewards in college and university careers depend on publication of a revised Ph.D. dissertation, followed as quickly as possible by a second book along similar, monographic lines. Only a bold and reckless young historian dares in the first ten years of teaching to raise his or her eyes very far from the turf defined by graduate training. After that, habits are fixed; frontiers for further detailed research multiply with the refinement of techniques; and the mists of world history, however enticing in themselves or important for a well-planned curriculum, seem better left to someone else.

This career pattern is clearly the chief determinant of historians' behavior and explains the professional disregard of the obvious questions about what we ought to expect undergraduates and citizens to know about the past. Intellectual disdain for textbook writers perhaps masks jealousy of the financial rewards a successful textbook can bring. But that sort of pettiness has serious consequences for the long-range health of the profession. By insulating academic research from questions of scale and proportion, subjects that are always critical for textbook writers and for teachers of any sort of introductory civilizational or global history course, the profession avoids grappling with what stubbornly remains the most important question before it: What can and should be taught about the past in schools and colleges to prepare our students for living in an ever more closely interacting world?

A second obstacle to professional concern with world history has been a heritage of unexamined assumptions about how historians elicit truth and meaning from the records of the past. The ideal of "exhausting the sources" was upheld in graduate schools as recently as the 1940s. That was supposed to make every dissertation permanently true, since no one could ever turn up a new source that would change the conclusions to which the fledgling historian had come. Such an ideal of course dictated ever-narrowing themes for research, since historians' perverse ingenuity kept on discovering more and new sorts of relevant sources. It also assumed that there was a prefabricated temple of historical knowledge that already existed, within which each new monograph could find its appropriate place spontaneously, correcting and thereby perfecting it, without disturbing the architectonics of the whole.

But as tacitly agreed-upon patterns of historical meaning lost definition in the post-war world, monographic gems, polished to perfection though they might be, no longer had a temple of knowledge awaiting them. Instead, monographic history began to drift toward meaninglessness for all but a small circle of experts whose latest work revised some fellow expert's work in the same field. Debates within the charmed circle of the learned could be lively and even amusing under these circumstances; and human ingenuity in extracting unexpected data from recalcitrant sources achieved flamboyant sophistication. Yet as debates proliferated, clusters of experts drifted apart, each intent on its own exploitation of particular kinds of sources. The history profession rapidly lost its cohesion under these circumstances. Up-to-date teaching of introductory courses, even within a national frame, became ever more difficult because the latest research had become so disparate and diverse that nations disintegrated into separate sub-groups, each pursued by its own cluster of experts with minimal concern for context of any sort. If national history became impossible, how much more absurd even to try to think on civilizational or global terms!

Yet meaning in history arises not from sources but from the questions historians ask of them—and of themselves. If historians ask trivial questions, they get trivial answers. If they ask big questions, they get big answers. And with changes of scale, new patterns and different meanings emerge. Everything depends on the inquiry the historian makes, and on the conceptual frame he brings to his task of interrogating sources.

Map-making offers an instructive parallel. A map that set out to "exhaust the sources" by recording every blade of grass would be true in a sense: true for a moment and for a square yard of turf. It would also be useless, for the same eye that surveys the map could just as well survey the original area that the map set out to reproduce. Similarly, if historians had ever really "exhausted the sources," they would merely have reproduced the original confusion by transcribing it onto their own pages.

Moreover, maps such as our imagined one, no matter how high they were piled in a cartographic laboratory, would not add up to a map of the world or even of a single country. Problems of projection would have to be solved first; and then the further question of what to leave out would arise if an intelligible, usable map is desired. Historians lack clear rules for projection; and they characteristically resist leaving things out, fearing thereby to lose their already tenuous grasp on truth. But truth is itself a simplification and interpretation of reality as experienced; and its power arises from the way verbal ordering of the world can focus attention on what really matters, while everything else in the sensorium fades into the status of background noise that can safely be ignored. In any case, to make either national or global history possible, an agreed-upon principle of exclusion must be employed. Otherwise total confusion prevails, since sources are effectively infinite and data from the past surpass all under-standing. Without such a principle, the more we know the more confused we become. That, it seems to me, is what the history profession has achieved in the past thirty years. Surely it is time for the best brains of the profession to think carefully about projection and relevance and to try to discern how history—knowable history—can be made to fit together into an intelligible whole.

Cynics and defeatists may say that history as a whole really and truly makes no sense. If so, why study tiny parts of a meaningless whole? Revisionism—our preferred posture—makes sense only when there is something to revise. If he has no general interpretation of history to modify, the monographic scholar has lost his occupation.

As actually experienced by men of affairs and the general public, the course of events constitutes one long, tumultuous emergency after another, adding up to much noise and repeated alarms and the general impression that no one is really in control. But the whole point of writing histories is, with the help of hindsight and whatever wisdom the historian can bring to bear, to sort out from such hurlyburly the things that really did matter, thereby giving order to what, as experienced, was conspicuously disorderly. That, in a nutshell, is the way intelligent action becomes possible. Human mastery of the natural world rests on an exactly parallel ordering of disorderly sensory encounters with the world around us. Scientists have worked wonders by leaving things out and directing attention to what really matters. Efforts to conduct ourselves wisely and well in the social universe can only build on the same intellectual capacity to simplify and generalize experience by the use of words, so as to become able to recognize what is important in the situation we confront by comparing it with what we know or believe about past encounters of a similar kind. And just as travellers need a map to tell them where they are, so human beings, as members of nations and other sub-groupings of humanity, need a mental guide to human diversity (and perversity?) if they are to avoid unpleasant surprises in encounters with others. That is the reason for insisting on world history, and in a world as interactive as ours, it is a very compelling reason indeed.

To get there, historians must know what to leave out. They have to decide what really mattered, what recorded history adds up to. Our predecessors of the nineteenth century did address this question, and came up with the idea that history turned upon the halting but uneluctable progress of liberty. This was what gave meaning to detailed researches into medieval and modern constitutional practices. It was also what governed the distribution of attention in the old Western civilization courses of the 1930s and 1940s. But the experience of World Wars I and II made the progress of liberty seem an implausible faith; and the proliferation of specialized historical research effec- tively obscured the nineteenth-century liberal idea without ever confronting it directly or finding a substitute criterion of relevance for understanding human history.

Since the debate on the structure and meaning of human history has scarcely been joined, this paper can only offer some sort of provocation. Let me therefore suggest that two alternative models for world history seem at hand. One is to survey landmarks of the increment of human power across time—power over nature and power over fellow human beings. This amounts to a modified version of the idea of progress, substituting power for liberty. The reason for the substitution is that liberty seems a waif in a world of massive bureaucracies, whereas the cumulation of human powers through technology, knowledge, and organizational skill seems unmistakable. Those with power usually prevailed; that is why it has accumulated so impressively across the centuries. Those without it tried to imitate and catch up with the most powerful of their day or else set out to strengthen their own different way of life by appropriate and necessary innovation.

The possibility of successfully resisting even powerful outsiders points toward the second available model for world history: that is, a sampling of the immense variety of human cultures that have divided the earth in times past, with attention to their most significant interactions across the centuries. This sort of history seeks however imperfectly to enter into the minds of human beings and see the world through their eyes as far as possible. It may therefore be labelled humanistic as against the colder, more external, analysis of human power.

The real question for either approach is to decide in detail what to emphasize and what to pass over. Technological, scientific, and organizational history can get lost in details as easily as a cultural survey can. Both approaches confront an infinity of possible sources and accessible subject matter. What really counted? That remains the critical issue. Prolonged debate and some successful trial runs may settle the matter, practically if not theoretically. In the meanwhile, let me offer a few tentative suggestions.

In the progress of human power, two principal thresholds seem obvious: the shift from hunting and gathering to food production, and the large-scale exploitation of fossil fuels that took place during what is somewhat inadequately referred to as the Industrial Revolution. (The transport and communications revolutions, resulting from the use of inanimate sources of power, are probably more important for humanity as a whole than the cheapening of consumer goods that industrial applications of power simultaneously permitted. But that is another story.)

Between these two principal thresholds lie two lesser but important landmarks. The first of these is the rise of what we call civilized societies, i.e., societies in which occupational specialization separated a considerable proportion of the population from those who spent their time raising food. Such specialists developed superior skills rather rapidly, and societies hospitable to such specialization came to enjoy enhanced wealth and power. Thus the rise and spread of civilizations in the ancient Near East and subsequently in China, India, the Mediterranean lands and then later in Mexico, Peru, Japan and sub-Saharan Africa ought to figure as an important step in the progress of human power.

A second landmark in that same history is the emergence in the course of the first millennium A.D. of transport and communication links among the previously more or less isolated civilizations of Eurasia and, after 1500, of America as well. As contacts multiplied in frequency and significance, a world system started to assert itself that can best be called ecumenical as against the civilizational structures of earlier times. The world system in turn achieved stronger definition with the exploitation of inanimate sources of power after the end of the eighteenth century because of cheapened transport and communication. This projects us into the contemporary world where reactions and adjustments to instantaneous communication and rocketry are still in their initial stages and where drastic disturbances to older demographic balances arising from an intensified dissemination of disease germs and of medical knowledge and skill are even more important disturbers of customary ways of use and want.

A course built along these lines ought to emphasize the double-edged character of power. Every increment to human ability to manipulate the natural and social world brings both gains and losses. Those possessing new instruments of power commonly acquire wealth and compel obedience, but achieve these goods only by interfering with or destroying customary ways of life that other human beings treasure. Moreover, new skills that allow more massive intervention in the earth's ecosystem often have unexpected and damaging side effects. The earliest agriculturalists, with their slash-and-burn techniques of cultivation, as well as modern chemical plants, with their pollution of the environment, ran into such side effects. Wise historians ought always to recognize and try to appreciate what is being destroyed as well as what is being created, holding a balance between power-wielders and their victims through all the centuries.

So much for power and progress and a possible framework for its pursuit in a world history course. I can be more cursory in describing the cultural alternative since my principal book, *The Rise of the West: A History of the Human Community* (1963) set forth my best effort at such an interpretation of the past *in extenso.*

Since tens of thousands of human cultures have existed and thousands still survive in more or less vigor and diversity among us, radical choices must be made to write a world history textbook around the record of separate cultures. First of all, one must seriously explore those early cultures that used writing. That means restricting our history to societies we call civilized, with only glimpses into the neighboring communities as reported by civilized and usually unsympathetic observers. Archaeology can do something to fill in gaps, of course; but garbage heaps as a rule tell little about the inner world of conscious meanings that gave ancient illiterate societies their reality.

Civilizations themselves are complicated and diversified, and the literary record, by and large, favors the privileged element within such societies. Only in recent times can the history of the poor be discerned, and even then imperfectly. Still, if one fastens on the central, governing ideas and institutions of the civilization in question, one can hope and believe that something of the distinctive character of life as experienced by the rich and poor alike in societies long vanished from the earth can still be grasped.

Human cultures do, after all, tend toward coherence. Otherwise too many encounters are indeterminant and embarrassing (as well as dangerous) to the sharers of the culture in question. Coherence is attained by fixing on one or two dominant values and institutions, making them override competing and conflicting considerations whenever necessary. That makes encounters with strangers within the society sufficiently predictable that life becomes bearable. What an historian then must do is to recognize from the literary record what are the central dominant ideas and institutions around which everyday behavior was organized.

This is not an impossible assignment. The Chinese family, Indian castes, bureaucratic empires in the ancient Near East, and territorial sovereignties in Europe each, in its own domain, enjoyed a kind of primacy over competing institutions. The diverse ideals of Chinese *li* (decorum), Indian transcendentalism, Near Eastern monotheism, and European legalism (law in society as well as in nature) have a similar centrality, and can be seen to complement the corresponding dominating institution. If each of these ideas and institutions is carefully explored (perhaps with the help of translations from original texts), I believe that a real insight into key diversities of the world's most enduring cultural systems can be achieved. And since diversity still survives with almost undiminished force, a good grasp of these organizing principles is practically important for the conduct of foreign affairs.

Other parts of the world where literacy is of recent origin can best be explored through anthropological reports perhaps, or by choosing from travellers' accounts. But in justice to the lands and peoples that remained apart from the civilizational structures of Eurasia until recent times, an effort to sample simpler and nonliterate cultures is called for, presumably in terms of their local ruling ideas and institutions.

Beyond this, to provide a base for a successful history course, cultural pluralism must somehow come to grips with interactions among cultures and civilizations. A simple way to do so is set forth in my book. My scheme recognizes one or another civilization entering on a phase of efflorescence during a period of several hundred years. After describing aspects of that efflorescence, I then set out to see how peoples round about reacted to the achievements of the dominating civilization. I expected to find that populations encountering new and superior skills would usually wish to imitate and catch up, while nonetheless retaining their own identity. A process of selective borrowing, often involving unexpected side effects and provoking new breakthroughs, was thus initiated. Borrowings and subsequent adjustment and readjustment sooner or later allowed some part of the earth, with a different civilizational heritage, to assume primacy through new efflorescence. Europe's recent world dominion thus became merely the latest in a series of similar pulses of world history, uniquely powerful thanks to intensified communication but not otherwise different from earlier Chinese, Hellenistic, Indian, and Moslem periods of efflorescence and expansion.

Perhaps these two models of world history could be combined, without cluttering the course with excessive information or excessively complex concepts. But I have not been very successful in my own efforts in that direction, and for the time being, at least, I judge it would be best for historians to work within one or the other model and see what they can do to educate themselves and their students within either the humanistic or the social scientific tradition. Chronologically abbreviated world history courses, beginning with 1500, 1750, or even 1950, often seem attractive and more manageable than efforts to take on the whole sweep of historic time. Yet I believe that such courses also require that the time segment chosen for intensive consideration be somehow set in a truly world-historical context by going back to the classical roots of each of the world's surviving civilizations. Flash-backs can do this, if teachers have available a well-digested understanding of the deeper past. So, first the spade work; then, if need be, and when preference or prudence dictate, chronologically abbreviated versions of world history courses may become practicable.

How much of all this is attainable today? Only by trying can anyone tell. And only when course planners and teachers are clear about how they must decide what to leave out can world history courses worthy of the name actually emerge. Serious debate and individual effort are only beginning; and rewards within the historical profession continue to discourage the undertaking. Consequently, the demand for world history in our colleges still comes mostly from academic administrators, legislatures, and the general public. But if enough historians take heed and accept the risks involved in leaving a particular field of expertise behind in order to read widely enough to reflect competently on questions of world history, then a global perspective will soon become possible in our society thanks to well-constructed and well-taught courses in world history. The time is not yet. Perhaps it will arrive within a decade. I sincerely hope so, for our country and the world at large badly need global vision, knowledge, and cross-cultural understanding.

Technology as a Central Theme for World History

L.S. Stavrianos

The Nobel laureate economist, Gunnar Myrdal, has noted that whereas his discipline traditionally had neglected the problems of undeveloped lands, since World War II there has been a "swelling flood of research" in this field. The shift, observes Myrdal, "has definitely not been an autonomous and spontaneous development." Rather it has been a result of political forces such as the cold war, the colonial revolutions, and the urgent need for economic development in the newly independent Third Word nations.[1]

Our discipline of history also is directly affected by the course of world events. Just as economists after World War II were impelled to work in the field of "development economics," so historians were impelled by the same global trends to turn from West-oriented to world-oriented history. The results of this shift are well known: new textbooks, new courses, retooling workshops, and the emergence of the World History Association.

Today we are entering another period of global turmoil and disruption surpassing even that of four decades ago. Inevitably it will leave its mark on the various disciplines. Economists from fifteen countries met in New York in June 1983 and agreed that "current economic concepts have nothing to do with present-day reality" and that these concepts need to be "modified or adjusted." The economists have launched a three-year project entitled "Adapting Economic Thinking to Changing Global Conditions."[2]

Historians are not so directly under the gun as are economists. We are not held responsible for fluctuations in GNP, in unemployment rates, or in Dow-Jones averages. But it would be wishful thinking for us to assume that we can ignore the storms that are transforming the world before our eyes. What happened after World War II was child's play compared to what is going on

L.S. Stavrianos is Professor Emeritus of History at Northwestern University and Adjunct Professor Emeritus of History at the University of California, San Diego.

today. In the late 1940s and 1950s it was colonial empires that were dismantled. Today it is the entire globe that is being turned inside out and upside down. All peoples and all societies are affected, capitalist as well as socialist, developed as well as underdeveloped, the First World *and* the Second World *and* the Third World.

In such a period of wholesale disruption, people look to the past for reassurance and guidance. Education inevitably is being affected, as is evident in the shift to "practical" courses that will meet the latest demands of the job market. A study based on 300,000 incoming freshmen in 500 colleges reveals that in 1967, 82.9% wanted to find in college "a meaningful philosophy of life." By 1984 the percentage had dropped to 44.1—a decrease of almost 50% in fifteen years.[3]

Ferment of such magnitude inevitably will affect the teaching of history. Rather than being caught up and tossed about by the changing tides, it is better that we decide for ourselves in what direction we want to go. We can begin by analyzing the nature of the global crisis confronting us. The extent of the crisis becomes self-evident by simply listing its principal manifestations: the overhanging mushroom cloud, depletion of natural resources, global structural unemployment, increasing hunger amidst plenty, growing inequity within as well as between nations, environmental degradation, and soul erosion accompanying soil erosion.

These global ailments obviously have diverse roots, but for the most part they are by-products of our current technological revolution. The problems we confront obviously would be qualitatively different if we had not undergone the first Industrial Revolution in the eighteenth and nineteenth centuries, and the current, second Industrial Revolution since the 1940s. This basic fact suggests an approach for understanding and teaching not only modern history, but the entire sweep of world history.

The linkage between technological revolutions and world history can be made because the industrial revolutions were not unique. Each heralding a new phase of human history, they were in their time but the latest of a succession of technological revolutions. Six such revolutions stand out, providing a skeletal framework on which we can sculpt the body of world history. These are the Human Revolution, when our ancestral hominid gave way to *Homo sapiens,* capable of making fire and using tools; the Agricultural Revolution, when humans shifted from food gathering to food production; the Urban Revolution that marked the emergence of civilization; the Commercial Revolution that heralded the rise of the technologically precocious West; the first Industrial Revolution, with its steam power, electrical power and labor-saving machines; and the current, second Industrial Revolution, with its nuclear power, labor-replacing machines and genetic engineering.

These technological revolutions have proven a blessing. They transformed humans from seemingly puny and defenseless creatures into the dominant species of this planet. But they have also been the source of much of the misery and peril that have disfigured human history. The reason for this ambivalent legacy is that each technological revolution not only raised productivity, but also caused social disruption, which necessitated changes in institutions, in ways of thinking and in interpersonal relationships. Thus each major technological revolution necessitated correspondingly major social change.

Unfortunately, human beings throughout history have welcomed technological change, which enabled them to live better, but have resisted social change, which was uncomfortable and threatening. They have consistently preferred the traditional, the familiar, the socially approved ways of thinking and acting. The resulting time lag between technological and social change has been responsible for much of the misery and violence that has stained human history from its beginnings to the present.

This analysis suggests the structuring of world history within the context of the above six technological revolutions. Each revolution might be studied under three headings: (1) its origins and nature, (2) its impact on various aspects of life; and (3) the lag between technological and social change, and the resulting disfunction and malaise that culminate in revolutionary upheavals or, much more commonly, in gradual evolutionary modifications and adjustments.

As an example of this approach, the Urban Revolution might be analyzed as follows:

1. Origins in increased productivity resulting from improved agriculture (irrigation and plow) and from new crafts (metallurgy, pottery, textiles, coinage, wheel).

2. Impact on various aspects of life, including productivity, growth of population, increased wealth, use of surplus to support specialists (priests, kings, courtiers, administrators, military, and merchants), resulting class differentiation that replaced paleolithic and neolithic classlessness, urbanization, emergence of regional civilizations (in East, South, and Southwest Asia; Europe; Africa; and the Americas), underlying similarities and distinctive characteristics of these regional civilizations.

3. Lag between technological and social change evident in class differentiation and class conflict, as reflected in new religions of social protest, periodic peasant uprisings, rise and fall of successive dynasties, and barbarian incursions into centers of civilization enfeebled by social turmoil.

The current, second Industrial Revolution might be analyzed as follows:

1. Origins in World War II developments in nuclear energy, computers, robots, space science, genetic engineering, and information revolution.

2. Impact on various aspects of life, including: "Green Revolution" export-oriented agriculture in Third World, agribusiness in First World, rise of multinational corporations, export of industries as well as goods, emergence of integrated global economy and global labor force.

3. Lag between technological and social change evident in ecological repercussions, depletion of natural resources, urbanization without industrialization in the Third Word, labor-replacing machines and structural unemployment, growing inequality between and within nations, crisis of values and cultural identity, reformist and fundamentalist religious responses, and the arms race threat to economic well being and to species survival.

These two examples may well arouse certain concerns among historians. One is the specter of technological determinism. I believe this bogey can be exorcised if the historical past is respected rather than distorted. "Machines make history," Robert Heilbroner informs us, but "they do not make all history."[4] Of course not. Technology simply creates parameters within which a society functions, but what is done within those parameters varies enormously according to the values of individual societies.

We find many examples of societies molding technology as well as the opposite. Steam power was known in Alexandria in the first century A.D., but because of the abundance of slaves it was harnessed only in a device that opened temple doors. Likewise, a Mexican priest invented the cotton gin in the eighteenth century, before Eli Whitney, but nothing came of it because it was cheaper to exploit fifty peons than to buy a machine that would put them out of work. More significant was the failure of Chinese society to exploit fully its inventions of gunpowder, compass, and printing, in contrast to their eager utilization by Western society, with far reaching global consequences. Perhaps the most fateful example of the impact of society on technology is the current focus of the second Industrial Revolution on war production, with implications as unthinkable as they are disregarded.

A technology-oriented approach to history may also cause concern that the end product will lack substance—that the complexity and richness of human life and history will not be adequately analyzed and appreciated. In this case also, I believe the substantive issue is not so much approach as it is good history or bad. If the approach outlined above is properly implemented, it will encompass fully as many phases of human experience as are treated in existing courses. Several examples illustrate that such an approach can give both focus and historical depth to the problems that students will face as adults.

Ecological Problems will be seen not as peculiar to our age—all past societies (including the paleolithic) had ecological repercussions, but the unprecedented power of modern technology has correspondingly magnified its ecological impact to its current intensity and global scope.

Demographics traditionally comprised maximum reproduction to ensure species survival, but today the problem is to attain birth control equal to the new death control—an unresolved problem, with global repercussions.

Daily Work, despite the technological revolutions, has become more onerous since the paleolithic food gatherers worked 15 to 20 hours per week, or since the Romans enjoyed 150 to 200 public holidays a year.

Sex Relations through history have been determined not so much by formal political action as by successive structural changes in society, resulting in oscillation between egalitarian and hierarchical relationships.

Inequity between and within nations has been accentuated rather than alleviated by each of the successive technological revolutions.

War has been utilized for millennia as a legitimate and often profitable instrument of policy, but it has become progressively more destructive until today it is mutually suicidal.

A course organized along these lines should leave students not blinkered and bedazzled by technology but more critical and realistic. I will give three examples of the reappraisal that can be expected. The first is that the constantly accelerating power and tempo of technology constitutes a threat as well as a promise. In 1899 the Commissioner of the Patent and Trademark Office recommended to President McKinley that his office be abolished because "Everything that can be invented has been invented."[5] In 1985, after 3.8 million subsequent inventions, the Patent Office was still functioning with 1,400 examiners. And it has begun a $300 million computerization of its operations in order to keep up with the swelling torrent of new inventions.

Not only is the tempo of technology increasing, but so is its power. Nuclear energy, computers, space ships, and genetic engineering obviously are infinitely more potent and disruptive than the spinning and weaving innovations of eighteenth-century England. Also the current technological revolution is unfolding on a global scale, in contrast to the centuries necessary for past technological diffusion from one region to another.

The leisurely tempo of earlier times afforded a time cushion that enabled our ancestors to ride out the adverse consequences of belated social change. The loss of such a cushion has made the traditional policy of muddling through obsolete. To illustrate this point, consider the avalanche of a neglected slagheap dating back to the first Industrial Revolution. Loosened by heavy rains, in

October 1966 it cascaded down on a schoolhouse in Aberfan, Wales, wiping out an entire generation of school children. Today we face not century-old slag heaps but the more formidable 50,000 nuclear bombs, plus contamination of global skies, lands, and seas. So we conclude that muddling through may have been a viable strategy in the past, but today it invites disaster.

A second example of needed reappraisal is the common assumption that technology has endowed us with unprecedented power and has made us the unchallenged masters of our planet. It can be argued that each technological revolution has decreased rather than increased the security of humans. Following the Agricultural Revolution, peasants found themselves more vulnerable because they depended on the few staples they grew, in contrast to their ancestors who had far larger and safer reservoirs of scores of plants and animals that they had gathered and hunted. Today our technology has enabled us merely to substitute non-renewable resources for renewables, which increases rather than decreases our dependence on the environment.

A third example of needed reappraisal is the faith that problems created by technology can be solved by more technology—a quick Technological Fix. But most of today's problems are impervious to technological remedies. "We know much about atoms," observes biologist Mary Clark, "something about inanimate rocks and gasses, less about the development and functioning of living organisms, very little about whole ecosystems, and practically nothing about culture, economics, politics, or the arms race. In fact, it is our on-going search for a scientifically based, technological solution to the arms race that continually makes it *worse* rather than better."[6]

This leads to the conclusion that technology can be a useful servant but also a terrible master. The problem we face is to make this unique product of the human brain serve us; we should not serve it. Our lack of success in doing so has led some distinguished scholars to conclude that technology has become unmanageable—that it has acquired a dynamism independent of its human creators. So we are asked to accept a modern animism that invests technology with the spirits once believed to inhabit mountains and trees. We are asked to prostrate ourselves before an idol labelled technology, even though technology itself is the incarnation of human rationality.

Confronted with these paradoxes, students may be stimulated to reconsider their current lack of interest in acquiring in college a "meaningful philosophy of life." Perhaps they will reflect on why Albert Einstein wrote as much about ethical and social issues as about science. "Knowledge and skills alone cannot lead humanity to a happy and dignified life," wrote Einstein,

> humanity has every reason to place the proclaimers of high moral standards and values above the discoverers of objective truth. What humanity owes to

personalities like Buddha, Moses, and Jesus ranks for me higher than all the achievements of the inquiring and constructive mind."[7]

Students may also reflect on the very similar "philosophy of life" expressed by an American Indian Chief in 1853:

> This we know: The earth does not belong to man; man belongs to the earth. This we know: All things are connected like the blood which unites one family. All things are connected.
> Whatever befalls the earth befalls the sons of the earth. Man did not weave the web of life; he is merely a strand in it. Whatever he does to the web, he does to himself.[8]

Notes

[1] Gunnar Myrdal, *The Challenge of World Poverty* (London: 1979), pp. 6-8.

[2] *New York Times*, June 21, 1983.

[3] UCLA Cooperative Institutional Reform Programs, *The American Freshman: National Norms for Fall, 1984.*

[4] R.L. Heilbroner, *Between Capitalism and Socialism* (New York: 1970), p. 147.

[5] New York Times, February 20, 1985.

[6] M.E. Clark and L. Holler, *The Dangers of Scientism* (forthcoming).

[7] Cited by T. Ferris, "The Other Einstein," *Science* (October, 1983), 36.

[8] Chief Seattle's message to President Franklin Pierce, cited in M.E. Clark, *Ariadne's Thread* (forthcoming).

The Comparative World History Approach

Philip D. Curtin

O ne of the most pressing problems for education in the final quarter of the century is the proliferation of knowledge. In history alone, fields of knowledge unrecognized in 1950 have new prominence. Some are new areas like Africa and much of Asia, which were either left out or kept subordinate in the typical Western civilization courses—and rarely offered in American universities as courses on their own merits. Others are new topical approaches like women's history, the history of the family, historical demography, or Afro-American history. If these are added to what we used to expect students to learn, something we once expected will be squeezed out. Students spend less time in history courses, in any event, than they did a quarter of a century ago. History itself, in short, has already shrunk to make room for new subjects in the university curriculum.

This problem at the broadest level recurs when one tries to put together a university course in World History. Three alternative approaches are now becoming common. One is a world history survey, often confined to a rather short period of time in order to make possible a genuine world-historical perspective without an impossible level of superficiality. "The World of the Twentieth Century" would be a typical title for such a course.

A second possibility is to try for a broader perspective but to limit that perspective to some defined part of the world. That, in effect, is what the old Western civilization course did. Another possibility is to take something broader—the Atlantic basin, for example, so that European history is balanced to some extent by bringing in North America, South America, and Africa. Another is to use the Indian Ocean world as a way of balancing the Middle East against India and southeast Asia.

Philip D. Curtin is Herbert Baxter Adams Professor of History at The Johns Hopkins University.

A third possibility is to try for a global perspective by pursuing themes that occur in several parts of the world. In effect, this approach combines extremely superficial reference to many aspects of world history with deeper soundings into particular topics that are seen to have particular importance. This is sometimes known as comparative world history, as opposed to the world history survey.

It is a little hard to describe how this approach works pedagogically. No texts have been written with this intent, though Eric Wolf's *Europe and the People without History*[1] would come close. Some book-length studies by historians who use the comparative world approach in their own teaching, however, illustrate the way they can pursue particular themes in a variety of cultural contexts. Michael Adas's *Prophets of Rebellion*[2] would be one example. My own *Cross-Cultural Trade in World History*[3] would be another.

Part of the problem is that a comparative course can follow a great variety of themes. The comparative approach is simply that—an approach, not a substantive body of information. Rather than talk in generalities let me illustrate *an* approach to comparative world history with a course I have been teaching since 1953 in one form or another. The course began as a one-semester offering, then evolved and changed as it grew to two semesters and altered with the times and the need to conform to the teaching requirements of three different universities—meanwhile passing itself off under four different titles.

The current name is "The World and the West," and its central point is that, by the end of the eighteenth century, the West had become the dominant culture in the world—and was to become still more dominant politically, intellectually, and militarily as the world entered the "European Age" of the nineteenth and twentieth centuries. This may sound like the older "expansion of Europe" approach, but it is not. It assumes some knowledge of European history, and sometimes deals with European motives and attitudes, but it is fundamentally concerned with the impact of Europe on other cultures. The emphasis is on culture change among the non-Europeans.

The present version is a two-semester course, the first semester with the sub-title "The Shifting Balance" being devoted to the rise of Europe in the period from about 1000 A.D. to the beginnings of the industrial age. The end of the pre-industrial world is not taken as a strict chronological line, but rather as a transition, as some institutions characteristic of the pre-industrial period are pursued well into the nineteenth century—plantation slavery, for example, being carried down to its abolition in Brazil in 1888. The second half deals with the impact of Europe in the industrial age itself, defined roughly as 1800 to the present.

The course rests on a theoretical framework of elementary, if not simple-minded, generalizations about culture change. One of the most basic is that aspects of culture can be transmitted on the initiative of the donor, that of the receiver, or both. The diffusion of technology across and between the "inter-communicating zones" of world history is a recurrent theme in both semesters in many different circumstances. With technology, the initiative was most often that of the recipients. Religions, on the other hand, have often spread through a missionary effort by the transmitters, as is fully evident not only with the spread of Christianity and Islam through overt proselytization but also in the spread of Buddhism along the trade routes of central Asia until it reached both China and Japan.

Less intentional culture change took place, of course, and especially in the colonial settings that emerged as European power began to make itself felt overseas. In this connection, the course organization uses a number of distinctions in cultural demography. In recent centuries the dominant Europeans have found themselves in control of societies having four distinct patterns of culture.

In one, called "territorial empire," Europeans ruled an alien society through relatively small cadres of administrators and soldiers. Typically, these cadres need not have been more than five percent of the local population. They were often much smaller. Examples would be the Netherlands Indies, any part of tropical Africa, or the British *raj* in India.

An opposite cultural-demographic pattern came into existence when the dominant power blanketed the native inhabitants with so many settlers that the settler culture became *the* culture of the new country. Overseas Europeans, in effect, carried their way of life with them as they moved. These territories can be labelled "true colonies." The obvious examples are the United States, Canada, Argentina, Australia and New Zealand, and large parts of Soviet Asia.

Between these extremes, two other patterns have some importance. One is sometimes called "plantation society." The crucial factor, however, is not the agricultural system but the fact that the dominant power introduced settlers—not European settlers, but settlers from a third society. The most obvious example is northeastern Brazil and the Caribbean islands, where the Europeans ran the plantations but Africans worked them. Even though the percentage of Europeans was in the range common to territorial empire, the mass of the people had come as uprooted individuals, without a community other than the one they joined as slaves. This made it very difficult to retain their original culture intact. The result was the formation of a new, mixed culture of a kind often labelled "creole."

The second cultural-demographic type lying between territorial empire and true colony is commonly called a plural society—that is, a society where two cultures exist side by side, each retaining its integrity over long periods of time. The obvious examples are places like Malaysia, where Malay and Chinese cultures continue to the present alongside smaller minorities of Arabs, Indians, and Europeans. South Africa, most of Soviet Central Asia, Andean Latin America, or Algeria before 1962 are all part of the same pattern. But these societies are not necessarily indefinitely plural. Cultural integration over the long term tends to produce a growing area of common culture, even though enclaves of originally separate cultures may persist. Mexico is a good example of this kind of cultural integration over the past couple of centuries. Most Mexicans now live with an integrated culture with both Indian and European roots, even though some Spanish and many Indian communities have kept their cultural integrity into the 1980s.

These categories, however, are not designed to provide an iron-clad theory or to carry much of the weight of explanation. They are a convenient framework for comparison, with the understanding that comparison will highlight differences as well as similarities. The categories are also useful as a guide to representative types of culture contact that need to be "covered" in a course that aims to achieve the perspective of world history.

The course outline proceeds through a set of topics—three to four per semester. It begins with a survey of relations between major societies over the period from about 1000 A.D. to the early sixteenth century, intended mainly to set the stage for a non-ethnocentric view of the world as it was then. Here and throughout the course, no textbook is available to carry the main thread of narrative. When good survey material is available, as it is in this period from the works of William McNeill and Eric Wolf, reading assignments can carry the burden of continuity, while lectures can deal in greater detail with problems needing more analytical treatment. For other topics, the lectures have to carry the main line, while readings provide material for case studies.

In the first section, lecture and readings together seek to examine the resources available to the major world societies in their agricultural systems, technology, political organization, and military power—and to survey intersocietal relations.

The second topic has to do with the impact of Europe on maritime Asia from Japan south and west along the Indian Ocean coasts as far as Ethiopia—over the period of the sixteenth century to the late eighteenth. Its aim is to look at culture contact in a period when the impact of Western culture came mainly through trade and the missionary movement. Students read large sections of my *Cross-Cultural Trade* along with parts of regional texts like Percival Spear for India[4] or Steinberg and others for Southeast Asia.[5] The lectures deal comparatively with particular themes—such as the successes and failures of the Christian missionary movement in sixteenth-century Japan, Timor, and Ethiopia, of the economic impact of improvements in maritime technology on freight rates, hence on the possibilities of trade between parts of maritime Asia—and on the agricultural adjustments that followed.

The third and final topic for the first semester is a return to the Atlantic basin for a seven-week examination of the "Rise and Fall of the South Atlantic System." The centerpiece is the complex of slave plantations in the tropical Americas, fed by the slave trade from Africa and intimately related to the Western societies of North America and Europe, as well as to the plural societies of nearby, non-plantation Spanish America. Although the core is culture-change within the "plantation" cultural-demographic type, the combination of lectures and readings makes it possible to survey Spanish American colonial history in a superficial way, while looking briefly at African history in the era of the slave trade and then in somewhat more detail at the revolutions that demolished the South Atlantic System. Jamaica and Haiti serve as case studies for the late eighteenth/early nineteenth century, while Brazil and Cuba are used to illustrate the final end of slavery in the Americas. One sidelight within this topic is a single lecture on the Spanish theory of empire in the sixteenth century, set alongside the English theory of empire in the early seventeenth. The purpose of this lecture is partly to bring in the importance of intentions and justifications, even when these are not in line with reality, and partly also to serve as background for two similar discussions of imperial theory in the second semester: one on the theory of overseas colonization in the early nineteenth century, a second on the theory of imperial expansion later in the century.

The second semester of this comparative world history course poses far more severe problems of organization, if only because the industrialization of western Europe and eastern North America created far greater power differentials between the West and the rest of the world. It also brought about a far more complex set of cross-cultural tensions and adjustments, as the Europeans created their territorial empires overseas.

The sub-title for the second semester is "The Revolution of Modernization." I must add a caveat immediately. I do not subscribe to the modernization theory that was so popular in social scientific circles in the 1950s and 1960s and for some time afterwards. The definition of modernization used here is strictly economic—the creation of a kind of society capable of high productivity and high mass consumption. "Industrialization" would have done just as well, but for the fear of leaving advanced agricultural economies like Denmark or New Zealand out of the picture.

The semester begins with some theoretical discussions of what modern-ization might and might not be taken to mean and then passes on to a four-week topic on European overseas settlement, the only topic focused directly on European activities. This approach has several purposes. One is to introduce the study of migration as a key fact of recent history—now seen on a scale more massive than the slave trade had been, and standing as background for the still more massive patterns of migration that were to follow the Second World War.

A second is to highlight the fact that cultures do not change *only* because of contact with alien societies. They also change in response to new circumstances, and culture change among the overseas Europeans is a case in point. This is approached through case studies. I first look at transfrontier cultures, those of Europeans who moved beyond the frontiers of the European way of life and adopted a new culture they either invented to meet their new circumstances or borrowed from the alien people they settled among. The examples used here are the *métis* of Manitoba up to the 1860s or so, the gaucho culture of the Argentine pampa up to the early nineteenth century, and the *trekboer* culture of eighteenth-century South Africa.

Transfrontier cultures serve to introduce a two-week comparative study of frontier–metropolitan tensions, using Argentina and South Africa in the first half of the eighteenth century as cases in point. Here, the main line of survey is carried by sections of texts on Argentine and South African history, while the lectures carry an analytical theme drawing from the geographers' ideas about central-place theory.

Just as the first topic for the semester focused on "true colonization," the second focuses on territorial empire, beginning with a quick survey of the patterns of imperial expansion and its possible causes, but concentrating on conquest and culture change from the point of view of the conquered. Four principal examples are used here, those of Soviet Central Asia, Bengal, Java, then Mexico, concentrating there on the Maya of Yucatan and the Yaqui of Sonora. As usual, some topics can be carried by readings—Elizabeth Bacon on Central Asia,[6] Nelson Reed on Yucatan[7]—while others are more easily presented in lectures.

The third topic is called "Conversion." It, too, comes from the introductory typology of culture change—in this case, culture change by intent, a thread already followed in the minor theme of Western missions and non-Western responses in the first semester. The nineteenth-century missionary movement now makes its appearance in a pair of lectures on the movement in Europe and on the ground in Uganda, while the students read Robin Horton[8] and J.D.Y. Peel[9] for sociological and anthropological comparisons between the *reactions* to the missions in Uganda and Nigeria. The use of Uganda illustrates one way comparative cases can serve several purposes. Using the same time/place context in different ways allows the students to work from a body of material that begins to be familiar. Uganda in the 1880s to about 1910 is used first to show how European missions operated, second as part of a two-case example of African reactions to missionary teaching, and finally to introduce the theme of non-Western borrowing from the West as a form of "defensive modern-ization."

This theme of cultural change on the borrower's initiative continues in the two weeks that follow, which take up Meiji Japan and Turkey from the nineteenth-century reform movement into the period of Ataturk.

The final topic of the course departs from the original typology to look at political and intellectual pressures in the mid-twentieth century non-Western world—at the independence movements as a political manifestation of a revolt against the West, but even more as subtle reactions of ambivalence in aversion to some Western manifestations and as a continued and avid effort to get at least the kind of material resources industrial technology seems to make available. The national revolts are given a week, just as conventional "imperialism" was given a week. The first of the remaining weeks is devoted to millennial movements of an anti-Western nature, combining lectures with readings from Michael Adas's *Prophets of Rebellion*. The final two weeks use Indonesia and Ghana from the early independence movement to the fall of Nkrumah and Sukarno, respectively.

A course of this scope creates some special pedagogical problems. It covers a lot of unfamiliar material in a fairly short period of time. For the past ten years or so, I have experimented with ways of doing this. One of these is the interplay of lectures and readings, so that one tends to carry the main or survey aspect of the course, while the other carries the analysis. This organization implies a different role for the lectures and readings, though the two work together. It also calls for a conscious effort to integrate the two, done with two periods of class discussion each week in addition to the two lectures that are normal at Johns Hopkins. To give the lecturer time to direct all class discussions himself, the lectures are on tape cassettes available in the library on loan. The readings tend to be about 100 to 150 pages each week. Each student is expected to produce at the beginning of the week a three-page "intellectual journal," giving his or her reactions to the current readings and just-past lectures. This exercise tends to prepare students for the discussions, and the students are compensated for the extra work by receiving four credits in place of the usual three. It is obvious that a course of this kind can achieve breadth, but only at the cost of coverage. It is also necessarily idiosyncratic. No two teachers putting together a course in comparative world history will do it quite the same way. This may not be altogether bad, but the particular course outlined here also leaves some serious gaps. It tells students far too little about the last fifty years. On the other hand, teachers probably teach better what they understand better. As long as they avoid the trap of staying too close to their own research interests, both they and the students probably learn more from eclectic and uneven breadth combined with depth in sample soundings than they would have learned from systematic superficiality.

Notes

[1] Eric Wolf, *Europe and the People without History* (Berkeley, Cal.: 1982).

[2] Michael Adas, *Prophets of Rebellion* (Chapel Hill, N.C.: 1978).

[3] Philip D. Curtin, *Cross-Cultural Trade in World History* (New York: 1984).

[4] Percival Spear, *India: A Modern History* (Ann Arbor, Mich.: 1961, 1972).

[5] David D. Steinberg, David K. Wyatt, John R.W. Smail, Alexander Woodside, William R. Roff, and David P. Chandler, *In Search of Southeast Asia* (New York: 1971; Honolulu, 1985).

[6] Elizabeth E. Bacon, *Central Asians under Russian Rule: A study in Culture Change* (Ithaca, N.Y.: 1980).

[7] Nelson Reed, *The Caste War of Yucatan* (Palo Alto, Cal.: 1964).

[8] Robin Horton, "The Rationality of Conversion," *Africa* 45 (1975), 219–35, 373–99.

[9] J.D.Y. Peel, "Conversion and Tradition in Two African Societies," *Past and Present* 7 (1977), 108–49.

World-Systems Analysis:
Five Questions in Search of a
New Consensus

Immanuel Wallerstein

The traditional general education in history in the United States (but also in western Europe) has laid emphasis on teaching the history of one's own country plus teaching the history of something that has been called the Western world (and/or civilization). In the U.S., the latter has generally meant some knowledge concerning the history primarily of Great Britain, France, and Germany in the nineteenth and twentieth centuries, of England from the sixteenth to eighteenth centuries, of the "Renaissance" and "Reformation" and also some dabbling in that of the Middle Ages as well as in that of classical Greece and Rome.

In the period since the Second World War, there has emerged some criticism of such curricula as being too "Eurocentric." Attempts have therefore been made, with very limited success, to add some instruction in what might be thought of as the "great civilizations of the East"—India, China, Japan, occasionally the Arab caliphates. Whatever gain has been achieved by this broadening of geography (which has not been too widely adopted) has probably been more than offset by the decline in standard history instruction, both at the college and high school levels. One cannot simply presume today that a college graduate has a working elementary knowledge of, for example, the French Revolution.

However, neither a plea for patchwork additions to the old curriculum (a smattering of Chinese history on top of Western history) nor a general deploring of lowered intellectual requirements in our educational system is really to the point. A more fundamental question is arising. The way we teach history today is part and parcel of the intellectual consensus that emerged in Europe during

Immanuel Wallerstein is Director of the Fernand Braudel Center at the State University of New York, Binghamton.

the nineteenth century in the wake of the social issues laid bare by the expansion of the urban-industrial sector and the heritage of the French Revolution. And this consensus itself is being called into question. The point therefore is to see what was the consensus and what were its social roots, why it has come to be questioned and in what ways, and what are the implications for instruction in "history."

The consensus arrived at in the nineteenth century is not too difficult to describe; by definition it is familiar to everyone, although (as is the case for most intellectual consensus) people tend to think of these presumptions as obvious or factual rather than as socially constructed perspectives. I will limit myself here to three basic premises, although they scarcely exhaust the picture.

Premise No. 1

The history of the modern (Western) world is the history of the rise of the "middle classes" (economically, politically, culturally) in the wake of the steady expansion of the market-centered organization of production and the slow but steady urbanization process. This phenomenon has been accompanied in the political arena by the steady decline in the arbitrariness of political authorities. It has involved in the social sphere an overall increase in human welfare and of popular participation in decision making. The slow process reached a decisive and positive turning-point in the twin key events of the late eighteenth century: the Industrial Revolution in England and the French Revolution.

Premise No. 2

The units within which these changes have occurred, and therefore the key units for historical analysis, were the (national) states. It was "England" that had an "industrial revolution" between 1780 and 1840; it was "Germany" which failed to have a bourgeois (or democratic) revolution in 1848–49. The explanations are to be sought in the prior history of these areas. We look therefore at "German" or "Italian" history of the eighteenth, and fifteenth, and even the tenth centuries to understand why "unification" of these two "nations" occurred so "late." In any case, the history of all national states has been a history of internal homogenization, of lessening loyalties of citizens to "traditional" entities or groups (e.g., "ethnic" or religious groups) and increasing loyalty to the "national" group.

Premise No. 3

The story told under premises 1 and 2 is a story of human progress. It is the story of the search for human freedom, a relatively successful search. Furthermore, the search for progress is continuing. If there seem to be setbacks, they are temporary. If there are phenomena which do not fit the picture, they are anomalous. Such progress is not only empirically real but theoretically inevitable. Finally, there was a derived proposition from these premises that concerned "world history." The story of human freedom was a discovery of (a product of the particular history of) the Western world. One of its consequences was the rise of a technology which enabled the Western world to expand "overseas." This expansion itself represented the progress of "civilization," since its basic impact was "civilizing."

To be sure, baldly stated like this, the viewpoint seems a bit caricatural, and no doubt there have been innumerable caveats, dissents, and nuances expressed. Still, a reading of high school textbooks in Western countries written between say 1850 and 1950 would doubtless confirm the generality of this consensus about how the modern world should be interpreted.

The social roots of this consensus seem very clear. The hegemony of Great Britain in the world-system in the mid-nineteenth century combined with the dramatic expansion of applied scientific technology, lent itself to this view of the world which might be seen to be a reasonable explanation of the existing realities combined with an ideological justification of the privileges of the powerful. Although many detailed changes in world realities occurred thereafter, it could be argued that the system continued to seem to thrive (even despite the two world wars of the twentieth century, and despite the Russian Revolution) until perhaps the 1960s. That being so, the particular intellectual consensus continued as a basis of both academic and public social analysis.

The ways in which this social reality began to change radically can be seen in the simultaneous occurrence of three seemingly separate developments in three different parts of the world. In the non-European zones of the world, the rise of nationalist movements did not in itself challenge the assumptions of the consensus, since it could be argued they represented the fulfillment of the process. There was, however, a fly in the ointment. It was the phenomenon of the so-called growing gap between industrialized and Third World countries. Political independence of former colonial areas did not seem in practice to overcome world inequalities or necessarily bring the automatic benefits of political and cultural "progress." Explanations that were sought in the prior "history" of the "nations" did not seem *to them* very satisfactory. They therefore pushed in two directions. One was to look for explanations in some supranational processes. The other was to raise "civilizational" questions, posing the concept of civilizations (plural) against that of civilization (singular), which translated into doubts about universalistic assumptions built into Western historical reasoning.

At the same time, that zone of the world with Communist governments, running from central Europe to east Asia, began to experience seismic internal political difficulties. In some way, the Russian Revolution of 1917, particularly once it came into its Stalinist phase, had not really challenged the premises of the consensus. In a sense, the Communists presented themselves as the heirs of the process that had occurred over long historical time in the Western world and as its logical fulfillment. What began to come into question, among the participants of the social movements in power in these countries themselves, was the degree to which progress had really been achieved (the issues of "revisionism" on the one hand and of "terror" on the other). Once again, explanations sought in the immediate or long-term history of these "nations" did not seem very satisfactory to the people there, and alternative explanatory schemata were sought. The impact of these developments was even greater perhaps elsewhere in the world. The "disillusionments" experienced were disillusionments in the face of predictions derived from the consensual framework of analysis. This led many to reappraise the premises.

Finally, in the Western world itself, the 1960s represented the institutionalization of a new kind of social turmoil which was not easily explained by the consensual premises. In particular, the premise of the reality and desirability of a process of national homogenization was called into doubt. Many groups proclaimed that they had been *entirely* left out of the process hitherto described as universal: women, all kinds of low-status "ethnic" and "national" groupings, persons of particular sexual inclinations, the handicapped, etc. To some extent, to be sure, this represented merely one more set of demands within the framework of the established process which could be accommodated, but to some extent it increasingly represented a challenge to the "assimilationist" model implicit in the old consensus, which is why these "new social movements" have aroused such strong emotional resistance. In order to pursue their objectives, these movements have consequently been forced increasingly to question intellectual premises and not merely current policies.

The intellectual outcome of the past twenty years has been to create a situation in which the premises described previously no longer represent a consensus, but merely one set of premises among actively contending sets. There is in some sense a search going on for a new consensus. This is one of the reasons why projects such as this one are being generated.

It is too early to institutionalize a new model in the university. Rather, what is incumbent on us in the present era is to construct curricula in which these premises are brought to the fore as open intellectual questions. Eminently feasible and desirable, such organization would entail a more "difficult" curriculum, of course, since it is always more difficult—for teacher and student—to discuss uncertainties rather than to learn "transmitted knowledge." But in fact there is considerable evidence in the real world that people are sufficiently uncomfortable about received verities to be somewhat willing to engage in this more difficult mode of learning.

In particular, I suggest that five open questions have to be incorporated into the basic teaching of history (first at the college level, later at the high school level).

1. What is the meaningful unit of social analysis? Does "Germany" have a history between 1500 and 1800? There are various alternative assumptions, for example. Between 1500 and 1800, "Germany" was merely a linguistic zone within the European world-economy. Or Prussia had a history, but not Germany. Or "central Europe" had a history. I am not debating this issue here. I merely wish to suggest that the debate should not be considered an esoteric one for advanced scholars but a fundamental one for beginning students.

2. Where is the "world"? Is "world history" the history first of the "West" which then came to encompass the globe? Alternatively, is it the sum of "high civilizations"—the West plus China plus India plus...? Is the concept of "civilization" properly speaking used in the singular or the plural?

3. What is appropriate periodization? This is of course an old debate. The original division of Western historiography into Antiquity, the Middle Ages, and Modernity reflects well-known premises. The breakpoints of the "Agricultural Revolution" and the "Industrial Revolution" reflect not too different ones. But insofar as questions 1 and 2 get discussed, a systematic discussion of alternative periodizations seems eminently on the agenda.

4. Are the "groups" we use to discuss history, particularly modern history, appropriate ones? "Middle classes" and "aristocrats" are obviously different groups. So are "workers" and "peasants." Is this distinction so sure? A good deal of the empirical work of the last twenty years has called precisely these two obvious categorizations into question. If they do not "hold," much of modern history has to be radically rewritten.

5. How can progress be measured, and within what units (question no. 1 again)? Was everything that occurred later progress over that which was earlier? and was it inevitable? A favorite for parlor philosophy, this question can be made empirical/theoretical, open to careful historical analysis.

The reader may be thinking: This is all very well, but can students discuss such questions without prior concrete historical knowledge? But the "prior knowledge" comes wrapped mostly in premises that presume answers to these questions. The trick is to wrap the knowledge in such a way as to leave the premises open. This will be harder for the professoriat than for the students. But it is the minimum necessary if one wants to give undergraduates a "global perspective," and it is attainable if we wish to do it.

Commonly Articulated Goals for World History Courses

Kevin Reilly

1. Geographical Knowledge of the World

In a recent nationwide test on "global understanding" conducted by the Educational Testing Service, 3,000 American college students were asked to circle the area where they were born on a map. About 150 students circled Central America or South America. "After some digging," according to the report, "the confused researchers discovered that those who had circled Central America had been born in the Midwest, and those who had circled South America were from Tennessee, Virginia, and other southeastern states." Student geographical knowledge varies widely. While one student can place Rangoon and Shanghai accurately on a world map, another places Canada in Siberia, the Mediterranean in Hudson's Bay, the Mississippi at Tierra del Fuego, and the Sahara in Alaska. An attainable goal might be the ability to locate ten to twenty of the world's major countries and perhaps a similar number of the world's major rivers, seas, mountain ranges, deserts and cities. Further, the student might be expected to locate areas, places, and routes that are referred to frequently as the course progresses.

2. General Awareness of the Age and History of the Earth

While it is difficult for students (or the rest of us) to conceive of geological and evolutionary processes lasting millions of years, students should not think as if there were no earth before 1960, 1900, or 4004 B.C. They should have some awareness that the earth is billions of years old, humans have existed for millions of years, and the origins of civilization go back thousands of years.

Kevin Reilly is President of the World History Association and Professor of History at Somerset County College.

3. Use of Vocabulary for Periodization of World History

The student should be able to speak of the distant past in terms more precise than "in caveman days" or "way back in the old days." While the instructor would be pleased with the effective use of such terms as paleolithic, neolithic, bronze age, urban revolution, ancient, classical, first millennium B.C., Shang dynasty, Hellenistic, Gupta or fifth century, the minimal expectation would be an ability to use some such terms (at least some of the time) in referring to the past.

4. Understanding the Impact of Technological Changes

The student should be able to say something about technological changes in human history. While an ability to distinguish between hunting-gathering, agricultural-pastoral, and industrial society would be minimal (at least so the student would not expect to find electrical batteries in ancient Egypt), one would also hope for some understanding of the impact of some such technologies as the following: the plow, irrigation, writing, printing, gunpowder, the clock, the railroad, atomic fusion, plastics, the computer, and others.

5. Ability to Categorize, Classify, or Compare Human Societies

Students should be able to make world history intelligible through the use of some social, political, or economic categories some of the time. Such terms as feudal, capitalist, pastoral, industrial, democratic, colonial, labor intensive, rice culture, and mining civilization only hint at the possibilities. The point is not which categories are used, but that some are.

6. Familiarity with Some of the World's Great Religious and Cultural Traditions

While it might not be possible to expect American graduates to distinguish between Shiite and Sunnite traditions of Islam, they should be able to say something about the world's major religions. At a minimum, students should be able to say something about Buddhism, Christianity, Confucianism, Hinduism, Islam, and Judaism.

7. Accessibility of Global Past

Students should be able to use information about the world's past when they face current problems. They should be able to draw on historical experiences (beyond their own lives and cultures) for understanding and insight. Their reference points and examples should transcend their own time and place.

8. An Understanding of the Rise of the West

Students should be aware of both the recentness and suddenness of the rise of the West. This might include some knowledge of the importance of other civilizations before 1500, an understanding of the causes and dimensions of the Western rise and revolution. It might include an understanding of some of the following developments: Renaissance, Reformation, exploration, colonialism, slavery, capitalism, scientific revolution, industrial revolution, middle-class political revolutions.

9. An Understanding of the Impact of Western Dominance World-Wide

Students should be aware of some of the ways in which this "rise of the West" has been experienced in other parts of the world, especially in colonies, former colonies, and "Third World" countries. This might include an understanding of some of the history of imperialism and anti-colonial revolutions. It might also include an understanding of American foreign policy, international agencies, or post-colonial tensions.

10. Ability to imagine and empathize with the foreign

Students should develop an awareness (even an appreciation) of cultural and human diversity. At the least, the student should not automatically assume that the foreign is similar or the exotic wrong. At best, this awareness will deepen the student's sense of human possibilities, and, thus, the student's own humanity.

POLITICAL SCIENCE

Political science offers two categories of international focus: foreign and comparative politics, and international relations and politics. These subfields of the discipline are closely linked, as explanations of international politics of many countries are influenced very considerably by international circumstances.

In contributing to the NCFLIS project, the American Political Science Association solicited essays in both categories. The first five chapters that follow—by Suzanne Berger, Leon Epstein, Gerhard Loewenberg, Susanne and Lloyd Rudolph, and Ole Holsti—offer perspectives on increasing the comparative content of political science, whose focus on national political systems has been very largely on the United States. Suggesting the desirability of engaging students in comparative foreign policy analysis, the Holsti essay provides a transition to the four contributions by Harold Jacobson, George Quester, Robert Keohane, and Kenneth Thompson. These international relations chapters survey concepts, approaches, theories, and teaching strategies within the subfield of international politics and international relations.

Subject only to series editor Kurt Müller's stylistic concerns that the essays appeal to non-specialist readers, the integrity of each of the following essays has been maintained. One exception, however, is that we have omitted the syllabus that accompanied Kenneth Thompson's essay because of a policy decision not to reprint syllabi in this book.

Politics: American and Non-American

Suzanne Berger

Considering how Americans compare their nation with others, Tocqueville observed that general ideas about politics testify to the weakness of human intelligence. "The Deity does not regard the human race collectively.... Such is, however, not the case with man.... Having superficially considered a certain number of objects and remarked their resemblance, he assigns to them a common name, sets them apart, and proceeds onwards."[1]

As it is for other human beings, so, too, for political scientists. And of the generalizations which have helped Americans and American political scientists organize the confusing mass differences and similarities between this country and others, none has been more important and enduring than the notion of the uniqueness of the American political community. This conception is reflected in the split within the discipline between those who study the U.S. political system and those who study comparative politics, a field understood to encompass various foreign countries. The rubric that in the *American Political Science Review* until the 1950s used to read "Foreign Government and Politics" has been replaced by a section of book reviews entitled "Comparative Politics." But today as in the past, it is rare to find teaching or research in political science that truly integrates the analysis of American politics within a comparative framework.

Why this conception should remain is difficult to understand, for over the past half-century there have been many shifts in the discipline and in the world that challenged the premises of research based on American exceptionalism. Already in the interwar period, significant work in political science was moving beyond configurative case studies of individual countries. Indeed, C.J. Friedrich's important *Constitutional Government and Democracy* (1937) included the United States in its examination of how well certain general political theories explained the experiences of major political systems. Whatever reser-

Suzanne Berger is Ford International Professor of Political Science at the Massachusetts Institute of Technology.

vations one might have had about the methodologies of comparative research on which Friedrich relied, the broad influence of his work promised a new integration of American politics into an expanded field of comparative politics.[2]

Other far-reaching changes seemed to point in the same direction. Simply to list them: the experiences of Fascism, Nazism, and Stalinism shifted intellectual attention away from what had been an almost exclusive focus on liberal democracies. These repressive regimes could not very well be analyzed by reference to their distance or proximity to American or British locations on the great universal trajectory of progress toward democracy. Rather, to account at all for the origins, mode of functioning, and the immediate postwar period, the appearance in world politics of a large number of newly independent, non-Western, less-developed countries had a similar impact on political science. It expanded the category of political phenomena that were seen to matter and broadened the scope of political analysis.

At the same time, theoretical developments within the discipline produced a frame within which the structures, processes, and values of heterogeneous political experiences could be compared. The conceptual apparatus of structural-functionalism offered the possibility of ordering and analyzing the vastly enlarged body of significant political facts. It also made it possible for American political scientists to transmit a science of politics that was no longer simply a knowledge of American political life and a vision of a kind of global progress to liberal democracy. Rather, structural-functionalism seemed both to redefine the status of the American political system—now simply one case among others (albeit still regarded in some ways, both theoretical and political, as more advanced)—and to raise the status of other polities—now to be understood as systems in their own right and not mainly as examples of blighted or incomplete democratic development.

Finally, the emergence in Western Europe and elsewhere of a highly sophisticated political science, increasingly independent of the juridical and historical traditions which had inhibited its growth in the past, also constituted a reason to hope that the gulf that separated political research on the United States from that on the rest of the world would at last be bridged. The younger political scientist abroad had in many cases been trained in American universities and shared the enthusiasm of their American counterparts for the new theories and methodologies of comparative research.

Despite these promising elements, the bifurcation of political science into American politics and non-American politics remained. There are exceptions, the most outstanding and influential of which remains Gabriel Almond and Sidney Verba's *The Civic Culture* (1963). But on balance, with respect to the central concepts of the discipline and the study of the core institutions and processes—parties, interest groups, representative assemblies, voting, governance—developments in each of the two main wings of political research were remarkably little affected by developments in the other. Alex Inkeles in 1949 had observed the excitement in American social science over research on foreign societies and had cautioned: "There cannot be one social science for the study of one's own country and a different one for the study of other nations."[3] Thirty-five years after this prescient warning, the scholar of comparative politics and the scholar of American politics who venture across the well-marked frontiers onto each other's turf still feel themselves to be traveling on *terra incognita*. It is indeed as if there were one set of conceptual maps—one social science—for U.S. politics and another for comparative, that is, "foreign," politics.

The changes at the core of the discipline have left the old boundaries largely intact, but on the periphery of the field, new approaches to comparison of U.S. and foreign experience are appearing. By "periphery" I mean the areas of intersection and overlap of political science with other academic disciplines. For those interested in the integration of American politics within comparative politics, there are three "zones" of intellectual ferment on the periphery of political science. First, in historical sociology, the great and controversial book of Barrington Moore, Jr., *The Social Origins of Dictatorship and Democracy* (1966) and the comparative research on Europe, Asia, and the U.S. that this work stimulated have had great influence within political science. A younger generation of sociologists is continuing to mine this rewarding vein. Exemplary of the intellectual concerns of this group is the work of Theda Skocpol, who has moved from a study of the role of state bureaucracies in accounting for different revolutionary outcomes, *State and Social Revolutions: A Comparative Analysis of France, Russia, and China* (1979), to a study of bureaucratic capabilities in the implementation of New Deal programs.[4]

The second zone in which new conceptualizations of American and foreign experience are being developed is that of political economy, a field that spans what had been a no-man's land between economics and political science. The work of such senior scholars as Charles E. Lindblom, *Politics and Markets* (1977), and a host of "middle" and younger scholars (to mention only a few: Peter Gourevitch, Charles Maier, Stephen Krasner, Peter Katzenstein, Michael Piore, Charles Sabel, John Zysman) all develop arguments in which the specificities of American experience are accounted for within a more comprehensive theoretical frame. The analysis of the patterns of relationships that emerge between state and economy in advanced industrial capitalist societies builds on comparisons of a number of countries, among which is the United States. The special features of the American case are conceived as phenomena that have to be explained by the theory, and not as barriers to comparison and generalization.

The third area in which there has been real change in the ways research on American and foreign political experience has been carried out is public policy. The study of the "common problems of industrial societies" has produced a large literature on how the U.S. and others identify problems, mobilize resources, politicians, bureaucracies to resolve them, and, then, implement solutions. This literature has been criticized with some justice as an atheoretical lining-up of superficially comparable events, with little or no reflection on the significance of the comparisons. The best of the work in this mode, however, has contributed not only to widening the range of options that can be imagined for a particular social problem, but also to a deeper understanding of the politics of the societies in which the problems appear. Exemplary of such work by a younger generation of scholars who have been interested in direct comparisons of the U.S. and a foreign society are the books of Steven Kelman, *Regulating America, Regulating Sweden* (1981), and Deborah Stone, *The Disabled State* (1984).

Even with all this activity on the edges of the discipline, what remains problematic is the transmission to and reception by the core. Those who toil in the zones of intellectual innovation on the periphery have developed more or less far-reaching hegemonic claims about the implication of their work for the discipline as a whole. But the writ of these claims barely extends beyond the group of those working within the same rather specialized intellectual province. The new ways of thinking about American politics that have appeared on the periphery of the discipline have had strikingly little impact on the great majority of political scientists who study U.S. political parties, elections, state and local government, bureaucracies, and so forth.

The temptation is great (especially for those working in a new way on comparative study of the U.S.) to conceive the present situation as a Kuhnian moment in which normal science is about to be overtaken by radical innovations. A more sober reading suggests that the objects of study—the puzzles—that fascinate those at the core and those on the edges are so different that all of these activities may well continue indefinitely on tracks that neither converge nor collide. The logic of the intellectual endeavors which engage the respective parties does not appear to lead to decisive confrontations. Whatever learning and transmission takes place between core and periphery will have to be the product of willed, planful intellectual creation.

Notes

[1] Alexis de Tocqueville, *Democracy in America*, vol. 2, trans. Henry Reeve (New York: Schocken, 1961), p. 14.

[2] Harry Eckstein, "A Perspective on Comparative Politics, Past and Present," in Harry Eckstein and David Apter (ed.), *Comparative Politics* (New York: Free Press, 1963), pp. 21–23.

[3] Alex Inkeles, "Understanding a Foreign Society: A Sociologist's View," *World Politics* 3(1950–51), 269. The article was based on a paper read to a joint section meeting of the American Political Science Association and the American Sociological Society in 1949.

[4] Kenneth Finegold and Theda Skocpol, "State Capacity and Economic Intervention in the Early New Deal," *Political Science Quarterly* 97:2(1982).

Cutting across the Institutional Grain: The Study of Political Parties

Leon D. Epstein

Having had a foot in each camp for over 30 years, I am acutely aware of our discipline's customary division of the study of political parties between American and non-American subjects. The division remains most apparent in teaching programs despite increasing cross-national research efforts during the last few decades. I doubt that merger is entirely feasible. The division is deeply rooted in the general development of political science in the United States, and something like it is characteristic of other subjects as well as of parties. Legislatures, executives, and courts readily come to mind. Significantly, they are governmental institutions so linked to a country's constitutional and historical experience that a national context for their study seems plainly appropriate. Although parties are not governmental institutions in the same sense as are legislatures, executives, and courts, they have become more than merely private political associations. Most notably in the United States, they are plainly quasi-governmental in many respects. Perhaps this helps to explain why American political scientists have treated our parties, along with governing agencies, as American institutions while leaving parties in other nations for treatment under the rubric of comparative government and politics. Much can be said on behalf of that institutional tradition, but one must grant that it ties our work to geographic units and thus keeps many political scientists closer to historians, in at least one methodological sense, than to economists or sociologists. For better or worse, we thus appear less scientific, conceptually, than the ambitious title of our discipline suggests.

In any geographical breakdown of specialties within political science, American government and politics is by far the largest of several area studies. The predominance dates from the first 15 or 20 years of this century when our discipline established itself on a fairly large scale in American universities. Before

Leon D. Epstein is Hilldale Professor of Political Science at the University of Wisconsin.

those years, it is true that general comparative analysis was emphasized by European-trained scholars who had been the pioneers of political science in late nineteenth-century America. But with the "Americanization" of the profession between 1904 and 1914, there came not only numerous scholars trained exclusively in the United States but also a greater interest in American political phenomena. By 1915, American government had replaced a "comparative government/general political science" offering as the most frequently encountered undergraduate course in departmental curricula.[1] Rapidly, too, political science departments developed courses devoted to particular American institutions and processes. Parties provided subject-matter for one of those courses. Books on American parties had appeared even earlier, soon after the famous British scholar Bryce called attention to the special importance of parties in the United States.[2] And by the 1920s there were first-class texts, resembling in intellectual quality the best texts now in use.

The study of American parties has thus long been a well-recognized field for scholarship as well as for teaching. When American political scientists say that they are parties specialists, most of them mean—and the discipline understands them to mean—that their work mainly concerns parties in the United States. A minority of these Americanists also occasionally study parties in another nation, especially Britain, and the minority is probably larger and more impressive now than a few decades ago. But most scholarly work on non-American parties, now as in the past, is the product of political scientists who specialize in the affairs of particular foreign nations. Although their field is called comparative, it is seldom any more or less so than the study of American phenomena. Systematic cross-national work on parties, as on other political subjects, remains exceptional although important and increasingly influential. Most often the research finds its way into academic courses on particular nations or regional clusters of nations. The courses, unlike those in the American field, do not include many devoted exclusively to parties. Rather, a foreign country's parties tend to be studied only along with a country's other political institutions and processes (as, of course, American parties are also included in introductory American government courses). Not only does each foreign country, or cluster of countries, have fewer topical courses than does the American field, but any topical breakdown that exists is less likely to be institutional especially in studying third world nations.

These general impressions are quickly confirmed by looking at university course catalogs. I checked ten of these, including the catalogs of five universities whose departments usually rank among the most prestigious, and found that every one of the ten listed an American parties course, but only one a comparative parties course. Several departments, however, had advanced courses, often intended principally for graduate students, with titles like "comparative group political behavior" that indicate the inclusion of parties.

I have already suggested that the considerably more salient study of American parties is not inherently more national, or parochial, than the study of non-American parties. Commonly, however, it is so regarded, perhaps partly because the most imposing efforts to transcend national boundaries in writing about parties have come not from Americanists but from scholars whose research (and their own careers) began outside the United States. Ostrogorski, Michels, and Duverger are the leading older cases in point.[3] Their work, despite even Ostrogorski's heavily American content, exerts influence chiefly among students (including American students) of European parties. So I expect will Sartori's monumental comparative parties work, now that it has begun to appear,[4] be more influential outside the American field although the work includes the United States in its universe of both Western and non-Western nations. Moreover, certain European scholars, though studying politics in their own countries, have begun to ask American-derived questions particularly about voting behavior.

The American parties field may also appear more parochial because the great bulk of its scholarship is a native product. Bryces have not been numerous. Nor have many of the talented European émigrés of the 1930s devoted themselves to American parties and politics as they have so notably to other areas of our discipline. To be sure, a predominance of native American scholarship in the American parties field has not precluded comparisons with parties in other nations. But few American specialists have made such comparisons a central concern even when they admired foreign models. Once the parties field itself developed, Americanists were seldom as systematically comparative as Lowell had been at the turn of the century.[5]

I was especially impressed with the Americanist character of the parties field, as it is ordinarily understood, when almost 20 years ago I wrote a chapter for a volume honoring V.O. Key, Jr., the field's preeminent scholar.[6] I had been asked to discuss the relation of Key's work to the comparative study of parties in other nations. Furnished with a full list of his numerous and distinguished publications, I noticed that it contained only one article about another country. It was on federalism and governmental grant policies in Canada. With respect to parties, Key's research was exclusively American. His references to foreign parties were parenthetical efforts to sharpen descriptions of American phenomena with contrasting examples. Yet neither 20 years ago nor now do I find anything pejoratively parochial about Key's works. In fact, within the American parties field, he was a pioneer in raising the study of state politics from a "How-it-is-by-us" character to a genuinely comparative level. Doing so was decidedly relevant, for example, to his exploration of the impact of the direct primary on party organizations. Like the subject itself, that exploration was distinctively American, but the method was comparative even without reference to non-American material.

At its best, as in the work of Key and many others, American parties scholarship is hard to fault because of its national attachments. It may well gain intellectual depth from those attachments insofar as American parties must be understood as responses to American historical and constitutional circumstances. A similar point can more readily be made with respect to teaching. Most of us do not detach parties from their national context (American, British, or whatever), so as to teach a course about parties generally. No doubt, we might do so successfully when we have students, probably at the graduate level, who have previously studied parties under American and other national rubrics. But, speaking for myself, I have not found it pedagogically advantageous to substitute an undergraduate comparative parties course for either the standard American parties course or the general British politics course that I teach. Two decades ago, I tried such substitution for juniors and seniors, and it failed even though my students were in an honors program. The failure, I thought, lay in the difficulty of comprehending the role of parties without knowledge of the political systems and societies in which they operated. Admittedly, the failure might have flowed also from intellectual limitations that I suffer as a result of the long-standing national division of subject-matter.

Given those limitations, be they permanent or only those of an older generation, the best that I have been able to do in my undergraduate teaching is to introduce a more concertedly comparative perspective than has been usual in courses related to particular countries. Thus, in an American parties course, while the subject-matter remains entirely American, I include not only the customary contrasting foreign examples, but also a conceptual framework in which, at the start and conclusion of the course as well as along the way, American parties are compared with parties in other Western democratic nations so as to emphasize their similarities and differences. This can now be done more effectively than a few decades ago because of the scholarship available in both American and non-American fields. Moreover, the scholarship reflects more consciously comparative concerns than used to be the case.

There are other signs as well of slow if undramatic change with respect to the geographical division of parties work. For instance, it used to be exceptional for APSA annual meetings to include American and non-American parties papers in the same section of panels or on the same panel; the custom was, and to a large extent still is, to have sets of comparative politics panels that included papers on non-American parties, and a set of American politics panels, under one name or another, that included American parties papers. But in 1983, in the section "Political Parties and Interest Groups," while six of eight panels were

115

entirely American, one was about a party in West Germany and another had papers about Britain and Germany as well as the United States. Significantly, too, the new APSA Organized Section, Political Organizations and Parties, has a membership reflecting some non-American and generally comparative interests along with the predictably predominant American specialists.

In summary, I see opportunities for a mutual enrichment of the American and non-American parties fields without anything like a merger that would cut across the institutional grain of our discipline. We are likely to have, and we should have, country specialists as long as we have countries with their own historical and institutional structures. But neither those specialists nor others are precluded from the intellectual advantages of cross-national comparisons for understanding political phenomena wherever they appear. For example, it is worth asking whether party decline, now so familiar a thesis in the American field, can be discerned in other Western democratic nations, or whether the decline is a distinctively American phenomenon. If the latter, at least with respect to the substitution of candidate-centered voting for party cues, can we attribute the decline of American party efficacy to television when other Western democratic nations also rely increasingly on television for political communication while their parties nevertheless continue to structure electoral behavior?

Notes

[1] Albert Somit and Joseph Tanenhaus, *The Development of American Political Science* (Boston: Allyn and Bacon, 1967), pp. 61–62.

[2] James Bryce, *The American Commonwealth* (Chicago: Sergel, 1891), Vol. 2.

[3] M. Y. Ostrogorsky, *Democracy and the Organization of Political Parties* (London: Macmillan, 1902); Robert Michels, *Political Parties*, trans. Eden and Cedar Paul (Glencoe, Ill.: Free Press, 1949); Maurice Duverger, *Political Parties*, trans. Barbara and Robert North (New York: Wiley, 1954).

[4] Giovanni Sartori, *Parties and Party Systems* (New York: Cambridge UP, 1976), Vol. 1.

[5] A. Lawrence Lowell, "The Influence of Party Upon Legislation in England and America," *Annual Report of the American Historical Association* (Washington, D.C.: GPO, 1902).

[6] Oliver Garceau, ed., *Political Research and Political Theory* (Cambridge, Mass.: Harvard UP, 1968).

The Division of Political Science into American and Non-American Politics: The Case of Legislatures

Gerhard Loewenberg

When undergraduates want to study legislatures, more often than not their choice is limited to a course on Congress, although they may find courses on the legislative process which includes attention to state legislatures.[1] This is hardly a cause for student discontent. The first, and often the only, ambition of political science students is to learn about the American system of government. That is why the introductory course in the discipline is usually a course in American government, why courses on state and local politics are entirely concerned with the United States, why courses on political parties are really about the Democratic and Republican parties, and why there are hardly any courses on the executive at all since the only subject in that area which is taught is the American presidency.

It was not always so. A century ago, as curricula in political science developed in American universities, a general, theoretical concept of politics predominated that derived from continental and particularly German approaches to the subject.[2] The focus on American politics came a full generation later, inspired by a concern for citizenship training and by the prospect of large captive audiences in classrooms of students fulfilling teacher certification requirements.[3]

America First was consistent with the mood of the United States in the 1920s, but less so in the 1930s and 1940s. In those decades student interest in non-American politics revived in response to the nation's involvement in world affairs, and this interest was expressed in the curriculum by separate courses, often misnamed "comparative government." These were frequently courses in a series of major foreign governments, shaped by the writing and teaching of

Gerhard Loewenberg is Dean of Liberal Arts and Professor of Political Science at the University of Iowa.

a new cohort of émigré faculty who revived the European influence on American political science. In this form the study of what was called "comparative government" gained a larger place in the curricula of departments of political science. But as a subfield of the discipline, comparative government remained too small, and the approach was too country-specific, to permit sub-specialization except by geographic areas. There was no place in it for courses on non-American legislatures, or executives, or political parties.

For at least a decade, the name "comparative government" was not widely recognized as a misnomer for a field which consisted of the study of foreign governments *seriatim*. When comparison did begin to be taken seriously, the methodological problems it raised generated an interesting, if at first quite esoteric, literature which impinged not at all on undergraduate curricula and only sporadically on graduate training.[4]

The bifurcation of the study of politics into American and non-American has had two kinds of costs for students of political science. First, while they learn about the politics of their own country in considerable detail, students are likely to remain baffled by the politics of other countries even as the actions of these countries impinge ever more specifically on American lives. Second, without systematic comparison, the general understanding of politics which students gain in our classrooms is shaped by that decidedly deviant case on which they will inevitably concentrate, that of American politics. As long as this is so, their notion of politics, of the sources of conflict and the institutions for coping with it, is badly skewed.

As an example of a legislature in world-wide perspective, Congress is highly aberrant. It has ten times the staff of any other national legislature. It has much weaker parties, far stronger committees, and immeasurably greater control over legislation and budgets than any other representative assembly in the world. It has members who are more independently entrepreneurial than other representatives anywhere. It is uniquely independent of the executive, and the executive, incidentally, is unusually independent of it. What can we learn about legislatures as political institutions from a study of such an example? How can we interpret Congress without knowledge of the generic type of which it is but a single, highly atypical example? How can we evaluate it, consider alternatives, assess reforms?

Continue with the example of this institution. One modest way of providing context and provoking generalization about legislatures is to stay within American boundaries but to compare Congress with legislatures in the states and localities. Variation, the prerequisite of generalization, is immediately available. Opportunities for observation are close at hand, even if systematic comparison across 50 state political systems is a daunting enterprise. But arousing student interest in legislatures across the river or the mountains is a problem. And theoretical problems abound: under what conditions can a national legislature operating in an autonomous political system be compared with state legislatures operating within a single national environment? Yet courses on legislative systems that consider varieties of American legislatures are more practicable than courses that include varieties of non-American assemblies. Excellent texts are available.[5] Comparisons of similar phenomena within the United States are attractive.

By contrast, cross-national comparison is less likely to enter into courses on Congress, or on any other American politics subjects. Course materials are sparse. Where they exist, they displace rather than supplement the standard texts. The intellectual challenge of setting a study of Congress within the context of the study of, say, examples of European, Latin American, and Asian legislatures, seems forbidding.

Concepts are abstract and elusive, data are spotty and lack equivalence, the appropriate level of analysis is unclear. The incentives for meeting such a challenge in the design of undergraduate courses are slight.

Yet the prospects of integrating the study of Congress and the study of non-American legislatures are not negligible. Quite appropriately, it is not student demand but scholarly interest that is likely to provide the motive. Curiosity about Congress on the part of the leading scholars in the field is promoting research on other legislatures just as curiosity about American voting behavior among its leading investigators inspired research on voting in other countries, by both Americans and non-American scholars.[6]

The division between American and non-American politics in our curricula occurred for institutional rather than for intellectual reasons. If the fields are gradually to be reunited, it will have to be for compelling intellectual reasons to which our institutional arrangements for teaching the subject may respond.[7] Intellectual curiosity, prompting scholars to ask questions about Congress which can only be answered in comparative perspective, will have to be the source. Unless scholars have that curiosity which leads them beyond the native horizon, their students cannot be expected to seek anything other than what they get: courses on Congress masquerading as courses on legislatures, courses on American politics purporting to be introductions to political science, courses on recent presidential politics appearing to offer instruction on political parties and voting behavior. However, in an increasingly research-driven discipline, there are reasons to believe that the expertise we have developed as teachers of American politics may well be channeled into an attempt to interpret the politics of our immediate surroundings in terms of the politics of the larger world community to which we also belong. A generation of undergraduates which is not only baffled but deeply worried by politics beyond the seas will be responsive to that direction.

Notes

[1] L. Sandy Maisel, "Teaching the Congressional (Legislative) Process, A Background Paper," presented at the Annual Meeting of the American Political Science Association, Denver, Colorado, September 2-5, 1982.

[2] Albert Somit and Joseph Tanenhaus, *The Development of Political Science* (Boston: Allyn and Bacon, 1967), p. 18.

[3] *The Teaching of Government*, report by its Committee on Instruction (Charles Grove Haines, chairman) to the American Political Science Association, New York, N.Y., 1916, quoted in Somit and Tanenhaus, op. cit., p. 62.

[4] Gerhard Loewenberg, "New Directions in Comparative Political Research: A Review Essay," *Midwest Journal of Political Science* 15(1971), 741–56.

[5] For example, Malcolm E. Jewell and Samuel C. Patterson, *The Legislative Process in the United States*, 4th ed. (New York: Random House, in press); William J. Keefe and Morris S. Ogul, *The American Legislative Process; Congress and the States*, 4th ed. (Englewood Cliffs, N.J.: Prentice-Hall, 1977).

[6] The state of scholarship on non-American legislatures will be apparent in the articles which Malcolm E. Jewell, Samuel C. Patterson, and I are editing for the *Handbook of Legislative Research* (Cambridge: Harvard UP, 1985); cf. Mogens N. Pedersen, "Research on European Parliaments: A Review Article on Scholarly and Institutional Variety," *Legislative Studies Quarterly* 9(1984), 505–29.

[7] This might be regarded as a particular application of the ideas expressed by Warren E. Miller in his presidential address, "The Role of Research in the Unification of a Discipline," *American Political Science Review* 75(1981), 9–16.

How Can We Get There from Here?
Thoughts on the Integration of
American and Comparative Politics

Susanne Hoeber Rudolph and Lloyd I. Rudolph

The bifurcation of political science into American and comparative politics impoverishes both. The division parochializes them by encapsulating the study of politics within national boundaries. The result is to deprive each of the theoretical contributions generated by the other and to cut them off from the institutional and policy alternatives each has devised. The loss to the study of American politics is probably the more severe because its practitioners have not been prepared to recognize the limitations of their "area specialty."

Historical and institutional determinants help explain the bifurcation. Because academic political science, that is, political science as a discipline and a profession is, as Bernard Crick has shown, American in its origins and early development, it has been less attentive to non-American contexts. More than other academic social science disciplines, political science lacks eighteenth- and nineteenth-century European masters. In the belief that America was showing the world its future, post-war behavioral political science like other aspects of the American way of life became an American export to Europe and the third world.

There were countercurrents. World War II followed by America's global role led many American political scientists to attend to European, East Asian, Soviet, and Third World politics in ways that infiltrated the study of American politics. The post-Sputnik decade (1958–1967) was the era of area and language centers. Comparative politics gained ground as graduate students were induced to study foreign languages and cultures along with their parent discipline. But escalating war in Vietnam led to cutbacks in international education from which

Susanne Hoeber Rudolph and Lloyd I. Rudolph are Professors of Political Science at the University of Chicago.

comparative politics has yet to recover. Spurious demands for relevance and the new isolationism led to the reduction of language teaching at both high school and collegiate levels. Within universities, surviving area and language centers lost the bargaining advantages that had enabled them to influence departmental appointments and curricula.

The bifurcation of political science into American and other politics is the result, too, of pressures on political science departments to educate citizens and prepare students for jobs or careers. These concerns are high on the agenda of the state legislatures that fund most political science education. They are more concerned to support education that seems to have a demonstrable connection to state needs than education whose global and international dimensions seem remote. The cuts of the 1980s in state-funded higher education have affected all areas of research and teaching, but cuts in international education have been particularly severe.

There are forces at work that tend to unite rather than to separate American and comparative politics. One is the changing role of America in the world economy. Until recently, the American economy was inward-looking, producing mainly for the domestic market and only marginally influenced by world trade. America's increasing involvement in the world economy, like its earlier involvement in world order, has generated interest in the politics of other nations. Knowledge of foreign tastes, social contexts, and political futures have become increasingly important for foreign sales, investments, and production.

Another force that tends to unite rather than to divide American and comparative politics is research methodologies and theories that approach political phenomena without regard to national boundaries. The recent resurgence of European-derived macro-social theory, including its Marxian and Weberian strains, has followed its founders in not separating America from the world. Similarly, the new political economy of Andrew Shonfield's *Modern Capitalism* and Charles Lindblom's *Politics and Markets* follow their mentors, Smith, Ricardo, Malthus, and Marx, by using concepts and frameworks that include the American variant.

But this comprehensiveness is not confined to the macro-social and political economy "revivals." In the more American behavioral research tradition, Stokes, Verba, Nie, and Eldersveld, to mention only a few, made the American "case" part of a wider investigation of political participation. More recently, the study of neo-corporatism has entered an arena dominated by American-- inspired pluralist conceptions, the organization and representation of interests. Together with pluralism, neo-corporatism provides a framework for the common study of interests in America and abroad.

Another promising countercurrent that opens the way to the integration of American and comparative politics is the study of state formation. When

Seymour Martin Lipset tried to integrate the study of American and comparative politics in *America, The First New Nation,* it was generally assumed that nation building preceded state formation. It now seems more likely that the reverse is true, that states create nations. Similarly, as Theda Skocpol has shown, revolutions are more likely to occur when states are weak than when classes are strong. The "American Liberal Tradition" avoided the study of state formation because it subordinated the state to an ideology that featured the individual and the community. To be sure, there was an earlier tradition of institutional analysis of the state but it had fallen victim to the behavioral attack on formalism and legalism. American experience with the welfare and national security state during the New Deal and after World War II once again made the study of the state plausible in the land of Lockean low stateness. The American state now accounts for about one-third of GNP and about one-fourth of employment, proportions that make it difficult to distinguish it from socialist states in industrial democracies.

America's recent historical experience encouraged research on state formation and the relationship of the state to society. Such research crosses the American-comparative divide by encompassing the Atlantic nations; the multinational imperial states, Russia, India, and China; and weak post-colonial states that often lack national integration. The state as an object of study is in search of a theoretical framework that can address all three of these types. State formation studies have led to a reevaluation of the American historical experience that reveals a statist aspect previously obscured by liberal and pluralist lenses. The history of the executive branch, the state's role in industrialization and the management of an industrial economy, and the New Deal's creation of a welfare state, for example, are subjects of recent studies.

The bifurcation of American and comparative politics has impoverished both. Their integration requires overcoming the historical and institutional forces that caused their separation and encouraging old and new countercurrents that recognize but transcend national boundaries.

The Bifurcation of American and Non-American Perspectives in Foreign Policy

Ole R. Holsti

The bifurcation of American and non-American perspectives in foreign policy analysis is a large topic to which justice cannot be done in limited space. To reduce the subject to somewhat more manageable scope, the focus here is on teaching and, more specifically, on undergraduate courses on American foreign policy. After examining some evidence that might shed light on the question, this essay will suggest some reasons, both within and outside the discipline, for this development, as well as some possible ways of avoiding undue parochialism by ensuring that non-American perspectives get some hearing.

This is not the place to undertake extensive content analyses of foreign policy texts, but even a cursory glance at several recent, widely used volumes indicates that many students are exposed almost wholly to American perspectives. Materials cited in footnotes and as suggested readings are overwhelmingly written by American authors. That pattern also extends to three of the best recent collections of readings on American foreign policy. The first includes 32 essays, not one of which is by a non-American, all nine chapters in the second are by Americans, and only one of 12 essays in the third is co-authored by a foreign scholar. In fairness, it should be pointed out that these materials hardly present a homogeneous viewpoint on the sources, conduct, and consequences of American diplomacy; a collection of readings that includes essays by George Kennan, Carl Gershman, Henry Kissinger, and Stanley Hoffman can hardly be accused of presenting a single outlook. Moreover, the diversity of choices

Ole R. Holsti is George V. Allen Professor of International Affairs at Duke University. The author acknowledges Joseph Grieco and Timothy Lomperis for their useful comments on an earlier draft of this essay.

among available texts provides a broad range of perspectives, from moderately hard-line to distinctly revisionist.

Of the several reasons for the bifurcation of American and non-American perspectives on foreign policy, perhaps the most general is a growing specialization, not only within the discipline but in its sub-fields as well. This trend is not, of course, confined to political science as it may be found in virtually all disciplines. As the literature to be mastered increases, there is an almost inevitable tendency for graduate training and research—and ultimately, teaching—to become somewhat narrower in scope. A related source of pressure toward greater specialization is the flood of documentary material available to the student of current foreign policy.[1] As a consequence of a seemingly inexorable trend toward specialization, most doctoral candidates sit for examinations in a smaller number of sub-fields than did their counterparts a generation ago with results that are almost certain to be reflected in many syllabi. But specialization does not seem a sufficient explanation. We also need to consider other contributing factors, more specifically, some developments, both within and outside the discipline, during the post-war period.

An important manifestation of the "behavioral revolution" in international relations was a series of challenges to supplement if not displace the reigning "realist" perspective. Among the central features of realism are the premises of "unitary rational actors" whose international behavior is guided by a relatively objective standard, "the national interest." These premises tend to direct the analyst's attention to features of the international system—structural anarchy, the existing distribution of power, alliance arrangements, and the like—as the most potent forces driving foreign policy. Domestic politics are to some extent viewed as a residual category that may, for example, be used to explain deviations from "rational" behavior.

Among the more important challenges to realist premises were several that can be subsumed under the label "decision-making" approaches. Drawing upon theories and findings from a wide range of disciplines—including but not limited to cognitive psychology, organizational behavior, and social psychology—the advocates of decision-making perspectives share the view that one needs to go beyond the premises of the unitary rational actor and to examine political processes within nation-states in order to understand their foreign policies. The decision-making literature is far too extensive to summarize here, but it is worth citing a few of its major manifestations.

- The seminal essay by Richard Snyder and his colleagues gave the decision maker's "definition of the situation" (which might or might not correspond to that prescribed by the logic of realism) a central role in foreign policy analysis.[2] Later contributions by Robert Jervis and John

Steinbruner, drawing heavily upon cognitive psychology, represented major additions to this aspect of the decision-making literature.[3]

- Recognizing that most foreign policy decisions take place within a group context, the psychologist Irving Janis undertook revealing studies that highlight aspects of small group dynamics that may enhance or erode the quality of foreign policy decisions.[4]

- The dramatic growth of foreign policy bureaucracies led a number of scholars, including Richard Neustadt, Morton Halperin, and Graham Allison, to examine the impact of politics within and between bureaucracies on making and implementing foreign policy decisions.[5]

Two things may be worth noting about these major contributions to theory and research. First, each of them directed the analyst's attention to some aspects of the domestic political arena, with at least some potential dilution of the impact attributed to the external environment, including the policy processes in other nations. Second, whereas realism has venerable and important roots in European thought (Thucydides, Machiavelli, Carr, Morgenthau, et al.), not only have decision-making perspectives largely been the work of American scholars, but many of its best applications are case studies involving U.S. decisions.[6] It is scarcely surprising, therefore, that they should have had a significant impact on teaching American foreign policy.

These developments within the discipline coincided with some others that may have reinforced the tendency to place greater emphasis on the domestic determinants of foreign policy. The "behavioral revolution" flowered during the period in which American political, military, and economic power reached its zenith. Even those who might have been skeptical about claims of "American exceptionalism" of a positive variety were inclined to argue that the nation's status as a democratic superpower rendered it relatively impervious to external constraints and, concomitantly, more sensitive to the dynamics of domestic politics. For example, a widely cited framework for the comparative study of foreign policy indicated that external factors ranked among the least potent explanations for American foreign policy.[7]

By the mid-to-late 1960s a radically different theory of "American exceptionalism" gained supporters in the wake of the nation's disastrous involvement in Vietnam. According to this view, not only was the United States an exceptionally malign international actor in southeast Asia, but virtually its entire history has been characterized by imperialist expansion. The corollary was that the driving forces of American foreign policy were to be found in structural flaws in the society, which, in turn, were usually linked closely to the putative imperatives of capitalism and its concomitants—class structure, repression, racism, and the like.[8] The validity of either the positive or negative variants of

"American exceptionalist" theories is beyond the scope of this essay.[9] For present purposes the main point is that both of them direct the foreign policy analyst's attention inward rather than outward toward the external environment. Consequently, non-American perspectives take on somewhat secondary importance.

If one assumes that neglect of non-American perspectives not only intensifies the almost universal parochialism of undergraduate students but also results in incomplete analyses, what remedies are available? Several come to mind.

One approach might be to embed the study of American foreign policy within comparative foreign policy courses. Whether because of habit, the time restrictions of a single semester, or other reasons, few have done so. A quick survey of catalogs at leading universities reveals the existence of relatively few such courses.[10] In any case, comparative foreign policy courses are no more likely to supplant those on American foreign policy than are introductory comparative politics courses to replace those on American government.

Assignment of readings by non-American authors is another possible remedy. Among the most trenchant insights about American diplomacy have been those of such foreign observers as de Tocqueville, Brogan, Aron, and others. Such assignments may also be valuable for another reason. Because a strong sense of history is a rare commodity among contemporary undergraduates, assignments in such works as de Tocqueville may be a healthy corrective against tendencies to believe, for example, that difficulties in developing coherent and continuous foreign policies are problems that originated with the Carter and Reagan administrations.

Recent issues of the annual *America and the World* volumes published by the Council on Foreign Relations have been marked by a notably better representation of foreign authors than earlier volumes in that series. Articles by leading European, Canadian, and other analysts provide important non-American perspectives on issues ranging from Soviet-American relations to debates on "no-first-use" of nuclear weapons, and from Euromissiles to Third World debt problems.

Finally, although many decision-making case studies focus on what took place in Washington, there are some that offer striking insights on how the issue was defined and dealt with abroad; Neustadt's study of the Suez and Skybolt episodes is a good case in point.[11]

When class size and resources permit, simulations, role playing exercises, and similar activities can provide some useful correctives to an excessive parochialism, especially if they are preceded by extensive research on how the issues in question engage political processes abroad and with what likely consequences.

Research paper assignments can also be structured to require the student to examine issues, processes, and outcomes from a non-American perspective.

Perhaps the most effective way to overcome the bifurcation of American and non-American perspectives on foreign policy is to employ a framework of the course in which both are integral to the entire undertaking. One of the many ways of doing so is to depict American foreign policy makers as operating in three arenas—domestic, alliance, and global—which serve as sources of challenges, opportunities, and constraints. Each issue can then be analyzed in terms of the political processes within and among the three arenas. The patterns will probably vary according to the issue area; we would not expect them to be the same for immigration policy, SALT, detente, and demands for a new international economic order. Such a framework forces one to examine issues not only from the perspectives of key actors in Washington, but also from those of leaders, parties, and institutions abroad. If students come away with at least some appreciation of the fact that policy makers abroad must also operate within *their* domestic political arenas as they cope with such issues as the Siberian pipeline embargo, the mining of Nicaraguan harbors, sanctions on Poland, or the sale of nuclear technology to China, and that the necessity of doing so may shape their policies vis-à-vis the United States, much will have been gained.

Decision-making and related approaches have significantly enriched our understanding of foreign policy, not the least by banishing such clichés as "politics stops at the water's edge" from our vocabulary, if not from that of Fourth of July orators or incumbent candidates on the hustings. They may even be necessary to any adequate theory of international relations.[12] Decision-making approaches have also enhanced more fruitful interaction between students of domestic and foreign policy. If they have had the unintended consequence of contributing to a bifurcation of American and non-American perspectives on foreign policy, the barriers to effective remedies are not inherently insurmountable.

Notes

[1] Ernest R. May, "Writing Contemporary History," *Diplomatic History* 8 (Spring 1984), 103–13.

[2] Richard C. Snyder, H. W. Bruck and Burton Sapin, *Foreign Policy Decision Making* (New York: Free Press, 1962). This book is based in large part on a monograph originally published in 1954.

[3] Robert Jervis, *Perception and Misperception in International Politics* (Princeton, N.J.: Princeton UP, 1976); and John D. Steinbruner, *The Cybernetic Theory of Decision* (Princeton, N.J.: Princeton UP, 1974).

[4] Irving Janis, *Groupthink: Psychological Studies of Policy Decisions and Fiascoes*, 2nd ed. (Boston: Houghton Mifflin, 1982). The first edition was published in 1972 under the title, *Victims of Groupthink*.

[5] Richard Neustadt, *Alliance Politics* (New York: Columbia UP, 1970); Morton H. Halperin, *Bureaucratic Politics and Foreign Policy* (Washington, D.C.: Brookings Institution, 1974); and Graham Allison, *Essence of Decision: Explaining the Cuban Missile Crisis* (Boston: Little, Brown, 1971).

[6] For example, Glenn D. Paige, *The Korean Decision* (New York: Free Press, 1968); and Allison, op. cit. For a fuller discussion of American domination of the discipline, see K.J. Holsti, *The Dividing Discipline: Hegemony and Diversity in International Theory* (London: Allen and Unwin, in press).

[7] James N. Rosenau, "Pre-Theories and Theories of Foreign Policy," in R. Barry Farrell, ed., *Approaches to Comparative and International Politics* (Evanston, Ill,: Northwestern UP, 1966), p. 48.

[8] For example, Richard Barnet, *Roots of War* (New York: Atheneum, 1972); Gabriel Kolko, *The Roots of American Foreign Policy: An Analysis of Power and Purpose* (Boston: Beacon, 1969); and Gar Alperovitz, *Atomic Diplomacy: Hiroshima and Potsdam* (New York: Simon and Schuster, 1965).

[9] For a further discussion, see George Quester, *American Foreign Policy: The Lost Consensus* (New York: Praeger, 1982); and Ole R. Holsti, "The Study of International Politics Makes Strange Bedfellows: Theories of the Radical Right and Left," *American Political Science Review* 68 (March 1974), 217–42.

[10] Eight of the 26 included courses that deal with the policies of more than a single nation (e.g., "Foreign Economic Policies of Advanced Industrial States," or "East Asian International Relations"), but only two offered courses entitled "Comparative Foreign Policy."

[11] Neustadt, op. cit. Allison's study of the Cuban missile crisis (op. cit.) also deals with Soviet decisions, but necessarily on the basis of relatively limited data. Neustadt, on the other hand, had access to substantial information, based on interviews and other evidence, concerning British decision making during the Suez and Skybolt episodes.

[12] On this point, see Benjamin A. Most and Harvey Starr, "International Relations Theory, Foreign Policy Substitutability, and 'Nice' Laws," *World Politics* 36 (April 1984), 383–406.

The International Component of Political Science Curricula

Harold K. Jacobson

Throughout the world, attaining peace and prosperity are clearly at the top of the agenda of human concerns; consequently, they are the most central and salient issues of politics and government. In the late twentieth century, however, no country can achieve these goals through its own actions alone. For all countries in this era of interdependence gaining peace and prosperity each require collective efforts. Thus domestic policies cannot be considered in isolation from foreign policies, and domestic politics are inextricably linked with international and ultimately world politics. Even if one were interested only in events within one's own country, these would have to be put in a larger context to be properly understood. But most individuals adhere to ethical beliefs that mandate that their concerns extend certainly beyond their own countries' borders, if not to all of humanity. For these reasons, any up-to-date and valid political science curriculum must have a vital international component. The implications and ramifications of this assertion merit exposition, then examination and consideration.

Interdependence and the Necessity of Collective Action

First, though, the prior assertion that countries cannot gain peace and prosperity acting on their own should be substantiated. For small countries the matter has never been in doubt, at least since industrialization began and probably since the origins of the state system in the seventeenth century. It is only with respect to large countries that plausible arguments have been made to support strategies of political isolation and economic self-reliance. Some small countries, it is true, have sought peace through neutrality, but the viability of such a course has always depended on their constant efforts to ensure the

Harold K. Jacobson is Professor of Political Science at the University of Michigan, where he is Director of the Center for Political Studies.

consent of their larger neighbors to their inviolability. Small countries have never been able to conceive of pursuing economic growth without substantial reliance on foreign trade.

If World Wars I and II did not provide conclusive evidence to squelch the belief that large countries could remain aloof from major international conflicts, the advent of nuclear explosives and missile delivery systems certainly has. No country, no matter how large, could escape the effects of a large-scale war fought with nuclear weapons. Even if a large country were not drawn into the conflagration as an immediate party to the conflict, its territory, population, and civilization would be seriously affected by the world-wide aftereffects of a large-scale nuclear war. All countries large and small must strive to prevent the tragic disaster of a nuclear holocaust. Large countries, such as China, India, the Soviet Union, and the United States, that historically have attempted to isolate themselves from broad and inclusive international conflicts, by this date seem to have fully absorbed this truth, and for some time now their governments have been actively engaged in efforts that they have argued were designed to preserve peace. However one might evaluate the wisdom or efficaciousness of these efforts, one cannot doubt that these countries fear large-scale nuclear war or that their leaders and populations realize that political isolation is not a realistic strategy for avoiding this catastrophe. Active policies to preserve peace are now a recognized necessity for all countries.

Evidence constantly surges to the fore to invalidate the belief that some countries are large enough so that their territories contain sufficient resources and their populations constitute markets of sufficient size to be able to gain prosperity through economic self-reliance, but this belief still claims adherents. Even those who hold this belief, though, admit that total economic self-reliance is impossible and accept the necessity of foreign trade for defined, limited purposes.

The Federal Republic of Germany, France, Japan, and the United Kingdom, all countries with relatively large territories and numerically sizeable populations, long ago accepted the fact that a strategy of economic self-reliance could not bring them prosperity and based their policies on this awareness. In contrast, during the twentieth century, China, India, the Soviet Union, and the United States have each either pursued or considered policies oriented toward economic self-reliance. However, autarky has become less and less viable as a strategy for these countries as well.

The present governments of China and India cannot grow at the pace that they desire unless there are substantial interactions between their economies and those of other countries. Both China and India need foreign capital to supplement domestic savings and access to technology that is developed mainly in the industrially advanced countries of the West (Western Europe, North

America, Japan, and Australia). To earn sufficient foreign currency to pay for this technology and to service the debts that they incur, both also need to ensure that their exports have access to the markets of the West. Since there is little prospect that this basic framework will significantly change even in the distant future, as long as China and India seek rapid economic growth, they will face the necessity of economic collaboration with other countries.

The situation is more nuanced and complicated with respect to the Soviet Union and the United States. As long as it can trade with its immediate neighbors in Eastern Europe that have communist governments, the Soviet Union is markedly less dependent on imports of basic raw materials than are Japan, the member countries of the European community, and, to a lesser extent, the United States. Furthermore, the Soviet system of central planning contains an inherent bias against reliance on economic factors that are not under the direct control of the planners: the plan could be jeopardized if such factors were assigned a substantial role and unforeseen changes occurred with respect to their availability or price. For some years, however, fulfilling Soviet economic goals has required significant imports of agricultural commodities and technology from non-communist countries. As long as this situation persists, and there are no signs of its abatement, the Soviet Union has no alternative to having at least limited economic exchanges with non-communist countries.

The United States historically has been ambivalent about being involved in international economic relations. From the first days of the establishment of a national government, the United States has sought access to markets for its exports and opportunities for investments abroad. But almost as early in its history, the United States sought to limit access to its own market through protectionist policies, policies that it pursued well into the 1930s. As World War II drew to a close, the United States took the lead in attempting to create an open world economy, but in the process it was careful to ensure that its own economy would be largely exempt from outside control. Three decades later, the United States now finds itself ensnared by the success of its own efforts. In the relatively open international economy that was created, world-wide economic growth has been unprecedented. One result has been that foreign trade has become an increasingly important component of the United State economy. Another result is that the economic importance of the United States relative to the importance of other countries has diminished; consequently, the ability of the U.S. to insist on having its own way in economic arrangements has also declined. By 1980 export earnings accounted for more than eight percent of the U.S. gross national product (GNP), a decade earlier the figure had been less than four percent. By 1980, one out of five jobs in the U.S. economy depended in some way on foreign trade, and 40 percent of U.S. cropland was devoted to production for export. As the involvement of the

United States in international economic affairs deepened, many individuals and groups within the United States became increasingly frustrated by their country's diminished control over its own economic destiny. At the same time that a strategy of economic self-reliance became less feasible for the United States, it paradoxically became more appealing for these individuals and groups. Even if they should come to control U.S. policy making, however, it would be impossible for them to extricate the United States from international economic affairs. Because the United States is more dependent on imported raw materials, it would be impossible for them to make it even as self-reliant as the Soviet Union.

If the Soviet Union is as self-reliant as a country can be in the present era and still realistically aspire to economic progress, it is evident that for the overwhelming majority of the world's more than 160 sovereign countries it is impossible to consider their domestic economies in isolation from the international economy.

If countries individually are to gain peace and prosperity, today and in the future they must seek these goals through the collective action of many, and eventually all, countries. Complete political isolation and economic self-reliance are strategies of the past, if indeed they ever were viable. Foreign policies must be an essential element of domestic policies. Because of this, the domain of political science analyses must extend beyond any individual country's border, and political science curricula must include an international component.

The Basic Characteristics of International and Global Politics

Providing an international component for political science curricula is not simply a matter of ensuring the inclusion and treatment of political relations among countries and of political systems of countries other than that where the academic institutions involved in the activity are located. It involves rather introducing consideration of types of political relationships that are basically different from those that are found within countries.

Since the seventeenth century, sovereignty has been the defining characteristic of the structure of the international system and consequently of international politics. Sovereignty is commonly understood to mean that the government of a territorial unit is supreme within its territory and is free from external control. Because all independent countries in the international system possess sovereignty, the international system lacks a central authority. The international system is a system of decentralized authority. Unlike domestic political systems, in the international system there is no central authority that can impose rules of conduct on countries, much less legal entities and individuals. Instead, rules have to be accepted voluntarily by countries, and if they are to be applied to individuals, the modality of doing this is for countries to apply them to individuals within their own territories.

The structure of the international system explains why political relationships among countries are fundamentally different from political relationships within countries. It also sets in motion dynamic forces that work against the realization of peace and prosperity. Because countries must rely on efforts that they themselves organize to provide for their own physical protection, the international system has been characterized as a self-help system; countries must create and maintain their own military forces, and if they conclude that these provide insufficient protection, they can supplement them by concluding alliances with other countries. The difficulty is that such a system appears to have a built-in propensity toward violence. If countries had irreconcilably incompatible objectives, violence would be the only way of settling the dispute, but even if countries' objectives were compatible, in a self-help system violence could be the outcome. Even if a country desired only to defend itself, given the difficulty of projecting exactly what level of military force would be required, the government would be likely to build in a margin of safety. The governments of other countries, of necessity forced to rely on their own military forces for intentions, and to ensure their own countries' safety are likely to build up their own military forces in response to whatever actions the first country may take. The first country, in turn, will respond to their moves. Thus even under the best of circumstances, when all countries merely desire to preserve their own political independence and territorial integrity, the international system has a built-in propensity toward arms races. For a variety of reasons arms races can lead to war: accidents can occur, a country could feel that it should attack to take advantage of its own military superiority, or a country could feel that the final moment had come before it would fall irretrievably behind.

The international system also has a built-in propensity toward a less than optimal division of labor within the world economy. Because countries must rely on efforts that they themselves organize to provide for their own protection, there is a tendency to shape their economies so as to minimize vulnerabilities; in more direct language, there is a propensity toward autarky, particularly among the larger countries. The larger countries seek to be as capable as possible of meeting their military and wartime needs without having to rely on others. Thus they seek to ensure that their economies include the basic industries and are self-sufficient with respect to the production of food, whether or not this is efficient by economic criteria.

Until the principle of sovereignty is abandoned or sharply curtailed, these dynamic forces set in motion by the structure of the international system can only be overcome by countries acting through voluntary agreements, agreements which often require countries to forego short-term benefits in the expectation or hope of achieving substantial rewards in the longer term.

To point out that the decentralized character of the international system sets in motion dynamic forces that work against the realization of peace and prosperity is not to argue that sovereignty is the main explanation for the failure to make greater progress toward these goals. Nor is it to condemn sovereignty as a principle for organizing the international system. There are numerous other explanations for violence and war and for shortcomings in promoting economic welfare, many of which, such as human aggression and greed, are also relevant to explaining failures within domestic systems. A balanced evaluation of sovereignty would require evaluation of its many virtues as well as the problems it causes. It allows diversity, and it permits political units to be small enough so that meaningful political participation is possible. Within the West, sovereignty has historically generally permitted and facilitated economic growth and development and the definition and protection of human rights.

The purpose is rather to show how the structure of the international system shapes both the processes and the substance of international political relationships. Any analysis of these relationships must take this structure as its starting point. Because of this structure, negotiation and bargaining and raw coercive power loom much larger in international than in domestic politics; electoral, legislative, and judicial behavior are of much less importance, and even can play no role at all. Any efforts at international public policy must have as its first task achieving voluntary agreement among those sovereign countries with the capacity to act in the relevant area; only if this is gained can the substantive issues be addressed. Moreover, the substantive issues of preventing or at least ameliorating arms races and tendencies toward autarky are constantly present, and they can never be resolved so long as sovereignly remains the organizing principle of the international system.

It is the structure of the international system that makes international political relationships different from domestic political relationships and thus determines what must be included in building an international component into political science curricula.

Ingredients of an International Component

Described in their generic form, the basic parts of an international component for political science curricula are a basic introductory course, advanced courses, and sections in courses in other subfields covering relevant material from this subfield. The basic course, which should serve as a prerequisite for whatever subsequent work a student might do in the subfield, must concentrate on the fundamental structural characteristics of the international system. Giving a list of advanced courses will indicate other topics for inclusion in the basic course as well as the range of substantive material that should be included in the international component and in courses in other subfields.

Delineations of courses inevitably involve issues of educational philosophy and goals. These issues therefore must be addressed briefly to put the list of courses in proper context. Courses dealing with international political relationships should primarily impart principles that will be useful for students understanding these relationships throughout their subsequent adult lives. Although current international issues have enormous fascination for students and can and should be used to engage their interest, courses that focus primarily on such issues are bound to be ephemeral and to have limited long-term impact. Principles must be the core of courses. To understand the principles properly, students must understand the framework within which they operate. They must also grasp historical trends so that they understand how this framework has developed and how it might be transformed in the future. Beyond principles, courses must also have a certain factual content so that students can place these principles in their dynamic historical context. Although the titles in this list of courses emphasize substantive concerns, the intention is, as will be evident in the discussion of the contents of the courses, that they should focus primarily on principles and basic factual material, not current events.

How many advanced courses can and should be included in a political science curriculum will depend on many factors including the number of faculty, the size of the student body, and the total number of courses required and permitted in a concentration program. The list presented here could be expanded or cut to fit particular situations.

Given the preceding discussions, the list will not be surprising. One course should deal with security, another with the political aspects of international economic relationships, and a third with international institutions and the efforts to add greater structure to the international system so as to facilitate achieving voluntary agreements among countries. All three of these courses approach the subject from the perspective of the international system. One or more courses should also be included that approach it from the perspective of countries, or more technically, nation states, the basic actors in international political relationships. This could be a comparative foreign policy course, or a course or a series of courses dealing with the foreign policy of the country in which the academic institution is located. This is especially true for the United States because of its unique importance in the international system. In the 1980s the U.S. gross national product (GNP) still was more than a quarter of the world product, U.S. exports and imports were more than 10 percent of the global exports and imports, and U.S. military expenditures were more than 25 percent of the world total. The Soviet Union, the country whose capacity for influence was nearest to that of the United States, had military expenditures that were almost as large as those of the United States, but its GNP was only half as large, and its exports and imports only about a third as large. The United States continues to have a unique capacity for influence in the international system.

The Basic Course in International or World Politics

Although the basic course in international or world politics should serve as a prerequisite to the advanced courses in the subfield and thus should introduce the subject matter of all these courses, its major subdivisions probably will not be accurately described by the titles typically given to any of them. The introductory course should have a logical coherence, and the best way to develop this is not simply to give, in sequence, synopses of advanced courses.

Before defining the contents of the basic course, however, its place in a political science curriculum needs to be considered. Often international or world politics has been considered an advanced course. The rationale has been that because of the complicated nature of international politics students should have a certain maturity and a substantial background in social sciences before tackling the issues. If courses in social science, including work in history, economics, and positive and normative political theory, are in fact taken before the course in international politics, the course can obviously be much more sophisticated. On the other hand, if a course in domestic government and politics is considered the only prerequisite, it provides little on which to build. Furthermore, given the importance of international issues, the wisdom of restricting the potential audience may be questioned. For these reasons, there is an increasing tendency to treat international politics as an entry-level course.

Basic courses in international politics need to cover five large areas of concern. First, the problems of studying and analyzing international politics need to be addressed. These include the role of normative judgments, the meaning and method of utilizing a scientific approach, and the problems associated with applying quantitative techniques of analysis to events that occur only infrequently and to actors that exhibit widely diverse characteristics. Beginning students can find such discussions mystifying and boring. They are better kept brief and amply illustrated to demonstrate that the epistemological and methodological choices that one makes have real consequences for one's understanding of the substance of international politics.

Second, the structure of the international system needs to be portrayed. This involves introducing the concept and consequences of sovereignty and showing how the decentralized character of the system sets in motion dynamic forces propelling states toward arms races and autarky. The point will emerge that nation states are the principal actors in international politics. Nationalism and national self-determination must be dealt with so that students can understand the physical shape of the territorial units or nation states in the international system, the spread of the system of sovereignty to virtually the entire globe, and the real potentialities for the merger of units and the creation of supra-national authorities. Although nation states are likely to be the principal actors in international politics for a long time to come, there are increasing numbers of non-state actors of some consequence, and they need to be introduced in this part of the course. Finally, it can no longer be assumed that countries will always act as coherent units in international politics; there are sub-state actors among them, governmental departments other than the foreign office that nevertheless conduct foreign relations and non-governmental associations taking actions outside their countries' borders.

Third, the factors that shape the foreign policy behavior of countries should be analyzed. Outlining the scholarly efforts to establish general categories of foreign policy behavior is an essential preliminary step. The tradition in international politics has been to dichotomize, dividing countries into those that seek to preserve the status quo, particularly the existing division of territory, and those that seek to change the status quo. In the period since World War II there has been a tendency for this dichotomization to fall from favor. One reason is that the post-World War II status quo did not have a broadly accepted basis in international law until the Helsinki accords were signed in 1975. Another reason is that the dichotomization is too blunt an instrument to capture the many facets of contemporary foreign policy behavior; among other reasons territorial issues are often an almost trivial component of foreign policy behavior. Modern scholarship makes extensive use of issue areas for the categorization of foreign policy behavior, and to the extent that there is dichotomization, it is usually based on a continuum with cooperation and conflict being the opposite poles.

In discussing the factors that shape countries' foreign policy behavior, the state system is an appropriate starting place; the decentralized nature of political authority in the international system establishes basic parameters for the foreign policy behavior of all countries. The state system also means that an action-reaction model has considerable explanatory power in analyses of foreign policy behavior, since much of foreign policy behavior is initiated as a response to an act taken by another country. The state system is the most general factor shaping countries' foreign policy behavior; others are more specific. This section of the course can be conceived as moving through a series of nested, more and more specific explanations. Next would be the physical environment of the various countries, their geographical position, and the level of their own and the worlds' technology. These factors set limits and incline countries toward particular behavior. U.S. and British emphasis on naval forces and Japanese concern about the security of its access to raw materials are examples of how geographical position affects foreign policy behavior. Among other consequences, the level of technology determines the significance of raw materials. Once external factors have been examined, it is appropriate to seek explanations within countries. Economic theories are one major category of such explanations; they should include Marxist and neo-Marxist as well as classical liberal explanations. Theories emphasizing differences among political systems and those stressing the consequences of organizational and bureaucratic behavior provide another category. The final category of explanations is comprised of those that are the most personal and psychological; they emphasize public attitudes and opinion, operational codes of elites and individuals, basic psychological predispositions of individuals and leaders, and perceptions and misperceptions in communications.

The fourth section of the course should deal with the instruments that countries use in pursuing whatever foreign policy goals they may have. Since, regardless of the instrument used, the object is to affect the behavior of other actors, this section should start with a general discussion of power and influence. Again, the impact of the state system is evident as it emphasizes the coercive aspects of power and influence. The basic instruments of foreign policy are diplomacy, economic blandishments and coercion, and military force. Game theory can be introduced during the discussion of diplomacy; it greatly enriches an otherwise largely atheoretical discussion. Placing the discussion of military force in this section of the course dealing with instruments of foreign policy implies that the issues of war and peace are treated throughout the course and that war is seen as having multiple causes. The character of modern weapons, the enormous destructive force of nuclear and thermonuclear warheads and the rapidity with which missiles can travel vast distances, sharply reducing warning times, needs to be stressed. This has altered decision makers' attitudes about the use of force and put issues of arms control and disarmament in a new perspective. Reluctance to use force and practical limitations on the possible gains from the use of force have elevated the importance of economic blandishments and coercion as instruments of foreign policy. These points need to be discussed in the course on a more abstract level as well as on this concrete level. There is an interplay between the instruments and the goals of foreign policy: goals are not sought regardless of costs, and at some level of costs, pursuit of a goal will be postponed or perhaps even abandoned.

The final section of the course should deal with the efforts that countries have made and continue to make to cooperate. International institutions are clearly involved, and the growing number of international governmental and non-governmental organizations in the international system is testimony to the tendency in the system toward increasing institutionalization. Organized and lasting cooperation, however, need not necessarily involve institutions, nor does the existence of an institution ensure that there will be cooperation. It is important that this section of the course not become bogged down in formalities. Stressing the concept of regimes is one way of avoiding this danger. Regimes have patterned behavior and expectations and demonstrate norms and accepted modalities for establishing and modifying norms.

Advanced Courses in International Politics

As stated above, a well-rounded curriculum in political science should include advanced courses in international politics in at least four principal areas: international security; international political economy; international organization and integration; and foreign policy. The course in international security should make students thoroughly familiar with the characteristics of existing and prospective weapon systems. In addition, it should analyze procedures that countries use for making decisions about security issues, classical and contemporary military strategy, and the theory and practice of disarmament and arms control. This course deals with the issue of peace in what has come to be called the negative sense; that is, in the sense of limiting the amount of physical violence in the international system. It must also deal with how countries use and threaten to use military force in efforts to obtain foreign policy goals. Though foreclosing the possibility of nuclear war is a universally shared objective, military force continues to be a major instrument of foreign policy. Furthermore, there are some objectives that are so important to countries that they would risk nuclear war rather than forego the pursuit of these objectives. Preserving their territorial integrity and political independence are objectives of this order for most countries.

International political economy is a relative newcomer to the repertoire of advanced courses in international politics even though there is a rich tradition of work in this special area. The overwhelming importance and the great urgency of problems of war and peace in the period when the study of international politics was developed—the period starting with the closing years of World War I and running through the onset of the Cold War—forced a concentration on security issues. Skepticism about Marxism in Western countries, where the study of international politics was strongest, was another reason for a lack of emphasis on economic issues. Whether it is because of the enormous destruction that nuclear weapons would cause, or for other reasons, as the post-World War II period has developed, the probability of major war seems to have declined, allowing other issues, particularly economic issues, to increase in relative salience. Starting in the 1960s, Western countries' interest in Marxism and more broadly in economic explanations increased. Both factors explain the growing popularity of international political economy.

Few courses in international political economy can require as prerequisites both an introductory course in international politics and sufficient courses in economics to include a basic economic treatment of international trade and international finance. Consequently, the course has the burden of presenting material that students need to know to deal with the basic issues of international political economy but which the instructor cannot assume that they learned in other courses. The principal challenge is to design an international political economy course that is in fact a course in international political economy and not just a watered-down course in international economics.

A course in international political economy should cover the basic issues of international trade and finance and the institutions and regimes dealing with these issues. It should also deal with what are termed North-South issues: problems of dependence and development. Other topics that should be included are raw materials and basic resources and multinational or transnational corporations. Although the concentration will inevitably be on economic relations among countries with market and mixed economies, the course should also deal with economic relations between market and centrally planned economies and among the latter. The course should treat Marxist, neo-Marxist, and structural, as well as classical liberal explanations. The main challenge for the instructor, as stated above, is to ensure that political variables are introduced and have a central place. Courses in international organization have been a part of the repertoire of advanced courses in international politics since work in international politics began because international organizations, and the League of Nations in particular, were seen as the most appropriate prescription for peace. Often these courses were taught by individuals whose original training had been in international law. Because they date from an era when political science was different from what it is today and because of the intellectual roots of the scholars who originally worked in the area, international organization courses have often been highly descriptive and normative, so much so that they sometimes seem passé in a modern political science curriculum. A variety of attempts have been made to infuse the study of international organizations with the spirit of modern political science. Some of these have been more successful than others. Those that have been least successful have been those that have involved the direct transfer of concepts and techniques of analysis developed in the context of domestic political systems. Because of the state system, international institutions are simply not identical to domestic political institutions. What is clear is that like domestic political institutions international organizations need to be understood in a conceptual framework of political power and influence, but in international institutions most of the actors are formally and in fact agents, and the output of the institutions seldom has legally-binding consequences. International institutions provide frameworks for organizing voluntary cooperation among sovereign countries; they are not hierarchical command systems. It should be stressed, however, that whatever their limitations, international organizations are the principal vehicles for organizing voluntary cooperation in the state system and thus must play a major role in the quest for peace and prosperity. A course should analyze both the limitations and potentialities of international organizations.

Foreign policy courses view international politics from the perspective of the principal actors: countries. Whether the course is one dealing with comparative foreign policy or with the foreign policy of a specific country, the key issue is to introduce a theoretical perspective to ensure that the course is not just a description of the foreign policy or policies of one or several countries. There is a growing consensus among specialists in the area that the factors listed in the description above of the basic course contents, those that contribute to shaping foreign policies of states, provide an organizing framework and thus something of a theoretical perspective. In courses that deal with a specific country, a diachronic approach will allow some comparative analyses. Inevitably courses in foreign policy will devote greater attention to domestic political processes than other courses in international politics. They will also usually devote some attention to the substantive content of foreign policies. To avoid this being contemporary history, it can be approached as the dependent variable, the matter to be explained by the factors that shape foreign policy, which can be seen—again to appropriate a technical term—as the independent variables.

Adding an International Dimension to Courses in Other Subfields

Traditionally, if political science courses went beyond process and dealt with the outputs of political processes or public policies, foreign policy was the last of the topics to be considered, a topic that would be included if time allowed. The argument here is that the international dimension is too important to be left to the specialists in international politics. Carrying this argument to its logical conclusion, the international dimension ought to be the first element of any course: the politics of a country can only be understood when the place of that country's security position and its economic relationships to other countries set basic parameters on possible government policies and thus on the nature of politics. The first point then is a plea to start discussions of the government and politics of particular countries by setting the international environment that surrounds and shapes the domestic situation.

A second argument is that virtually all countries are involved in such extensive relationships with other countries that discussions of public policy must take these into account. Even for the United States, a discussion of macro-economic policy that does not include a consideration of U.S. foreign economic policy is incomplete. A third argument is that even political processes are susceptible to outside influences. In some cases this is now a matter of legal obligations. For instance, for the countries of Western Europe that have adhered to the European Convention for the Protection of Human Rights and Fundamental Freedoms, civil and political liberties protected by the convention are subject to the jurisdiction of the European commission and court, as well as domestic courts. External influences are less obvious in matters of electoral and legislative behavior, but they are nevertheless there. They ought to be included in analyses. The influences come from the fact that countries in varying extents and with respect to various issues cannot solve matters alone. Thus relationships with external actors are bound to impinge on domestic disputes.

A final argument is that courses that supposedly deal with political science broadly should include treatments of international issues. This stricture applies particularly to courses in political philosophy, methodology and techniques of political analysis, and modeling. These courses should not be limited to domestic concerns. Courses in political philosophy should deal with war and interstate violence; those in methodology, with the analysis of aggregate data and of small samples; and those in modeling, with game theory. The study of both international and domestic politics will be enriched if they draw on a common core of normative theories, analytical techniques, and deductive propositions.

The central thrust of this essay has been that since international and domestic politics are inextricably linked, the study of the two should be tightly intermixed. An array of international politics courses would be one way of ensuring such a mixture, but this approach leaves the integration to the students. Including international issues in courses about domestic politics would move toward helping students with this task. Adequate attention to international issues in general political science courses would make this integration a permanent feature of the discipline, if not during the period of this generation of teachers, surely during that of the next. Developments in the real world require that political science move in this direction.

References

William C. Olson, "The Growth of a Discipline," in B. Porter, ed., *The Aberysthwyth Papers: International Politics, 1919–1969* (London: Oxford UP, 1972), pp. 3–29.

James N. Rosenau et al., "Of Syllabi, Texts, Students, and Scholarship in International Relations," *World Politics*, 39, No. 2 (1977), pp. 263–340.

Robert O. Keohane and Joseph S. Nye, *Power and Interdependence: World Politics in Transition* (Boston: Little, Brown, 1977).

Kenneth N. Waltz, *Theory of International Politics* (Reading, Mass.: Addison-Wesley, 1979).

Teaching International Relations to American Students

George H. Quester

The teaching of international politics within the United States has been buffeted about a great deal in the past decade, reflecting shifting trends in social science analysis, reflecting also some major rethinking and "moments of truth" about America's role in the world.

The end of World War II had seen a widespread acceptance of *Realpolitik* analysis, as exemplified in the writings of Hans Morgenthau, generally responding to the unprecedented degree of United States participation in world affairs in the resistance to Hitler's Germany. This new realistic interpretation contrasted itself with an original, more idealistic, liberal position attributed to Americans in general for the earlier and more naive times before 1939, an idealism attributed in an extreme form to Woodrow Wilson in his approach to the outcome of World War I.

The years of the Vietnam War then brought in a strong third contender in various forms of Marxist or radical interpretation of international events, as many students, and many of their instructors, concluded that American capitalism was somehow to blame for this most unpopular war. Yet the same years also saw a number of other perspectives introduced, not strictly liberal, radical, or power-politics, with each perspective perhaps explaining a portion of what unfolds before us, but none explaining enough to win any kind of central role.

It will be argued here that as many as six distinct perspectives are now regularly brought to bear in the advanced study of international relations, each of which could be accused of conveying an agenda (hidden or otherwise) of its own, each of which should be brought to the surface for the students in a course.

George H. Quester is Professor of Government and Politics at the University of Maryland.

Power-Politics

We might as well begin with the power-politics perspective, for it is perhaps the one still used most often in basic texts, and it was central in fostering the establishment of international relations as a distinct subject at the end of World War II.[1] This is an interpretation that all nations are basically alike in their foreign policies, motivated by a quest for power, just as individual entrepreneurs in economics are motivated by a quest for monetary profit. The United States, in this view, should thus be seen as an ordinary country, no better or worse than other nations, and the perspective is billed as a useful antidote to naiveté and hypocrisy, for American students might otherwise see their own country as too high-minded and generous. A Woodrow Wilson or a James Monroe or Henry Kissinger is thus to be interpreted just as a Bismarck or Metternich or Clemenceau.

The difficulties of international politics, in this view, are largely attributed to the inherent anarchy of the international situation, resembling the "prisoner's dilemma" situation of game theory, rather than to the failings of particular political regimes and societies, or to the evil character of any individual politicians. The analog is often drawn to the writings of Hobbes, as international politics looks like "the state of nature," in which no one can dare trust anyone else. Machiavelli's concept of service to one's own state is endorsed as perfectly natural under the circumstances, supplanting any higher morality derived from traditional religion or from the more generally humanistic strains of political philosophy. The power-politics approach is thus basically pessimistic in many ways, but it is a relaxing pessimism, guarding against disappointments, since the moves of an adversary's statesmen look less pathological and more natural.

This would also be a view stressing how important it is to study the international arena as a separate area of politics, since the rules are so substantially different (perhaps there really are no rules because there is no world government). If Hobbes loses his relevance to domestic politics, once men take his advice and submit to a ruler, he would still be very relevant to an international arena which looks so much like "the state of nature."

All the perspectives we will outline here may lead to the conclusion that international relations is too important to leave out of any balanced political science curriculum. How can matters like nuclear war, the international energy crises, and the future of Lebanon and Israel, not deserve attention? Yet this first perspective would underline such importance by stressing how *different* international politics is from ordinary politics (so different that it belongs in a separate department?), while the others might be inclined to question such a difference, finding the root explanations for international politics back in our domestic arenas.

American Liberalism

The second perspective on our list is substantially different and can be labelled the "American liberal" outlook; a view which begins by seeing traditional international relations as needlessly anarchic and powerminded, thus interpreting American foreign policy as striving for the reform of international as well as domestic politics around the globe.[2] Wilson's phrase about "making the world safe for democracy" captures a great deal of the spirit of this view, for Americans saw themselves as intent on spreading political democracy to countries around the world, thereby making war much less likely. According to this outlook, the United States is an unusually good and benign country, rather than an ordinary country; and it has a great deal to offer and teach the ordinary countries of this world.

Rather than ever concluding that war and international conflicts are natural, this perspective expected more from international law and the spreading of democratic institutions. (International law was indeed a central part of what was taught in international affairs at American universities *before* World War II.) Americans with this perspective thus tended to blame other countries for wars, in particular non-democratic countries. One would in fact have great difficulty in finding any instances of political democracies—governments elected by their people—fighting wars against each other. Americans with this liberal perspective thus tended to think of Woodrow Wilson as wise rather than naive, while such foreign statesmen as Clemenceau seemed short-sightedly selfish. The United States, in this view, had little or nothing to be ashamed of in its role in international politics, as the biggest mistake we could make would be to try to emulate the tired old power-politics of the old world. America was still "the new world" in this perspective, a source of hope and useful example.

Radical Interpretations

The third perspective on our list, which we would label Marxist or radical, is almost exactly the obverse of the second, for it would view the United States as an unusually bad nation on the world scene (rather than as unusually good or even as merely ordinary). In this perspective, capitalism is pathological and in decline for the domestic half of life. It is also pathological in its impact on international politics, as outlined by Lenin's application of Marx to the analysis of international politics and illustrated in armed conflicts over markets and in the self-indulgences of military-industrial complexes. Since we remain the most capitalist country in the world, it is no accident, by this interpretation, that we are the most troublesome nation—needlessly provoking most of the Cold War,[3] inflicting war on Vietnam to delay or prevent the establishment of a Marxist regime, followed by a half-hearted détente, a stoking up of new arms acquisitions and another Cold War.

The radical view shares with the liberal view an assumption that wars are not to be blamed simply on "prisoners' dilemma" situations and the preemptive opportunities of the anarchic international system, but should be blamed instead on the character of nations themselves. The liberal would have blamed war on non-elected regimes, whether they be monarchies, Fascist, or Communist. The radical would blame wars and arms races instead on the economic imbalances of a capitalist regime, whether it be in Nazi Germany or in the United States. Just as the liberal has difficulty in imagining that liberal regimes (political democracies) could fight wars against each other, the radical long remained convinced that truly socialist regimes would never war with one another. The recent armed conflicts between China and Vietnam must come as something of a shock for this interpretation.

The words of analysis often enough become the words of propaganda and political argument. The liberal and the radical would both claim to attach great international significance to an attainment of democracy, with realists such as Hans Morgenthau correspondingly attaching very little importance to this domestic attribute of regimes. Yet there are two very different senses of democracy in use here; partisans for either side could avoid needless misunderstanding by adding qualifying phrases to identify political democracy and economic democracy.

The American liberal regards it as most important, first and foremost, that governments serve by the consent of the governed, that they be elected (facing the prospect of being defeated in bids for reelection), that the opposition be allowed to campaign, and the press be free to criticize the performance of the incumbents. The latter freedoms are essential to making elections meaningful in the first place. Government by consent of voters, in free, uncoerced, elections is what is at stake. We could label it *political* democracy, amid a contention that this contributes to good behavior in foreign affairs, and thus leads to peace.

The radical correspondingly cares much more about whether economic resources are distributed evenly, with the poorest of persons not being markedly poorer than the rich, with little or no economic domination of one man by another, and everyone having as much access to food, education, medicine, and housing as he is judged to need. Since this *economic* democracy amounts to a more egalitarian sharing of the good things of life, it might come into conflict with the liberal notion of free elections and political democracy. If so, the radical would choose to dispense with such liberal institutions as free elections and free press, for it would be democracy in the economic sense that is more important and more conducive to international peace.

Transnational/Ecological Perspectives

A fourth perspective on international politics took its cue from concerns about ecology, and about generally unmanageable global trends, concerns emerging at the beginning of the 1970s. This perspective stressed how much more there was to international politics besides issues of war and peace, and argued that the transnational impact of common material problems and complex interactions markedly reduced the role of the state in international affairs.[4]

This perspective discounts any picture of states behaving as single actors, the picture basically shared by the first three perspectives. Portions of states have to deal with portions of other states, partially because states are internally divided against themselves, but largely because the material problems of a technologically more complicated and polluted world make it impossible for issues to be handled any other way. In this perspective the problems we share are huge and unmanageable, and man must assign far less importance to the winning or even the deterring of wars. Global relations encompass much more than inter-state or international relations, since all share the same problems on "spaceship earth."

Such a reinterpretation of global politics seemed quite consistent with the fractionation of alliances and the emergence of detente which many observers anticipated at the end of the Vietnam war in the 1970s. War, and military matters in general, receded in the curriculum, no longer having a special status as "high politics," which issues such as acid rain were no longer dismissed as "low politics."

Unfortunately, for this particular analytical perspective, and unfortunately for mankind, the military fraction of international dealings did not decline as much as predicted in the 1970s. This seemingly made it easier for instructors of international relations courses, not having to shrink the military portion of their curriculum to make room for new weeks of lectures and analysis on ecology, but it caused a global apprehension that wars are returning in greater frequency and incurring less international condemnation. Even as wars continue, a major portion of the transnational/ecological perspective remains valid, since some very complicated global interaction problems have also not abated or gone away, and they impose a growing burden on all governments involved.

Some issues overlap the radical and the transnational perspectives, and there are a number of other overlaps in the initial list of perspectives. The workings of international trade and commerce, amid the growth of multinational corporations, might be dismissed as relatively unimportant by power-politics analysts, and viewed as generally benign by the traditional liberals. In contrast, Marxists see the "dependencia" of such extensive investment and trade as basically a part of the sickness of capitalism. Transnational/ecological analysts would also see such "dependencia" or "interdependence" causing complications, although perhaps offering a solution; these same complications keep states from focussing only on such traditional questions as national sovereignty and war and peace.

Bureaucratic Politics

A slightly different, fifth interpretation of foreign policies merging into the stream of international interactions stresses the bureaucratic self-interests of individuals and portions of governments. This "bureaucratic politics" view has some of the same attributes as a number of the views already outlined.[5]

It overlaps with the transnational/ecological emphasis in stressing that governments are not unified rational actors, but rather congeries of separately operating agencies. These two viewpoints differ when the bureaucratic focus stresses the selfish intentions of separate bureaucrats, pursuing their own career futures, rather than interests of the public at large. The transnational focus would stress the fractionation produced by the new multiplicity and complexity of problems.

The bureaucratic politics approach also shares some assumptions and conclusions with the radical perspective, and many students find the two simultaneously congenial. Each perspective assumes that the military-industrial complex, and the entire foreign-policy apparatus of the United States, fails to serve the interests of the American people; instead serving vested interests, in a manner making wars and arms races much more likely. The major difference would be that the bureaucratic perspective imputes very similar behavior to the government officials and military-industrial complex of the Soviet Union and all Communist countries as well, seeing such behavior as the inherent self-interest of bureaucrats, rather than as a reflection of the economic stages in the development of capitalism.

This tendency of seeing all countries as behaving very much the same also gives the bureaucratic perspective a lot in common with the power-politics view. Being cynical about what men pursue, as compared with what states pursue, the perspective is once again a hedge against naivete and disappointment. While *Realpolitik* analysts assume that all states seek power, the bureaucratic view simply fractured this assumption and concluded that all individuals seek career advancement.

This is analogous to the economist's assumption that all businessmen seek to maximize profit. The important difference is that the Morgenthau analysis presents a picture of basically unified states, using phrases like "Germany sought," "Russia feared," "Britain offered," etc., while the bureaucratic politics analysis imputes such rational behavior to the U.S. Navy versus the U.S. Air Force, etc.

It probably is the most difficult to find anything in common, in logic or in basic student appeal, between the American liberal view and the bureaucratic politics model. The normal American liberal believes that people enter government to serve their country, rather than to pursue a form of profit for themselves. The idea of a fractured, internally-divided, foreign policy apparatus thus comes as a shock.

The one strand that might unify these two views is found in the basic liberal perspective that wars and international dealings are *per se* something that should be eliminated and avoided. Asking Americans to have a unified front when a foreign enemy opposes us conflicts with liberal ideas of pluralism and free discussion and explains nostalgic longings for an earlier isolation and the hoped-for spread of pluralistic democracy to the entire world, making the confrontations of a combative foreign policy unnecessary.

The American liberal view traditionally distrusted government just as much as foreign policy. It might regard it as natural that people in government and foreign policy could not be harnessed monolithically to serve a single set of national interests; problems would not arise from bureaucratic behavior, but from harsh conformist demands of an active foreign policy in a hostile world environment.

Human Error

A sixth interpretation of international politics might seem quite parallel to that of American liberalism, but would come as a broader perception that international problems are largely the result of various kinds of mis-analysis and mistakes. Rather than assuming that the United States has some uniquely insightful advice to offer the world (namely that countries should institute free elections and thereafter let peaceful international exchange take care of itself), this view involves a more general collection of approaches stressing human error. These errors occur in democracies as well as non-democracies, causing crises to get out of hand, resulting in wars, or allowing long-term problems of population, ecology, and economic distribution to go unsolved.

Some of this becomes a discussion of standard operating procedures governing bureaucracies everywhere, leading such structures to be insufficiently adaptable to new problems, insufficiently attuned to the signals other countries are transmitting, etc.[6] In other cases, the errors analyzed are not so much in organizational procedure, but more in the individual human being's inability to handle large amounts of data and decision-burden. The insights brought to bear here are drawn from cybernetics and psychology, as well as from sociology, business, and public administration.

The humanities and philosophical or religious moralities offer broader suggestions of fundamental error as the essence of international relations problems. Suggestions are advanced that man's most fundamental error is to be insufficiently aware of the human costs of war, or insufficiently compassionate—unaware of the needs of other nations or the possible justice of other nations' claims. The problems of the international system, in this broad perspective, cannot be blamed on the simple anarchy of the international arena, or on capitalism or dictatorial governments. They also cannot be explained simply by the complexity of transnational politics, or by the self-service of career-pursuing government officials. Rather the problems are seen in one way or another as fundamental defects in intellectual analysis. Men simply make mistakes in the international arena, mistakes that can be far more deadly than in ordinary politics.

Introspection

Any such division into categories of perspective is arbitrary, of course, with some substantial overlap from category to category. Many students or analysts of international politics would not recognize themselves as fitting into any one of these perspectives in particular, or would not acknowledge any significant overlaps between their own analytic category and any of the others. Yet it will be contended here that this taxonomy captures many of the tensions besetting anyone now teaching a course on international relations, amid waves of new data and new impressions that began flooding American campuses during the Vietnam War, followed by concerns about energy shortages, ecology, and complex interdependence.

Above all, it is always important to allow the initial impressions and value premises of students to surface. Most of them were quite interested in politics before they plunged into international politics, developing definite preferences about the domestic governance of whatever country is their home. Most of these students already have strong views about political philosophy, even if they are more implicit and subliminal than explicit and well footnoted. Part of selecting categories of analysis will depend on the hidden linkages between students' assumptions about ordinary life and their assumptions about world politics. It is unusual for someone who sees Marxism as the appropriate system for domestic life to regard communist states as the cause for tension and war. And it is unusual for an American liberal to blame capitalism or democracy for increases in the likelihood of war.

At its worst, a tendency emerges toward relating all the good things of the world on one side and all the bad things of the world on the other, degenerating into a wing interpretation of history—a sorting out of historical and other evidence converting everything into a contest between the good guys and bad guys. A tendency to tie all progress or decadence together is particularly normal for liberals and Marxists, as they both agree that war and arms races are evil, though they are separated by drastically different definitions of domestic good and evil. In contrast, the realism of *Realpolitik* pessimistically stresses how there is always a necessity for choice among goods, for lesser evils, since what advances mankind on one dimension sets it back on another.

The transnational/ecological perspective and the bureaucratic politics perspective are much more likely to emerge among professional analysts within the political science community than from the man on the street or the college sophomore. These perspectives are also a little more likely to be free of broad good–evil connections. Yet, some of the literature on bureaucratic politics also offers a picture of domestic pathology (i.e., a selfish, competitive career advancement pattern of admirals around the world) leading to an international pathology (i.e., resulting naval arms races to obtain the most battleships and aircraft carriers, and the wars that may result). Life becomes simple: eliminate one problem, and you have eliminated another in the process.

Viewpoints stressing general overall error come from various directions. This perspective may find the proclivity toward error almost irreducible; in other versions, the problem may be eliminated if the world can be educated on a few simple points. As academics, we can hardly escape our own career interest in touting and performing education, and this sixth perspective is one found at least as much on campus as off.

Analysis of War and Peace

What subspecialties of subject matter are logically required to break out of these conflicting perspectives? One essential building block, implicit in most of these categories (though perhaps not in the ecological perspective), is the basic logic of conflict. Students need to be taught a rudimentary amount of applied game theory, including the general outlines of "prisoners' dilemma," and "chicken,"[7] perhaps with homely illustrations going back to Rousseau's "hare and the stag." Depending on which of the perspectives is found most congenial, greater or lesser attention is assigned to military variables, including concepts of stability and instability in armed confrontations, the impact of massive countervalue instruments introduced with nuclear weapons, the special logic of limited war, and its varieties: local war, guerrilla war, terrorism, etc.

Concepts of the balance of power need to be explored, helping students understand varying uses of the term in newspaper editorials, idle chit-chat, or even in international relations textbooks.[8] Of considerable use to students would be a listing of plausible ways of keeping the pack; systems found over the known history of mankind, specifying the time periods when they were in effect, and the circumstances that brought them down. As a modest proposal for such a list, one might include: (1) the balance of power system in the Greek city-states, and the system's emergence in Italian Renaissance city-states extending through France under Richelieu and the continuing efforts of Britain thereafter; (2) the accomplishments of a single world empire by military conquest, for instance the Pax Romana; (3) the extreme local defensive strength of feudalism, (4) a general fear of insurrection, which at least once has produced enough inter-state cooperation to make inter-state war unlikely—as in Metternich's Holy Alliance system after the defeat of Napoleon; (5) the establishment of a League of Nations system specifically intended to prevent war *per se*, by rendering judgment on those initiating violent hostilities, directing sanctions and punishment against such criminal acts; and (6) the "balance of terror" system of today, relying on the ability of two superpowers to inflict massive retaliatory destruction on each other's cities, no matter who may win wars fought on ordinary battlefields.

In stressing the incidence of war or peace as the major dependent variable, all such discussion would be somewhat biased toward the first three perspectives, perhaps in particular toward power-politics, since most of the independent variables cited are characteristics of the overall system rather than defects of one or several of the domestic structures. Yet the significance of war and peace as output will be considerable for most students and for most Americans; the presumption about detente that led scholars to predict that war and peace might become moribund or secondary considerations was very short-lived.

International Law and Organization

Because they were always part of the traditional package, or because they have had real lives of their own, some discussion of international law and organization should also be threaded in at an early stage. To avoid sounding naive or out of touch, international law should probably not be discussed or taught in the matter-of-fact manner of domestic law. A realistic focus would instead begin with why nations find it in their interest to sign and adhere to treaties, perhaps quoting Frederick the Great's aphorism that "the only reason we keep our promises is that no one would otherwise ever trust us in the future."

International law is often ignored and evaded, but it is also often observed and adhered to, even in time of war (viz., the "laws of war"). The logic of an exchange of promises, matched by exchanges of threats, does much to explain why international law has a real life of its own, just as it explains how there are "limited wars," in which some weapons are used and others are not.

International organization is best brought in with references to the real leverage and bureaucratic momentum of launched organizations rather than to idealistic blueprints of how they are meant to function on the drawing board. At this point we can usefully thread in some insights from the bureaucratic politics perspective. If the admirals of all the world's navies are best explained by a model which presupposes that they wish to add ships to their fleets, can we not adduce a parallel model to explain the bureaucracy of the United Nations or the International Red Cross? Rather than writing off the impact of international organizations as irrelevant to international politics, because they do not have enough guns and power of their own, perhaps we should take note of the power any bureaucracy can exercise once it has been brought into being—even a multinational or international bureaucracy. We can introduce a bit of history on the evolution of some practices and precedents for international organization, dating back to Metternich's years when European regimes began coordination efforts to prevent the Rhine or Danube from flooding, to head off liberalism, etc.[9]

Material Factors: Economics and Science

Analyses of the impact of military weapons and technology on international politics might, on reflection, be viewed as just a special case of the broader impact of all science and technology in this area and the more general impact of economics and material factors. We previewed this already with the perspective emphasizing the ecological unity of the globe.

Any good basic course on international politics will have to devote several weeks to the impact of economic factors, ranging from resource shortages and damaging externalities stressed by the ecologists to Marxist issues of international economic dependence and interdependence and to economic leverage as a form of power, even a tool of deterrence—as in the protection of West Berlin or Hong Kong against attack. The broader impact of science in foreign policy sometimes will include the role of scientists, introducing the sociology of science. Some basic discussion of central issues of international economics *per se* will also inevitably be germane, covering transitions from the gold standard to the reliance on sterling, the predominance of the dollar, and the system of free-floating exchange rates applied since the 1970s.[10]

One way to sort this economic impact is by using geographical categories with "North–South" issues including dependencies seen by either Marxist or transnational interpretation, with "East–West" issues being assayed within the power-politics framework in an attempt to measure whether either ideological side is restrained by trade or freed for adventure and then with "North–North" issues being argued among and within industrialized democracies, amid complicated patterns of inflation, unemployment, and economic growth.

National Culture and Psychology

"National character" theories were fashionable during World War II; the war was blamed on personality defects allegedly widespread among Germans or Japanese. These theories rapidly dropped into disfavor, since the entire exercise resembled Fascist ethnic and cultural generalization too much. Yet most students enter international affairs subjects intuitively assuming that there is truth in some generalizations, since "Russians are different from Latin Americans, who in turn are different from Chinese, or from Australians, etc." Getting these to the surface, to be tested or criticized, will probably remain an important part of any international relations course.

We have hinted at two "national character" explanations for international events already, views blaming American capitalism or Russian Communism for world tensions. In a sense, any course on international politics taught with the United States becomes an introspective study of American national character, since students relate their own background and country to the premises and expectations they advance about international relations.

When a nation becomes involved with culture as a component of its foreign policy, perhaps even as the main component, it makes a greater difference. The contemporary French government's commitment to encouraging speaking French around the globe is a minor illustration of this, a commitment not sufficing to undo the growing preeminence of English. Like earlier times, the Basques, Flemings, or Bretons resist the preeminence of French, and are matched by the resistance of French Canadians to the preeminence of English.

For the sake of history, and because ethnic factors are undergoing a resurgence in motivating electoral publics and governments, a broader survey of such forms of ethnic nationalism and imperialism would be appropriate here. The phrase "imperialism" has more recently been appropriated by radicals to describe the foreign policies of any capitalist state, but students need to be acquainted with its earlier connotation in the decades before World War I. Then Europeans took pride in teaching Africans and Asians to speak French or German or English, and the ethnic future of small portions of Europe or of any other continent seemed important enough to be worth risking war. After 1945, the atrocities of Hitler and Mussolini put ethnic nationalism under a cloud, with the "nationalism" phrase much more often applied simply to the desire of any European colonial possession for national independence. Students need to be reminded of how much more it meant before World War I and after, amid various endorsements of ethnic self-determination as the solution for irredentist disputes, amid the interpretations of such self-determination offered by the various strains of Fascism.

"Cultural imperialism" can now mean almost as many things as "imperialism" itself. It can mean deliberate efforts to advance a particular culture, or (not quite the same thing) a policy of political imperialism motivated by concerns for culture. It might refer to an inadvertent spread of one culture at a loss to another, as when Hollywood's movies and television programs make young people around the world more inclined to learn English, or to emulate what they think is the American way of life.[11] Consistent with the transnational focus, the interpenetration of societies via such mass culture is now very great, and tends to have a life of its own, not controlled or regulated by any particular government's edicts.

History

The American student taking an international relations course typically has not developed any deep knowledge of history in his years in high school. Since some of the possible workings of the international system are demonstrated by the ebbs and flows of civilization, the instructor (in what is ostensibly a political science course) will nonetheless have to sketch in the outlines of this history.

History can be used in many ways here. For the purposes of illustrating points about the diplomatic process, anecdotes from real life often have more human interest and more appeal than an abstract discussion of "country A" and "country B." Bismarck, Clemenceau, and Churchill were certainly quotable enough in their time, and the drama of international politics includes a lot of this.

History is illuminating not only at this microcosmic scale, of course, but also in the broader macrocosmic form that we open when listing systems which have prevented war and produced peace in the past. Students ought to be able to tell the difference between the Roman Empire and the Holy Roman Empire. They ought to be able to relate the purest form of "balance of power" to the social conditions of the days of Frederick the Great and understand how other conditions after the French Revolution produced a very different international result.

Going beyond using macrocosmic states of play as static models, an international politics theorist might possibly be able to deduce a "political development of the international system" very comparable in theories of momentum and change and dialectical evolution to the "political development" theories that have been so much elaborated for domestic politics.[12] This would then be part of drawing international politics a bit more into the mainstream of the rest of political science.

The more perceptive student might well ask why international politics is grouped in with all the rest of political science (the other slices usually being American government, comparative government, political philosophy, and perhaps the methodology of political analysis), since the cast of mind of people choosing this area is often so different from those fascinated by ordinary politics.

Many instructors are indeed fond of opening a course on international politics by stressing how very different this subject area is, given its overarching anarchy, its lack of transcendent morality, and its enthusiasm for Machiavellian attitudes of "my country, right or wrong." Much of this emerges from the power-politics perspective, of course, stressing the traps laid by the prisoners' dilemma and the security dilemmas of international relations. This environment produces an ambient possibility of widespread violence and war, making secrecy normal rather than abnormal, thrusting government officials into an inherently adversarial relationship with their counterparts in other countries.

Some of the differences also stem from the multidisciplinary nature of the subject (illustrated in the course outlined here), including healthy doses of economics, history, psychology, sociology, anthropology, and philosophy, as well as physics and chemistry. Some instructors will remember the time, immediately after World War II, when universities established entirely separate and independent international relations departments, with the decision coming only later in the 1950s to blend them back into the political science departments.

The multidisciplinary approach can teach students to look for a steady evolution of the international system, linked for hundreds of reasons to the evolutions of domestic political life, to discover what is common and unifying through all of political science.

Mathematical Approaches

The more serious political science students will of course want to have a try at applying to international politics some of the more modern and quantitative methods regularly used now in the analysis of domestic politics. The willingness to try such methodology sometimes presupposes a slightly mathematical cast of mind, producing enthusiasms among some students, while others handicapped by "math anxiety" lump all such approaches together as needlessly difficult, adding nothing to what their intuitions tell them.

However, it is important to call students' attention to the great variety of possible mathematical approaches to the study of international relations. An application of Game Theory, for example, returns to one end of the spectrum of perspectives (that of power politics pitting entire national units against each other as rational actors), while the application of statistical inference techniques often takes the student and researcher into the subject from a very different perspective (indeed almost from a calculated absence of perspectives, as the social scientist using such techniques may be deliberately disallowing all prior intuitive premises and assumptions, hoping that an objective process of coding data and sampling correlations will separate true relationships from those that are simply folklore).

Critics of such applications of statistical inference to international politics might contend that the international system never gives us a large enough "n" of data; perhaps there are not enough comparable crises, wars, or international events to let mathematical approaches of this sort offer better insights than those supplied by naive intuition. Such approaches can indeed tell us a great deal about the swings of masses of voters in domestic elections, but the votes of the United Nations General Assembly may never involve large enough numbers or have enough relevance to real politics to be comparably susceptible to such analysis.

The instructor should offer some positive examples of statistical analysis of the variance in internationally important events, along with some discussion of the pitfalls.

Introspection Once More

At the very end of the course, the instructor should probably once again alert students to all the international debates about the international relations subject. For example, is the phenomenon of war to be the central output variable or is this being supplanted? Is international politics mostly different from ordinary politics, or is it in many respects the same? Has economics in some sense—Marxist or otherwise—become the central determinant of international relations? Is there a major trend of development in the international system, or is it cycling in a repeated and predictable pattern, a pattern with nations behaving the same from continent to continent, and century to century?

Unless an instructor is extraordinarily lucky or prescient, he will encounter some international current events during the semester which amount to a surprise, upsetting predictions and confusing students as well as faculty. A way of converting this from a liability to an asset is by comparing the extent to which the various perspectives outlined could predict such events. Implicit in each bias are premises about the likelihood of wars and alliances and crises, about the likely behavior of different kinds of foreign countries, etc.

Social science analysis is accustomed to the "fact-value" distinction. Another way of comparing the contending perspectives in an international relations curriculum is to sort them by whether they mainly address the appropriate values and end-goals of foreign policy (perhaps this comparison most distinguishes the liberal and Marxist analyses, although pitting them against each other), or whether they mainly address factual descriptions of opportunities (with the power-politics approach and the transnational/ecological perspectives mainly warning of the inherent choices to confront although differing substantially about which forks in the road are likely to loom largest).

Issues of epistemology will also rear their ugly heads. How would a Marxist interpret all the other perspectives, except (in a somewhat *ad hominem* fashion) to argue that they are themselves, just like American foreign policy, the products of capitalist nurture. "If you do not see how capitalism caused the Vietnam War, you have been brainwashed by Madison Avenue, Wall Street, and the American way of life."

And how would a liberal interpret contrary perspectives? Perhaps similarly responding in an *ad hominem* manner, accusing the Marxist of yearning to govern others without their consent, accusing the power-politics school of enjoying international intrigues and wars for their own sake. To ask anyone to introspectively question their motives somewhat changes the nature of argument. It may be an unfair debate technique, but necessary, nonetheless, to round out the full nature of our international relations problem.

And finally, how much social science analysis could be accused of being a self-conscious social science, political science for the sake of analysis, rather than for relevance to any policy maker? Are not some interpretations of foreign policy, international interdependence, or international politics in general always going to have more appeal for the graduate student in political science or the faculty member than for the undergraduate, the man-on-the-street, or the career foreign service officer?

As academics, we might be inclined to trust those views which reflect extra years of graduate study, but the same *ad hominem* doubts which various schools of thought direct at each other should be directed at ourselves. Are we too inclined to be cynical about the motives of those who make a career in the foreign service or military service? Are we too much in a hurry to make international politics resemble the rest of politics? This critical question might never come to the forefront of student thinking about an international politics course; but it is something the instructor must contemplate in preparing curriculum and lecture notes, and it is a question that might even be profitably brought into the open, at some stage of the lectures or discussion in this course.

Notes

[1] Still one of the best examples is Hans Morgenthau's basic textbook, *Politics among Nations*. 5th rev. ed. (New York: Knopf, 1978).

[2] A clear statement of this position, as presented before events of the 1960s brought the ideological issue and contending interpretations more into the open can be found

in Thomas Cook and Malcolm Moos, *Power Through Purpose: The Realism of Idealism* (Baltimore: Johns Hopkins Press, 1954).

[3] For a good example of such a radical interpretation, see Gabriel and Joyce Kolko, *The Limits of Power* (New York: Harper and Row, 1972).

[4] A collection opening up a great deal of the transnational perspective is that by Robert O. Keohane and Joseph S. Nye, ed., *Transnational Relations and World Politics* (Cambridge: Harvard UP, 1972). See also, by the same authors, *Powers and Interdependence: World Politics in Transition* (Boston: Little, Brown, 1977).

[5] Perhaps the most often cited single work in the bureaucratic politics interpretation is Graham T. Allison, *Essence of Decision: Explaining the Cuban Missile Crisis* (Boston: Little, Brown, 1971).

[6] Two very interesting works that could be loosely grouped into this area are Robert Jervis, *Perception and Misperception in International Politics* (Princeton, N.J.: Princeton UP, 1976) and John Steinbruner, *The Cybernetic Theory of Decision* (Princeton, N.J.: Princeton UP, 1974).

[7] For a good, clear introductory discussion of the applications of game theory, see Anatol Rapoport, *Two-Person Game Theory: The Essential Ideas* (Ann-Arbor: U of Michigan P, 1973).

[8] Still one of the better distinctions among definitions is Ernst B. Haas, "The Balance of Power: Prescription, Concept, or Propaganda," *World Politics* 5, No. 4 (1953), pp. 442–77.

[9] On the role of international law in international politics, see Adda B. Boxeman, *The Future of Law in a Multicultural World* (Princeton, N.J.: Princeton UP, 1971). On the role of international organization, Leland M. Goodrich and David A. Kay, ed., *International Organization: Politics and Process* (Madison: U of Wisconsin P, 1973).

[10] One book I have found very useful on these issues is Joan E. Spero, *The Politics of International Economic Relations*. 2nd ed. (New York: St. Martin's, 1981).

[11] For a discussion of some of the issues raised in the category of "cultural imperialism," see Herbert I. Schiller, *Mass Communications and American Empire* (Boston: Beacon Press, 1971).

[12] For an interesting attempt in this direction, see F.W. Hinsley, "The Development of the European States System since the Eighteenth Century," *Transactions of the Royal Historical Society* 11(1961), pp. 69–80.

Teaching How to Ask Questions about International Relations

Robert O. Keohane

Contemporary world politics is a matter of life and death. Studying international relations means studying war—a traditionally tragic subject that has become existentially overwhelming today—and peace. Orthodox theories of international relations proclaim the inevitability of periodic warfare; modern science informs us of the likelihood that human civilization at our present standard would not survive an all-out nuclear exchange.

Since they are aware that the world is a dangerous place, it is not difficult to persuade eighteen-year-olds of the importance of studying world politics. The prospect of nuclear destruction can powerfully concentrate the mind. So can the possibility that America's ruling class would once again send young men to fight in jungles on behalf of ill-defined causes combining ideology with a peculiar version of *Realpolitik*. On somewhat greater reflection, they can see the relevance to their own lives of changes in the world political economy, whether these involve oil embargoes, trade protectionism, or Third World debt. The more sensitive students may be troubled by the contrast between how they live and the near-subsistence conditions that still face most people on this planet.

The contradictions between the conditions of their own lives and what they see around them provide us, as teachers of international relations, with a great opportunity. Most of our students have led remarkably privileged lives: rich, secure, with a great deal of personal freedom. If they were sufficiently near-

Robert O. Keohane is Professor of Government at Harvard University. The author is grateful for comments on an earlier draft of this article to Nannerl O. Keohane and Susan Moller Okin, and for the point about the Romans' propensity for warfare to an unknown author. The quotation from Richard Southern and the story about Robert Maynard Hutchins and William Howard Taft come from the notebooks of his late father, Robert E. Keohane, who did not include references to sources, but whose textual scholarship was meticulous and whose anecdotes usually reflected the essence of the reality being described.

sighted, the world would be their oyster. But if they look toward world politics, they see inequality, deprivation, violence, and danger—possibly for themselves, certainly for others. We can easily point out these inequalities and challenge them to think about them.

Students may come to us for answers, but the most we can do is to help them enrich and organize the questions that they ask, and to provide them with the analytical tools and historical knowledge needed to discover provisional, partial answers for themselves. We cannot provide our students with well established theories that explain the past, much less predict the future. World politics is characterized by intense strategic interaction, hence by the indeterminacy of outcomes. Clear causal patterns are difficult to discern because it is so hard to keep "other factors equal" while examining the effects of selected forces on the behavior that we wish to explain. A multitude of influences, from personal psychology to world system-structure, affects the behavior of states, and even more complexity is introduced when we take transnational actors such as multinational corporations into account. Prospectively, we are unable to predict events, retrospectively, they appear overdetermined.

Stanley Hoffmann's characterization of theory in international relations as "a set of questions" rather than an array of answers remains timely, especially for undergraduate teaching (Hoffmann, 1960, p. 40). Our answers tend to be ephemeral—Robert Gilpin (1981, p. 227) doubts that we know more than Thucydides about the great issues of war and peace—but old questions endure and new ones multiply. The chief task we face in teaching undergraduates about international relations is to provide them with the capability to ask the right questions—now and twenty or forty years into the future—about world politics.

We need to think about how to do this on two levels: that of the introductory international relations course and of the international relations curriculum as a whole. Most students who are enrolled in an introduction to international relations will never take another such course in their lives. In introductory courses we should not seek to teach them fragments of half-developed and problematic theories that we debate with one another, but rather to pose fundamental questions. We should keep in mind not so much what they will know at the end of the course—as reflected in the final examination—but how much our teaching will help them analyze events when they pick up newspapers in the future to discover that the superpowers are negotiating an arms control agreement, an oil embargo has been declared, or a war has broken out in an obscure area of the world. For these people, the questions we teach them to ask in one term will provide the basis for the questions they ask as citizens throughout their lives.

Such a course in international relations seems indispensable for all students of politics today. This is obvious for people interested in comparative politics, who will be lost if they cannot situate the countries that they study within the world system (Katzenstein, ed., 1978). It is true also for students of political theory, whose theories of justice must increasingly come to grips with problems of international inequality, intervention, and warfare (Walzer, 1977; Beitz, 1979). But it is also the case for students whose primary interests lie in American politics and policymaking. Many of the pressures on the United States, as well as some of its opportunities, come from abroad. Two world wars, an apparently interminable Cold War, and wars in Korea and Vietnam have shaped the national consciousness and altered the nature of political institutions. The American political economy has been transformed by rapid increases in foreign investment, exports, and bank lending, as well as by the impact of the Military-Industrial Complex. "Domestic policies" such as those having to do with energy, taxes, and antitrust have become internationalized. To study American politics today as if the United States were isolated from the rest of the world would be like trying to explain the internal structure of a corporation without looking at its competitive environment.

Some of our students will become majors in international relations, if this option is available, or will concentrate on world politics as political science majors. They should have deeper knowledge of history, of varieties of world cultures, and of analytical techniques than students who take only the introductory course. Thus they should be able to ask better questions and to devise more sophisticated provisional answers. But few even of these will ever become professors of international relations or State Department policy analysts. Their task, like that of those who took only one course, will be of individual evaluation and capability for intelligent discussion, not sustained research. Vaguely remembered fragments of a half-forgotten research methodology and arcane terminological distinctions will not be particularly helpful to them.

Designing Introductory Courses

The design of our courses and curricula should reflect our urgent search for the right questions to ask, comparatively and historically, about our scientifically recalcitrant but existentially overwhelming subject. In my view, we should begin with the problem of war and peace. To construct an international relations curriculum or even an introductory course, without trying to understand war—and why the absurdity of nuclear war is possible—would itself be absurd.

Yet is it frightening to teach about nuclear war—to "think about the unthinkable." As professional students of world politics, we are naturally and properly reluctant to deal with such a subject in the naive and emotional way characteristic of much public debate and many of the pronouncements made by our well-meaning colleagues in academic institutions. Somehow we need to confront this "hot" topic analytically—with sufficient detachment to be able to analyze as well as to agonize, but with enough emotional integrity and passion not to make the subject turn cold in our hands. Thinking about nuclear strategy requires concentrated brainpower, not just good will and feelings. It is important to remind ourselves, and our students, that it is not a game.

Nuclear diplomacy cannot be understood without some knowledge of pre-nuclear diplomacy, nor can the contemporary "balance of power" be comprehended without both an analytical and historical awareness of what that phrase has meant over the last several hundred years. The relevance of nuclear war does not mean that we focus most of our attention on it. Since we fortunately have no direct experience of a nuclear exchange—only of the unilateral use of atomic bombs by the United States against a country armed solely with conventional weapons—the analysis of nuclear strategy is hypothetical and abstract. Its logical essentials, as reiterated most recently in a new book collectively authored by six Harvard scholars, *Living with Nuclear Weapons* (Carnesdale et al., 1983), are not excessively complicated, and should be taught. However, to dwell on their esoteric refinements would be to detract attention from our experiences of war and crisis, as well as to give too much credence to the speculations of defense planners and policy critics alike.

Nuclear war is the central problem of contemporary world politics, but the circumstances in which it could arise, or the means by which it could be prevented, can only be understood by examining the world into which nuclear weapons were delivered. World politics, as an historical fact of the human condition, needs to be understood if we are to think clearly about this pressing problem.

Few eighteen-year-olds care much about history for its own sake, or for the intellectual puzzles that it provides. But we can demonstrate that they need to study history to comprehend world politics in the nuclear age. They need an historical perspective in order to understand the major forces that affect their lives through world politics: the competition for dominance and the security dilemma between the superpowers; the permanent war economies and military bureaucracies of the United States and the Soviet Union; how pressures from expansionist states affect what constitutes prudent action for status quo powers; the combination of uneven development and increased interdependence promoted by the operation of capitalism on a world scale; the effects of intense nationalism and nationalist radicalism in Vietnam, Iran, or Nicaragua; and the difficulty of reconciling ideals with self-interest in a treacherous world. It is not difficult to persuade them that to understand these forces and these dilemmas they need to study major recent events—the onset of the Cold War, the Cuban Missile Crisis, and Vietnam. All these raise as many questions as answers, about their antecedents and about the supposed historical parallels seized on by perplexed policymakers or considered reflectively by scholars. So we lead our students backward through time, to the arms races and crises that preceded World War I or even to the struggle for hegemony between Athens and Sparta in fifth century B.C., searching for the right questions and for threads of meaning.

Yet history is not enough. To make world politics intelligible, analytical categories and theories are also necessary. We can combine history and analysis by teaching introductory international relations as comparative history, using comparative case analysis, or "focused comparison," as Alexander George (1979) has called it. Since only one global system exists at any given time, comparative analysis in international relations must necessarily be historical. Major events can be taught both as history—providing essential background to students who, unfortunately, often know little of the past when they enter college—and as case studies illustrating major analytical puzzles. This avoids two pitfalls: either trying to teach theory first, postponing historical interpretation to the second half of the course (which leads to aridity and a lack of understanding of historical context by students) or concentrating on modern history in a theoretical way, only introducing concepts from political science rather lamely as afterthoughts. History and analysis can be intertwined in dialectical fashion. The onset of World War I raises questions of technology and force, the relationship between domestic structure and foreign policy, and the unintended consequences of strategic interactions among states. The Munich crisis forces one to confront the disjunction, which is at the core of the tragic subject of world politics, between peaceful intentions and actions having peaceful consequences. The Cuban Missile Crisis allows one both to analyze conditions for effective crisis management and to raise questions about organizational and bureaucratic politics as constraints on rational choice.

It probably does not make a great deal of difference what cases one chooses. In my course on the Twentieth Century, I concentrate on the origins of World War I, Munich, the Cold War, Korea, the Cuban Missile Crisis and Vietnam, the contemporary arms race, the oil embargoes of the 1970s, and the debate over a "new international economic order." As students read about these topics, I stress fundamental analytical concepts in lectures.

Some of these concepts deal with macro-level causal analysis: how to categorize causes of war as individual, national, or system-level phenomena, and what the characteristic difficulties are with each of these "images" (Waltz, 1959); how to think about causality over time in terms of increasing constraints on choice, rather than as an issue of "free will and determinism," how to assess claims about conditions for equilibrium (as in balance of power theory) and about spirals of instability (as in action-reaction theories of wars and arms races); and how to draw connections between economic interdependence and political power. I emphasize the differences between world politics and domestic politics, otherwise beginning students will too readily view the unfamiliar subject of world politics in terms of their more benign personal experience.

It is particularly crucial to stress that in world politics, intentions may be perversely related to outcomes: unanticipated consequences are the rule rather than the exception. Not only may those who desire preponderance be destroyed, but those who seek peace in unwise ways may find themselves confronted by wars that could have been avoided with greater firmness, or more thorough preparedness. The Right Wing characteristically refuses to admit that our belligerence can stimulate antagonism in others; the Left Wing often seems to believe that foreign leaders who have demonstrated their willingness to rely on force would respond positively to sweet reason.

These dilemmas cannot be resolved with simple recipes. Proponents of "peace through strength" quote the Romans' injunction that those who seek peace should prepare for war—forgetting that Imperial Rome was involved in almost constant warfare. Preparing for war affects both our own attitudes and others' expectations about our intentions. Conversely, those who uniformly advocate military cutbacks and political concessions ignore at their peril the danger that powerful, ambitious adversaries will thereby be emboldened to demand more and to take more risks. Even policies of appeasement—invoked by interventionists as symbols of folly—are not necessarily mistaken. Chamberlain failed to deal effectively with Hitler; but an American policy in Vietnam that sought peace even at the expense of a friendly government would have been superior to the strategy actually followed—a strategy devised by admirers of Winston Churchill who thought they had "learned the lessons of Munich." Those who fail to learn the lessons of the past are destined, as Santayana said, to repeat them; but those who take their historical analogies too seriously are likely to make the opposite errors from those they are striving to avoid (Jervis, 1976, Chapter 6). In a course on world politics it is important to point out the shortcomings of all simple formulas for peace.

The complexity of links between intentions and outcomes provides a bridge between analysis of world politics at the systemic level and foreign policy analysis. Much of my introductory course is devoted to the latter, since it permits a focus on concrete events rather than abstractions, and since American students—imagining themselves as future presidents and secretaries of state—are fascinated with the problem of superpower decision making. How are decisions made, and what standards should we construct for making them better? Having seen how difficult it is even for a perfectly rational individual to make correct decisions under conditions of strategic uncertainty, we may be even more disturbed by the recognition of how poorly actual crisis decision making meets the usual criteria of rationality. Even the Cuban Missile Crisis—

often taken on the American side as illustrating an exemplary decision making process—raised the prospect of an unwanted war. The most popular event in my introductory course at Stanford was an annual debate between Alexander George and the historian Barton Bernstein on the subject of whether Kennedy's behavior in the Cuban Missile Crisis, risking war with the Russians, was justifiable. The students were gripped by the powerful arguments on both sides and by the foreign policy dilemmas illustrated by the fact that even 15 years after the event, the best-informed scholars in the country could not agree on whether decisions made during the course of a single week were prudent.

Taking a foreign policymaker's perspective on an issue such as the Cuban Missile Crisis provides a natural point of entry into a discussion of ethical issues in world politics, for the citizen as well as the leader or expert. Both the question of nuclear weapons and the experience of United States involvement in Vietnam raise issues of morality as well as those of explanation. Should our ethical standards emphasize intentions or consequences? In what respects should the moral code of government officials be different from that of individuals? Under what conditions is intervention in the internal affairs of another country legitimate? Is the threat to use nuclear weapons justifiable? If so, what about the actual use of such instruments of mass killing? These questions should be raised in a course on international politics, even if they cannot be answered.

No time remains in my introductory course for the issues on which I conduct my own scholarship: changes in the international political economy of the advanced countries, problems of interdependence, the decline of hegemony, and prospects for international economic cooperation. In part I slight these for variety's sake, since I teach them elsewhere. But there is a more important reason. After giving priority to questions of war and peace, I think that it is necessary to give some sustained attention to inequality and poverty. This is a pervasive and pronounced feature of world politics, as compared with domestic society. For most of the human race, it is arguably a more serious problem than the risk of nuclear war, and certainly a more pressing one. It is also a question from which our students, in their own lives, are almost completely shielded.

In my discussion of inequality I focus on its relationship to political power. Economic inequality is not a natural fact, and it is not simply a result of the distribution of resources worldwide. As we know, it is an artifact of human institution. It reflects patterns of dominance and subordination, now and in the past. Perhaps radical critics point this out best, but the most forthright and honest conservatives, such as Robert W. Tucker (1977), acknowledge it as well.

The sources and effects of these patterns of dominance need to be described and, insofar as possible, explained. This positive analysis takes on life when counterposed to a normative analysis of inequality since disparities in standards of living between rich and poor countries are so great they challenge justification by any moral theory applied on a worldwide basis. Students need to understand why governments of wealthy countries—and perhaps why they, themselves—are unwilling to take the risks of supporting fundamental changes in these conditions. Since fundamental change in the Third World will necessarily involve basic changes in political power as well as economic structure, we need to ask about the political and economic costs to the rich countries of supporting revolutionary movements that are inherently uncontrollable by faraway great powers. The Brandt Report on world development problems (1979) illustrates through the force of moral appeals that the rich countries should do much more and that such actions are in their own self-interest. But its fate as a virtual dead-letter demonstrates the difficulty of persuading powerful governments to act on the basis of long-term visions if they are not forced to do so by immediate pressures.

War and inequality are the two most life-threatening problems of our era. My introductory international relations course is designed to ensure that students are aware of these vital issues and that they can ask some intelligent questions about the causes of each threat and about proposed cures. Since broad surveys often reduce everything to superficiality, I concentrate on these two problems. Students who learn, in discussions of war and inequality, to ask the right questions about historical causality, decision making, and connections between wealth and power, can ask similar questions on their own about other aspects of world politics and the international political economy.

Designing An International Relations Curriculum

Again I will write from personal experience. I went to Stanford University from Swarthmore College in 1973 not just as a member of the political science department but as chair of an interdisciplinary international relations committee led by the political scientist Alexander George and several historians, including Gordon Craig. My role was to set up an undergraduate program in international relations, which was later to become a major.

My colleagues and I believed that the diversity of the field of international relations constituted our chief challenge. We defined the field not only to include parts of the traditional disciplines of economics, history, and political science, but also to incorporate aspects of those humanistic and social scientific disciplines that study the interaction of cultures rather than polities or economies—anthropology, comparative literature, comparative religion, even classics—and those that discuss evaluative standards of action, such as moral philosophy. This approach made intellectual sense (as well as being mandated by the terms of a grant from the National Endowment for the Humanities) since political and economic organization depend on, and affect, culture, that is, the "the webs of significance" that human beings have spun (Geertz, 1973, p. 5). But it raised organizational problems since the very diversity of the subject could lead one to believe that virtually everything constituted international relations.

Our solution to this problem was to introduce structure into the curriculum without imposing rigid requirements. All students had to take the quarterly introductory course. They also had to complete two years of a foreign language and , unless exempted (which was rare), spend a significant period of time working or studying abroad. We did not want to graduate majors in international relations whose only first-hand exposure to a foreign culture was tourism. Since Stanford had an extensive foreign studies program, it was easy for students to make the necessary arrangements. Finally, students had to do work in each of the three "clusters" into which we grouped our courses: political-historical, political-economic, and cultural-humanistic.

These requirements could be met by a variety of combinations of courses and independent work. Without further specification,there would be no guarantee of coherence since a student could have taken a random selection of courses ranging from arms control to the economics of underdevelopment to the ways in which Europeans and Americans viewed each other through 18th and 19th century literature. In addition to meeting our formal requirements, therefore, each student had to select a theme for his or her own work in international relations. It could be geographical, as long as interaction between societies was stressed: focusing on Soviet–German or East Asian–North American relations was all right, whereas an emphasis simply on the internal politics of the Soviet Union, Germany, or China would not be accepted. It could be problem-oriented, stressing a subject such as the international and domestic aspects of underdevelopment in the Third World or superpower security problems and arms control. It could also deal with a non-geographically defined sub-system, such as the international political economy of modern capitalism. There had to be a theme, but students were free to choose their own. We did not demand, ethnocentrically, that everyone take courses on American foreign policy just because these are conventionally part of an international relations program; nor did we pay much attention to the nominal disciplines from which a student's courses were drawn, as long as the two basic requirements—some breadth (ensured by the requirement of doing work in each cluster) and some depth(ensured by the requirement of having a theme) were met.

Having chosen a theme, each applicant to the program had to write a brief essay justifying it and showing how the courses that he or she planned to take related to one another. The director of the program and another academic advisor looked over the essay and discussed it, insofar as necessary, with the student, but it was essentially the student's responsibility. Students thus had to take charge of their own lives and think about what they wanted to learn. We believed, with Richard W. Southern, that people learn "by being puzzled and excited, not by being told," so we tried to get them puzzled and excited about their own curricula rather than to tell them what to do.

It is difficult to implement such a curriculum successfully. At Stanford we had a particularly hard time maintaining the humanistic and cultural components of our program since they were regarded by many students and faculty as not being integral to the field. Without continuing effort, entropy sets in; the curriculum tends to revert to the familiar triad of history, politics, economics. Departmental pressures may hinder even such modest attempts at inter-disciplinary synergy. Yet it is often worthwhile to try. The richness and range of history and the analytical clarity of economics are as important to students of international relations as the attention to the sources and exercise of power that characterizes political science.

To construct an international relations program with rigid requirements might be worse than to undertake no curricular initiatives at all. I do not believe that we should prescribe a single curriculum that every student of international relations must study. The best curricula have few requirements but many incentives for students to think for themselves. Just as our courses pose more questions than answers, so our curricula should be open-ended enough for students to discover new connections among apparently separate aspects of our highly diverse subject. Unless we are willing to engage in curriculum development in this spirit, we would be wiser simply to allow students to pick and choose internationally oriented courses within the rather mild constraints typically imposed on their majors by political science departments.

The argument of this essay is well summarized by a story (perhaps apocryphal) about a meeting in late 1920s between Chief Justice William Howard Taft and Robert Maynard Hutchins. Hutchins was not yet thirty, but already dean of Yale Law School; Taft had been president and was an eminent conservative. Meeting Hutchins, Taft is said to have asked, "Mr. Hutchins, do you teach your students at Yale that all judges are fools?" to which Hutchins is reported to have replied, "No, Mr. Chief Justice, at Yale we teach them to find *that* out for themselves." If we design international relations courses and curricula so that students will learn to ask the right questions and find their own answers to the existential moral, political, and economic problems with which we struggle, we will have met the demands of our calling.

References

Beitz, Charles, 1979. *Political theory and international relations* (Princeton, N.J.: Princeton UP).

Brandt, Willy, et al., 1979. *North-South: A program for survival* (Cambridge: MITP).

Carnesdale, Albert, et al., 1983, *Living with nuclear weapons* (New York: Bantam).

Geertz, Clifford, 1973. *The interpretation of cultures* (New York: Basic Books).

George, Alexander L., 1979. Case studies and theory development: The method of structured, focused comparison. In Paul Gordon Lauren, ed., *Diplomacy: New approaches in history, theory, and policy* (New York: Free Press).

Gilpin, Robert, 1981. *War and change in world politics* (Cambridge: Cambridge UP).

Hoffmann, Stanley, 1960. "Commentary," in Hoffmann, ed., *Contemporary theory in international relations* (Englewood Cliffs, N.J.: Prentice-Hall).

Jervis, Robert, 1976. *Perception and misperception in international politics* (Princeton, N.J.: Princeton UP).

Katzenstein, Peter J., ed., 1978. *Between power and plenty: Foreign economic policies of advanced industrial states* (Madison: U of Wisconsin P).

Tucker, Robert W., 1977. *The inequality of nations* (New York: Basic Books).

Waltz, Kenneth N., 1959. *Man, the state and war: A theoretical analysis.* Institute of War and Peace Series (New York: Columbia UP).

Walzer, Michael, 1977. *Just and unjust wars: a moral argument with historical illustrations* (New York: Basic Books).

Political Science Concepts in the Study of International Relations in an Introductory Course

Kenneth W. Thompson

The most compelling argument for including international relations within political science is that its focus and core principles are found in the dominant concerns of political science.

Until the late 1930s, approaches to the study of international relations were those of diplomatic history, international law, or current events. History for a time had a monopoly on the study of international relations and the classic works of Harold Nicolson, Webster, Mowat, and Butterfield were the center-pieces of the subject. Diplomatic history was a branch of historical studies, and its rigor and systematic approach earned the admiration of university leaders.

International law competed with diplomatic history and added a new dimension of hope for change and reform. In the interwar period, most of those who held major chairs in international studies were international lawyers: Jessup, Briggs, Wright, Wilson, Wild, Berdahl, and Hyde. They brought not only high scholarly standards to the subject but deep commitment that never again would Americans turn their back on international cooperation. The terms for filling several leading chairs reflected a missionary spirit. Not only were professors to teach and convey knowledge; they had the responsibility as well to inculcate respect for international law and organization.

The current events and contemporary problems view was a third approach. It put stress on what had happened the day before as reported by *The New York Times*. If its methodology was not always rigorous, its output was surely relevant.

When political science moved into the study of international relations, it was with a mission of its own. The map of international relations had been all

Kenneth W. Thompson is Professor of Government and Foreign Affairs at the Woodrow Wilson Department of Government and Foreign Affairs, University of Virginia.

inclusive from the study of agriculture to xenophobia. Frederick S. Dunn had argued that full comprehension required a grasp of twenty-one separate disciplines. However, to cast the net so broadly, promoting interest in everything, left the field devoid of a central focus. Political scientists filled this vacuum by bringing forward some of the historic and traditional concerns of those who study politics. These included power and interest, political groupings and alliances, authority and sovereignty, as well as law and organization. Politics and power were not the sole elements of international relations, but they provided the conceptual framework for subordinating other elements to concerns that were fundamental to conflict and cooperation.

Political science helped bring unity and coherence to international studies. It made possible the formulation of a unifying set of questions and concerns. Who were the dominant powers in a region or the world, who were the minor or subordinate powers? What accounted for that influence and power or its lack? What were the elements of national power? What were the currently prevailing patterns of the balance of power and the patterns in other eras? What normative and institutional means existed as limitations on power? What prospects existed for transforming present day patterns of international politics?

It would be wrong to claim that some of these questions had not been asked by historians, lawyers, or students of current events. The persistent character of international politics through the ages assured that others had addressed at least some of the questions within a different discipline and framework.

The fact that all these questions and more were appropriately political science questions made for a coherent whole. Moreover, the tendency of scholars in the discipline to emphasize analysis rather than mere description gave further shape to the field. The study would not have been lacking in some of these characteristics if political science had not entered the field, but the overall pattern surely reflected politics as the dominant and coordinating concern.

For these reasons—historical, analytical, and intellectual—international relations has come to occupy a central position in the study of political science. The growth of substantive concerns has followed the directions of the discipline: national institutions, policymaking, national security, and conflict management. It would be false not to point to the differences—the lack of a sovereign authority and conflict domestically has not been entirely irrelevant for an understanding of world modalities. In any event, a case can be made for keeping the study of international relations squarely in the center of the study of politics and power.

Introduction to International Relations

The introductory course in international politics and relations at the University of Virginia has three objectives which crisscross one another and determine its structure and content. First, through lectures and readings, the instructor attempts to supplement and reinforce and, for some students, supply the substantive knowledge needed to understand contemporary international relations. Certain students initially require historical knowledge, though other needs include economics, geography, politics, and sociology. It would be wrong to conclude that the first objective is to provide remedial assistance for all students: for some the purpose of the introductory material is to supplement existing knowledge, and for others to provide a missing historical background.

Second, an introduction to international relations must assist the student in formulating a theoretical framework to give meaning and coherence to the unfolding of contemporary international events. The legacy of the study of international politics beginning with such figures as Frederick L. Schuman, Hans J. Morgenthau, Harold and Margaret Sprout, and Grayson Kirk can be found in their respective emphases on a broadly inclusive and overall framework for understanding the patterns of world politics. Without such a framework, international studies remains forever condemned to approaches that have each in turn proved insufficient. Diplomatic history, a forerunner of the study of international politics, made notable contributions to the accurate description of past international politics. In the words of certain distinguished historians, the aim was "to get the story right." But diplomatic history has suffered from its concentration on unique events at the expense of broader ideas and principles. While paying tribute to history and historians, the Virginia course has therefore sought to encompass philosophers of history more attuned to the search for principles. We have introduced students to the histories of Arnold J. Toynbee, Oswald Spengler, Edward Gibbon, and Jacob Burckhardt as variants of historical studies that are sometimes close in approach to theories of international politics.

In the quest for a theoretical framework, the Virginia program has also sought to transcend a mere concern with current events. Latter day versions of international relations theory have often wandered from the realities of current events. So determined have such theorists been to construct abstract formulations uncontaminated by concrete realities of any kind that they have shunned all current events. The opposite tendency, more apparent in the earlier days of international relations theorizing, was for critics to make *The New York Times* their Bible and never go beyond the discussion of current events. A consequence of this approach had been to make every professor of international relations his or her secretary of state. In fairness one must note that some earlier professors of international relations such as Harvard's Payson S. Wild forced students to grapple with the most demanding foreign policy decisions by asking the question: "What would you do if you were secretary of state?"

During the interwar period, professors of international law and organization moved the study of international politics into a stage of attention to the role of world institutions and world law. Virtually every professorship of note had as its purpose the promotion of respect for world organizations such as the League of Nations. As with the other approaches, such as current events, no one can responsibly criticize the moral and intellectual qualities of the occupants of the major professorships in the interwar period. Quincy Wright, George Grafton Wilson, Philip Jessup, Herbert Briggs, Hardy Dillard, and Illinois' Berdahl were men of commanding presence and influence. Indeed, the success of the American movement that culminated in the San Francisco conference testifies to their impressive contributions to broadening the vision of young Americans. It is questionable whether the political science community has ever had so direct an impact on American foreign policy. But the reformist and evangelical character of the approach spawned a reaction within the movement spearheaded by figures such as Nicholas J. Spykman and Hans J. Morgenthau. At the Carnegie Endowment Conferences on International Law and Organization and Related Subjects in the 1930s, Spykman and Morgenthau put forward minority viewpoints which sought to push their colleagues in the direction of greater attention to the inter-relationship of international law/organization and international politics. Harking back to his earlier work on Simel, Spykman argued for a sociological approach, and Morgenthau recapitulated what he had written earlier in his career on a functional approach to international law and organization. Neither completed his work on international law as both turned to full-time concern with international politics, but each left a body of thought and questions that forced students of international relations to consider issues that reformers had suggested belonged primarily in the past.

The Virginia course has sought to marry international politics and international law and organization concerns within a framework that did justice to both continuity and change. In the Quincy Wright Library, students are able to consult the best writings from the earlier tradition, a tradition which Wright himself sought to redefine in his *Study of International Relations* (see discussion of Wright's life's work in my *Masters of International Thought*.) At the same time, the student explores the school of thought that owes a lasting debt to Spykman, Morgenthau, and the early architects of theories of international politics.

Third, the test of a theory in the social sciences is the extent to which it brings order and meaning to the diverse subject matter of a segment of human experience. In the present example, does the theory help the student relate the raw stuff of international politics to some coherent view of past and present events? Is it able to provide a map which guides both the policymaker confronted with a succession of foreign policy choices and the student who looks over the decision maker's shoulder? A third section in the Virginia course examines contemporary diplomatic problems in the light of a particular theory of world politics. One of the lacunae in social science theory stems from the failure to put the theory to work. Medical and biological research rests on the premise that the researcher must not be too far from the patient in the bed. Observation over a period of weeks of the work of physicians and surgeons in a surgery ward confirms the extent to which biological research is tested and employed in practice. In a similar vein, the test of such theories as national interest depends on its use in contemporary crises such as Lebanon, Grenada, and Soviet–American relations. There is an element of escapism in a theoretical endeavor which never holds up the importance of a theory for the understanding and amelioration of political problems.

Given the threefold emphasis on history, theory, and contemporary foreign policy problems, a further question which confronts the professor is how he or she can bring the student to the point of comprehending what a given approach has to offer. One alternative is to expose the student to a wide range of differing viewpoints falling within or beyond a given intellectual tradition. In the first years of the Virginia course, such an approach was followed by bringing the student into contact with fragments of thought representative of all the different perspectives on international politics, e.g., American realism, British pragmatism, and continental jurisprudence or decision-making theory, systems theory, transnational theory, and integration theory. Apart from the difficulties facing any given professor in doing justice to these differing viewpoints, he confronts a more serious problem in pedagogy. A former colleague at the University of Chicago was wont to observe: " If I succeed in communicating one large idea in a semester's course, I consider that course a success." Inspired by Leo Strauss' viewpoint, the Virginia course has moved in the direction of a more concentrated approach. In order to communicate "one large idea," I have given the students a heavy dose of the writings of Hans J. Morgenthau, Reinhold Niebuhr, George F. Kennan, Walter Lippmann, Louis Halle, and my own, thus bringing more unity of thought into their study. Their required readings have been drawn from such works as Morgenthau's *Politics Among Nations*, Niebuhr's *Structure of Nations and Empires*, and my *Political Realism*.

Yet I am all too aware of the perils of narrow indoctrination such an approach entails and have sought to combine diversity with unity through a variety of broadening experiences. The most successful technique has been to introduce students to different approaches incarnate in presentations by living exponents of differing philosophies. For example, my colleague I.L. Claude delivers the lecture on international law. Until his death, Hardy Dillard presented his views on international law, prefaced by a spirited comment to the effect: "Don't believe everything Ken Thompson tells you." Building on his concept of the *Anarchical Society* (required reading), Hedley Bull has given the lecture on international society. Ambassador Adam Watson lectures on the balance of power, Tony Leng on China, Ruhi Ramazani on the Middle East, Paul Shoup on Eastern Europe, John Armitage on arms control, Alfred Fernbach on collective security, and Whittle Johnston on pluralism and universalism.

A second route for broadening the universe of discourse has been through introducing students to a diversity of viewpoints through selected readings linked with particular lectures. When I.L. Claude lectures on international organization, students read portions of his classic text, and a similar practice is followed with other lectures. Moreover, my book, *Masters of International Thought*, introduces students to the writings of some eighteen "men of large and capacious thought" and provides the basis for introductions to other perspectives. Students use individual chapters, which combine analyses of important thinkers with bibliographies of their major works, as background for required papers. They write either about approaches in general or approaches reflected in views on a particular problem. The span of thought of the "masters" range from Herbert Butterfield or John Courtney Murray to Arnold Wolfers or Karl Deutsch. Cold War studies center on Walter Lippmann, George F. Kennan, or Raymond Aron. International law approaches include Quincy Wright and Charles de Visscher. Historians whose work is discussed are Arnold J. Toynbee, Louis J. Halle, Jr., and E.H. Carr.

Another technique which has proven useful is the periodic presentation of key studies introduced in my lectures with what amount to a paragraph or two of verbal annotations. I have found that this way of bringing studies to the attention especially of the best students is more effective than simply listing them in a long bibliography which students may or may not consult.

As important as any other aspect of the course is the role of teaching assistants. Ideally, these are carefully chosen advanced graduate students who have passed comprehensive exams in "International Politics and Theory." Once a week students meet in groups of eight or ten with a teaching assistant who guides discussions and helps generate answers to outstanding questions. Lectures delivered to upwards of three hundred students serve to map broad principles and ideas. Discussion sections fill in the gaps left by mass lectures. It is no exaggeration to say that effective one-on-one instruction takes place in the discussion sections. Here, with their individual teaching assistants, students seek answers to their most troublesome questions. The discussion sections are also ideal laboratories for teaching assistants to hone their skill as young professors. They constitute a corps of junior faculty who promise to become a new generation of scholars, and they hold in their hands the future of international studies.

SOCIOLOGY

The essays by sociologists Edward Tiryakian, Immanuel Wallerstein, William Foote Whyte, and J. Michael Armer present powerful reasons for internationalizing their discipline. Each of the four essays addresses the question: What should sociology majors learn about the world in their undergraduate years? Their approach focuses particularly on macrosociology and comparative sociology, including attention to historical social systems, the interdependence of social systems, and the relevance of sociological knowledge for foreign policy analysis. Special concern is noted for a sociology-of-knowledge approach to the conceptual models and paradigms brought to the undergraduate years by students emerging from secondary schools and exposure to television.

As part of the NCFLIS project and as a complement to these essays, Michael Armer has prepared a volume, *Syllabi and Resources for Internationalizing Courses in Sociology* (1983), which includes 22 course syllabi in nine mainstream undergraduate sociology courses as well as specifically international courses and a major section compiled by Neal R. Goodman on teaching aids and resources for internationalizing courses. Edited for the American Sociological Association's Committee on World Sociology, it is distributed by the association's Teaching Resources Center. The Committee on World Sociology has devoted attention to a variety of initiatives to increase the comparative and area studies content of North American sociology curricula and the annual meetings, to broaden and deepen crossnational linkages among sociologists, and to sensitize members to the ethic of research in foreign societies.

Sociology's Great Leap Forward: The Challenge of Internationalization

Edward A. Tiryakian

This paper takes as given that (a) the level of international competence in the United States, even among America's elites (in both the private and the public sector), is substantially less than it should be in terms of our national interest as a competing world power, one whose hegemony is under severe pressure, economically as well as politically, and (b) the level of international competence among American students of sociology (graduate and undergraduate) is considerably below what might be an acceptable figure, given the nature of sociology as a comparative discipline that seeks to present systematic information and theoretically grounded interpretations of modern societies.

By "international competence," a term that has received some recognition (Commission on International Education, n.d.), I will mean a general knowledge of the world scene so as to be able to have an environmental context for actions, events, and situations that receive world recognition and that have world import. By "general knowledge of the world scene," in turn, I mean a basic knowledge of world geography, world demography, world history, world economy (including gross parameters of the international division of labor and/or the interrelatedness of regional economies), world politics, and inter-societal processes and exchanges. If we take all these aspects together, it will be few individuals indeed who have international competence. We might loosen the criteria to signify by international competence: knowledge (geographical, demographic, historical, etc.) of two or more regions other than the one in which the actor's country of origin is located, or perhaps, to dilute the standards of competence even more, knowledge of one region other than that of the actor. No matter which of the above standards are invoked—and we might call them "high," "medium" or "low" levels of international competence—I suspect that

Edward A. Tiryakian is Professor of Sociology at Duke University and Vice-President of the International Association of French-Speaking Sociologists (AISLF).

the majority of undergraduate majors, graduate students, and quite likely, the sociology faculty in the United States, would fall below the threshold mark.

If I have mentioned graduate students and faculty in the same breath as undergraduates, it is because the three are interrelated. The point is obvious but deserves to be made. The problem of increasing international competence in sociology is not simply a question of introducing more comparative materials in the undergraduate curriculum. It is that, but it is more than that. It is also increasing the international competence and awareness of graduate students who will be tomorrow's teaching and research faculty. And, of course, it is also increasing acceptance and support among the majority of American academic sociologists that international competence is and ought to be of vital importance to the discipline, not simply an exotic frosting.

My academic career has been limited to the university setting, but of course, sociology is also taught at colleges, either four-year or two-year ones. I will try in this paper to make recommendations that may be useful to the spectrum of institutional settings in which sociology is taught, but it does make a difference whether the undergraduate program is given in a college or in a university where graduate training is also part of the setting. Where the latter is the case, increasing the international competence of the undergraduate curriculum may be facilitated or obstructed by graduate teaching assistants. If the graduate students either are from other countries or have done field work outside the United States, they can add in classroom discussions an important cross-national perspective to substantive materials; further, the instructor in charge of the course would do well to invite such a teaching assistant to give a lecture to the course on comparative aspects of a given topic, to complement readings that pertain to the United States. On the other hand, if the ethos of the department is such that graduate students are implicitly steered to doing research solely on American data sets and discouraged from doing overseas field research, then they are of little assistance in increasing awareness of the global scene among undergraduate majors.

Perhaps, by virtue of the experience of being a teaching assistant in a course where the instructor can make the comparative emphasis a salient one, a graduate student may be proselytized to the merit of developing an international or cross-national perspective in her research. At this point, the faculty person will have the question of providing adequate support, intellectual and financial. Intellectual support means not only encouraging a graduate student to think comparatively about a project or theme that might be of interest as doctoral research, but also to facilitate an informal on-going intellectual exchange between students and possibly faculty, and not just in sociology but from other departments (anthropology, political science, perhaps history and economics). Financial support will mean seeking external funding that provides travel and support for an overseas stay. My limited experience in recent years has been that contrary to what one might think, given severe cutbacks in social science programs in federal agencies, finding financial support for students wishing to do research outside the United States is not an acute problem. What is a problem is to find adequately prepared and trained sociology graduate students! Most of our graduate students lack language facility to do research abroad (except in English-speaking areas) and lack knowledge of the social milieu for which funding may be available; this gap reflects the elimination of the language requirement from graduate training. Worse, they lack professional motivation to do research overseas.

So much for a digression on graduate students, but they are a key link between undergraduates and faculty, and attention about upgrading the international competence of undergraduates should give consideration to these background intermediaries. But let me concentrate on the undergraduate side of internationalizing the sociology curriculum, since that is my main concern.

My first recommendation is that in planning how to internationalize sociology, the faculty make an assessment of available resources. Resources may be grouped under three categories: material, institutional and human. Under "material resources," I include on-going programs at one's institution that may facilitate students' obtaining overseas experience (e.g., study-abroad programs, exchange programs with foreign universities, etc.). I also include, of course, the compilation of instructional materials, syllabi, readers, and other such printed matter that can be used in course preparation (e.g., Adams and Waldman 1983; Armer 1983). These should be thought of as initial stimuli that can be used once the crucial decision of internationalizing the sociology curriculum has been reached.

By "institutional resources," I mean resources available both within one's academic institution (e.g., the presence of an international-studies center, films available for classroom use, etc.) and outside the academic institution (e.g., corporations in the town, city, or state where the college is located that have an international dimension, or, in the public sector, state agencies that seek foreign investments or foreign markets.

By "human resources," I mean persons at one's institution who may have specialized knowledge of social conditions in foreign regions or specific countries, or if not specialized knowledge, then first-hand experience in the everyday life of persons living in such regions or countries. Such persons may be thought of as potential "informants." Again, human resources may well include persons living in proximity to the academic institution who have first-hand knowledge of some areas or countries—for example, refugees from Southeast Asia, immigrants/refugees from Central America and the Caribbean, and so forth.

If I suggest such an inventory of resources, it is because these will be an important support system for whatever academic attempt one will undertake. To devise a course having an international component or focus is not difficult, but to develop an interest and a commitment among undergraduate students (or graduates for that matter) does involve the ability to mobilize certain resources other than sheer intellectual ones, such as reading assignments. In my judgment, if one does bother to assess the three sorts of resources that should be mobilized or utilized, then practically anywhere in the United States a considerable latent support system can be identified that would undergird curriculum innovations of the sort to be discussed here.

Internationalizing the Sociology Curriculum

In the face of the enrollment crisis which has beset sociology nationally, there are different adaptive modes of response which departments have tried. One mode is to weather the storm by doing "business as usual," not seeking structural changes in the undergraduate curriculum, and simply doing (better) what one has been doing before the enrollment inflation of the late 1960s to early 1970s, and before the enrollment deflation of the late 1970s to early 1980s. A second mode has been to adapt the curriculum to students' concern that what they take be instrumental in landing a job, and this may mean reorienting the curriculum to better training in research methods and applied sociology (Watts, Short and Schultz 1983:47-61). A third mode that I know of, but with just a few brave souls attempting it, such as Farganis at Vassar (1983), is to upgrade the introductory course by making it an introduction to the most exciting theoretical issues and figures of the discipline (such as the classical triumvirate of Durkheim, Weber, and Marx).

What I wish to suggest here is a fourth mode, namely, to provide an international comparative concentration within the sociology major. I will only sketch out what this concentration might have as its key components; of course, modifications would have to be made according to departmental circumstances, availability of resources, and the like.

Let me begin by following up a proposal made by Gerhard Lenski (1983, 1984a) that introductory sociology be (like Gaul and so many other things) made into three. In this formulation, Lenski suggested (1983:157) there be separate (a) *macro* (the study of total societies and of the world system), (b) *micro* (the impact of societies on the individual) and (c) *meso* (the student's own society and its institutions) courses. I would like to focus on just the macro introductory, leaving aside the merit and feasibility of the tripartite scheme and of the other two avenues of introducing sociology.

As a preliminary consideration let me suggest, to be mildly provocative, that sociology's distinctiveness as a discipline rests upon two great insights/premises, fashioned by a host of our tribal ancestors. At the micro level, sociology posits the internalization of society in the development process of the human being (without which self-reflexivity would be impossible). At the macro level, sociology posits the systemic nature of social institutions, that is, the interrelatedness and interdependence of units into an on-going whole whose properties cannot be deduced from any one single unit and whose properties are subject to transformations over time stemming from endogenous and exogenous factors. Perhaps we can summarize both of these insights/premises into a single compound statement: "No man is an island unto himself; and neither is any social institution." By extrapolation, if in a given physical setting social institutions come to cohere so as to form a recognized nation-state (i.e. a socio-political actor recognized as such by other such actors having political legitimation), then macro sociology may be viewed in a complementary manner. On the one hand, it may be viewed as dealing with the processes operative within nation-states that interrelate these structurally and dynamically into a social system, either by voluntary or coercive means or a combination thereof.

On the other hand, macro sociology may have a more encompassing, "global" perspective, namely, as dealing with the structure and dynamics of relations between clusters of countries (such clusters having a certain collective identity, political, cultural, or otherwise) and, ultimately, with relational structures between clusters tending in the modern period to develop into one broad, interrelated global system. It follows that if this is the case, important features of social phenomena occurring within a given country or nation-state must in part be accounted for by "exogenous" factors, that is, by interrelationships between those phenomena, their societal setting, and those of other societies. I trust that these remarks will be seen, upon reflection, as sociological "common sense," for they are simply an extension of the customary sociological standpoint. The only radical aspect of this is that I am suggesting we make this the basis for introducing sociology to students.

What might the syllabus of such an introductory course look like? The aim or purpose of the course is to introduce students to the field of sociology, which deals with large-scale social phenomena and their global interdependence and manifestations. The course intends to give students a sociological orientation to the contemporary world scene, viewed as an evolving network of nation-states, and to provide students an orientation to the comparative nature of sociology, its theoretical and methodological traditions. Other such statements indicating the macro dimension of this introductory course should be stated.

Regarding textbooks, this is of course a matter of preference. As far as I am aware, there is not presently a textbook structured along the lines of a global orientation. But some introductory textbooks have more of a macro and/or comparative emphasis than others. To be suggestive, and only suggestive, one might consider as an appropriate text—if one is inclined to use a textbook in introductory sociology—Lenski and Lenski, *Human Societies* (1982) for its macro/evolutionary emphasis, or two texts having more comparative materials than most: Westhues, *First Sociology* (1982) and Spencer and Inkeles, *Foundations* (1985). This may reflect that Westhues and Spencer reside in Canada. Actually, I would encourage alternatives to textbooks, unless by unanticipated good fortune the macro introductory course drew such large numbers of students as to warrant multiple sections and make a textbook a desirable, readily accessible, uniform reading assignment. Let me suggest some alternatives to having a textbook as the mainstay of the course.

First, I think it might be important to spend the initial meetings in laying out the conceptual frame of reference of macro sociology, in particular, that emphasis dealing with transnational and international components of the world scene. In some ways, Wilbert Moore's paper of 20 years ago (Moore 1966), if not programmatic of the new macro sociology, is at least mildly prophetic and could be used as a lead-off reading assignment. Following this initial orientation to sociology as a study of interrelated social systems, it would seem well to spend three or four weeks on giving students the broad parameters of the *spatial-temporal* context of the world scene, since human action, including the action of large-scale social systems, is always framed or grounded in a spatial-temporal context. Concretely, I mean exposing students to the rudiments of world history and human geography. Readings might be selected from such works as McNeill (1971), for world history, and De Blij (1971), for geography. It is here that human resources of one's institution can be involved in the form of guest lectures by historians, geographers, demographers, and others. Historians would be invited to provide concisely an orientation to the world's major historical doings, on an area or regional basis, at least in the past 500 years, which is, in terms of Weberian and Marxist orientations alike, the temporal frame of the "modern" period. Geographers and demographers (if instances of both can be located within one's institution or nearby) would be asked to provide an orientation to the major human ecosystems of the world, population distributions, their habitats, their resources and major modes of adaptation to the environment.

It is only after such an orientation that a sociological approach to the international scene should be undertaken. If a text is not used, it might prove rewarding to use a macro orientation that is consistent and integrated. Daniel Chirot's *Social Change* (1977), which has affinity (but not identity) with a world-system, political-economy approach, is eminently readable and would provide useful reading materials for a couple of weeks. This can be complemented, supplemented, or foiled by a work with a different, more "idealistic" orientation than that of political economy, namely, Parsons' *The Evolution of Societies* (1977).

Both these works have a tacit Western emphasis, and do not give major attention to a very salient fact about the modern world, namely, the rather systematic intrusion in and domination of non-Western peoples and societies by Western nation-states (and here I would include Russia). That is, a very major aspect of the transformation of the modern world is the effective colonization of the Middle East, Asia, Africa, and the Western Hemisphere by Europeans and their progenies overseas. The modern world has been fashioned by the interaction of relatively economically advanced, predominantly industrialized, politically unified and autonomous Western nation-states with, for the most part, (outside Asia) small-scale, agrarian, predominantly rural societies; this interaction, backed up by technological and military superiority of the former forced the latter into varying states of dependency. Formally politically dependent social units became linked with Western nation-states in a colonial system.

The above remarks may seem banal, if not a truism of modernization. But perhaps less obvious is that the social systems which resulted from this interaction, that is, colonial societies, have *sui generis* characteristics that cannot be deduced from the properties of Western countries or non-Western countries *ante* modern colonialism. The nature of economic, political, religious, and other institutions, even the nature of social identity, differs in colonial societies from comparable sets of social and socio-psychological phenomena in either Western "modern" societies or in non-Western "traditional" societies. Since this is not the occasion to discuss colonial societies as such, I will refrain from the temptation of a long digression. But I will not refrain from saying that if we want sociology majors to have an understanding of the world scene, they must have an awareness that most of the world bears a heavy imprint of a colonial burden or legacy. Naiveté on this topic is not only an affliction of undergraduates, it is also a common undiagnosed ailment of most sociologists who write introductory textbooks.

To rectify this at the very beginning of a student's introduction to sociology, I would recommend that an important section be devoted to the colonial situation, the colonial social system, and how this has an effect on the nature of social relationships. The sort of readings which might be used here would be at the psycho-social level: the first work of Fanon, *Black Skin, White Masks* (1967) and the more recent, brilliant study of Said, *Orientalism* (1979). Both of these can be used to show how the "construction of reality," and more specifically, the "construction of personality" has a societal function in a colonial context of (Western) domination; more structural readings of colonial and post-colonial situations might be found in the early but still useful volume edited by Wallerstein (1966) and later works by Goldthorpe (1975) and Alavi and Shanin (1982).

At this point in the introductory course, I would provide students with a learning experience of a different nature, but one that will assist them in learning to pay attention to the world scene from a standpoint other than is customary, namely, to view the world scene from the perspective of other world actors besides the official American stance and that provided by major mass media. The single experience which I have found over the years provides students with an ineluctable appreciation and awareness of "the other" (and after all, the etymology of sociology is derived from the science of "the other") is the field experience.

By that I mean students spending for a week or two several hours (say, in lieu of class contact hours) in the town, city, or village near the academic institution and trying to do some participant observation of persons or different lifestyles or social class or ethnicity than the student's familiar world. It was very effectively put in the year-long introductory course in social relations at Harvard (then called "Soc.Rel. 10") by Leon Bramson when he was in charge of organizing the course, many years ago. Readings were done in the classic study of William Whyte, *Street Corner Society,* and students then had the task of finding their way to the North End of Boston, spending several hours in this Italian neighborhood, writing up their observations and interactions with the urban dwellers and discussing their notes in class. Having participated in that course as a faculty associate, I have been sold ever since on giving under-graduates field experience not only in introductory sociology but in almost any substantive course above it. I find this is one of the best ways of getting students to be ego-involved with the materials, that is, to have a feel for being producers of sociological knowledge, not simply passive consumers.

In terms of field experience in an introductory course which might be instrumental in relating to the international scene, one could use vintage participant observation studies of a very varied kind: Laurence Wylie's sensitive *Village in the Vaucluse* (1974); and Banfield's *The Moral Basis of a Backward Society* (1958) are community studies done in Europe by American social scientists, while Gans's *Urban Villages* (1962) and Liebow's *Tally's Corner* are equally fine domestic studies also done with a participant observation orientation. Any one of these, or any other current favorites, can be used as back-ground models to give students a grasp of the sort of information and data that may be gathered in the field. The experience itself will sensitize students to seeking to understand how the everyday world is structured, perceived, and understood by actors operating in a different cultural, physical, and socio-economic environment from that of the everyday world of students.

I would also propose that the introductory course appeal to the student's past. Before expanding on this, let me suggest that if we want sociology undergraduates to become more competent in international affairs, we must appeal to their own interest, and not simply to some vague idealistic line that "it is part of a liberal arts curriculum to have knowledge of the world scene, etc." And what I want to indicate is that a concentration in macro/global sociology should make the case that such a concentration is to the student's interest—past, present and future. The introductory course may be a useful vehicle for tapping at the student's past.

Every person in the United States, with few exceptions, has a socially identifiable ethnic and/or racial status. This entails the carrying of social baggage which may be more or less burdensome, more or less in the consciousness and awareness of the actor. I would suggest that as a project for an independent paper, one that would provide an important component of the term grade, each student seek to find something about (a) the society and social milieu from whence originated her/his ancestors at the time of coming to the United States, (b) that society and social milieu today (in terms of regime, economy, social stratification, etc.) and (c) the major intervening social processes and structural changes that took place in the society or setting of origin from the period of emigration/immigration to the present. This, of course, is a task which might well be appropriate for a master's paper or even doctoral research, and in making the assignment in an introductory course, one must be realistic as to what one expects students to be able to achieve. But it should give students an experience of major importance. It may give them an exposure to oral history, if they have parents or grandparents who can provide information about the locale from which they emigrated to the United States. In the case of students whose families have been here for more than, say, three generations, it will still provide them with the occasion to learn about social history.

As a result of this assignment, students should also gain familiarity with an area of the contemporary world setting and its situation today—whether that are is Hong Kong, Ireland, Mexico, Norway, Pakistan, Poland, Puerto Rico, Quebec, West Africa, etc. In uncovering their ethnic roots, students will find relational ties with other parts of the globe today. This activity should lead to a sustained interest and increased awareness in at least one other part of the world.

I would also recommend wherever appropriate the use of films to sensitive students to the everyday life in the modern world as it is experienced in other geographical settings, preferably not anthropological films of exotic settings and peoples living in a "primitive" environment seemingly cut off from the world historical process. I mean films more like "The Battle of Algers," "Xala," or even "Gandhi," that can depict colonial and neo-colonial situations, but by no means do I wish to suggest they be confined to the Third World (domestic or overseas). In my opinion, sociology has to catch up with anthropology in making effective classroom use of films and other visual media.

These, then, constitute my major recommendations for what might go into an introductory course in sociology having the international scene as its emphasis.

A second course in the global concentration I am proposing is a topical course on major international issues and problems. This course would be particularly effective when co-taught by a sociologist and a colleague from a different department, such as a political scientist or a macro economist. Such a course has been successfully given at Duke University by my colleague Gary Gereffi, and a description of the syllabus is available in Armer and Goodman (1983: 123-134). I am sure that a great many colleagues and universities have developed or are developing similar interdisciplinary courses on global issues (Soroos 1983; Tulchin 1984), but I am not sure if sociologists are everywhere taking the lead in having the chief responsibility for organizing such a course. I am advocating that they do so and that such a course would be a very logical part of an undergraduate curriculum in sociology: essentially it would be the macro/global equivalent of courses in "social problems." In fact, it may be quite possible to take the typical content of a "social problems" course and make it comparative and global. For the purpose of illustration, if one of the social problems treated is that of "drug addiction," a global perspective would situate that problem historically and cross-nationally (e.g., the forcible introduction of opium in China in the nineteenth century), examine global variations in the nature and incidence of drug addiction today and consider economic and social structures involved in the international traffic in drugs, etc.

I would suggest that such a topical course on global issues and problems might begin with the theme of "the global crisis," both because of the real urgency of having Americans understand deteriorating socio-economic conditions abroad as much as at home, and because the theme of "global crisis" is one which will indicate to students that sociology is alert to real-life concerns. Among core readings that could be assigned here would be the volumes put out, respectively, by The Brandt Commission (1983); by Amin et al. (1982); and by Tiryakian (1984).

Finally, irrespective of the contents, this course would do well to get students to start reading some of the informed, non-specialized journals that deal with world affairs, such as *Foreign Affairs*, *World Policy Journal*, and *World Press Review*. If possible, students with some linguistic ability should be encouraged to make oral reports or prepare written papers that would document some global issue by means of periodicals written in languages other than English. An important learning experience comes from seeing how a certain global issue is perceived and formulated in other countries, hence the merit of encouraging students to read papers published outside the United States. Even English-language editions of newspapers and periodicals published abroad will generate an international awareness that students would not have if they stick to the American press and television for their way of looking at the world.

The first two courses sketched out in the preceding pages are intended for underclassmen (albeit they should be attractive electives for students concentrating in other departments). For sophomores and junior concentrators in sociology, I would propose a required course that might be entitled "Comparative Analysis in Sociology" or just "Comparative Sociology." This course would have as its basic purpose imparting to students methodological training in large-scale comparative research in diachronic and synchronic analysis. It would be a complement to standard undergraduate courses in "Research Methods," which usually do not examine the societal or historical matrix of sociological data gathering and analysis.

Much of the orientation readings in such a course can be taken from several volumes explicitly devoted to comparative sociology as such, beginning with Marsh (1967) and going on to Vallier (1971), Armer and Grimshaw (1973), and Armer and Marsh (1982). Students can then be exposed to more recent comparative materials and methodological discussions, for example, those found in Lenski (1984b) and Hopkins and Wallerstein (1982). Depending on the caliber of students and their motivation, I would also urge the assignment (in part if not in whole) of major substantive sociological studies that make extensive use of historical data. The classic figure is Max Weber, particularly his comparative studies of religion, civilization, and modernity. As a bold step, why not assign *The Protestant Ethic and the Spirit of Capitalism* alongside *The Religion of India* or *The Religion of China*? (of course, one student can be assigned *The Protestant Ethic*, one *India*, and a third *China*, with the entire class discussing the comparative features and logic of Weber's specific studies). On the contemporary scene, Eisenstadt's study of empires (1963) and the more recent ones of Skocpol (1979) on endogenous and exogenous factors common to successful revolutions and Baltzell (1979) on differentials in the development of Boston and Philadelphia, are the sort of first-rate studies that illustrate the richness of comparative sociology. During this course, students should either get specific assignments or be asked to do independent readings in journals that have a comparative focus, for example, *Comparative Studies in Society and History* and the *International Journal of Comparative Sociology*.

Let me add that if at one's institution there is available to students a secondary major in international studies, comparative area studies, or the like, then the comparative analysis course in sociology should get visibility outside the department as a course that can give students a methodological training they would not otherwise obtain. This will attract students who already have some interest in the international sphere and majors who might otherwise be attracted to other departments; it will also give students regardless of major conceptual tools and technical skills that will appeal to prospective employers and professional schools. If the "Comparative Sociology" ("Comparative Methods of Analysis," etc.) course can be cross-listed, it might make it an even more stimulating classroom situation if the course can be co-taught with a colleague from another department, such as history, anthropology, or political science. A substantive topic might be the focus for some weeks, one that would allow comparisons between the incidence and nature of a social phenomenon in the United States and the same phenomenon in another setting. Again, just to be suggestive, one might look at the industrial setting in Japan and the United States to account for differences in productivity, or national policy toward autochthonous populations in the United States, South Africa, and Australia, and the sociologist and her/his colleague could make explicit how each would approach the topic methodologically.

The methodological training of students concentrating in the international sphere should not be limited to the course I have just indicated. They should be encouraged to take a course in field research, if available, in anthropology, historiography, history, and, of course, courses in research methods and statistics for the social sciences (presumably available in sociology). These opportunities may not be available and may be best thought of as further training for a master's degree (which I will briefly touch on later).

Before we get to the senior year, there are a couple of aspects of the concentration in the macro/global sociology curriculum that I would like to mention. First, it is my observation over the years that a good number of students at college like to spend some time abroad, usually in their junior year; however, unless my perception is erroneous, most of those who go abroad are in the humanities rather than the social sciences, and in any case very few if any sociology majors take a junior-year abroad program. I like to think that the new introductory course and the global issues course would stimulate interest in students to spend time abroad and experience a different setting. The person(s) responsible for the concentration in macro/global sociology should encourage and assist in this, not only providing information, but also in assistance to the students. By "assistance to the students," I mean several things. One is that the department should be willing to give course credit to students who might do some supervised research in the course of a summer semester or year abroad (even if the supervision is done at a distance, with the student writing up his/her experiences in the form of a journal or gathering some quantifiable data that can be analyzed on his/her return). Second, the coordinator for macro/global sociology, or some other departmental figure (such as the director of undergraduate studies) should seek to find for undergraduate concentrators training experience outside the classroom with firms or agencies that have some interest in the international scene. The training experience could be either remunerated (e.g., summer employment) or not (e.g., internships). It is here again that making an extensive inventory of locally available resources can prove rewarding. For example, an internship may be worked out with a state agency that sends trade missions abroad or acts as host for trade missions from abroad; a multinational corporation may have its headquarters in the state in which the academic institution is located and may provide summer employment in its branch office in Mexico or in Scotland; the municipality may have a social welfare bureau that requires part-time workers to interview families recently arrived from the Philippines, Hong Kong, or Vietnam. It is these and myriad other possibilities of relating students to different socio-cultural settings, either during the academic year or during summers, that should be thought of as part of the total experience a sociology department can offer its international concentrators. As to the senior year, I would propose here a seminar, on a topic of the instructor's choice, which would be required of all concentrators (but open to others). It would be well if the seminar allowed the opportunity, perhaps in the early weeks, for students who have gathered data in the field over the summer or during their junior year abroad to address the topic in terms of how the topic might appear to persons in the setting where they did their work. The topic might have comparative and timely aspects and allow for student research.

Again, let me suggest a couple of possibilities. Suppose that the academic institution is located in a state marked by growing unemployment in the steel or textile industry, and suppose further that various figures (spokesmen for the industry, political representatives, etc.) have been saying that there is need to restrict imports if further cuts in the domestic labor force are to be avoided. This situation could well provide the basis for a sociology seminar in the international sphere, since obviously the unemployment of American factory workers is interrelated with economic development outside the United States. The seminar could spend some time discussing the nature of the American industrial setting, factors of productivity, management-worker relationships, and so forth; it would also consider the exporting countries and their industrial circumstances. Students in the seminar should have the experience of using not only aggregate data available from published sources (World Bank reports, Department of Commerce publications, etc.) but also data that might be obtained directly by interviewing management and union officials, factory workers, unemployed workers, etc.

A second possible topic might be one like "Migrants and Refugees," which would examine domestic and transnational aspects of the subject. As of this writing (1984) there is pending in the United States a major legislation concerning the regulation of migration into the United States (the Simpson-Mazzoli Immigration Reform and Control Act). In several states there is an important seasonal migration of farm workers, with a labor force consisting of a considerable number of alien migrant workers. Students in the seminar might collaborate on a study of the problem of foreign migrant workers and their relation to local communities, not only in the state in which the academic institution is located, but also nationally and cross-nationally (for example, the status and situation of alien or "guest" workers in different countries in Western Europe, or in the Middle East).

Further, the seminar should also examine the economic and political situation of migrant workers (and other immigrants) in their country of origin. After all, some persons who leave one country to go to another may do so for economic or political reasons or both. Consequently, the seminar should examine not only economic immigrants to the United States, but also political refugees, or persons seeking political asylum. An important variable here is how the United States government defines certain groups. Thus, if the United States has friendly ties with country X in Central America, it may deny "refugee" status to persons seeking entry under that rubric, but allow this to persons coming from country Y, defined officially as unfriendly.

In dealing with these and related aspects of the general topic, including international aspects of migration and refugee problems, students would learn a lot about the agricultural business in the United States, about the politics of legislation, and about the nature of linkages of the United States to various other countries who are, wittingly or not, "exporting" population to America. I think this is an excellent way of making undergraduates appreciate the significance of the many facets of the sociological study of migration.

Perhaps not all topics for a senior seminar can exploit local resources, but in any case, the senior seminar should give students the opportunity of writing a term paper which allows them to explore analytically and empirically an aspect of the interdependence of the modern world. Preferably, the seminar topic and the term paper should drive home the point that global interdependence and interrelatedness have real consequences on the lives of people, including real people with whom students have had contact.

Conclusions

Earlier, I mentioned that internationalizing sociology by means of a concentration in sociology should appeal to students' interest in terms of their past, present, and future. The past, I have suggested, may be personalized in the focus on ethnicity and the interrelationships between the United States or the North American setting and the historical societies from which students' families originated. The present should come out of courses on global issues and the senior seminar (as well as getting students to read regularly journals and magazines that have a heavy content of global affairs). What about the future?

Besides the obvious point that the interrelatedness and interdependence of the world means that the well-being and survival of one part of the world affects the well-being and survival of all parts, including the United States, and besides the corollary that as a world power the economic and political activities of the United States have a disproportionate impact on other parts of the world, there is a more personal consideration that pertains to the future of students. I would here invoke a material interest, namely that majoring in sociology with a concentration in the international/global sphere can provide strong assets and background skills for employment in companies and agencies that have a vital stake in international matters. These are bound to increase in coming years, whether the domestic economy is on an upswing or a downswing, whether liberals or conservatives are in office.

I have no doubt that there would be a demand for undergraduate majors who have had an international concentration. What is needed is for the sociology faculty to realize that this is one way of revitalizing the undergraduate curriculum and in getting bright and socially aware students to take sociology courses that they might otherwise shun. But it will entail some serious work and coordination with other departments, perhaps even with some other professional schools that might be part of the academic institution (e.g., a business or law school).

Whether the work entailed in developing such a concentration is worth it is, to be sure, a gamble. To add to the stakes, let me suggest that if the academic institution in question has a graduate program, the sociology department might think of offering a combined B.A./M.A. degree for those undergraduate concentrators in macro/global sociology who opt for a fifth year, one in which they would prepare a master's thesis and take graduate courses that might complete their methodological and theoretical training in both sociology and ancillary departments. The advantage of this degree would be to enhance employment opportunities in the public or private sector by providing a higher level of supervised training than just the B.A.

One last point to be raised is why the sociology profession should encourage the internationalization of the curriculum. Quite aside from the fact that sociology ought to play an important role in the social science curriculum of any academic institution, there is a fundamental reason. I would argue that the sociological concepts we have been brought up with, our tools of analysis, our basic frame of reference, have been developed in the context of a certain historical epoch, the epoch of industrial and state formation. The major actors on the scene were actors on the domestic scene, public and private actors. The social landscape on which they moved, cooperated, and struggled for a place in the sun was the landscape of the self-contained nation-state. But that landscape is rapidly changing today, certainly in part because of technological revolutions that are interrelating the world, but also because of economic and cultural changes that increase international networks and interrelatedness.

All this leads me to my ultimate conclusion. If the cause of the enrollment crisis in sociology is the perception that our field is not "relevant" for undergraduates, there is a more serious side to the problem. Touraine (1984) has very cogently exposed the relevance of sociology in general today in representing social life and modernity. We are near the point of exhausting our intellectual capital based on "modern" Western industrial societies and of the everyday life contained in these entities. If macro sociology is to be relevant in the next century, it must drop the parochialism of implicitly confining itself to intra-state phenomena. It must also develop the concepts and the grammar to deal with the transnational scene and transnational structures and processes of change. In its graduate training and professional research, it must commit itself to a "great leap forward."

References

Adams, Jan. S., and Waldman, Marilyn, ed. 1983. *Transnational Approaches of the Social Sciences.* Lanham, Md. New York and London: UP of America.

Amin, Sami, Arrighi, G., Frank, A.G., and Wallerstein, I. 1983. *Dynamics of World Crisis.* New York and London: Monthly Review Press.

Armer, Michael, and Grimshaw, Allen D. ed. 1973. *Comparative Social Research: Methodological Problems and Strategies.* New York: Wiley.

Armer, J. Michael, ed., and Goodman, Neal R., comp. 1983. *Syllabi and Resources for Internationalizing Courses in Sociology.* Washington, D.C.: ASA.

Armer, J. Michael, and Marsh, Robert M., ed. 1982. *Comparative Sociological Research in the 1960s and 1970s.* Leiden, Netherlands: E.J. Brill. (Originally published as Volume 22 of the *International Journal of Comparative Sociology.*)

Baltzell, E. Digby. 1979. *Puritan Boston and Quaker Philadelphia.* New York: Free Press.

Banfield, Edward C. 1958. *The Moral Basis of a Backward Society.* New York: Free Press.

Brandt Commission. 1983. *Common Crisis North–South: Co-Operation for World Recovery.* Cambridge, Mass: MITP.

Chirot, Daniel. 1977. *Social Change in the Twentieth Century.* New York: Harcourt.Commission on International Education. n.d. *What We Don't Know Can Hurt Us.* Washington, D.C.: ACE.

De Blij, Harm J. 1971. *Geography: Regions and Concepts.* New York: Wiley.

Eisenstadt, S.N. 1963. *The Political Systems of Empires.* New York: Free Press.

Fanon, Frantz. 1967. *Black Skin, White Masks.* New York: Grove Press.

Farganis, James. 1983. "Social Theory as Introductory Sociology: A Humanities Perspective." National Endowment for the Humanities. Education Division, Grant 20015.

Gans, Herbert. 1962. *The Urban Villagers. Group and Class in Life of Italian-Americans.* New York: Free Press.

Goldthorpe, J.E. 1975. *The Sociology of the Third World. Disparity and Involvement.* Cambridge: Cambridge UP.

Hopkins, Terence K., and Wallerstein, Immanuel, ed. 1982. *World-Systems Analysis, Theory and Methodology.* Beverly Hills: Sage.

Lenski, Gerhard. 1983. "Rethinking the Introductory Course." *Teaching Sociology,* 10:153–68.

———. 1984a. "Sociology, Anthropology, and the Study of Human Societies." *Teaching Sociology,* 11:335–40.

———. 1984b. *Current Issues and Research in Macrosociology.* Leiden, Netherlands: E.J. Brill.

———, and Lenski, Jean. 1982. *Human Societies: An Introduction to Macrosociology.* 4th ed. New York: McGraw-Hill.

Liebow, Elliot. 1967. *Tally's Corner.* Boston: Little-Brown.

McNeill, William H. 1971. *A World History.* 2nd ed. New York: Oxford UP.

Marsh, Robert M. 1967. *Comparative Sociology: A Codification of Cross-Societal Analysis.* New York: Harcourt, Brace.

Moore, Wilbert E. 1966. "Global Sociology: The World as a Singular System." *American Journal of Sociology* 71:475–82.

Parsons, Talcott. 1977. *The Evolution of Societies.* (Ed. with an introduction by Jackson Toby.) Englewood Cliffs, N.J.: Prentice-Hall.

Said, Edward W. 1979. *Orientalism.* New York: Vintage/Random House.

Skocpol, Theda. 1979. *States and Social Revolutions.* Cambridge: Cambridge UP.

Soroos, Marvin S. 1983. "The Study of Global Issues." *SASASAAS (South Atlantic States Association of Asian and African Studies) Review,* 8:n.p. (Published at Appalachian State U, Boone, N.C.).

Spencer, Metta, and Inkeles, Alex. 1985. *Foundations of Modern Sociology.* 4th ed. Englewood Cliffs, N.J.: Prentice-Hall.

Tiryakian, Edward A., ed. 1984. "The Global Crisis: Sociological Analyses and Responses." *International Journal of Comparative Sociology,* special issue. 25. Nos. 1–2 (Also published as a paperback by E.J. Brill, Leiden, Netherlands.)

Touraine, Alain. 1984. "The Waning Sociological Image of Social Life", in E.A. Tiryakian, ed.: "The Global Crisis: Sociological Analyses and Responses."

Tulchin, Joseph S. 1984. "Global Issues." *Office of International Programs Newsletter,* Spring issue. n.p. Chapel Hill, N.C.: U of North Carolina.

Vallier, Ivan, ed. 1971. *Comparative Methods in Sociology. Essays on Trends and Applications.* Berkeley: U of California P.

Wallerstein, Immanuel, ed. 1966. *Social Change. The Colonial Situation.* New York: Wiley.

Watts, W. David, Short, A.P., and Schultz, C.C. 1983. "Applied Sociology and the Current Crisis." *Teaching Sociology.* 11:47–61.

Westhues, Kenneth. 1982. *First Sociology.* New York: McGraw-Hill.

Sociology for Undergraduates: Social Systems as World Systems, World Systems as Historical Systems

Immanuel Wallerstein

For a group of scholars who have throughout most of their organizational history emphasized the careful compilation of empirical data, sociologists have been remarkably casual about time-space specification. There are countless sociological monographs whose location in time and space are unknown or downplayed. There have been two reasons for this somewhat surprising attitude. One was the protection of privacy. *Middletown* was not identified by its real name because it was thought that to do so would intrude on the rights of the individuals the researchers had interviewed. But *Middletown* was not identified also because it was thought to be in some sense "typical"—in this case, typical of small-town America. That is to say, the universalizing assumptions of most sociological analysis meant that space-time specificity was often not very salient.

When sociology sought to become self-consciously "historical" because it was dealing with larger-scale phenomena, it traditionally became "comparative." By a curious paradox, to become comparative in turn meant to become in fact anti-historical, since it was regularly presumed that one could "fill boxes" with "comparable cases" across all of time and space.

The most fundamental expression of this refusal to make time and space salient was to be found in the most basic term in the sociological lexicon: society. Introductory sociology textbooks have classically struggled to offer a definition of this term. If, however, one looks at these definitions, one will rarely discover that either time or space coordinates are included.

Yet, if one then proceeds to read the textbooks in the descriptive segments that follow the exercises in definition, one notices that quite often there are

Immanuel Wallerstein is Director of the Fernand Braudel Center at the State University of New York, Binghamton.

spatial (if not temporal) adjectives linked to the noun, "society." They may talk of *Japanese* society, *Dutch* society, etc. They also occasionally talk of *Navajo* society, *Pygmy* society, etc. Sometimes even, they will talk of something like *Moslem* society. Thus it turns out *implicitly* that societies are thought to exist either within the boundaries of modern nation-states or within the boundaries of the "tribes" or "civilizations" which anthropologists were presumably studying.

Either of these implicit assumptions has enormous empirical problems which were seldom explored. The boundaries of modern nation-states have constantly changed over time. Do the "boundaries" of a society change with each change of juridical boundaries of a state? If not, are there criteria other than juridical, such as language, or even more vaguely "values," to fix the boundaries? But if so, is there such a thing as Dutch society in the Frisian-speaking zones of the Netherlands? As for the "tribes," are Navajos a "society" within American society? or only a society before they were included in the United States? In Egypt, is there both a Moslem society and an Egyptian society?

Finally, in addition to these ambiguities which might be said to be a besetting sin of sociology throughout the world, there is an extra problem with U.S. sociology. Much of it has been written as if the U.S. were in fact the world. The data all tend to be drawn from research about the U.S., often without this fact entering into the analysis in any specific way.

Many sociologists have been aware of these difficulties for a long time, and a certain amount of effort has been taken in recent years to overcome these limitations by "adding" a comparative-historical dimension to our research, our scholarly meetings, and our textbooks. "Adding" a comparative-historical dimension however may not remedy the malady. It may even compound it by the fact that such an exercise accepts, indeed legitimates, the very assumptions that created the problem.

The most important change we need to make is the most fundamental: to make time and space central to sociological analysis and not secondary; to define issues, frame research designs, and provide explanations through time and space. One does not "add" something called an "historical-comparative" dimension. That something (which we should in fact rename) is what defines sociology.

To be sure, this means restructuring much (if not most) of our research, reconstructing our pedagogy, and recasting fundamentally our elementary textbooks. It even means rethinking our premises about methodology (and this involves more than a question of improving and/or changing our techniques). I shall therefore present the argument for seeing social systems as world systems, and seeing world systems as historical systems. I shall then draw the implications for the definitions of social boundaries, for data and evidence, for the object of the sociological enterprise. Finally, I shall discuss what we may expect under-graduates to know already, to learn in the course of their studies, and the pedagogical conclusions to draw.

Social Systems as World Systems

A social system, if it means anything, presumably refers to a relatively self-contained entity driven primarily by its internal dynamic. Obviously any entity, once specified with time-space coordinates, faces two uncertainties as to whether the boundaries were specified appropriately. Since normally there are social zones beyond its presumed outer boundaries, is it really the case that the social system in question is "autonomous" vis-à-vis some discernable larger entity of which it might be thought to be merely a "part." At the same time, for any given entity, there are normally smaller entities discernible within its boundaries. Are none of these smaller entities in fact "autonomous" vis-à-vis the presumed social system in question?

The answer to these two quite legitimate queries cannot be deduced theoretically and therefore is impossible to know *a priori*. They are empirical questions. To know whether "Dutch society" is a "social system" we must ask about its "autonomy" vis-à-vis something larger. Were we to decide it stood up to this test, we would then ask whether the prison in Hilversum could be said to be, as some have argued about prisons, a "total system" and therefore in fact "autonomous" vis-à-vis Dutch society? While the query is empirical and not theoretical, there are some relatively straightforward guidelines for our judg-ment. For a social system to be "autonomous," and therefore to be a "system," we do not have to prove it is hermetically sealed off from outside pressures or totally homogeneous internally. We have only to be able to argue that there are essential equilibrating mechanisms of the presumed system sufficiently effica-cious to respond to and absorb these external and internal pressures according to the rules that govern this presumed system. Since in fact all systems are eternally evolving, the "equilibrating" mechanisms that succeed today may not succeed tomorrow. But to the extent they do not succeed, the system is ceasing to be a system.

With this guideline (which, if straightforward, is no doubt difficult in practice to make operational) we can look at human history and ask if we find any patterns of social systems. While many sociologists have done this, few have done this with this set of guidelines. My own reading of the mass of historical data out there is that thus far in human history we have known three kinds of social systems, though I can imagine a potential fourth.

There seem to have existed what I call "mini-systems," that is, systems whose boundaries include a single division of labor, a single political structure, and a single cultural pattern, and are not in fact located in some larger system. This comes close to what anthropologists have thought of traditionally as the "pre-contact tribe." I say that there "seem to have existed" such entities because I believe that scholars have rarely if ever actually visited such systems and virtually no one who did so put anything in writing about it, nor apparently did members of these systems. Most of our data about "primitive peoples," "tribes," etc. come from observations by scholars (and at an earlier period by travelers) whose study visit was made possible precisely by the fact that the group in question was in fact not (or no longer) autonomous from a geographically more extensive social system. Thus our "observations" have been inferences drawn from a quite particular situation, that of a relatively homogeneous small group of rural persons living within (typically) a colonial state to a hypothetical mode of functioning at an earlier moment of time (the so-called pre-"contact" moment). The fact is we really don't—and never will—know very much about how such mini-systems really functioned. We know more or less, though, that they existed in relatively large number across historical time. How large a number depends on doubtful speculations about the temporal survivability of such mini-systems. Did they typically last 100, 1,000, or 10,000 years? Let the scholar who has serious evidence present it.

I do not in consequence dismiss the reality of such mini-systems, but I do feel there is a built-in limit to our potential knowledge and therefore a real limit to what we can teach undergraduates about them. What we do know something about and therefore can teach something about are social systems that are "world systems." The definition of a world system is very simple (but the virtual opposite of what has often been used to define a social system). It is a system which does not have a single set of cultural practices or values but in which are located several or multiple cultures, by whatever criterion one wishes to define culture (*Weltanschauung*, language, religion, rules of social behavior, etc.).

If it is not the uniqueness or the integratedness of the cultural sphere which defines the system, what does? It seems to me that clearly what is crucial is the ability to reproduce the structure collectively, and this depends on the collective ability to produce and distribute the material means necessary for collective reproduction over time. This is what is really meant by that classic sociological concept, the social division of labor. A division of labor is bounded by the physical area and the peoples that are linked together in an ongoing set of productive activities which makes possible their collective reproduction. When we have located this set of activities and its boundaries, we have located a social system. Such zones (of land and peoples) are discoverable as historical, empirical realities. We can investigate when and where they have existed, and we can designate with more or less confidence their effective boundaries.

A mini-system is of course a social system in this sense, but so are many other entities which do not have the cultural homogeneity of mini-systems. These latter are the world systems. People living in world systems have been the real subject matter of the social sciences over the last 150 years. But we have failed to conceptualize it in that way.

If now we investigate the empirical instances of such world systems we discover that there have been two major variants of world systems. One has an overarching political structure, and we may call that variant a world empire. A second variant does not have this overarching structure, but rather contains multiple political units whose relations one to the others are regulated by some rules but not by any (or much) organizational structure. This variant we may call a world economy (because the absence of an overarching political structure allows much greater freedom for contenders in the market to pursue their ends).

World Systems as Historical Systems

World systems are historical systems. That is to say, they come into existence, they "develop" over time, and at some point they cease to exist. None is or can be timeless, because social systems always contain internal contradictions in their dynamic processes and are always subject to exogenous forces such that eventually they cannot reproduce their essential features. They then may "disintegrate" or be absorbed into another social system, or "transform" their nature in some fundamental way. For both world empires and world economies, we can actually "observe" these historical evolutions. Mini-systems no doubt are also historical systems but, for reasons already suggested, scholars have almost no way of observing what were their particular historical evolutions, which is why we know so little about them.

To some people, the phrase "historical system" sounds paradoxical. They argue that if something is "historical," it cannot be "systemic" because it is constantly changing; and that if something is "systemic," it must be equilibrated and therefore is in some sense unchanging. De facto, this is the view of the holders of the two extreme positions in the classic nineteenth-century methodological debate between the so-called idiographic school (who emphasized the uniqueness of all social occurrences) and the so-called nomothetic school (who emphasized the laws that govern all social behavior). The position argued here is squarely in the middle of this continuum and at odds with both of these views. The argument is that all social structures are simultaneously historical and systemic, eternally evolving and yet retaining for some significant length of time some essentially unaltered structural features. Another way of putting this is to say that all of social reality consists both of cyclical rhythms, in which equilibrating mechanisms constantly bring behavior back from its oscillations away from some mean, and secular trends, in which the very equilibrating mechanisms create systemic changes, and that over time such changes make it impossible to reproduce the equilibrium.

If we wish to translate these notions into something more concrete, we must approach analyses of social reality by trying to see the social whole which is a particular historical system, analyze its mode of functioning and therefore its cyclical rhythms, and discover its contradictions and therefore its secular trends. On the one hand, each historical world system is particular, but within its boundaries there are generalizations that can be made about its mode of operation. We have thus a large but not infinite time-space scope for our generalizing instincts. For example, most of sociology has in fact been written about one particular historical system, the capitalist world economy that came into existence in the sixteenth century, expanded its frontiers over time to include the whole world, and still exists. This particular system does not encompass all of historical social reality, but it encompasses a part that has traditionally absorbed most of our scholarly attention. We may of course call this traditional allocation of our attention into question, and no doubt should. It remains true to say that much of what has been asserted to be lawlike statements uncovered by sociologists have in reality been observations about the mode of operation of one particular historical system.

But can there then be no history or sociology of historical systems as a whole? Yes, there can, though traditionally sociologists have paid very little attention to what might be termed, in somewhat cumbersome form, the historical sociology of historical world systems. Given the little work that has been done on this matter, we can at present say little. Nonetheless, we can make one very important observation, starting with our perception of three types of historical systems: mini-systems, world empires, and world economies.

Somewhere before 8000–10,000 B.C. there probably existed nothing but mini-systems, or so our limited archaeological knowledge seems to indicate. How many coexisted on the earth at any one time is a matter about which we could at best hazard a guess.

Then came the "agricultural revolution," and larger historical systems began to come into existence—and, of course, go out of existence. From this time forward to circa 1500 A.D., historical evidence indicates the coexistence on the planet Earth of the three kinds of historical systems, although once again we might be hard-pressed to draw a map showing numbers and locations for any given year or century of all these systems side by side.

We know something more. From the work of historians and others who have worked on such topics as "empires" and "civilizations," it becomes clear that, of the three types of historical systems, the world empire was the strong form in this period (that is, approximately 10,000 B.C. to 1500 A.D.). By this

I mean that world empires seemed to expand and contract over time by the operation of dynamics internal to them (and which can be specified). While any given world empire was in its expansionary phase, it would "absorb" surrounding mini-systems and world economies (which thereby ceased to exist as historical systems). When these world empires began to contract, they would leave "voids" in "abandoned" zones within which new mini-systems and world economies began to grow.

Thus, from a planetary point of view, world empires were the "strong" form; their internal dynamics determined the fate of the mini-systems and the world economies far more than the other way around.

Circa 1500, this situation changed in a rather dramatic way. For some reason (which needs to be explained, and can be), a particular world economy located in Europe proved to be unusually durable. It was therefore able to consolidate itself in such a way that all of a sudden it became the "strong" form on the planet. Instead of being absorbed by some world empire, its internal dynamic pushed it to expand over time and absorb all the world empires with which it came into contact and, of course, all the mini-systems. Indeed this particular historical system, the capitalist world economy, proved so strong that by the late nineteenth century it had expanded to the outer geographical limits of the planet, having absorbed all other historical systems.

Now, for the first time in the history of the planet, instead of a multiplicity of temporally coexisting historical systems on the planet, there was only one, which created a qualitatively new situation. This then opens the question of the future. Since we have already argued that all historical systems eventually come to an historical end, this one will too, and indeed it is not too difficult to describe the dynamics of that development. However, when it does, with what will the "void" be filled?

Hypothetically, we might return to a pre-1500 pattern of multiple coexisting historical systems. Or we might see the creation of a structure closer to that of a world empire in that there would be a single global political structure. Yet, in the absence of neighboring zones, the dynamics of such a structure would have to be very different from those which governed the multiple world empires whose dynamic involved territorial expansion and contraction. This is my possible fourth type of historical system, which is hard to foresee and impossible to describe since it does not yet exist.

The Science of Social Systems
that Are Historical Systems

From the premises adumbrated in the previous sections, I shall proceed to review the implications for our traditional views of scientific activity in sociology.

They do not cause one to throw out any of the accumulated data or wisdom about methods of research. They do raise questions about three rather serious issues which have far-reaching implications for future work.

The first and most obvious is the question of appropriate boundaries of analysis. All systemic analysis (and sociology has always largely been that) operates on a metaphor of internal/external spheres. It is clear from what has been argued heretofore that a world systems perspective calls into question the usual defined boundaries of social action, and in most cases substitutes for the society/state the boundaries of a world system.

What is often misunderstood are the practical implications of such a stance. It no more follows that one cannot study meaningfully some relatively small-scale institution or group (e.g., a local school administration, a "street corner society," or strangers in a supermarket engaging in conversation) than is true under our present dominant assumptions. We presently assume that such institutions are located in a particular state with laws affecting the group in question, that there is an official language, etc. That is, we intrude a whole set of "constraining factors" in our analysis that derive from our (often merely implicit) set of the relevant boundaries of social action. All that is suggested—but that of course is very much—is that another set of social boundaries (usually wider in space and longer in time) be this frame of reference.

The wider-longer boundaries immediately affect the analysis of "social change." Much that passes for social change suffers from a too close-up look at social reality; quite frequently, the so-called change turns out to be spurious newness when seen in the light of the appropriate set of boundaries. Since undergraduates are inherently and notoriously prone to the ailment of rediscovering the world and called it new, it is particularly important that their mentors be somewhat armed against this distorted view.

The second implication is our appreciation of the existing accumulated "data," particularly the data that are numerical in form and sit in the libraries and archives of the world. Let us never forget that the word "statistics" derives from the word "state." According to the *OED*, "the earliest use of the adjective in anything resembling its present meaning is found in mod. L. *statisticum collegium*, said to have been used by Martin Schmeizel (professor at Jena, †1747) for a course of lectures on the constitutions, resources, and policy of the various States of the world."

No doubt, as a set of mathematical techniques, statistics has come a long way from this eighteenth-century origin. But in terms of the statistical data that we have at our disposition, we are not all that far removed. I would hazard the view (no one to my knowledge having collected statistical data on this question) that at least 95 percent of the world's accumulated statistical "data" are numbers collected by states about parameters of their own activity or numbers collected by scholars and then generalized to universes which are state-bounded.

This of course makes eminent sense if the modern state is the crucial arena of social action of the modern world. It makes considerably less sense if we alter the boundaries of social action we utilize and substitute those of a world system. We then immediately realize that the numbers applicable to the world economy as a whole are not simply a sum of the national figures (which the statistical operations of the United Nations and similar institutions seem to imply) but are a set of numbers which have largely been uncollected heretofore, either (a) because they involve relationships at the level of the world system as a whole, or (b) because they involve compiling simultaneously and combining data about some transactions which occur only within a single state and other transactions which transcend state frontiers, or (c) because they involve comparing geographical entities which are in general smaller than and different from the states.

Of course one can say, "Go out and collect such data." To be sure this is good advice and essential. But much of our present analyses depend (at least in part) on secondary analysis of what has already been collected. It must therefore be taken into account that primarily one variety of "data" has been widely collected for 150 years, and a considerable bank of this variety of data therefore exists. The "new" kind of quantitative data needed for world systems analysis has not been widely collected and it will take a minimum of 30 years or so to build up a reasonable bank of such data.

The third implication is perhaps the most controversial. It has to do with the metamethodological assumptions of sociology as it has been taught and practiced. These assumptions were built into the nineteenth-century nomothetic-idiographic debate to which reference has been made. The nomothetic school had a model of science in which, from a base of empirical observations (which were normally "messy" since the real world "mixes together" large numbers of particular factors), scientists drew out the essential features (abstracting them) in order to analyze cause and effect. In a crude sense, one was supposed to go from complexity to simplicity which was clarity. The best statement was considered to be the most abstract, the widest in scope, the one which used the fewest variables. This was seen as a difficult but ultimately possible task. This was also seen as following in the footsteps of the physical sciences.

No doubt not everyone agreed with this objective, but this was/is a dominant view. If, however, (a) all systems have both cycles and trends, (b) our systems are such large-scale entities that we have very few cases (and for the variety of a long-surviving world economy there is only one), and (c) the historical sociology of historical world systems by definition deals with a single case, unreplicable even theoretically, then our conventional metamethodology hardly speaks to the intellectual issues involved in the scientific analysis of such systems.

What might work, if we can translate it into careful, controlled procedures, is the inversion of our usual treatment of data. Suppose we started with the most general, the simplest formulations, those with the fewest variables (which is essentially what we do when we observe cyclical rhythms), crosscut these with other simple statements in order to arrive at more complex and "messy" ones, slowly working our way forward to the ultimate point of a "coherent historical interpretation" of a large-scale, long-term social phenomenon. This is not, be it noted, the traditional attempt of idiographic historians to empathize with a particular social reality but rather an attempt to utilize theory in order to interpret what in fact did happen in the way it did, and which therefore enables us to project, in the light of how persons have acted facing real historical alternatives in the past, how other persons might conceivably act facing real historical alternatives in the present or future.

Pedagogical Possibilities

The approach suggested here is often criticized paradoxically for two opposite pedagogical reasons. It is suggested, on the one hand, that this approach makes sociology too "easy" for the student (and scholar), too "journalistic," too "polemical," too "subjective." On the other hand, we are often told it makes it too "hard" for the student, requiring him/her to read and know about a very wide range of historical phenomena, described in multiple languages, about an endless number of particular topics. What was called journalism at the beck and call of any amateur suddenly has become transformed into such vast scholarship (and exotica) that it is available only to a rare genius.

Neither image is in fact correct. There is no need for analysis at the level of a world system to be any less systematic or rigorous than analysis at the level of a state. Indeed, if correctly done, it requires considerably more rigor since it calls into question many things which other analysts assume and can therefore take for granted.

On the other hand, simply because one expands the boundaries of social action over wider space and longer time does not normally inflate the real social energy a particular piece of social research requires. Has the astronomer an inherently more difficult task than the microbiologist? I cannot believe this. It is a pure red herring to say that world-systems analysis is "beyond" the researcher or the undergraduate.

Still, it does mean we have to teach our courses somewhat differently. We must cease "tacking on" historical background in the first week of class and "social change" in the last. The whole course is nothing but historical background cum social change. This is the topic, no matter what the title of any "substantive" course. It requires the students to observe exactly what is cyclical and what is secular, since both processes are constantly present. It requires comparisons that are both broader and narrower than we often now practice. On the one hand, the wild comparisons over all of time and space of an abstract institutional structure (the family, bureaucracy, etc.) have no meaning and negative utility because such "structures" cannot be intelligently defined and demarcated except as integral parts and products of a given historical system.

On the other hand, even when our comparisons are made within a single historical system, we too frequently compare one phenomenon under close scrutiny with another whose features are considered "so well known" as to obviate the need for such close scrutiny. The introductory sociology course cannot rely, as it too frequently does, on the generalizations about major phenomena (let us say the French Revolution or immigration to the U.S. in the late nineteenth century) which are part of the knowledge the student brings from previous education. A comparison must always be between two empirically analyzed situations, not between one so analyzed and another retrieved in summary, idealized form. This seems so obvious it may seem pointless to mention it. A quick review of textbooks should convince one that the problem is real. The problem is real because the problem is structurally based. Our state-based view of reality has been well institutionalized. Once one redefines the boundaries of social action, however, many obvious truths cease to be so. We are then forced to be more wary, more empirical, more tentative in our theorizing.

The question remains, who will educate the educator? The answer is surely not other educators. In the long run, the origins of the world-systems perspective was not located in some internal evolution of the intellectual arena but in the fact that our previous approach was pushing us increasingly into culs-de-sac within which we found much of contemporary reality puzzling and/or anomalous. Changes in the real world forced changes in our ideas. This reality is educating the educator. On the other hand, it is the scientist who is called on to clarify this reality by theorizing it and then to bring others to be able also to interpret it. This is very feasible, but it requires a genuine intellectual effort by the professoriat.

An Intercultural Context for Economic, Political, and Military Relations

William Foote Whyte

If Americans are to understand our international economic, political, and military relations, we must be able to place political issues in the context of the cultures and societies in which they arise. This requires not only some understanding of other nations; it also calls for an understanding of American society and culture, which tend to shape decision-making processes in Washington.

Beyond a general comprehension of cultural and social factors at home and abroad, we need to develop ways of learning about the relations between beliefs and behavior at the individual and group level and also at the macro-level where we are concerned with the relations between political ideologies and governmental decision making.

Sociology focuses on the conceptual tools and schemes of analysis designed to help us to understand behavior in groups, organizations, and communities. In the early years of the discipline, American sociologists concentrated on studies of our own society. In recent years, sociologists have broadened their horizons through reading the research reports on their own societies of foreign sociologists and through engaging in their own field work abroad. The internationalization of sociological research has been immensely stimulated by the work of social anthropologists, whose discipline has led them to concentrate heavily on studies of cultures different from our own.

To make more concrete what students should learn from sociology (and social anthropology), I shall concentrate on what can and cannot be accomplished, by various means, in critical areas of international confrontation. I will focus on our relations with Soviet Russia, and also on our relations with developing nations, particularly in Latin America, the foreign area I know best.

William Foote Whyte is Research Director of Programs for Employment and Workplace Systems of the New York State School of Industrial and Labor Relations at Cornell University.

I believe college students need to learn:

1. The difference between political ideologies and national governments.
2. How a few deceptively simple concepts shape our foreign policies.
3. The role of private enterprise in international development.
4. The role of communal (religious and ethnic) conflicts in civil and international strife.
5. The limited powers of U.S. military assistance and involvement.
6. What can and cannot be accomplished through economic and technical assistance.

I shall concentrate on these problem areas because there is much confusion and misinformation on all these points.

Distinguishing between Political Ideologies and National Governments

Years ago at the time of the U.S. invasion of the Dominican Republic, I was startled to hear a radio commentator report, in a voice filled with alarm, that "In the Dominican Republic there is not one Communist Party but there are three Communist Parties." By attaching the word "Communist" to these parties, the commentator made it appear that the situation was three times as dangerous as would have been the case if there had been a single Communist Party.

Suppose the commentator had conveyed the same idea but without using the label: "In the Dominican Republic the most radical opposition is divided into three small parties." That message would have indicated that extremist opposition was not only weak in numbers but badly divided.

Since I had always admired Eric Sevareid, I was surprised to hear him fall victim to the popular confusion between ideology and political power. That so thoughtful a person as Sevareid could speak such nonsense suggested the importance of considering how we can help people learn the difference between a political ideology and a government.

The problem is that when a political commentator or politician uses the words "Communism" or "Marxism," he conjures up in the public mind a body of people not only committed to a rigid political ideology but also dominated by the Soviet Union. This myth appears able to withstand any amount of contradictory evidence. When Yugoslavia broke away from Soviet political domination and established a highly democratic system for the governance of its industrial plants, cold warriors could disregard this ideological and political rupture because Yugoslavia did not seem to be a very important country. There was still the "Sino-Soviet Bloc." When the rupture of cooperative relations between Russia and China occurred, cold warriors were at first unable to believe what had happened. They sought to explain the obvious political conflict as simply a ruse designed to deceive western democracies.

When it at last became evident even to State Department policy makers that the split between the Soviet Union and the People's Republic was real and deep, the implications of this change were only partially taken into account. To be sure, Richard Nixon recognized the political realities sufficiently to enable him to establish some degree of cooperation with that enormous nation. However, the political ruptures involved in the defections of Yugoslavia and the People's Republic from Russian domination have been set aside in a sealed compartment of the brains of some of our most prominent policy makers as they continue to confuse communism with the government of the Soviet Union.

The effects of this confusion can be illustrated particularly in recent and current policy-maker efforts to interpret Latin American politics. During the fourteen months (1961–62) I spent there I learned that Peru also had three communist parties. There was a Stalinist Party composed of those who, no matter what happened internationally, still were committed to the party line as interpreted from Moscow. There were the Maoists, committed to following the gospel as preached by Chairman Mao. And then there were the Trotskyites, who were still committed to the belief that the wrong man had emerged to control Russia following the death of Lenin. Yes, Leon Trotsky was still alive and well in the politics of at least a few dedicated followers in the Peru of that era—and, for all I know, Trotsky's interpretation of communism may still be alive somewhere in Latin America.

I have not kept up with leftist politics in Peru in recent years, but I recently read that, in the campaign for mayor of Lima, there were seven candidates who called themselves Marxists. A more recent research report indicates that there are now nine Marxist parties. For all I know, some of them may call themselves socialists rather than communists. Indeed, in the 1960s there were several very small socialist parties that also expressed a commitment to Marxism.

What does this all mean? When we think of communism or Marxism—the two terms seem to be equated in the public mind—if we pay attention to the doctrines espoused by Karl Marx, we are dealing with a body of writings which, for the variety of interpretations to which it is subject, can be compared with the Holy Bible. The religious fundamentalists of the far right and the most liberal churchmen—regarded as covert communists by the far right—can all find support for their theological interpretations in Bible passages. So it is with the ideological theologians of the far left.

Latin American Marxists appear to be united on only one point: opposition to "Yankee imperialism." They have not been concerned with the brutal actions of the Soviet Union in crushing independent and popular leaders in Czechoslovakia or Hungary. They don't worry about the brutal control of Poland by the Soviet Union nor about the bloody war Russia is waging in Afghanistan. Those countries are far away. It is in the western hemisphere that for many years they have experienced dominance of private companies, mainly owned by U.S. interests, and the frequent interventions, economic, political, and military, of the United States to help conservative governments put down popular opposition.

I never heard a Latin American Marxist express the view that it was a good idea for his country to become an economic and political satellite of Russia. Links with Russia have generally been considered, in these circles, a matter of expediency. The United States was clearly seen as the enemy of popular and progressive reform movements, and Russia, being the only strong declared enemy of the United States, was therefore the only nation that could be looked toward for help in the political and economic struggles to build a strong, progressive, and independent nation. But that does not mean that they welcome dependence on Russia. In fact, when I was briefly in Nicaragua several years ago, it was widely believed that Fidel Castro himself had advised the leading Sandinistas to try to avoid becoming too dependent on Russia and to seek some modus vivendi with the United States.

In the last half century, there have only been two periods in which hostility toward the United States did not have great popular appeal. During the years of Franklin D. Roosevelt's "good neighbor" policies, there seems to have been some tendency of radicals on the left to think that it might be possible to transform their societies, to achieve greater economic and social justice, with the tacit support or even encouragement of the United States. Years later, after his Bay of Pigs fiasco, when John F. Kennedy mounted his "Alliance for Progress," Latin American liberals and radicals were again encouraged to believe that they could achieve progress with the encouragement of the United States. In fact, it was extraordinary the popularity that Kennedy attained in Latin America during his all-too-brief presidency. Friends in Lima told me that they cried when they heard the news of his assassination.

In this context, the actual or potential linkages of leftist governments or leftist political factions to the Soviet Union should be regarded as more a matter of expediency than ideological conviction. Since they see their country as under hostile economic, political, and military pressure from the United States, they naturally look for help in the only corner where they see possibilities of finding it. If U.S. policies became less ideologically muscle-bound and more open to the realities, the United States could find openings for building friendly relations with leftist governments in the developing world.

This conclusion was expressed by Frank Church, former chairman of the Senate foreign relations committee:

... the root of our problem is not, as many Americans persist in believing, the relentless spread of communism. Rather, it is our own difficulty in understanding that Third World revolutions are primarily nationalist, not communist. Nationalism, not capitalism or communism, is the dominant political force in the modern world. (*Washington Post*, March 26, 1984)

How Concepts Shape Foreign Policy

It would be comforting to believe that foreign policy decisions were based on an intellectual analysis of the relevant information. If that were the case, then the problem would be to choose smart leaders and see to it that they had access to the information. The fallacy in that assumption is illustrated by David Halberstam's book on the Vietnam War. Its title, *The Best and the Brightest*, states the basic lesson. Halberstam argues that the key foreign policy advisors to Presidents Kennedy and Johnson were generally regarded as intellectual superstars, and yet they led us into the worst foreign policy disaster in our history.

Nor was the problem a lack of access to relevant information. On any foreign policy question, the volume of information potentially available is overwhelming. The leaders and their staff have the enormous task of sorting out the information flow to distinguish between information and misinformation and to determine what information is most relevant for policy making. The sorting process depends on guidelines established by certain key concepts. To understand foreign-policy making, it is important to probe beneath the publicly stated arguments in order to discover the key concepts that shape decision.

In recent years, U.S. foreign policy has been shaped by concepts that equate Marxism with communism and communism with the foreign policies of the Soviet Union. In this framework, any serious political conflict in a Third World country is likely to be seen as reflecting the trouble-making involvement of Russia. It is not that policy makers deny all indigenous roots of such conflicts, but they see the Soviets taking advantage of internal problems to exploit existing grievances.

How should the U.S. respond to such Soviet trouble making? A fundamental rule is that we must avoid "appeasement." Ever since Neville Chamberlain sold out Czechoslovakia to Hitler for "peace in our time," the appeasement concept has been a major influence on foreign-policy thinking. It can be and has been applied to almost any situation where Russia has appeared to make an aggressive move. If we do not confront the Russians, we are guilty of appeasement, regardless of how far-fetched the analogy between the case in question and the pre-World War II situation in Central Europe.

The Vietnam War gave us the "dominoes" concept: if we give way of appeasement and fail to confront the communist menace, then the fall of one nation to the communists will inevitably be followed by the fall of its neighbors. As Frank Church commented,

> Vietnam did fall to the communists, but only two dominoes followed—Laos and Cambodia, both of which we had roped into the war. Thailand, Malaysia and Indonesia continue to exist on their own terms. The Peoples Republic of China, for whom Hanoi was supposed to be a proxy, is not engaged in armed skirmishes against Vietnam. (*Ibid.*)

The dominoes concept is currently being applied to Central America, although the leaders of none of the potential domino states appear to be as worried over their impending fate as the U.S. policy makers.

Making policy in terms of such concepts yields high costs in human and material terms, yet paradoxically the costs themselves tend to support current policies. Here the key concept is "credibility." If the decision makers commit us to a policy that is costly and produces no obvious benefits, nevertheless we must "stay the course" because otherwise we would lose credibility with our opponents and our allies. Supporters of our current policy claim we lose credibility only if we fail to exercise our military power consistently. Opponents see a loss of credibility if our actions fail to match our professed ideals.

In the business world, decision makers follow a different logic. When the leaders of Ford Motor Company finally had to recognize that they could not make a profit with the Edsel, they decided to stop producing the Edsel. In the foreign policy field, Edsels survive because they are not subjected to pragmatic tests. The more our policy makers have invested in a policy, the more they see U.S. credibility at stake, and the more committed they are to pursuing the policy.

The Role of Private Enterprise
in International Development

When I began my research in Peru in 1961, with the aim of studying the relations of Peruvian managers with Peruvian workers and union leaders, I soon learned that the pure cases I was seeking were few and far between. With very few exceptions, the well-established companies were either foreign owned or else had been created by immigrants or the sons of immigrants. By the third generation in the country, industrial entrepreneurship was a calling with low value in Peruvian culture.

Following this analysis, the dominance of foreign and particularly U.S. owned firms in Peru cannot be explained simply in terms of the aggressiveness of U.S. managers and entrepreneurs and the support of our government, with the connivance of their government. To a large extent, the sluggish development of Peruvian industry can be attributed to social and cultural factors which have made the role of the industrial entrepreneur unappealing.

As I looked beyond Peru to other countries in Latin America, I learned that the same general conditions prevailed. Predominantly, it was immigrants or sons of immigrants who had been the national industrial entrepreneurs. The elite of these countries appear to have taken over traditional Spanish values and attitudes toward work. In these terms, a respectable (and respected) person does not work with his hands.

This interpretation was brought home to me when I was arranging for Peruvian publication of my report "Culture and Industrial Development: The Case of Peru" (1963). In this article, I recounted briefly the origins of three major Peruvian industrial enterprises. Luis Banchero, the son of an Italian immigrant, had started work as a gasoline station attendant and had gone on to become the fish meal king of Peru. Alfredo D'Onofrio's family had come from Italy when he was one year old. He had started work with a pushcart, selling candy and ice cream, and had gone on from this beginning to build a fortune based on manufacturing and distributing chocolates, cookies, and ice cream. Oscar Ferrand had come over from France while a young man and had established himself precariously as the owner and operator of a corner grocery store. His son had built the leading glass manufacturing company, owned the Ford agency for Lima, and was a major figure in one of the leading banks.

When I discussed the translation with Graciela Flores, who had worked on this research with me, she urged me to leave the personal histories out of the article. I asked her, "Why shouldn't we tell the story? Aren't the facts well known in Lima?" She replied, "Of course the facts are known, but it would embarrass the children and grandchildren of the original entrepreneurs to be reminded of the family's humble beginnings." In other words, far from taking pride in the hard work and upward mobility of the founder of the family fortune, the descendants would like to nourish the illusion that their families had always been socially prominent. (See also Whyte and Braun, 1966.)

I find that Latin American intellectuals are not inclined to deny the facts on which my interpretation is based, but they resent the implication that their industrially backward state is not simply the result of exploitation by the multinationals, backed by the U.S. government. Of course, there is no practical value in laying the blame either on U.S. multinationals or on the traditional cultures of Latin America. However, recognizing the cultural roots of industrial underdevelopment helps us understand the basis of hostility of Latin American intellectuals on the left to private enterprise in their country. I shall never forget the comment made by Julio Cotler, one of Latin America's leading sociologists, who said to me "The armed forces are practically the only large organizations in Peru that are owned and managed by Peruvians."

With this situation prevailing in many Latin American countries, it is not simply political propaganda when politicians on the left argue that the economic and financial policies of the nation are controlled in large measure by interests based outside their country. In fact, this can serve as an issue where people on the right and on the left find themselves in agreement. For many years, the owners and editors of Peru's leading conservative newspaper, *El Comercio*, were the most vociferous proponents of the nationalization of International Petroleum Company, then owned by what is now Exxon. It is hardly surprising to a student of Latin American affairs that Latin Americans over a broad political range from the left to the right failed to react with enthusiasm to the Reagan policies of stimulating U.S. private investment in their countries.

During my first year in Venezuela (1954–55) when I was engaged in industrial relations research with Creole Petroleum Corporation (then part of what is now Exxon), I assumed that, if the expatriate executives of the company could just learn how to adjust better to the prevailing culture and social structure so as to make positive contributions to the economic and social development of the country, U.S. firms and Latin American businessmen and politicians could live happily ever after. I long ago lost that faith. I was not disillusioned by evidence of exploitation and oppression by U.S. management people, though there has been plenty of that. On the whole, I suspect that, if we compared the social and economic programs and personnel policies of U.S. companies in Latin America with companies in the same line of activity owned and managed by nationals, we would conclude that on balance the U.S. management record has been more enlightened and humane. However, that argument holds little weight in Latin America. There are some aspects of domination by foreign owned and managed companies which cannot be met by any dispassionate balancing of the objective social and economic facts. If we think back to the American Revolution, we will understand how Latin Americans feel on this question. Modern historians are now inclined to argue that, economically speaking, the American colonies were reasonably well off while under control of the British. There were, of course, real economic grievances, but the basic issue was that the colonists were not in control of their own destiny. Such is the case today in Latin America.

In reaction against foreign economic and financial dominance, many Latin American politicians and intellectuals are inclined to favor government owner-ship and operation of the means of production. We may try to persuade them that, if they have this kind of economic system, eventually they won't be satisfied with it and will have to consider other options—whether private ownership, employee ownership, or worker cooperatives—but they will have to find this out for themselves. We cannot expect to impose the answers. I am not arguing that it is impossible for U.S. companies to play constructive roles in developing countries. Such countries would be terribly handicapped if they had to depend entirely on their own human and natural resources for the development of technology, manufacturing methods, and management systems and techniques. I am simply arguing that the traditional pattern of a wholly U.S. owned company in a developing nation involves serious and unavoidable political problems. In fact, many leaders of U.S. industry have come to this conclusion. We now see increasing cases of joint ventures in which ownership is shared 50-50 between the U.S. company and national investors—or even 49-51, with the nationals holding the controlling interest. We also see the growth of contractual relationships in which the U.S. firm forgoes ownership altogether but profits from supplying technology and technical assistance in engineering, manufacturing, and marketing. Students should be led beyond the traditional pattern to explore new forms of international business relations, even though the literature is still sparse on such recent developments.

The Role of Communal Conflicts
in Civil and International Strife

Ideologues on the right are inclined to see violent conflicts within a developing nation in terms of the struggle between communism and the free world. Ideologues on the left are inclined to explain the same phenomenon in terms of the class struggle within the nation. Neither set of ideologues has been able to find a plausible explanation for the violent communal conflicts involved in the Iranian revolution and its aftermath or for the strife among the many religious and ethnic factions of Lebanon.

The religious-ethnic bases in these cases have been too obvious to ignore, but the ideologues have tried to force the conflicts into their own cognitive frameworks. For Lebanon, the rightist ideologues argue that Russia and Syria are stirring up trouble to prevent the factions from getting together. In the past, leftist ideologues argued that such strife represented "false consciousness" on the part of workers, which would be overcome when they recognized their true class interests. Currently they can claim that this false consciousness is exacerbated by the intervention of the imperialist powers, the United States and Israel. Such arguments only lay the blame and make it more difficult to understand the internal dynamics of communal conflict. Unless we can open the minds of our students to the study of communal conflicts, they will be ill prepared to understand international crises now and in the future.

215

The Limited Powers of Military Assistance and Involvement

I find it striking how the lessons that should have been learned through U.S. military assistance and involvement in Vietnam have not been applied to our current Central American policies. In fact, the same strategies that failed in Vietnam are now being applied in El Salvador and Nicaragua. What the Reagan administration was undertaking in Nicaragua presented even greater political and military problems than the U.S. encountered in Vietnam. In that war at least we were supporting a government in place and an army, some of whose units were willing to fight. In Nicaragua, the CIA had the task of organizing, training, and financing a rebel army led by experienced Nicaraguan military officers— whose experience, however, had been gained while they led the hated National Guard under the Somoza dictatorship. Then, to make the project more palatable to U.S. public opinion, the CIA undertook to set up a political directorate including some members with authentic democratic records.

We began our involvement in Vietnam sending advisors, who were expected to orient and train the South Vietnamese Army. In fact, the problems of the South Vietnamese armed forces had very little to do with the quality of their training. They were serving under top political leaders and military commanders who had earlier been allied with the French military and political leaders who had fought to maintain French control of what was then a colony. Although Presidents Eisenhower and Johnson sought by fiat to make the government of South Vietnam part of "the free world," this rhetoric could not wipe out the memories of the colonial past. And no amount of military training could instill in the South Vietnamese forces a willingness to fight and die for the country that was governed by the remnants of the colonial power.

At this writing, a similar situation prevails in El Salvador. To be sure, El Salvador is not a colony of a foreign power (yet), but it has been dominated economically and politically by a tiny elite of enormous wealth, supported by "death squads" that make a practice of assassinating anyone who might be suspected of being disloyal to the government. Top officers in the military have been closely allied with the dominant economic and political elite, and the rank and file soldiers are predominantly conscripts, forced into service, who have shown a notable reluctance to re-enlist when their compulsory service is terminated. With the exception of some units, the government troops have appeared more concerned with their personal safety than with fighting and winning battles. They have been opposed by military units made up of volunteers committed to fight for victory, no matter how long it takes and how difficult the struggle.

All this appears to be known to our State Department, and yet the U.S. government continues to display its blind faith that military training will convert the government troops into an effective fighting force.

Our political leaders also display an inordinate faith in military hardware. The assumption seems to be that if we just provide the government we support with enough weapons, eventually that government will prevail. As happened in Vietnam and as is happening today in El Salvador, the U.S. is supplying substantial hardware to both sides. Various observers have estimated that from 20 to 50 percent of the munitions we supply to the government forces end up in the hands of the insurgents. Nor is this simply a matter of arms captured in battle. There have been various reports of government officers selling U.S. munitions to the rebels.

The administration justifies our massive flow of munitions to government forces on the grounds that, as the President stated, the guerrillas are being "armed to the teeth" by Nicaragua, Cuba, and Russia. The validity of this claim is difficult to test because the administration will only provide evidence to congressional committees in secret hearings, from which the legislators emerge with a variety of opinions, some being impressed with the evidence, others considering it unconvincing.

Whereas at other points the administration seems to ignore the parallels with Vietnam, it is important to recognize here that the parallel breaks down. To be sure, the North Vietnamese forces captured large stores of U.S. munitions, but they also had a steady supply coming to them from Russia and China, down the Ho Chi Minh Trail. Since North Vietnam bordered on China, there was no way that the U.S. could block this flow at the source, without making war on China, and U.S. bombing on the Trail only served sporadically to interrupt the flow. The geography of Central America presents a much more difficult situation for foreign supporters of the guerrillas. Nicaragua and El Salvador do not share a common border. In fact, El Salvador is surrounded by Honduras and Guatemala, whose governments are hostile to the guerrilla forces. Given the geographical situation and the testimony of independent observers, it seems reasonable to believe that the military assistance received by the guerrillas from foreign powers is only a small fraction of that flowing into the government of El Salvador from the United States. Since the weapons used on both sides of the conflict are predominantly those supplied by the United States, our arms traffic is simply increasing the level of violence.

Problems with Economic and Technical Assistance

Since the United States is a rich country and we would like to consider ourselves a generous people, we are naturally inclined to want to share our good fortune with people of the poorer countries of the world. Nor are our leaders simply motivated by altruistic considerations. There is a widespread belief that, if we can help poorer countries toward economic and social progress and democracy, this will make those countries better customers of the United States and more friendly toward our international policies. The problem is not with these assumptions but rather with the difficulties in providing economic and technical assistance that will enable those countries to fulfill our expectations for them.

I believe our policy makers were misled by the spectacular success of the Marshall Plan and have only gradually come to recognize that comparable successes in the poor developing countries are much more difficult to attain.

The problem was well stated recently by Luis Burstin, Costa Rica's secretary of information from 1974 to 1978.

In the last ten years, Latin America received more foreign credits than Europe obtained under the Marshall Plan. In Europe, American magnanimity and European political wisdom combined to produce reconstruction and the consolidation of democracy. Here in Latin America, larger amounts of money have produced only economic crises, bankruptcy and problems of liquidity. Democracy is fragile or nonexistent, and poverty runs rampant. The differences between Latin America and Europe are obvious. Europe needed reconstruction. In Central America, we still have to construct our economies from the ground up. In Europe, there was a tradition of learning, discipline, science and technology. There is nothing of that sort in Latin America—and there is a long tradition of corruption and political desolation. But that is only the beginning of the problem.

> Here in Latin America, a large part of what goes in through the front door goes out through the back. The flight of capital drained more than half of the foreign credits obtained by Mexico and Venezuela in the last three years and one-third of those obtained by Argentina. In the same period, some $15 billion was invested in real estate or deposited in foreign banks by Central Americans. This is nearly twice the sum that the Kissinger mission proposed for the region—$8 billion in five years. (*New York Times*, February 9, 1984)

To focus the problem, let me concentrate on agricultural research and development, for two reasons. This is a field where it was generally assumed, when President Harry Truman announced his Point Four program, that the United States had an ample store of "know how" that could be exported so as to raise the standard of living of the rural poor. This is also a problem area to which I have devoted many years of study.

Judging from U.S. experience, in agriculture the best vehicle for exporting know-how was an extension service. As I argued in an earlier publication (Whyte, 1975),

> The deficiencies of extension are well documented in an impressive study of *Extension in the Andes*. From the end of World War II until 1970, the U.S. government placed its major agricultural development emphasis on the creation and financing of an extension system modeled after that of the United States. The support of this program for Latin America by the U.S. government was $30 million and the 12 host governments included in this study spent $55 million. This study, financed and published by AID, is especially noteworthy because it documents in great detail the failure of the organizational model and strategy that AID itself supported for so many years: "The lesson...of field investigations is clear: that sort of independent extension operation developed, not always intentionally, by the U.S. advisors and their counterparts is practically useless; extension only succeeds in improving productivity if it offers a profitable new technology in an economic regime that reduces risks, guarantees prices and/or offers credit." (Rice, 1971)

It is now clear why this massive extension effort yielded negligible results. In the first place, the program was based on a number of false assumptions. It was generally believed that when peasants or small farmers failed to adopt improvements recommended by agricultural professionals, it was because they lacked information regarding the improvements, and they were locked into their traditional culture and were resistent to change. This assumption dictated a strategy of improving communication between professionals and small farmers and devising strategies and tactics to overcome this resistance to change. Research has now led us to call these assumptions "the myth of the passive peasant."

The traditional strategy also assumed that the initiation of changes in behavior must go in one direction only, from the professional to the small farmer. It was widely assumed that in his 20 to 40 years or more of experience in farming, the small farmer had learned little about agriculture and that all the solid knowledge was possessed by the professionals.

Research now indicates that an effective development program must be based on the initiation of changes in ideas and behavior in both directions, from the small farmer to the professional as well as from the professional to the small farmer. We have found many cases in which the small farmers have actually adopted the recommendations of extension agents—with disastrous results. Such outcomes cannot be explained simply in terms of the incompetence of the extension agents or problems in communication, though these factors can be involved. The more basic problem is that until recent years people engaged in agricultural extension in developing countries tended to underestimate the enormous variability in soil, water, and climate conditions within a given country and even within certain areas of the same country. It is now well recognized that recommendations for seeds, fertilizer, and cultivation practices effective in parts of the United States cannot simply be exported to developing countries. Furthermore, even in developing countries, there is generally an enormous social and geographical gap between the experiment station and the farms on which the extension agents seek to apply the lessons learned on those stations. Experiment stations are universally located in areas where the soil and climate conditions are relatively favorable, where there is an ample supply of water, and where the required inputs can be readily supplied. The large majority of small farmers who have generally been left behind so far in the advances of the "green revolution" are working under far more adverse physical and economic conditions.

In recent years, agricultural professionals and agricultural policy makers have begun to recognize the need for basic changes in programs and policies. We now find increasing tendencies to conduct agricultural experiments outside the experiment stations under conditions common to the small farms, and the leaders in these changes are also recognizing the importance of incorporating small farmers as active participants in the experimentation and change program. Professionals have come to respect the farming systems evolved over the years through experience and trial and error by the small farmers themselves. They now recognize that small farmers are not likely to be any more resistant to change than the agricultural professionals themselves. The problem therefore is first to understand the farming system actually practiced by the farmers of a given area. As agricultural economist Randolph Barker puts it, "The baseline is not zero. The baseline is the farming system in current use" (personal communication). Unless the agricultural professionals understand the nature of this system, they will not be able to devise ways to improve it. And they will not understand it unless they are willing to learn from the small farmers.

Since the traditional one-to-one relationship between extension agent and small farmer is far too expensive to be applied throughout any developing country, the agricultural research and development strategy now coming into practice involves the professionals working with groups or organizations of small farmers. In other words, a simple person-to-person diffusion strategy is replaced by efforts to work with and through organized groupings of farmers.

There is also a more fundamental structural problem involved in many developing countries. Land ownership is highly concentrated in the hands of small elites. The large mass of farmers have such small plots in such disadvantageous physical locations that no program of technical assistance can provide them with much economic improvement. The need for land reform has long been recognized by political leaders in the U.S. and in developing countries, but government-sponsored reform programs that really effect basic changes in land tenure have been very scarce. Since those large landowners who stand to lose the most from land reform tend to be closely allied with leaders of their governments, it is difficult enough for those governments to carry out basic structural changes even in peacetime. When a government is pressured by the United States to proceed with land reform in the midst of a civil war, it is hard to imagine a successful program emerging.

Our foreign policy makers are inclined to believe that when a government we support is under attack by insurgent forces, beyond military aid, the problem must be solved through helping the government become more democratic. Thus we urge the government to hold elections. Under the obvious influence of our own culture, we are inclined to believe that elections are a necessary means for a government to establish its legitimacy and win the support of its people. When critics point out that elections held in Vietnam or El Salvador during the civil wars have their obvious defects, the policy makers reply that it is unrealistic to expect people who have not experienced democracy to be able to hold a democratically ideal election but that even imperfect elections are to be preferred to communist domination under which there would be no elections at all. Thus it was that our policy makers pushed the South Vietnamese government to hold elections and argued for their value even though the political leaders fighting in the opposition were not candidates, and the most popular candidate who wished to run against government leaders was ruled off the ballot. In fact, election laws ruled off the ballot anyone who had ever been arrested for a political offense by the French colonial government!

In El Salvador, a similar situation has prevailed. The political forces engaged in fighting the government have had no candidates on the ballot, but the U.S. administration has taken great pride in the fact that over 80 percent of the eligible voters went to the polls in 1982, even against threats on their lives by the guerrilla forces. The weight of this argument depends on general ignorance in the United States regarding the nature of election laws and practices in El Salvador as well as in a number of other Latin American countries. I find it extraordinary that none of the political correspondents reporting on the 1982 election in El Salvador mentions the fact that, under the laws of that country, voting is compulsory. Furthermore, to enforce this law, the government requires every citizen of voting age to carry for personal identification a *cedula,* which is stamped in the polling booth at the time the citizen votes. Under present conditions, at any time and at any place, the military or the police can demand that the citizen show evidence that he or she has voted. If the citizen cannot show the voting stamp, he is automatically considered to be out of sympathy with the government, and this makes him a prime target for the right-wing death squads. (A similar condition prevailed for South Vietnamese elections.) Under these conditions, the high voting turnout may simply indicate that the citizens were more fearful of reprisals from the government than from the guerrilla forces. This case illustrates not only the readiness of U.S. government officials to believe in elections under any conditions, but also the tendency of reporters to be satisfied with reporting simply what they observe, rather than investigating the conditions that create the behavior they report. (By the time of the 1984 Salvadoran elections, some of the facts noted here had been reported by journalists—two years late.)

The lessons here are not that the U.S. should terminate our economic and technical assistance to developing countries. The lesson is that enormous amounts of time and money and blood have been expended in past efforts, with meager results. Therefore, it is important for students to study the record so as to learn more about the limitations of exporting economic and social development and also explore the possibilities of new and better ways of helping poorer people around the world.

Implications for Curriculum and Teaching

In order to understand the difference between a political ideology and a national government, students need not only some familiarity with Marxism as a body of political literature but, more importantly, some exposure to the widely varying ways that Marxism has been interpreted in different countries by different factions or political parties. Since it is so widely assumed by political leaders and the general public that any party that calls itself communist or Marxist is dominated by the Soviet Union, it is important for students to learn that this has applied only to certain communist parties at certain times and places. Students should learn that in most places at most times political leaders who call themselves communist, socialist, or Marxist are likely to be more committed to the welfare of their own country (as they define it) than to advancing a worldwide communist movement. Students should consider under what conditions and to what extent the U.S. policy makers can influence foreign Marxist leaders through means other than threats of force or military intervention.

Regarding the relations between private enterprise, both foreign and domestic, and national governments, students should not be allowed to cast the problem simply in terms of debates as to whether private enterprises or government owned and operated enterprises are more efficient. The cultural and social factors that have inhibited the growth of industrial entrepreneurship in developing nations and the natural resistance that people have to domination of their economy by foreign private interests must also be taken into account.

In terms of more basic social theory, students should have to grapple with the relationship between political ideologies and behavior. Our policy makers seem to assume a one-way causation from political ideology to behavior. If people believe in Marxism, they will behave as Russia dictates. This simple-minded view contradicts social research findings regarding the relationship among attitudes, values, and behavior. Here I should not go beyond a general statement since I am not expert in this literature, but let us at least assume that the students should recognize the extent to which political attitudes and ideologies are shaped by personal experience—which means by past behavior which has led either to punishing or rewarding results.

It is also important to recognize that people in other countries do not see the world in simple terms of competition or conflict between political ideologies or between nations espousing opposing ideologies. Lebanon is a prime case in point. Students would not need to understand in detail the nature of religious and ethnic groupings in order to appreciate the folly of treating that troubled nation simply in terms of international power politics.

Regarding the limitations of military assistance and military intervention in developing nations, it is important for students to study the Vietnam War. Not only was this the greatest foreign policy disaster in U.S. history. The nature and causes of that disaster have now been well documented so that the lessons of Vietnam can be learned on the basis of solid research and documentation. Cornell political scientist and Southeast Asia specialist George Kahin has found great student interest in a course he has given on "The Vietnam War." (Sociologist José Moreno reports the same student enthusiasm for such a course at the University of Pittsburgh.) It seems to me especially important to study Vietnam not simply as history but as a means of drawing lessons that may—or may not—apply to current U.S. foreign policy problems.

It might also be useful to direct the attention of students to our CIA interventions in Iran and Guatemala as well as to the repeated involvement of the U.S. Marines in Nicaragua. The CIA interventions were hailed as great successes in the 1950s, and they were attained at relatively little financial cost to the United States at the time. Now, years later, the balance sheet, even in terms of U.S. interests, appears much more negative. Our Guatemalan intervention overthrew a democratically elected government and produced a series of brutal military dictatorships. Our intervention in Iran deposed the leader who was intent on nationalizing foreign oil companies and established the dictatorship of the Shah. When he was finally overthrown by the followers of a religious fanatic, our involvement with the Shah produced a virulent anti-Americanism that led to the holding of Americans hostage in our embassy and may well have been a determining factor in the election of Ronald Reagan over Jimmy Carter.

Obviously, our relations with Nicaragua today cannot be understood without examining the history of U.S. intervention there.

So as not to load the dice, I would encourage teachers and students to look for cases in which U.S. military intervention has appeared to have favorable outcomes both in the future development of the nation where we intervened and also in relations between that nation and the U.S. However, such cases may be hard to find. Grenada might be considered, but, at this writing, the record is too short for any firm conclusion. The Dominican Republic might be considered, since it appears that democratic governments continue to rule in that country, and there seems little evidence of the virulent anti-Yankee sentiment found elsewhere where we have intervened. Still, we may question whether this intervention served the interests of the U.S. or of the Dominican Republic. As a student of that nation has written,

> In the Dominican intervention, the United States found itself drawn into a factional struggle among Dominican military and civilian figures, among whom communist activists played an insignificant role. Washington, obsessed by Castro's Cuba, interpreted all ambiguities as part of an international communist master plan....
>
> Having committed U.S. forces, Johnson quickly raised the stakes. He declared that "what began as a democratic movement was seized, really taken over, and placed in the hands of a band of communist conspirators." Subsequent efforts by CIA and FBI investigators to document the President's claim were fruitless. (Abraham Lowenthal, *Washington Post*, April 10, 1984)

José Moreno (personal communication) points out that a later president and some of the key power figures in his cabinet and in the legislature were active in the rebel government of Colonel Caamaño.

> These men...are not basically different from what they were in 1965. Then and now they are nothing more than middle class liberals who advocate the implementation of a democratic system under a constitutional process.

Beyond the money it took to support several thousand U.S. troops for almost 18 months, Abraham Lowenthal argues that

> the costs of the Dominican intervention should not be forgotten. It dealt a severe blow to the Alliance for Progress, killed off the useful notion of an inter-American peace-keeping force, exposed the OAS as a mere fig leaf, and alienated many Latin Americans. It helped open a domestic "credibility gap," soon to be reinforced by Vietnam, that has complicated U.S. foreign policy ever since. (*Ibid.*)

Regarding the potentialities and limitations of programs to aid developing countries economically, socially, and politically (toward democracy), it is important to develop courses and seminars that would focus on the U.S. and other bilateral and multilateral assistance programs. Students should gain some understanding of the complexity of the aid process. They should also recognize that the knowledge required for the mounting of an effective aid program is necessarily multidisciplinary. Here I can speak particularly from experience in studies of the agricultural research and development process. I learned over the years that it was not good enough to integrate knowledge from the social science disciplines; we social scientists needed also to grasp some of the essential principles in the plant, animal, and soil sciences and in agricultural engineering. Over a period of more than six years, I was involved in discussions and writing projects across this range of disciplines within the Rural Development Committee of Cornell University's Center for International Studies (Whyte and Boynton, ed., 1983). This project brought together from a broad range of disciplines those who had become convinced from experience and research that the traditional answers regarding agricultural research and development did not provide useful guidance to those seeking to administer programs designed to benefit small farmers.

It would also be useful for political scientists or political sociologists to develop a course focusing on an international comparative study of elections. The aim should not be to determine whether it is a good or a bad thing to have elections but rather to explore the conditions under which elections can yield reasonably stable governments that have the support of their people.

Conclusion

Concepts such as culture, social structure, and ideologies will mean little to students when presented in the abstract. They will take on meaning as students are led to relate them to current issues in international relations. This focus will enable students to go beyond media summary reports to gain a framework for better understanding of other nations and of our own. This, in turn, should lead to a better understanding of the dynamics of U.S. international relations. Such a sociological approach to the study of issues in international relations can greatly enrich the college educational experiences.

Works Cited

Rice, E.B. 1971. *Extension in the Andes: An Evaluation of Official U.S. Assistance to Agricultural Extension Services in Central and South America.* Washington, D.C.: U.S. Agency for International Development.

Whyte, William F. 1963. "Culture, Industrial Relations, and Economic Development: The Case of Peru." *Industrial and Labor Relations Review*, 16:4.

———. 1975. *Organizing for Agricultural Development.* New Brunswick, N.J.: Transaction Books.

———, and Danon Boynton, ed. 1983. *Higher-Yielding Human Systems for Agriculture.* Ithaca: Cornell UP.

Whyte, William F., and Robert R. Braun. 1966. "Heroes, Homework and Industrial Growth." *Columbia Journal of World Business*, 1:2.

References for U.S. Intervention Studies

Note: The country studies cited below tend to be highly critical of U.S. policies. For the study of any country, the instructor should try to find one or more references supporting U.S. policies, so as to expose students to a range of conflicting interpretations.

Central America

Diskin, Martin, ed. 1983. *Trouble in Our Back Yard.* New York: Pantheon.

Feinberg, R.E., ed. 1982. *Central America: International Dimensions of the Crisis.* New York: Holmes and Meier.

LaFeber, Walter. 1983. *Inevitable Revolutions: The United States in Central America.* New York: Norton.

Dominican Republic

Gleyeses, Piero. 1978. *The Dominican Crisis: The 1965 Constitutional Revolt and American Intervention.* Baltimore: The Johns Hopkins UP.

Lowenthal, Abraham. 1972. *The Dominican Intervention.* Cambridge: Harvard UP.

Gutierrez, C.M. 1972. *The Dominican Republic: Rebellion and Repression.* New York: Monthly Review Press.

Moreno, J.A. 1971. *Barrios in Arms: Revolution in Santo Domingo.* Pittsburgh: U of Pittsburgh P.

———. 1975. "Intervention and economic penetration: The case of the Dominican Republic." *In Summation* (Michigan State U), 5:1-2 (Fall).

Guatemala

Cook, Blanche Weissen. 1981. *The Declassified Eisenhower.* New York: Doubleday.

Kinzer, Stephen, and Arthur Schlesinger, Jr. 1983. *Bitter Fruit: The Untold Story of the American Complicity in Guatemala.* New York: Doubleday.

Immerman, Richard H. 1982. *The CIA in Guatemala: The Foreign Policy of Intervention.* Austin: U of Texas P.

El Salvador

Montgomery, Tommy Sue. 1982. *Revolution in El Salvador: Origins and Evolution.* Boulder, Colo.: Westview.

Arnson, Cynthia. 1983. *El Salvador: A Revolution Confronts the United States.* Washington, D.C.: Institute for Policy Studies.

Nicaragua

Booth, John. 1983. *The End and the Beginning: The Nicaraguan Revolution.* 2nd ed. Boulder, Colo.: Westview.

Fagen, Richard R. 1983. *The Nicaraguan Revolution.* Washington, D.C.: Institute for Policy Studies.

Walker, Thomas W. 1981. *Nicaragua, the Land of Sandino.* Boulder, Colo.: Westview.

————. 1982. *Nicaragua in Revolution.* New York: Praeger.

————, ed. 1985. *Nicaragua: The First Five Years.* New York: Praeger.

————. 1986. *Nicaragua: Profile of the Land of Sandino.* 2nd. ed. Boulder, Colo.: Westview.

Iran

Rubin, Barry. 1980. *Paved with Good Intentions.* New York: Oxford UP.

Note: For the accounts of U.S.-Iran relations, see Iran sections of the memoirs of three key figures in the Carter administration:

Brzezinski, Zbigniew. 1982. *Power and Principle: Memoirs of a National Security Advisor.* New York: Farrar, Strauss, and Giroux.

Carter, Jimmy. 1982. *Keeping Faith: Memoirs of a President.* New York: Bantam.

Vance, Cyrus. 1983. *Hard Choices: Four Critical Years in Managing American Foreign Policy.* New York: Simon and Schuster.

Vietnam

Halberstam, David. 1969. *The Best and the Brightest.* New York: Random House.

Herring, George C. 1979. *America's Longest War: The U.S. and Vietnam, 1950–1975.* New York: Wiley.

Kahin, George McTurnam. 1986. *Intervention: How America Became Involved in Vietnam.* New York: Knopf.

Porter, Gareth. 1981. *Vietnam: A History in Documents.* New York: New American Library.

Acknowledgement

For helpful criticisms and suggestions on an earlier draft, I am indebted to George Kahin, Walter LaFeber, Dennis Gilbert, and Jose Moreno.

The Deparochialization
of American Sociology

J. Michael Armer

O ver two decades ago, in his 1965 presidential address to the American
Sociological Association, Wilbert Moore stressed the need for a more
global perspective in American sociology. Even earlier, Everett Hughes
(1961) and others had lamented the "ethnocentricity" of American sociology.
It was Moore, however, who brought the parochial character of American
sociology briefly to the center of sociological attention. He argued that much
of substantive sociology by American scholars was concerned primarily with
American phenomena and demonstrated little apparent awareness of either
the boundedness of evidence and interpretations nor the impact of foreign
influences on these phenomena. From the structural-functionalist perspective
prevailing at that time, he called attention to the importance of viewing the
world as an interdependent system of interacting structures and processes.

Although there has been a shift in theoretical paradigms toward more social
conflict and political-economy perspectives during the ensuing decades,
American sociology has remained largely culture-bound and non-comparative.
There remains the "myth extant that 'society' begins at Maine and ends at Miami
Beach, begins again in New York and ends in California" (Horowitz 1964:32).

The evidence of this continuing parochialism is present in both teaching and
research within the discipline. With respect to teaching, the proportion of
sociology departments that include regular offerings of comparative, world--
system or global sociology courses in their curriculum, much less courses on
sociology of the Third World or of particular regions or countries, is small. A
phone survey of 25 randomly selected departments from the 1986 *Guide to
Graduate Departments of Sociology* turned up six (24%) with two or more such
courses included in their total undergraduate curricula. A survey mailed by the
ASA Committee on World Sociology in 1981–82 to chairpersons of all 869

J. Michael Armer is Professor of Sociology at Florida State University.

sociology departments listed in the 1981 *Directory of Departments of Sociology* (ASA, 1982) requesting names of faculty with international or comparative interests and/or who taught courses with any comparative or international content yielded responses from only 86 departments (10%). Follow-up correspondence with faculty names provided by the chairs generated 213 syllabi (an average of one course with international content out of every four departments contacted). These figures may well underrepresent the actual proportion of curricula and courses that incorporate cross-cultural content and attention to international forces or global processes, but they lend credence to the concern that American training in sociology remains ethnocentric.

Of course, as noted by the President's Commission on Foreign Language and International Studies (1979), American education in general provides students little exposure to the world beyond U.S. boundaries. The social sciences are no exception. But compared to anthropology, political science, economics, history, and geography, there is reason to believe the waggish assertion that sociology is "the queen of the provincial sciences."

The evidence with respect to research reaffirms this judgment. Gareau (1986:49–50) summarizes the results of ten studies that list the most important scholars based on citations in American sociology journals and textbooks. Of the total 222 modern scholars (i.e., excluding "the old masters such as Durkheim") listed in the samples, the nationality of all but two was American. He concludes that these findings "smack of nationalism/ethnocentrism" in American sociological research.

My more recent review of 84 research articles in the 1985 volumes of the *American Sociological Review* and the *American Journal of Sociology* shows only one third (34.5%) contain evidence from outside the United States or reference to international influences (Armer, 1987). This percentage has increased little from research published in the 1965 volumes of the same two leading journals. In comparison, almost two thirds (65.8%) of research articles in the two major British sociology journals (*Sociology* and the *British Journal of Sociology*) include international content and/or attention to foreign or global influences.

Explanations and Prospects

There are numerous possible explanations for the parochialism of American sociology ranging from geographical isolation of the nation to publication pressure within the profession. The most systematic analysis by Hollander (1981:27) suggests that the source of this preoccupation with American society "include the traditional, idealistic American exceptionalism (i.e., that in this society lofty ideals could and should be realized and so forth); the practical, problem-solving, ameliorative bent; the concern with scientific precision and methodology; and since the 1960s the intensification and institutionalization of social criticism." In addition, one might add the influence of geographical and geopolitical factors of size and physical insularity, natural resource sufficiency, cultural homogeneity, and last but not least, political, economic, and military power.

> Protected by geography that has provided us with oceans to the East and West and blessed with abundant resources in between, Americans have been conditioned to define their identity in terms of our separation from the rest of the world. As a nation of immigrants believing in America as a land of new opportunity, a place to escape from tyranny, poverty, and oppression, it is not surprising that we have sought to leave the rest of the world behind us. (Wong 1985:104)

From a political-economy perspective, Gareau (1986) interprets the parochial emphasis as the result of the dominant role of the United States in the contemporary world system. As the most powerful and wealthy post-war nation, the eyes of the world, including those of American sociologists, were focused on American society. American sociology (and other fields of study) had tremendous influence throughout the world, and American theoretical perspectives and methods of sociological practice were paramount. However, in more recent decades, he suggests, divergent national sociologies have emerged and have begun to replace or challenge the imported American sociological perspectives. A "multinational version" of sociology is emerging.

Changes in the content and practice of sociology outside the United States have been noted and described by other authors as well (e.g., Mohan and Martindale 1975; Hiller 1979). Comparative and historical case studies by foreign sociologists often generate data which do not fit patterns and processes predicted by conventional theories of American origin. Critical sociology, dependencia theories, socialist views, and other alternative perspectives have developed to interpret the new evidence abroad while American sociology apparently has remained substantially provincial. In other words, international sociology *has* become less Americanized even if American sociology has not yet become internationalized.

There are reasons to believe, however, that greater internationalization of American sociology is inevitable. As Hiller notes, the differentiation of national sociologies from American sociology itself should contribute to the deparochializing process by calling attention to divergencies in sociological patterns and processes in different sociohistorical settings (Hiller 1979). Also, the emergence of over 100 independent nations into the world political system and the economic development or underdevelopment experience of these nations have focused attention increasingly on imperialist or dependency relations between nations rather than on internal evolutionary or systemic processes. Finally, the growth of global communication capabilities, international data sources, and international travel opportunities in recent decades has made foreign events and international linkages more visible and accessible to all. It is reasonable to expect that these various world developments and technological advances will expand international horizons of sociologists and promote greater research and teaching attention outside U.S. boundaries in the future.

Indeed, there already is some evidence that American scholars are abandoning preconceptions based on experience and evidence from the United States alone and beginning to work toward more universalistic and global conceptions of social process and human behavior. The spread of dependency and world-system perspectives among younger generations of American sociologists, expanding interest in political-economy analyses, and increasing numbers of comparative historical studies, even if not yet strongly reflected in the discipline's two major journals, signal a nascent reduction in culture-boundedness of American sociology. Indeed, the focus on comparative sociology for the theme of the 1987 annual meetings of the American Sociological Association is further evidence of increasing attention to international data and influences. It is as if the ASA has finally acknowledged the wisdom of Horowitz' early advocacy of comparative studies and claim that "You can no longer settle any major sociological problem within the boundaries of the United States" (1964:32).

Much of the sociological impetus for this increasing attention to world interdependence and global processes stems from the work of scholars in less developed regions of the world seeking to understand developments in their own societies. Underlying this new interpretive framework of interdependence and globalism is the theme that sociologists must begin "to explain the structure and development of the capitalist system as a whole and to account for its simultaneous generation of underdevelopment in some of its parts and of economic development in others" (Frank 1966:17). Indeed, studies by American sociologists of social institutions, structures and behavior patterns in Third World societies now frequently stress the historical influence of economic, political, and social relations with external metropolitan countries and transnational corporations. Often overlooked by these scholars and the discipline as a whole is the logical extension of world system and interdependency arguments to the analysis of characteristics and developments within the United States itself: understanding American society (and other advanced societies) requires attention to international influences and external relations just as does understanding of less developed societies. Sociologists must pass on to their students a recognition that life in American society cannot be explained without greater attention to global processes and international developments. American economic trends, political processes, class structure, urban developments, demographic patterns, family life, ethnic relations, health, environmental protection are all intimately affected by external forces and interests.

In short, sociologists can no longer hope to understand American society, much less the world at large, by focusing exclusively on the U.S. It is not simply a case of being interested in teaching our students how things differ in other societies but of comprehending how things operate in our own society that necessitates attention to the world around us.

What Sociology Students Need to Know

The implications of this new reality for sociology teaching is important to consider. What is it that our students must learn? First, our students have to gain awareness that human society is not static. It has evolved historically into larger, complex, industrial, scientific communities that bear little resemblance to life in earlier centuries. Unfortunately, most of our introductory sociology textbooks are largely ahistorical and limit themselves to anthropological examples about exotic cultures, rather than solid data on the past. An effort must be made to familiarize our students with history—that of the United States, that of other developed countries, particularly European countries whose fate has been intertwined with that of the United States, and that of underdeveloped countries whose history we have so often determined.

Second, we need to make more salient to our students that human society has various forms and that none of them, including our own, is inherently superior nor destined to be the model toward which other societies change or even aspire. Of course, at one level of awareness, these truisms are "known" to all students, but at a deeper level, they are often ignored when interpreting world events, interacting with foreigners, or understanding societal structures or processes. Students often assume that civilized people in other areas of the world see things, hold values, and live lives pretty much the same as we do. This naive ethnocentric assumption of common social conditions and human experiences paralleling our own masks the question of what in fact is or is not shared and leads to simplistic analyses of social issues.

Students need to learn that American society is not typical. Indeed, in many respects the U.S. political system, economic structure, history, laws and legal procedures, geography, population composition, consumption patterns, and so forth are highly atypical and hardly a reasonable basis for world-wide generalization. Just as students at a younger age come to recognize that their own families, neighborhoods, or communities are not typical of families, neighborhoods, or communities elsewhere, they need exposure to other cultures and societies to appreciate the rich diversity at this level of social order. To the extent that American sociology fails to expose students to historical and foreign materials, it fails to educate them in a general science of human behavior and instead teaches twentieth-century American human behavior. As such, it neglects a major concern of sociological inquiry, the identification and explanation of universal patterns and processes of social interaction and, where not universal, the spatial-temporal limits of such patterns and processes. Information from other historical periods, sociocultural settings and political-economic contexts extends the range and variety of social phenomena beyond that found within a single society. Foreign area and comparative data thus provide interpretive insight and empirical evaluation of propositions regarding these phenomena and are essential to the discipline's claims of scientific status.

Third, our students need to develop an appreciation of the interdependence among nations of the world and the bald fact that the social, political, and economic order of advanced industrial societies like the United States are directly affected in profound ways by policies and events in other societies. Because debt-ridden Latin American countries cut U.S. imports by almost 50 percent between 1981 and 1983, over 400,000 Americans became jobless (Hamilton 1986, p.4). The taking of American hostages by foreign groups in the Middle East has served to undermine the reputation and effectiveness of two U.S. administrations. Admitting Spain into the European Common Market threatens the livelihood of thousands of American wheat farmers. In short, in an increasingly interdependent world, the national security and economic interests of nations rest in part on knowledge about and successful dealings with people, governments, and organizations in other nations. The advantages, costs, and challenges of such interdependence and interpenetration need to be understood by American students. Government, business, science, and other segments of society will need an ever-expanding flow of information and expertise about other nations and peoples in order to cooperate and promote our interdependent interests. The cultural boundedness of American sociological instruction limits the preparation of our students to live in this increasingly interdependent world and to contribute to these national and international interests.

Fourth, our students need to become aware of the importance of transnational systems and forces for an understanding of social phenomena in their own society. The growth of world system theory as an analytic paradigm in recent decades has made many sociologists more aware of the extent to which international realities shape social relations and processes within nations. In other words, sociologists need to incorporate international data or global analyses in our teaching because social relations and processes at an *inter-*

national level help explain *intra*national social structures and social change over time.

As an example, Portes and Walton (1981) describe how the social class structure of the United States has been transformed by participation in a global economy based increasingly on international concentration and centralization of capital, primarily via the activities of multinational corporations. "Exigencies of the world economy are coming to have a greater bearing on the intranational organization of social classes than uniquely indigenous conditions" (p.141). As the movement of capital and people has become easier through the development of communication and transportation facilities, there has been an increasing shift of capital investment to the periphery (cf., Bluestone and Harrison 1982). Internationalizing production through setting up production plants abroad and breaking up the production process has led to diminishing certain kinds of labor (e.g., blue collar, manual) and expanding other kinds (e.g., white collar, service). In short, sociological knowledge of the world at large is often necessary to make sense out of social institutions and processes at home. Domestic sociology can be better understood from the standpoint of an interdependent, international political economy. (For other illustrations, see Feagin's 1985 study of the changing character of an American city or Wirt and Harmann's 1986 comparative analysis of educational systems.)

Related to interdependence among nation-states but even more important is the growth and international impact of multinational corporations. These semi-autonomous entities form a world-wide web of economic transactions that greatly influence the economy and polity of virtually every society of the world. The rate of employment, class structure, goods and services available, trade balances, and other factors are all directly affected by decisions by multinational corporations over which state and local governments have little control.

Thus, comparative research and international data are increasingly important in sociology teaching not as exotica or as "how they do it differently" in some other place, and not just as aspects of comparative sociology, social change, or national development, but rather as the study of interdependent global processes that affect the daily lives of people in the United States as well as elsewhere.

Finally, our students need to gain a greater sense of the world as a global community rather than as a collection of nations. Weston (1979–80:74) calls this "world order education" which refocuses student vision from an inter-nation state perspective to a global or planetary perspective. In particular, global problems facing humanity often are largely ignored or greatly diminished from a purely national or international perspective. Our competitively premised and operating nation-state system dominates attention and in many ways contributes to the arms race, nuclear proliferation, exploding populations, pollution, dwindling resources, spreading authoritarianism, social injustice, and deprivation which increasingly threaten the existence and quality of life. As a result, new planetary arrangements and mechanisms are needed and are beginning to emerge. Under these circumstances, Weston argues, enlightened self-interest requires that societies begin to educate people about both the global forces and problems mentioned above and the burdens and benefits of global change. Holistic in perspective, informed by humanistic values, oriented to the future, and committed to fundamental change, world-order education is the optimal response to this challenge, argues Weston, who provides guidelines and references for such education (Weston 1979–80: 75–95; also Parker 1984).

Course of Action

The question is how to achieve these objectives in designing our sociology courses. There are two basic ways to approach the lack of international content in undergraduate sociology curricula. The first is to introduce new courses in comparative sociology, national development, and/or global sociology in the sequence of introductory-level or required courses. At the upper-division (junior and senior) level, new courses in specialty areas such as comparative family, political economy of education, and international stratification can be added. One problem with this approach is that academic departments may not have sufficient faculty or students to offer such courses on a regular basis. The second and perhaps more feasible approach is to incorporate more international and comparative content into existing standard introductory-level courses (especially Introductory Sociology, Social Problems). Indeed, there is a growing belief that the second approach needs greater emphasis, i.e., that an international perspective needs to be developed throughout the curriculum in most, if not all, courses offered. This view is consistent with the remarks made by Groennings to the American Council on Education:

> The core problem now being addressed is that most students have little exposure to international perspectives because these perspectives are not well integrated in the undergraduate curriculum.... The prevailing thought now is that the international dimension should not be a smattering of courses at the periphery of the supermarket curriculum but part of a basic shared educational experience—not only for experts but for all undergraduates. (quoted in Doeringer 1985:128)

More specifically at the immediate level of standard sociology courses, how can we incorporate international content and perspectives? There are several possible options depending on instructors' expertise and interests. First, one or more sections of the course can be devoted to comparative data from other societies and/or to international influences on U.S. patterns as well as U.S. influence on foreign societies. For example, an introductory sociology course might contain an initial section covering basic concepts of social structure and institutionalization followed by a historical/comparative section dealing with evolution from simple and isolated societies to complex societies connected into world-wide economic, political, and cultural systems. (For illustrations of this and subsequent course suggestions, see Armer, *Syllabi and Resources for Internationalizing Courses in Sociology,* 1983.)

A second option is to bring international data and influences to bear throughout the course as different topics (economy, urbanization, education, marriage and family, etc.) are covered. The more international content there is and the more focused the attention on a common set of societies throughout the course, the more it may approximate comparative sociology (or a comparative course in a particular specialty area).

A third option is for sections of a topical course to be devoted to international issues. For example, a social problems course could be divided into four or five problem areas, some of which would be international or global in focus, such as world depletion of resources and environment decay, global poverty and hunger, and inequality between nations.

Fourth, the course topic can be progressively considered at different levels of analysis from the individual level to the community, institutional or societal, and eventually international or global levels. One can imagine a sociology of education course dealing progressively with individual, classroom, school, community, national, comparative, and international issues, or a social psychology course dealing with individual behavior, social interaction, group dynamics, collective behavior, comparative psychology, and international movements and ideologies.

In addition to incorporating international content and perspectives into existing courses, entire courses can be structured around international themes or global concerns. For example, at the University of North Carolina, a course entitled "Human Societies" is one of three introductory courses from which students choose as a prerequisite to other sociology courses. (The other two are "Society and the Individual" at the micro-level and "American Society" at the meso-level.) The course is divided into sections on ecological-evolutionary theory, development from prehistory to industrialization, life in contemporary (capitalist, socialist and Third World) societies, and the future.

Another model would be to focus a whole course on case studies and comparisons of contemporary societies. For example, an introductory sociology course could focus on "contemporary societies" and compare social structures and processes in major world powers such as China, Japan, Russia, the United

Kingdom, and the United States, or in major blocks such as Western, Eastern, and Third World nations.

A third model of organizing an entire course around international or global concerns is to join other faculty with specializations in other fields or disciplines and offer a team-taught course on global problems. For example, at the University of West Florida, an interdisciplinary course was launched in 1983 entitled "Humanity and Global Resources: Education for Tomorrow." Edmisten (1985–86:11) reports that "fifteen professors, representing twelve departments and three colleges, addressed the global issues of food, population, energy, environment, arms and security, cultural differences, and world trade."

Finally, the entire course might involve analysis of relevant topics from the perspective of global or transnational forces. An illustration of this approach would be a course that treats social problems from a global perspective (e.g., world poverty, population problems, multinational corporations). As I have suggested, the growth in recent decades of world-systems theory as an analytic paradigm has made many sociologists more aware of the importance of transnational systems and forces in understanding social phenomena *within* nations. They have begun to see how social relations and processes at an international level help explain internal social problems and processes. Sociological knowledge of the world at large is often necessary to make sense of the American social institutions and social changes that are covered in introductory sociology courses.

Conclusion

As we have seen, there are a variety of reasons for increasing the international content in sociology courses and a variety of strategies for doing so. The choice is guided by the academic level and the substantive focus of the course as well as the time, experience, and resources available to an instructor. Obviously, developing course material of a global nature is only one way of giving students "greater insight into foreign societies and international issues," as called for in the report by the President's Commission (1979:16). In addition, the Commission advocates a requirement of two or three courses in international studies as well as a foreign language requirement, a "domestic junior year abroad" at major international studies centers for students at institutions with limited resources in this area, greater opportunities for faculty to acquire or strengthen their international skills, and expanded institutional commitment to international studies. Though not emphasized in the report, universities can also promote global awareness by making provisions for a large international student population, expanding study abroad programs, and fostering a worldwide exchange of scholars.

The National Assembly on Foreign Language and International Studies (1980) noted that a strong commitment by the university administration is central to any efforts to develop and expand the international dimension of undergraduate education along these lines. Chief academic officers and governing boards must make significant institutional decisions regarding organizational structures, budget allocations, and faculty assignments. Sociologists have a role to play here as well. In addition to taking initiatives with respect to their own courses and curricula, they can help encourage the administrative involvement and institutional commitment necessary for successful internationalization of university education.

For too long American sociology has remained inwardly focused. While the world has grown increasingly complex and interdependent, while communications have become increasingly rapid, while international travel has become as much a part of life as holiday visits to relatives was in earlier generations, the internationalization of sociology has lagged behind. In our research and teaching, we are only beginning to recognize that what happens in one part of the world has effects, often immediately, on other parts of the world. Third World nations are not being recreated in the image of the West but are asserting their own versions of agrarian and/or industrial society. As the world becomes technologically advanced and grows interdependent, it begins to share a global awareness that our major problems are universal and require international cooperation for resolution. These tendencies are becoming increasingly apparent to sociologists and to others in society, and they portend the increasing internationalization of American undergraduate education. The discipline and society will both benefit from the inevitable deparochialization of American sociology.

References

American Sociological Association. 1982. *Directory of Departments of Sociology 1981.* Washington, D.C.: ASA.

Armer, J. Michael, ed. 1983. *Syllabi and Resources for Internationalizing Courses in Sociology.* Washington, D.C.: ASA Teaching Resources Center.

———. 1987. "Provincialism and Internationalism in Contemporary American Sociology." *International Sociology* 2 (September): 315–324.

Bluestone, Barry, and Bennett Harrison. 1982. *The Deindustrialization of America.* New York: Basic Books.

Doeringer, Franklin M. 1985. "International Perspectives on Campus." *Liberal Education* 71(Summer):127–133.

Edmisten, Patricia Taylor. 1985–86. "Bringing Global Education to the University and the Community." *Journal of Environmental Education* 17(Winter):11–13.

Feagin, Joe R. 1985. "The Global Context of Metropolitan Growth: Houston and Oil." *American Journal of Sociology* 90(6):1204–1230.

Frank, Andre Gunder. 1966. "The Development of Underdevelopment." *Monthly Review* 18(4):17–31.

Gareau, Frederick H. 1985. "The Multinational Version of Social Science with Emphasis upon the Discipline of Sociology." *Current Sociology* 33(3):1–165.

Hamilton, John Maxwell. 1986. *Main Street America and the Third World.* Cabin John, Md.: Seven Locks Press.

Hiller, Harry T. 1979. "Universality of Science and the Question of National Sociologies." *American Sociologist* 14(3):124–135.

Hollander, Paul. 1981. "Comparative Sociology in the United States and Why There Is so Little of it." *Current Perspectives in Social Theory* 2:21–29.

Horowitz, Irving Lewis, ed. 1964. *The New Sociology: Essays in Social Science and Social Theory in Honor of C. Wright Mills.* New York: Oxford UP.

Hughes, Everett 1961. "Ethnocentric sociology." *Social Forces* 40(1):1–4.

Mohan, Raj P., and Don Martindale, ed. 1975. *Handbook of Contemporary Developments in World Sociology.* Westport, Conn.: Greenwood Press.

Moore, Wilbert E. 1966. "Global Sociology: The World as a Singular System." *American Journal of Sociology* 71(5):475–482.

National Assembly on Foreign Language and International Studies. 1980. *Toward Education with a Global Perspective.* Washington, D.C.: Association of American Colleges.

Parker, Walter. 1984. "Globalizing the Social Studies Curriculum." *Educational Leadership* 42(October):92.

Portes, Alejandro, and John Walton. *Labor, Class and the International System.* New York: Academic Press.

President's Commission on Foreign Language and International Studies. 1979. *Strength through Wisdom: A Critique of U.S. Capability.* Washington, D.C.: GPO.

Weston, Burns H. 1979-80. "Contending with a Planet in Peril and Change: An Optimal Educational Response." *Alternatives* 5:59–95.

Wirt, Frederick M., and Grant Harmann. 1986. *Education, Recession and the World Village.* Philadelphia: The Falmer Press.

Wong, Frank F. 1985. "Pilgrims and Immigrants: Liberal Learning in Today's World." *Liberal Education* 71(2):97–108.

PSYCHOLOGY

Like sociology, psychology is international in its roots and became, in the United States, overwhelmingly American in its focus. Increasing attention to the discipline's international dimensions is being stimulated by concern that psychology must be more international as a science and in its applications.

In contributing to the NCFLIS project, the American Psychological Association commissioned the following essays by Michael Cole, Harry Triandis and Richard Brislin, Roger Russell, Virginia Staudt Sexton and Henryk Misiak, and Judith Torney-Purta. Urging that their discipline become more internationally oriented, the authors focus especially on cross-cultural study within developmental and social psychology. Sexton and Misiak contend that non-North-American psychology can be incorporated into almost every course in the psychology curriculum.

It is the complex cultural variable, especially in its impact on perception, cognition, motivation, and interpersonal behavior, that causes other disciplines, e.g., political science and sociology, to be keenly interested in the international dimension of psychology; their concern with cultural explanations of behavior links all these disciplines to anthropology. Since the rise of Nazism, there has been interdisciplinary attention to the social psychology of international relations.

The World beyond Our Borders: What Might Our Students Need to Know?

Michael Cole

I have been asked by American Psychological Association to discuss the relevance of the rest of the world to American psychology students. This assignment grows out of a new wave of concern about America's place in the world. Economic and political events of the 1970s have increased the conviction in many circles that American students are not obtaining a realistic picture of their place in the world from their college education.

There is no doubt that there is widespread ignorance among our citizenry of world events that are vital to their interests (Barrows, Klein, and Clark, 1981). The question is, what do we do about it? More particularly, what should we be doing in our classrooms to ensure that our students enter the adult world with an increased appreciation for the world beyond our borders? This is not an easy question for American psychologists to answer. Nor are we all likely to answer in the same way. The real question, it seems to me, is, "Why bother?" What, in particular, should we be teaching as psychologists? I will address this problem in three parts. First, I will survey three areas of interest to psychologists in which some knowledge about international matters is already represented in our curricula. Next, I will recount the effect on my work of my coming into serious contact with psychology and life in other countries. Finally, I will describe a few of the techniques that I use to pass on some of my own experience to my students.

The History of Psychology

An obvious place to start is to examine how we teach the origins of our ideas about psychology. Virtually all psychology curricula contain some material on the historical development of the discipline. Even if no special course on history

Michael Cole is Professor of Psychology and Communication and Director of the Laboratory of Comparative Human Cognition at the University of California, San Diego.

is taught, many textbooks begin with a brief history of the ideas and people considered most germane to understanding the current state of the field.

During my undergraduate career, I was introduced to the ideas of prominent scholars from many different countries. I read about Galton, an originator of the correlation coefficient and of the study of individual differences; Binet and Simon, who gave us intelligence testing in its nearly modern form; Kohler, Koffka, and other German psychologists who said provocative things about problem solving and perception; and Pavlov, who gave us a scientific model of learning. I was also introduced to philosophers like Locke, Rousseau, Mill, James, and Dewey as important contributors to contemporary (1950s) psychology. Freud made his appearance in the personality course. What relationship his ideas had to any of the other courses in the curriculum was not made clear, but it was clear that most of my teachers considered Freud unscientific and therefore of dubious character.

Overall, this historical background did not seem especially relevant to my training as a psychologist, although I found the discussions interesting. It was far more important that I master the right methods for obtaining appropriate data and make myself familiar with an area of research within which to ply my skills. I was too preoccupied with mastering the techniques of constructing Markov models to spend much time on the history and metatheory they represented. Until after I obtained my Ph.D., my main impression was that the history of psychology was best understood by examining the contemporary achievements of its most developed branch, American experimental psychology. From this perspective, history was the story of the past, an antiquarian hobby in which dusty artifacts gave testimony to the errors of our forebears.

Contemporary Theories

Another obvious area in which international influences make themselves felt in the undergraduate curriculum is that of psychological theory. It is my impression that the shifting role of the United States in world affairs is roughly paralleled by a shifting relationship between basic approaches to theorizing in different countries. In the mid-1950s the supremacy of American technology set the target all industrialized countries attempted to achieve. Our modes of psychological theorizing and the methods they generated were studied and emulated in many different countries. To a large extent this is still the case. Countries as different from us as the Soviet Union and Japan, each with long intellectual traditions in psychology, have undergraduate psychology curricula that bear a startling resemblance to our own. American textbooks have been widely translated and used as the basis for undergraduate education, and American research topics are carefully followed.

For a number of years, American dominance in prestige and numbers of psychologists (APA is by far the largest national association) meant that theoretical discourse was likely to be very much on American terms. It did not appear that we had very much to learn from the rest of the world.

Things have changed. While APA membership is still large in numbers and English still dominates international conferences, the enormous asymmetry in numbers and prestige that American psychology enjoyed in the 1950s has been substantially reduced, although the changes have not been uniform. As to relative numbers of psychologists, the enormous efforts of other industrialized countries to train research psychologists have clearly born fruit. Within foreign universities psychology faculties have been created with substantial support for basic research. Large research establishments exist within the military and in industrial firms. When American specialists go to international meetings, their counterparts are designing human-machine systems for the exploration of space and for efficient production of human resources. The mutual relevance is obvious, but American technological preeminence has given us less to learn, or so it has seemed until recently.

Americans have also discovered lines of research originating in other countries that were poorly attended to in the decades immediately following World War II. The work of Jean Piaget, which was by no means unknown to American students of the 1930s, became a dominating influence in developmental psychology of the 1970s. The work of the German ethologists, which at first appeared no more significant than a parlor trick (the image that comes to mind is a bearded Lorenz followed by ducklings), began working its way into the superstructure of associationistic learning theories. In the area of clinical psychology, the methodology of which has always been suspect in university circles, ideas from Eastern philosophy and a variety of interactional theories from Europe began to be debated. At the very time when foreign ideas in psychology seemed least relevant on technical grounds, some of the basic ideas of psychologists in other countries were beginning to change the assumptions of many American psychologists.

Two interwoven threads are discernible in the tangled tapestry of these events. First, the rest of the world has joined the United States in making psychological sciences an integrated part of the apparatus for running an industrialized state. This integration has meant acceptance of the basic analytic devices for making sense of, and evaluating, human behavior. These methods can be, more or less, standardized. They contribute to production and the creation of new social institutions to embody the proper conditions for efficient running of the system. A number of societies are now faced with common difficulties. These difficulties arise from the fact that all engage in similar sorts of industrial production and compete within a single economic arena. And there is now a large international community of psychologists whose work is mutually relevant because their societies share these concerns.

Second, we have seen the United States join the rest of the world in acknowledging the limitations of assuming that people can be understood entirely according to the kind of scientific laws that permit us to exploit the physical world. This acknowledgement, although uneven, has taken several forms.

Some claim that the limitations of physical models are a technical problem and that, with sufficiently powerful computers, we will someday be able to represent basic psychological processes in physical systems in all their essential features. Others deny even the possibility of reducing living matter to mechanical control. Whether one accepts the mechanistic goal for psychology or not, work in artificial intelligence and human-machine systems requires, at the very least, that we acknowledge the systemic nature of human psychological processes. The current work in cognitive systems renders relevant the work of Europeans whose ideas Americans found impenetrable two decades ago: Piaget, Lacan, Vygotsky, Luria, Lewis, Cassirer, and many others.

Americans are also becoming aware of the human costs associated with too much success at organizing society to exploit modern technology efficiently: school failure on a large scale, creation of social classes separated by huge information gaps, worker alienation, changes in family socialization patterns, and isolation of the handicapped and aged. In dealing with these common affronts to the sufficiency of existing psychological theorizing, psychologists from different countries have often found common cause. This is true, for example, of Japanese, Russian, Chinese, and American psychologists whose task it is to figure out the human consequences engendered by industrial success.

Contemporary Variability

Thus far, my discussion of the relevance of international information to undergraduates has been very much discipline bound: Who were the important thinkers; what theories can help us solve specific common problems? There is a second way, however, in which we can think of an internationally based understanding being important to psychologists, and that is by asking how people in other countries experience life as individual people living in communities. How do they react to their life circumstances? How do their experiences shape their understanding of human nature?

These are by no means new questions, but they took on a special character following World War II because of the wide acceptance of the idea that psychologists could be useful in solving important social problems, of which education and national economic development were two primary examples. A worldwide commitment to industrialization meant worldwide commitment to modern education. Education is expensive. Psychologists, it was hoped, would find ways to reduce the cost and to help speed social and economic change, not only by increasing educational productivity, but also by finding a great variety of ways to bring broad masses of people into the modern world.

As a consequence of these beliefs, and the policy directives that followed, an unprecedented number of trained psychologists found themselves working in very distant parts of the world, where they encountered religions and political systems that strained their ideas of how people could organize their lives together. They encountered individuals and whole societies that operated with virtually no literacy, schooling, or industrialized work patterns. These psychologists worked not only in schools, but also for mining firms, ministries of communications, and international agencies.

It might be thought that this commitment to the utility of psychology abroad would result among Americans in a great flowering of interest in the study of psychology among diverse peoples. In fact a large number of research studies have been carried out in a variety of countries by American psychologists interested in figuring out how cultural variations produce psychological variations. Many monographs have been written summarizing this work, and specialized journals have been formed to handle the volume of new data.

However, it is not clear that psychological research making systematic use of cultural variation has penetrated very far into the undergraduate curriculum. A sampling of introductory texts yields some well-known studies: infant motor development in Africa, day care in Israel, infant temperament in Japan, theoretical thinking in Uzbekistan. But no overall understanding informs the examples. They are selected to illustrate particular points derived from a quite restrictive scientific tradition. The countries, activities, and processes they sample change from one example to the next because there is no overall framework, with an appropriate methodology, to guide this form of inquiry.

Cross-cultural psychology is very often treated as a slightly miscreant stepchild or perhaps as just a specialized method by the mainstream of psychology. Like clinical psychology, its methods are suspect. The basic idea is simple enough: The fact of variation can be used to find out which parts of human experience are universal and which are subject to environmental control. The difficulty for psychologists arises from the inability to create the clean, analytical situation that the basic idea seems to promise and require. Because the proper conditions of psychological observation could not be demonstrated at the turn of the century, the conclusions of the psychologists who went to the Torres Straits near New Guinea to get comparative data on visual acuity were vulnerable, and Titchener (1916) was unable to accept them. So, too, contemporary psychological methodologists mistrust research carried out in varied cultural circumstances. Too often such research violates the most fundamental rules of the experimental method without offering compensating safeguards to constrain theoretical claims (see Cole and Means, 1981).

As a consequence, cross-cultural work is ghettoized; its results only rarely inform the dominant activities through which psychologists strive for a general theory. I do not intend here to debate the actual merits of cross-cultural research. It is enough to say that, for whatever reasons, knowledge of the basic psychological characteristics of people living in other parts of the world makes up a very small part of our undergraduate curricula. We can draw on anthropological accounts that are often accepted as reasonable descriptions. But we have to keep in mind that these descriptions are themselves theory-bound and often the source of controversy (for example, note the current controversy over Margaret Mead's early work in Samoa). We can draw on cross-cultural research, but it is easily disregarded on methodological grounds. Faced with these unsatisfactory alternatives, teachers of psychology most often are left to depend on their own backgrounds.

A Midpoint Summary

Up to this point, I have presented what I believe to be an oversimplified, but generally accurate, picture of the way in which information about people living in other parts of the world enters the undergraduate psychology curriculum. I have suggested three ways in which such information might be relevant—in history, comparative theoretical approaches, and cross-cultural research. Using my own education and an informal survey of contemporary textbooks at the freshman and sophomore levels as my database, I have concluded that, by and large, American psychology does not make a great deal of use of historical or comparative information to go about its chores. Moreover, I have argued that these characteristics of our science are not perceived as a problem because psychology has fit relatively well into the social orders of which it is a part: the absence of such information is only seen as a problem on rare occasions by a few people.

Efforts to extend current practices can be criticized for various weaknesses. But, realistically, it is difficult to see the situation changing much until events force even more attention to be paid to the international sphere as a source of important social knowledge.

Until that time comes, the best evidence we have of the potential usefulness of information from abroad to the education of American psychologists comes from the results of the work done in those relatively few cases where Americans have been deeply involved in other countries. Here I will draw on my own experiences, both as a source of evidence of improvement of my own research and as a means of making such improvements available to my students.

Sputnik

Halfway through my undergraduate education, the USSR launched the first Sputnik satellite, an event that galvanized public attention. Except for reading the headlines, I did not pay much attention to Sputnik. I was not planning to be an engineer or an astronaut, and no one seemed to be throwing money in my direction, so it was not clear how I was to be affected. Eventually, Sputnik profoundly changed the course of my career.

One pressure generated by Sputnik was for language training, especially Russian language training. When I entered graduate school at Indiana University in 1962, that institution required that doctoral candidates pass two language examinations. I was flabbergasted. I could read French passably well, although I knew nothing about French work in psychology. The idea of learning a second foreign language when my whole education had taught me that foreign thinkers were of purely historical interest struck me as a clear indication of Indiana's isolation from reality. I wanted to learn Fortran.

A mimeographed wall poster offered an intriguing solution—"How would you like to study in Russia?" Now *there* was an interesting idea; Pavlov, politics, and adventure. Moreover, all I had to do to follow up the idea was to visit the Indiana University history department, the location of the academic head-quarters of the Soviet–American academic exchange program. Many things fell into place. The exchange was short on scholars in several disciplines, and psychology was one of them, and the people in charge were interested in me. But I would have to learn Russian and something about the USSR. Just to make the possibility really attractive, a fellowship was offered that would compensate me for the extra work.

At first I thought of this educational strategy purely in opportunistic terms. I had been going to school for about 18 years without respite. I had never been out of the country. In order to be supported to live in another country for a year, I "had" to take the language courses but I got paid well in the bargain. I also had an opportunity to learn a lot about the modern world.

Of course the Russian language and Russian area studies were extraneous to my real education. They could be viewed as an academic expedient with a year's exotic adventure as a bonus. The rest of my education pursued the historical interests of my own society. Indiana University and my mentor, William K. Estes, provided me with fine training in quantitative and analytic methods for the study of learning. I was privileged to watch a master theoretician at work; a firm foundation was set for my future in American psychology.

247

My experience was not unique among members of my generation. Sputnik made a difference. Although relatively few psychologists learned the Russian language or Russian psychology, hundreds of young doctorate holders from many fields studied in the Soviet Union, absorbing to varying degrees the life of the people with whom they worked. Their writing has been crucial to enriching America's knowledge of its most prominent international competitor. (I do not seek to answer the question of who, in general, profits more from these exchanges. Personally, my professional work has gained enormously.)

Dealing with Soviet Psychology

My entering understanding of Soviet psychology was strongly shaped by the historical links between Pavlovian neurophysiology and American behaviorism. During the 1950s a good deal of Russian research had come to the attention of American psychologists. Figures such as Eugene Sokolov and Alexander Luria were seen as formulators of more sophisticated stimulus-response theories that would accommodate factors such as attention and language into the basic stimulus-response, associationistic theory of learning. Even the Russians' diagrams looked the same as ours, and I arrived in Moscow hopeful that I could get something more from the experience than a vacation abroad by finding out about research on semantic conditioning and mediated stimulus-response learning.

The situation that greeted me was recognizable as a kind of shabby version of the image that I had built up from my reading. Consistent with a long-standing complaint about European psychology in particular, I found that experiments were conducted in a fashion that paid less attention than I thought proper to the issue of design and procedure. Equipment was often held together by baling wire or glue, and a good deal of the work seemed to depend on a young man with expertise in jury rigging electromechanical devices. To make matters worse, Luria no longer showed much interest in semantic conditioning. I was 10 years late.

People were very polite to me. They did their best to create the conditions I thought appropriate for the work, and all of us worked at not getting upset when things did not pan out too well. We collected semantic conditioning data. At the same time, my hosts made it clear that I was going through a lot of wasted motion. Their basic orientation to theories and data collection seemed different from mine. They were interested in the news that I brought them about mathematical models as descriptive techniques, but what they really wanted to know was what theory of human psychological functioning was the model a part of; how did it help explain aphasia or prescribe an educational program for the classroom? In other words, what was my work about? My distrust of their observation was neatly matched by their amusement at my naive, model-based empiricism. Just as I found a lot of their work mushy and unscientific, they found mine peculiarly abstract and inaccessible.

I came away from the USSR without any real feeling that I had learned something useful for application later to my career. I had encountered interesting research ideas and some very impressive applications of research in school, clinical, and work settings, but had no conviction that Soviet psychology offered a paradigm worth the effort of changing directions. Of course, I subsequently spent three years conditioning dogs...to test a mathematical model based on techniques invented by a Russian named Markov and used imaginatively by an American psychologist named Estes.

My own professional commitment was to put the experience to some useful purpose. So I agreed to edit the *Handbook of Contemporary Soviet Psychology* (Cole and Maltzman, 1969) and to edit *Soviet Psychology,* a journal in which translations of articles representative of Soviet psychological research and theory are published. That would fulfill my obligation.

Encountering Variability

One thing, as they say, leads to another. Spending a year in Moscow is one way to get past the postdissertation doldrums, and it certainly changes one's notion of how the world works. But it is a lousy place from which to hunt for a job in an American university: The mail is unreliable and transportation to interviews a little expensive. I was saved from exile by Bill Estes, who arranged for me to spend a year at Stanford as a lecturer in order to gather my wits and get on with my career. Here, again, the power of Sputnik made itself felt as the move for educational reform initiated in 1957 spread into the underdeveloped countries of the world.

From the late 1950s well into the 1960s, American scientists received support from the government to revise basic science curricula in hope of improving our ability to build our own Sputniks faster and better than the Russians. According to existing evidence (Wahlberg, 1983), this effort has made a real difference in American schools. However, I did not experience the new math in American schools, but as part of an assignment in a tiny West African village. My selection for this assignment is an outstanding example of that elusive concept, serendipity. I was at Stanford because, in part, Estes liked working with Patrick Suppes. Suppes was involved as an advisor to a project to extend the new math into anglophone Africa. I had a passport and a willingness to travel. What was more, I had a degree as a mathematical learning theorist; I was an expert on learning. On this pretext, I was sent as an advisor to John Gay, a missionary mathematician with an interest in elementary education.

In Russia no one had ever asked me to account for the processes by which people thought in their everyday lives. As a psychologist, all I had to account for were the laws by which word meaning is expressed in involuntary and objectively measurable ways. The tasks I set up in Russian took little account of the way that word meanings are organized as part of everyday thinking. It took a little time to get adjusted to the situations we constructed to enable us to present stimuli to Russian subjects and to record responses. But, in essence we taught the subjects how to provide a calm and organized background against which we could make our recordings. I could have stayed home and run the same experiments a little more cleanly.

In Africa the situation was completely different. It was not clear that I would be able to address the problems that greeted me there with any of the techniques I knew. The situation, in a nutshell, was the following. As roads opened up new areas of contact with the outer world, children living in the jungle areas of Liberia were being exposed to schooling. Despite large expenditures of money, the schools were considered a failure because the dropout rates were very high and the final achievement levels very uneven.

Gay was looking at this problem from the perspective of a mathematician-educator whose college students amazed him with their difficulties in learning mathematics. This dismay took him to nearby Kpelle villages to observe mathematics instruction. He was appalled by the situation that greeted him. Liberia is a very poor country with many distinct tribes and tribal languages. In 1964 the country had very few miles of all-weather road. Education had been very limited in the country prior to World War II and was still very limited. The teachers were a mixture of graduates of missionary schools or very limited public schools and Peace Corps volunteers who did not speak the local dialects well enough to teach in them. The textbooks were from American school systems, discards of the prior decades.

In all this chaos, what fascinated Gay was the great difficulty that students encountered with problems of measurement and arithmetic reasoning in school, even though people seemed to manage their daily affairs and keep track of their possessions well enough. He was taken with the most elementary principle of education, that you must begin where the student is in order to guide the student through the system. But Gay did not know where to begin. He did not have any idea what the students already knew when they came to school, nor did he know what adults who had not been to school knew. My job was to help him find ways to figure out what the Kpelle people understood about mathematics.

It amazed me that anyone took seriously the idea that I could be of use in such an enterprise. Somehow people, John Gay in particular, had mesmerized themselves into believing that a mathematical learning theorist knew how mathematics is learned, not only in America, but in Liberia as well! So, no sooner had I recovered from the trip than I found myself in a tiny village, an eight-hour walk from the nearest road. (I, of course, being an important expert, flew into the village.)

The most immediate consequence of this encounter was that I spent the next 15 years commuting on an irregular basis to and from Liberia, where, first under the caring hand of John Gay and then on our own, my colleagues and I worked on the problem of culture and thought. The results of this work have been published in various places and need not be summarized here. In the present circumstances, the following, rather general summary of this cross-cultural research experience seems relevant. In order to find a coherent way to deal with the problems posed to us on that first field trip, we had to rethink the disciplinary division of labor that put culture and thought into different scientific categories at the end of the past century (Laboratory of Comparative Human Cognition, 1982a, 1983). This reassessment motivated new lines of research, sometimes serving as a critique of existing conceptions, sometimes offering new concepts and methods to replace the old (Cole, Gay, Glick, and Sharp, 1971; Scribner and Cole, 1981). Eventually we were led back home, where we sought to apply what we had learned in our own cultural settings to the problems that cultural variations pose us (Cole and Traupmann, 1980; Laboratory of Comparative Human Cognition, 1982b; Newman, Griffin, and Cole 1984).

An especially rewarding aspect of the cross-cultural work was that it gave me a whole new basis on which to interact with Luria and an entirely new way to deal with basic problems of learning, my starting point and my anchor in all that wandering. Until I began to fashion an interest in cross-cultural psychology, Luria did not have much to learn from me. I was friendly, and I obligingly helped with translations of his work, but I did not know anything special. By 1966 my status in this regard had changed. Luria was *very* interested in cross-cultural comparisons.

Remembering that Luria had once told me a little about his research in Central Asia (long before I thought of going to Africa or could take a special interest), I pressed him for more details on what he had done and why. He, in turn, pressed me for information about my own work in a nonliterate society. We struck a bargain. He would tutor me in his cross-cultural methods, working through his old data, if I would help with preparations for the International Congress of Psychology, to be held in Moscow that year. So I spent most of my mornings in the summer of 1966 working through musty data protocols and listening to Luria's account of his work.

What amazed me about Luria's approach to culture and mind was not so much his specific methods, although they were often very ingenious, but rather, it was the assurance with which he applied a relatively small set of concepts that I knew were important to his earlier theorizing about brain functions as well. I was really struggling to find a coherent framework to fit the pieces of empirical work together. Luria did not seem to have any problem at all. He had clearly worked out a very coherent viewpoint, but I was having trouble understanding it.

Perhaps the safest thing to say is that I am still learning. At this writing, my research is deeply influenced by the psychological framework that Luria and his colleagues constructed more than 50 years ago in the burst of humanistic enthusiasms released by the Russian revolution. At the same time, I am from a different culture and a different generation, so the way I interpret his ideas cannot be considered a copy of the original. Luria and I disagreed about the interpretation of his cross-cultural theories, and I have never been an expert in neuropsychology; frameworks are analytic devices, not straitjackets. Perhaps one of the most important things that I eventually learned through my attempts to reconstruct a sociocultural theory of mind was a way in which I could unite my interest in psychology as a discipline with my interest in people's use of their minds in a wide variety of social endeavors. It allowed me to gain a new sense of my own education.

So What?

For what it is worth, I have presented my brief sketch of how a crash program in international education affected one psychologist. The larger value of my experiences to American psychology and American society is well beyond my power to evaluate. It does seem like a very good strategy though, for a society to send some of its members to live for a while in the other fellows' town in order to come to know, more or less, what those fellows are up to. The news the travellers bring back might seem strange or impenetrable, but it might also bring answers to some nagging questions. If it is indeed the case that American technological supremacy is in doubt and that our security as a nation rests in part on our ability to deal intelligently (as contrasted with forcibly) with the rest of the world, the news we can get from abroad may well be crucial to our future.

On a personal level, there is no doubt in my mind about the value of my experiences. They have fundamentally changed the way I think about the world, the way I teach, and the way I conduct my research. All aspects of my professional life have been made much more enjoyable than I can imagine them being otherwise.

Applications to Teaching

As what I learned from my involvement in West Africa began to connect with the way of theorizing that I had encountered in the Soviet Union and the canon of research that I had learned in America, I found myself perplexed about the best way to teach. It was especially difficult to formulate comparative findings because they could so easily be criticized on methodological grounds that any good experimenter knew by heart. I began to teach using experimental techniques as a basic medium. It was not clear how nonexperimental evidence was relevant, except perhaps as local color. When I used nonexperimental material to question the experimenter's cross-cultural data, my curious criticisms seemed like nitpicking.

Over time I have worked to find ways to convey the experience of growing up in a very different culture. Now, dissatisfied with what I can communicate through experimental results, I reach into other disciplines and other historical eras for material. I also find myself reaching into other media. Videotape, film, novels, and even music come into my classroom as I seek communicable replicas of some of the experiences I have had.

So, for example, a film like *Dersu Uzala* directed by the great Japanese film maker, Akira Kurosawa, but shot in Siberia, illustrates to an incredible degree the nonliterate peasant of Luria's Central Asian trips. François Truffaut's *Wild Child* helps students understand what civilization meant to our forebears during the Enlightenment. Many fine ethnographic films make the vast range of human adaptations more palpable.

Novels and memoirs are another medium of source material. Camara Laye's, *L'Enfant Noir*, Chinua Achebe's novels about Ibo life in the early days of colonialism, and many current Japanese novels all offer informative glimpses of very different ways of experiencing the world. In this category, I would also include ethnographies and fictionalized accounts of Europeans' dawning understanding of another culture (such as Elizabeth Bowen's searching reconstruction of her own initiation into anthropology, *Return to Laughter*).

Materials like these cannot stand on their own in a psychology class. Because they are of interest to students for reasons institutionally quite separate from their interest in psychology as a discipline, the instructor must show how they are relevant. That is a big challenge because as data, films and novels are pretty hard to reconcile with experimental procedures. My own response to this dilemma is to use that need for reconciliation as a wedge into discussing the methodological assumptions of our taken-for-granted procedures so that students have the best possible chance of using the materials to good advantage.

Because a lot of invention is required, I cannot imagine trying to create an "international knowledge" curriculum in psychology. But I can see those psychologists who find that they want to put more effort into exploring the international context of their work organizing workshops at the annual APA convention and preparing a compendium of materials found useful by individual members. Perhaps publication of relevant sources in specialized APA journals or the *American Psychologist* would be appropriate. The sources of information are legion. It is only the will to organize them that is lacking.

References

Barrows, T.S., Klein, S.F., and Clark, J.L.D.(1981). *What college students know and believe about Their World.* Princeton, N.J.: Educational Testing Service.

Cole, M., Gay, J., Glick, J., and Sharp, D.W.(1971). *The cultural context of learning and thinking.* New York: Basic Books.

Cole, M., and Maltzman, I (1969). *Handbook of Contemporary Soviet Psychology.* New York: Basic Books.

Cole, M., and Means, B. (1981). *Comparative studies of how people think.* Cambridge, Mass.: Harvard UP.

Cole, M. and Traupmann, K. (1980). Learning from a learning disabled child. In W.A. Collins, ed. *Minnesota symposia on child psychology* (Vol. 14). Hillsdale, N.J.: Erlbaum.

Laboratory of Comparative Human Cognition. (1982a). Culture and intelligence. In R. Sternberg, ed., *Handbook of human intelligence* (pp. 642-719). Cambridge: Cambridge UP.

Laboratory of Comparative Human Cognition. (1982b). A model system for the study of learning difficulties. *The Newsletter of the Laboratory of Comparative Human cognition, 4,* 39-66.

Laboratory of Comparative Human Cognition. (1983). Culture and cognitive development in W. Kessen, ed., *Mussen handbook of child development* (Vol. 1, pp. 295-356). New York: Wiley.

Newman, D., Griffin, P., and Cole, M. (1984). Social constraints in laboratory and classroom tasks. In B. Rogoff and J. Lave, ed., *Everyday cognition: Its development in social context* (pp. 172-193). Cambridge, Mass.: Harvard UP.

Scribner, S., and Cole, M. (1981). *The psychology of literacy.* Cambridge, Mass.: Harvard UP.

Titchener, E.B. (1916). On ethnological tests of sensation and perception. *Proceedings of the American Philosophical Society, 55,* 204-236.

Wahlberg, H.(1983), April) *A comparative study of Japanese and American school achievement.* Paper presented at the Conference on Child Development in Japan and the United States, Stanford U, Palo Alto, Cal.

Cross-Cultural Psychology

Harry C. Triandis and Richard W. Brislin

The general goal of this paper is to contribute to a more internationally oriented education for undergraduates. Psychologists can and have contributed to this goal in several ways (Landis and Brislin, 1983:chapters by Mestenhauser and Hughes). For instance, there are classroom exercises that encourage students to take into account the viewpoint of people in countries other than their own. Foreign students have been employed as guest lecturers, and programs have been established that encourage learning through intercultural contact. All of these could be the focus of an article, and indeed contributions from these areas will occasionally be referred to in this article. Space limitations, however, limit our coverage to what is probably the best known area, which combines psychology and internationalism: the activities collectively call "cross-cultural psychology."

Studying Culture

Definitions of psychology usually include the phrase, "the scienctific study of human behavior." A direct implication of this definition is that human behavior in all parts of the world must be investigated, not just those aspects of behavior conveniently available to investigators in highly industrialized nations with a long history of scientific endeavor. Cross-cultural psychology refers to the collective efforts of researchers who work among people who speak various languages, live in societies ranging from technologically unsophisticated to highly complex and industrialized, and who live under different forms of political organization. Ideally, various aspects of people's culture are carefully identified and related to important theoretical issues in psychological theory, resulting in conclusions about the culture's influence on behavior. In turn, these conclusions improve the theory.

Harry C. Triandis is Professor of Psychology at the University of Illinois. Richard W. Brislin is Research Associate at the East/West Center, Institute of Culture and Communication, University of Hawaii.

As with many highly complex concepts, such as intelligence, personality, or emotion, research involving culture proceeds vigorously despite the lack of widespread agreement on an exact definition. Formal definitions have numbered in the hundreds (Kroeber and Kluckhohn, 1952), leading to the joke that culture is defined by the latest anthropological monograph. For the purposes of this presentation, we shall attempt to identify those aspects of the definitions that indicate best what psychologists actually do when they carry out research in various parts of the world (see Brislin, 1983, and Triandis, 1972, for more material on definitions.)

Anthropologists have written most extensively about culture. Kroeber and Kluckhohn (1952, p. 181) concluded their influential review by suggesting that many definitions contained these common elements: "patterns, explicit and implicit, of or for behavior transmitted by symbols, constituting the distinctive achievements of human groups ... [and] ideas and their attached values." It is interesting to note that the concept of "patterns transmitted by symbols" predate the current psychological concern with "scripts" as a method of how people organize information in their memories (Abelson, 1981). Scripts are like short dramatic presentations with guidelines to characters, settings, props, and even dialogue. Scripts also clearly differ across cultures: how one approaches potential marriage partners; how one behaves toward female subordinates; or how a person calls a meeting for important decision-making activities.

Melville Herskovits(1948) proposed the important generalization that "culture is the man-made part of the human environment" (p. 17). Triandis (1972)benefited from Herskovits's contribution and made a distinction between physical and subjective culture. The former would include objects made by humans, such as houses, tools, and gardens, and the latter would include people's cognitions, attitudes, and behaviors associated with those objects in the form of values, roles (for example, who has a right to build a house), and beliefs (for example, when is the best time to plant). Culture should not be defined so broadly that it is all-encompassing and thus indicative of nothing very much in particular. Earthquakes are not best conceptualized as part of a culture, even though the written or unwritten record of a society may indicate their frequent occurrence. However, people's beliefs about how best to prepare for earthquakes, or their tendency to deny the possibility of earthquakes in their lifetimes, *are* part of their culture.

Although early attempts at cross-cultural research too often imposed the framework of the researcher's own culture on other people, current standards demand that evidence be presented that indicates how concepts are seen and experienced by the people in the culture under study. Given this goal, the influence of work in cognitive psychology as well as cognitive anthropology has been strong. Psychologists have studied people's knowledge about their world, the ways in which this knowledge is passed on to future generations, and the conflicts experienced when various cultures within the same country have very different interpretations of events. Clifford Geertz's (1973) definition captures this major research area: "Culture denotes a historically transmitted pattern of meanings embodied in symbols, a system of inherited conceptions expressed in symbolic forms by means of which men communicate, perpetuate, and develop their knowledge about and attitudes toward life" (p. 89).

There are a number of benefits to the study of human behavior that can accrue by carrying out research in various cultures. Such research, however, is difficult, given the physical demands of field work, language differences, and varying norms toward participation in research exhibited by members of different cultures. The benefits of cross-cultural research lie largely in better theory development and better conceptualization of important variables. The difficulties are largely based on added methodological burdens. We shall discuss both benefits and difficulties.

Benefits of Cross-Cultural Research

Behavioral scientists have discussed the advantages of cross-cultural research over investigations carried out within any one country (Brislin, 1983; Naroll and Cohen, 1970; Strodtbeck, 1964; Triandis, 1972; Whiting, 1968). Space limitations permit examination of only a few.

Theory Expansion

Most theories are based on a limited set of observations carried out in the theory developer's own country. Only after rigorous testing in various parts of the world, carried out among people varying along dimensions relevant to specific hypotheses, can a theory be called robust. A good example is Piaget's work on cognitive development (Dasen and Heron, 1981; Piaget, 1973). A basic aspect of this theory is that children approach problems that challenge their thought processes in ways different from adults. The approaches are summarized by a set of four identifiable stages through which children pass as they grow out of infancy, through childhood, and into early adolescence. The invariance of the stage sequence is a central research question. If the sequence is invariant, then biological factors must play a key role. If the stage sequence varies widely among children in different cultures, then biological factors must play a much smaller role. Piaget (1973) wrote: "This is the first fundamental problem, the solution of which requires extensive cross-cultural studies"(p. 300).

Increasing the Range of Variables

By doing cross-cultural studies, investigators can often increase the range of variables beyond what is obtainable in any one study. The age at which an event occurs in people's lives provides a good example. Assume that a researcher is interested in the relationship between the age at which a child is weaned and some aspect of that child's personality (Whiting, 1968). If a researcher studied this variable in only one country, there might be a very narrow range of ages at weaning across different babies because the norm for the "proper" weaning age is often widely accepted. For instance, most babies in the United States are weaned before they reach one year of age. But by gathering data in different cultures where the norms for age at weaning are quite varied, the researcher can find children who were not weaned until they were four or even five years old.

Another example involves the effects of population density on people's reactions to others in their environment. Using a now common distinction between density (number of people in a specified area) and crowding (people's reaction to the density), Munroe and Munroe (1972) studied several societies in Africa that varied in density from 250 to 1,400 people per square mile. Higher densities led to more responses indicative of withdrawal from others, such as norms against holding hands with friends and less favorable evaluations of family members. Combined with other studies of behavior in highly dense environments (for example, Anderson, 1972, studied Chinese in communal dwellings in Malaysia), significant advances have been made in our knowledge about how people cope with density so as to minimize negative effects. See Altman and Chemers (1980) for a longer review.

Unconfounding Variables

Perhaps the most intriguing use of cross-cultural studies is the unconfounding, or taking apart, of variables that occur together in any one culture. Assume, for instance, that a certain ethnic group has a high rate of alcohol use. There are at least two possible explanations: (a) a biological factor associated with membership in the ethnic group and (b) attitudes and values concerning alcohol learned during an individual's socialization into a culture. By studying members of that ethnic group who live in their culture of birth and by comparing them with others of the same ethnic background who have moved and assimilated themselves in other cultures, these two explanations can be tested. This was the approach of Sue, Zane, and Ito (1979), who studied Americans of Japanese ancestry (AJAs) who had reached various levels of acculturation in the mainstream middle class of the United States. Acculturated AJAs showed the greatest use of alcohol, a finding that favored a cultural explanation over one designating a biological propensity toward alcohol use.

Many times, the complex variable "culture" itself has to be unconfounded. Too often, the word is used in a vague manner and refers to some combination of differences in skin color, country of origin, language, customs, socialization practices, and sometimes socioeconomic class. Fontaine and Dorch (1980) were interested in studying marriages among people from very different backgrounds, but they felt that "cross-cultural marriage" was too vague a term. They disentangled the vagueness by gathering data from couples whose marriages were interethnic, involving a skin color difference; international, with two countries of origin but no difference in skin color; and interreligious. They found different dynamics among the various categories of couples with respect to coping with stress. For instance, interethnic couples were more likely to interpret problems as being due to factors external to themselves. Perhaps this interpretation is attributable to the greater visibility of interethnic couples to members of the larger community. Community-wide reactions (stares, gossip, discrimination) may be used as explanations for marital stress.

Study of the Context for Behavior

A basic theoretical point in social psychology is that behavior is a function of the person and the environment. However, the environment, or the social context in which behavior occurs, has proven very difficult to conceptualize and to study. One reason is that researchers are most often themselves members of the culture under investigation. They find it difficult to separate themselves from their environment or to pick out and analyze aspects of their own culture that they have always experienced as a totality. But the separation of self from environment is not as difficult when researchers work in other cultures. Researchers can often see aspects of the social context that may be influencing people's behaviors, perhaps because those aspects contrast with what is similar in the researchers' own culture. Cross-cultural studies, then, can lead to more insights into how general principles are affected by contextual factors. The designation of such contextual factors and the interaction of general principles with these factors have been identified as one of the great challenges for modern psychology (Cronbach, 1975).

Cross-Cultural Methodological Issues

Although these and other advantages of cross-cultural studies have enriched psychological theory (other examples in Brislin, 1983; Munroe, Munroe, and Whiting, 1981; Triandis et al., 1980-1981), progress has not been without difficulties. Many problems beset cross-cultural researchers, including the additional stresses brought on by doing work outside the familiar confines of their own society. Imagine a rather typical scenario. Researchers have to adjust to life in another culture without their familiar, sometimes extensive, support groups. Residents are perhaps distrustful of researchers, equating well-dressed outsiders with intrusive governmental officials. Residents speak a different language, have different norms concerning everyday interpersonal interaction, and are participants in long-term networks in which researchers have no place. Some residents may have a status in the community that might be threatened by research results. These and other research-generated stresses are beginning to receive attention (Goodenough, 1980).

Same Concept, Different Meaning

Problems from the standpoint of research methodology have long received attention (Brislin, Lonner, and Thorndike, 1973; Frijda and Jahoda, 1966; Triandis and Berry, 1980). A very frequent complaint is the following: "I developed a scale to measure what I thought was a well understood concept. But the people in the other culture think differently about the concept. We weren't talking about the same thing."

Rather than giving up in frustration, current thinking in cross-cultural research starts with the presumption that concepts will not have the same meaning across cultures. There may be some identical aspects to a concept, but there will also be a culture-specific meaning. This presumption is part of what has been called the *emic-etic* distinction (see Berry, 1969, 1980; Pike, 1966; Starr and Wilson, 1980, for longer reviews.) The terms are borrowed from linguistics, where a phon*emic* system documents meaningful sounds specific to a given language. A phon*etic* system organizes all sounds which have meaning in any language. For psychology, then, the emic-etic metaphor suggests that culture-common (etic) and culture-specific (emic) aspects of concepts should be expected and sought.

A good example can be found in the need for achievement. McClelland (1961), working in the United States, originally identified aspects of the broad concept, involving individualistic striving for goals that were neither too easy (ensuring a trivial success) nor too difficult (ensuring failure). Working later among Pacific Islanders, specifically Hawaiian Americans, Gallimore, Weiss, and Finney (1974) found that some aspects of the broad concept had to be modified to understand the need for achievement in other cultures. Pacific Islanders would work hard to achieve goals, but the emphasis on individualistic striving was not as strong as among the original samples in the United States. Islanders would work hard with others on tasks or would work hard if the outcomes could be clearly shared with others. Thus the aspect of the need for achievement does not have to be discarded. Rather, there seems to be an etic core (for example, having a goal-setting standard of excellence, affective reactions to success and failure, etc.) and an emic coloring of that core depending on cultural factors. Maehr and Nicholls (1980) add the interesting and important examples of Iran and Japan to the cross-cultural view of the need for achievement.

Translation

The problem of different meanings for what seems to be the same concept also arises when attempts are made to translate from one language to another. Researchers complain that it is difficult to phrase certain concepts central to one culture (Japanese *amae*, Doi, 1973; Greek *arete*, Triandis, 1972) in the language of another. Again, this fact should be a starting point for research rather than a frustrating end to one's aspirations for data collection. Translation has received a great deal of attention (Brislin, 1976; Sechrest, Fay, and Saidi, 1972), and a few points can be made here.

The decentering technique (Werner and Campbell, 1970) allows identification of materials that are relatively easy and relatively difficult to translate. Material is prepared in an original language version, and it passes through the efforts of several bilinguals. Some translate from the original to the target language, and others translate back from the target to clarify it as in the diagram below (figure).

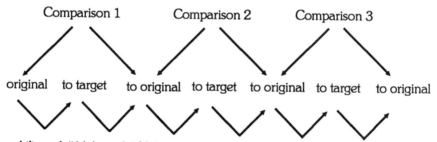

After other checks for quality, analysis can be done of the versions represented by the extreme ends of the diagram (the first version, and the third back-translation). Each comparison should show more convergence. If the same or similar working is present in these two versions, a hypothesis for further testing is that the concepts are easily expressible in the two languages. There would have to be words in the target language for the concepts to "survive" the translation into and out of the target. If the wording is different, then there may be emic coloring of the concepts. For instance, Brislin (1970) studied translation into Chamorro, the language of Guam and the Northern Marianas Islands. He found that the original test item, "I like to gossip at times," came out of the de-centering procedure as, "I sometimes like to talk about other people's business." Further investigation led to the recognition that there is no general word for *gossip* in Chamorro: There must be a distinction made between a male and female gossip. This fact is of importance for understanding interpersonal communication among speakers of Chamorro. Other investigators have obtained insights from translation results. Phillips (1960) could not have the sentence stem, "Sometimes a good quarrel is necessary because..." (p. 302) translated into Thai. "After much discussion, the translators decided that, although it was conceivable that an American might enjoy a quarrel for its cathartic effect, the notion would be incomprehensible to a Thai" (p. 302). Translators should often play a role more like collaborators in research, with important contributions to make to the substance of the research program, rather than as hired help.

Multiple Methods

A frequent criticism experienced cross-cultural researchers make is that a certain study suffers from single-method (also called "mono-method") bias. This means that problems with a method are confounded or confused with the substantive topic of study. For instance, a test to measure personality through self-report very often suffers from an identifiable method bias: In some cultures people flatter themselves, and in others people are self-deprecating. Mono-method bias is dealt with by gathering data using as many different techniques as possible (Webb, Campbell, Schwartz, and Sechrest, 1966). Confidence in results increases as the number of different methods yielding those results increases. For instance, the study of the tendency to conform to the view of others has benefited from investigations using a variety of methods (Mann, 1980). These include people's judgments about perceptual materials, reactions to statements of opinions and attitudes of others, and actual behavior, such as contributions to charity. Studies have been carried out in laboratories, in the guise of man-on-the-street interviews and in cultures in which the strength of social norms regarding conformity varies (e.g., Berry, 1967; Huang & Harris, 1973). Another way of introducing the field of cross-cultural psychology is to review its contributions to psychology as a whole. This can be done by looking at a number of cross-cultural contributions to both general and applied psychology.

Contributions to General Psychology of the Study of Culture

Perception

Environment and culture have important influences on perceptual processes. These can occur both through modification of physiological mechanisms and through learning. For example, Bornstein (1973) has reviewed the links between environmental factors (radiation levels found in high altitudes and near the equator) and physiological changes (development of a filtration mechanism that blocks out shortwave radiation), which result in increased visual acuity in those environments.

Perhaps the most important of the demonstrations of the effects of experience on perception is by Segall, Campbell, and Herskovits (1966), who showed that those raised in "carpentered environments" are susceptible to certain visual illusions, such as the Müller-Lyer. People raised in carpentered environments are more likely than those raised in noncarpentered environments to interpret nonrectangular junctions (such as one finds in the Müller-Lyer illusion) as two-dimensional objects. Numerous studies have refined this conception (e.g., Jahoda, 1966) and have identified additional relevant factors (e.g., pigmentation of the fundus oculi) that may decrease illusion susceptibility (Berry, 1971; Jahoda, 1971).

There is also evidence that learning is necessary for the perception of pictorial depth and thus the ability to gain information from pictures. Hudson (1958, 1960) suggested that unschooled African subjects lack the ability to perceive pictorial depth; it is acquired through education. Numerous publications have both criticized and supported this argument. Experience with stimuli of a particular type increases the speed of accurate responses to such stimuli (Deregowski, Muldrow, and Muldrow (1972).

These and many other studies were reviewed by Deregowski (1980), who also reviewed cross-cultural work with constancies, the perception of color and form, binocular disparity (e.g., Bagby, 1957), eidetic imagery (e.g., Doob, 1966, 1970), the perception of time, as well as auditory, olfactory, and cutaneous perception, among other topics.

Cognition

The relationship of culture and cognition (Triandis, 1964) has been approached from three perspectives (Shweder and Bourne, 1982): the universalist (e.g., Lonner, 1980; Osgood, May, and Miron, 1975), the evolutionist (e.g., Luria, 1971), and the relativist (e.g., Price-Williams, 1980). The first identifies similarities in cognition; the second focuses on changes in cognitive functioning that can be traced to the activities a group engages in; the third examines differences among cultural groups. All perspectives have some validity from certain points of view. First there are universals: all people categorize; they use opposites and associations; and they group evaluative, potency, and activity attributes together. Synesthesia and phonetic symbolism suggest common human behavior patterns. Although there are universals, there are also deviations from these universals. For example "literacy makes some difference to some skills in some contexts" (Scribner and Cole, 1981, p. 234), as does familiarity with the stimuli subjects have to process (Pick, 1980). Social and cognitive stimulation, nutrition (McKay, Sinisterra, McKay, Gomez, and Lloreda, 1978), and education (Jahoda, 1981; Rogoff, 1981; Scribner and Cole, 1981; Sharp, Cole, and Lave, 1979) all influence intellectual performances. Finally, there is specificity and relativism. Humans classify experience differently (Price-Williams, 1980), as ethnoscientists have documented (e.g., Tyler, 1969).

Thus it appears that our task is to sort the universal from the culture-specific, because both elements are present in most cognitive performance. Recent treatments of language development (Bowerman, 1981) and memory (Wagner, 1981) have focused on both. In discussing Piaget, both universals, such as his stages of development, and cultural specificities such as the role of magic in interpreting conservation task results, must be examined (Dasen, 1977; Dasen and Heron, 1981).

The components of cognitive systems (categories, association, memories, syllogisms, encoding and decoding, semantic integration, verbal explanation) can be found in all cultures, but they are related to each other in complex systems of cognitive processes. Luria (1971) used the concept of the functional system, a flexible and variable organization of cognitive processes, which Cole and Scribner (1974) found useful in dealing with the question of the universal versus the specific in cognition. According to Cole and Scribner, basic processes are the same, but functional systems are different and are influenced by cultural variables. The same component, for example, categorization, enters many different functional systems. In their study among the Vai, Scribner and Cole (1981) found that English schooling had some effects on almost all cognitive processes. The use of the Vai script produced differences in a few cognitive processes, such as categorization, encoding, and semantic integration, whereas Quranic literacy had few effects (affected recall). The use of Arabic also had some effects (changes in categorization, recall, writing). Thus, it is possible to link specific experiences with specific cognitive performances. Because cultures provide unique patterns of experiences they do have effects on specific configurations of performance.

It is important for psychologists to be aware that specific findings are likely to include both universal and culture-specific elements and to avoid over-generalization, lest a finding *appear* universal because it was obtained in only one population! Although the finding may have universal elements, one should not conclude that it is universal until it has been obtained in more than one setting and with diverse populations. Or, to use the language introduced previously, etic concepts may have emic colorings.

Motivation

One of the earliest useful discussions of motivation was Klineberg's (1954) analysis of the dependability of motives. He employed three criteria: (a) continuity, that is, whether the particular form of behavior in humans was also found in apes and other biological species; (b) psychological bias, that is, whether there was a biochemical basis for the behavior; and (c) universality, that is, whether the behavior occurred in all cultures. Motives that met all criteria were called absolutely dependable, and different levels of dependability were established. Thus, hunger, thirst, need for rest and sleep, the elimination of waste products, and activity and esthetic drives were classified as among the most dependable. Sex, postmaternal behavior, and self-preservation were thought to be of somewhat lower dependability. Aggressiveness, flight, and self-assertiveness were even less dependable, whereas gregariousness, the paternal motive, filial motive, acquisitiveness, and self-submission were classified as least dependable. Of course, this list does not exhaust behavior patterns that could be identified. It is interesting because it required cross-cultural investigations for the classification to take place.

The history of the cross-cultural study of such motives is one of increased differentiation. For example, starting with one concept, such as achievement, one finds numerous distinctions. Cultures differ in their attributions for success and failure (Weiner, 1972), in their value orientations (Kluckhohn and Strodtbeck, 1961), definitions of success, criteria of success, individual versus social evaluations of achievement, time perspective, and so on. Cultures also differ in what goals are considered important. This broad research area has been reviewed by Kornadt, Eckensberger, and Emminghaus (1980).

Interpersonal Interaction

Both universal (Lonner, 1980; Triandis, 1978) and culture-specific elements (Hall, 1959) can be found in interpersonal interaction. Social behavior is perceived to occur along certain universal dimensions, such as association-disassociation, superordination-subordination, intimacy-formality, and overtness-covertness (Triandis, 1977, 1978). As a result of interaction, individuals develop stereotypes that probably follow universal laws (Campbell, 1967; Davidson and Thompson, 1980) such as cognitive consistency (Brewer and Campbell, 1976; Triandis, 1968). However, both the content and degree of endorsement of stereotypic elements tend strongly to be culturally specific.

In interpersonal interaction, cultural groups differ in (a) the perceptual differentiations they make—for instance, in the extent to which they use particular cues such as age, sex, or social class in social perception (Davidson and Thompson, 1980); (b) how they use the information extracted from such differentiations, for example, how they evaluate others; and (c) how they interact, for example, whether association, superordinate, intimate, or overt behaviors are frequent or infrequent (Triandis, 1980).

Among the more important dimensions of perceptual differentiation in social interaction is the definition of the other as a member of the in-group or out-group and the identification of ascribed versus achieved attributes of the other. The information may be placed in broad or narrow cognitive frameworks and is abstracted, in different degrees, in different cultures (Glenn, 1981). A number of value orientations (Kluckhohn and Strodtbeck, 1961) are brought to bear on the evaluation of the information. Cultural differences in the amount of touching, eye contact, orientation of bodies, loudness of voice, and physical distance have been identified. Wolfgang (1979) has edited a set of papers summarizing and describing studies of nonverbal behavior. Triandis (1977) summarized much of the literature on interpersonal behavior and integrated it with cross-cultural data.

Group Dynamics

Group life is an attribute of the human species. There are no cultures where the majority of the population lives alone (Naroll, 1983). However, groups differ in the attributes used to define in-group membership. In some cultures the in-groups are relatively narrow (for example, just family and friends) and in other cultures much wider (Triandis, 1972). It is probable, though not yet established, that cultures with narrow in-groups have clearer norms and impose sanctions for deviation much more severely than cultures with broad in-groups. The extent to which individual behavior is predictable from norms, roles, interpersonal agreements, and other such group influences as opposed to from the affect toward the behavior itself or the perceived consequences of the behavior—as specified by models such as those of Fishbein and Ajzen (1975) or Triandis (1975, 1977, 1980)—is most likely to vary with culture. For example, Davidson, Jaccard, Triandis, Morales, and Diaz-Guerrero (1976) found that educated Mexican women and most American women used the perceived consequences of having one more child as the major determinant of their intention to have another child, whereas the intentions of lower class Mexican women conformed to social pressures. Thus lower class Mexican women conformed to differ from American women in their perceptions of fertility behavior.

Most cross-cultural research on small groups failed to distinguish behavior toward in-group members from behavior toward out-group members, and thus just replicated U.S. or European results. People in cultures with small in-groups behave toward out-group members in more or less the same way subjects in Europe and North America behave toward confederates in laboratory settings. Thus, for instance, the rates of conformity to the Asch (1956) procedure were similar for the majority of countries. Mann (1980) has reviewed studies from Brazil, Hong Kong, Germany, Japan, Lebanon, and so on. Conformity is somewhat higher in subsistence societies engaged in agriculture (Berry, 1967, 1974) and in tribal societies (Whittaker and Meade, 1967), but overall the Asch results replicated well, Similarly, in most studies of cooperation-competition, reviewed by Mann, there are few cultural differences, though there are some well established differences on this dimension with samples of children. The few deviations from Western findings suggest differences in preference for autocratic and centralized styles of leadership (Meade, 1967; Misumi, 1972).

However, the few studies that did consider the difference between behavior toward in-group and out-group members have uncovered important differences. For example, Leung (1983) found that Chinese subjects behave quite differently toward a friend than toward an unknown person (student of the same university). In general, with a friend they allocate rewards according to the equality principle, particularly when their own contribution to task success was high. With the unknown person they allocate according to the equity principle. American subjects allocate according to the equity principle in both conditions and follow equity rather than equality even more faithfully with a friend than with and unknown person. Marin (1981), working only with out-group members, found that Colombian subjects allocated according to equity even more extremely than American subjects.

Applications of the Study of Culture

Cultural Variables in Selection and Employee Appraisal

The importance of construct validation of selection procedures in each of the cultures in which they are to be used is the key argument of the cross-cultural psychologist asked to participate in personnel selection. Too often in the past, procedures that had been validated in one culture were applied in other cultures without further validation. Irvine and Carroll (1980) have provided several practical guidelines for the use of tests across cultures. Their suggestions are essential reading for those who use tests with culturally heterogeneous populations.

When a supervisor from one culture appraises the performance of a subordinate from another, the accuracy of the appraisal is likely to be lower than when these individuals come from the same culture. We know from research in social perception (see Triandis, 1977, pp. 106–114) that appraisal is highly inaccurate. However, this problem is compounded across cultures because the observer is often not aware of norms in the other culture that require certain behaviors. An observer who has learned to make "isomorphic attributions" (Triandis, 1975) concerning the behavior of a member of another culture (from that member's viewpoint) may avoid the inaccuracies in social perception associated with differences in culture. Thus when the supervisor assigns the same causes to the behavior of the subordinate that the subordinate assigns to his or her own behavior, some of the difficulties of interpersonal interaction across cultures are eliminated.

In any case, the situation is likely to result in unfair evaluations of the subordinate because appraisal requires apprehension storage, recall, and integration of information into a final evaluation. At each of these stages cultural differences are likely to introduce errors in judgment. First, in terms of apprehension, people from different cultures have different personal constructs (Kelly, 1955) and different ideas about what constitutes "good" noteworthy behavior. Second, stereotypes and implicit personality theories influence the storage of the information that has been noted. Third, stereotypes and culture-linked notions of what is the prototype "good employee" influence recall. Finally, the unpredictability, complexity, and status-incongruity associated with social perceptions of persons from other cultures is likely to influence the process of integration unfavorably for the subordinate. To reduce these negative effects it is important to provide cross-cultural training.

Cross-Cultural Training

In an increasingly interdependent world the demands for cross-cultural training are growing. Several reviews (Brislin, 1981; Brislin and Pedersen, 1976; Landis and Brislin, 1983) are available. A quick overview can be obtained from Brislin, Landis, and Brandt(1983). These authors set the goal of cross-cultural training as producing "significant change in the judgments of the actor's social or skill competence by people from *another* cultural background" (p. 3, italics in original). They describe six kinds of culture training in some detail and give references to publications where these kinds of training were employed.

Information or fact-oriented training. Trainees are presented with facts about the other culture through lectures, videotapes, and reading materials.

Attribution training. This training used programmed learning books, called culture assimilators (Fiedler, Mitchell, and Triandis, 1971) designed to teach a person to look at social behavior from the point of view of members of another culture—what we previously called isomorphic attribution.

Cultural awareness. Trainees focus on the values of their own culture so as to become sensitive to cultural differences and acquire the ability to absorb information from other cultures. The "contrast American" (Kraemer, 1969; Stewart, 1966) is one of the approaches that does this.

Cognitive-behavior modification. The well-documented principles of learning are used to shape trainees to extract more reinforcements from other cultures and to avoid punishments (David, 1972).

Experiential learning. Participants experience another culture (e.g., through field trips) or simulations of life in that culture (see Trifonovitch, 1977).

The interaction approach. In this type of training, participants interact with members of another culture. An aspect of experiential learning, but without the elaborate simulations, this approach is less expensive than experiential learning.

Evaluations of these approaches are few. Only the culture assimilator has been tested extensively. The data suggest that people learn a great deal, but the changes are more frequently cognitive rather than attitudinal or behavioral. Thus it appears that a combination of methods is required. The costs, benefits, and ethics of each training approach must be evaluated.

Psychology courses designed to provide students with information about life in other cultures may well use some of the above approaches. This may be one of the most promising ways to internationalize the teaching of psychology.

Psychopathology

Marsella (1979) and Draguns (1980) have provided useful overviews of the relationship of culture and psychopathology. Mental disorders range from minor disturbances (Tseng and Hsu, 1980), sometimes traceable to alienation (Guthrie and Tanco, 1980), to disorders of clinical severity (Draguns, 1980). The antecedents of psychopathology have been reviewed by Sanua (1980) and those of depression by Marsella (1980). Variations in therapeutic procedures have been examined by Prince (1980).

There are many commonalities in disorders across cultures. Usually some imbalance (physiological disturbance or interpersonal trauma, or behavior inconsistent with a moral code) increases anxiety; an interpretation of the imbalance is often available in cultural myths or folk medical terms; and personal habits, shaped by particular culture-specific patterns of socialization, are used to reduce the anxiety. Such conditions often result in unusual behaviors or strange beliefs, which nevertheless temporarily reduce the level of anxiety and hence are reinforced and occur more and more frequently. The therapeutic experiences employed in different cultures, whether by drugs, shock, talking, or isolation of the patient, are attempts to eliminate the unusual behaviors and/or beliefs.

Cultures differ in their myths, themes, concerns, wishes, illusions, and world views. Because the behavior of psychiatric patients often shows affinities to the stereotypes of the cultural group and reflects conceptions of the patient's role, measures of psychological disturbance may serve as social indicators of the culture in which they occur (Draguns, 1980, p. 125). There are, moreover, cultural differences in what behaviors are considered normal, in the frequency of diagnosis of disturbances, and in the expression of the disturbance (Marsella, 1979). Overall, the presence of a highly integrated social life, social cohesion, and relative ease in extraction of resources leads to lower levels of depression, crime, substance abuse, suicide, and interpersonal aggression (Naroll, 1983).

Conclusions

Current standards of cross-cultural research require evidence concerning the way the topics under investigation are conceived by the populations in the various cultures. The benefits of cross-cultural research lie largely in better theory development and better conceptualizations of important variables. For example, Piaget's stages of cognitive development appear in many cross-cultural studies, but the attainment of a stage at a particular age depends on cultural factors (Dasen, Lavallee, and Retschitzki, 1979; Price-Williams, Gordon, and Ramirez, 1969).

Cross-cultural studies increase the range of variables, help unconfound variables, and allow an assessment of the effects of context on bahavior. Cross-cultural work can often identify a universal core of meaning of a theoretical construct, as well as variations of the meaning of the construct in different cultures. Culture has important influences on many fields including perception, cognition, motivation, interpersonal behavior, and group dynamics. For optimal treatment of these topics, it is helpful to indicate both the limits of certain generalizations and the culture-linked variations.

The hope is that in the future a natural science will be developed that will link attributes of cultures to attributes of individuals and behaviors.

Applications of cultural information to problems of employee selection and appraisal, such as helping a supervisor from one culture make correct attributions concerning the behavior of a subordinate from another, can reduce interpersonal conflicts. The "correct" attributions are those that match the attributions that supervisors from the subordinate's own culture usually make. Culture-relevant information can be used in training programs when people experiencing face-to-face contact are from very different cultural backgrounds. The information about supervisory styles is illustrative of the findings from research that have been used by practitioners.

Cross-cultural training has taken many forms, but only a few evaluative studies have been completed so far. Culturally appropriate psychopathology are important frontiers of future research.

References

Abelson, R. (1981). Psychological status of the script concept. *American Psychologist, 36,* 715–729.

Altman, I., and Chemers, M. (1980). Cultural aspects of environment-behavior relationships. In H.C. Triandis and R.W. Brislin, ed., *Handbook of cross-cultural psychology: Vol 5. Social psychology* (pp. 335–393). Boston: Allyn and Bacon.

Anderson, E.N. (1972). Some Chinese methods of dealing with crowding. *Urban Anthropology, I,* 141–150.

Asch, S. (1956). Studies of independence and conformity: A minority of one against a unanimous majority. *Psychological Monographs, 70* (9, Whole No. 416).

Bagby, J.W. (1957). A cross-cultural study of perceptual predominance in binocular rivalry. *Journal of Abnormal and Social Psychology, 54,* 331–334.

Berry, J.W. (1967). Independence and conformity in subsistence level societies. *Journal of Personality and Social Psychology, 7,* 415–418.

———. (1969). On cross-cultural comparability. *International Journal of Psychology, 4,* 119–128.

———. (1971). Müller-Lyer susceptibility: Culture ecology and race. *International Journal of Psychology, 6,* 193–197.

———. (1974). Differentiation across cultures: Cognitive style and affective style. In J. Dawson and W. Lonner, ed., *Readings in cross-cultural psychology* (pp. 167–175). Hong Kong: U of Hong Kong P.

———. (1980). Introduction to methodology. In H.C. Triandis and J.W. Berry, ed., *Handbook of cross-cultural psychology: Vol 2. Methodology* (pp. 1–28). Boston: Allyn and Bacon.

Bornstein, M.H. (1973). Colour vision and colour naming: A psychophysiological hypothesis of cultural difference. *Psychological Bulletin, 80,* 257–285.

Bowerman, M. (1981). Language development. In H.C. Triandis and A. Heron, ed., *Handbook of cross-cultural psychology: Vol. 4. Developmental psychology* (pp. 93–185). Boston: Allyn and Bacon.

Brewer, M., and Campbell, D.T. (1976). *Ethnocentrism and intergroup attitudes: East African evidence.* New York: Wiley-Halsted.

Brislin, R. (1970). Back-translation for cross-cultural research. *Journal of Cross-Cultural Psychology, 1,* 185–216.

———. (1976). *Translation: Applications and research.* New York: Gardner.

———. (1981). *Cross-cultural encounters: Face-to-face interactions.* New York: Pergamon.

———. (1983). Cross-cultural research in psychology. *Annual Review of Psychology, 34,* 363–400.

———, Landis, D., and Brandt, M.E. (1983). Conceptualization of intercultural behavior and training. In D. Landis and R. Brislin, ed., *Handbook of intercultural training. Vol. 1. Issues in theory and design* (pp. 1–35). New York: Pergamon.

Brislin, R.W., Lonner, W., and Thorndike (1973). *Cross-cultural research methods.* New York: Wiley.

Brislin, R.W., and Pederson, P. (1976). *Cross-cultural orientation programs.* New York: Gardner.

Campbell, D.T. (1967). Stereotypes and the perception of group differences. *American Psychologist, 22,* 817–829.

Cole, M., and Scribner, S. (1984). *Culture and thought.* New York: Wiley.

Cronbach, L. (1975). Beyond the two disciplines of scientific psychology. *American Psychologist, 30,* 116–127.

Dasen, P.R. (1977). *Piagetian psychology: Cross-cultural contributions.* New York: Gardner.

————, and Heron, A. (1981). Cross-cultural tests of Piaget's theory. In Triandis and Heron, *Handbook. Vol 4.* (pp. 295–341).

Dasen, P., Lavallee, M., and Retschitzki, J. (1979). Training conservation of quantity (liquids) in West African (Baoule) children. *International Journal of Psychology, 14,* 57–68.

David, K. (1972). Intercultural adjustment and applications of reinforcement theory to problems of culture. *Trends. 4,* 1–64.

Davidson, A., Jaccard, J.J., Triandis, H.C., Morales, M.L., and Diaz-Guerrero, R. (1976). Cross-cultural model testing: Toward a solution of etic-emic dilemma. *International Journal of Psychology, 11,* 1–13.

Davidson, A., and Thomson, E. (1980). Cross-cultural studies of attitudes and beliefs. In Triandis and Brislin, *Handbook. Vol 5.* (pp. 25–71).

Deregowski, J.B. (1980) Perception. In H.C. Triandis and W. Lonner, ed., *Handbook of cross-cultural psychology. Vol 3. Basic processes* (pp. 21–117). Boston: Allyn and Bacon.

————, Muldrow, E.S., and Muldrow, W.F. (1972). Pictorial recognition in a remote Ethiopian population. *Perception, 1,* 417–425.

Doi, L.T.(1973). The Japanese patterns of communication and the concept of amae. *The Quarterly Journal of Speech, 59,* 180–185.

Doob, L.W. (1966). Correlates of eidetic imagery: A cross-cultural will-o'-the wisp? *Journal of Psychology, 72,* 13–34.

————. (1970). Correlates of eidetic imagery. *Journal of Psychology, 76,* 223–230.

Draguns, J.G. (1980). Psychological disorders of clinical severity. In H.C. Triandis and J.G. Draguns, ed., *Handbook of cross-cultural psychology. Vol 6. Psychopathology* (pp. 99–174). Boston: Allyn and Bacon.

Fiedler, F.E., Mitchell, T., and Triandis, H.C. (1971). The culture assimilator: An approach to cross-cultural training, *Journal of Applied Psychology, 55,* 95–102.

Fishbein, M., and Ajzen, I. (1975). *Belief, attitude intention and behavior: An introduction to theory and research.* Boston: Addison-Wesley.

Fontaine, G., and Dorch, E. (1980). Problems and Benefits of close intercultural relationships. *International Journal of Intercultural Relations, 4,* 329-337.

Frijda, N. and Jahoda, G. (1966). On the scope and methods of cross-cultural research. *International Journal of Psychology, 1,* 109–127.

Gallimore, R., Weiss, L., and Finney, R. (1974). Cultural differences in delay of gratification: A problem of behavior classification. *Journal of Personality and Social Psychology, 30,* 72–80.

Geertz, C. (1973). *The interpretation of cultures.* New York: Basic Books.

Glenn, E.S. (1981) *Man and mankind.* Norwood, N.J.: Ablex.

Goodenough, W. (1980). Ethnographic field techniques. In Triandis and Berry Handbook Vol. 2. (pp. 29–55).

Guthrie, G.M., and Tanco, P.P. (1980). Alienation. In Triandis and Berry, Handbook Vol. 6. (pp. 9–595).

Hall, E.T. (1959). The silent language. Garden City, N.Y.: Doubleday.

Herskovits, M. (1948). Man and his works. New York: Knopf.

Huang, L, and Harris, M. (1973). Conformity in Chinese and Americans: A field experiment. Journal of Cross-Cultural Psychology, 4, 427–434.

Hudson, W. (1958, December). The African in industry. Engineering and Foundryman 39, –40.

———. (1960). Pictorial depth perception in sub-cultural groups in Africa. Journal of Social Psychology, 52, 183–208.

Irvine, S., and Carroll, W.K. (1980). Testing and assessment across cultures: Issues in methodology and theory. In Triandis and Berry, Handbook Vol. 2. (pp. 181–244).

Jahoda, G. (1966). Geometric illusions and environment: A study in Ghana. British Journal of Psychology, 5, 193–199.

———. (1971). Retinal Pigmentation, illusion susceptibility, and space perception. International Journal of Psychology, 6, 199–208.

———. (1971). The influence of schooling on adult recall of familiar stimuli: A study in Ghana International Journal of Psychology, 16, 59–71.

Kelly, G.A. (1955) The psychology of personal constructs. New York: W.W. Norton.

Klineberg, O. (1954). Social psychology. New York: Holt.

Kluckhohn, F., and Strodbeck, F. (1961). Variations in value orientations, Evanston, Ill.: Row Peterson.

Kornadt, H.J., Eckensberger, L.H., and Emminghaus, W.B. (1980). Cross-cultural research on motivation and its contribution to a general theory of motivation. In Triandis and Berry, Handbook. Vol. 3. (pp. 9–595).

Kraemer, A.J. (1969). The development of cultural self-awareness: Design of a program of instruction (HumRRO Prof. Paper 27–69). Alexandria, Va.: Human Resources Research Organization.

Kroeber, A., and Kluckhohn, C. (1952). Culture: A critical review of concepts and definitions. Cambridge, Mass.: Peabody Museum.

Landis, D., and Brislin, R. (1983). Handbook of intercultural training. (Vols. 1–3). New York: Pergamon.

Leung, K. (1983). The impact of cultural collectivism on reward allocation. Master's thesis, Department of Psychology, University of Illinois at Urbana-Champaign.

Lonner, W.J. (1980). The search for psychological universals. In H.C. Triandis and W.W. Lambert, ed., Handbook of cross-cultural psychology. Vol. 1. Perspectives (pp. 143–204). Boston: Allyn and Bacon.

Luria, A.R. (1971). Towards the problem of the historical nature of psychological processes. International Journal of Psychology 6, 259–272.

Maehr, M., and Nicholls, J. (1980). Culture and achievement motivation: A second look. In N. Warren, ed., Studies in cross-cultural psychology (Vol. 2, pp. 221–267). London: Academic Press.

Mann, L. (1980). Cross-cultural studies of small groups. In Triandis and Brislin, Handbook. Vol. 5. (pp. 155–209).

Marín, G. (1981) Perceived justice across cultures. Equity vs. equality in Colombia and in the United States. *International Journal of Psychology. 16*, 153–159.

Marsella, A.J. (1979). Cross-cultural studies of mental disorders. In A.J. Marsella, R.G. Tharp, and T.J. Ciborowski, ed., *Perspectives on cross-cultural psychology* (pp. 233–262). New York: Academic Press.

———. (1980). Depressive experience and disorder across cultures. In Triandis and Draguns, *Handbook. Vol. 6.* (pp. 237–289).

McClelland, D. (1961). *The achieving society.* Princeton, N.J.: Van Nostrand.

McKay, H., Sinisterra, L., McKay, A. Gomez, H., and Lloreda, P. (1978). Improving cognitive ability in chronically deprived children. *Science, 200*, 270–278.

Meade, R.D. (1967). An experimental study of leadership in India. *Journal of Social Psychology, 72* , 35–43.

Misumi, J. (1972). *Group dynamics in Japan.* Fukuoka, Japan: Kyushu University.

Munroe, R.L., and Munroe, R.H. (1972). Population density and affective relationships in three East African societies. *Journal of Social Psychology, 88*, 15–20.

Naroll, R. (1983). *The moral order.* Beverly Hills, Cal.: Sage.

———, and Cohen, R. (1970). *A handbook of method in cultural anthropology.* New York: Natural History Press.

Osgood, C.E., May, W., and Miron, M. (1975). *Cross-cultural universals of affective meaning.* Urbana: U of Illinois P.

Phillips, H. (1960). Problems of translation and meaning in field work. *Human Organization, 18* (4), 184–192.

Piaget, J. (1973). Need and significance of cross-cultural studies in genetic psychology. In J. Berry and P. Dasen, ed., *Culture and cognition: Readings in cross-cultural psychology* (pp. 299–309). London: Methuen.

Pick, A. (1980). Cognition: Psychological perspectives. In Triandis and Lonner, *Handbook. Vol. 3.* (pp. 117–153).

Pike, K. (1966. *Language in relation to a unified theory of the structure of human behavior.* The Hague: Mouton.

Price-Williams, D.R. (1980). Anthropological approaches to cognition and their relevance to psychology. In Triandis and Lonner, *Handbook. Vol. 3.* (pp. 155–184).

———, Gordon, W. and Ramirez, M. (1969). Skill and conservation. *Developmental Psychology, 1*, 769.

Prince, R. (1980). Variations in psychotherapeutic procedures. In Triandis and Draguns, *Handbook. Vol. 6.* (pp. 291–349).

Rogoff, B. (1981) Schooling and the development of cognitive skills. In Triandis and Heron, *Handbook. Vol. 4.* (pp. 175–236).

Sanua, V.D. (1980). Familial and sociocultural antecedents of psychopathology. In Triandis and Draguns, *Handbook. Vol. 6.* (pp. 175–236).

Scribner, S., and Cole, M. (1981). *The psychology of literacy.* Cambridge, Mass.: Harvard UP.

Sechrest, L., Fay, T., and Zaidi, S.M. (1972). Problems of translation in cross-cultural research. *Journal of Cross-Cultural Psychology, 3*, 41–56.

Segall, M., Campbell, D.T., and Herskovits, M. (1966). *Influence of culture on visual perception*. Indianapolis, Ind.: Bobbs-Merrill.

Sharp, D., Cole, M., and Lave, C. (1979). Education and cognitive development: The evidence from experimental research. *Monographs of the Society for Research in Child Development. 44* (1–2, Serial No. 178).

Shweder, R.A., and Bourne, E.J. (1982). Does the concept of the person vary cross-culturally? In A.J. Marsella and G.M. White, ed., *Cultural conceptions of mental health and therapy*. (pp. 97–140). Dordrecht, Holland: D. Reidel.

Starr, B.J., and Wilson S. (1980). Some epistemological and methodological issues in the design of cross-cultural research. In M. Hammett and R. Brislin, ed., *Research in culture learning: Language and conceptual studies* (pp. 143–153). Honolulu: UP of Hawaii.

Stewart, E. (1966). The simulation of cultural differences. *Journal of Communication, 16,* 291–304.

Strodtbeck, F. (1964). Considerations of meta-method in cross-cultural studies. *American Anthropologist, 66,* 223–229.

Sue, S., Zane, N., and Ito, J. (1979). Alcohol drinking patterns among Asian and Caucasian Americans. *Journal of Cross-Cultural Psychology, 10,* 41–56.

Triandis, H.C. (1964) Cultural influences upon cognitive processes. In L. Berkowitz, ed., *Advances in experimental social psychology* (pp. 1–48). New York: Academic Press.

———. (1968). Some cross-cultural studies of cognitive consistency. In R.B. Abelson, E. Aronson, W.J. MCGuire, T.M. Newcomb, MJ Rosenberg, and P.H. Tannenbaum, ed., *Theories of cognitive consistency: A sourcebook* (pp.723–730). Chicago: Rand McNally.

———. (1972). *The analysis of subjective culture*. New York: Wiley.

———. (1975). Culture training, cognitive complexity, and interpersonal attitudes. In R. Brislin, S. Bochner, and W. Lonner, ed., *Cross-cultural perspectives on learning* (pp. 39–77). Beverly Hills, Cal.: Sage.

———. (1977). *Interpersonal behavior*. Monterey, Cal.: Brooks/Cole.

———. (1978). Some universals of social behavior. *Personality and Social Psychology Bulletin, 4,* 1–16.

———. (1980). Values, attitudes and interpersonal behavior. In. H. Howe and M. Page, ed., *Nebraska Symposium on Motivation 1979* (pp. 195–260). Lincoln: U of Nebraska P.

———, and Lambert, W., Lonner, W., Heron, A, Brislin, R., or Draguns, J., ed. (1980–1981). *Handbook of cross-cultural psychology* (Vols. 1–6). Boston: Allyn and Bacon.

Trifonovitch, G. (1977). On cross-cultural orientaition techniques. In R.W. Brislin, ed., *Culture learning: Concepts, applications, and research* (pp.213–222). Honolulu: UP of Hawaii.

Tseng, W., and Hsu, J. (1980). Minor psychological disturbances of everyday life. In Triandis and Draguns, *Handbook. Vol. 6.* (pp. 61–97).

Tyler, S.A. (1969). *Cognitive anthropology*. New York: Holt, Rinehart and Winston.

Wagner, D.A. (1981). Culture and memory development. In Triandis and Heron, *Handbook. Vol. 4.* (pp. 187–232).

Webb, E., Campbell, D., Schwartz, R., and Sechrest, L. (1966). *Unobtrusive measures: Nonreactive research in the social sciences.* Chicago: Rand McNally.

Weiner, B. (1972). *Theories of motivation: From mechanism to cognition.* Chicago: Rand McNally.

Werner, O., and Campbell, D. (1970). Translating, working through interpreters and the problem of decentering. In R. Naroll and R. Cohen, ed., *A handbook of method in cultural anthropology* (pp. 398–420). New York: Natural History Press.

Whiting, J. (1968). Methods and problems in cross-cultural research. In G. Lindzey and E. Aronson, ed., *Handbook of social psychology.* Vol. 2. (pp. 693–728). Reading, Mass.: Addison-Wesley.

Whittaker, J.O., and Meade, R.D. (1967). Social pressure in the modification and distortion of judgment: A cross-cultural study. *International Journal of Psychology, 2,* 109–113.

Wolfgang, A. (1979). *Nonverbal behavior: Applications and cultural implications.* New York: Academic Press.

Psychology in Its World Context

Roger W. Russell

A n invitation to discuss a topic such as "Psychology in Its World Context" is flattering but also rather frightening. The world is a big place, and any human activity can be expected to differ considerably from region to region, from language to language, from culture to culture. I was aware of this when the invitation came to me. I have been fortunate enough to be employed as a psychologist in universities on three continents, and I have visited with former students and undertaken projects (e.g., Moghni and Russell, 1968) with colleagues in three others. Although common threads run through the formal disciplines of psychology as they are practiced in all these areas, there are differences in definitions of "psychology," in formal qualifications for psychologists, in the roles psychologists play, and in what various societies expect of the discipline in return for their support of it.

As I review my decision to accept the invitation I wonder how much it was affected by a comment from an undergraduate student at one American university where I was visiting at the time. Upon learning that I am from Australia he replied, "Vienna must be a lovely city." That started me thinking about how little some people know of what takes place outside their own region and about the exciting and intellectually challenging experiences they miss as a consequence. Great pleasures can come from discovering how well one can understand and fit into another culture, even if one does not intend to remain in it.

In this article, I have attempted to paint a realistic picture of psychology in its world context and of perceptions psychologists in other parts of the world have of American psychology. (The latter are not always laudatory, just as American perceptions are not always flattering.) It is important that, with but a few very short periods of exception, psychologists throughout the world have kept their communication channels open (Rosenzweig, 1979). In my opinion all have benefited as a result, just as undergraduate and graduate students in psychology can benefit from a more comprehensive understanding of

Roger W. Russell is Emeritus Professor at the Flinders University of South Australia.

psychologies in other countries. It is my hope that many who read this article will see a place for some study or work abroad as an important part of their career structures (Russell, 1962, 1967).

This article is organized around four basic topics. The first is concerned with factors affecting psychology in other countries and with roles psychologists can play in international affairs. Americans who have not yet had opportunities to see psychologists at work in other countries are often surprised to learn that what psychologists do and how they conceive of their discipline may differ considerably from the American model. What factors are responsible for such differences? A companion question may be: Why should Americans be concerned? This is the kind of question that characterized American isolationism prior to World War II. The discussion in the first of the following sections will at least start a reader thinking about the influences on American psychology that psychology abroad has had and will continue to have in the future. It seems reasonable in the second section to look at American psychology as viewed by psychologists in other countries and then in section three to consider psychology from an international perspective as affected by interests common to psychologists generally. These latter two topics will provide an opportunity to suggest ways in which an interested student may make contacts at the international level.

Factors Affecting Psychology in Other Countries

"The conditions in which psychology is growing and the demands made upon it, and even the definitions of psychology and psychologist, show a wide range from one country to another" (Rosenzweig, 1982, p. 117). To understand psychology in its world context it is important to appreciate the nature of these conditions, demands, and definitions.

Who May Be a Psychologist?

The term "psychologist" is generally defined by educational and training background, by membership in a scientific and/or professional society, or by certification under legislation. Obviously such criteria are not universal absolutes but may vary among nations as educational systems and perceived cultural needs differ. As psychology began to organize internationally, it became apparent that accommodations would have to be made because definitions of psychology and psychologist varied from country to country. The decision at the time was to accept definitions as they were formulated by responsible groups, usually national psychological societies, within each country. This orientation gave rise to very broadly inclusive terms. It meant that a psychologist in country X might not qualify as a psychologist in country Y. It also meant that psychologists were engaged in activities in some places that were not practiced in others. It called attention to the fact that psychologists everywhere had to be aware of a world community of psychology that was broader than any internally oriented perception of the discipline within their own culture. Such awareness may lead to greater sensitivity and a better understanding of both the nature of differences between national psychologies and the factors that affect the roles other psychologists have within their own cultures. Lack of such understanding has sometimes led to allegations that some national psychology express "feelings of superiority" that are not only unbecoming among scientists and professionals generally but can result in failure to recognize important new developments. It will be useful at this point to consider briefly those factors that have affected the development of psychology in other nations.

Economic Factors

"Psychology is a discipline cultivated mainly in the industrialized countries ... and not so much in other nations" (Ardila, 1982b, p. 120). All human activities draw on a nation's resources. Indeed, one very important source of reinforcement that shapes and maintains human behavior is the support it receives from society. The number of psychologists in a country is related to opportunities for training and for employment. Decisions about manpower needs affect resource allocation, which, often in a remarkably short period of time, is reflected in the number of young people undertaking education for careers in a given science or profession. A relation between economic conditions and the development of psychology has been illustrated during the present century by the differential growth in a number of psychologists in various parts of the world. Information provided by Rosenzweig (1982) indicates that the total number of members in the 36 national societies affiliated with the International Union of Psychological Science (IUPsyS) in 1970 increased from 53,219 to 101,521 ten years later. The increases for individual societies ranged from 0% to over 200%, but the growth occurred almost entirely within industrialized nations. The distribution of psychologists within the United States also demonstrates the operation of economic factors: They are found especially in the wealthier states, in the highly urbanized states, and where centers of higher education are located (Richards and Gottfredson, 1978).

Geographical Factors

Although the great strides taken in modes of transportation during the present century have helped greatly to alleviate the problem, geographical distance between nations has had an influence on the world-wide development of psychology and, hence, on roles open to psychologists. "The tyranny of distance" was a general complaint of those who sought to bring Western

European psychology even to those "colonies" speaking the same language and practicing similar culture patterns. Circumstances were much more complicated when different languages and cultures were involved. On the one hand, geographical separation might have provided a buffer against intervention from Europe and North America and thus might in some cases have enabled greater freedom for the development of indigenous psychologies amid a less heavy-handed domination by Western psychology. On the other hand, because of its early development, Western psychology tended to become firmly entrenched once it did arrive in other parts of the world. Some in Australia claim that this has been the state of affairs in that country and that, as a consequence, there still are no distinctive "Australian" contributions to psychology despite the generally recognized excellence of its psychologists (Nixon and Taft, 1977).

Linguistic and Semantic Factors

English has become accepted, not always gracefully, as a universal language in psychology as in other sciences. The older among us can recall the time when very significant portions of the world's literature in psychology appeared in French or German. I still have clear recollections of examinations in these two languages (in some universities each lasted a full day) as the most difficult parts of my doctoral requirements. The major difficulties were semantic in nature: What was the "true" meaning in English of a term in the other language? It should not be surprising that the current predominance of the English language may affect development of psychology in non-English-speaking countries by placing constraints on the meanings of concepts and on the tools for discovery and analysis. Even when translations into indigenous languages are provided, meanings are likely not to be precisely the same. A.V. Lagmay (1984) has illustrated the potential effects of such semantic factors in a recent discussion of "Western Psychology in the Philippines," in which he has described limitations placed on the development of psychology in his country by the establishment of an educational system based on the English language: "the current practice is one of adoption and assimilation, with revision, modification and translation wherever it is feasible, of concepts and tools ... as they are in English" (p. 42). The usual reaction of Americans when effects of such semantic factors on psychology in other countries are mentioned is one of surprise, a reaction that is also elicited by the comment that "American psychology disregards almost completely research done in other countries and particularly in other languages" (Brandt, 1970, p. 109).

Cultural Factors

"Interest in psychology is worldwide, but as long as the discipline is so much influenced by one culture (and it does not matter which culture), there cannot be a truly international psychology" (Ardila, 1982a, p. 328). At international congresses of psychology in the past the contributions of all participants appeared to fit quite readily into familiar packages regardless of the country from which a participant came. The nature of the problems studied, the methods of study, and the general conceptual frameworks within which they were discussed had commonalities that were generally taken for granted, as if they were structurally inherent in all psychology. However, more thorough examination reveals that the organization can be identified with that which characterizes Western psychology, that is, it is not necessarily indigenous to all national psychologies.

Although able to implant its concepts and methods onto other national psychologies, Western psychology has sometimes had its difficulties in trying to understand behavior in other cultures. "When a psychologist looks at a non-Western culture through Western glasses, he may fail to notice important aspects of the non-Western culture since the schemata for recognizing them are not provided by his science" (Azuma, 1984, p. 49). Psychology in Japan provides an example of the blending of Western psychology with the concepts and needs of a non-Western country. Hiroshi Azuma of the University of Tokyo has analyzed the stages through which the development of psychology in that nation passed in coming to grips with non-Western cultural phenomena without forcing them into a Western mold: a "pioneer period" when the potential relevance of psychology was realized and the discipline was introduced at a textbook level; an "introductory period" during which psychology was accepted as a significant discipline for study; the "translation and modeling period" characterized by detailed transplantation of concepts and methods in their Westernized forms; a more sophisticated "indigenization period" when new ideas and approaches appropriate to the local culture were introduced; and an "integration period" when "psychology gets freed, to a certain extent, from the rigid but otherwise unnoticed mold of traditionally Western concepts and logic" (Azuma, 1984, p. 54).

National Interests and Priorities

Clearly the establishment and the stability of national goals are two of the major issues presently confronting society the world over. Relatively rapid changes in social concerns during the past half century have been reflected in changes in the roles for psychologists that a society is willing to support. What has been acceptable during one decade has received highly emotional criticism in the next. It is very difficult for any science or profession to respond to so dynamic a state of affairs. The sciences and professions have been described as "pipeline industries." They cannot be turned on or off suddenly. It takes years for a systematic body of knowledge, for example, a discipline of psychology, to develop and for psychologists to add to it or to put it to work. Some stability of national interests and priorities is required, perhaps in the form of a long-range plan for systematic change or pressures toward conformity to the status quo. Western psychology has fortunately become increasingly sophisticated in finding ways to contribute to national interests. Psychologists in developing countries are becoming well aware of the importance of being "relevant," given the particular sociocultural conditions and development policies of the environment in which they function (Serpell, 1984). This is exemplified in the People's Republic of China, where national planning now expects psychologists to lend their knowledge and skills to achieving the goals of the "four modernizations." "To do so ... a culturally specific psychology must be created to meet the demands of our own national conditions" (Ching, 1984, p. 63).

Throughout recent analyses by indigenous psychologists of the development of psychology in Africa, Asia, and South America, there runs the common theme of "relevance" (see Sinha and Holtzman, 1984). Psychology needs to demonstrate relevance to the particular sociocultural conditions and developmental policies of the Third World. From a psychologist in Turkey comes the observation that developing countries have "inherited the field ready made from the West rather than having participated actively in its development" (Kagitcibasi, 1984, p. 146). In the opinion of another psychologist in Zambia,

> revitalization of endogenous cultural development is essential for developing a valid and socially acceptable psychology. This requires both sensitivity to the cultural load of Western psychology and systematic exploration of distinctive indigenous concepts (Serpell, 1984, p. 179).

National Expectations

Expectations of the roles of psychologists in supporting national interests and priorities have significant effects on the development of psychology. Pressures toward preservation of present policies in some countries and toward economic and social change in others keep questions about the roles of psychologists as psychologists very much alive.

Melikian (1984) has summarized the impact of psychology in five Arab Gulf oil-producing states as follows: "As of this date, psychology has not left a noticeable impact on industry or government. It has not been recognized as a potential contributor to development planning. Whatever consulting role psychologists have played has been primarily restricted to ministries of health" (p. 74). A wider view of the responsibilities of psychologists is implied in the recent comments on American psychology of a psychologist from Iran, who believes that psychologists should, but do not, "think about the ways and means of inducing changes in the attitudes and practices of those who control the bulk of economic resources needed for dealing with poverty and injustice prevailing in the Third World"(Mehryar, 1984, p. 166). Within the extremes represented by these two examples, differences of opinion have long existed on the extent to which psychology has knowledge, skills, and sophistication that can be validly applied in support of national goals (Russell, 1972).

In a sense, national expectations of psychology are reflected in the nature of the positions psychologists achieve in society. During the period 1958 to 1966, the prime minister of South Africa, a former professor of applied psychology at one of the national universities, rigorously applied a policy of apartheid, which was perceived by his constituents as supporting national policies. Were his actions those of a "psychologist"? Psychology has received social recognition in other parts of the world where, for example, psychologists have served as cabinet ministers, members of national, state, and local legislative bodies, and even as army chief of staff (Salazar, 1984). In all such capacities their activities may have been relevant to the goals and policies of the societies they served, but the question is whether the activities were "relevant" when judged in terms of the special competencies of psychologists.

As indicated in my earlier comments on "relevance," opinions differ as to the extent to which current psychological knowledge and methodology can be soundly put to work in the interests of national and international affairs. What have psychologists to contribute that is different from the intelligent citizen, public official, or specialist in some other discipline? Put in another way, what *special competencies* can the psychologist as a psychologist—in contrast to the psychologist as an intelligent citizen—bring to bear on issues of national or international affairs? During recent years the opinion has been expressed strongly that psychologists have methods and techniques, sophistication about relevant variables, and some well founded information that may serve as bases for useful contributions both to national and international affairs. The first step toward any such contribution must be to analyze the issues involved for their psychological components. Most of us are not accustomed to thinking about national and international affairs in terms of their psychological content, but if such content can be found, the psychologist has a role to play. A second step lies in compiling and integrating information already available and immediately relevant to the identified psychological dimension of the issue being addressed. This step is really the familiar one of summarizing current knowledge on the question. Where the state of the art is inadequate to solve the problem at hand, a third step may have to be taken, that of undertaking research. This is an area in which the academically trained psychologist is likely to feel at home. Research may be targeted at the areas of social action (patterns of group conflict and strategies for conflict resolution), individual motivation (bases of aggression in the personality), cognitive structure (national images), social processes (dynamics of public opinion), and social structure (psychological bases of nationalism). These and related research orientations are not new (e.g., see Katz, 1961; Pool, 1961; Snyder and Robinson, 1961). A fourth general area for the psychologist's contribution to national and international affairs lies in the application of current knowledge and skills. This requires that information about psychological knowledge and skills reach policy makers who can put it to use. That psychologists have not always been successful in this regard has been attributed in the past at least as much to difficulties in communication as to the public's perception of their capabilities. Recently, psychologists have become more skillful in conveying information to persons in strategic policy positions at the national and international levels.

Psychologists and their organizations have become increasingly involved at the international level. Individuals have served as advisors to international bodies such as the United Nations Educational, Scientific, and Cultural Organization (UNESCO), the World Health Organization, and the International Labor Organization. The International Union of Psychological Science (IUPsyS) has undertaken several special research programs at the request of UNESCO. Recent co-ventures have included studies on woman's role and status (with the International Social Science Council) and on television and the child (with UNESCO), and conferences under UNESCO auspices on the psychology of the child, trends in social science research on children, and, most recently, the impact of psychology in the Third World.

Perceptions of American Psychology

In interacting with persons from another country, we benefit very significantly from information on how we are perceived. How is American psychology viewed from abroad? It will be obvious to a reader that the brief comments to follow are not conclusions from an exhaustive study but are intended to indicate that American psychology is perceived as neither saint nor sinner, neither the ultimate sage nor the persistent fool.

Professor E.G. Boring, when chairperson of the department of psychology at Harvard University, once commented about the growth of psychology in the United States using linear extrapolation of the membership list of the APA. He concluded that not long after the turn of the 21st century the number of psychologists would just equal the world's population. In the perceptions of many psychologists living abroad this caricature of American psychology is not without some basis. The growth in size of the discipline in the United States has dwarfed its counterparts elsewhere—and with this fact have come some attitudes that are welcomed and others that may be disturbing to Americans. "Over the last 75 years, American psychologists have earned the abundant gratitude of the rest of the world. But like all parents of ambitious children ... they had better not expect much in the way of thanks" (Berlyne, 1968, p. 452).

Perceptions of American psychology by neighbors to the north sometimes center on its provincialism. "American psychology can thus be said to be truly American. It reflects the American emphasis on doing (experimentation) and making (quantification of data and publications), as well as the contradictions inherent in American society, and the feeling of general superiority" (Brandt, 1970, p. 1093). Another Canadian writing at about the same time suggested that the relative dominance of American psychology could be expected to change, as, indeed, has the earlier dominance of psychology in Western Europe: "The United States has been the principal guardian of psychology during a vital formative period.... But this custody cannot be expected to last forever, and it is no doubt a good thing that it cannot" (Berlyne, 1968, p. 452). Efforts by the American and Canadian Psychological Associations have already moved to redefine "American" as "North American" psychology, perhaps raising the question of whether the new amalgam will be any less provincial.

Views expressed by good friends from south of the border have also been quite frank. I recall an incident several years ago when, in toasting colleagues at an international dinner, a Mexican psychologist commented, "We Mexican psychologists are very humble because we are so far away from God and so close to the United States." Such remarks may be made only partly in jest. In his 1982 analysis of "international psychology," Colombian psychologist Ruben Ardila concluded that

contemporary psychology is largely an Anglo-Saxon discipline that shares the values and assumptions of English-speaking countries, particularly of the United States; some of these values and conceptions seem to be alien to the Latin-American way of thinking (Ardila, 1982b, p. 120).

Over a quarter century ago an American psychologist viewing psychology from the vantage point of his affiliations with the Arab Near East joined with a colleague in commenting, "There is some suspicion that psychology is an instrument of Western imperialism, but there is reason to hope that this suspicion will be overcome as increasing numbers of Arabs become psychologists" (Prothro and Melikian, 1955, p. 309). In the quarter century since then the number of psychologists has, indeed, increased, and fuller communication has developed between Arab psychologists and psychologists in other regions (Melikian, 1984), although the Western model of psychology still comes under some attack (e.g., Mehryar, 1984).

Further examples of perceptions of American psychology as stated by psychologists from abroad are reported in a 1984 number of the *International Journal of Psychology* (Sinha and Holtzman, 1984), which is worthy of reading as long as a reader looks at the comments objectively, recognizing that a few come from the adrenal rather than the cerebral cortex.

The past quarter century has seen very significant changes in perceptions by Americans themselves of the roles of American psychology. From being a discipline very closely affiliated with institutions of tertiary education and expressing strong feelings about the "purity" of its academic goals, American psychology has descended from its ivory towers and gone to work. Today only about 35% of American psychologists teach in universities and other tertiary institutions. The number of "applied" psychologists in the American Psychological Association first exceeded the number of "academic" psychologists in the late 1950s. Now career specialization entices the largest numbers into clinical or educational/school psychology or into the field of counseling and guidance (Rosenzweig, 1982).

Concern about possible consequences of provincialism in American psychology is being expressed by many American psychologists. Early among these were Murphy and Kovach (1972), who concluded their *Historical Introduction to Modern Psychology* with the observation that

> there are some consequences that need to be faced. An obvious one is that the American psychologist, with so many rich facilities at his command, seldom thinks it necessary to read much of the newer psychology from other lands. Almost everything which he regards as important is available in English—in fact, in several translations (p. 484).

On the other hand, writes a representative of UNESCO,

> The output produced by the West impresses by its neatness and precision, but often disappoints scholars from the Third World by its artificiality, triviality, and lack of relevance to the real-life psychological situations confronting them (Schwendler, 1984, p. 14).

Psychology will be wise to adopt a global orientation if the best of both is to come from interaction.

An International Perspective

The authors of *What College Students Know and Believe about Their World* write

> A nation now so irrevocably immersed in global complexities [cannot] endure for long the fashionable academic obsession with micro-knowledge refined to fit on the point of a needle. (Barrows, Klein, and Clark, 1981, p.1)

The monograph summarizes a 1980 nationwide survey of freshmen and seniors in four-year colleges and students in two-year institutions. The survey was designed to study their understanding of the world and of world issues. Myopic views also characterize perceptions of the sciences and professions with which students and, indeed, their more senior colleagues identify. Psychology is not without its provincialism. It is possible that the very success of North American psychology has led to what the survey has described as a "general lack of interest in other nations and world issues among these students" (Barrows, Klein, and Clark, 1981, p. 38). One lesson of the 20th century has been that no one society in today's world can long exist in isolation—nor can its sciences or its professions. Expanding the focus of undergraduate and graduate education and training in psychology to include an understanding of the discipline in other parts of the world can make for better-educated graduates and for a better psychology at home.

No nation has a monopoly in modern psychology. It is true that by several criteria American achievements in many areas of psychological endeavor have become dominant in world psychology. Estimates of numbers of psychologists in various nations place those in the United States at between 70,000 and 120,000, with the next largest number in Brazil at about 20,000 (Rosenzweig, 1982). In terms of the number of psychologists per million of population, North America stands first at an estimated 424, Western Europe second with 322, Australia-New Zealand third with 235, and Latin America fourth with 120. Such statistics reflect national interests, for individuals are encouraged to enter those scientific and professional pursuits that are reinforced by the societies in which they live. The so-called Western psychology developed in industrialized societies that were characterized by science and technology as understood by their physicists, chemists, evolutionary biologists, and eventually by their social scientists as well. Objectivity and empirical verification in the study of psychology have come to achieve high prestige in some other societies, for example, in Japan, but not in all.

That the relevance and appropriateness of the values and concepts of Westernized psychology for the interests and needs of developing nations should be questioned is not surprising. Similar queries gave rise to the processes by which modern Western psychology evolved, most of which derived from the revival of Greco-Roman conceptualizations during Medieval and early modern times. But there were other civilizations that also showed a high standard of inventiveness. For example, during a period of several centuries B.C., the search for an understanding of human behavior in India and other areas under its influence led to the development of a psychological system of a nature quite different from that of the Greco-Roman renaissance. This system focused on the basic psychophysical nature of emotion, memory, perception, and thinking, and it was concerned with applying its general principles for practical purposes (Murphy and Kovach, 1972). Such different systems of psychology were the products of social interests of the times and influenced the nature of cultural traditions that continue to affect the direction in which psychology is evolving.

Those who wish to understand changes in psychology occurring during any particular period require familiarity with the background from which these developments emerged. Similarly, one must look at social and cultural developments in order to anticipate directions in which further changes may be expected. Herman Ebbinghaus, one of the pioneers of modern experimental psychology, once commented that psychology has a long past but only a short history. The long past involved innovative efforts in several parts of the world. The history is very much in the making today and cannot but have significant influences on the scientific and professional career of students now electing psychology as their life's endeavor.

Effects of Common Interests

The diversities apparent in the emergence of psychology in various areas of the world suggest several related questions. What interests do psychologists have in common? Are cultural, regional, or national psychologies so different from each other as to have little, if any, overlapping objectives? Are they so mutually exclusive as to make familiarity with more than one not even worthwhile? Evidence that, indeed, there are interests in common comes from several sources, all of which involve communication across the boundaries of national psychologies.

Exchanges of Persons

Common interests bring together individuals from different countries. Histories of modern psychology (e.g., Boring, 1950) record the attractions that Wundt's laboratory at Leipzig and other European centers of early development in modern psychology had for scholars from abroad, who studied in them and took their knowledge back home. Analogous education and training fostered common interests both in the subject matter of psychology and in the methods by which the frontiers of that subject matter could be enlarged. As knowledge in psychology grew, new centers of excellence were recognized and in turn became involved in the exchange process.

Much international communication in psychology still takes place on a person-to-person basis. Opportunities for individuals to take advantage of exchange programs have increased greatly during the past half century. Both governmental and private organizations have come to recognize that much is to be gained from the exchange of information about matters of common interest, as well as from the better intercultural understanding that comes as a side effect of such exchanges. Support for study abroad is now available from a number of different sources for the serious young scholar with sufficient insight to appreciate that there is something of value to be gained from examining the same basic questions from the vantage point of more than one cultural setting.

Internationally Oriented Publications

Further evidence that there are common interests among national psychologies is to be found in scientific and professional publications that provide media for psychologists from all nations to exchange ideas and information. Such communication is vital to the development of a systematic body of knowledge. It makes information public and provides opportunities for its verification by others, for its assimilation into the existing body of psychological knowledge, for stimulating further investigation, and for putting what is known to work toward some practical end. Unfortunately language differences place constraints on the extent to which common interests are served by this method. Despite the fact that English has become widely accepted as a universal language in science, lack of facility in other modern languages still imposes limitations on American students. Translations are helpful, but they often lose many of the nuances of the original. Volumes like the *Trilingual Psychological Dictionary* produced by IUPsyS are helpful to those who wish to study an original work, but such dictionaries are of limited scope.

An incident at the 1957 International Congress of Psychology in Brussels, which still is very clear in my memory, illustrates the importance with which archival publications are viewed as a means of furthering common interests among national groups. As executive officer of APA, I was approached by A.R. Luria, representing the Society of Psychologists of the USSR, who requested an informal meeting with American representatives to discuss the exchange of publications. He expressed concern not about Soviet psychologists receiving American publications (which were translated by his government for those of his colleagues who could not read English), but about the fact that very few Soviet publications were available in translation for American consumption. Of obvious importance to Luria and his colleagues was the two-way exchange of information about matters of common interest. The Brussels exchange was followed 20 years later by an article in the *American Psychologist* comparing American and Soviet approaches to clinical neuropsychology, which demonstrated that Luria was, indeed, very serious about the exchange (Luria and Majovski, 1977).

289

International and Regional Meetings

Without efficient means for communicating information about matters of common interest there would "certainly be unnecessary duplication of activities and research which the world community cannot afford and would slow down the application of science for the benefit of humanity" (International Council of Scientific Unions, 1982). Realization of the validity of this point of view led psychologists to organize the first International Congress of Psychology in 1889 in Paris, under the presidency of T.A. Ribot. Ninety-five years later, in 1984, the 23rd Congress was held in Acapulco, Mexico; in 1988 participants journeyed "down under" to meet in Sydney, Australia, for the first such meeting in Australia. The years have seen an increasing interest in these special events, which bring together several thousand psychologists from all parts of the world to discuss scientific and professional matters of common concern. The interests of psychologists from many nations in applications of psychological knowledge and methodology are the special focus of international congresses arranged by the International Association for Applied Psychology (IAAP). Other more limited meetings encourage the exchange of views about matters of common interest to psychologists within a geographical region (e.g., Inter-American), within a cultural area (e.g., Islamic), and within a language grouping (e.g., French-speaking).

Regional and International Associations

Rapid development of psychology following the turn of the 20th century encouraged the formation of national societies to stimulate the internal growth of the discipline. But again, as with the other evidences of common transnational and cross-cultural interests just described, strong motives appeared that led beyond national boundaries to the establishment of regional and international associations.

Most prominent among these associations is the IUPsyS, referred to above. Founded at the Thirteenth International Congress of Psychology in Stockholm in 1951, the union is a federation of national psychological societies. Several individual-member associations are affiliated with IUPsyS., for example, the International Association of Applied Psychology and the International Council of Psychologists (ICP). From its founding IUPsyS was designated as a nongovernmental organization in consultative relations with UNESCO, its main channel of communication with that organization being through the social sciences department of UNESCO and now through the International Social Science Council. In 1982 the union was voted to full membership in the prestigious International Council of Scientific Unions, thus gaining recognition for the commitment modern psychology has always had to the biological as well as the social sciences. The main goals of IUPsyS include encouraging the exchange of ideas and information among psychologists in different countries; contributing to communication through psychological documentation generally; aiding the exchange of scholars among the world's institutions; and supporting international projects of special current interest to psychologists and to society. Students interested in IUPsyS and its activities can obtain information from the union's Secretary-General, whose name and address can be found in the union's official publication, *The International Journal of Psychology*.

Some Concluding Comments

Understandably the attention of students in psychology is directed toward those activities that, in their judgement, have the highest probability of leading to a successful career in their chosen profession. But attention to psychology in its world context can add a significant dimension to career planning at undergraduate and graduate levels. The history of psychology has shown that development of the discipline has been influenced by contributions from several regions of the world. Psychologists who are not aware of what is happening elsewhere than in their microcosm run the risk of being left behind as the discipline continues to change. Communication with colleagues from other countries also provides opportunities to be a part of —possibly to influence— that change. And, not to be forgotten, are the challenges, excitement, and pleasure that come from interactions with persons of other cultural backgrounds who are equally identified with the successes of psychology as a science and as a profession.

References

Ardila, R. (1982a). International psychology. *American Psychologist, 37*, 3, 323–329.

———. (1982b). Psychology in Latin America. *Annual Review of Psychology, 33*, 103–122.

Azuma, H. (1984). Psychology in a non-Western country. *International Journal of Psychology, 19*, 45–55.

Barrows, T.S. Klein, SF., and Clark, J.L.D. (1981). *What college students know and believe about their world.* New Rochelle, NY: Change.

Berlyne, D.E. (1968). American and European psychology. *American Psychologist, 23*, 447–452.

Boring, E.G. (1950). *History of experimental psychology.* New York: Appleton-Century Crofts.

Brandt, L.W. (1970). American psychology. *American Psychologist, 25*, 1091–1093.

Ching, C.C. (1984). Psychology and the four modernizations in China. *International Journal of Psychology, 19*, 57–63.

International Council of Scientific Unions. (December 1982). *Newsletter No. 12*, Annual Report.

Kagitcibasi, C. (1984). Socialization in traditional society: A challenge to psychology. *International Journal of Psychology, 19,* 145–157.

Katz, D. (1961). Current and needed psychological research in international relations. *Journal of Social Issues, 17,* 69–78.

Lagmay, A.V. (1984). Western psychology in the Philippines: Impact and response. *International Journal of Psychology, 19,* 31–44.

Luria, A.R., and Majovski, L.V. (1977). Basic approaches used in American and Soviet clinical neuropsychology. *American Psychologist, 32,* 959–968.

Mehryar, A.H. (1984). The role of psychology in national development: Wishful thinking and reality. *International Journal of Psychology 19,* 159–167.

Melikian, L.H. (1981). The transfer of psychological knowledge to the Third World countries and its impact on development: The case of five Arab Gulf oil-producing states. *International Journal of Psychology, 19,* 65–77.

Moghni, S.A., and Russell, R.W. (1968). Application of new educational technology to literary training in Pakistan: A research project. *International Journal of Psychology, 3,* 209–212.

Murphy, G., and Kovach, J.K. (1972). *Historical introduction to modern psychology,* New York: Harcourt, Brace, Jovanovich.

Nixon, M., and Taft, R. (Ed.) (1977). *Psychology in Australia.* Sydney, Australia: Pergamon Press.

Pool, J. de S. (1961). *Communication and values in relation to war and peace.* New York: Institute for International Order.

Prothro, E.T. and Melikian, L. (1955). Psychology in the Arab Near East, *Psychological Bulletin, 52,* 303–310.

Richards, I.M., and Gottfredson, G.D. (1978). Geographic distribution of the U.S. psychologists: A human ecological analysis. *American Psychologist, 33,* 1–9.

Rosenzweig, M.R. (1979). Promoting international communication in psychology: The program of the IUPS Committee on Publications and Communication. *International Journal of Psychology; 14,* 285–286.

———. (1982). Trends in development and status of psychology: An international perspective. *International Journal of Psychology, 17,* 117–140.

Russell, R.W. (1962). Psychology and international affairs; Can psychologists contribute? In G.S. Nielsen (Ed.), *Psychologists and society: Role and responsibility* (pp. 48–58). Copenhagen: Munksgaard.

———. (1967). Planning and supporting foreign area research. In *Foreign area research:A conference report* (pp. 13–18). Washington, DC: National Research Council, National Academy of Science.

———. (1972). Academic and applied psychology: A rapprochement. *Professional Psychology, 4,* 232–237.

Salazar, J.M. (1984). The use and impact of psychology in Venezuela: Two examples. *International Journal of Psychology 19,* 113–122.

Schwendler, W. (1984). UNESCO's project on the exchange of knowledge for endogenous development. *International Journal of Psychology, 19,* 3–15.

Serpell, R. (1984). Commentary on the impact of psychology on Third World development. *International Journal of Psychology, 19,* 179–192.

Sinha, D., and Holtzman, W.H. (Ed.) (1984). The impact of psychology on Third World development [Special issue]. *International Journal of Psychology, 19,* 3–192.

Snyder, R.C. and Robinson, J.A. (1961). *National and international decision-making.* New York: Institute for International Order.

American Psychologists and Psychology Abroad

Virginia Staudt Sexton and Henryk Misiak

> Can we seriously entertain the possibility of growing isolation in the light of the truly international character of our general scientific endeavor? Does not man's quest for understanding his world and himself stem from a common origin of shared needs and curiosities? Are not the objective methods and theories of science truly supranational, perhaps even supracultural?
>
> —Murphy and Kovach, 1972, p. 484

It is a truism that the growth and expansion of American psychology has been phenomenal. At the same time, it appears that as American psychologists grew more conscious of their accomplishments, progress, and influence, their interest in psychology outside their country waned and communication between them and psychologists in other countries faltered. As a result, American psychologists were often unaware of important new developments and achievements in other lands. Moreover, they were not aware of how their own achievements and theories were perceived and judged by foreign psychologists. This article addresses itself to these problems.

The Foundation of American Psychology

The roots of American scientific psychology were formed in Europe, particularly in Germany. Early experimental psychology, transplanted to the United States, was modeled after the psychology of Wilhelm Wundt and his Psychological Institute at Leipzig, and the majority of the American pioneers of psychology studied in Leipzig. In time, other European influences, especially British, were felt in America and were pervasive almost until World War I.

Virginia Staudt Sexton is Distinguished Professor of Psychology at St. John's University and Henryk Misiak is Professor Emeritus of Psychology at Fordham University.

After World War I, less and less attention was paid to foreign literature as American psychologists produced their own. As American psychology advanced, it placed greater emphasis on the objective, nonphilosophical, quantitative, and practical aspects of psychology than did European psychology. The volume and significance of American contributions steadily grew, and as productivity in America eventually outdistanced that in other countries, the history of psychology was actually being made in the United States, particularly after 1930.

Nevertheless, in the tradition of William James, James Baldwin, James McKeen Cattell, and others who enriched American psychology by what they had learned in Europe, psychologists from the United States continued to visit European universities and maintain contacts with European psychology and philosophy—although with increasingly less intensity. R.M. Ogden, G.W. Allport, R.B. MacLeod, and many others studied in Europe and returned fertilized with new ideas that they subsequently implemented in America.

It must be remembered that psychological statistics, intelligence testing, Pavlovian conditioning, psychoanalysis, Gestalt psychology, the Rorschach test, and many other theoretical approaches, methods, and tools came to America from Europe. The influx of European psychologists in the 1930s (Jahoda, 1968; Mandler and Mandler, 1968) and during World War II had a powerful impact on the discipline in America by introducing American psychologists to new problems and tasks, as well as by initiating new directions of thought and activity. In 1972 Murphy and Kovach stated that "the major psychological ideas of today, as taught in American universities, are ideas which arose in Europe between the time of Darwin and World War II" (p. 484).

Isolationism in American Psychology

As American psychology acquired a dominant position in world psychology, it ceased to keep up with psychological advances in other countries and became increasingly isolated. American psychology became, in the words of Kahn (1962), "vague," "fragmented," "lacking goals," and "suffering from inbreeding" (pp. 706–707).

Brandt (1970) wrote that "American psychology disregards almost completely research done in other countries and particularly in other languages" (p. 1092). He also stated that "there is no English-language market for foreign research that does not fit into the American way of life. Many foreign language psychological publications containing research that conflicts with American psychology have never been translated into English even though they are so widely accepted outside English-language psychology that several editions have already been published" (pp. 1092–1093). The following example illustrates Brandt's point. A European psychologist coming to the United States in 1944 was shocked that the name, research, and theories of Jean Piaget were practically unknown to American psychologists and psychology students, except to a few developmental psychologists. He was shocked because in Europe, long before 1939, Piaget was regarded as one of the most prominent psychologists, and his research commanded the attention of psychologists in every European country. Every psychology student knew and had to know Piaget. A decade or so later in America, Piaget, inevitably, became widely known and his ideas influential.

Foreign psychologists also criticize American psychologists for not knowing, not even caring to know, about their contributions and activities. In 1977 a prominent psychologist from Mexico, Rogelio Díaz-Guerrero, challenged the universality of the psychology of Canada and the United States. According to Díaz-Guerrero (1977), none of the three "philosophico-political" forces of American psychology today—psychoanalysis, behaviorism, and humanistic psychology—"can lay claim to universality" (p. 934). He further stated

Actually, all three forces of American psychology appear overly satisfied with their basic tenets. As a result, I believe that the average American psychologist, in spite of having the greatest resources and possibly the highest levels of technical training, may be much more ethnocentric and parochial than others. Isolationism and the blindness of power may partially account for this (p. 935).

Consequences of Isolationism

American isolationism, whatever its cause, has resulted in ignorance of some important developments in other countries that could have enriched and fertilized American psychology at an earlier stage and would have opened new vistas, theoretical and practical. To illustrate this point, we can mention a few new areas of psychology, developed in other countries a long time ago, but noticed in America quite late.

With respect to theoretical psychology, American psychologists in general were long unaware of the impact of dialectical psychology, a psychology in keeping with the doctrines of Marxism-Leninism, on several European countries, not merely on the communist ones. It was only in the 1970s, thanks to a handful of psychologists with a European background, that American psychologists learned about dialectical psychology (Riegel, 1976). There have been some noteworthy movements in West Germany, such as the *Kritische Psychologie* and the Frankfurt School, which have not been widely known by Americans.

Among the applied fields let us mention, by way of illustration, three: clinical neuropsychology, defectology, and sports psychology. Clinical neuropsychology had long been practiced in France, Italy, and especially Russia before it became popular here. Defectology, a well established and successfully practiced specialty in Russia and Eastern Europe, was overlooked, and the term was not to be found in American psychological dictionaries (Sexton and Misiak, 1976). Similar to American psychology of the handicapped, defectology in Eastern Europe has a much broader scope. It is the borderland of clinical psychology and pedagogy, and it deals with children who have sensory, motor, speech emotional, and intellectual defects. There is a voluminous literature on this subject. Although sports psychology has been a lively area of research and practice in Europe for decades, it has caught the attention of America, where it is becoming popular, only relatively recently.

The fact that American psychology has gained so much from European psychology "may be a telling argument," wrote Murphy and Kovach (1972),

> against allowing young psychologists to become too provincial. If the current European psychology becomes for Americans so remote that it is not even worthwhile to get acquainted with it, we shall have succeeded in creating an insular psychology, the applications of which even within our own provincial boundaries will have had an insufficient human "working through," an insufficient systematic testing before the general bar of science, and of civilization. And we shall be fortunate indeed if we can still hear the international and intercultural voices as the din of our own chorus continues in its confident intensity (p. 484).

Concluding his review of American and European psychology, Berlyne, in 1968, warned, "Most of the important advances in psychology of the next few decades will, it is safe to predict, grow out of American psychology. But many of these will take place outside the United States." (p. 452).

In the last few years, we have seen among American psychologists a growing awareness of the need for closer contacts with psychology and psychologists in other countries.

Toward Internationalism

It is obvious from the preceding comments that considerable consciousness raising is demanded if American psychologists are to develop a world view of their science and profession. This broadening experience should include exposure to the research of foreign psychologists through literature and, possibly, through international meetings, travel, exchange programs, and cooperative research. The contribution each of these can make to widening knowledge of psychology in other countries is substantial; however, to be effective the process must begin with undergraduate training through direct exposure to, and contact with, psychology abroad. It must involve the education of both teachers and students if American psychologists are to extricate themselves from the provincial rut into which they have fallen. It is the teacher's responsibility to familiarize students with non-North American psychology, which can be incorporated very well into practically every course in the psychology curriculum (Russell, in this volume). It is especially appropriate in the history of psychology, systems of psychology, and cross-cultural psychology courses and in seminars on international psychology.

Literature

Literature is a primary resource for both students and teachers. Inspection of post-World War II volumes of *Psychological Abstracts* reveals abundant psychological literature, books and articles, of many countries. Recently, for example, in Europe a highly significant 15-volume multiedited work was published, *Die Psychologie des 20. Jahrhunderts* [*Psychology of the 20th Century*], (Strube, 1976–1980). North American students and psychologists cannot afford to ignore this massive compendium of psychological scholarship, or any literature of this type.

Ideally, reading assignments from foreign literature should be made in traditional courses. Regrettably, students and faculty with foreign language expertise are rare in American colleges today, and they threaten to become rarer because of the declining interest in foreign language study among American students. Students might well heed the admonition of Otto Klineberg: "If there is one piece of advice I feel capable of giving to young psychologists, particularly if they want to work abroad, it is that there is no substitute for being able to talk to people" (cited in Lindzey, 1974, p. 177). He also quotes Wallace Lambert of McGill, who says that "people are successful in learning foreign languages when they are interested in the human beings and the cultures involved, not usually because they have a gift for languages" (cited in Lindzey, 1974, p. 177).

The Europeans have learned this lesson well, perhaps too well. The use of English as the principal language of international communication in psychology has generated lively debates in Europe, for example, in Germany between Traxel (1975, 1979) and Lienert (1977). Smith (1981) reviewed this particular debate and took the position that "a one language psychology may have more disadvantages than advantages for an international psychology" (Smith, 1983, p. 123). However, psychologists in many countries, some of which have little-known languages, have been eager to have access, as users and contributors, to the largest body of psychological literature, and they frequently choose to use English to communicate their ideas and report their research findings, often in American journals (Eysenck, 1980).

Those students who have foreign language expertise should be encouraged to read original sources. Unfortunately, most of our college and university libraries subscribe to only a few foreign journals. However, the knowledgeable and ingenious teacher can come to the rescue. The teacher can cull articles from various foreign journals and loan these articles to students for their study. The article by Judith Torney-Purta in this collection gives a wealth of suggestions in this regard. In addition, there are several publications that provide up-to-date information for English-speaking readers of literature and current trends in psychology in various non-English-speaking countries.[1] In particular, *The Psychological Reader's Guide*, published in the Netherlands, is an easy-to-scan bibliographic monthly that lists the contents of more than 200 journals in psychology throughout the world.

Psychology teachers should familiarize themselves with foreign publications so that they can discuss research and theoretical psychology being developed abroad. They should also incorporate such material into the textbooks they write. North American psychology textbooks show a conspicuous lack of references to the psychology of other countries. Moreover, if teachers become more knowledgeable, they will be more effective role models for their students and help them develop a world view. In addition, they will be better prepared to confer with their non-American colleagues on the psychology of other countries. Most North American psychologists have discovered, to their embarrassment, that foreign psychologists, no matter what their country, are familiar with American psychology and read American journals and books. The reverse is rarely true. As Smith (1983) in his reply to Ardila (1982) pointed out, "Psychologists in other lands have access to a wider literature because of the common multilingualism" (p. 123). He argued that it may not be the scientist publishing in French or German who is isolated, but rather the English-only reader. Smith suggested that "it might behoove educators of North American psychologists to once again take the doctoral foreign language examination seriously" (p.123).

Among the publications of particular usefulness teachers will find the following: the *International Review of Applied Psychology* (IAAP quarterly); the *International Psychologist* (ICP quarterly); the *Revista Interamericana de Psicologia* (SIP quarterly); and the *Journal of Cross-Cultural Psychology* (IACCP quarterly). The *International Journal of Psychology*, published by the International Union of Psychological Science, is also important. Each issue is devoted in large part to scientific and theoretical papers in all areas of psychology, with emphasis on topics where social or cultural context is important. An added feature in some issues is the "International Platform for Psychologists," which offers an opportunity to exchange views and opinions on psychology as an academic and applied profession.

International Meetings

The importance of international meetings and congresses of psychology for exchange of information and ideas was recognized quite early in the history of the discipline. Convening an international congress of psychology was first suggested in 1881 but did not come about until 1889, in Paris. Since then numerous international meetings have been held in various countries, and large numbers of international societies of a specialized nature have been established. In recent years, as Bouvy, Wilpert, and de Wolff (1982) have pointed out, because of the explosion of international scientific congresses in terms of scale, frequency, and cost, the opportunity to communicate informally with seniors or peers is somewhat diminished, especially for junior scientists.

Generally, however, attendance at most international meetings provides an opportunity to establish actual contact with non-American colleagues. It is important to note that international meetings and congresses often convene in the United States, so that, from time to time, even students on limited budgets can attend. It is the teacher's job to inform students about such meetings and to encourage them to attend.

Among the international societies and associations to which many American psychologists belong and whose meetings they attend regularly are the following: the International Association of Applied Psychology (IAAP; founded 1920); the International Council of Psychologists (ICP; founded 1942); the Inter-american Society of Psychology (SIP; founded 1951); the International Association for Cross-Cultural Psychology (IACCP; founded 1972); and Cheiron, the International Society for the History of Behavioral and Social Sciences (ISHOBSS; founded 1968). The most important international association is the International Union of Psychological Science (IUPsyS; founded 1951). A federation of 44 national member societies, IUPsyS sponsors international congresses every four years.

A more complete listing of various specialized societies can be found in the *Encyclopedia of Associations*. In addition to the address, telephone numbers, and size of the organization, each description includes the scope and purpose of the organization and lists the location and date of annual conferences and the organization's publications.

Travel and Study Exchange Programs

Perhaps one of the most broadening experiences is traveling to foreign countries to visit psychologists and their institutions. Several programs facilitate travel, work, and study abroad. SHARE (Sharing Home and Round-the-world Experience) is a program designed to advance psychology by providing opportunities for members of various groups to make personal contacts, in the course of international travel, with colleagues of similar psychological interests (Jacobson and Reinert, 1980). Psychologists from all over the world who are willing to host colleagues from other countries register with SHARE. Some psychologists offer office visits or tours of local facilities; others offer overnight home stays.

Founded in 1975, SHARE is a joint project of psychological associations with members who have international interests, cosponsored by the International Council of Psychologists, the Interamerican Society of Psychology, the school-psychology and humanistic-psychology divisions of the American Psychological Association, the International School Psychology Association, the National Association of School Psychologists, and the International Association for Applied Psychology. As of 1983, more than 200 psychologists in 32 states or territories of the United States and in 28 other countries around the world were registered as interested in hosting psychologists from other countries. More detailed information about the SHARE program can be obtained by writing the Chair of the planning committee, Frances A. Mullen, 4014 Cody Road, Sherman Oaks, CA 91403.

The Fulbright program is perhaps the best known federal program. The Fulbright Act of August 1946 authorized the financing of educational exchange for the purpose of enabling "the government of the United States to increase mutual understanding between the people of the United States and the people of other countries" (Council for International Exchange of Scholars, 1984, p. 1). Under the Fulbright program, grants are made to U.S. citizens and nationals of other countries for university lecturing, advanced research, graduate study, and teaching in elementary and secondary schools. It is also possible in the terms of this program for United States colleges and universities to invite foreign scholars to lecture on their campuses to strengthen the international dimension of their programs. For those interested in applying, the available awards in the various disciplines by geographic area are published each year. Application details may be obtained from the Council for International Exchange of Scholars, 11 Dupont Circle, Suite 300, Washington, DC 20036.

In a series of three articles in *Teaching of Psychology*, Calhoun and his associates (Calhoun and Long, 1982; Calhoun, Selby, and MacFarlane, 1980; Calhoun, Toner, and Selby, 1980) discussed their experiences as well as specific problems of implementation and their personal reactions to their department-by-department faculty exchange. They offered many valuable suggestions to those interested in developing a similar type of faculty exchange program.

Students and teachers will also find *The Learning Traveler Series* and other publications of the Institute of International Education (IIE) helpful. Based on an annual survey by the Institute, these books describe a multitude of study and travel opportunities. The directories present all the essential information required for enrolling in programs overseas: program dates, locations, and lengths; course descriptions, including prerequisites, credit, teaching methods, and language instruction; housing; costs; scholarships; work-study; and program evaluation. Programs included are sponsored by U.S. colleges and universities, foreign institutions, and private U.S. and foreign organizations.

The National Science Foundation (NSF) offers a variety of programs: cooperative research, joint seminars, regional seminars, and long-term research visits. Considered visits, cooperative-research proposals are for a primarily domestic research project from which special benefits are expected to accrue. NSF defines as benefits sharing facilities of the research environment; joining complementary skills in experimentation or theoretical analysis; and combining the use of resources. Cooperative-research projects must be designed jointly and conducted collaboratively by scientists of the United States and the cooperating country. Joint seminars enable scientists in the United States and in cooperating countries to confer on areas of mutual interest. These conferences may be on any scientific subject within the general purposes of the National Science Foundation's programs. Ordinarily the seminars convene in either country and involve small groups of scientists. Such seminars facilitate the exchange of information and ideas, as well as foster increased cooperation.

Regional seminars enable U.S. scientists to confer with colleagues from various countries on topics of particular regional interest. They also provide for the mobilization of competence in a special research area from among several countries, particularly when such mobilization promises mutual benefits. Long-term research visits support research conducted primarily in a host laboratory or at a research site in a foreign country. Typically lasting four to twelve months, the visit is intended to focus on a program of research conducted in collaboration with a scientist from the host country.

Other efforts are also being made. For example, the Institute of International Education (IIE) operates a computer-based referral service, the Register for International Service in Education (RISE), designed to help developing countries locate educators (of both secondary and university levels), specialists, and researchers in various fields, including the health professions and the social sciences. RISE's dual purpose is to facilitate the use of U.S. higher education resources by educational systems of developing countries and to promote understanding of these countries among U.S. nationals.

Conclusion

The value of knowing the state of psychology in other countries and the need to maintain close relations with colleagues abroad cannot be over-emphasized. There are many alternatives for enlarging and maintaining such contact, of which the ideal outcome is a truly international psychology from which all countries would profit. It is particularly important that psychologists in the United States and in other developed countries be especially sensitive to the scientific and professional concerns of the Third World and that they respond to them as well as they can (Giorgis and Helms, 1978).

Speculating about psychology in the year 2000—quite appropriate to our theme— Gardner Murphy wrote

> If psychologists mean quite seriously that man, as man, is richly intertwined with his ecology, it follows that the psychology of the next two decades will depend enormously upon the discovery of new forms of cross-cultural, cross-national communication. Indeed, it follows that unless there is very broad cross-national communication and action, there will be no human race to investigate. It will not do for American psychology, now having about 92% of the world's psychological personnel and about 92% of its published communications, to undertake a bland and supposedly disinterested study of the rest of the world in order that the wise and productive science, which they represent, can convey appropriate knowledge to those struggling along in less enlightened paths of endeavor. The study of the human predicament can come from a human race familiar with the method of science, but a human race speaking many tongues, regarding many values, and holding different convictions about the meaning of life sooner or later will have to consult all that is human (1969, p. 528).

Note

[1]English-language publications specializing in the presentation of research done in other countries include the *International Journal of Psychology*; *Soviet Psychology*, a quarterly journal of translations; the *German Journal of Psychology*, a quarterly of abstracts and reviews; *Psychologia, the International Journal of the Orient*; *Japanese Psychological Research*; the *Indian Journal of Psychology*; and the *Polish Psychological Bulletin*. In addition, most foreign-language books and journals in psychology publish abstracts in English, French, or German.

References

Ardila, R. (1982). International Psychology. *American Psychologist, 37*, 323–329.

Berlyne, D.E. (1968). American and European psychology. *American Psychologist, 23*, 447–452.

Bouvy, A., Wilpert, B., and de Wolff, C.J. (1982). International scientific conferences; the psychologists' blind spot. *International Review of Applied Psychology, 31*, 317–326.

Brandt, L. (1970). American psychology, *American Psychologist, 25*, 1091–1093.

Calhoun, L.G., and Long, G.T. (1982). International exchange in psychology: Personal reactions. *Teaching of Psychology, 8*, 103–104.

Calhoun, L.G., Selby, J.W., and MacFarlane, J.B. (1980). Faculty exchange in psychology: Faculty development without most of the costs. *Teaching of Psychology*, 7, 111–112.

Calhoun, L.G., Toner, I.J., and Selby, J.W. (1980). International exchange of faculty: Specific problems of implementation. *Teaching of Psychology*, 7, 185–186.

Council on International Exchange of Scholars. (1984). *Fulbright senior scholars: Awards abroad 1984-1985*. Washington, DC: CIES.

Díaz-Guerrero, R. (1977). A Mexican psychology. *American Psychologist, 32*, 934–944.

Eysenck, H.J. (1980). A comment on the Traxel-Lienert discussion regarding publication in English by German psychologists. *Psychologische Beiträge, 22*, 372–376.

Giorgis, T.W., and Helms, J.E. (1978). Training international students from developing nations as psychologists: A challenge for American psychology. *American Psychologist, 33*, 945–951.

Jacobson, E.H., and Reinert, G. (Ed.). (1980). *International directory of psychologists* (3rd. ed.) Amsterdam: North Holland Publishing Co.

Jahoda, M. (1968). The migration of psychoanalysis: Its impact on American psychology. In D. Fleming and B. Bailyn (Ed.), *Perspectives in American History: Vol 2. The intellectual migration: Europe and America 1930–1960* (pp. 420–445). Cambridge, Mass.: Charles Warren Center for Studies in American History, Harvard U.

Kahn, T.C. (1962). Evaluation of United States of America psychology by the "four-years-absent method." *American Psychologist, 17*, 706–708.

Kennedy, S.B. (1982) Resources for planning undergraduate study abroad in psychology. *Psi-Chi Newsletter, 8*, 7–8.

Lienert, G.A. (1977). Über Werner Traxel: Internationalität oder Provinzialismus zur Frage: Sollten Psychologen in Englisch publizieren? [Internationalism or provincialism: Should psychologists publish in English?]. *Psychologische Beiträge, 19*, 487–492.

Lindzey, G. (Ed). (1974). *A history of psychology in autobiography. Vol. 4.* Englewood Cliffs, N.J.: Prentice-Hall.

Mandler, J.M., and Mandler, G. (1968). The diaspora of experimental psychology: The Gestaltists and others. In D. Fleming and B. Bailyn (pp. 371–419).

Murphy, G. (1969). Psychology in the year 2000. *American Psychologist, 24*, 523–530.

———, and Kovach, J.K. (1972). *Historical introduction to modern psychology.* (3rd ed). New York: Harcourt, Brace, Jovanovich.

Riegel, K.F. (1976). Dialectics of human development. *American Psychologist, 31*, 689–700.

Sexton, V.S., and Misiak, H. (Ed.). (1976). *Psychology around the world.* Monterey, Cal.: Brooks/Cole.

Smith, R.J. (1981). On provincialism and one-language psychology. *Psychologische Beiträge, 23*, 293–302.

———. (1983). On Ardila's international psychology. *American Psychologist, 38*, 122–123.

Strube, G. (Coordinator). (1976–1980). *Die Psychologie des 20. Jahrhunderts* [*Psychology of the 20th Century*]. Vols. *1–15*. Zurich, Switzerland: Kindler Verlag.

Traxel, W. (1975). Internationalität oder Provinzialismus? Über die Bedeutung der deutschen Sprache für deutschsprachige Psychologen [Internationalism or provincialism? Concerning the importance of the German language for German-speaking psychologists]. *Psychologische Beiträge, 17* , 584–594.

―――. (1979). Publish or perish!—auf Deutsch oder auf Englisch? [in German or in English]? *Psychologische Beiträge, 21*, 62–77.

Annotated Bibliography of Materials to Add an International Dimension to Undergraduate Courses in Developmental and Social Psychology

Judith Torney-Purta

For centuries cross-cultural comparisons have contributed to attempts to understand human behavior (Herodotus being an often quoted early example). Specialized journals for publishing cross-cultural psychological studies have been in existence for less than 20 years, however. The founding of the *International Journal of Psychology* took place in 1966. The first *Annual Review* article on culture and psychology was published only about 10 years ago by Triandis, Malpass, and Davidson, although the *Annual Review* had previously devoted some attention to psychology in other countries (e.g., the 1964 edition had an article on psychology in the Soviet Union). In the past decade courses devoted to cross-cultural approaches to psychology have increased, although they are still offered in a relatively small percentage of departments. Attempting to stimulate cross-cultural awareness among undergraduates who are taking nonspecialized courses (introductory psychology, developmental psychology, social psychology) is even less common. Fostering this awareness through such courses requires an infusion approach—looking for places in the established course of study where a cross-cultural example is appropriate or where readings that illustrate psychological processes in other cultures can be used.

Writing in 1980 in the *Journal of Cross-Cultural Psychology* to commemorate its tenth anniversary, M.H. Segall noted a readiness on the part of those who teach undergraduate psychology to foster global awareness by using international resources. Such teaching could, he felt, reduce students' ethno-

Judith Torney-Purta is Professor of Human Development at the University of Maryland.

centrism about the field they were studying (and perhaps in their own lives as well) and help them deal more intelligently with cultural relativism.

Approach and Purposes of the Review

Most undergraduate psychology syllabi are already crowded. Instructors are most likely to add materials to foster a cross-cultural perspective if they are made aware of international resources that can help meet the existing objectives of courses: readings useful for the preparation of lectures, for assignment to students, for in-class discussion or participation exercises, and for out-of-class assignments. This article will provide an annotated bibliography of such resources, assuming that the instructor has already been convinced of the value of incorporating international materials. (Although films are also an excellent resource, because of space limitations they will not be reviewed.)

International or cross-cultural resources can serve several functions. They can illustrate the generality (or lack of generality) of psychological theories or laws. They can illustrate the presence or absence of ecological validity. They can help the student understand how social and cultural factors influence behavior and psychological development, factors that may be difficult to recognize in personal experience limited to one culture. They can highlight both universal and culturally relative aspects of human experience. Discussions of cross-cultural resources can sometimes illuminate a student's own stereotypes and ethnocentric biases. Experience with cross-cultural resources in psychology may make a student more sensitive when dealing with individuals from other cultural groups (either in a domestic context or during international travel). Some resources can inform a student about global issues with psychological dimensions (e.g., immigrants' adjustment to new cultures or individuals' problems in rapidly modernizing societies).

In describing materials that may bring a cross-national or international dimension to undergraduate psychology, I will follow several principles: First, I will attempt to highlight up-to-date material. A basic resource summarizing materials through the late 1970s is the *Handbook of Cross-Cultural Psychology*, edited by H. Triandis and a series of co-editors in the specialized fields covered by the six volumes—perspectives, methodology, basic processes, developmental psychology, social psychology, and psychopathology—and published in 1980 by Allyn and Bacon. Many of the chapters from these volumes will be cited, as it is a basic source. A single-volume *Handbook of Cross-Cultural Human Development* was edited by R.H. Munroe, R.L. Munroe, and B.B. Whiting and published by Garland STPM Press in 1981. A three-volume *Handbook of Intercultural Training* was edited by D. Landis and R. Brislin and issued in 1983 by Pergamon Press. Because cross-cultural psychology is such a rapidly developing area of study, the interested instructor is advised to take full advantage of new materials by using PsycSCAN or *Psychological Abstracts*, scanning new issues of periodicals such as the *Journal of Cross-Cultural Psychology*, and examining the chapters on topics such as cross-cultural psychology and psychology in other nations that appear in the *Annual Review of Psychology* (e.g., by Brislin in 1983). Many periodicals, such as the *International Journal of Psychology, Journal of Personality and Social Psychology, Child Development, Developmental Psychology, Human Development, European Journal of Social Psychology,* and *Canadian Journal of Behavioural Science* (to mention only some of the periodicals in English) carry articles written by non-American psychologists or including cross-cultural comparisons. This article will concentrate on books and selected chapters because they are more likely than journal articles to present the type of integrated perspective suitable for undergraduate instruction.

Second, I will attempt to balance illustrations of cultural differences with a discussion of cultural universals. Cross-national studies (usually defined as involving countries that share a European tradition) will be examined, as will cross-cultural studies (focusing on more primitive cultures or on developing countries).

Third, I will include exercises in which students can actively participate, questions that they can discuss, materials to which they can apply psychological theories or research, and sources of data that they can use in exploratory analysis. These principles will guide the selection of material to make the bibliography useful to an undergraduate psychology instructor. The researcher in this field would probably make a different selection.

Techniques Useful across Subareas of Psychology

Several resources will be noted as useful as the basis for a simulation or role-playing exercise. One structure for such a simulation is that six or seven students (usually members of a small advanced undergraduate class) each be assigned a chapter or an article written by a non-American psychologist. It is preferable if this article is a review rather than the report of a single study. Each student is assigned to play the role of the author as if he or she were in attendance at an international meeting where the paper is to be presented. Other students serve as discussants. The specific out-of-class assignment for presenters is first to find out basic information about the author's country (where it is, its level of economic development, and how it is governed) and then to abstract the article or chapter so that it can be presented in ten to fifteen minutes. At the beginning of the class session each individual is introduced as if he or she were the international psychologist, and each in turn presents a paper. Following the presentations, the "delegates" are asked to address a series of questions concerning plans for future research conducted cooperatively. When using papers from developing countries, students may also find it useful to discuss the politics of research as well as the relative emphasis that should be placed on basic research and on the application of research to improving life situations. See, for example, the questions raised by D.P. Warwick writing on the politics and ethics of cross-cultural research in the first volume of Triandis and Heron (p. 380). As in all role-playing exercises, it is important to discuss the experience with the students. A number of the collections of chapters, which are described under the specific headings, are suitable as the basis for use in such a simulation.

A second general technique could be used in any of several areas within psychology. Students read journal articles reporting research conducted in the United States (either assigned by the instructor or found by themselves in an area of interest). The students then rewrite the articles as proposals for cross-cultural study. In one section of each proposal the students must give reasons the problem for study would be clarified by cross-national or cross-cultural study.

Organization of the Bibliography

The major sections are devoted to resources useful in developmental psychology (many also appropriate for educational psychology) and resources useful in social/organizational psychology. Except for three books that are suggested as supplementary texts for student purchase, the sections describe materials that would be used in the library.

This organization is not intended to exclude the possibility that some instructors may wish to concentrate on theories, research, and practice of psychology in some particular region of the world (a kind of "area studies approach" to cross-national psychology). Such an approach would require the use of resources from other disciplines, such as anthropology and comparative political studies. The following resources in psychology might be useful in such an approach. *Psychology around the World*, a book edited by V. Sexton and H. Misiak and published by Brooks/Cole in 1976, describes the status of psychology in 40 countries on six continents. *Psychology in Africa*, a book by M. Wober published by the International African Institute (London) in 1975, includes sections on research in developmental, cognitive, and perceptual processes. Descriptions of psychology and current research in Japan can be found in the 1966 and 1972 *Annual Review of Psychology* and in the *American Psychologist* for November 1977, as well as in Japanese psychology journals available in English. Descriptions of psychology in Latin America can be found in the 1982 *Annual Review of Psychology* and in a wider literature available to those who read Spanish. Discussions of Eastern European psychology are in various sources including the somewhat dated 1964 *Annual Review* chapter on the Soviet Union; the 1980 *Annual Review* chapter on the German Democratic Republic; *Soviet Developmental Psychology: An Anthology*, edited by M. Cole and published in 1977 by M.E. Sharpe (White Plains); as well as translations of the works of Luria and Vygotsky. Studies of psychology that take advantage of the cultural variety and collective living arrangements in Israel include the chapter by C.W. Greenbaum and S. Kugelmass in *Studies in Cross-Cultural Psychology* (Vol. 2) edited by N. Warren and published by Academic Press in 1980.

Resources Useful in Developmental Psychology

Supplementary Text for Courses in Developmental or Educational Psychology

Wagner, D.A., and Stevenson, H.W. (1982). *Cultural perspectives on child development.* San Francisco: W.H. Freeman.

This paperback text, consisting of 20 chapters of 20–30 pages each, primarily by North American psychologists, would be an excellent supplementary text in a child psychology course. Each chapter could be keyed to a chapter of a developmental text. The book not only provides material for judging the universality of developmental processes but also gives an international context for assessing the influence of culture on development and for placing research findings from Western cultures in perspective. Most of the chapters include details about research in more than one non-Western culture (Latin American and African countries are especially well represented). The book is not a dry recitation of methods and findings of cross-cultural research; it transmits a sense of excitement by including several challenges to previous research (especially Jahoda and McGurk's chapter on the perception of depth in two-dimensional pictures). Super and Harkness's chapter on affect in infancy and early childhood is an excellent starting point for discussion of universals in the mother–child interaction. The chapter by Ciborowski and Price-Williams on animistic cognitions provides some examples of interviews that undergraduate students could replicate with children in their own communities. The chapters on informal and formal education and its influence on cognitive development (by Greenfield and Lave and by Stevenson, respectively) not only summarize important recent cross-cultural research but also provide a starting point for students to consider how informal education and formal education serve separate and complementary functions in their own society and in other societies at various levels of development. The Pope chapter, which raises the issue of the universality of Kohlberg's stages of moral development, could also be used to discuss problems with the notion that a higher stage of moral development is necessarily better. The book also contains excellent chapters on cognition, nutrition, Piagetian approaches, and personality development.

This book will serve many of the same functions as *Cross-Cultural Child Development* by E.L. Werner, which recently went out of print. Werner's text, however, included a chapter on peer–peer relations and another on problems of parent–child relations in modernizing societies that are not as well represented in the Wagner and Stevenson volume.

Placing Cross-Cultural Research in Context

Bronfenbrenner, U. (1979). *The ecology of human development.* Cambridge, Mass.: Harvard UP.

This book provides a framework for analyzing the ways in which different levels of a social and cultural system have an effect on human development. Students who can judge the presence or absence of ecological validity in laboratory studies conducted in the United States can more easily understand why cross-cultural studies of psychological processes are important. The book can provide an important bridge between laboratory and field studies. Several of the chapters use cross-cultural examples to illustrate the importance of the exosystem and the macrosystem to the understanding of human behavior. Students can be asked to think of other examples. The article by Bronfenbrenner in the *American Psychologist* (1977, *32*, 513–531) contains many of the same ideas and may be more accessible to undergraduates.

The Study of Infancy

Kay, M.A., ed. (1982). *Anthropology of human birth.* Philadelphia: F.A. Davis.
Leiderman, P.H., Tulkin, S.R., and Rosenfeld, A. (Ed.). (1977). *Culture and infancy: Variations in the human experience.* New York: Academic Press.
Super, C.M. (1980). Cross-cultural research on infancy. In H.C. Triandis and A. Heron, ed., *Handbook of cross-cultural psychology: Vol. 4. Developmental psychology* (pp. 17–54). Boston: Allyn and Bacon.
Super, C.M., and Harkness, S. (1982). The infant's niche in rural Kenya and metropolitan America. In L. Adler, ed., *Cross-cultural research at issue* (pp. 47–55). New York: Academic Press.

Cultural variations in infant behavior and parent–infant relations are well summarized here. Students can give reports on the birth event and on early infancy from material to be found in Kay's book on Benin, China (both Taiwan and the People's Republic), Egypt, India, Ireland, Japan, Malaya, Indians in Mexico, Nigeria, St. Kitts, and various American subcultures. They can make reports based on descriptive material and research summarized in chapters in

Leiderman et al.'s book concerning infancy in Botswana, urban Great Britain, Guatemala, Israel, Kenya, Mexico, Uganda, and Zambia. These reports could also be used as the basis of a simulation of an international meeting described previously. In discussing such reports it is important to draw attention to both the similarities and the differences of experiences of mothers and infants in these cultures, lest the students remember only the exotic nature of some of the details of birth rituals.

The Universality of Piaget's Theory

Dasen, P.R., ed. (1977). *Piagetian psychology: Cross-cultural contributions.* New York: Gardner Press (Wiley).
Dasen, P.R. (1982). Cross-cultural aspects of Piaget's theory: The competence-performance model. In L.L. Adler, ed., *Cross-cultural research at issue* (pp. 163–170). New York: Academic Press.
Dasen, P.R., and Heron, A. (1980). Cross-cultural tests of Piaget's theory. In Triandis and Heron, *Handbook, Vol. 4.* (pp.295–342).
Edwards, C.P. (1981). The comparative study of the development of moral reasoning and judgment. In R.H. Munroe, R.L. Munroe, and B.B. Whiting, ed., *Handbook of cross-cultural human development* (pp. 501–530). New York: Garland STPM Press.
Greenfield, P. (1976). Cross-cultural research and Piagetian theory. In K. Riegel and J.A. Meacham, ed., *The developing individual in a changing world.* Hague: Mouton.

Discussing ways of giving an international dimension to the presentation of Piaget's theory may appear to have a certain irony, because the major theoretical works have their basis in the study of Swiss children and have been written in French. Dasen, who is at the University of Geneva, has written several chapters in English examining research testing Piaget's theory cross-culturally and has edited a major collection of these studies. The set of resources listed above could provide most of the material for one or two undergraduate class sessions to examine evidence for the universality of Piaget's theory. The following subtopics are suggested for summarizing cross-cultural research regarding the issue of universality: (a) the sensorimotor stage; (b) conservation; (c) kinship concepts; (d) concrete operational functioning in adults; (e) formal operations; (f) the role of schooling and of ecocultural demands in cognitive development in the Piagetian model; (g) training cross-nationally; and (h) the special importance of the competence–performance distinction in studies of the theory's application. Basic information on all these topics is available in the listed resources; students should be encouraged, however, to consult abstracts and journals for original research reports.

The Study of Child–Parent and Child–Peer Relations

Lambert, W., Hamers, J., and Smith, N. (1979). *Child rearing values: A cross-national study*. New York: Praeger.

Rohner, R.P. (1975). *They love me, they love me not*. New Haven, Conn.: HRAF Press.

Tapp, J. (1980). Studying personality development. In Triandis and Heron, *Handbook. Vol. 4*. (pp. 343–424).

The Tapp chapter, an introduction to and an overview of studies of personality development and child-rearing correlates cross-culturally, also presents a framework for analysis. Tapp includes in-depth studies of a single culture, some of which would fit under the almost abandoned "national character" model, and comparisons of another culture with the United States (such as that of the USSR by Bronfenbrenner in *Two Worlds of Childhood,* published by Russell Sage in 1970, and of England by Barker and Schoggens in *Qualities of Community Life,* published by Jossey-Bass in 1973).

The books listed above summarize extensive data collections involving parents (primarily mothers) in several different societies, and they could be used in many ways in an undergraduate course. The Rohner book presents data from the Human Relations Area Files (101 cultures) to examine the universality of effects of parental rejection on children. Lambert, Hamers, and Smith report a collection of data on child-rearing values from working- and middle-class parents in 17 cultural groups. Students can develop their own hypotheses about parent socialization and child behavior and can test out those hypotheses using the data tables in the book or (when such tables are not available) suggest what additional measures or analysis would be necessary. Students could also administer in their own community the instruments used by Lambert, Hamers, and Smith and speculate about the sources of the differences they observe.

Morsbach, H. (1980). Major psychological factors influencing Japanese inter-personal relations. In N. Warren, ed., *Studies in cross-cultural psychology. Vol. 2*, (pp. 317–342). London: Academic Press.

This is one of several possible sources to illustrate recent attempts to account for personality characteristics that appear typical of a culture by using a combination of observations of mother–child interaction and other socialization factors. I have listed this chapter because of widespread current interest in Japan. One could also find books in most libraries with titles beginning "Child Rearing in ..." as the basis for student reports.

Seymour, S. (1981). Cooperation and competition. In R.H. Munroe, R.L. Munroe, and B.B. Whiting, ed., *Handbook of cross-cultural human development* (pp. 717-738). New York: Garland STPM Press.

Sutton-Smith, B., and Roberts, J.M. (1980). Play, games, and sports. In Triandis and Heron, *Handbook, Vol. 4*. (pp.425-471).

The area of children's play and peer relations is of special interest to undergraduate students. Play behavior is also easy to observe. One can give undergraduates brief training in time-sampled or event-sampled observations and instruct them to find a public setting in which to observe children in leisure-time activity (a video arcade, a swimming pool or beach, a carnival with games of skill, a shopping center, a playground, or a museum). Using the references suggested in the two listed chapters, as well as finding others available by scanning abstracts or recent journals, the student could draw up a format for observing children that could be suitable for use both in the local public setting chosen and in another culture (or cultures). After completing the observation in his or her own community, the student reports on that observation and then suggests what would be expected if the observation had been conducted in a different cultural context. It is probably easiest, if the behaviors chosen for observation are some that would be expected to differ in another cultural context. For example, if the setting were a competitive game, the student might hypothesize that cooperative behavior would be more common in some other cultures. If the setting were one in which adults and children were participating in activities together, the student might hypothesize that there would be different kinds of interactions in another country.(Some recent descriptive material on childhood in the Soviet Union or in the People's Republic of China could also be used in making these comparisons.)

The Study of Adolescent Development

Kandel, D.B., and Lesser, G.S. (1972). *Youth in two worlds: United States and Denmark*. San Francisco: Jossey-Bass.

Tallman, I., Marotz-Baden, R., and Pindas, P. (1983). *Adolescent socialization in cross-cultural perspective*. New York: Academic Press.

Young, H.B., and Ferguson, L.R. (1981). *Puberty to manhood in Italy and America*. New York: Academic Press.

Although there has been considerable recent interest in adolescent development (indexed by publications such as the *Handbook of Adolescent Psychology*), the work has paid little attention to cross-cultural study. That situation is ironic because so many aspects of adolescent development seem to be influenced by cultural factors. The three listed volumes each represent a comparison of adolescents in another culture with those in the United States.

The Kandel and Lesser volume is written at a level suitable for under-graduates, and either the book or an article reference in it that reports part of the study might be assigned as a supplementary reading. Based on a study of 14-to-18-year-olds in Denmark and the United States, it is an excellent context-setter for discussion of adolescent development. The authors conclude that Danish families are more democratic and Danish parents set fewer rules than families in the United States. An instructor could stimulate an interesting discussion of that finding and of other findings about relations with friends and attitudes toward secondary schooling.

The Young and Ferguson volume could also be used as a supplement, but it relies somewhat more on psychological tests with which undergrad·:ates may be unfamiliar and on tables that may be difficult for some students to interpret. Students from some ethnic backgrounds will find the volume intriguing because the adolescents studied currently live in Boston, Rome, or Palermo, but all their grandparents had been residents of Southern Italy.

The volume by Tallman and his collaborators contains the most extensive theoretical framework and is the most useful for helping students understand the dilemmas of modernizing societies. Data were collected from 11-to-15-year-olds in Mexico and the United States using a simulation played by both parents and children regarding life plans. Some classes will try to replicate the simulation; others will be interested in further exploratory analysis of the many detailed tables; still others will want to discuss the authors' conclusion that U.S. parents are stimulating narcissism and self-indulgence among their children, whereas Mexican parents are overly concerned with helping their children better themselves using material goods as the index of success.

Massey, J.A. (1976). *Youth and politics in Japan.* Lexington, Mass.: Lexington Books.

Torney, J.V., Oppenheim, A.N., and Farnen, R.F. (1975). *Civic education in ten countries: An empirical study.* New York: Wiley.

These volumes report studies of the political socialization of young people. The first is an in-depth study of attitudes toward government and democracy in Japan. The second describes research on the knowledge and attitudes concerning politics (including support for civil liberties and for women's rights) among 14- and 17-year-olds in Western European countries and the United States. Both could provide material for lectures or special reports. Political values, especially cross-national differences in the meaning of democracy and related political institutions, are a topic of considerable interest to under-graduates.

A Collection of Chapters by Non-American Psychologists Summarizing Developmental Research in Other Nations

Hartup, W., Ahammer, I.M., and Pick, H.L., ed. 1982). *Review of child development research. Vol. 6.* Chicago: U of Chicago P.

This recent and excellent collection of 20 chapters includes the work of psychologists in ten nations (primarily from Eastern and Western Europe). It presents many resources for lecture preparation for courses in child psychology, for research for papers by juniors or seniors, and for the simulation exercise described.

The chapters written by Eastern Europeans are of special interest. Lisina, a Soviet, describes research in which the child's "need for interaction with adults" and "need for interaction with peers" are described as the only routes toward proper self-concept development. Students' attention can be drawn to the way in which the design and interpretation of research may be shaped by the political and educational ideology of the country in which it is conducted. Students can also consider the way American researchers design and interpret their work based on a more individualistic perspective. Linhart, a Czech, describes Eastern European approaches to the study of self-regulation and refers to Lenin in describing "developmental dialectics" in which "learning plays the role of a formative process which 'runs ahead of mental development,' being oriented to changes in ... society" (p. 496). Venger, a Soviet, elaborates on the role of education and training in organizing and directing the activity of children and forming their abilities in a purposeful way. Less stress is placed on waiting for ontogenetic development to make a child ready for learning, and training that shapes cognitive growth is emphasized. These chapters could provide a stimulus for comparing the assumptions in other theories, such as Piaget's, concerning the role of training versus the role of development. (These chapters would be as useful in an educational psychology course as in a developmental psychology course.)

This volume is not limited to the Eastern European perspective, however. Two French psychologists, Mounoud and Hauert, review works from several French-speaking countries. They compare Piaget's theory with that of Wallon (who also wrote in French during the 1940s on the subject of infant intelligence). From their own laboratory they include recent work concerning the role of posture, muscle tone, and prehension patterns in early infant development, and they focus on the importance of proprioceptive and olfactory cues provided by the individual caring for the child. The chapter is relatively abstract in its theoretical discussion, but it presents a way of integrating some of the material on motor and perceptual development currently found in undergraduate developmental texts with theory about intellectual development during infancy.

A chapter by Serpell reviews recent studies of perceptual development and intelligence in developing countries. In an undergraduate developmental psychology course this chapter could be a starting point to question the existence of a universally applicable definition of intelligence; whether the observation of self-managed activities by natives might be more useful than standardized tests of intelligence; and the effects on intellectual development of play or work (in contrast to school) experience.

Three chapters in the Hartup volume are by German authors and summarize work on achievement motivation, cognitive development, and the effects of schooling. Heckhausen's chapter could introduce a discussion of the meaning of achievement motivation in Western Cultures from early in life and the ways school experience changes that motivation. The chapter by Trudewind examines the ecology of achievement behavior, including measures of home and school environment. Included in the Weinert and Treiber chapter are summaries of the International Association for the Evaluation of Educational Achievement (IEA) studies of achievement conducted in 22 countries. Equally appropriate to an educational or developmental psychology course for relatively advanced undergraduates, these chapters could serve as the impetus for considering the impact on school achievement of multiple influences, which may be more obvious when students view nations other than their own.

The Study of Aging

Cowgill, D.O., and Holmes, L.S., ed. (1972). *Aging and modernization.* New York: Appleton-Century-Crofts.

Finley, G.E. (1982). Modernization and aging. In T.M. Field, A. Huston, H.C. Quay, L. Troll, and G.E. Finley, ed., *Review of human development* (pp. 511–523). New York: Wiley.

Fry, C., ed. (1980). *Aging in culture and society.* New York: Praeger.

Lyell, R. (1980). *Middle age, old age: Short stories, poems, plays and essays on aging.* New York: Harcourt.

Myerhoff, B.G., and Simic, A. (1978). *Life's career—aging: Cultural variations on growing old.* Beverly Hills: Sage.

Today's undergraduate has grown up in a youth-oriented culture that values self-reliance and progress. Promoting an examination of these values, an introduction to cross-cultural studies on aging might stress universalities and differences in treatment of and expectations for older people, followed by reports organized by theme or country. The books listed above provide useful introductory material along with a wide range of descriptive chapters on aging in countries as diverse as Colombia, Ethiopia, France, India, Japan, Mexico, Norway, Tanzania, the USSR, and Yugoslavia. The Myerhoff and Simic book also includes some comparisons involving American ethnic groups—Polish-Americans compared with Poles living in Poland. Topics that can be addressed using these materials include (a) relation between the elderly and their families; (b) the role of traditions and rituals in shaping the lives of the elderly; (c) characteristics of groups and communities in which the elderly live; (d) value differences between youth and the elderly, for example, dependency; and (e) the ways in which the process of modernization influences life for the elderly. Although these books of readings (primarily by anthropologists) are excellent sources, students should also be directed to related articles in psychology journals.

The Lyell collection of short fiction has several pieces that depict aging in other societies—China, India, Israel, Japan, and Russia. The following novels also portray the experience of the elderly in other cultures: Kawabata, *Sound of the Mountain* (Japan); Achebe, *Arrow of God* (Nigeria); Clavel, *Fruits of Winter* (France).

The Study of Policy as It Influences Children and Families

Kammerman, S.B., and Kahn, A.J., ed. (1978). *Family policy: Government and families in fourteen countries.* New York: Columbia UP.

Many instructors include the study of government policy as it influences children and families as part of courses in developmental psychology. This volume, which reviews policy in Eastern and Western European countries, is an excellent means to add a comparative dimension to such study. The individual chapters provide material for student reports and for discussion of the values that underlie U.S. policy.

Resources Useful in Social and Organizational Psychology

Supplementary Text for Courses in Social Psychology
Segall, M.H. (1979). *Cross-cultural psychology: Human behavior in global perspective.* Monterey, Cal.: Brooks/Cole.

This hardbound text (approximately 250 pages) could easily be keyed to most textbooks in social psychology. Six of the eight chapters deal with topics in such courses: e.g., cultural differences in motives, beliefs, and values; change and modernization; and out-group values and stereotypes. The author has included exercises for student participation and has reviewed an extensive amount of research.

Differing Orientations to the Study of Social Psychology in Other Nations

Moscovici, S. (1972). Society and theory in social psychology. In J. Israel and H. Tajfel, ed., *The context of social psychology* (pp. 17–68). London: Academic Press.

Strickland, L.H. (1979). *Soviet and Western perspectives in social psychology.* Oxford: Pergamon Press.

Tajfel, H. (1981). *Human groups and social categories.* Cambridge: Cambridge UP.

The contrast of North American social psychology with Western European (Moscovici and Tajfel) and Eastern European approaches (Strickland) is highlighted in these volumes. The argument made by Moscovici and Tajfel (and by many other Europeans)—that American social psychology is not "social" at all because it retreats to explanations at the individual level—is not one that the average undergraduate is likely to understand. Because many undergraduates define social psychology as "what is included in a text with that title," their instructors must place the subject in a broader context. One part of that context is the view of critical theorists who criticize the positivistic research tradition for its blindness to the effects of political ideology. These theorists stress that research about social facts is unlike research about physical facts because its results can be used to protect the interests of those holding economic and political power.

Moscovici describes U.S. research as the "social psychology of the nice person" and cautions European psychologists against adopting social psychology as defined in the United States because it has concentrated on problems that may not correspond with social problems in Europe. Tajfel presents similar arguments that social psychology should deal with the relation between the individual and society. When, for example, does interindividual behavior become intergroup behavior? In other words, when does a negative relation between a white individual and a black individual become an issue of negative group relations. The instructor who has an able class interested in such issues will find a wealth of materials, especially by British, French, and German social psychologists.

A set of positions that may be even more difficult for undergraduates to understand is the exemplification of Marxist thinking in Soviet social psychology. The Strickland book contains papers primarily by Russians and by Canadians and includes a fascinating description of the approach taken in teaching social psychology in the USSR. Unfortunately, the Russian papers are very short.

Universality in Social Structure and Morality in Their Influence
on Social Problems

Naroll, R. (1983). *The moral order: An introduction to the human situation.*
Beverly Hills, Cal.: Sage.

An anthropologist, Naroll presents data from a worldwide set of cultures
relating to understanding universal components of a moral and social order. In
particular he is concerned with the effects of "moralnets" or strong social
networks often found in societies with extended family structure. He presents
data demonstrating that the existence of moralnets is related to lesser incidence
or severity of ten social problems, including sex discrimination, child abuse, and
alcoholism. An instructor can present his method and ask students to explore,
from a psychological point of view, the specific social problems Naroll discusses.
The entire volume can supplement a text on social problems, and individual
sections can be used for specific topics in social or developmental psychology.

Cross-Cultural Differences in Values

Klineberg, O., Zavalloni, M., Louis-Guerin, C., and BenBrika, J. (1979).
Students, values, and politics: A cross-cultural comparison. New York:
Macmillan.

Mann, L. (1980). Cross-cultural studies of small groups. In H. Triandis and R.W.
Brislin, ed., *Handbook of cross-cultural psychology: Vol. 5. Social psychol-*
ogy (pp. 155–209). Boston: Allyn and Bacon.

Osgood, C.E., May, W.H., and Miron, M.S. (1975). *Cross-cultural universals*
of affective meaning. Urbana: U of Illinois P.

Stewart, E.C. (1979). American assumptions and values. In E.C. Smith and L.F.
Luce, ed., *Toward internationalism: Readings in cross-cultural communica-*
tion. Rowley, Mass.: Newbury House.

Triandis, H. (1972). *The analysis of subjective culture.* New York: Wiley.

Zavalloni, M. (1980). Values. In Triandis and Brislin (Ed.), *Handbook. Vol. 5.*
(pp.73-120).

Much of the content in undergraduate social psychology courses deals with
values and attitudes. The Zavalloni chapter includes a detailed discussion of
Kluckhohn's work on values in other cultures. The chapter by Mann raises the
issues of cross-cultural differences in group conformity as well as of competition
and cooperation in small groups. The Stewart chapter describes some of the
commonly ascribed aspects of the U.S. value system, which can be compared
with other value systems; the Smith and Luce book has additional chapters with
some useful material on other nations. This material can be used to view in a
comparative framework the role of individualism, competition, faith in social

and technical progress, equality, respect for education, religious faith, and so on in the United States.

The book by Klineberg and his collaborators is an excellent source for students to use in exploring the findings of a cross-national data collection (the book has extensive presentations of data) and even in replicating some of the research (they can use the questionnaire in the book). Data were collected from approximately 10,000 university students in 11 countries (both Western European and developing societies). A variety of topics were included: domestic political orientations, views of the ideal society, nationalism, career and life goals, perceptions of university education, the role of women, protest movements, morality, and religion. The books discussed in the previous section on adolescent development also have material related to these topics.

The Osgood and Triandis books include extensive reports from a large study of subjective culture (e.g., values, beliefs, attitudes, and roles) conducted in 25 countries (including Eastern and Western European, Asian, Middle Eastern, and Latin American countries). Both books have extensive material in tabular form available for student reports. The Triandis book makes some interesting cross-cultural comparisons of emotional experience (e.g., anger, courage, and freedom) that could serve as the basis for student discussion.

The comparative study of values using these resources could lead into a study of ways of improving intercultural communication, a topic to which psychologists have devoted extensive attention.

Supplementary Text for Courses in Social Psychology Dealing with Cross-Cultural Differences and Intercultural Communication
Samovar, L.A., and Porter, R.E., ed. (1982). *Intercultural communication: A reader* 3rd ed. Belmont, Cal.: Wadsworth.

This paperback selection of short readings from the fields of cultural anthropology, social psychology, sociology, and communication theory covers various topics: subject culture viewed as a matter of shared perception; sex roles in the Middle East; Japanese social experience; American nondominant cultures; verbal and nonverbal interaction; and ways of improving intercultural communication. Each section is followed by a brief annotated bibliography, suggested additional readings, and discussion questions (some of which are general and others quite specific). The book would be useful as a supplement in courses in social psychology or in courses targeted on intercultural issues.

Intercultural Communication and Training

Brislin, R.W. (1979). Orientation programs for cross-cultural preparation. In A.J. Marsella, R.G. Tharp, and T.J. Ciborowski, ed., *Perspectives on cross-cultural psychology* (pp. 287–306). New York: Academic Press.

Brislin, R.W. (1981). *Cross-cultural encounters*. New York: Pergamon.

Landis, D., and Brislin, R. (1983). *Handbook of intercultural training Vols. 1–3.* New York: Pergamon.

Pedersen, P. (1979). Non-Western psychology: The search for alternatives. In Marsella, Tharp, and Ciborowski, (pp. 117–135). New York: Academic Press.

Brislin's chapter focuses on techniques used in programs designed to improve intercultural communication and contrasts training based on self-awareness, information or cognitive approaches, attribution training, behavior modification, and experiential learning. In *Cross-cultural encounters*, Brislin presents both extensive background concerning individual and group factors and suggestions concerning ways of improving the quality of contact between individuals of different cultural groups. The "cultural assimilator," a method used to acquaint Americans who are to live in another culture with attributions made by individuals in social situations in that culture, is described in each of the Brislin references and in a chapter by Albert in the Landis and Brislin handbook. This technique could be used in a class as an example of what is involved in intercultural training. The instructor would probably need to obtain more complete copies of a cultural assimilator and instructions for its use (see listing in the Albert chapter).

A large variety of programs and techniques for intercultural training are described in the three-volume Landis and Brislin handbook. The contribution to the handbook by Pedersen and his chapter listed above are useful sources for discussions about differences in concepts of personality and how the underlying assumptions of counselors may stand in the way of communication between individuals from different cultural groups, especially in counseling situations.

Simulation Game Useful for the Study of Intercultural Communication

Shirts, G. (1979). *Bafa Bafa*. LaJolla, Cal.: Simile.

The purpose of this simulation is to give students the experience of being a member of a culture based on different value assumptions and to create a situation in which problems of intercultural communication and even culture shock arise. In this game, which can be played and discussed in about 90 minutes, a class of 12 to 35 students is divided into two "cultures" that operate from different assumptions about social behavior. After spending a few minutes "learning their own culture," a process of visiting between cultures begins, and students try to learn as much as they can by observation and interaction about the other cultural group. This extremely interesting exercise can be used to introduce many concepts relating to the cross-cultural study of psychology.

Stereotypes and General Problems in Intergroup Relations

Brewer, M.B., and Campbell, D.T. (1976). *Ethnocentrism and intergroup attitudes: East African evidence*. New York: Wiley.

Davidson, A.R., and Thomson, E. (1980). Cross-cultural studies of attitudes and beliefs. In Triandis and Brislin, *Handbook. Vol. 5*. (pp. 25–71).

Tajfel, H., ed. (1982). *Social identity and intergroup relations*. London: Academic Press.

The Davidson and Thomson chapter gives an excellent summary of the acquisition of stereotypes and can serve as the starting point for discussion of the students' own stereotypes about other racial or national groups. One way of organizing such a discussion is to ask students to write a one- or two-page intercultural or interracial autobiography addressing questions such as: What was your image of people from other cultures and racial groups when you were five or six years old? When you were an adolescent? Is this image different now? What information or experience formed or changed these attitudes? Do you remember ever feeling like a member of an "out-group?" Can you think of any ways to change those stereotypes or prejudices? The students then exchange their autobiographies in pairs and orally summarize them. Thus individual A's autobiography can be summarized by individual B, while B's is summarized by A. This situation is more satisfactory than if each person presents his or her own autobiography, as students will often be hesitant to discuss their own negative feelings. The instructor summarizes and interprets the material presented to illustrate the pervasiveness of stereotypes and the difficulty of modifying them. Any student who is hesitant to have his or her autobiography considered should have those feelings respected, but even in racially mixed classes few students choose not to participate.

The Brewer and Campbell volume as well as the Tajfel collection can be used to illustrate the extent to which ethnocentrism and strong in-group feelings (based on various characteristics of group membership, including race, religion, national origin, tribe, and language) shape interaction. The role of cognitive factors, personal contact, and shared cultural elements can be discussed using these materials.

Stereotypes and Problems in Intergroup Relations: The Special Case
of New Migrant Groups
Coehlo, G.V., and Ahmed, P.I. (1980). *Uprooting and development: Dilemmas
of coping with modernization.* New York: Plenum.
Emecheta, B. *Second-class citizen.* (1983). New York: Braziller. (paperback).
Matthews, E. (1982). *Culture clash.* Chicago: Intercultural Press.
Schonbach, P., et al. (1981). *Education and intergroup attitudes.* London:
Academic Press.
Watson, J.L., ed. (1977). *Between two cultures: Migrants and minorities in
Britain.* Oxford: Blackwell.

U.S. undergraduates are likely to have little awareness of the number of
workers and their families from Southern Europe (especially Turkey, Italy, and
Greece) who have migrated to Northern Europe as "guest workers" and the
extent to which British society now includes large numbers of migrants from
former British colonies. Much of the renewed interest on the part of European
social scientists in intergroup attitudes results from the problems of education
and social services that have resulted. This situation is therefore an excellent
concrete illustration of the pervasiveness outside the United States of negative
intergroup attitudes that are not exclusively racial in character. The Schonbach
volume, which reports research on German secondary school students' attitudes
toward Turkish and Italian migrant workers, is probably too complex for
assignment to students, but it does suggest topics for discussion, for example,
the role of socioeconomic conditions and personal contact in intergroup relations, as well as home and school factors.

The Coehlo and Ahmed volume discusses mental-health issues and coping
strategies in the adaptation of immigrant groups from Asia, India, and Latin
America to the United States, as well as immigrants to Israel. This book can
serve as a resource for student projects or reports. The book by Matthews, a
reconstructed diary of an American family that served as sponsors to a Vietnamese immigrant family, provides a first-hand account of some of the problems
discussed in the Coehlo and Ahmed volume.

Another source for student reports would be the Watson volume, which
describes the history of migration to Britain from China, Greece, India, Pakistan,
Poland, Turkey, West Africa, and the West Indies. The material presented in
the chapter on West Africa would be read in conjunction with the Emecheta
book. Although classified as fiction, this book appears to have an
autobiographical basis. The main character is a Nigerian woman who follows
her husband to London, has five children, and copes with many problems
associated with being "a second-class citizen"—both a migrant to England and
a woman. The book raises issues of modernization and sex roles in African

cultures, problems of assimilation faced by migrants in a second culture, the meaning of children and family in African cultures, the role of social networks, and alternative views of morality. It raises the further questions of how the experience of this character (or of those from the various groups discussed in the Watson volume) relates to the current experiences of immigrants to the United States and the kinds of prejudice they encounter. If the college or university is situated in or near a community where groups of recent immigrants live, students can use that topic for a paper based on observations or interviews. If students have no such direct access, they can use recent newspapers and magazine articles that have presented extensive analyses of the problems of migrants.

American attitudes toward new immigrants and toward immigration policy is an excellent focus for students to design, administer, and analyze an attitude survey for adults or other students. Questions might include the following: What should be the basis for immigration restrictions that would both be fair and protect U.S. interests? Another question is whether the following factors should be taken into account in deciding whether a group or an individual would be allowed to immigrate: ability to speak English, agreement not to take a job displacing American workers, possession of a needed occupational skill, proof of ability to be financially independent for one year, residence in a country practicing political repression, residence in a country threatened by famine, residence in a country friendly to the U.S. government, and so on. This project can simultaneously give training in survey skills and expose students to a current policy issue with international ramifications.

Sex Differences and Sex-Role Stereotypes

Ember, D. A cross-cultural perspective on sex differences. (1981). In R.H. Munroe, R.L. Munroe, and B.B. Whiting, ed. *Handbook of cross-cultural human development* (pp. 531–580). New York: Garland STPM Press.

Williams, J.E., and Best, D.L. (1982). *Measuring sex stereotypes.* Beverly Hills, Cal.: Sage.

Two basic issues in the study of sex roles are the extent to which there are culturally universal differences between the sexes and the extent to which these differences and other characteristics are reflected in beliefs about the sexes (sex-role stereotypes). The Ember chapter is a source for considering the universality of sex differences. A very lively discussion could be stimulated in an undergraduate class based on the criteria and framework Ember sets out.

The Williams and Best book is an excellent resource for reading by more able students and for exploration of hypotheses using the extensive tables the authors present. They have collected data (using an adjective check list) from male and female university students in 28 countries and from children in 24 countries. All major areas of the world except the Middle East and Eastern Europe are represented. The authors described both cross-cultural similarities and cross-cultural differences in sex-role stereotypes. Questions for discussion might include the following. To what extent do stereotypes found in the Williams and Best study match the sex differences described by Ember? Are sex-role stereotypes more or less characteristic of societies with a Western European orientation (when compared with African, Asian, or Latin American groups)? What is the role of religion in forming sex stereotypes? Because many sex stereotypes appear in different cultures, should we become less concerned about their existence in the United States? If it is not possible for students to read the entire book, several articles describing this project are available in the journals (and are referenced in this book).

Blumberg, R.L. (1976). Fairy tales and facts: Economy, family, fertility, and the female. In I. Tinker and M.B. Bramsen, ed., *Women and world development.* Washington, D.C.: Overseas Development Council.

Schlegal, A., ed. (1977). *Sexual stratification: A cross-cultural view.* New York: Columbia U.

Tiffany, S.W. (1979). *Women and society.* Montreal: Eden Press.

In considering the influences of culture on sex roles, instructors have many opportunities to broaden students' interests in developing world areas by considering women's status. Lumberg presents and refutes ten myths and stereotypes about women and development. Students could use other chapters in the Tinker and Bramsen volume, as well as materials from the country-by-country presentations in the Schlegal and Tiffany books to suggest other stereotypes and myths about women and the ways psychological research might be used to evaluate those myths and stereotypes. Other questions for discussion might include the following. What evidence is there that modernization improves the status of women? Concerning a country in which women's options are severely limited, how could one answer a husband who argues that his wives are well taken care of and would not want more equality? The Emecheta book previously cited is also an excellent source for this topic.

Achievement Motivation

Kornadt, H.-J., Eckensberger, L.H., and Emminghaus, W.B. (1980). Cross-cultural research on motivation and its contribution to a general theory of motivation. In H. Triandis and W. Lonner, ed., *Handbook of cross-cultural psychology: Vol. 3. Basic processes* (pp. 223–321). Boston: Allyn and Bacon.

Maehr, M.L., and Nicholls, J.G. (1980). Culture and achievement motivation. In N. Warren, ed. *Studies in cross-cultural psychology* (Vol. 2, pp. 221–267). London: Academic Press.

discussed in many social psychology courses, achievement motivation is of special interest in West Germany. The chapter in the Triandis handbook was written by three West Germans. It presents McClelland's theory relating need for achievement to entrepreneurial behavior and economic development and considers the relation of this motive to child-rearing processes. The authors present evidence for a kind of universal achievement motive; however, they argue that this motive should be studied within the context of the subjective cultures of different nations (as suggested by Triandis).

The Maehr and Nicholls chapter presents a somewhat more critical view of McClelland's theory. It argues that his conceptualization was based on an individualistic American model of achievement. In other countries, such as Iran or Japan, views of success and motivation to achieve may be tied into the subjective culture in different ways. The authors also comment on the extent to which schooling practices (which probably have a determinative effect on motivation to achieve, especially in developing countries) have been ignored in favor of the study of child-rearing practices. They use cross-cultural evidence to expand the conceptualization of achievement motivation and also discuss problems with the assumption that any test (even a projective test) has cross-cultural validity. Students have their own ideas about why they are motivated to study and to excel. Their own reflection on those motives and how they have been shaped can be stimulated by the cross-cultural similarities and differences Maehr and Nicholls present. These readings can also be integrated into a study of traditional and modern attitudes in developing nations. If some students in the class have taken their primary and secondary education in another country, they can be asked to discuss the motivation differences they have experienced.

Aggression

Goldstein, A., and Segall, M. (1983). *Aggression in global perspective.* Elmsford, N.Y.: Pergamon.

Aggression and its sources are often considered in social psychology courses. This work includes a wide-ranging collection of chapters reporting psychological and sociological research on that topic in Brazil, Hungary, Nigeria, and Peru, as well as in several countries in Asia (including China) and Western Europe. The volume illustrates the extent to which common factors predict aggressiveness across nations and the widespread concern about this problem. Students might be asked to read recent U.S. research on aggression and then search this volume for corroborating or conflicting information.

Work Organizations

Bass, B.M., and Burger, P.C. (1979). *Assessment of managers: An international comparison.* New York: Free Press.

Hofstede, G. (1980). *Culture's consequences: International differences in work-related values.* Beverly Hills, Cal.: Sage.

Tannenbaum, A.S., et al. (1977). *Hierarchy in organizations.* San Francisco: Jossey-Bass.

Tannenbaum, A.S. (1980). Organizational psychology. In Triandis and Brislin, *Handbook. Vol. 5.* (pp. 281–334).

These works are closely related to the previous topics of value differences between countries and of achievement motivation. The Bass and Burger book contains materials from 12 countries (primarily in Japan, Latin America, and Western Europe); in addition to paper and pencil measures, it includes performance on organizational behavior exercises. The Hofstede book contains detailed material, suitable either for lecture preparation or for student reports, comparing values of managers in 40 countries (covering every major area of the world). The book by Tannenbaum and his associates reports research on organizational hierarchy in Austria, Israel (a kibbutz), Italy, the United States, and Yugoslavia. The Tannenbaum review chapter covers the area more broadly.

The concluding chapter of the Hofstede volume summarizes differences by world area in the way individuals are motivated and the preferred style of organizational hierarchy. These summaries could be a starting point for considering the formation of work-related values and the ways organizational design might be adjusted to them.

Work Organizations and Careers in Japan

Cole, R. (1979). *Work, mobility, and participation: A comparative study of American and Japanese industry.* Berkeley: U of California P.

Plath, D., ed. 1983). *Work and lifecourse in Japan.* Albany: State U of New York P.

These two books could be used very effectively to contrast the social psychology of working life in Japan with that in the United States. The Cole book suggests contrasts that can be illustrated from the case studies of career development in various Japanese organizations presented in the Plath volume. This approach will give students a more realistic sense of working life in Japan than data from the social sciences alone.

Conclusion

There is much recent cross-culturally relevant literature in other areas of psychology, especially in perceptual, cognitive, and personality psychology. Several of the resources cited in the previous two sections could be used in these areas as well. For example, the Segall book, *Cross-Cultural Psychology*, includes visual perception and cognition, and Wagner and Stevenson's, *Cultural Perspectives on Child Development* has a number of relevant chapters.

In summary, a surprising amount of recently published material is suitable for infusing an international dimension into undergraduate psychology courses. This bibliography is intended to provide useful suggestions for resources both to individuals who regularly take a cross-cultural point of view and to others who have not previously used international materials in their undergraduate courses.

JOURNALISM AND MASS COMMUNICATION

Journalists convey a pragmatic attitude that used to be reflected in the adage "local news is news and foreign news is foreign." In recent years, there has emerged a set of very practical reasons for developing the international dimensions of journalism: world news often has local implications, and in many cases local news can only be explained in an international context.

In contributing to the NCFLIS project, the Association for Education in Journalism and Mass Communication solicited the following essays by Bonnie Brownlee, Crocker Snow, Jr., Mary Gardner, Lowndes Stephens, John L. Martin, Richard Critchfield, Sharon Murphy and James Scotton, John Maxwell Hamilton and Susan Siltanen, and George Krimsky. The authors focus on the incorporation of international components into the journalism curriculum and consider journalists' development of international coverage and the contribution of media research to knowledge about other countries. These essays emphasize ways of learning and reporting as well as international knowledge and cross-cultural communication.

Several authors point out the inadequacy of American reporting on the Third World. The Sigma Delta Chi Foundation, an affiliate of the society of Professional Journalists, undertook a project in which newspapers in towns and cities across the country made nearly two dozen different kinds of connections between their communities and the Third World. In doing so, they utilized a variety of reporting techniques. The products appear in a book by John Hamilton Maxwell which bears the same title as his chapter in this book, *Main Street America and the Third World* (1986).

Internationalizing the Journalism Core: What's Being Done

Bonnie J. Brownlee

Bringing international issues to the journalism curricula in U.S. colleges and universities, as the articles in this book make clear, will require a change in mindset for most instructors. Neither our standard stock of textbooks nor our traditional way of thinking about journalism education is geared toward the world beyond the U.S. perimeter. For the most part, we concern ourselves with teaching our students to cover a city council in a story with a tight lead and a smooth inverted pyramid style. We strive to make certain the young journalists-to-be can spell correctly most of the time—or at least we hope they know enough to use the dictionary when in doubt. We insist on accuracy, we talk of the glory of seeking truth and exposing falsehood, and we cajole these young people into carrying their stylebooks wherever they go.

This is all well and good. After all, many journalism instructors have worked extensively in the media; they know what it takes to succeed. Yet, the world today is becoming smaller as it becomes more complex. Satellites bring the blood of an assassination in India, the beauty of New Zealand's rolling countryside, the horrifying tragedy of a Shuttle explosion to the screens of our television sets. As John Maxwell Hamilton and Susan Siltanen point out in their article, no U.S. town, however small and remote, is isolated from the effects of world events. One could well argue that any perceived isolation remaining in the heads of U.S. citizens represents a failure of both the education system and the news media of this country. In journalism education, the two are linked. If journalism programs don't stress the importance of understanding world affairs, world events, and just plain geography, journalism graduates and, later, journalists are not likely to work very hard to make such issues understandable to the general public.

Bonnie J. Brownlee is Assistant Professor of Journalism at Indiana University.

A Study of Journalism Curricula
In an effort to find out the extent to which international issues are taught in college journalism curricula, I mailed two letters of appeal to members of AEJMC: one letter to members of the international division and another to all other members. Sent in June 1984, the letters asked for copies of syllabi and general commentary on ways in which international issues were taught. I was especially interested in hearing from those who teach mainstream courses—history, communication law, reporting, editing, ethics, mass communication and society—the courses least likely to be international in outlook.

Results
I received syllabi representing 122 courses: 56 international communication courses, and 66 non-international courses. The non-international courses are of interest here, and Table 1 ranks the most common courses represented.

Table 1. Non-International Journalism Courses

Course	No. of Syllabi
Mass media and society	17
History	7
Reporting	5
Editing	4
Ethics	3
Public opinion	3
Communication law	3
Broadcasting	2
Economics of mass media	1
Public relations	1
Advertising	1
Others	19
Total	66

Topics by Course

Mass Media and Society
Although it's not always clear from the syllabi precisely what the course units entail, the bulk of the topics seems to deal with pointing out differences between the U.S. press—in theory and practice—and other press systems around the world. Four courses looked at what might be called the "nature of foreign press,"

and two others addressed Siebert et al.'s "four theories of the press." Two more looked at the historical background of the First Amendment; another, at the perceptions others gain of the United States by attending to our media.

History of Journalism

International issues seem not to be addressed to any great extent in journalism history courses. One course included a segment on the New International Information Order; one took a historical view of coverage of international affairs in U.S. papers; another compared the development of mass media in different countries; two others at the "antecedents"—philosophy—of the U.S. press.

Reporting

Though only five responses were submitted for courses on reporting, these showed several innovative approaches. Two courses had units that looked at the difference between the work of U.S.-based and foreign-based reporters. In an attempt to localize international news, one professor has his students write stories about foreign investment in the state and region. Another asks students to cover TV programs on international affairs.

Editing

Several professors said that they make use of news and map quizzes to focus on international issues. Two looked at "international news values." One said he does this to alert students to potential biases and stereotypes that may creep into news stories. One person said she specifically seeks stories with international datelines for her students to edit, with the hope that the exposure and subsequent discussion of the issues will interest the students in foreign affairs and drive home the theme of an increasingly interdependent world.

Other Journalism Courses

Two faculty members teaching ethics included units comparing press systems, and both said they make an effort to bring in foreign journalists and other foreign visitors on campus to talk to the class about issues faced by journalists. One person teaching communication law compared the legal and constitutional processes in the United States and other countries. A professor teaching public relations included a segment on polling in different countries; another, a discussion of the role of propaganda worldwide.

Among the syllabi were several for specialized readings courses. One looked at U.S. press coverage of the Grenada incident and the Falklands/Malvinas war. Another had current newsmakers and events as its focus.

Textbooks

A review of the syllabi reveals that the topics covered and methods used come with minimal aid from textbooks. A number of professors require their students to read "global" newspapers, such as *The New York Times* and the *Christian Science Monitor*. With the most frequently cited books listed no more than twice, texts in use by this sample are Hachten's *World News Prism*; Rosenblum's *Coups and Earthquakes*; Siebert et al.'s *Four Theories of the Press*; Agee, Emery, and Alt's *Maincurrents in Mass Communication*; and Katz and Wedell's *Broadcasting in the Third World*. *The Associated Press Stylebook and Libel Manual* is listed on many syllabi and it, of course, is a source of many things international.

Conclusions

Simply by studying a stack of syllabi, it is impossible to tell exactly what is being taught about the world and how topics are presented. But this examination indicates that international affairs play significant roles in quite a few non-international journalism courses. The way in which issues are presented varies with professor and course; there certainly is no text on internationalizing any given course. The most frequent subjects appear to be the New International Information Order, some variation on the "four theories of the press," and historical background of the U.S. press. The most frequently used textbooks, it seems, are not the standard reporting and editing books, but rather books that specialize on international matters: Hachten's, Rosenblum's, Siebert et al.'s.

A paper by Kurt Kent of Florida, presented at the AEJ convention in Houston in 1979, laments the state of editing and reporting texts in their lack of focus on international affairs. (See Kurt A.M. Kent, "Reporting and Editing Courses Need International Emphasis," 1979, and N. Riley Kirby and Kurt A.M. Kent, "Basic Texts Score Low on International News Reporting, Editing." 1979.) At that time, few of the 10 texts studied included more than a few examples of international origin or devoted more than a few paragraphs to international aspects.

The study presented here does not attempt to look at the specific texts, and such a study certainly would be worthwhile—expanding from recent editions of editing and reporting texts to texts for law, broadcasting, advertising, ethics, and history of journalism. Still, it seems fairly clear that what is international in the classes represented here comes primarily from the experiences and ideas of the professors teaching the courses and/or from a select few specialized texts.

Have we advanced any since the National Symposium on the Study of International Communication, a meeting sponsored by the International Communication Division in 1969? Has the "undergraduate professional curriculum" been internationalized, as recommended at that time, rather than new international courses added? Have members of the division developed packaged "practical professional exercises" and encouraged others to use them, as suggested by Kent in 1979? Have authors been encouraged to include international affairs in their textbooks?

Based on the evidence from the current study, we still have a long way to go to reach these goals. Indeed, all sorts of international topics are taught in specialized and general courses labeled "international." (This study garnered 56 international communication course syllabi from 36 universities and an array of titles, from "The Marxist and Socialist Press" to "Mass Media Systems in Latin America" to "Mass Communication in Communist Systems" to "The Role of Communication in Development.") The point, however, is that not all students take international communication classes. A U.S. public poorly versed in world affairs can be traced—at least to some extent—to poorly trained journalists. A reporter or editor who neither knows where El Salvador is nor why it might be important to U.S. citizens is not likely to handle a story from that small Central American country with any great insight or interest.

With the current encouragement of the U.S. Department of Education, this is an opportune time to reaffirm the concern and to restate the unfulfilled recommendations made in earlier studies of the journalism curriculum. This collection of essays, we hope, will provide some ideas and incentives to those who specialize in international communication and, especially, to those who teach core journalism courses.

We still need a systematic look at the texts. We still need some generally accepted and widely publicized principles or topics that should be covered in the various core courses. We still need to expose our students to journalists from other countries and to journalists from our country who report on the world. Unless U.S. journalists have an appreciation for the interdependence of the world and for the historical, cultural, religious, social, and political differences and similarities among nations, we can scarcely expect the general public of the United States to be adequately informed.

Going Global

Crocker Snow, Jr.

A dozen years or so ago, the British Broadcasting Corporation aired a much-praised television series titled *Civilization* that was hosted by Sir Kenneth Clark. Highly educational in content, it was an impressive and informative series, but the "civilization" portrayed stopped geographically at Mesopotamia. None of the history of the East—gunpowder, codification of law, Japanese feudalism, the first literature—was cited. In its own way the series was a little like the lead headline from the infamous days of Boston journalism: "Three Boston Dead in Philly Train Crash, 32 Others."

Journalism, of course, is largely a function of attitude and perspective. It is also a function of the writer's or editor's sense of the audience. The two cases cited, the one sublime, the second a little ridiculous, are extreme examples of journalism accommodating the primary concerns of the audience being addressed. The British and American television audiences were most interested in and cognizant of the roots of Western civilization, and this is what Sir Kenneth Clark's writers gave them. The Boston newspaper readers of yesteryear were presumably interested if any "locals" were involved, and this is what the headline writer told them.

But if the world we inhabit, a world in which borders, time frames, and horizons are shrinking, the journalistic perspective must expand to remain relevant. Our point of view must broaden to capture more of those elements that "impact," to use the terminology of the social scientists, on us all.

The concept of international interdependence is no longer one of fancy, but of fact. The lesson of an interdependent world is constantly before us all. It comes, for instance, from the variation in the "El Niño" ocean current off Peru over the past few years and its disastrous effects, both climatic and otherwise, observed throughout the world. It comes from the ever-less fanciful writings of Buckminster Fuller about "Spaceship Earth" and the now immortal words of Neil Armstrong as he first set foot on the moon: "That's one small step for man,

---

Crocker Snow, Jr., is Publisher and Editor-in-Chief of WorldPaper.

one giant leap for mankind." It comes from the cold statistics showing that the proportion of U.S. gross national product involved in exports and imports has risen from 6.8 percent in 1980—and from the consequent realization that "buying American" would be almost impossible to do.

Today, exchange rates between the dollar, the yen, and the pound sterling fluctuate in minutes not days. Fortunes are won and lost on the basis of instantaneous reactions to the Federal Reserve Bank's latest hint about the prime rate, or the latest announcement from an OPEC meeting in Vienna. Today, an epidemic such as AIDS emerges, apparently out of Africa, and is quickly transmitted to people all over the world. The eruption of Mount St. Helens endangers not only local inhabitants and the local timber industry, but new dust in the atmosphere affects temperature gradients—and crop harvests— in almost one-quarter of the globe for six months thereafter.

We as a nation have a reasonable head start for developing global perceptions. Throughout its history, our country has been a melting pot for different bloodlines, cultures, and races. How many of us were thrilled when a Cambodian refugee, Linn Yann, made the regional finals of a national spelling bee last year? How many of us are made proud by the worldwide pressures for immigration into this country? It's no coincidence that the U.N. headquarters is in New York, or that the head of the World Bank has always been from the United States, or that the annual meeting of the International Monetary Fund and the World Bank takes place in Washington every September. Is it any surprise to discover that the International Advertising Association, with members in 70 countries and a membership of nearly 3,000, has headquarters on Fifth Avenue?

In spite of all this, the United States is slow on the international uptake, resistant to foreign issues and events. The major media of this country devote scant space to news and views from places beyond our shores. We are also resistant to foreign languages: James Reston properly pointed out that while the United States does fine in the "hardware of high tech," we are truly an underdeveloped country in the "software of language." We are meddlesome and parochial at the same time, and can pay the price for this in many ways.

A few years ago, I attended a meeting of 20 Japanese and American newspaper editors who were experts on each other's country. One discussion leader tested our understanding and empathy with a quiz. He asked for a show of hands on the question, "How many of you believe the Japanese economy is open to foreign trade competition?" Ten people—all the Japanese—raised their hands; the 10 Americans did not. Next he asked, "How many believe that Japanese economic success is partly due to a free ride for the last 30 years with virtually no defense spending?" Again it was a 10-to-10 breakdown—except the other way around. The third question: "How many believe America would support Japan if there were a nuclear threat against her by China or the Soviet Union?" Once more, the vote was 10 to 10, with the U.S. editors believing the United States would support Japan and the Japanese not believing this. Only the response to the final question—"How many believe that if there were an embargo on oil going into Japan, the United States and the major oil companies would transfer sources of oil to support Japan?"—broke down the national lines. In this case, 18 of us thought there would be support for Japan.

At the risk of belaboring the point, here were 20 people with extensive trans-Pacific experience who were as sympathetic to the other country's concerns as any group could be; yet, our perceptions of these key bilateral concerns were diametrically different, split along national lines. That's an important lesson to remember when we, as consumers of international news and suppliers of the technology to transmit it, pursue our workaday affairs.

Information, of course, is a key. It is the central foodstuff of the globalism for which I argue, but it isn't all protein-rich or fat-free. One reason is that most international news to which we have access is dominated by one's own point of view. It is, for the most part, prepared by Western writers for a Western audience and therefore reflects a Western perspective and value system. This imbalance is a root of the current debate about the New World Information Order. Indeed, it is a fact that much Western writing about the developing world is superficial and simplistic, emphasizing the proverbial "fires, coups, and earthquakes."

Information alone, then, is not enough. Understanding is necessary, too. We're all aware that the world is changing faster than any of us can comprehend. The option of putting our heads in the sand and trying not to be bothered is really not an option at all. Being international isn't only a realization that there's a lot going on out there that's mysterious and important, coming from different wellsprings; it's an understanding that there's a lot of value there, too. It isn't just a recognition of the exotic, but an awareness of the essential.

In the care and feeding of young and aspiring journalists, this recognition can come not only from preaching but from practice. It can come in humdrum, workaday ways from focusing on the essentials of perspective and attitude.

One place to begin is in the subscription lists and the type of media being used in the classroom. A good sampling of foreign publications—dailies, weeklies, and periodicals—can spice up course curricula. When the dateline, the nationality of the reporter, and the audience are different, suddenly the story selection, tone, and editorial conclusion differ too. Using the likes of the *World Press Review*, a monthly magazine that reprints key stories that have appeared in the press around the world, or *WorldPaper* can underscore just how vital perspective and point of view can be. Introducing some foreign journalists, the

Washington correspondents of Japanese or German media, for instance, in some guest lectures can accomplish the same thing.

The world has never looked quite the same to me since my first trip abroad in 1958, when, in the summer after my freshman year of college, I traveled with a friend to Russia for several weeks. It was a baptism of foreign sights, sounds, and smells—a first time to harbor passport, travelers checks, and a bagful of preconceptions and prejudices. And where more interesting than Moscow and Leningrad during the first summer they were open to American tourists?

I was playing junior reporter then, writing a series of student-adventures-in-Russia features for *The Boston Globe*. My friend and I probed and poked, sold socks on the black market, and had our camera confiscated when we took pictures of off-limits sites. But, of course, we survived and learned—learned that the world isn't quite so round or smooth as we had seen in the classroom, nor that the Russians were as evil or hostile as we had been led to believe.

It's been a nonstop course of continuing education ever since, a journey without any end in sight, but one with more and more familiar landmarks in Asia, Europe, Latin America, and the Middle East. The background music has remained the same: a refrain reminding one that people all over the world have similar preoccupations and problems, but because of different social, economic, and political conditions, they have different methods of dealing with them. That fact underscores how much there is to learn from others—a truism that everyone dealing in the international arena should absorb and act on.

At a May 1984 conference in Washington entitled "Global Crossroads: Educating Americans for Responsible Choices," the soft-spoken Indonesian Soedjatmoko, head of the U.N. University, put it all succinctly:

> I see the world ahead as one where we will be hearing increasing insistence by non-Western cultures on the need and right to maintain their own cultural identity. It would be wrong to assume that we are moving toward a single world culture—a pluralistic global society is an inevitable reality to which we must learn to adjust.

We need also recognize the relativity of one's own culture—it is but one way of dealing with reality and the organization of society, in light of the vision one may have about the ultimate meaning of human existence, individually and collectively. There are many other cultures with visions no less valid. We need to see that such cultural pluralism enlarges the options open to all of us in making our choices about the future, both for our own societies and for the world at large.

As I look to the next century, I am more and more convinced that it will be the capacity to learn—and, in particular, to learn from each other—which, more than any other single factor, will determine the viability, autonomy, and integrity of all societies. I am speaking here of a new kind of learning—one that will enable us to survive, in humane fashion, in a world undergoing profound transformation. We will have to adjust ourselves to living in a world of 10 billion, a world in which science and technology are triggering rapid social and value changes.

To put it another way, going global is both a state of mind and an attitude of humility. Journalists entering the international arena should remember that the sound of one hand clapping is no sound at all.

Revamping the Journalism Curriculum

Mary A. Gardner

I t's easy to criticize the lack of interest of many "Americans," if I may use that term, in learning a foreign language and learning how people of another culture think, live, and work. Yet if we are to understand others, we must first understand why we think and behave the way we do, and why we tend to be parochial.

We forget far too easily that we're a very young nation, one that evolved during the communication revolution, and one in which the English language has been considered the essential melding force for nation building and unity.

Julio Camba, the Spanish journalist, marveled in the early 1900s that a country filled with immigrants from all over Europe could develop into "Americans" so rapidly; they began to look and act the same, he said, no matter what country they came from. The development of a firm and resolute jaw, he decided, was the outstanding characteristic that identified the American physiognomy. And he noticed that wherever he met them, Americans were chewing gum—in subways, at sports events, or standing in line at theaters.

"Aha," he said to himself, "that's what builds that strong, resolute jaw, turning Italians, Germans, French, and even Spaniards, into identifiable Americans. In this nation of diverse people, it's really chewing gum that forms and holds the people and the country together. They really are 'Los Estados Unidos Gomados.'"

I regret this rather loose remembrance of a chapter in one of Camba's many books, the title of which has been lost to me because I shared his humor with a friend who never returned the book. Nevertheless, it does illustrate his wonderment at how such a diverse group of people could be forged into a nation. In retrospect, however, I'm sure that Camba would have agreed that it was not chewing gum alone that bound the United States together but, among other things, our common language—one that newcomers strove mightily to conquer. We shouldn't forget this when we complain of our tendency to look

Mary A. Gardner is Professor of Journalism at Michigan State University.

at English as the only essential language for our survival. It has always been largely so.

Neither should we forget the happenstance of the period in which we evolved as a nation. When I lived in Austria from 1948 to 1951, I was always struck by the many dialects I encountered throughout the country. Here was a nation slightly smaller in area and population than Ohio; yet, a person from Vienna couldn't understand a person from Styria (and vice versa) unless they both spoke "high German." And this was true throughout various "lands" and villages of Austria. It's as if natives of Columbus, Ohio, couldn't understand those of Toledo if they didn't speak the lingua franca of the state.

Why didn't we develop the same problem in the United States? I suspect in part because newcomers wanted to become Americans and for their children to learn English and because communication technology was evolving during our country's growth. We didn't have pockets of population isolated for great periods of time because communication lines followed our people as they moved west.

In 1807, the steamboat was invented. Though short-lived, canals were built in the 1830s. Steam railroads began carrying passengers and freight, and by 1869 the transcontinental railroad was joined at Promontory, Utah. In the meantime, the pony express operated from 1860 to 1861. Then came the telegraph, rotary press, and typewriter. In the short span between 1870 and 1925, the telephone, linotype machine, phonograph, motion picture, subway, zeppelin, airplane, radio telephone, first transcontinental airmail route, and radar were developed. This flurry of invention occurred as our shores were welcoming more immigrants who sought a new life as Americans. Thus, except for a few citizens isolated here and there, communication facilitated the growth of a nation in which people generally spoke only one language, albeit with regional accents.

Also, communication technology and popular education in the United States evolved in a somewhat parallel manner (as did journalism education), furthering the spread of the English language. Thus today, we have a nation where one may travel for 3,000 miles and speak only one language. Perhaps this is also possible in one or two of our Latin American neighbors by size if not population, but even there many isolated population pockets exist. In Europe, it is possible to travel 500 miles and speak five different languages. No wonder we are a people of little language sensitivity.

My father, a veterinarian, learned German in college in the early 1900s and then moved to a small Ohio town, where he never had the opportunity to use the language again. Today, of course, more young people have the wherewithal to travel and study abroad; yet most will return to jobs and locales where, unlike in Europe, they will have little chance, if any, to use their newly acquired language skills. Their experience, of course, will help enlarge their cultural awareness and international interests, but on their return many will simply preoccupy themselves with that which obviously affects them directly—local affairs. This is unfortunate at a time when we have a great need for people in government and business who can work in the language and culture of another country.

Journalists Need a Foreign Language

In spite of this gloomy picture, I suggest that studying a foreign language has a particular value for students of journalism, and not just because they might someday become foreign correspondents. The study of a foreign language brings many fringe benefits that students may not appreciate until much later. Almost 10 years ago, I argued in vain against dropping the two-year foreign language requirement from our Michigan State curriculum, because I thought— and still think—it taught students self-discipline and persistence (especially needed among journalists) and gave them insights into another culture.

Furthermore, learning a foreign language generally forces students to learn English grammar—certainly they have to know about infinitives and subjunctives in English before they can understand them in another language. In short, a foreign language program provides a rare opportunity for our students to strengthen their English, in addition to learning a foreign language, gaining some cultural sensitivity, and losing some of their parochialism.

People of such a huge country, however, naturally have local concerns and regional preoccupations, and we must constantly strive to keep parochialism from crippling our relationship with the rest of the world. This isn't easy, especially when people are faced with critical problems at home. Nor can we be sure that important international stories will receive adequate attention of our readers or listeners.

During a conference on world tensions, held in Minneapolis, a well known political science professor from the University of Minnesota took a journalist from the Minneapolis *Star* to task because, he said, the *Star* hadn't prepared its readers for the intertribal warfare that erupted when Nigeria received its independence.

"Why, professor," the journalist replied, "my paper sent me there before independence, and I wrote a series about what problems were likely to occur— including tribal conflict."

The professor looked somewhat startled.

"The problem, sir," the reporter observed, "is that when I wrote that series, you weren't interested in Nigeria and didn't bother to read it."

The professor had the grace to blush.

Communication at best is difficult. People don't always attend to a text or conversation unless it particularly interests them at the moment, and international communication particularly is fraught with uncountable problems. All the more reason, we may argue, that we need to make more students aware that our community is becoming increasingly global and that we all need to understand it better if we are to survive within it. And, certainly, universities have the obligation to broaden cultural understanding and to help students hone intercultural communication skills.

Internationalizing the Journalism Curriculum

What pragmatic means might we use to "internationalize" our journalism curriculum and broaden our students' vision beyond those elective international communication courses we offer? I'd like to step outside our discipline for a moment and suggest that we first need to require students to study a language for two years at the university level. I know that I'm fighting windmills, but somehow we need to recognize the importance of this primary step before we take the secondary one. Without it, it seems to me, any program will be meager at best.

Of course, the classroom provides us with many opportunities to encourage, and even force, our students to understand that they are not living in isolation. Let's then consider some of the basic courses in journalism and how we might add an "international" dimension to them.

Introductory Mass Media Courses

- Introduce students to theoretical concepts of the press, illustrating them with international examples, stressing their roots, evolution, restrictions, advantages and disadvantages, and why they have evolved as they have.

- Discuss U.S. news values, the agenda-setting functions of the mass media, and how the media are viewed by the Third World.

Basic Reporting Courses

- Resort to weekly current-events quizzes, ensuring that they are up to date and include questions about what is happening on the local, national, and international scene. Students then will have to read newspapers and listen to news broadcasts.

- Assign news stories that require students to tie a local story in with a similar problem in another country. For example, farmers in the area may be losing their land because of the economic situation. How does their problem compare to that in another country? Can the similarities and differences be compared? Could a sister community of the state offer a comparison?

- Bring foreign correspondents into classes and have them discuss the problems of newsgathering in another culture and what they have learned from living and working abroad. It may be more difficult to locate such correspondents if the campus is outside a metropolitan area, but other sources—the local or regional AP or UPI bureau, or the regional newspapers or broadcasting stations—may be helpful.

- Invite local business people and legislators who have traveled abroad in behalf of the city or the state, or on personal business, to tie their experiences and opinions in with a local story on business or economics.

- Discuss stereotyping of women and minorities and of nationalities. Note that women, in a sense, are the third world of the United States—that their complaints about how they are covered are quite similar to those voiced by people in the Third World. Use examples from both worlds.

Undoubtedly there are professors on campus who have done research overseas. Their information gathering and cultural problems are often similar to those experienced by journalists, even though their profile in the country is likely to have been lower. Depending on their field of experience, the professors may be able to place in context a recent news event that has occurred in the country of their research. They may also be able to give a local angle to an event. For example, if we have a teacher shortage in our schools and we're hiring teachers from other countries, does that mean we might help create a similar shortage abroad? This, of course, might add an international angle to a local story.

Foreign students provide another classroom resource. Sometimes they have worked on newspapers or in broadcasting even though they may be studying for an advanced degree in another field. Often they are avid consumers of the media. Even non-journalists can talk about what is taking place in their own countries and provide a view of U.S. media that our students may never have encountered. They may be pleased to talk about how their countries have, or have not, been covered by the local news media in our city. The resulting discussion will most likely be a challenging and lively one. Some balance must be provided by the instructor, of course, because foreign students do have the tendency to equate the local paper of our university town with their best national paper—an unfair comparison.

Photography

- Assign students to photograph a spread on culture groups within the community, illustrating where they are, what traditions they preserve, how hard they have worked, and what difficulties and benefits they have encountered. For example, Lansing has a Vietnamese restaurant and a Korean restaurant, both started by refugees, whose owners should make interesting profiles.

Public Affairs Reporting

- Have students examine the impact of legislative action on overseas trade, why and how local companies operate abroad, and how state and federal legislation affects the state and local work force and that of the foreign country involved.

- Have students examine the cultural groups in their community and their impact on the political life of the city. Let reporters struggle with trying to gather information from sources who speak little English and whose culture is distinct from their own. For example, we have a Hispanic population in Lansing that has its own community center and monthly newspaper. Ironically, in spite of the fact that our students are always seeking publication outlets, very few have volunteered to work for *El Renacimiento*, the monthly newspaper, even though its editor has spoken to our classes and tried to recruit reporters, editors, and advertising sales people. In short, most students must be assigned stories through their classes if they are to poke their noses into the community.

Editing

- Provide stories for editing that involve international issues or events that can be related to, or placed in context with, the local or state scene. Include stories that require geographical knowledge and will force students to use atlases and almanacs.

- Include editing exercises that stereotype nationalities, races, the handicapped, and women. Such exercises provide the opportunity to draw comparisons cross-culturally on stereotyping and to sensitize students to language use.

History

- Include sketches of the history of the principal world news agencies, why they came about, our reliance on them, and how they differ.

- Discuss briefly the coverage of the United States by the British during the Civil War, and how and why our coverage of World War I, World War II, Korea, Vietnam, and Grenada differed.

Law

- Include the differences, positive and negative, between our legal system under common law and that of other countries under the Napoleonic code or other legal systems.

Further Suggestions

Of course, similar techniques may be used in magazine writing courses, electronic news courses, and even newspaper editorial management courses. For example, a class can examine the differences between the U.S. concepts of management and those of Japan or how *Le Monde* of France is managed compared to most U.S. newspapers.

No mention has been made of the videotapes available on foreign reporting or the documentaries on other countries. Some of the latter might be shown in beginning reporting courses with the requirement that students turn in stories based on the tape content.

Of course, all the suggestions above require extra work and imagination by the instructor if they are to be developed into viable means to add an international touch to courses that usually are parochial. We may never know how effective such ideas are, but studies could be devised to measure short-term benefits, if not long-term ones.

Whether we can help lead students into a world beyond their immediate one is uncertain, but teachers who truly wish to stretch minds and enlarge students' vision and understanding should dare to try.

Journalism in a University's International Program: The South Carolina Experience

Lowndes F. Stephens

Most members of journalism faculties in accredited programs are committed to a strong liberal arts education for journalists and for other students pursuing careers in the mass media. Even as the Accrediting Council for Education in Journalism and Mass Communication moves to give schools some flexibility in interpreting the requirement for 75% of course work to be in liberal arts and sciences, the council has made it clear that schools should increase the number of hours required for graduation, if more skills courses are needed, rather than reduce the number of courses in liberal arts and sciences.[1]

The international communication division of the Association for Education in Journalism and Mass Communication is especially interested in seeing that the journalism education curriculum introduces students to the global implications of journalism practice. Unfortunately only a handful of journalism students take an elective course in international communication or an advanced seminar in communication and national development, typical offerings in departments/schools of journalism and mass communication. Many programs no longer require students to take a foreign language or "area studies" courses; thus, many graduates can meet their liberal arts and sciences requirements without exposure to comparative political, economic, social, and mass media systems. We introduce students to politics and economics in the public affairs reporting courses, to statistics and the scientific method in our research methods courses, to logic in our communication theory courses. So, too, must we consciously acquaint them with the international implications of journalistic practice, and with the political, economic, and cultural constraints that influence journalistic practice in other parts of the world.

Lowndes F. Stephens is Professor of Journalism at the University of South Carolina.

What follows are some experiences at internationalizing the journalism curriculum at the University of South Carolina.

Institutional Support

James B. Holderman, president of the University of South Carolina since 1978 and former chairman of the U.S. Commission to UNESCO, has made internationalism the signature of his administration. Under his leadership the university has established affiliation programs with colleges and universities in the Middle East and China and has built a growing presence in Latin America. The university has become a popular site for such important international meetings as President Reagan's summer 1984 Caribbean conference on the Future of the Western Community and an International Monetary Fund conference of some 20 finance ministers and dignitaries in November 1985.

The president also has established a special assistant for international development and a system vice president for intercultural affairs and professional development. Further, he has reorganized the International Center to expand its visibility and effectiveness; a former undersecretary of the Department of State (Eagleburger) directs the office. Other related offices include the Office of International Services, which coordinates relations with new foreign faculty members and new foreign students, and the Institute for International Studies, which organizes approximately 15 symposia a year. The U.S. Ambassador to South Korea is on leave as director of the Institute for International Studies. Journalism faculty regularly participate in these symposia.

The university's Office of Sponsored Programs and Research supports efforts on the part of faculty and academic units to work on international and intercultural affairs projects. For example, the office supported a College of Journalism and School of Public Health affiliation program proposal in 1984 with Cairo (Egypt) University.[2] Several units, including journalism, have had long-range contracts with governments of the various African states to train students at the undergraduate and graduate levels.

South Carolina's master's degree in international business is a nationally recognized program and faculty members who teach in the program have assisted journalism students whose theses have focused on international advertising and international public relations issues.

The University of South Carolina also gave birth in 1973 to a program called the Freshman Seminar Experience-University 101, recognized throughout this hemisphere for improving the survival skills of college students. The University 101 program annually hosts a national conference attended by about 900 faculty members from colleges and universities in North America. International and ethnic-minority students are encouraged to take a three-credit, pass-fail course that orients students to the demands of college-level academic work and to the support services on campus that can help them survive. Four journalism faculty members teach in this program; one senior member is co-director.

Six campus resource agencies are especially helpful to international students: Academic Skills Development Center, Writing Center, Career Planning and Placement Center, English Program for Internationals, Academic Computing Center, and Office of International Studies.

The Academic Skills Development Center offers reading and study skills development to students. When journalism faculty direct students to the center, the consultants encourage students to use materials related to their classes, such as the foreign newspaper stacks in the college library.

The Writing Center offers free tutorial sessions to students in all aspects of writing and free workshops on sentence structure; organization; term paper, thesis, and dissertation writing. Journalism students at all levels are encouraged to use the center. Instructors receive post cards indicating students have visited the center. International students, regardless of how well they may have done on the Test of English as a Foreign Language (TOEFL), find these services especially helpful.

The Career Planning and Placement Center provides international students and those interested in working outside the continental United States the opportunity to research prospective careers. Services include individual and group counseling, a career library with interactive computer, and community referrals for information and experience.

The English program for internationals is an intensive English program serving about 70 students each semester. Each student devotes 23 hours a week to English classes, grammar and reading practice, and writing and listening skills. Some students are sponsored by their national governments or by businesses. Government sponsors for fall 1985 included Kuwait, Oman, Qatar, the Saudi Arabian Education Mission, and the United Arab Emirates. Students can live in the International Village on campus or make their own living arrangements.

The academic computer-services office supports students who want to apply computers to their academic work. Frequently, international students seek computer accounts in the journalism school because they recognize word-processing skills can cut the considerable editing time they spend polishing term papers and theses. Students take short courses on various computer programs and then may be eligible for a computer account.

Finally, the Office of International Services serves as the most significant resource for internationalizing the journalism curriculum on campus. OIS supports foreign scholars working or studying at the university. The office publishes an international handbook for foreign students;[3] organizes international coffee hours, a host family program, a program for international wives and children; and supports various international student clubs. OIS also provides information on academic programs offered outside the United States and on international students studying in the United States.

Special Event Example: World Food Day

The university demonstrated its broad support for increasing the international awareness of members of the local and university communities when it hosted an international teleconference as part of World Food Day Activities, October 16, 1985. Participants were invited to observe national and local panels discuss world hunger and potential solutions to this global problem.

The national portion of the program was projected onto a large-screen television. Panelists included Peter McPherson, administrator of the U.S. Agency for International Development; Barbara Huddleston, chief of the Food Security and Information Service of the U.N. Food and Agriculture Organization; Marie Angelique Savane, president of the Association of African Women for Research on Development and international vice president of the Society for International Development; and Sen. Paul Simon of Illinois.

The national panel discussion was followed with a local discussion by a panel of experts in a variety of related fields. The national panelists then returned for concluding remarks.

Journalism instructors took advantage of the event by assigning students in reporting courses to cover various aspects of World Food Day. Students in skills classes were given assignments based on this event.

Initiatives by the College of Journalism

The college maintains contact with 30 to 40 recent foreign student alumni who encourage their associates interested in studying in the United States to consider attending South Carolina. We have an alumni association in Hong Kong, for example, and our Chinese students tell us they have come to the university because of recommendations from these alumni. Further, our faculty, when traveling overseas, often visit graduates and foreign members of AEJMC. These contacts assist faculty in their own research and assist us in identifying potential students for our program.

The College of Journalism encourages student participation in the annual AEJMC convention and helps with the costs of attending the convention for any student in the program. We encourage foreign students to compete for the travel grants sponsored by the Institute of International Education and to take advantage of other special opportunities for international students. For example, our students have recently served as summer Voice of America fellows and have attended special workshops sponsored by USIA.

We make a special effort to assign to international students advisers who are themselves interested in international issues and who have traveled extensively outside the continental United States. These advisers get a briefing from the university's international services office. Further, we prepare a kind of press kit for all our graduate students and emphasize certain items for international students. For example, in addition to our graduate student handbook, we include

- a brochure developed by the international communication division of AEJMC.

- a flier listing opportunities for financial aid and travel (such as IIE convention travel grants and VOA fellowships).

- a copy of *Journalism Abstracts* and other AEJMC publications to encourage student membership in AEJMC. *Journalism Abstracts* gives students good ideas on thesis and dissertation topics.

- a biographical sketch on other program graduates from the same country or region of the world with information about the placement of these students after they have finished our program.

- a list of library holdings of special interest to international students and scholars (such as foreign newspaper holdings, Foreign Broadcast Information Service reports, UNESCO documents, *World Press Encyclopedia, World Press Review, Gazette*).

International students pursuing graduate studies also complete a detailed questionnaire before admission to the program. The questionnaire includes basic biographical information and work-history data, scores on the Graduate Record Exam and on the TOEFL (we look for scores of 580 and higher), and a statement of purpose.[4]

We emphasize oral presentations in our graduate seminars and encourage a mix of foreign- and native-born students in all courses. All students, including our international students, must pass a typing test and complete remedial core-skills courses before they are admitted as candidates for a graduate degree. In our graduate courses, we encourage international students to challenge our press philosophies on whether they are appropriate models for their own societies and to share with us how they are able to separate the skills training from the ideological training they also receive as students in American programs of journalism and mass communications.

Our U.S. students are encouraged to travel abroad and develop an international view. Students who study abroad work with appropriate faculty members and complete a detailed written project report to earn three semester hours of credit.

We also "flag" potential members of Phi Beta Kappa when they are college sophomores. Those with high grade point averages are interviewed and are encouraged to take a foreign language and develop an "area studies" emphasis. These students also become a pool of potential prospects for significant university-wide scholarship programs: the Fulbright Research Grant; the Mellon Fellowship; or the Truman Scholarship. Our college has placed and received Rotary and Fulbright awardees.

We ensure that faculty with little apparent interest in international communication will have opportunities to work with foreign students by requiring all our students to take remedial skills courses. Many of the faculty who teach these courses end up on foreign students' thesis committees. Our graduate students must complete a four-hour written comprehensive exam. The college graduate council gives foreign students the option of preparing the written exam in their first language; they are given 24 hours to have the written exam translated into English.

Future Initiatives

Several initiatives might be considered for fostering internationalism in the journalism curriculum. First, the Accrediting Council for Education in Journalism and Mass Communication might start training a pool of team members who are qualified to advise and evaluate the efforts of journalism schools in expanding the international scope of their curricula. Second, the United States Information Agency should continue to encourage faculty exchange and affiliation programs. Third, journalism and mass communication programs should form regional consortia and develop "exportable" programs for countries in need of more journalism education initiatives. Our own college is working with institutions in Jamaica. Perhaps we could work with the University of North Carolina-Chapel Hill in developing a reciprocal degree program with countries in Central America. Part of the program could include faculty and student exchanges. Students could get skills training in our program and theory, research, history, and law from North Carolina. Faculty from Central America could teach our students courses in contemporary issues and international communication and development.

Fourth, journalism programs should make more extensive use of existing networks to expand the exchange of foreign scholars and students. Our South Carolina Fulbright Society is very active. We need to establish a stronger network of journalism faculty/students who have held Fulbrights, who are members of the International Association for Mass Communications Research, the International Communication Association, and the international division of AEJMC.

Fifth, faculty development initiatives are required to make U.S. professors more effective in teaching foreign students and teaching U.S. students about international issues. Moreover, we must help develop foreign faculty members who have difficulty in relating to our students, who are prone to challenge the authoritarian teaching styles of many faculty members.[5]

Finally, journalism programs should commit financial aid to students who show promise in developing an international perspective. Scholarship applications should include information about foreign language proficiency and foreign travel.

Summary

Schools of journalism and mass communications in the United States need to emphasize internationalism in their curricula. The accrediting council, central administration, and journalism units must set the stage. At South Carolina, the central administration has made internationalism a critical element of its administration, and the journalism unit has launched its own initiatives. The accrediting council has done little in this area and may see no demand on the part of the professoriat or professions for internationalizing the curricula. Individual faculty members and students can develop their own international skills. Particularly in institutions with strong traditions of faculty governance, the faculties must first be sold on the importance of internationalization.

Notes

[1] Joe Shoquist, who heads the AEJMC, made this clear during a recent visit to the College of Journalism, University of South Carolina.

[2] Unfortunately, several proposals from the university were turned back by the United States Information Agency because the *summary* sections of the proposals were too long. The SPAR office protested vigorously but none of the proposals, including our own, was put back into the review process.

[3] The International Communication Division of the Association for Education in Journalism and Mass Communication published *Advising International Students: Model Advisement Kit* as its 1984–85 service project. This 18-page booklet was prepared by the author in July 1985 and distributed to each department/school/college of journalism and mass communication program in the United States in August 1985. The author is especially appreciative of the advice provided by the International Studies Association, the Office of International Services, and the International Business Studies program offices at the University of South Carolina-Columbia. Copies are available for $1.50 by writing Professor Lowndes R. Stephens, College of Journalism, University of South Carolina, Columbia, SC 29208.

[4] A copy of a prototype questionnaire is contained in *Advising International Students: Model Advisement Kit.* See previous note.

[5] Useful resources in this regard are Ohmer and Associates, *On College Teaching* (San Francisco: Jossey-Bass, 1978); Ohmer Milton, *Alternatives to the Traditional: How Professors Teach and How Students Learn* (San Francisco: Jossey-Bass, 1976); and Sally S. Gaff, Conrad Festa, and Jerry G. Gaff, *Professional Development: A Guide to Resources* (*Change* Magazine Press, 1978).

Integrating International Perspectives into the Research Methods Course

L. John Martin

Mass communication research has in recent years become an essential part of the curriculum in the study of journalism and mass communication, wherever it is taught. Its usefulness in public relations, advertising, and marketing is obvious, but the news side, both of print and electronic media, has found that research can help build audience.

Research helps reduce the risk of making wrong predictions. It is human nature to try to minimize uncertainty. We normally hope fervently that things will evolve in a predictable fashion. We may say, "Surprise me" but we like our surprises to be within predictable bounds. That is why in the modern world, most of us who accept empiricism as the key to the reduction of uncertainty depend on research to help us explain and predict our environment. But such acceptance is by no means universal. Even in societies that are technologically most advanced, research to some still smacks of sorcery or, at the very least, mirrors. Such people confuse theory, which is probabilistic, with laws, which are deterministic, and when an outcome is not predicted by the theory, they throw out the baby with the bath water.

Here I will assume that research is the mechanism whereby we can learn the rules that govern our environment. Further, I will assume that although different methods may have to be devised to study the communication process and effects in some countries or cultures, mass communication research is as relevant in Africa or Europe as it is in the United States. Findings, of course, may have to be interpreted differently from country to country. Beveridge points out that experimental results, for example, are valid only for the precise conditions under which an experiment was conducted[1]. He notes that an influenza virus could be made to spread from one mouse to another in an American laboratory, while in a lab in England it could not be accomplished, even though the strains of

---

L. John Martin is Professor of Journalism at the University of Maryland.

mice and virus, the cages, and the techniques were identical. If one knows of or suspects possible differences between two countries, those differences become essential experimental variables that need to be controlled in an international study.

A variety of skills, techniques, and procedures are taught in mass communication research courses in the United States. Most of the same methodologies are also taught in other countries. But although the application of quantitative methods to the social sciences was first suggested by such nineteenth-century European mathematicians, economists, and sociologists as Adolphe Quetelet, Emile Durkheim, John Stuart Mill, and Max Weber,[2] communication research has received most attention and has seen its greatest development in the United States in the past 50 years.

One reason for the lack of much *cross-national* communication research is its cost. Among the earliest international communication studies were those sponsored by UNESCO and conducted soon after World War II by Hadley Cantril, a Princeton psychologist.[3] The few truly international studies that have been undertaken since those early days after the war have generally been sponsored by UNESCO, the International Press Institute, the U.S. Information Agency, the BBC, or some major foundations and organizations in the wealthier countries of the world. A few studies have been done cooperatively by communication scholars in various countries.[4] Cooperative research may be one solution to the cost barrier.

Typically, mass communication research methods courses cover differences among the purpose, methods, and uses of qualitative and quantitative research; the concept of measurement; scientific method; collection of data of various types; statistical methods for the reduction, comparison, linkage, classification, and analysis of data; and possibly the use of computers in performing these functions. While some of the premises of researchers in other cultures may be different from those of Americans, so that the theories that are formulated may be different, the scientific method for building and testing the theories remains constant.

Measurement concepts are arbitrary and other cultures might well develop different classifications and yardsticks. But, so far, no new measurement models have emerged in modern times. Cultures that have a tendency toward inductive reasoning rather than deductive will, I believe, tend to favor qualitative and holistic approaches over quantitative and micro analyses. Thus, the Chinese and several other cultures are inclined to move from the general to the specific, the whole to the part, rather than from the part to the whole, the specific to the general, as in the United States and in many other Western cultures.[5] As for statistical methods, these are universal, and the world is rapidly emulating the more-developed countries in the use of computers. What is left is data collection, and it is to this that the greatest attention is generally given in attempts to internationalize the teaching of research methods. The rest of this paper will, therefore, focus on this topic.

Survey Research

Because journalism involves individuals in society and survey research is a method of collecting data from, and generalizing about, people in a group (referred to as a population or universe), surveys are probably the most common method of data collection in journalism. And Robinson says that surveys are the most frequently used research method in public relations.[6] It is appropriate, therefore, to see in what ways surveys can be and are used in international settings and what special methods, rules, and caveats need to be observed.

Pollsters

The U.S. Information Agency, the BBC, and Deutsche Welle—to name a few of the organizations that conduct surveys abroad—seldom if ever use their own personnel in data collection. Even international pollsters, such as the Gallup organization or International Research Associates, use local affiliates or contract the field work to a local firm or a university professor. In some countries, this is the only permissible way to go; in all countries, this is the only intelligent way to conduct a survey. In addition, certain authoritarian and communist states simply do not permit surveys to be conducted. In many non-Western countries, the survey topic, questionnaire, and design must be approved by the government.[7] Some topics are simply taboo, especially attitudinal studies. In such countries one usually must limit oneself to media-habits studies or to the collection of demographic data. Specifications for local pollsters must be carefully written and field work closely monitored. Analysis of data depends on certain methodological assumptions that cannot be made in countries with totally different cultural traditions.

Questionnaire Construction

One must distinguish between foreign surveys and cross-cultural surveys. The former is difficult; the latter often looks almost impossible. Questionnaires are hard enough to write in one's own language and even after numerous pretests turn out to be invalid or, at least, unreliable. In international studies there are, in addition, problems of (1) different ambiguities in the languages of the research and of the respondent, (2) differences in the connotations of words in the two languages, (3) non-existence of certain concepts, and (4) idiomatic confusions. Nida illustrates problems of translation of the Bible with examples of each of these difficulties. There is no word for "brother" or "sister" in Mayan, for example, but one must indicate whether the person is an older or younger brother or sister. A sower does not scatter seed in many parts of the New World but uses a dibble-stick for planting. In many places, cities don't have gates and the term "door" has to be used instead. "From the uttermost part of the earth to the uttermost part of heaven" (Mark 13:27) is no distance at all in the Totonac language, which considers heaven (the sky) and earth to be like the rind and the flat part of a half orange. The fig tree in Yucatan not only bears no fruit, but puts out its leaves after the rainy season rather than just before the summer, as in Mark 13:28. The Semitic idiom "children of the bridechamber" (Matthew 9:15) must be translated "children of the house of the man who marries the woman."[8]

It is normal practice to write the questions in the language of the researcher, get them translated into the language of the respondents, and then have a second person translate them back into the language of the researcher. While this ensures linguistic correspondence as far as dictionaries go, it fails to take care of connotations and the absence of concepts in the target culture. The problem is bad enough in single-country studies; it is compounded in cross--cultural studies in which comparability is a prerequisite of analysis.

Sampling

The existence of census data, maps, lists, and other sampling frames is often taken for granted. In most countries these items are either unreliable or nonexistent. The rationale of sampling is that if *every* individual and *every* combination of individuals in the population have an equal or known chance of being selected, a sample scientifically (randomly) drawn from the *entire* population will be representative of *that* population. It is necessary to emphasize both "entire" and "that," since when the population is unknown, there is no way one can tell what population to project to. Yet that is the situation in many developing countries.

Other methods have been tried to achieve sampling frames. Aerial photographs have been used instead of maps, with a grid being placed over the photograph and either individual homes or clusters of houses being selected for sampling.[9] Another form of area sampling in villages is the random walk, which involves starting at a random point and zigzagging according to a prearranged random plan through the village, picking every *n*th home for interviewing.

Data Collection

Nowadays in the United States, most surveys are done by telephone. While this may mean that 8%–10% of the population cannot be reached because they have no phones, non-coverage is a problem by any method, and the economy of telephone surveys must be balanced against the dubiously higher accuracy of face-to-face interviews.[10]

The same cannot be said of other countries, where the proportion of the population reachable by telephone may be much lower. Added to this are the problems of many more non-working phones, greater sharing of phones, and the unreliability or even non-existence of telephone directories. This leaves face-to-face interviewing and mail surveys. Mail delivery is not altogether reliable in some countries, and where literacy is low, the problems are compounded. This brings us back to face-to-face interviewing.

Interviewing

The training of interviewers is important everywhere but in countries where the population has not been interviewed a great deal except, possibly, by government troops or tax collectors, it is essential. Usually, the class, education, and sex of the interviewer cannot be haphazard. In South Asia, for example, interviewers must generally be of the same class as the respondent, and in most Moslem countries, the sex must be the same. A male cannot interview a female or vice versa, especially not alone.

In many countries, people are suspicious of strangers asking questions. Interviewers in Thailand are told to approach a home or a compound calling out, "This is scientific!" Courtesy bias is strong in Asia. The respondent doesn't want the interviewer to lose face and will tell him or her anything the respondent thinks is expected. The only way negative comments could be elicited in Southeast Asia, we found in USIA, was by saying that the sponsor was anxious to learn what was wrong with the product—obviously biasing the responses.[11]

Interpretation

Almond and Verba say that the problems of cross-national surveys are no different from the problems of surveys within a nation. "Just as the 'Italian' interview situation may differ from the 'British,' so may interviews with upper-class respondents differ from those with respondents of lower status with the same nation," they say.[12] The differences lie, rather, in the magnitude of the problems faced, according to Holt and Turner.[13] Almond and Verba further point out that "if we say that Britons and Mexicans differ in a particular attitude, this does not mean that all Britons think one thing and all Mexicans something else; there is usually a substantial overlap between the nations, as well as great variation within each one."[14]

There is a difference, however, and it is that the important variable of community homogeneity is not controlled. True, there will be some Britons who are more similar in some respects to Mexicans than they are to other Britons, but this is because culture is not necessarily coterminous with nationality. There are many cultural traits that are shared by peoples in different nations.[15] Comparability for purposes of the interpretation of survey data must be tackled in terms of the variables that are being studied. Each variable must be ascertained in the different cultures and an index found for each in terms that are comparable.[16]

Content Analysis

Survey research is the obvious method to use in the study of the communicator, the audience, and the effects of the media. For a study of the message, the most appropriate method is content analysis. Since the generation of messages is central to the profession of journalism, content analysis is a peculiarly "journalistic" methodology. Probably more theses and dissertations use it than any other method, principally because it is cheaper, faster, and less frustrating than, say, survey research.

Content analysis is particularly favored in international studies, since it is much more convenient to take the samples to be studied (newspapers, broadcast tapes, etc.) to the researcher than to transport the researcher to the subjects of a survey. Content analysis is, therefore, the preferred data collection technique in the international communication field. Moreover, it is probably the most common method of international intelligence collection. In spite of this, little has been written about the peculiar problems of comparative content analysis.

The technique is especially useful when political restrictions make it impossible to observe developments in a country directly. Thus, Carl Beck at the University of Pittsburgh analyzed the content of media in East European countries and by counting the frequency with which the names of Communist labor leaders appeared over time, he was able to chart their rise and fall in the communist hierarchy.[17] In the same way, Kremlinologists figure out the hierarchical structure of the Politburo: by analyzing photographs of Soviet leaders at official functions. The closer a person is to the center of the lineup, the more power he or she has in the Kremlin.

Content analysis is also appropriate in following the political vacillations of an inaccessible foreign leader. The speeches of Gamal Abdel Nasser of Egypt were closely monitored and analyzed to determine whether he was edging closer to the Soviet Union or to the United States. The frequency with which he used such key words as "imperialism" and "socialism" tended to signal his leanings some time before he made his moves. Content analysis can similarly be used to study communicators of all types—political, social, economic, media, church, educational, and other leaders—for a number of characteristics. Content analysis of their speeches and writings provides a possible substitute for direct interviews, especially in the international field, where such leaders are often inaccessible.

In making comparisons among media in different languages, including those that use different scripts from the Roman characters used in English, certain adjustments must be made. In a study of the Indian press conducted by USIA in 1962, which included content analysis of newspapers in both English and vernacular languages, three correction factors were used by which to multiply the number of column inches of space devoted to a particular story. One was a factor that corrected for differences in column width. This varied from paper to paper and sometimes even within a single paper. The second was a factor to correct for the idiosyncrasies of language: Certain languages could say the same thing in much less space because the language typically used more inflections than prepositions, adverbs, and conjunctions; fewer or no definite or indefinite articles; affixes instead of pronouns; and so forth. The third factor corrected for typographical variations, since the type in some languages necessarily took up more space than in others.

Scaling

One cannot discuss international communication research methodology without making some reference to the semantic differential. This is a scaling technique that was almost tailor-made for cross-cultural studies. In developing an *Atlas of Affective Meaning* for 620 concepts in 23 cultural communities, the authors say that "although languages do display superficial uniqueness in phonology, grammar, and semantics which render them mutually unintelligible, at a deeper level they display certain universals which render them mutually translatable."[18]

The semantic differential extracts the affective (as opposed to cognitive) meaning of concepts so that one can compare their emotive locations in semantic space.[19] This can be done across cultures and Osgood and his associates have found that one can characterize any concept in at least the 23 cultures they have studied by means of three or four dimensions of meaning. Thus, one might compare the concept of freedom in different cultures by asking people to rate it on seven-point scales using polar adjectives that measure an evaluative dimension, a potency dimension, and an activity dimension. In a few cultures, it has been found that other dimensions measure more of the meaning than the potency and activity dimensions do in English. But on the whole, these two, and especially the evaluative dimension measure most of the meaning of concepts in all cultures.

Through scales, one can usefully make cross-national comparisons. Hadley Cantril, a Princeton psychologist, developed a self-anchoring scale to circumvent the problem of the non-comparability of individual ratings. He used a ladder with 10 rungs and asked individuals to say where on the ladder they saw themselves in terms of their happiness or freedom or future, etc. Then they were asked where they believed they had been five years earlier and where they saw themselves five years in the future. Averaging these scores for each country or culture not only showed people's state of mind within the country or culture but enabled the researcher to make comparisons between and among cultures.[20]

It has been suggested that Likert scales must be used carefully in cross-cultural studies because of response sets.[21] It is quite conceivable that responses of a certain type may be more common in certain cultures than in others. One of my graduate students—a USIA employee—speculated on the basis of personal observation, that people who live in countries around the Mediterranean would tend to check extreme responses, while people in Scandinavia and northern Europe would tend to be more moderate in their responses. This was not borne out in an examination of dozens of surveys done by USIA in Europe. While this finding is not conclusive, it illustrates the danger of generalizing from limited observation, especially in international communication research.

Notes

[1] W.I.B. Beveridge, *The Art of Scientific Investigation* (New York: Random House, 1957), pp. 34–35.

[2] See L. John Martin, "The Genealogy of Public Opinion Polling," *The Annals*, Vol. 472 (March 1984), pp. 12–23.

[3] Richard L. Merritt and Stein Rokkan (ed.), *Comparing Nations: The Use of Quantitative Data in Cross-National Research* (New Haven: Yale UP, 1969), pp.14–25.

[4] See Stein Rokkan, Jean Viet, Sidney Verba and Elina Almasy, *Comparative Survey Analysis* (The Hague: Mouton, 1969).

[5] I owe to Dr. Diana Kao, professor emeritus of linguistics at CCNY, an example that illustrates this. She points out that the Chinese address their letters by starting with the country, followed by the city, street address, and name of the addressee. In the United States, of course, one goes from the specific to the general.

[6] Edward J. Robinson, *Public Relations and Survey Research* (New York: Appleton-Century-Crofts, 1969), p. 9.

[7] There are some borderline countries, such as Turkey. When, as chief of the Near East and South Asia Division of USIA's Office of Research, I recruited an advertising agency to undertake a survey, I urged the agency to have the questionnaire cleared by the government. I was told that this would be unnecessary. The agency never cleared anything with the government, and it would only make the government suspicious if the questionnaire were sent in for clearance.

[8] See Eugene Nida, "Linguistics and Ethnology in Translation-Problems," in Dell Hymes (ed.), *Language in Culture and Society* (New York: Harper and Row, 1964), pp. 90–97.

[9] Martin Bulmer, "Sampling," in Martin Bulmer and Donald P. Warwick, *Social Research in Developing Countries: Surveys and Census in the Third World* (Chichester: John Wiley, 1983), pp. 92–96.

[10] Robert M. Groves and Robert L. Kahn, *Surveys by Telephone* (New York: Academic Press, 1979), p. 6.

[11] See Emily L. Jones, "The Courtesy Bias in South-East Asian Surveys," in Bulmer and Warwick, *op.cit.*, pp. 253–260.

[12] Gabriel A. Almond and Sidney Verba, *The Civic Culture* (Princeton: Princeton UP, 1963), p. 56.

[13] Robert T. Holt and John E. Turner, *The Methodology of Comparative Research* (New York: The Free Press, 1970), p. 6.

[14] Almond and Verba, *op.cit.*, p. 51.

[15] See L. John Martin, "The Contradiction of Cross-Cultural Communication," in Heinz-Dietrich Fischer and John Calhoun Merrill (ed.), *International and Intercultural Communication* (New York: Hastings House, 1970), pp. 424–434.

[16] Holt and Turner, *op. cit.*, p. 14.

[17] Presentation at the Foreign Service Institute.

[18] Charles E. Osgood, William H. May, and Murray S. Miron, *Cross-Cultural Universals of Affective Meaning* (Urbana: U of Illinois P, 1975), p. 4.

[19] See Charles E. Osgood, George J. Suci, and Percy H. Tannenbaum, *The Measurement of Meaning* (Urbana: U of Illinois P, 1967).

[20] Lloyd A. Free and Hadley Cantril, *The Political Beliefs of Americans: A Study of Public Opinion* (New York: Simon and Schuster, 1968), pp. 94–96.

[21] See A.N. Oppenheim, *Questionnaire Design and Attitude Measurement* (New York: Basic Books, 1966), pp. 117–18, 119; C.A. Moser and G. Kalton, *Survey Methods in Social Investigation* (2nd ed.) (New York: Basic Books, 1972), pp. 362, 374.

Covering the World from Villages

Richard Critchfield

L ooking back today, we seemed remarkably confident at the start of America's post World-War II imperial era. CBS correspondent Eric Sevareid, in the spirit of the times, wrote in a 1946 book that Americans had gone off to war carrying our country's "bright tools and great muscles, her giant voice and will." Now, he said, "America was involved in the world ... and neither the world nor America would ever be the same." Sevareid felt it was America's destiny to "create a world in its own image."

That was close to 40 years ago. Today we have V.S. Naipaul, a gloomy but penetrating observer, attributing "all the trouble in the world" to the need of all of its people to adapt to the West and its ways, particularly to American ways. "Not adapting to its tools," Naipaul has said, "but trying to fit in with its ideas."

How did Sevareid's bright promise become Naipaul's bleak reality? History marches to its own drummer, but I think we can say one thing: The big failures of the past 40 years have been failures, not of U.S. power, but of knowledge. In Africa, in Vietnam, in East Asia's economic challenge or Islam's counterreformation, we have repeatedly looked at events in terms of the politics of the surface and not deeply enough at the economic and cultural trends beneath the surface that were actually deciding things. What makes other people tick? If Naipaul is right and the world's trouble is coming from everybody else trying to adapt to our ways, it's as though a great big drama is going on all over the planet in which countless individuals are making choices and taking actions to learn, adapt, grow, and survive. With something so fast and kaleidoscopic—all the little parts moving different ways at once—how can we observe, much less report, what is going on?

The Importance of Villages

My own feeling is that you have to go to villages. There you find small, relatively simple, groups of people living on the land and growing food. It's the

---

Richard Critchfield is a journalist with University Field Service International.

easiest way to learn about any culture and to get some idea of how that culture is changing. You have to look at individual people and see them in a sort of anthropological way.

What do I mean by this? Let's take a reporter based in a Third World capital such as New Delhi or Cairo or Mexico City. Say he wants to find out what an ordinary person thinks. He goes out to the countryside and Abdul or Natu or Juan says he is very poor, fatalistic, and not hopeful about the future. Yet right away we can sense the superficial quality about what is said. A stranger from the rich, Western world has swooped down and is told, if it is a good interview, what Abdul or Natu or Juan feels to be true. But it is not what he will tell his neighbor when the two are working side by side in the fields by themselves. And that is what we need to know.

In *Under the Banyan Tree*, a new collection of short stories, Indian novelist R.K. Narayan quotes his watchman as wanting him to remove his own name from the gate. The man says

> All sorts of people read your name aloud while passing down the road. It is not good. Often urchins and tots just learning to spell, shout your name and run off when I try to catch them. The other day some women also read your name and laughed to themselves. Why should they? I do not like it at all.

Just a few lines of dialogue and India comes alive. For the words are spoken within their own cultural context, not, as in the journalist's interview, as one culture speaking to another. Any reader with sensible and discriminating ears can tell the difference right away. Naipaul himself is, of course, a master of dialogue, too: gently and humorously in his portrait of life in his native Trinidad, *A House for Mr. Biswas*, or terrifyingly in *A Bend in the River*, which tells us a great deal about modern Africa when things go wrong. My favorite example of how dialogue tells a story are Chekhov's short stories, especially "Peasants" and "The Steppe." Writers of fiction often articulate the universal elements in human lives to teach us more than any formal theory.

Learning from the Social Sciences

Yet the reporter also has much to learn from the social sciences. Every time I go out to a village, I apply ideas gleaned from anthropologists. Margaret Mead and Oscar Lewis defined culture as a set of rules, or solutions to problems, handed down from father to son (or, more commonly, mother to son), so that each generation doesn't have to start from scratch. Robert Redfield, another pioneer in anthropology, contributed the key finding that people who live by growing food share the same values—property, the family, mutual help, a work ethic—except when it comes to abstract ideas or religion.

Philosophy also helps reporters, particularly the work of Aristotle, who saw plainly 2,300 years ago that human culture is decided by how individuals get their food. Reporters may also be helped by the work of somebody like Richard Leakey, who has traced human origins back two million years. Leakey, whom I interviewed in Kenya a few years ago, has concluded, "Human beings are cultural animals and each one [human] is the product of his particular culture." Leakey says that man is not innately anything but is capable of anything and that he evolved a cooperative society because his hunting-collecting economy and later the invention of agriculture required it. This notion that culture has an economic basis is also given great importance by Marx.

Ideas, I find, have value in reporting only if they work in a practical, concrete situation. For example, after watching Stephen Jay Gould on television not long ago, I jotted down several things he said: "Change may often be sudden; stability is life's history." "Stability is the essence and change is stress—not continuously accumulating, but rare and episodic." "It's systems that change, not individuals." When it comes to change brought to culture by technology, I ask myself whether these observations hold in a practical village setting.

As Senator Pat Moynihan once told me, everything leads to everything. I've just spent most of the last three years researching and writing a book on how Americans adapt to technological change. I found that from the disappearance of the frontier in the 1880s until World War II, we made a dizzyingly quick shift from country to city, farm to factory, horses to cars and tractors, kitchen surgery to scientific medicine, fundamentalism to Darwinism, revival meetings to Hollywood movies. As we made these shifts, we quite naturally shed some of our old-time religious faith, family ties, work ethics, sense of mutual help, and other values that are rooted in necessity among groups of people who live on the land and grow food.

At bottom, this is a confrontation (not necessarily a conflict) between religion, the core of any culture, and science (technology simply being its application to human affairs). This is not clearly understood, as I found in a recent trip to the rural Middle West. Millions of Americans are plainly trying to reconcile the continued industrialization of agriculture and what it is doing to our society with a deep sense of cultural loss.

So while we're still ahead in the game of adjusting to technology, we're not all that much ahead. As with people in the Third World, we, too, have to make our ideas fit in with the new tools, our deepest religious beliefs fit in with all the changes brought by science. Elsewhere in the world, the agnostic Confucians— Chinese, Japanese, Koreans—roar ahead, followed more hesitatingly by the Malay-Javanese, with the caste-ridden Hindus in doubt as a minority modernizes while a deprived subclass still makes up half of India's population. Cultural adjustment is coming most slowly among the deeply religious Moslems; feudal postcolonial Latin society with its inequitable land ownership, military juntas, and peasant uprisings; and the sub-Saharan Africans, plagued by extremely high human fertility and an exhausted soil, leached of its minerals.

Going to the Village

Armed with a few basic teachings of anthropology, history, and philosophy, one sets for the practical laboratory to try them out: a village. Knowledge of a country—its politics, geography, economics, and history—is needed, too, but more important, I think, is knowledge of the local culture, whether it be Confucian, Malay-Javanese, Hindu, Buddhist, Hebrew, Christian, Islamic, or tribal African. Language helps, and one quickly picks up some phrases. But to stenographically record dialogue as it is spoken, often in some rural dialect, is extremely difficult for a foreigner. It is advantageous, in any case, to be accompanied by an interpreter from the local culture and—as often happens—race. It doesn't hurt to have the moral support of a working companion.

Then, to understand villagers especially, one needs to live intimately with them, sharing some of their struggle and idleness, the losses and the gains. In a few weeks, one comes to identify with them.

Anthropologists have what they call the "participant-observer" method, which in villages can mean rolling up your sleeves and doing the same daily work as the people you want to write about. There is much to be said for this. Hard physical labor is the central fact in the lives of most of mankind. In the 21 villages where I've stayed since the late 1960s, this has meant herding sheep and cattle; diving for fish and octopus with harpoon guns and spears; cutting sugarcane; threshing sorghum; digging up cassava root and milling it into flour; and, mostly, sowing, weeding, harvesting, and threshing wheat, corn, and rice. Housing might be a black-tent Bedouin encampment, a Punjabi cattle barn, a bamboo cottage, or African grass hut. Sleeping is on string cots, carpets, straw mats, the occasional bed, or, in Brazil, in a hammock. Most of the earth's inhabitants, two-thirds of whom still live in these villages, eat mostly bread or rice and a few vegetables and a little meat. They wash it all down with tea, coffee, beer, rum, or homemade liquor (enough village living can turn you either into a vegetarian or an alcoholic).

Common work, common food, common discomforts soon break down any barrier of reserve. It soon becomes a kind of mutual commitment. In my experience, within a few weeks, whoever was being written about would come to take our mutual enterprise very seriously.

For my interpreters and me, it got to be a routine: Usually he (rarely she, except in cities, though I did use women interpreters in Kenya, South Korea, and Brazil) jotted down as much dialogue as he could during the working day, while I pitched in as a fairly mute co-worker. Then we'd relax with the villagers in the evening; if anything of interest happened, we'd write it down the next day. With such a narrow focus, day in and day out, week after week, I got to know people extremely well.

By the end of a stay, I'd end up with a stack of notebooks filled with dialogue, all copied down in longhand. What I like to do, after four or five weeks in a village, is to go back to a city hotel room and type it all up. Then I begin to see what sort of a story is emerging (rarely what I expect) and what oft-repeated phrases no longer need to be recorded.

In Berat, a village in Upper Egypt, high on the Nile, where I devoted almost two years to a book-length village story, published as *Shahhat,* we had the best system. Shahhat, a fellah, and I worked together in the fields each morning (when we started, he knew no English and I no Arabic). At noon Nubi, my interpreter, bicycled two miles from Luxor, where he had a government job. We all ate lunch together and spent several hours every afternoon going over who said and did what the previous morning and evening. I wrote down all the dialogue in great big ledgers and eventually had more than 700 pages of typed single-spaced notes. Equally long studies were done in a Sikh Punjabi village, tracing one family's fortunes from 1969 and in a village in central Java, my longest continuing village study since I began this work in 1967.

Commonalities among Villages

Daily routines vary from one village to another and within a village depending on the season, but I try to time my stays to coincide with harvests, when villages are liveliest and the fields are full of people. There are a few constants. Villagers tend to rise with the sun and go to bed an hour or two after it sets—except for the Javanese, who, with all-night shadow plays and dance performances, do with less sleep than anybody I ever saw.

Invariably, the first person in a household to stir in the morning is a woman, who may get up about 4 a.m. to wash, to make a fire to boil water for tea or coffee, and to milk the cows and buffalo. Moslem men, if devout, will rise at 4 a.m., too, to say the first of five daily prayers, kneeling in the direction of Mecca. In the Sikh Punjabi village, we'd be rocked out of our beds at 4 a.m. by the amplified cacophony of a few pious old men praying loudly over the Sikh temple's loudspeaker. This, for most people, was the signal to wrap up in a blanket, huddled and anonymous, and make their way to the fields under cover of darkness to, as the Punjabis invariably put it, "answer the call of nature." Then back to bed for a couple more hours of sleep until sunrise. Except during threshing, when we took our cots right to the fields, most village men got up about 6 a.m. or 7 a.m., as did older women, once they had a daughter-in-law in the house to do the early chores.

If the family has cows, buffalo, donkeys, or other animals, somebody, usually a young man, cuts fodder: in Egypt twice a day, in Punjab and Morocco just in the evening. Aside from harvesting with a sickle, this was my favorite work, particularly in Punjab, when I'd ride back to the village each night, half dozing and tired to the bone, on a cartload of freshly cut clover. The rest of the day might be filled with sowing, weeding, harvesting, or threshing, or, once a week, marketing in a nearby town, or, in slack times, just sitting around. Only African women actually cultivate land from start to finish, but in many villages women do a little field work. Most of the time they stay at home, preparing meals; washing clothes and dishes; mending; sewing; perhaps weaving cloth, blankets, or rugs; caring for the children; raising chickens or maybe a few sheep and goats; fetching water on their heads in earthen jugs or tins; or going to the village shopkeeper to buy on credit a few matches, some salt, or other necessity.

What really makes village living so easy and pleasant is its sense of time. Time seems to expand so that each day seems much longer than it is. The only sound one may hear all day is the call of birds, a donkey's bray, or other human voices. Since one's destinations tend not to be great, getting there may be a walk or a bicycle ride. One tends to lose track of what time it is or even what day of the week it is; every day is very much like the next. It's far from our Western kind of stress.

The Village Method

One is, of course, working the whole time: watching, listening, and taking notes. When I go to a village for the first time, I begin with its ecological and economic system, its agriculture: the plowing, sowing, weeding, harvesting, and threshing of crops. Gradually this look at farming leads naturally to an under-standing of systems of marketing or converting crops to food for the family. I begin to see the way the village and its social structure are organized. From here I move into family life and religion and the way people think and feel. In common with the social scientist, I study the larger civilization in which a village finds itself: its history, religion, art, philosophy, literature, and present-day politics and economics. (There are two ways to do this: the conventional way of reading books by authorities or the unconventional way of concentrating on how things look solely from the viewpoint of the villagers. I have tried it both ways.)

If possible—a switch from a social scientist's approach—I then try to interview the nation's political leader. I want to fit the villager I'm writing about into a larger, more topical frame of reference. In this way, I'm doing a kind of news story.

Such a story can be about social upheaval (the caste system versus modern farm science in India) or urban migration (a rice peasant who becomes a pedicab driver in Jakarta) or criminal alienation (an uprooted Moroccan villager who robs foreigners and ends up in prison). Politics is the stuff of journalism, but it is commonly just a surface reflection of these other things. For example, one can argue that India's agricultural revolution has decided its national politics, the changes brought by high-yield dwarf wheat in the Sikh-populated Punjab creating a chain of reaction that ultimately led to Indira Gandhi's murder. A village stay can be aimed at learning more about some big global issue (overpopulation as seen in a fishing village on the densely-populated island-state of Mauritius, the Green Revolution in several of the villages).

The purpose of my work in villages has been to tell a story, based on actual dialogue, so as to capture a changing moment in time as a way of shedding light on an event or situation. In newsroom usage, I write "situationers." Or put another way, a reporter using this village method of reporting is engaged in a kind of portraiture. The reporter is relying on intuition and impression to convey a picture to readers. Often the story is most convincing when it is most personal. I learned this subjective—as opposed to objective—style of journalism in India when in 1962 I did a profile of Indira Gandhi for A.M. Rosenthal, who had flown in to cover India's Himalayan war with China. "Don't describe her the way you think *The Times* would," he said. "Write how she really looks to you." This has proved sound advice over the years. The idea is to produce, being honest and keeping to the facts, as true a portrait as the reporter can perceive and write.

Bringing the Village Approach to Reporting in the U.S.

The same approach also works in the United States. In 1971, after I'd spent two years living in villages in India, Indonesia, Iran, Mauritius, and Morocco, and writing all five up as book-length stories, each illustrated with 50 to 60 pictures, I returned to the staff of *The Washington Star* for what became my final year with the paper.

One day my editor said, "Why don't you try the same techniques with the people in the Washington area? Just go out and observe and write about them as if they were Asian villagers." My editors, Charles Seib and Burt Hoffman, assigned various "types" of people to profile: "a middle-aged bureaucrat," "a redneck construction worker," "a pretty, single girl living alone." In scavenger-hunt fashion, I'd go out to find such people. The original series, "How We Live," consisted of nine individual profiles. In time, we published the stories of 20 or more individuals or families. They ranged in age from a first-grader to a 73-year-old woman who had just run out of money and was going to have to seek public assistance. There was a Marine, a garbage man, a black car thief who spent 11 years in prison, a middle-aged "overqualified" executive who'd lost his job and couldn't find another, a Puerto Rican grandmother, a rich and activist Jewish family with a dropout son who'd become a rock musician, old Washingtonians, suburbanites, slum dwellers. For the family interviews, I moved in for a week, going to work with the husband one day, staying with the wife the next, accompanying the children to school or to college, and so on.

Again I tried to avoid interviews; instead, I simply observed and wrote down what the people said. In the U.S. homes, there was much less dialogue than in a village. I found Americans spend much more time physically alone—watching television, driving, reading. Another striking difference was the amount of stress in Americans' daily lives, with all the electronic voices, the fast speeds of cars, and the expectations for being busy and punctual. Stress is such an inescapable aspect of modern city living. But though stress can lead to high blood pressure, heart attacks, and nervous breakdowns, it also produces benefits. The flights to catch, cars to drive, traffic rules to obey, elevators to summon, television to watch, latest news to follow, goods to buy, deals to make, appointments to keep all produced stress in these people's lives, but were central to their vitality. The American mentality is to *do*; a villager's is often just to *be*.

It is also true that in our lives, just as in villages, most stress comes from interpersonal relations. "Hell," Jean-Paul Sartre said, "is other people." What strain and anxiety there is in villages tends to come from personality conflicts. But fun is other people, too. All people, villagers and Americans alike, are fascinated by each other's doings. One advantage of the village is that there is little competition. Unlike Americans, no villager must come to terms with diminished career expectations or must learn to live with his or her limitations. It takes opportunity to cause striving. We tend to be rich, and they to be poor.

One thing I have learned by studying both villagers and Americans is how relative a term that is—poor. In a village, to be poor is to go without the necessities, not the comforts. A villager who fills his belly twice a day and has a roof over his head may not *feel* poor. Almost everybody he knows is in the same fix. If anybody suffers social isolation in villages, it is the few richer families. Not so in the United States, where a poor person not only suffers indigence and want in comparison to the majority, but is made to feel crummy.

In my 1981 book, *Villages*, I expressed a conviction that inconspicuous individuals may comprise as much a story as headline events:

As a reporter, I'm very conscious that the sensational or tragic or catastrophic political and economic events occupy the headlines of our newspapers and the foregrounds of our minds. They loom up all out of proportion when they happen, but are quickly reduced to size with the perspective of time. This is true of most wars, revolutions, massacres, terrorist acts, famines, gluts, slumps, or booms. We are only vaguely aware that something might be going on in villages. One reason I took up this work was curiosity; after all, two-thirds of the people on this planet aren't just sitting on their hands. Now I'm convinced that it is the unconscious, obscure, and overpowering drives of millions upon millions of ordinary individual men and women that is the real stuff of history. Modern heads of state, like Tolstoy's king, are history's slaves. It hasn't got much zing, but the biggest story of the late twentieth century could well be the sum of countless small decisions and actions by unnoticed humble little nobodies out there in their villages.

I'm convinced this is equally true of Americans. A reporter's real wealth is the inexhaustible amount of story material all around us—ordinary people. Find a way to take part in their lives, watching what they do, writing down what they say, and a story worth the telling will always be there.

Learning from African Models

Sharon M. Murphy and James F. Scotton

Those serious about putting some "international" elements—or perhaps just examples—into journalism education in the United States can learn from several African models. Despite chronic shortages of material and funds when setting up their schools, the major journalism programs in Africa have built in—not added on—international examples, books, staff, and even students.

One can argue that this is of necessity. Journalism programs in Africa and other developing areas must look abroad for materials and funds unavailable locally. Although necessity can account for some internationalizing of journalism education in Africa, there are clear signs that a growing commitment to international journalism independent of need has developed.

At the school of journalism at the University of Nairobi, for example, the 1985–86 diploma course enrolled 20 students. Competition for places was intense; some students were not admitted until their fourth annual attempt. At least one student denied admission has made seven applications to the program and had the strong support of the government office that employs her. Despite this strong pressure from Kenyans for admission, the school of journalism gave two places to foreign students, one a U.S. citizen and the other a New Zealander. In the past, the journalism school has attracted students from Tanzania, Uganda, Zaire, and Zambia. This year two places were allotted to Ugandans, but they failed to arrive from that strife-torn country.

As with most journalism programs around the world, Nairobi's has only enough funds to do some of the things it wants to do. Its reading room subscribes to all the Kenyan dailies published in English and Swahili. The Kenya News Agency wire comes directly to the journalism school. In addition, though, the reading room gets the daily *International Herald Tribune* and the *Sunday Times*

Sharon M. Murphy is Professor and Dean of the College of Journalism at Marquette University. James F. Scotton is Professor of Journalism and Director of the graduate program in journalism at Marquette University.

of London. At about $1.50 and $2.50 a copy, respectively, this represents a large commitment from slim resources.

Of the 189 Kenyan students in the 1985–86 program, six are fluent enough in a second European language (French) to work with it professionally. One of these is also fluent in Italian. Of course, all these Kenyans know English (the East African lingua franca), Swahili, and one or two local Kenyan languages learned at home. All the class members said they would commit themselves to learning another language—some specified Russian or Arabic—if it would help them professionally.

This international outlook is also found in all faculty members at the school of journalism. Each of the six faculty members has at least one degree from a U.S. university and one is planning to take a Ph.D. at Britain's University of Leicester. At this time there is no graduate degree program in journalism or mass communications in Kenya, so graduate degrees must be from foreign universities. Still, Kenyan faculty members are committed to maintaining their international ties. Nairobi's school of journalism is working to develop a long-term student–faculty exchange program with New York University and possibly other mass communication programs outside Kenya. A similar program with the department of mass communication at the University of Lagos in Nigeria has been developed.

African Textbooks

Perhaps the major new and independent effort being made to internationalize journalism training in Africa is in textbook production. Twelve years ago, there was not a single text or even substantial manual that focused on African journalism among resource materials in the Institute of Communication at the University of Lagos. Graham Mytton and Michael Traber in Zambia and Zimbabwe had produced some useful material, but it was not comprehensive enough and the distribution was poor. Richard Aspinall's African experiences, particularly in Nigeria, resulted in a good UNESCO radio program production manual in 1973, but other UNESCO publications were judged inappropriate by the Lagos faculty.

We are now seeing the first texts produced directly out of the African setting by Africans. One is written by a U.S.-educated Nigerian, Ralph A. Akinfeleye. Another is an edited collection with contributions from 15 journalists of African nationality and/or wide professional experience in Africa. These two texts, both appropriate for newswriting and reporting courses, are being used in Nigeria and in Kenya, the two anglophone African nations with the most developed university-level journalism training programs. Both texts stress the international nature of African journalism and both stress the need to consider non-African commentary and criticism in training programs for African journalists.

Akinfeleye's book, *Essentials of Modern Journalism*, was first published in 1982. A second edition is planned for 1986. Nigeria has three university-level journalism training programs, at Lagos, Nsukka, and Kano. It also has the most diverse press and most extensive media system in Africa, serving an estimated population of 80 million. Still, Akinfeleye decided to bring as much of an international perspective as possible to what would basically be a text for Nigerian journalism students. He visited journalism training programs in Ghana, Kenya, Senegal, and Tanzania and met with faculty and students before writing the book. A major section of the book shows how different journalism programs in Africa, both in the university and non-university setting, carry out their training missions.

With three degrees from U.S. universities, Akinfeleye was aware of his inevitable American bias. He accepted that U.S. journalism programs were the best models for Africans at the time but he emphasized non-U.S. sources as well. Material from Great Britain, India, Sweden, and other countries went into the makeup of the book. Still, the text was produced primarily for Nigerian journalism students, and any student using it would be aware of other points of view and practices but would also clearly see the emphasis on Nigerian journalism.

A more recent text, *Reporting Africa*, edited by Don Rowlands and Hugh Lewin and published in 1985, allows each contributor to use his or her own professional experience and national/international setting as a base. The chapter "Covering the Courts," for example, is written by two Zimbabweans. Their examples are from court coverage by the Zimbabwe media. The chapter on feature writing is by Juby Mayet, one of South Africa's best-known journalists. Her examples come from her South African publications, primarily in the internationally circulated *Drum* magazine.

The editors of *Reporting Africa* found little difficulty in accommodating philosophical differences among the anglophone African countries. In the introduction, the Zimbabwean minister of information calls for African journalists to be "committed to the African revolution." However, he simply asks that this be a commitment of reporters and editors in Africa to present the facts and to try to do so with the African reader and listener in mind. As he says, "The African journalist must be committed to the independence and sovereignty of Africa, just as British, Russian, Japanese, or American writers are committed to their countries and national sovereignty."

In the same way, the individual contributors present the lesson of their own specialty without any but professional biases. Mayet, for example, in a chapter on feature writing, uses stunning examples from the South African publications, some of her own, and others by outstanding colleagues in South African journalism. Even though she knew she was writing for students in independent Black African nations, she never mentions the South African racial situation. She doesn't have to. The examples tell it all in their vivid personal portraits of South Africans.

Reporting Africa shows that journalism—at least outside the Communist world—has basically the same set of professional ethics. Michael Traber's listing of the elements of "news" timeliness, prominence, proximity, conflict, the unusual—could be transferred to Mencher or any of the other newswriting and reporting texts found in U.S. journalism classes. His consideration of "alternative" factors in the African setting is straight out of the "new journalism" arguments heard everywhere.

One of *Reporting Africa*'s most interesting and most valuable chapters—particularly to a non-African reader who wants to know more about Third World journalism's point of view—concerns news-agency journalism. It is written by Paul Fauvet, a Mozambican journalist who worked with the independence movements for Angola, Guinea, and Mozambique.

Despite his background, his employment by the government news agency in Mozambique, and his clear support for the New World Information Order, Fauvet says all journalists must strongly resist government efforts to insert propaganda into the news. National news agencies in Africa do need government support. They could not survive without it, Fauvet points out. However, since such agencies start with a certain credibility gap in the eyes of the outside world, they simply must treat the news in an accurate, straightforward fashion.

Fauvet says there is nothing unprofessional about giving prominence to a government program or statement. He says that you can also support such programs or statements—but in clearly identified editorial comment separate from the news. Government suppression of bad or embarrassing news is simply out of the question, says Fauvet. Sooner or later someone else will probably break the story and then the agency as well as the government will be discredited.

What we have, then, in *Reporting Africa*, is a remarkably international textbook on newswriting and reporting: newswriting chapters by a Kenyan and a Zambian, a section on using news sources by a Ghanaian, interviewing techniques by a Liberian, economic coverage by a German native who worked as a journalist in South Africa, and so on. From the traditional first course, African journalism students are getting an international view of the professional field. The 190-page text is produced simply, with word processor and photo-offset printing. But through its international list of contributors and their examples, it presents journalism as a profession with skills and ethics that apply across many nations and societies.

The need for relevant and culture-based texts is not confined to the news area. In 1977, a public relations text was begun at the University of Nigeria at Nsukka in response to needs there. The faculty was dissatisfied with the limitation imposed by public relations materials available, all of which had been prepared in the United States or the United Kingdom. While these texts could offer a wealth of information and could build on decades of successful practice, both in U.S./U.K. enterprises and throughout the world, the context was decidedly non-African, the examples not applicable in many instances, and the experience with them is often frustrating.

The goal with the text, currently nearing completion, was to gather examples and models from the African experience, and to prepare a book that would deal with political, economic and developing realities that young public information and public relations practitioners would need to understand to perform successfully within the African government. And those realities are most assuredly different from the context within which most of the best-selling texts are set.

Improving U.S. Journalism Education

For whatever reasons and out of whatever needs, journalism education in Africa is exposing students to the professional world on an international basis. On the contrary, in the United States it is rare for any but specific courses and seminars in international communication to include international content unless it comes from a student or guest speaker with overseas experience. A mass communications and society course may have John Merrill, Jeremy Tunstall, or the John Martin-Anju Chaudhary collection on the supplemental reading list, but in our experience, nothing outside the U.S. journalism framework gets into any of the basic courses.

It is possible to make students aware of the "world" of journalism. However, it will require a commitment to new values in our profession and development of faculty and teaching materials or at least new syllabi. It will also require some breakdown of the comfortable professional compartments most journalism educators enter during doctoral studies and leave only on retirement.

To start with, AEJMC's international division should break some of its own frontiers. Almost all "international" papers at AEJMC conventions, for example, are on panels with other "international"—meaning non-U.S.—papers. This hardly makes sense unless international equals "foreign." If the division is truly international, then the effort should be to bring together researchers who can present different points of view on all scholarly and professional areas of journalism and mass communication. We need not abandon international-division panels, but we should make an effort to let potential panelists know that we want to include relevant papers on the U.S. media and on U.S. research projects. In the same way, we should solicit international points of view—be they from U.S. citizens or non-citizens—on panels in all other divisions. There are so many graduates of U.S. programs on the faculties of overseas journalism programs that we have a long and accessible list of potential panelists. There are also many U.S. faculty members whose experiences—sometimes jarring to their own professional point of view—on overseas assignments can bring insights and challenges to almost any division's panels.

Better, however, would be to attract the professional and/or academic with little or no U.S. experience. His or her views of much accepted wisdom in our field could be refreshing as well as possibly upsetting to some.

Since many members of the International Division hold membership in other AEJMC divisions, it should not be difficult to set up what is really an interdivision liaison program. Each year specific members, particularly those who hold leadership positions in the other divisions, could be asked to seek some international component in each division's convention program, preferably within presentations on general academic and professional topics.

Though many U.S. journalism educators have taught or conducted research overseas, only a few have worked as journalists outside the United States, especially if you exclude those who worked for American organizations. Since undergraduate journalism education in the United States focuses strongly on professional training, opportunities to apply overseas insights in class may not arise often or easily. There are all sorts of possible ways of working on this problem—the international division can promote papers and panels based on overseas media experience, for example. On a one-year or two-year overseas assignment, a U.S. researcher or teacher might be encouraged to spend at least a portion of his or her time working with the local media.

There are also student exchange programs, of course. The most successful ones seem to be in foreign language studies. Others in the arts have developed, but we seem only to have just started student exchange programs in the communications fields. The feeling seems to be that a student needs a specific reason—language learning, access to art or literature collections, for example—to justify a semester or year away from the standard four-year U.S. under-graduate program.

This is where journalism education may require some commitment to new values. For one thing, it is time to start recommending substantial doses of foreign languages, international relations, non-U.S. history, and even inter-national communications to all journalism majors—not just to those few who know by the sophomore year that they are going to wind up as foreign correspondents. This may mean some tough curriculum choices.

Rethinking the Curriculum

Beyond this, however, we may require a rethinking of what journalism education on the undergraduate level is all about. Given the limited number of courses in the typical journalism curriculum, particularly in a semester format, we have tended to concentrate on the professional skills areas. After all, this is what both the students and their potential employers cried for. Within the journalism programs themselves, at least, there was little real commitment to a world view except perhaps in the introductory course.

In short, we may have to challenge the philosophy behind 700-page news reporting and writing texts that try to teach the journalism major everything from obituary writing to the APME Code of Ethics. We must also be ready to challenge the local editors who want journalism graduates—even interns— "ready to go to work." We simply cannot provide all this professional training and exposure in the limited number of journalism class hours available and still work in such things as a "world view" of what we and the media are all about.

This may not be possible, we admit. In Britain the media for years have provided almost all the professional training a journalist received. Even university graduates, increasingly joining British newspapers of all sizes, went into a training program. Some were formal programs while others consisted of colleagues and editors assigned to develop raw talent. All represented a commitment of time and money by the employer to professional training of new staff members.

This situation is changing in Britain. The Thomson Foundation, for example, has been reducing the numbers of students in its Newcastle training program. One reason, a Thomson executive admitted, is that editors and publishers see the possibility of shifting training costs to the journalism education programs developing in London, Cardiff, and elsewhere. These programs, like those in U.S. journalism departments, are organized so they can make the students and taxpayers pay the cost of professional training.

Even if we find the time in our undergraduate skills courses to bring in international points of view and examples, we will need to work out some kind of system of rewards and perhaps penalties to make it happen. As we all know, teachers teach what they know and use material that is easily available in convenient formats. A survey of a dozen journalism programs a few years ago, for example, showed that all the calls for a "media writing" course to accommodate the diverse professional goals of "journalism" majors failed to produce an effective course. Few instructors had experience across newspapers, broadcasting, advertising, and public relations. There was also no text available.

We could try to monitor professional programs—perhaps through accreditation—to see that they included international components. This is unlikely to be welcome, particularly by an accrediting agency that has had more than its share of criticism in recent years. It is also possible to develop workshops in the various divisions to show how teachers can easily and effectively improve their courses with international examples and points of view. This is something that international-division members with overseas experience could do throughout the year, particularly at regional AEJMC conferences.

It is unlikely that U.S. journalism educators will be taking more of their education at overseas universities. The U.S. journalism/mass communication education structure is so well developed that it would be difficult to persuade many graduate students that overseas institutions offered more opportunities. It is also unlikely that many from the United States will be able to work in overseas professional experience, except with U.S. organizations.

What may be necessary is an infiltration of the basic professional courses—from newswriting to ethics to law—by international points of view. This can come in the form of teaching materials, preferably attached firmly to the normal course with which instructors are familiar and comfortable. It is very unlikely, at least for the present, that we will get anywhere advocating such a radical approach as an international text similar to *Reporting Africa*. That could be a project for the future. Booklets, slides, and tapes, however, could be used as part of the normal courses in reporting, photography, and ethics.

The key requirement, we believe, is effort to develop a close link between the normal course work and the international material. For example, the first chapter of Mencher's widely used *News Reporting and Writing* is on "The Reporter at Work." It would not be difficult or expensive to include some international examples. Foreign correspondents in this country could be an initial source although at least some embassies or overseas news organizations might well be able to provide films, tapes, and other materials.

The change we're suggesting will not come easily or quickly, even with support from the AEJMC leadership. A commitment to a goal is only the beginning. Specific programs and individuals willing to devote a substantial portion of their professional efforts to such programs are essential.

As we have pointed out, U.S. journalism programs are justly proud of the stage to which they have developed. They are the models for most of the rest of the world. Changes, such as adding international points of view and materials to the curriculum, will take effort. To us, the international division of the AEJMC seems the likely body to mount that effort. With some imagination and hard work, the effort can bring more of an international view to journalism students in the United States.

Main Street Hattiesburg and the Third World

John Maxwell Hamilton with Susan A. Siltanen

For would-be journalists studying at universities, the prospect of covering foreign news is a distant thrill. Professors and editors are quick to caution students not to think about foreign stories until they have mastered local ones. Beginning journalism textbooks underscore the same point. As one primer puts it, foreign correspondence is "another of those journalism jobs not handed out to beginning staffers."[1]

As fair as the point is, U.S. educators have reason to ponder the implications. No doubt editors are wise to send seasoned reporters abroad. But are they correct in thinking that only foreign correspondents cover foreign news? Have journalism schools done an adequate job of teaching aspiring reporters and editors that foreign news is important precisely because it touches the everyday lives of Americans? Is there, indeed, a way of using local U.S. settings to make foreign news come alive for the newspaper reader, the radio listener, the television viewer?

Throughout much of U.S. history such questions would have seemed frivolous. U.S. citizens have traditionally had the luxury of looking inward. Oceans have buffered the country from foreign threats. Abundant natural resources have permitted an extraordinary degree of self-sufficiency.

Unfortunately, those early advantages have become a liability. The tradition that has sprung from them ill prepares our citizens to anticipate or cope with such modern developments as nuclear delivery systems that can reach the United States from any spot on the globe in a matter of minutes or with foreign manufacturers, whose output now competes with 70% of U.S. industrial production.

John Maxwell Hamilton is Public Affairs Specialist at the World Bank and Susan A. Siltanen is Professor of Speech Communication at the University of Southern Mississippi.

U.S. recognition of interdependence is nowhere more blinkered than with respect to the poor countries of the developing world. Having been educated to think of the United States as an extension of Europe, few realize that the developing world—the Third World—is our fastest-growing market, accounting for more of our trade than Western Europe and Japan combined. Few recognize that all military conflicts since World War II have come in developing nations.

Few, in fact, realize how quickly the developing world, consisting mostly of nations emerging from colony status, has grown. At its founding in 1945, the United Nations had 31 Third World members. Today it has 118. The Third World, which holds 51% of the world's population, will account for nearly 80% by the end of the century, according to one estimate.[2]

Unfortunately, at just the time that foreign news is most important to us, the cost of sending foreign correspondents abroad is increasing dramatically. Editors justifiably wonder if it is worthwhile to shoulder such expenses for stories about faraway and seemingly irrelevant places.

Foreign News in Hattiesburg

In an effort to address these legitimate editorial concerns while increasing U.S. understanding of the developing world, one daily newspaper in Mississippi, *The American*, tested a new approach. The results of that experiment show that communities do, indeed, have Third World news waiting to be covered right in their own backyards, that young reporters can gather it, and that readers want to know about it. The experiment opens new possibilities for journalists— and for educators who must prepare aspiring reporters to interpret the complex world that has grown up around the United States.

The thrust of the experiment, carried out in the fall of 1984, was simple. *The American*, with its 25,000 circulation, looked in its own southeast Mississippi community for stories tracing local connections to the Third World. The result was a series of five articles that ran in the paper. A poll conducted under the auspices of the University of Southern Mississippi School of Communications subsequently looked at whether the articles were read and whether readers' perceptions about interdependence changed.

Few states provide a better testing ground than does Mississippi. The state is what sociologists have called a "closed society," and often as not Mississippians like it that way. Only one state, New Mexico, has a higher percentage of people who have lived all their lives in the same home. The state college board maintains higher university admission standards for foreigners than for U.S. citizens. And the traditional Southern suspicion of the federal government and reverence for states' rights is perhaps nowhere stronger. Government foreign aid programs, for example, have all the appeal of portraits of General U.S. Grant.

Despite this, *The American* produced a five-day, front-page series of stories with sidebars that showed Third-World ties to virtually every segment of life in Hattiesburg.

Trade

Most large businesses and many smaller ones in the Hattiesburg area do business with developing countries. For some, such business has been matter of life or death. The largest employer in town, the Hercules, Inc., chemical plant, cut its work force by one fifth in 1982 when it decided to import rosin from the People's Republic of China. The company had been making rosin locally at twice the cost. The Johnson Music Co., a long-time Main Street Hattiesburg firm, had recently built a regional wholesale business on South Korean guitars, drums, and pianos. A number of firms reported that they used foreign parts and equipment to keep their plants going. The nearby Chevron refinery imported more than two thirds of its petroleum from the developing world.

Growing trade connections are not one-way, however. Hercules also exported to developing countries and, said its management, was able to remain competitive precisely because it could buy rosin at lower prices. The Hattiesburg plant of Miller-Picking exported about half its custom-made heating, ventilating, and air conditioning units to developing countries. Local farmers sold nearly all their wheat and soybeans to developing countries.

In many cases, improved sales to developing countries depend on seemingly subtle events. Expecting to export 60% of its pulp, the newly built Leaf River Forest Products plant, had targeted Indonesia as one of its best potential customers. Indonesia had recently passed a compulsory education law. Better education means more books; more books mean more paper.

Migrants

Migrants who have escaped political upheavals and wrenching poverty in developing countries contribute to Hattiesburg as physicians, federal meat-plant inspectors, special-education teachers, and business people. Even in this small community, where everyone seems to know everyone else, there are illegal immigrants working at menial jobs.

Migrants have added such new cultural options as Oriental restaurants in a community that once thought of dining out only on country-fried steak and potatoes. The influx of migrants has embellished traditional pastimes, adding soccer to the sports program at the local university and giving the queen, the daughter of a Nicaraguan woman, to the 1979 Hattiesburg beauty pageant.

Students

Despite rigorous admission standards for foreigners, enrollments of young people from developing nations have increased at the local university, even as USM enrollments in general have declined. At the time the newspaper series was written, USM was about to enter into a sister-university relationship with a South Korean university.

Often missed by local readers, faculty have major foreign involvements. One political science professor, it was discovered, played a key role in mediating constitutional disputes between the Turks and the Greeks in Cyprus.

Foreign Aid

Hattiesburg may now have a low regard for federally run charity overseas, but the community has plenty of its own foreign aid programs. Local Baptist churches regularly contribute to overseas missions and have made large special contributions for famine relief in Africa. Mississippi Catholics sponsor a mission in Saltillo, Mexico, to which they provide 30 tons of beans a month. Hattiesburg parishioners drive to Saltillo annually to build homes and to nurse the sick.

Local businesses do their part, too. Some have made contributions simply out of altruism. Some have seen in such acts long-term material benefits. "Like my daddy used to tell me," said a local executive who recently invited two Chinese to Hattiesburg for training in his company, "I never made a plug nickel off my enemies, but I've made a fortune off my friends."

Even a five-part series with sidebars has its limits, and many topics deserving in-depth treatment received only passing attention. Several examples: At least one local bank had outstanding loans to Third World countries; environmental problems in Panama caused low water levels in the canal and held up shipping from the Mississippi Gulf Port; local drug problems started in developing countries where poor farmers, desperate for a cash crop, grew coca used in making cocaine; a recent rash of farm failures was attributable in part to decreased buying power of indebted developing nations and in part to Third World countries competing in the international agriculture markets to earn foreign exchange.

Reader Interest

Proving that community newspapers can write such stories is, of course, not enough. The test of success is whether readers care, a question addressed in the readership survey carried out by the USM School of Communications.

The results of the poll exceeded expectations. According to the USM poll, about half the newspaper subscribers in Hattiesburg reported having read each of the main stories. This compared favorably with readership for any topic and enlarges on previous polls showing higher readership for breaking foreign news than most editors believe exists.[3] Strong readership for feature stories about the developing world is especially significant because the most important Third World news, generally speaking, lends itself to softer analytical pieces, such as those in *The American* series describing trends, rather than to spot news with thundering climaxes.

The survey, conducted before and after the series ran, also showed changes in readers' attitudes toward the developing countries.

In the initial survey, more than 90% of *The American* subscribers in Hattiesburg agreed with the general proposition that it is important to understand events in developing countries, but only about one half that number thought that those events really made any difference in their community. The second poll, taken after the series ran, showed that the percentage of people who agreed that political upheavals in developing countries made a difference in Hattiesburg increased by almost one fifth (from 41% to 48%); the percentage who agreed that economic growth in poorer countries promotes economic growth at home increased by almost one third (from 42% to 55%).

Less scientific but equally impressive was local enthusiasm for the series. *The American* received five times the local telephone calls it normally receives for its hottest stories, according to the newspaper's editor, Frank Sutherland. One of the most frequent comments was, "I didn't know we had such connections with the Third World." Another was that readers wanted more such articles.

Extending the Hattiesburg Experiment

Journalists looking for ways to educate U.S. citizens about the Third World have already begun to adapt the *American* experience to their needs. Helping this along is a project by the Sigma Delta Chi Foundation, an affiliate of the Society of Professional Journalists. The project, funded by the Carnegie Corporation and the Ford and Benton foundations, is developing additional models for local Third-World reporting and organizing workshops for journalists. As the Hattiesburg experiment shows, every community—indeed every campus— has ties to the developing world, and these can be described vividly. Moreover, several early experiments in the classroom show that student reporters can take on such stories provided they are given a few pointers.

Under the overall direction of Dennis R. Jones, chairman of the USM journalism department, advanced reporting and photography classes researched Hattiesburg's Third World ties. Those exercises produced information that *The American* was able to use in its series. At the University of Wisconsin, John Fett, a professor of agricultural journalism, asked students in his public relations class to develop stories publicizing an upcoming local conference on the developing world.

These two efforts show that though students can benefit from such an exercise, many are not adequately prepared to deal with Third-World issues. They have little concept of the developing world or its connections with the United States. Few seem to know where to begin to get background to prepare them to find and successfully complete stories.

Consequently, instructors should provide adequate time for students to learn something about the subject. Moreover, students will need some instruction in the use of local information centers and interviews to acquire background. Students should not concentrate on a specific story—an immigrant family, for example—until they have a good sense of the general immigrant situation. Otherwise the tendency is to report specifics without being able to put them in context.

Students' general unpreparedness can be turned to good advantage if teachers use the occasion of these stories to teach how to prepare for assignments with which they have little familiarity. In addition, these stories give students a change to dig and find stories in areas of their community—social services, churches, business—they might otherwise ignore.

More classroom experimentation is clearly needed. That task will be taken on by the Medill School of Journalism at Northwestern University. Under the direction of Medill dean Edward Bassett, the school will investigate ways to use classes on public affairs reporting to teach students about the Third World.

If these efforts continue, the next generation of U.S. journalists and the population in general may better recognize that local news is foreign news and improve coverage of our increasingly interdependent world.

Notes

[1] M.L. Stein, *Getting and Writing the News: A Guide to Reporting* (New York: Longman, 1985), p. 204.

[2] George Thomas Kurian, *Encyclopedia of the Third World* (New York: Facts on File Inc., revised, 1981), pp. ix–xii.

[3] See "Record," *The Quill*, April 1978, p. 7. Charles Lehman, "Meeting Reader's Multiple Needs: Content and Readership of News and Feature in the Daily Press," *Research Report* (New York: Newspaper Advertising Bureau, 1984). See also Leo Bogart, "The Public's Use and Perception of Newspapers," *Public Opinion Quarterly* 48 (Winter 1984).

A Two-Way Street in Reston

George A. Krimsky

The United States shrank a little the day its universities stopped requiring students to learn a foreign language. So did U.S. journalism. We are recovering somewhat from the Age of Relevancy, but provincialism remains the curse of American culture and adversely affects U.S. relations around the world.

By now we could have raised a full generation of internationalists from the postwar yearning for global unity. Instead, we still have kids who think geography stops when you memorize capitals; grown-ups are called "specialists" if they master a second language.

To journalism, this means that the pool of potential foreign correspondents is considerably smaller than it should be for a nation wielding such power beyond its borders as we do. One result is inadequate reporting from abroad, an unfortunate irony in the so-called Age of Information.

One of the worst-kept secrets of American journalism is that there are still powerful news organizations in this country not fully convinced that their reporters need to know the language of the country they are covering; useful, yes, but not necessary. This view is anathema abroad. One would be hard pressed to find any of the some 1,000 foreign reporters covering this country without a strong command of English. We could wait, of course, until the whole world learns English, but that would just intensify the problem.

Despite evidence to the contrary, this is not a sermon on the merits of language lessons. Rather, it concerns an attitude. To be fair, however, it is essential to point out that the U. S. does some things better than anyone else, and one of them is the practice of journalism. So, maybe we have the makings of a trade-off: a discipline for an attitude.

The possibilities of such an exchange prompted the establishment of an institution in Reston, Virginia, known as the Center for Foreign Journalists. Its title suggests its main purpose: to share with foreign journalists the skills and resources of the U.S. media. But it has an additional task, perhaps more difficult,

George A. Krimsky is Vice President and Executive Director of the Center for Foreign Journalists.

of helping raise the consciousness of members of the U.S. media about life and work in the developing world, where journalists labor in the same kind of impoverishment as do their societies.

Need it be said that journalists the world over (with some notable exceptions) harbor the same standards of honesty and responsibility as their more advantaged colleagues here? Need it be said that journalists in the Third World yearn for the same opportunity to work in an open society, with modern tools and expertise? Need it be said that journalists who believe their primary mission is to improve their nation (one definition of "development" journalism) can still be good journalists?

Perhaps we wouldn't know that from the transcripts of UNESCO conferences, but then again, not many journalists attend such gatherings. "Information ministers" speak for the profession back home and that has seriously tarred the image here of Third World journalism. The profession indeed is in a sorry state in many less-developed countries, but it is not a self-inflicted wound.

Perhaps history could have turned out differently. If the colonial press had made a more serious effort to train and employ local nationals, there could have been a significant cadre of professionals better prepared to cope with the pressure to come. Instead, the expatriates left little more than a generation of stringers, copyboys, and chauffeurs to run things after independence.

It didn't take long for the new leaders to realize the usefulness of a nationalized media. With good party members in charge, ill-equipped reporters and editors were left with the lonely prospect of having to sort out for themselves whether they were actually working for the good of their country or simply acting as toadies for an arbitrary regime. Instead of being rewarded with decent facilities, opportunities, and salary for their service, they paid the price of servility: a loss of respect and self-respect, not to mention more concrete forms of compensation.

All this borders on dangerous generalization, but the pattern has been appallingly similar in diverse regions of the Third World. The African continent provides ample examples. Not one African country has a truly independent broadcast system or news agency. More than 90% of Africa's newspapers fall under some form of government control. Yet, government status for the press does not bestow the privilege of sharing power and resources, as in, say, the Soviet Union, where the state-controlled media enjoy considerable benefit. Rather, the reverse is true in most of Africa.

The call for a New World Information Order has created a false sense of pride in the Third World media by pointing the finger elsewhere. But, all the access and technology sought from the developed world will not eliminate the uncomfortable reality back home of hobbled, degraded, and enervated media that are hardly capable of making use of tools so casually enjoyed in the West.

An Alternative: Center for Foreign Journalists.

The Center for Foreign Journalists has been established to address some of these problems. The main goal of the Center will not be concerned with issues of press freedom but rather with the sharing of know-how. Our focus is such basic services as workshops in reporting, writing, and editing techniques and an information clearinghouse on modern media advances applicable to a less-advantaged environment. Our hope is that by sharing the tools of good journalism—and, yes, the tools of a vibrant free press are of the finest quality—we can make a small contribution toward not only strengthening our profession worldwide but strengthening the reliability of information that is so vital for mutual understanding.

People ask us what good we hope to accomplish by sharing tools that simply cannot be used in a state-controlled environment. Worse yet, it is suggested that we imperil colleagues who would try to put their lessons to use.

We have some faith in the survival instincts of our colleagues in the Third World. They are masters at skirting disaster. If U.S. journalism schools were to ever conduct a course called "How to Say It without Saying It," it would have to be taught by a Third Worlder.

The journalistic tools we have in the United States, which we sometimes don't use enough, may not be fully applicable in most Third World settings, but they can certainly help turn "development" reporting into a more professional enterprise than hand-out journalism.

Are we raising frustration levels, particularly by introducing our high-tech culture to those unlikely to benefit from it for years to come? Yes, we probably are, but we can offset this by reducing the intimidation element, emphasizing that good journalism doesn't come from a computer and by introducing strangers to the more user-friendly technology.

Specifically, our center largely follows the workshop model of the American Press Institute, where our offices are located: We bring in experts from the working press and journalism education to conduct five- to 10-day career development sessions on subjects ranging from editorial skills to modern management techniques. The participants are foreign journalists already visiting this country on a variety of private-sector and government programs. Such journalists number in the thousands each year.

For those unable or disinclined to attend group sessions, CFJ has a library and computer databank of information on a broad range of media facilities, equipment, institutions, opportunities, and literature. In this way, we expect to act as a central repository of media resources and a "broker" to help make contacts for foreign journalists interested in improving the level of journalism back home.

Where do the U.S. media (the second lane of that two-way street) come in? First, U.S. media are providing the bulk of our financial support. CFJ is a non-profit organization that hopes to demonstrate concretely to a sometimes skeptical outside world that the independent media in this country are willing to share some of their good fortune. Second, every workshop program planned at the center includes a seminar component in which U.S. and foreign journalists sit side by side to exchange experiences, knowledge, and opinions.

In our broker role, we hope to assist current internship programs place foreigners at American newspapers and broadcast stations. Foreign intern programs aren't working particularly well in this country, and we hope to improve this by helping to better orient interns to our media realities, expand the base of U.S. news organizations willing to take interns, and make a better fit between guest and host. We have also been asked to help orient U.S. journalists to media and cultural realities abroad by conducting seminars for media delegations headed overseas. Our purpose is not to duplicate university education or existing visitor programs but to augment them, to fill a void in the very practical arena of sharing know-how.

PHILOSOPHY

Philosophers generally have detached themselves from contemporary issues, as they focus on the principles underlying all knowledge. Yet there are traditions in philosophy of examining the relevance of ethical theories internationally and cross-culturally, focusing on political philosophy, and offering courses on Oriental philosophy.

In joining the NCFLIS project, the American Philosophical Association commissioned the following articles by Peter Caws, Anita Silvers, Virginia Held, Bernard Boxill, Ofelia Schutte, and David Hoekema. In addition to addressing the relationship between philosophical study and international issues, they indicate how philosophical analysis may be applied to problems of international justice and discuss ways in which an international perspective can enhance students' philosophical understanding.

The Case of the Athenian Stranger: Philosophy and World Citizenship

Peter Caws

P hilosophy began where it did, no doubt, because of a couple of national characteristics of the Greeks: they were curious, and they liked to talk. "All the Athenians and the strangers which were there spent their time in nothing else, but either to tell, or to hear some new thing," comments the narrator of the Acts of the Apostles, setting St. Paul up to exploit Greek modesty about knowledge of the Gods in favor of his own immodest conviction. And not only did the Athenians like to talk about new things and new ideas, they turned talk itself into a social form. Some of the highest manifestations of this form, in which it is raised to the level of art, are to be found in the dialogues of Plato, where "the argument" appears as a constructed object to be passed from speaker to speaker, each treating it with respect, according to rule, and required to contribute something to it.

When American students learn philosophy in this tradition, they step automatically across their own national boundaries into another society and another epoch. This is not always made clear, since we often tend to assume our right to beliefs and habits that have their roots elsewhere without too much curiosity about those roots, like the preacher who is alleged to have said, "If English was good enough for Jesus Christ, it's good enough for me." Comfortably ensconced in the "Judaeo-Christian tradition" (a label whose omission of any reference to the Greeks says something about the continuing opposition between belief and reason), we give little thought to "international" questions involving the subsequent histories of Jerusalem or Rome or even Wittenberg. I will come back to this. But to stay with the Greeks for a moment: remembering that Athens was the first home of philosophy, it may strike us as significant that the chief interlocutor in Plato's last major dialogue, the *Laws*, should be an Athenian stranger. The action of the dialogue takes place in Crete, it is true, so

Peter Caws is University Professor of Philosophy at George Washington University.

it might just be that the Athenian is a foreigner there. But we must give Plato credit for the multiple significances of his text, and the conjunction of the two terms is suggestive in a deeper way than that. One defensible reading of it, I think, is as meaning that the philosopher must be a stranger, even in Athens.

The reason for this is clear enough: truth and rightness—to the clear understanding (if not to the practice) of which philosophy is committed before everything else, even if it turns out to be finally unreachable—cannot be exclusively or specifically Athenian virtues, nor can they belong to any particular culture or outlook. It must be possible to ask, even of Athenian beliefs, whether they are true, and even of Athenian policies whether they are right. This is a form of what has been called the open-question argument. And note that it will particularly be Athenian beliefs and policies that the Athenian philosopher will challenge; the Athenian who criticized only Sparta would be suspect, not because it might not be the case that Athenian institutions were genuinely better than Spartan ones, but because philosophical criticism, like charity, begins at home, and in an imperfect world there is always work to be done there.

This doesn't exempt Sparta from Athenian criticism, although it should be said that such criticism could only be brought to bear by Athenians thoroughly familiar with Spartan institutions *from a Spartan point of view*. But the right strategy for Athenian philosophers who want to improve matters in Sparta might rather be to give encouragement and support to *Spartan* philosophers, who, although they may in fact be suppressed by the Spartan authorities, will have a better chance of being heard in Sparta in the long run. And meanwhile the Athenian who is too self-congratulatory about Athens, especially to the Athenian authorities, will strike us as self-serving, as Rousseau does, for example, when he says "Heureux, toutes les fois que je médite sur les Gouvernements, de trouver toujours dans mes recherches de nouvelles raisons d'aimer celui de mon pays!" [happy, every time that I meditate on governments, to find always in my researches new reasons to love that of my country!][1]

All this talk about Athens and Sparta (not to mention Geneva) could of course easily be translated into contemporary terms, referring to the United States and the Soviet Union, and the lesson of our example must already be clear enough. American philosophers ought, it seems to me, be critically attentive to American beliefs and policies. It is far more important, in the first instance, to teach the methods of such critical attention than to show the superiority of democracy to communism or of capitalism to Marxism. Not, again, because that exempts the Soviet Union from American criticism, but if that criticism is to become part of the curriculum, it will have to be on the basis of close reading of Marxist and Soviet writings. And, similarly, the way to help benighted Russians (or Frenchmen or whomever—I have dealt elsewhere with the notorious problem of the split between Anglo-Saxon and "continental" philosophy, but it is still with us)[2] to become better philosophical critics is to make friends with Russian (French, etc.) philosophers and discuss philosophy with them, not just to tell one another how benighted they are. Just meeting a live philosopher from another part of the world and another tradition can do wonders for students' international awareness, even if it does reinforce their sense of privilege at the freedom and rigor of the philosophical argumentation they are used to (even, indeed, if it only awakens this sense).

I do not wish to deny that there are many philosophical tasks—in logic, metaphysics, the philosophy of science, even ethics and social philosophy—that are quite independent of this sort of international awareness. I speak of one responsibility among others, though it is one that I believe every philosophy department should assume. But if part of the philosopher's job is to bring critical attention to bear on the beliefs and policies of his or her own society, then he or she must be prepared to take a standpoint outside that society, to be, in other words, a stranger in it. And a responsible carrying out of the job will imply the availability of one or both of the following: a thorough knowledge of the beliefs and policies of other societies, actual or ideal, and/or a set of standards independent of and as it were higher or more authoritative than the standards of any particular society. The first desideratum will encourage comparative studies, an exposure to views and systems other than those the scholar (or, as I might as well say from now on, the student) has grown up with. The case is similar to the case for foreign languages: nobody who knows only one language can see that language from the outside, as it were, or can appreciate how thought is a prisoner to it, how its apparently most straightforward expressions are loaded with metaphors; just learning how to order dinner in French won't do much to relieve the parochialism of the monolingual, but it is a step in the right direction nevertheless—in the direction, that is, of a realization that there is a whole set of alternative schemes of expression. This realization induces modesty about the scope of one's own conceptual grasp of things, the exactitude of available meanings in the mother tongue. There is philosophical parochialism, too, which needs to be overcome by a similar exposure to alternatives (although it is to be noted that learning a second language does not necessarily mean that one stops speaking the first one).

It might be argued that the sort of exposure that is at issue here is not a matter for philosophy, that it is taken care of by courses in history and Western civilization and international relations, not to mention foreign and comparative literatures. All that is splendid, but it does not relieve philosophy of its special task. Other societies don't just exist but are and have been articulate about their own philosophical principles—and indeed the United States itself has been more explicit than most, as witness the writings of the eighteenth-century founders. So students might read, for material preparatory to reflection on their own society, not only Locke, Montesquieu, and the other precursors (along with Jefferson and the *Federalist* papers), but also More, Campanella, Swift, Butler, Morris, and Orwell among others, and not only Marx but also Lenin—and even, as far as that goes, Hitler himself and other racists and totalitarians who have used the forms if not the standards of rational argument. It is in other words reasonable for students of political and moral philosophy to know how other societies have behaved and misbehaved, how they have been governed well or badly, and how they or their leaders have rationalized or justified such government and behavior, as a comparative and empirical basis for their own analyses.

These analyses need to be pursued beyond the comparative stage, for having varied *objects* of criticism does not necessarily clarify the *principles* of criticism. This is where the second desideratum comes into play: finding a perspective independent of any society or culture (or for that matter language) from which to analyze and criticize social and cultural forms. This, it will be said, is just a special aspect of the task of philosophy in general, which is to do the same for all forms of thought, not just social and cultural but logical, epistemological, metaphysical, and the rest. And there is nothing wrong with that remark if it is taken seriously. For it has become commonplace to allege that we are all captives of the language and the conceptual structure we speak and employ in our everyday dealings, so that success in this general task would mean liberation from that captivity, and hence again a kind of alienation from the linguistic and conceptual habits of our own society or nation. Of course the idea that a conscious understanding of ourselves involves alienation is by now classical, at any rate in its Hegelian form—and Hegel is certainly one of the philosophers students ought to read in their search for analytic tools for the understanding of their own society, along with Plato, Aristotle, Hobbes, and other political philosophers (up to and including Rawls and Nozick), less tied than some of the apologists, polemicists, and Utopians to the virtues and defects of particular systems.

There is something that Hegel did not do, but that Plato did, which puts this set of considerations potentially at least on the level of what might be called internationalism or world citizenship rather than on the level of abstract theory. Hegel tied his system to the historical emergence of Spirit, which manifested itself in individual nation-states; for the individual *person* there was no higher duty than allegiance to his or her own state, no question of an international or transnational attachment. Despairing of the emergence of any actual state, Plato could not consider even Athens (or perhaps, after the death of Socrates, especially *not* Athens) as the collective embodiment of reason, and he concluded that the only thing for the individual to do was to become a citizen of an ideal state—ideal in the strong sense, in that it could exist only as an idea, perhaps never as a reality. There is a striking passage in Book IX of the *Republic* in which Glaucon suddenly catches on to this. Socrates has pointed out that the right thing for the "man of understanding" is to acquire goods and power only on condition that they do not "unsettle the constitution set up in his soul," on which Glaucon observes:

> Then, if that is his chief concern, he will have no wish to take part in politics.
> Indeed he will, in the politics of his own commonwealth, though not perhaps in those of his country, unless some miraculous chance should come about.
> I understand, said Glaucon: you mean this commonwealth we have been founding in the realm of discourse; for I think it nowhere exists on earth.
> No, I replied; but perhaps there is a pattern set up in the heavens for one who desires to see it and, seeing it, to found one in himself. But whether it exists anywhere or ever will exist is no matter; for this is the only commonwealth in whose politics he can ever take part.[3]

I want to conclude by asking whether there is any sense in which Plato's recommendation is reasonable for contemporary students of philosophy, and if so whether it might correspond to a valid "international" component of philosophical instruction.

In recent philosophical and political discourse, the term "international" evokes powerfully the several Internationals to whose deliberations Marx contributed in the nineteenth century. For him the proletariat was the genuinely international class, since the very idea of a national state involved the dominance of a property-owning bourgeoisie that required power to protect its interest. The "international" therefore was *against* anything national (which explains among other things why international interests have often been construed as anti-American). We would be more inclined to think that international interests should be able to transcend and criticize without destroying the national communities and characters that severally exist in the world. And for this something like Plato's strategy is still appropriate.

The *Republic* obviously made possible a conception of the rational life for human beings to which individuals could subscribe and which they could strive to realize, independent of any other individual characteristics. In this respect, Stoicism, whose chief exponents were an emperor and a slave, was a true if partial heir of Platonism. A possible consequence of this conception was, equally obviously, a new community of citizens of the "commonwealth in the realm of discourse," who would recognize one another precisely *through* discourse and who might as it were constitute a rational leaven diffused through the agglomeration of states, each impelled and governed by more or less irrational considerations, that made up the known world. It was something of a tragedy for the West that this conception had no secular realization in antiquity but was taken up by St. Augustine in the service of Christianity and turned by him into the City of God, whose principles of citizenship and whose potential for transnational realization (although not international, since nations were automatically to come under other-worldly judgment) were just those expressed and foreshadowed by Plato.

We ought not, however, allow the appropriation of good ideas by vested interests to discourage us from trying to realize them correctly. What would it mean, now, for individuals to live according to a revised version of the *Republic*, taking into account what has been learned about psychology, economics, etc., in the intervening 2500 years? What sort of transnational community might this make possible? Not a church, certainly; and not a United Nations at the government level, since we are talking about individuals and not governments. The individuals in question—and this is where the teaching of philosophy comes in, since its function on the Platonic model is precisely to produce them—would have to think not only of education and national government and poetry and the rights of women but also of world resources and class conflicts and terrorism and the risk of nuclear annihilation. They would need to confront the question of history—which could hardly exist for the *first* full civilization— and of the nature of civilization itself, now that it has spread from the cities, in which it originated, into the remotest corners of the globe. They would need to realize that their countries, as Plato uses the term, really co-exist in a real world which they jointly exhaust, so that there can be no question of colonization (the conceptual context of much Greek speculation about ideal states) nor even of retreat behind secure borders out of reach of the economic or ecological influence of other countries. They would further need to understand that the histories of particular countries, within the context of the extension of the works if not always the spirit of civilization, have been determined to an unpredictable degree by ideological commitments and conflicts, the roots of which lie largely in prejudice and unreason—a judgment to be brought where necessary against one's own fellows, ancestors, and traditions, but which can only be brought in the light of an actual acquaintance with the histories in question.

Most of this goes well beyond anything that Plato could have had in mind and argues against the detachment—though not the alienation—that he recommends for the man of understanding. There is, however, no inconsistency here. For the continued existence of philosophy in Plato's sense now depends on at least a standoff, if not a permanent accommodation or agreement, between countries having different ideological histories and traditions, which can no longer be treated calmly as possible enemies in war after the manner of Book V of the *Republic*. Since it seems unlikely that the ideal of that Book, of "rulers ... sufficiently inspired with a genuine desire for wisdom," will ever be generally realized, it will be up to the philosophers of each country to join with others—for the profession has no corner on wisdom—to try to rectify the deficiency. (I have suggested elsewhere how I think they should go about it.[4]) Here, however, we are concerned with the international rather than the national aspect of the problem, and the obvious recommendation to emerge from the foregoing is that philosophers (and their students) should come quite deliberately to think of themselves as members of a community—not to say citizens of another Republic—whose principles of membership transcend national and ideological considerations, consisting rather in a commitment to wisdom in social and political practice or, in other words, to philosophy itself in its practical (and not only in its contemplative) mode.

An obvious objection, among those that will immediately spring to mind, is that this looks like a call for a dogmatic conception of what philosophy is, for a metaphilosophical closure that would have totalitarian implications and would tend to put philosophy at the service of the most powerful ideology. However, it seems to me possible for philosophers from different traditions to agree, not on the content of metaphysical (let along ideological) doctrines, but on the necessity of criteria for the judgment of such doctrines and on the need for philosophical openness.[5] Many years of involvement with international activities in the profession have convinced me that even in Sparta (if I may summarize many particulars under a return to this metaphor) there are today numbers of philosophers whose language and methods and whose conception of rigor in argument are not so far removed from our own and whose interest in the sane behavior of their governments may be more urgent and sometimes more effective, in spite of repression, than the corresponding interest on our part. (We don't, collectively, take this very seriously, and that is a professional defect.) These are people it would be worth meeting and talking to, not just at an occasional international congress, or when they happen to come on official missions, but by repeated private (but perhaps collective and organized) visits and by regular correspondence, and not just to find out how things are done elsewhere but to inquire how they might be done together. To do this might require actually learning their languages, but that would be all to the good. (We might at least begin by putting substance into the language requirements for the Ph.D., perhaps by adding to the graduate curriculum reading courses using journals from other countries.)

In a way it is too bad that everyone doesn't still speak Latin. In a way I am recommending a return, not to a universal language but to a universal mode of discourse, to philosophy itself, as a possible basis for the kind of internationalism that, in an earlier and simpler age, the conduct of intellectual affairs in Latin used to represent. The stakes are higher now. It would be worth an effort on the part of the profession (and its association) to realize its international potential, even if that means a more deliberate adoption of the stranger's role.

The Latinate scholar may not always have felt at ease in the vernacular, but the compensation was access to the whole world of scholarship. Similarly for the philosopher: potentially at least, to be a stranger in Athens is to be at home in the universe.

Notes

1 Jean-Jacques Rousseau, *Du contrat social*, in *Oeuvres complètes*, 3, Paris: NRF/Gallimard (Bibliothèque de la Pléiade), 1964, p. 351.

2 *Sartre*, London: Routledge and Kegan Paul, 1979, pp. 5–6.

3 Plato, *The Republic*, tr. Francis Macdonald Cornford, London: Oxford UP, 1941, pp. 319–20.

4 "Reform and Revolution," in Virginia Held and Charles Parsons, ed., *Philosophy and Political Action*, New York: Oxford UP, 1970, pp. 72–104.

5 See my "Address to the Closing Plenary Session," *Acts* of the 17th World Congress of Philosophy, Varna, Bulgaria, 1973, pp. 847–50.

Reflections on the Mutual Benefits of Philosophical and Global Education

Anita Silvers

Significant energy in the education community is devoted to promoting the objectives of global education. No energy, I believe, is devoted to the teaching of isolationism, the antithesis of global education. This phenomenon is odd.

One explanation that comes readily to mind is the compelling need to remedy students' appalling ignorance about global issues. But students do not appear to be more ignorant about the subjects promoted by global education than they do about many other matters. For every survey displaying students' absence of knowledge about global affairs, there is another survey displaying their equal ignorance of national affairs. So students may be as appallingly ill-prepared to be isolationists as they are to be globalists.

Why, then, is there not a faction supporting isolationism, which is as vociferous as that favoring global education, just as there are vociferously antagonistic factions supporting evolution and creationism and factions promoting and opposing sex education? Although isolationism and globalism are antithetical, they do not typically manifest themselves as opposing theses or principles, asserted by opposing groups. Once again, I draw attention to the oddness of any proposal to teach people either to be isolationist or to understand and appreciate isolationism. Why do not isolationists need to insist that their point of view be taught, and what does this reveal about the value of global education?

Isolationism and Globalism Defined

The first step in exploring this question must be to clarify how isolationism and global education should be understood. Both positions, as I shall sketch

Anita Silvers is Professor of Philosophy and Chair of the Academic Senate at San Francisco State University.

them, will be caricatured in some respects. I do not contend that my sketches are constructed from claims typically advanced by those who favor global education and those who oppose it. Rather, my sketches represent the ends of a spectrum of opinion about what is important to teach children about their world. In fact, they represent antithetical views about what there is for children to know.

It is only by exaggerating both views a bit that we can comprehend the perspectives from which global education is promoted and from which it is ignored. Consequently, I shall distinguish the globalist and isolationist perspectives by means of certain oppositions in epistemic, ontological, and axiological commitments. Having identified some philosophical features that distinguish isolationism from globalism, we may be better able to explore what philosophy is capable of contributing in this area of instruction.

Globalists tend to disconcert at least some philosophers by presenting globalism as the view that we must remedy our students' (and our general population's) ignorance of the world. In philosophical terms, of course, "the world" is everything there is. Thus, in one sense, it is hardly likely that students are ignorant of the world; were they totally devoid of information about anything at all that is, they would be such empty slates that one would hardly know where to begin their education. In another sense, no human can possess a global knowledge, for presumably no human can know everything there is.

A serious point lurks behind this caricatured account. If students knew nothing about the world in the philosophical sense, the motivation for teaching them about the world would be the desire to teach them about what is. Advocacy of global education would reduce to general support in favor of remedying students' ignorance *per se*. Thus, advocacy of global education would reduce to advocacy of education in general, regardless of the content or focus of instruction. So, in this reduced sense, to propose that anyone favoring educating children should favor global education is to propose a truism. The benefits of global education in this sense are difficult to deny.

But globalists characteristically do not present themselves as concerned with education *per se*. Globalists appear to believe that instruction should provide information about communities, societies, or nations (depending on whether one adopts the methodology of anthropology, sociology, or international relations) other than the one in which students reside and with which they identify. In this characteristic stance, globalists oppose isolationists, who urge that students be allowed or even encouraged to ignore communities, societies, or nations not their own.

In its characteristic form, isolationism maintains a "we/they," "inside/outside" conceptual structure that is expressed through a variety of linguistic and cultural devices. These include languages which have one word for members of the group (names like "the people" or "Americans" or "civilized") and another name for humans who do not belong to the group (names like "the others" or "aliens" or "barbarians"); attitudes such as conceiving one's own culture to be so rich that others will be grateful to learn its language (so one's education need not include instruction in other tongues); and social, political, and economic structures that prevent or protect the members of a group from having to operate as if the interests or practices of other groups condition their own interests or practices. Because isolationism both creates and depends on the force of conceptual barriers that impede members of one community, society, or nation from appreciating—that is, from conjointly understanding and valuing—the culture of other communities or societies or nations, isolationism can be construed as a kind of solipsism, a philosophical position which claims that we are barred from appreciating communities, societies, or nations outside our own.

In the foreign-policy context, isolationism means a policy of non-intervention in affairs outside our national borders. But the philosophical sources and forces driving such isolationist policy perspectives derive from attitudes grounded in conceptions extending far beyond those relevant to the foreign-policy context alone. Isolationist perspectives constitute a world-view, complete with ontological and epistemic commitments, which sites the central reference point for formulating both beliefs and actions in the isolated agent.

However, isolationists normally are not committed-enough solipsists to deem insupportable the belief that the agent is not the sole inhabitant of the world. Instead, isolationists typically try to resolve the inconsistency between admitting that the agent shares the world with others and, nevertheless taking the agent as the sole reference point for judgment, by acknowledging in this shared world only those who resemble the agent in relevant respects. If those who share the world with the agent all are taken to resemble the agent in respect to all characteristics relevant to social and political judgment, then the agent's being the sole reference point for judgment does not obviate that judgment's also being appropriate to others in the world, since others in the world are interchangeable with the agent in all the relevant respects.

This is an awkward way of saying that isolationism overcomes solipsism's inability to recognize any social dimension by admitting that persons other than the agent exist while denying that they are differentiated from the agent in any relevant respect. Once again, this account inclines towards being a caricature of isolationism. But, in doing so, it illuminates epistemic and ontological sources of the isolationist's tendency to ignore all those who do not share his or her geographical location, language, history, government, culture, and beliefs about what is valuable.

Globalism adopts isolationism's ontological frame, but globalism threatens isolationism by rejecting its epistemology and, consequently, its goals in education. The rhetoric of global education is replete with imagery which contrasts the isolated individual with what is supposed to be external to the individual—namely, the world. For instance, the sponsor of the APA's global education project, the National Council on Foreign Language and International Studies, proposed to participating professional associations the propriety of addressing such issues as "what undergraduate student majors ought to learn about the outside world."[1]

Presumably, the "outside world" does not exhaust what undergraduate majors should learn about, so the "outside world" is just part of the world. This suggests that there is an "inside world" which, if it extends outside the student, resembles or is of a piece with the student's interior. Note the similarity of structures assumed by the globalist's imagery and by the isolationist's solipsistic view. Both isolationist and globalist distinguish between inner and outer worlds, but the former counsels ignoring, while the latter promotes exploring, the expanse of things which are beyond the boundaries of the inner world.

Philosophy as a Prophylactic against a Dangerous Tendency in Globalism

Having introduced arguments leading to solipsism, Descartes propelled philosophy into a struggle to account for how persons can cognize what is not part of—what is, in fact, dissimilar to—themselves. The subsequent epistemic moves are familiar. As long as monism is denied and dualism or pluralism presides, the link between knower and known remains fragile and subject to the eroding influences of relativism. Insofar as it is inherently dualistic, dividing but assigning equal importance to "inside" and "outside" worlds, globalism invites relativistic results.

Globalism challenges isolationism by introducing students to communal, social, and national attitudes, practices, and histories which are not their own. For example, the State of California History-Social Science Framework decrees that ninth and tenth grade students:

> should have opportunities to compare and contrast philosophies, language, literature, religions, the arts, and drama of different cultures, as well as to become more knowledgeable about the historical events which are of significance.

Throughout this Framework, typical of such documents across the country, differences between cultures are stressed. Even direct historical predecessors are made to seem alien by placing emphasis on the discontinuities and diversities which differentiate them from what typifies the student's own time and place:

Human values are not based on a single standard, but are inherently diverse from time to time and from place to place and from group to group.

Note that by emphasizing distance in time, place, and group, the California Framework leaps to embrace a position which encompasses the crudest aspects of relativism.

Although no tenet of globalism necessitates the leap to relativism, piling cultural difference upon cultural distance seems to precipitate a rush over this precipice. I recall, for instance, attempting to describe some of the basic standards of good reasoning to those who design the California education frameworks and meeting a curious kind of objection. It was objected that in different cultures, different significance may be attributed to the same behavior. The instance given was the practice, in Taiwan, of serving a fish to an employee at the New Year if one intends to fire him. This example was supposed to establish that different standards of reasoning prevail in Taiwan than in the U.S., because Taiwanese and Americans would draw different conclusions if served a fish by their employer at the New Year.

Almost anyone well educated philosophically is aware of the many difficulties which beset versions of relativism that take descriptive or cultural relativism as their basis. First, it is not clear how one could demonstrate that different cultures actually possess different beliefs or values. Given the presumption of different conceptual schemes which descriptive relativism adopts, it does not seem possible to decide whether different cultures possess the same or divergent values and beliefs. To determine that they do, it would have to be possible to show that the same act or the same state of affairs normally is the subject of inconsistent beliefs or evaluations. But if the cultures' conceptual schemes really differ, then their methods of identifying acts or states of affairs also are culturally relative. Thus there is no method for establishing the commensurability of individuations of acts and states of affairs across cultures, under the assumptions of cultural relativism. Nor can it be established that different cultures hold different beliefs or assessments about the same act or state. Consequently, the presumptions required by cultural relativism render cultural relativism impossible to prove.

Even if we accept *prima facie* that different cultures differ fundamentally in their judgments of value or belief, the mere fact of descriptive relativism does not entail that criteria of truth, obligation, permission, or goodness also be relativized to place or time. At first glance, it does appear that we may be inclined to accept as obligations within a society whatever that society depicts its members as obligated to do. For instance, to take a famous example, if a society is so structured that its members are expected to dispose of their aged parents while the parents enjoy good health, our first inclination might be that indeed this is what members of the society ought to do. However, a second look suggests that the case is more complex.

For one thing, it is not clear whether, in this case, we really are inclined to hold that the obligation to dispose of healthy aged persons exists, or whether we simply are inclined to think we understand why persons in certain social circumstances might feel obligated to effect such disposals. It also is not clear how we would be inclined to respond if afforded the opportunity to intervene. Would we refrain from fulfilling what we believe to be our own obligations to preserve life in the aged as well as the young because in doing so we would block someone from fulfilling what is considered a duty according to another culture's lights? While exposure to cultural differences may lead us away from accepting beliefs and values unreflectively and toward demanding rational support for the choice of some and the rejection of other beliefs or values, such a reaction to the facts of cultural diversity and distance is not tantamount to concluding that what one ought to believe and do is relative to the preponderant norms of each time and place.

As I observed earlier, these considerations should be quite familiar to those well educated in the fundamentals of philosophy. This is not to say that philosophers have resolved the problems of relativism. Such matters as whether and how communal, social, or national circumstance, by affecting the knower, also influence the nature of what there is to know, continue as subjects of intense and stimulating philosophical debate. But the very recognition of the propriety of such debates is a prophylactic against the hasty conclusions so often invoked when globalism confronts us with a diversity of cultural and natural perspectives.[2]

As Relativism Is to Globalism, so Reductionism Is to Isolationism

There are several philosophical problems and fields which should serve well in preparing philosophy students for encounters with globalism. In addition to the standard study of epistemology and ethics, students might benefit from acquaintance with such methodological positions as historicism. Exposure to the methodological struggles of those embracing historicism is illuminating. Historicists incline toward a methodology which, on the one hand, acknowledges that cognition and evaluation occur in the context of processes of historical change, but, on the other hand, avoids the self-defeating consequence of treating historical change as a ground for intellectual and moral skepticism.

In refining their positions, historicists are drawn to debate such matters as whether the method of comprehending things in terms of their places or roles in developmental processes in order to understand and assess them requires that the objects of understanding be considered to be reiterable or, alternatively, requires they be construed as unique. Vico, Hegel, Marx, Troeltsch, Croce, and Popper all make significant contributions to this discussion. And, because globalism vies with its opponent, isolationism, about such matters as whether the world which students are educated to confront should embrace what does not reiterate or resemble the student's inner or communally extended self, the consequences of adopting the various versions of historicism can also serve to illuminate the conceptual outcomes of commitments to globalism or isolationism.

Earlier, I suggested that the main difference between isolationists and globalists had to be epistemological rather than ontological because both appear to accept the division of what exists into outer and non-outer worlds. The globalist insists that we explore, while the isolationist believes we must ignore, whatever is in the outer world's extension. But what determines the population of inner and outer worlds?

The determining factor, I believe, is whether an object's attributes are construed to make it a reiteration or a semblance of the student's inner or communal self, in which case it counts as part of the inner world, or whether, on the other hand, the object's attributes are presented so as to make it seem unique. In the latter case, its difference from the student is emphasized, and it is relegated to the outside world. Note that the definitive characteristic of what populates the outside world for both globalists and isolationists is that external entities are delineated in terms of differentiating, or individuating, characteristics, whereas the entities of the internal world are described by focusing on how they resemble each other or are mere segments of a single whole.

An epistemic consequence of the conceptual scheme that frames both isolationism and globalism thus is indicated. Cognition of inner-world entities can employ devices such as analogies, generalizations, and laws, all of which rely on resemblance and reiteration, while what is definitive of external entities is precisely what resists such cognition. Consequently, in the scheme I have been using to sketch these positions, something like the following is likely to occur: to the extent that cognition is encouraged to proceed on principles which presume similarities of objects in the world, cognition will be impeded or proscribed in respect to any population of the outside world.

This process has a peculiar dynamic. If objects are acknowledged as properly cognizable, they are also accounted as inside the knower's world. On the other hand, if a decision depicting objects as foreign to the knower's world predominates, judgments regarding them are likely to be so insecurely based as to invite relativistic or skeptical arguments to undermine claims of cognition.

The intricate relationship between globalism and isolationism illustrates this point. One might expect, for instance, that learning a second language inherently bears the mark of a global perspective, for a foreign language should be intractably a recognition of an external world where there is a culture or community different from one's own. Indeed, this is the perspective adopted by globalists, who stress that to acquire a foreign language is to learn about alien cultural and conceptual modes. But other perspectives on language-learning exist, including one according to which languages are tools for extending economic, political, or cultural domination over those who speak them. This is an isolationist perspective, for, on it, language learning is simply one more tool to help the knower organize the world along her preferred lines.

What might be considered to be a clear example of globalism thus can develop into an instance of isolationism, depending on whether the instance is drawn under a rubric that emphasizes difference or under one that drives toward homogenization. This explains why isolationist education need not be advocated actively as globalism so often is. Supposing any knower to know anything at all, it seems plausible to suppose that knowers most easily learn what is least strange to them. Isolationism, which delimits knowers to knowing what resembles them and that adjures them to ignore what does not (should it be inescapably obvious to them that such things exist), does not need positive promotion or advocacy because learning what is not strange is thought to be a self-initiating or self-perpetuating inclination. To illustrate this view, recall how Plato relies on the resemblance between the rational part of the soul and the Forms to account for how persons acquire knowledge.

Of course, to preserve the isolationist base, anti-globalist efforts may demand some energy. Anti-globalism is simply voice opposition to learning about anything dissimilar from the knower. Note that ignoring what is dissimilar is a less forceful stance than opposing acknowledgement of what is dissimilar. The weaker position suffices only as long as dissimilarities and dissonances remain obscured from attention. But anti-globalism merely supports and is supported by isolationism. To advise ignorance or avoidance of global knowledge is not to advocate that students make an effort to know their inner selves.

Anti-globalism is a recognizable constituent of education-policy politics. Efforts to prevent learning about contrasting communities, societies, or nations are more typical accompaniments to isolationism than are efforts to promote learning what reiterates the substance of the learner's existing knowledge. For example, it was only recently that two apparently anti-global congressmen objected to the use of NEH state program funds to fund a "Russian Awareness" project, even though anyone who listens loyally to President Reagan's speeches could hardly claim that the President is opposed to awareness of Russians. Such phenomena are odd or rare, however. Typically, inertia suffices to impede the expansion of global education—the inertia induced by the facility of restricting one's learning to what resembles what one already knows.

Although it is easier to account for learning if one adopts a reductionist focus on that reduces what is to be learned to a semblance of the learner or of what she already knows, a reductionist focus makes it harder to account for the motivation to learn. The desire to learn seems more plausibly explained on a nonreductionist rendering that has the power to accord an air of mysteriously seductive otherness to the objects of knowledge. Isolationists do not deny that what is alien has the capacity to tempt. They merely remind us that the pleasure of having apple pie is insufficient recompense for the other, less beneficial, consequences of the serpent's success in introducing Adam to an alien fruit.

Reductionism is to philosophy what sand is to a pearl—an irritant that stimulates an iridescent result. Many of the supreme moments in philosophy have been either monumentally reductionist, or else have been equally grand constructions meant to deflect reductionist thrusts. To the extent that isolationism is reductionist, it holds both the fascinations and the danger of such systems: the fascination of achieving total intelligibility by subsuming under a single explanatory scheme everything that exists and the danger of overlooking or distorting anything intransigently unsubsumable. And to the extent that globalism permits what there is to be itself, globalism can be a source for anti-reductionist stands.

Globalism as a Prophylactic against a Dangerous Tendency in Philosophy

The foregoing considerations suggest why globalism, despite its proclivity for inspiring relativism, is a worthwhile component of a philosophical education. Out of its commitment to permit whatever there is to be as it is, globalism offers an arena in which philosophical analyses and theories can be subjected to vigorous tests. Philosophers learn about the concepts they study both by examining the logic of model structures and by observing what they take to be expressions of the concepts' actual structures, as these affect linguistic and other practices. Globalism offers philosophers views of a variety of practices, drawn from the contexts of different cultures, that enrich the set of samples and examples on which we can draw.

As it is pursued in our educational institutions, philosophy attends primarily to subject matter dominated by the ways of Greek thought. Indeed, the influence of Greek thought may be even more widespread than some philosophers realize, for there is reason to believe that a substantial component of Oriental philosophical thought was influenced by the Greeks.[3] Therefore, philosophical education as we provide it may be falling prey to the reductionism of isolationism by identifying itself with Greek thought and acknowledging, in the curriculum, only what resembles or reiterates itself.

American philosophical education thus may be isolationist, although it is isolated to the perspectives of another country and another time. This isolationist inclination in philosophical education has the bizarre consequence that, in American educational institutions, American philosophy is accorded the neglect reserved in other disciplines for alien ways of thought because it diverges in some important respects from the Platonic-Cartesian tradition. Globalism has the fortunate consequence of promoting philosophical engagement with concepts embedded in practices that, by our lights, are not familiar ones, although they may seem ordinary to those who practice them.

I do not pretend to know how philosophically effective global education can be. Perhaps the nature of philosophical reflection precludes philosophers from thoroughly understanding concepts that are not their own and are not reflected in the practices of their own culture. That is, proper use of a concept (or of its practical expressions) may be the requisite touchstone for judging one's philosophical treatment of a concept. If this is so, it may not be possible to address alien concepts philosophically. So, for example, philosophical analyses of the Navajo concept of causality, and of the Eskimo obligation code, may be reserved for those who actually use these concepts.

On the other hand, we need not conclude that a concept is alien unless attempts to comprehend it have been launched and then sunk. The potential for discovering whether seemingly strange practices express foreign concepts or turn out to be inspired by familiar ones) and the concomitant potential for enhancing our comprehension of philosophical methodology weigh in favor of expanding to global dimensions the field from which philosophers draw the content of their studies. Global education offers philosophers an opportunity to illuminate their own methodology and to learn how being sited in one rather than another community, society, or nation may affect how the philosopher does her work.

Thus, philosophy and globalism can provide safeguards for one another. For the non-philosophy major newly exposed to information about communities, societies, or nations whose perspectives apparently cannot be reduced to his own, philosophy can serve as a prophylactic against mistakenly inferring that certain kinds of relativism are true. For the philosophy major already well-imbued with the philosophical methods of the Platonic-Cartesian tradition, globalism may counter the reductionist tendency to attend only to one's own munities, societies, or nations whose perspectives apparently cannot be reduced to his own, philosophy can serve as a prophylactic against mistakenly inferring that certain kinds of relativism are true. For the philosophy major already well-imbued with the philosophical methods of the Platonic-Cartesian tradition, globalism may counter the reductionist tendency to attend only to one's own individual or communal practices to reveal the conceptual structures the serious philosopher seeks to understand.

Of course, if globalism is to render such benefits to philosophy, and if concomitantly philosophy also is to play its prophylactic role, globalism and isolationism must be addressed as epistemic stances, not as views about what subject matter to teach. As I have indicated, subject matter that superficially seems to be global nevertheless may be reduced to accommodate the isolationist perspective. So, for globalism's advocates, and for itself as well, philosophy has another lesson.

Those who promote global education would do well not to rely on the exotic flavor of materials about other peoples and other lands to make their case. Subject matter that seems brightly exotic can as easily be made to seem palely repetitive of familiar things. It is an epistemology, a view about what we can know, not a syllabus or a list of things that may be known, which bears the educational value globalism can provide.

Notes

[1] An extract of the report issued by the Council on Learning for its Education and the World View Project ("College Students' Knowledge and Beliefs: A Survey of Global Understanding") helps define "global education":

> [T]he ETS staff ... had to proceed on the assumption that global understanding is more than a knowledge (or cognitive) concept; that it also involves feelings (affect). The survey, therefore, would have to touch on students' attitudes and interests as well as knowledge and abilities, and to measure both....

[2] Joyce Hoy has pointed out to me that students in a typical philosophical survey course, introduced to a variety of alternative metaethical positions, for instance, might be inclined toward relativism by studying philosophy rather than protected against it. I think, though, this experience is more likely to produce skepticism, the view that no philosophical position can be demonstrated to be the correct one. If this is the case, philosophy still can serve as a prophylactic against crude relativism, as long as students agree that crude relativistic theories have not been shown to be correct simply because different cultures have different practices.

[3] I am grateful to my colleague John Glanville for bringing this point to my attention. He teaches about the interfaces of Greek and Oriental thought in a course called "Great Thinkers East and West," an exemplary instance of philosophical global education.

Philosophy and International Problems

Virginia Held

From the perspectives of most standard treatments of moral issues offered in undergraduate courses, nations are irrelevant. The student is presented with a variety of views of individuals. These individuals have desires, interests, and beliefs. They can but sometimes or often don't act rationally. And these individuals can be in or can enter into various relations with other individuals. These relations are commonly seen as contractual. On some theories, even morality itself rests on contractual relations. Morality advises the student that one should universalize one's moral judgments. One should be guided by universal moral norms, or one should base one's choice between alternative actions on a calculation of the benefits and burdens likely to result for all those who will be affected by one's actions, or one should act on enlightened self-interest.

Almost nowhere in all these familiar discussions do nations appear. And yet nations are utterly salient in our lives, determining whether we live or die, exerting the strongest influences on our futures, claiming our political loyalties, and focusing our identity.

Despite Marxian views that class is a more fundamental determinant of social conditions than is state, any number of recent developments confirm the overriding influence of nationalism. The conflicts between the Soviet Union and China, the nationalistic priorities of Marxist-Leninist governments throughout the world, and the inability of capitalist states to adopt unified policies for dealing with a variety of dangers demonstrate the extent to which national concerns still dominate the decisions of nations on the international scene.

I

What is a nation? Standard philosophical analyses have a very hard time taking this question seriously, much less offering even moderately successful answers to it. Of course we have not yet successfully clarified what persons are, or what minds and bodies and wills are or are not. But we provide students with

Virginia Held is Professor of Philosophy at Hunter College and the Graduate School of the City University of New York.

a variety of possible views with which to make sense of their experience, and we focus their attention on consciousness, perception, deliberation, and memory. We deepen students' awareness of what it may be to be a person.

Nations, in contrast, may remain unmentioned. Or they may be dissolved in entirely unsatisfactory ways into the persons supposedly composing them, or the leaders supposedly acting for them, as if they had no further reality. And the societies and social roles and social relations nations represent or embody or shape are often treated as of only marginal significance. The corporations and multinational conglomerates and bureaucracies that affect our lives in more fundamental ways than do many smaller states likewise receive little recognition within the frameworks of many philosophical treatments of moral problems. Collective entities are often neither acknowledged as existent nor even considered as perhaps having an existence that could be reduced to that of persons acting in their name. They are simply overlooked.

Students are exposed to questions about moral responsibility and the connections between claims about responsibility and other issues such as determinism. It would be helpful if they would more often consider such issues as the moral responsibilities of nations and corporations, and of the persons occupying the roles composing or creating or created by such collective entities. They should also be encouraged to consider the connections between alternative possible realities and such issues.

In some ways it is appropriate that we downgrade the importance of nations. They have not always been with us, and for the good of humanity should have their influence severely diminished. But philosophers will not contribute to limiting the excessive power of nations by simply ignoring them. For the foreseeable future we weaken our ability to overcome the dangers of nuclear confrontation, global upheaval, widening hunger, and environmental disaster if we fail to attend to the realities and responsibilities of nations and of those acting in, through, and for nations on the international scene.

Philosophers should also pay far more attention than they now do to developments that may lead the world beyond its present overdeveloped nationalism.[1] Such developments include more than just international law, which is important but limited and somewhat less likely to be overlooked. They should include also the growth of transnational movements, local self-help groups, and regional problem-solving mechanisms.

II

Inhabitants of the Third World sometimes now see themselves in a position somewhat comparable to that of the proletariat in earlier periods in the developed world.[2] Poor countries are demanding changes in the "world economic order" if it can be called that.[3] Such economic order as now exists leaves the gap between rich and poor countries widening at an accelerating pace rather than shrinking. Members of the poor countries have learned from history, even if the privileged and entrenched elites of the rich countries have not, that the poor can demand, and sometimes win, an improvement in their condition. If talk does not succeed, they may resort to harsher methods of winning concessions. An increase in violence is predictable, and it may be no less justifiable than that which some consider to have contributed significantly to the progress that has occurred since the nineteenth century toward less injustice for the working class.

Moral theories applied to international issues can suggest guidelines for deciding when violence may be justified and what limits on its use are required by morality.[4] Although violence should be avoided under almost all conditions, it is primarily the responsibility of those in power to see to it that the conditions in which violence might be justified are never present. In the world as it exists, it cannot be plausibly maintained, unfortunately, that there are no excuses for violence. We ought to be able to say that there are always morally better and more effective ways than the use of violence to make progress toward a more just and peaceful international order and toward greater respect for human rights. We cannot now convincingly do so. But we can create conditions that will make the use of violence less justifiable than at present.

Connections should be explored between morality and national security. We do not improve our standing in the world, nor even our security, by supporting the morally worse rather than the morally better side of historical change, as we have so often done in recent years. As Richard Ullman writes, "When death squads spread lawless violence with the tacit approval of governments that Washington supports, as they have done in El Salvador, Guatemala, and several [other] South American states, U.S. allies among advanced, industrialized states will find it more difficult to generate domestic consensus for following American initiatives.... And governments whose human rights' behavior Washington would like to influence will be even more likely to reject American criticism: double standards make weak platforms."[5]

Much more attention needs to be devoted to the *forms* in which developmental assistance ought to be offered. Ways of transferring commodities need to be found that will not decrease the welfare of the recipient countries, as does investment in Third World countries by high-income groups from developed countries. And transfers need to be made in ways that will avoid increasing inequalities within donor countries.[6]

Among the worst gaps of all are those between the rising successful few and the many left behind in the developing countries. Connections should be examined between different forms of developmental assistance and the fostering of this gap. In preventing or modifying the growth of this gap, non-capitalist development can be more successful than that resulting from corporate investment but may lead to entrenched bureaucracies. This does not mean *nothing* can be done about the problem as it is convenient for many to suppose. It means, among other things, that more attention should be given to understanding the forms of development that deserve support. And the goal should not only be to end poverty, enormous as that problem is. The goals should also be to *empower* people to work, to participate in shaping their lives, and to express themselves.

A large part of the appeal of the libertarian argument that universal egoism effectively benefits all depends on the assumption that the poor of the world are a bottomless pit, an infinite drain. Libertarians claim that if we were to recognize, even within our own society, that the poor have rights to enough to eat, we would have to prepare ourselves for horrendous reductions in our standard of living, as the poor of the world would pull everything down with them. Hence the libertarian slogan that needs do not generate rights. The frightening image promoted is of *everyone* reduced to poverty, instead of the present situation of some comfortable and some poor.

To counter such false threats, it is useful to consider contrary views. Some suggest that the poverty of the world could be rather painlessly ended by a simple transfer. Roger Hansen has calculated, for instance, that $10 billion–$13 billion per year for 15 years from the rich countries could wipe out world poverty. He writes that:

> a two percent annual transfer from the upper classes to the bottom 40 percent of the populations of the developing countries could successfully finance both the short-term and long-term goals of the strategy over a twenty-five year period."[7]

Although useful as a corrective to the claim that recognizing the basic needs of the world's poor would bankrupt us all, there is danger in the intriguing images of how easy it would be to alleviate the present suffering. They draw attention away from the complexities of the problem. The difficulties of getting capital to the countryside intact, and of investing it in ways that will meet the needs of the poor, are immense. Ways have to be devised to deal with deficiencies in infrastructures and to generate the right kinds of productive growth. Exploitative relations are often so powerful and so entrenched as to make progress for the poor impossible. Where the capital-allocation process is dominated by growth-oriented technocrats and profit-oriented urban industrial capitalists, the problems of dealing with the structural difficulties of rural development are severe. But then efforts to deal with the basic problems should focus on Third World allocations of investment that would produce development to serve human needs rather than profits for local as well as distant elites.

415

Moral discussion should address these issues, and discussions should include enough details and specific factors to preclude the easy dismissal of these problems as "beyond solution." If the average privileged member of a developed society is encouraged to believe that there is nothing that can be done about even flagrant global economic injustice, moral concern for such problems will be easy to avoid. Undergraduates who might like to ignore such issues should be made aware of the moral questions that can be raised about the disproportionate use of scarce resources by the rich countries of the North, relative to their population. The ratio may be approximately 15:1 on a per capita basis.[8] Consumption at this level affects economic conditions everywhere, reducing the availability of resources to meet the needs of other populations.

Philosophical discussion should also show why a satisfactory set of basic human rights must include economic and social rights, especially rights to basic necessities such as food, shelter, and clothing, along with the civil and political rights recognized by the liberal tradition. No one is in a better position to argue this case than are philosophers.[9]

III

Among the most difficult issues of contemporary international relations is the question of when intervention by one state into the affairs of another may be justified and the prior question of what intervention is.[10] Total non-intervention can seem morally irresponsible; as Michael Walzer notes, "against the enslavement or massacre of political opponents, national minorities, and religious sects, there may well be no help unless help comes from outside."[11]

On the other hand, for something to constitute intervention, it must, like rape, be "against the will" of the recipient. To request assistance is very different from having a solution imposed by an external power using force or threat. And one of the moral positions on which there is broad agreement is that people should be permitted to deal autonomously with their own problems without outside intervention. This is a view shared by the most divergent of nations and by groups within nations claiming to be more representative of the people in them than are their governments.

To try to sort out the moral requirements for dealing with such issues, we need an understanding of moral theory as well as a sound understanding of the relevant facts. But we also need intermediate principles at the level of inter-state behavior and criteria to determine whether governments truly represent people. Undergraduates should be assisted in thinking about these issues, on which they will almost certainly not be able to escape acting, either as citizens or as soldiers.

The dominant view of some earlier decades was that we should not apply morality to the domain of international relations. Influential statements of this view were made by Hans Morgenthau:

There is neither morality nor law outside the state.... The appeal to moral principles in the international sphere ... is either so vague as to have no concrete meaning that could provide rational guidance for political action, or it will be nothing but the reflection of the moral preconceptions of a particular nation.... Whenever the appeal to moral principles provides guidance for political action in international affairs, it destroys the very moral principles it intends to realize.[12]

He advocated foreign policies straightforwardly based on national interest alone.

In reaction to such views, many of those struck with the immorality of much that goes on in the international arena have tried, in contrast, to apply abstract moral theories directly at the international level. Or they have placed exaggerated hopes in a system of international law ill-suited to deal with many of the realities of international injustice and power. The results have often been disappointing.

The appropriate combination of realism about the likely behavior of states and moral concern with how state behavior can and ought to change is extremely difficult to achieve. Richard Falk notes, "it is naive to make proposals for drastic change that violate statist logic dependent on voluntary adoption by entrenched elites."[13] On the other hand, he notes, "the rationalism of realism makes it almost impossible to take seriously challenges that exceed the problem-solving capacities of the state system," as many current challenges do.[14] Neither realists nor their neo-realist successors can deal adequately with the problems arising from nuclear technology, ecological dangers, and the global gap between rich and poor. Both realists and neo-realists fail to address themselves to the right questions.

What we need is the development of normative international relations. As Falk sees this need, "values are critical elements of *analysis*, as well as of advocacy." To make the actual system of relations between nations work tolerably well,

requires the significant realization of a series of values: peace in the sense of minimum direct violence ...; economic well-being in the sense of satisfying the basic needs of all peoples; social and political justice in the sense of satisfying the basic claims of human rights; ecological balance in the sense of achieving environmental quality consistent with health and safety and of conserving the necessary stock of renewable and nonrenewable resources; and governance in the sense of achieving effective and humane structures of authority at all levels of social organization. Normative international relations aspires to promote disciplined inquiry into the ways in which such values can be realized, as well as to expose the value failures of the present and past arrangements of authority and the adverse consequences of "muddling through."[15]

Surely philosophers ought to be contributing, in the classroom as well as in their studies and elsewhere, to the development of normative international relations. And students of philosophy should become aware of what sincere moral inquirers might best look for and be guided by in the domain of international conflict and global injustice.

Notes

[1] See e.g., S. Mendlovitz, ed., *On the Creation of a Just World Order: Preferred Worlds for the 1990s* (New York: Free Press, 1975); and Richard Falk, *The End of World Order: Essays in Normative International Relations* (New York: Holmes and Meier, 1983). See also Elise Boulding, "Ethnic Separatism and World Development," in Louis Kirnesberg, ed., *Research in Social Movements, Conflicts and Change,* Vol. 2 (Conn.: JAI Press, 1979).

[2] See, e.g., Julius Nyerere, "The Economic Challenge: Dialogue or Confrontation?" *International Development Review* 1 (1976).

[3] See A. Carter, W. Leontief, and P. Petri, *The Future of the World Economy* (Oxford: Oxford UP, 1977).

[4] See Virginia Held, "Violence, Terrorism, and Moral Inquiry," *The Monist,* 67:4 (October, 1984).

[5] Richard Ullman, "Both National Security and Human Rights Can Be Served Simultaneously," *The Center Magazine,* 17:1 (March-April 1984), p. 25.

[6] See Graciela Chichilnisky, "Basic Goods, the Effects of Commodity Transfers, and the International Economic Order," *Journal of Development Economics* 7 (1980) 505–519.

[7] Roger Hansen, "Major U.S. Options on North-South Relations: A Letter to President Carter," in John Sewell et al. *The United States and World Development: Agenda 1977* (Washington, D.C.: Overseas Development Council, 1977), p. 68.

[8] Richard Falk. *The End of World Order,* p. 247.

[9] See, e.g., Henry Shue, *Basic Rights: Subsistence, Affluence, and U.S. Foreign Policy* (Princeton, N.J.: Princeton UP, 1980); Virginia Held, ed., *Property, Profits, and Economic Justice* (Belmont, Cal.: Wadsworth, 1980); James Nickel, *Making Sense of Human Rights* (typescript); and Jorge Domingues et al., *Enhancing Global Human Rights* (New York: McGraw Hill, 1979).

[10] See Virginia Held, *Rights and Goods. Justifying Social Action* (New York: Free Press-Macmillan, 1984), Chapter 14.

[11] Michael Walzer, *Just and Unjust Wars* (New York, Basic Books, 1977), p.87.

[12] Hans J. Morgenthau, *In Defense of the National Interest. A Critical Examination of American Foreign Policy* (New York: Knopf, 1951), pp. 84–85.

[13] Richard Falk, p. 11.

[14] *Ibid.,* p. 12.

[15] *Ibid.,* p. 16.

Theories of Justice and the UN Declaration on the Establishment of a New International Economic Order

Bernard Boxill

I n May of 1974, in its 2229th plenary meeting, the General Assembly of the United Nations issued its famous Declaration on the Establishment of a New International Economic Order.[1] Endorsed overwhelmingly by the "Third World" states of the United Nations, the declaration stressed the material poverty of many developing nations and the widening gap between these nations and the developed nations of the West, traced this gap to unjust policies of the developed countries, and called for massive transfers of wealth to the developing countries. Not made in the name of charity, or even of prudence, this call was made repeatedly and unambiguously in the name of justice. Thus it presupposed a theory of international distributive justice. But is there such a theory?

My theme in this essay is to illustrate the pedagogical value of an attempt to devise a theory of international distributive justice to support the declaration's claims. Theories of justice are commonly classified as utilitarian theories, contractarian theories, or theories based on natural rights. If there is a theory of international distributive justice, presumably it can be derived from such theories. The attempt to do so not only leads naturally to an examination of the UN declaration and to the international issues it raises but also throws certain of the difficulties of utilitarianism, contractarianism, and natural rights theory into bold relief. These difficulties, it will become evident, have seemed minor and manageable because they were assumed to apply only within the nation-state. When that assumption is dropped, the difficulties are seen to be more serious. The attempt to resolve them should cure any tendency toward over-simplification in normative theory, improve our grasp of domestic distributive

Bernard Boxill is Professor of Philosophy at the University of North Carolina.

justice, and deepen our appreciation of the difficulties and perhaps the limitations of a theory of international distributive justice capable of supporting the demand for a new international economic order.

Among other things, the UN declaration demands systems to "correct inequities" and "eliminate the widening gap between the developed and the developing countries." The normative theory which most obviously supports this demand is utilitarianism. According to utilitarianism, individuals and nations have an obligation to maximize the total happiness of mankind. For the utilitarian, this obligation implies that each person's happiness is as important as any other's. The happiness of a countryman is, in itself, no more important than, and counts for no more than, the happiness of an alien. In particular, the misery of an alien dying of starvation on the other side of the world is not discounted one whit because he is alien and distant. This egalitarianism fuels utilitarianism's demands for international redistribution and no doubt adds political appeal to the call for a new international economic order. For if we assume a diminishing marginal utility of goods and services—that aiding the poor produces more happiness than enriching the already well-to-do—this egalitarianism easily and naturally leads to the conclusion that inequalities are usually odious and widening gaps especially so, and accordingly that rich nations should give poor countries massive assistance in food, technology, and education.

Now the stringencies of utilitarian justice—that it requires equalizing incomes up to the point at which further equalizing will diminish total happiness—have long been well-known. But these stringencies were at least moderated by the tacit assumption that they applied only within the nation-state. Dropping that assumption reveals how stringent utilitarianism is. Given the poverty of the vast majority of people in the world, the rich minority and, more generally, the well-to-do probably have to give up a lot if utilitarianism is to be satisfied. We must remember that we are not speaking here only of famine relief or even "foreign aid." We are speaking of transfers from the rich countries to the poor up to the point at which further transfers diminish total happiness.

The utilitarian who wishes to avoid these stringencies is not without recourse. He can argue that an invisible hand leads private greed to promote the general welfare, not only within nations, but internationally; and, as a corollary, that maximizing happiness requires a certain level of productivity, that that level of productivity requires incentives, and that these incentives are, more or less, the income advantages enjoyed by the rich countries. Or he can argue that increasing happiness requires reducing total world population, but that massive transfers from the rich countries to the poor countries would increase total world population.

Unfortunately, these essentially laissez-faire arguments are not compelling. It may be that a laissez-faire policy best secures liberty, but it is the sheerest fantasy that it best secures happiness—even if we add, as the utilitarian must, "in the long run." It is not enough to argue, as certain conservative development economists argue, that European colonialism, a product of laissez-faire policies, brought the wheel and an increase in material prosperity to backward countries.[2] It is also necessary to argue that no other policies could do better. In particular, while it may be that productivity depends on incentives and even that productivity depends on the material incentive of higher income rather than on the moral incentives of exhortation, it is surely false that it requires the present inequalities between rich and poor countries. Similarly, while it may be that increasing total world happiness requires reducing population, it is questionable whether the way to reduce total world happiness is to let the people of the poor countries starve to death. Before utilitarianism allows resort to this desperate measure, it must be demonstrated that measures not causing so much misery (e.g., getting the people of the poor countries to practice birth control) cannot succeed.

It would seem, then, that utilitarianism may well be an attractive normative theory to one who welcomes the egalitarian redistributive measures called for by the UN declaration. But to one who finds these measures unjustifiably stringent, this only shows the wrongheadedness of utilitarianism. In any case, applying utilitarianism to the world as a whole leads naturally to a discussion of the demands for redistribution in the UN declaration and compels the student to take a long, hard look at utilitarianism.

Utilitarianism is not the only normative theory whose egalitarian presuppositions support the redistribution measures in the call for a new international economic order. Indeed, the egalitarian presuppositions of contractarianism are stronger than those of utilitarianism, and it may therefore supply a stronger basis for the call for a new international economic order than does utilitarianism. For example, although the utilitarian counts each person's happiness or misery equally, he is prepared to sacrifice one person's happiness if this will increase total happiness. The contractarian, however, will have none of this.

In John Rawls' contractarian theory, for example, the principles of justice are the principles which people engaged in social cooperation would choose to determine the division of social benefits and to regulate their claims against one another.[3] To prevent anyone from designing principles to favor his particular condition, Rawls further stipulates that the choice of principles must be made "behind a veil of ignorance," that is, that no one may know his position or status in the scheme of social cooperation nor his natural assets and abilities. Under these conditions, the choice of principles would be made as if by free and equal people and would, as Rawls maintains, be "the result of a fair agreement or bargain." Now, if this is the way that principles of justice are derived, then, assuming that the parties to the bargain are rational and self-interested, it appears that, in opposition to what utilitarianism teaches, no principles of justice will require that anyone be sacrificed merely to increase overall happiness. For each person knows that he or she could be the one to be sacrificed, but since each is self-interested, no one is prepared to be sacrificed. In this way, Rawlsian contractarianism probably provides a stronger argument against inequality than does utilitarianism.

It does not follow, however, that this contractarianism excludes all in-equalities, since inequalities can lead to larger shares for everyone. Assuming self-interest, for example, even the least advantaged members of a scheme of social cooperation will agree to inequalities if without these inequalities they would have even less. At the same time, however, and for the same reason, they will reject inequalities if without these inequalities they would have more. Putting these two considerations together, Rawls argues that because each party to the bargain knows that he or she could be in the least advantaged position, self-interest and rationality lead them all to agree to the principle that inequalities are to be permitted if, but only if, they are to the advantage of the least advantaged. Accordingly, on the contractarian ground that the results of a fair agreement are just, he concludes that this principle is one of justice and labels it the "difference principle."

Contractarian theory as formulated by Rawls lends itself easily and plausibly to a defense of certain claims in the UN declaration. Recall that for Rawls the principles of justice are those that people engaged in "social cooperation" would choose to determine the division of social benefits and to regulate their claims against one another. Now the UN declaration stressed the "interdependence of all members of the world community" and the "close interrelation between the prosperity of the developed countries and the growth and development of the developing countries." Assuming that "interdependence" and "interrelation" amount to "social cooperation," it seems natural to suppose that although Rawls applies his contractarian argument most elaborately to derive principles of domestic distributive justice, that argument can also be applied to derive principles of international distributive justice. Further, if this extension is justifi-able, it seems natural to suppose that just as the parties to the contract which resulted in principles of domestic distributive justice were all members of the nation-state, the parties to a contract resulting in international distributive justice should be all members of all states. Finally, assuming that the possibility of being in the least advantaged nation-state is as clear to the parties to the international contract as the possibility of being in the least advantaged position was clear to the parties to the national contract, it would seem that precisely as self-interest and rationality led the parties to the national contract to insist on a national difference principle, the same motivations should lead the parties to the international contract to insist on an international difference principle.

Radically egalitarian, the difference principle requires transfers from the rich to the poor up to the point at which further redistribution will reduce the incomes of the poor. Assuming that point has not been reached in the international distribution of wealth, Rawls' version of contractarianism yields a theory of international distributive justice requiring large transfers from rich countries to poor ones and therefore supports the redistributive demands of the call for a new international economic order.

Like the utilitarian, the contractarian who wishes to avoid these apparent stringencies of his theory is not without recourse. For example, he can accept the idea of an international difference principle but argue that present international inequalities are more or less to the advantage of the least advantaged and therefore more or less consistent with an international difference principle. Or, somewhat more plausibly, he can reject the idea of an international difference principle, arguing that such a principle would undermine national sovereignty and that the parties to an international contract would not agree to it because they would recognize the absolute necessity of national sovereignty.

The first of the above arguments is hardly serious, but the second is. The UN declaration insisted that "every country has the right to adopt the economic and social system that it deems to be most appropriate for its own development and not to be subject to discrimination of any kind as a result." If the declaration is correct in thus laying great stress on national sovereignty, it would seem that, being rational and self-interested, the members of the international convention would reject anything that would undermine national sovereignty, including an international difference principle.

It is possible that such an argument underlies Rawls' own rejection of an international difference principle. In Rawls' application of the contractarian argument to the international sphere, the parties to the contract are only representatives of states, and they agree only to principles of self-determination and non-aggression, not to redistributive principles. Though Rawls does not canvass the argument, it is possible that he took this position because he believed that national sovereignty was essential to both economic and cultural development and that any international principle more ambitious than self-determination and non-aggression—perhaps especially an international difference principle—would undermine national sovereignty.

It may be objected, of course, that an international difference principle does not have to undermine national sovereignty. Moreover, the UN declaration would obviously endorse that objection since its demands for transfer of wealth are made in conjunction with an insistence on national sovereignty. But it is far from clear that the declaration is consistent on this point. The economic and social policies a country autonomously adopts strongly affect its development and can conflict with a domestic difference principle. But it is inconsistent for a country to demand transfers of wealth from other countries in the name of an international difference principle while at the same time claiming the right autonomously to pursue policies which conflict with a domestic difference principle.

One way to avoid the inconsistency is to adopt Rawls' view that the parties to an international contract are the representatives of states, not all members of all states, but to argue, in opposition to Rawls, that those parties would agree to an international difference principle applying to nation-states as wholes, not to individuals. On this account international redistribution would not undermine national sovereignty. Rich nations would be obligated to transfer resources to poor nations up to the point at which further transfers would make poor nations even poorer, but poor nations would have the sovereign right to dispose of these resources as they saw fit. This, in effect is the position of the UN declaration. It calls for the rich countries to transfer resources to the poor countries with "no strings attached." The rich countries, however, argue that they will transfer resources only with strings attached. Who is right? On the side of the declaration it can be argued that transfers with strings undermine the good of national sovereignty which poor countries precariously, and in the case of ex-colonies, only lately, enjoy. On the side of the rich countries it can be argued that transfers without strings often serve to prop up corrupt and inefficient governments.

The issue is not resolved in favor of the declaration by a demonstration that some kinds of collectivities can have rights and can, in general, be owed justice.[4] One must also demonstrate that every poor nation-state in the modern world is the right kind of collectivity; that the members of its government are its true representatives to which resources owed to it should be turned over to dispose of as they see fit; and finally, that rich nations should obey the dictates of a collectivist difference principle when this undermines the dictates of an in-dividualist difference principle.

I do not propose to try to settle the issue here one way or another. My purpose is to illustrate how applying contractarian theory to the international issue of the economic inequality between nations leads both to a deeper appreciation of the complexities of contractarian theory and to a deeper appreciation of the difficulty of formulating a theory of international distributive justice to support the UN declaration.

Besides its indirect appeal to utilitarian and contractarian considerations, the UN declaration claims the right of each state to its natural resources. Thus, it emphasizes the "Full permanent sovereignty of every state over its natural resources," and, as a corollary, that each state is "entitled to exercise effective control over [its natural resources] and their exploitation with means suitable to its own situation, including the right to nationalization or transfer of ownership to its nationals, this right being an expression of the full permanent sovereignty of the state. No state may be subjected to economic, political or any other type of coercion to prevent the free and full exercise of this inalienable right."

As a political document, it is understandable that the declaration would make such a claim. The less industrialized, developing countries that largely supported the declaration are primarily producers of raw materials. In the past, the developed countries turned them into colonies and took raw materials from them with little or no payment. In the present, they continue to be cheated by what they consider to be unfair terms of international trade for raw materials. To support demands for compensation for past injustices and for changes in the terms of trade, it was therefore politically expedient that they claim that each state has inalienable rights to the natural resources within its boundaries. But in considering the fundamental question of a theory of international distributive justice, we must set political expediencies aside. What moral theory underlies the declaration's claim that states have inalienable and apparently nearly absolute rights to the natural resources within their borders?

The theory which comes most immediately to mind is natural rights theory. Natural rights theory emphasizes the natural and nearly absolute right of each person to his life, person, talents, and property. It is therefore easy to suppose that natural rights theory can be extended to justify the claim of a natural right of each state to its natural resources. Unfortunately, this is an illusion. Even at the level of individuals, natural rights theory has a difficult time explaining how individuals come to acquire rights to virgin material. John Locke said that we do so by mixing our labor with it. But whatever one thinks of this argument, it offers no support for the claim that states have rights to the natural resources within their boundaries. This claim is not founded on the premise that the state or its members have mixed their labor with the resources to which the state is alleged to have a right. Indeed, such a premise is denied by the fact that the resource in question is "natural," i.e., virgin. Nor do I think that it is possible to construct a less derivative argument for states' rights to natural resources on an analogy with the individual's right to his natural talents. There is something highly appealing about the claim that, although an individual with great talents has done nothing to deserve them, he nevertheless has an absolute right to them. Behind that appeal is no doubt the argument that denying that right would be to invite violations of his personality. But whether or not this argument is sound, a parallel argument to support states' rights to natural resources is far less appealing. Collectivities or groups of individuals may certainly have personalities, and foreign exploitation of natural resources within the natural boundaries of such groups may certainly violate these personalities. What is less certain is that the natural boundaries of these groups coincide with the conventional boundaries of the state.

Further, if natural rights theory provides little support for the claim that states have inalienable rights to the natural resources within their boundaries, it provides far more support for the claim that people have rights to what they have produced by their labor. Locke's solution to the problem of how people acquire rights to virgin material is that they do so by mixing their labor with it. But if this is so, the people of the industrialized, richer, more productive states have rights to their products and no obligation to transfer any of these products to the people of the less industrialized, poorer, less productive states.

I have not tried to rebut the claim in the UN declaration that states have inalienable rights to the natural resources within their boundaries. Consistently with my theme, I have tried to show how the attempt to use natural rights theory to support this claim both throws the difficulties of natural rights theory into bold relief and deepens our grasp of international issues. This is similar to what we found when we tried to extend utilitarianism and contractarianism to the international sphere in order to devise a theory of international distributive justice to assess and judge the proposals in the United Nations' Declaration for the Establishment of a New International Economic Order. The exercise of going from normative theory to international issues is thus doubly fruitful. On the one hand, it clarifies and deepens students' understanding of international issues. On the other hand, it does the same for their understanding of normative theory. Indeed, on the particular normative question of justice, I venture to say that the issue of international redistribution is the great testing ground of normative theory, serving to eliminate theories that are either inconsistent or incomplete.

Notes

1 United Nations, General Assembly. Resolution 3201 (S-VI). May 1, 1974.

2 See, for example, Peter Bauer "Western Guilt and Third World Poverty" in *Equality, the Third World and Economic Delusion*, (Cambridge, Mass.: Harvard UP, 1981), p. 72.

3 John Rawls, *A Theory of Justice* (Cambridge, Mass.: Harvard UP, 1971).

4 See Ali Mazrui "Panel Discussion" in *The New International Economic Order*, Jagdish N. Bhagwati, ed., (Cambridge, Mass.: MITP, 1977), p. 372.

Overcoming Ethnocentrism in the Philosophy Classroom

Ofelia Schutte

A recent study sponsored by the Council on Learning and supported by the Department of Education and the National Endowment for the Humanities raises some provocative questions regarding the average college senior's knowledge of international affairs.[1] How well do students graduating from U.S. colleges and universities understand international issues? What is their attitude toward other countries and cultures? How close to reality is the students' perception of their own knowledge or lack of knowledge of world affairs? To this set of queries our task is to add another concern, namely, is there anything that can be done in philosophy classrooms to improve students' understanding of world affairs? What can philosophy add, in particular, to the development of "global awareness"? And finally, is it really important for philosophers to address this issue, given the many issues that philosophers must teach and otherwise address?

At first glance, the results of the ETS survey conducted by the Council on Learning appear disappointing. College seniors did not perform significantly better than freshmen: the average variation was less than ten percentage points. Foreign language majors fared worse than social science majors. No correlation could be established between learning a foreign language and increasing the level of awareness of world events.[2] Most distressing of all was the response given to one question regarding students' geographical background. A small proportion of the students indicated that they were from Central America and South America when in fact what they meant was that they resided in the midwest or in the southern areas of the United States.[3] These students obviously did not realize that America, as in "United States of America," refers to a hemisphere that includes North, Central, and South America as well as the Caribbean. In this context, the United States, which generally refers to itself as

Ofelia Schutte is Professor of Philosophy at the University of Florida.

"America," constitutes only one part of America's vast land mass, as of its cultural heritage.

In terms of the arguments to be developed in the present essay, the results of the ETS survey need not be taken as the last word on the measurement of North American students' awareness of world events. The ETS survey is shaped by current concerns in political economy. In particular, many of the questions emphasize population and energy trends. It was these questions that students found most difficult to answer correctly. Therefore, it is no surprise that students in the social sciences fared better than students in the humanities. Literary knowledge was not counted as an aspect of knowledge of international affairs. Of all the humanities disciplines, history and religion received the most attention. The selection of religion is related to the fact that religious conflict is an important factor leading to war and to international confrontation. History, an indispensable discipline for acquiring knowledge of international affairs, achieves this status in great part because it provides a record of past conflicts and treaties.

The conclusions that can be drawn from the survey, therefore, are limited. Among the implications of this educational tool we must include not only the results of the test but also the cultural, political, and economic factors that guided the inclusion or exclusion of survey questions. It is not my task to evaluate the survey as such, but I take it as a point of departure for raising the question of what can be done to enhance students' global awareness in the context of the teaching of philosophy.

On Determining a Sufficient Understanding of World Affairs

The prerequisites for reaching an adequate understanding of world affairs are not easy to determine. The "international reality" in need of investigation is highly complex. From a philosophical standpoint, however, there are two fundamental conditions for understanding global reality that cannot be bypassed, no matter what else we add to the package. These two conditions are the development of critical thinking and of ethical awareness. Without critical thinking, we simply absorb whatever information or values we are given, with few or no questions asked. Without ethical awareness we may be able to gather impressive data, but our understanding of reality will fall short of the full potential attainable by human consciousness.

In claiming the two categories of critical thinking and ethical awareness as essential, I need to press the most sophisticated meaning available into these terms, to place the values and categories posited within the context of a concrete historical and cultural perspective. Thus we must not only posit the notion of ethical awareness, but question the historical and cultural parameters within which the very notion of ethical awareness can acquire meaning for North American philosophers. Similarly, we must not only recognize the desirability of critical thinking but observe its historical and cultural determinations. In using this category I am not referring to some absolute notion but to critical thinking as it is possible to understand it today, given our historical and cultural development as well as the current state of affairs that will either reinforce or challenge our concepts.

Whatever may be the role of other disciplines, then, I suggest that the role of philosophy in developing students' awareness of international events will be mediated in and through our traditional task of enhancing the students' capacity for critical thinking and ethical awareness through the study of philosophy. Apart from these broad mediations there are other, more specific ones, depending on the philosopher's area of specialization and current pedagogical interests. These more particular mediations range from a course in philosophy of culture or economic philosophy to introductory courses in ethics or social theory. As we consider the most specific ways of mediating the methodologies and the particular material to be used in enhancing and broadening the students' awareness of global affairs, we must not lose sight of the two most basic mediations that are properly and specifically related to the nature of our discipline. That is, we are dealing here with a metalevel of instruction as well as with the actual content of each course, where problems related to global awareness may be approached from a wide variety of perspectives.

Paradigms of Global Awareness

Recently the national media have focused attention on how well foreign nations achieve control over their economy, including control over the natural resources of their territories. For example, when a Third World country owes money to U.S. banks, media reports describe the conditions affecting that country's repayment of its foreign debt. The focus of interest in these reports is kept on the repayment of the debt. If problems arise regarding repayment, the responsibility for meeting the terms of the loan is assumed to lie with the debtor country.[4] When these considerations become the focus of attention, other equally important factors are left out of the picture, e.g., the circumstances that make some nations poorer and others wealthier and the responsibilities the more developed nations have toward the less developed. As consumers of the national media, our knowledge of world affairs is shaped by the information made available to us. If some questions do not receive sufficient national attention, our understanding of international affairs undoubtedly remains quite limited.

One basic difficulty with our attitude toward the rest of the world is the implicit belief that our way of life in the United States is superior to any other. A topic receiving national attention, the protection of the environment, is an issue that can easily be used to discredit Third World countries for exhibiting lack of control over their natural resources.[5] If another country faces problems due to overpopulation, one of the first questions that occurs to the U.S. audience is, "Why can't people in overpopulated, underdeveloped countries use contraception?" In contrast, an effort could be made to portray foreign people favorably in terms of their own cultural traditions and survival needs. In other words, our understanding of other cultures is so filtered by the assumptions implicit in our contemporary North American lifestyle that it is almost impossible for a reader of even the most reputable press reports to put herself or himself in the situation of the foreign person whose life is being analyzed. My thesis, then, is that this approach may teach us two or three things about what goes on in other parts of the world, but it fails to break the cultural barrier that keeps us from genuinely understanding the other.

It is difficult to break out of the conceptual frameworks that operate in the national media, which comprise the principal source of information regarding world affairs. The cultural and sociohistorical assumptions implicit in media reports move into the classroom, affecting the presuppositions and attitudes of teacher as well as student. Although reactions may vary in accord with liberal or conservative political opinions and preferences, there is much less disagreement regarding the assumption that our way of life is the best in the world and deserves to be exported to others. This attitude, which forms part of the general set I shall label "ethnocentrism," may be benign, or it may reach a fanatical level. One encounters its more extreme manifestations in the conviction that our way of life ought to be adopted by others whether they like it or not—either because it is in our national interest for this to happen or because it is "good for them, even if they don't know it." Finally, one encounters this attitude in its most irrational form when a student declares with pride and conviction that it would be better for all life on earth to end in the wake of a total nuclear war than for the current lifestyle of this generation of U.S. citizens to have to be modified in any significant way.

There are many forms of ethnocentrism, and I do not mean to suggest that the culture which dominates our everyday existence is the only one guilty of this practice. It may be helpful to offer a more specific account of the particular variety of ethnocentrism that rules our lives as well as the particular dangers it brings with it. I have already mentioned its worst danger—the attitude that this nation is justified in destroying the whole world if things do not fit the "bottom line" of its expectations. According to Freud, this attitude may be analyzed as a specific form of anxiety resulting from knowing that one has acquired an overwhelming amount of control over nature. The last pages of *Civilization and Its Discontents* (1930) offer a sketch of Freud's argument:

Men have gained control over the forces of nature to such an extent that with their help they would have no difficulty in exterminating one another to the last man. They know this, and hence comes a large part of their current unrest, their unhappiness and their mood of anxiety.... The fateful question for the human species seems to me to be whether and to what extent their cultural development will succeed in mastering the disturbance of their communal life by the human instinct of aggression and self-destruction.[6]

If we assent to the hypothesis that we are living under a pervasive belief that our way of life in the U.S (whether we are rich or poor, liberal or conservative) is better than life anywhere else on earth and, moreover, if Freud is correct and we in the advanced industrial and technological world are suffering from a type of anxiety dependent on the degree to which we can control the forces of nature, then the current preoccupation with the subject of how other countries are controlling their natural resources is less puzzling than it appears. Critics charge the U.S. with desiring world dominance: Freud points to the tendency of technological culture to perceive whatever it cannot fully control as a threat or as something "destabilizing." And such destabilization, whether real or imagined, is so deeply feared that some would rather destroy all life than give up the will to have total control over nature.[7]

It is not my goal in this brief essay to construct alternative models to ethnocentrism or alternative theories regarding the relationship of human consciousness to nature. Yet, sketchy as these observations are on the relationship of human consciousness to what it posits as "Other" than itself, they are both relevant and appropriate if our goal is to develop a genuine form of global awareness. The principles of critical thinking and ethical awareness suggest the way whereby one can reach the type of observations and critical remarks I have advanced so far. We need to be aware that the Other, who deserves our respect, sometimes appears before our consciousness in the guise of that much feared "nature," e.g., as a starving third world child, as a peasant woman in need of work or shelter, as the poor, as those whose skin is not white, as those who are the color of the earth. Having made these general remarks, in the remaining part of the essay I will address more specific forms of mediation between the subject matter of philosophy in some of its special fields and the possibility of raising students' awareness of our contemporary international predicament.

Specific Approaches and Options

At the introductory, lower-division level, let me compare two courses I have taught in the last four or five years: Contemporary Moral Issues, and Philosophical Origins II (a sequel to an introduction to ancient and medieval philosophy). At the University of Florida each of these courses counts equally toward graduation requirements in the humanities. The typical student in such a course enrolls in order to fulfill an area requirement. He or she has chosen philosophy from several options in the humanities and probably will not go on to take another philosophy course. The two courses differ in content and orientation. In Contemporary Moral Issues, such topics as world hunger and poverty, nuclear arms control, environmental protection, and the morality of war and peace may be discussed. In contrast, Philosophical Origins II is historically oriented. Its readings are selected from the works of thinkers such as Descartes, Galileo, Locke, Rousseau, Marx, and Nietzsche.

I have no formal data to assess students' comprehension of world affairs in conjunction with their taking these specific courses. But I have found, somewhat unexpectedly, that students enrolled in the historically oriented course have attained a much more solid comprehension of current world events than those enrolled in the course that specifically addresses such events. The historical course does not center on international affairs; it does not propose to involve itself even peripherally in such matters. Yet my experience has shown that if the class is reading Locke or Rousseau, for example, the students arrive at paradigms of political theory that they immediately apply to their contemporary experience, including the analysis of current world affairs. On the other hand, in the course on contemporary moral issues the students develop little or no historical awareness. While they are able to discuss the pros and cons of nuclear disarmament, for example, their understanding of this issue, as of others, tends to shift, depending on the "latest" argument heard.

These remarks are not meant to undermine the validity of the issues-oriented course. Students find these courses valuable. Moreover, I am sure that there are excellent ways of teaching such courses—ways that I have not yet discovered and that other philosophers may be practicing with a great deal of success. As I mentioned earlier, many different mediations may be employed in reaching a specific objective, and I can report only on what has worked best in my experience. Having made these reservations clear, I should add that after a few years of teaching at this southern institution (in enrollment, possibly the largest in the South), I am convinced that unless I begin with history, it is virtually impossible for me to get class discussion to a level where one may set the conditions for understanding today's world. Even more important than any specific historical content is the ability students acquire to take some distance from our cultural preconceptions, without which we remain unable to get to know the "other" who is unlike "us."

The argument for taking the other seriously as someone worthy of respect has been made by Beauvoir with respect to women and by Fanon (among others) with respect to blacks.[8] But it has not yet been made with respect to the *foreign Other*. The best work in this area, to my knowledge, is now being done by Latin American philosophers.[9] This work carries important implications for us. World conflict needs to be averted and nations need to live in peace, or at least strive toward peace. If these goals are to be realized, it is essential to develop the appropriate skills and sensibility not only to know the foreign "Other" (as the Council on Learning advocated) but to refrain from culturally and economically dominating other peoples and nations. Economic domination is a form of cultural domination, as are military domination and the notion that we have a right to impose our way of life on this whole continent, or, if possible, on the whole world. If anything undermines international law and order, it is this attitude. In order to counteract it effectively, it is important not only to engage in a critique of domination, but also of ethnocentrism.

In upper-division philosophy courses, I have consistently made it a point to incorporate a culturally diverse selection of reading materials as long as the subject matter of the course allows it. Thus, in Existentialist Thought, in addition to reading the usual figures—Kierkegaard, Nietzsche, Heidegger, and Sartre—I generally include Frantz Fanon's *Black Skins, White Masks* and Mary Daly's *Beyond God the Father*.[10] Writing assignments cover the possibility of creating a dialogue between writers of different cultural perspectives, on issues of common concern to both. Students will write on Kierkegaard and Daly, or on Sartre and Fanon. The differences among writers are approached not only from an abstract rational standpoint but also by taking into account the cultural and historical situation in which the writers are placed. In more advanced courses, especially at the senior level, I have also focused on criticisms of Western rationality, as in Nietzsche or Foucault, or on criticisms of the manner in which rationality has been applied to structure the relations of production governing our lives, as in Marx or Arendt.[11]

The idea behind these different approaches is to open up dialogue with the repressed, silent, or excluded Other who is such relative to the power that controls the discourse in which she, he, or it is framed. According to Western reason, the Other is unreason (or, alternatively, it is Eastern thought); for the capitalist, the Other is the Marxist; for the North American mind, the Other is the South American mind; for the masculinist philosopher, the feminist philosopher; for the American, the foreigner; for the white, the black; for the rich, the poor; and for the well-situated, the homeless. In all these pairs, in our culture the discourse of the former has overpowered that of the latter. If philosophy is the love of wisdom, then its function cannot be merely to reproduce the discourse and assumptions of the established powers. On the contrary, its function is to penetrate through to the other side and to create favorable conditions for the Other to come forward and express concerns, cares, disquietudes, and aspirations. In this process of recognizing and respecting the oppressed Other, the legitimacy of the Other's discourse must first be established.

This task of legitimation is already well under way in feminist theory and in other liberation-oriented theories, such as critical Marxism, psychoanalysis, and Afro-American philosophy. Each of these fields opens a new vision of reality, and the theoretical perspective of each redefines the terms through which our understanding of reality takes place. To this list we may add a new field—Latin American philosophy—in which there are yet more breakthroughs occurring with respect to the critique of domination. The study of Latin American philosophy represents a challenge (in some contexts directly, in others indirectly) to U.S. hegemony in this hemisphere and, in general, to the superpowers' will-to-power over the so-called Third World. In this context there is much for us to learn from these philosophers who, as Latin Americans, live both near to us in terms of shared philosophical and ethical interests and far from us in terms of their awareness of the hardships and pain suffered by their people due to past and present U.S. foreign policy. It is important for those of us who live in North America to hear their interpretation of the history of philosophy, their theories of ethics and rationality. Otherwise, we remain closed to the reality and actual needs of the other; we remain narcissistically bound to hear only what we are used to hearing, only our own voice.

Conclusion

Whether it is ultimately desirable for philosophers to give priority to international issues and concerns over the others that claim our time and attention, I leave it for the reader to decide. If these issues are addressed, however, then the questions of ethnocentrism and the national will-to-power need to be faced seriously. We have come very far in the progress of knowledge, yet we have not succeeded in guaranteeing the conditions for world survival. International conflict, much of it needless and all of it tragic, cannot be fully resolved unless our behavior toward the foreign Other undergoes radical change.

Notes

[1] See T.S. Barrows, S.T. King, and J.L.D. Clark, *What College Students Know and Believe about Their World* (New Rochelle, N.Y.: Change, 1981). Results of an Educational Testing Service (ETS) survey contracted by the Council on Learning are published in this report.

[2] *What College Students Know*, p. 36.

[3] *What College Students Know*, p. 27.

[4] See the lead story in the August 6, 1984, issue of *Time* (pp. 24ff), "Mexico City: The Population Curse." In this article, cited only as an example of a much broader phenomenon, the reader may find the types of value judgment currently appearing in the media regarding underdeveloped countries.

[5] *Ibid.*

[6] *Civilization and Its Discontents*, tr. and ed. James Strachey (New York: W.W. Norton, 1961), p. 92.

[7] On this topic see two works by Susan Griffin: *Women and Nature* (New York: Harper Colophon, 1978) and *Pornography and Silence: Culture's Revenge against Nature* (New York: Harper Colophon, 1981).

[8] Simone de Beauvoir, *The Second Sex*, tr. H.M. Parshley (New York: Vintage, 1974); Frantz Fanon, *Black Skins, White Masks*, tr. C.L. Markmann (New York: Grove, 1967) and *The Wretched of the Earth*, tr. C. Farrington (New York: Grove, 1963).

[9] Most of this work remains untranslated. On a theme indirectly related to this one and dealing with pedagogical theory the reader may consult Paulo Freire, *Pedagogy of the Oppressed*, tr. M. Bergman Ramos (New York: Seabury, 1970).

[10] Mary Daly, *Beyond God the Father* (Boston: Beacon, 1973).

[11] Among the books I have used by Foucault are *Madness and Civilization* (New York: Vintage, 1973) and Volume I of *The History of Sexuality*, tr. R. Hurley (New York: Vintage, 1980).

Socrates, Meet the Buddha

David A. Hoekema

Several of the other essays in this collection are concerned with the way in which the study of philosophy at American colleges and universities can contribute to students' awareness of global issues and problems. I shall take a different approach: I propose to reflect instead on the ways in which the opportunity to study philosophy in an unfamiliar cultural context can alter students' perceptions of the world and of philosophy itself.

To set the background for discussion, let me describe briefly a teaching experience which brought these issues forcefully to mind. In the fall and winter of the 1980–81 academic year I had the enviable opportunity to serve as Field Supervisor of an overseas study program, the St. Olaf College Term in the Far East. Eighteen students, my family, and I spent four and a half months traveling and studying in Hong Kong, Japan, Taiwan, and Thailand, studying the arts, history, and culture of Asia under the instruction of faculty members at local universities. Together with Susan Bosma Hoekema, who served as Assistant Field Supervisor, I taught a course, "Symbol and Reality," which brought together readings and exercises in philosophy of religion, philosophy of the arts, and cultural anthropology.

The program of study of the Far East Term included a course in Chinese art, taught at Soochow University and at the National Museum in Taipei, Taiwan, by members of the faculty and staff of those institutions. In Chiengmai, Thailand, where we spent three and a half of our five months abroad, three courses were offered to the American students by faculty members at Chiengmai University: an intensive course in spoken Thai, a course on the history and practice of Buddhism, and a survey course in Southeast Asian history.

The course which Susan Hoekema and I taught was designed to complement the other courses offered and to provide occasions for critical reflection on students' experience, both academic and extracurricular, of Asian society

---

David A. Hoekema is Associate Professor of Philosophy at the University of Delaware and Executive Director of the American Philosophical Association.

and culture. Assigned course readings therefore included Western philosophical and anthropological studies of the nature of symbolism (drawn from writers such as Ernst Cassirer, Susanne Langer, and Clifford Geertz) and examples of religious and literary texts that made use of symbolic forms (e.g., the *Tao Te Ching* and classical Buddhist, Christian, and Hindu texts). Our hope was that this course would foster a more critical and inquiring attitude both toward Western philosophy and toward Eastern culture than students might otherwise adopt.

For a variety of reasons that hope was fulfilled only in part. Logistical problems proved far more serious than we had anticipated; library resources in English were meager, and even though "Xerox" has become a familiar common noun in Thai, it was difficult to gain access to a photocopier. Competition for students' time and energy was intense. The example of Thai university students, many of whom regard serious study as a regrettable necessity to be put off until exam week, proved infectious.

All the same, the juxtaposition of the several courses mentioned brought out clearly the distinctive character of Western philosophical teaching, whose emphasis on critical analysis and explicit methodological awareness contrasted sharply with the pedagogical approach of the other courses. The contrast between the philosophy course and the course in Buddhism was particularly marked. The instructor in that course was a highly qualified and respected scholar of Buddhist studies who has traveled widely and has studied in Asia and in the West. Yet the course followed traditional patterns in its emphasis on assimilation rather than analysis. The instructor's goal was to provide both intellectual and experiential knowledge of Buddhism as it is taught and practiced, not to demand a critical assessment of its distinctive features. Such an approach, despite its limitations, is an instructive complement to the pedagogical approach of most Western instruction in philosophy and religious studies.

As a result of their intercultural academic experience, students gained a deeper knowledge of the world in several ways. First, and most obviously, they gained a greater understanding of the history and culture of several regions of Asia through both academic study and group trips to historic sites, with both American and local faculty members serving as guides. At the same time they developed a deeper understanding of their own culture and tradition as they were repeatedly forced not only to notice its many differences from the culture in which they were temporarily immersed but also to explain and defend Western thinking and customs to fellow students and members of Asian host families, with whom they lived for two months.

The emphasis in the course we taught on Western as well as Eastern texts proved helpful in enabling students to relate their experience to more familiar categories. The study of Western religious texts alongside Eastern texts, and the comparisons frequently drawn in class discussions between literary and artistic works from various cultures, proved to be valuable in more ways than we had anticipated, deepening students' awareness of both cultures. Perhaps most important of all, philosophical reflection on the specific topic of the course, symbolism, was enormously enriched by the many experiences which showed us all how little understood are the complex symbolic systems which are the very fabric of a culture. Thai society has been less pervasively influenced by Western values than have some other Asian societies, including those of urban Japan and Taiwan. We were therefore forced to learn—slowly and with many regrettable lapses—to cope with a culture in which a vast range of behaviors and expressions have meanings that differ sharply from their meanings in contemporary Western societies.

It seems hardly necessary to emphasize the last point, and yet the depth of the differences we found in interpersonal behavior surprised us all. Some of the differences in symbolic meaning are relatively obvious and straightforward, such as the Thai strictures on touching another person's head or turning the sole of the foot toward a person or a religious image. More surprising and more perplexing than such customs and rules of social courtesy were the words and gestures that took on unexpected and unwanted meanings in Thai eyes. To live in perpetual uncertainty whether the simplest social action, such as a gesture of irritation or an invitation to a meal, may cause offense or be misinterpreted is a powerful means of opening one's eyes to the diversity of ways in which persons of different cultures relate to each other and to the world in which they live.

If we take the experience I have described as an example of international study in philosophy, what does it suggest about the contribution which such experiences can make to philosophical education? I shall identify three areas in which it can enhance students' philosophical understanding: in their understanding of the self, of political relationships, and of education itself. I do not wish to overstate either the significance of study abroad or its specific relevance to philosophy. Certainly many of the fruits of overseas study can be gained within the borders of one nation, and it would be impractical to insist that a philosophy curriculum without an international component is radically incomplete. Moreover, there are other areas of undergraduate study, including history, anthropology, and the study of languages, in which the relevance of international experiences is more direct than in philosophy. All the same, I believe a persuasive case can be made for the appropriateness of such a program in an undergraduate philosophy curriculum—and for the appropriateness of philosophical topics and materials in an overseas program.

The Self

More than any other contemporary philosopher, Heidegger has treated, as the fundamental topic of philosophical reflection, the nature and status of the self as a concrete individual related to others in complex ways. But Heidegger's reflections on the way in which the self is constituted through the unnoticed and unacknowledged and his insistence that our concept of the world is disclosed less clearly in our moments of Cartesian doubt than in our use of a hammer to pound in a nail may initially seem strained and implausible. Heidegger's relentless emphasis on the concrete can take on a paradoxically abstract air, since the result seems to be to make bewildering complexity out of what is inherently simple.[1]

The experience of living and studying in a culture radically different from one's own persuasively refutes this initial response to Heideggerian reflection. For, whatever judgment one may eventually come to concerning the correctness of Heidegger's own hermeneutic theory, one is forced in a foreign culture to recognize that our concept of ourselves is not an *a priori* universal but is radically dependent on cultural patterns and expectations. The autonomous individual whose perception and whose rights compose the basis of Western epistemology and political philosophy seems to Thai students and scholars not an intuitive given but a puzzling invention, imported in large measure from the West.

To live in an Asian culture is to be reminded many times each day of the divergence between Western and Eastern conceptions of the self and its significance. Many Asian customs, ranging from the elaborate expressions of deference to social superiors to the valuing of politeness over literal truth in responding to direct questions, both puzzle and irritate Western visitors. If we begin asking Heidegger's questions about the nature of the self, we discern the ways in which these customs reflect not simply a different history but an emphasis on the social and communal rather than the autonomous nature of the individual. The experiences of the students who participated in the Far East Term provided many examples of the ways in which the challenge of living and studying in an unfamiliar culture led to a changed and deepened awareness of the dependence on social and cultural influences of understandings of the self.

Political Relationships

Closely linked to divergent conceptions of the self and its significance are sharply different understandings of the relationship between the individual and the state. In a sense, this second topic of philosophical reflection is an expression of the first. Just as the modern Western conception of the state is built on the foundation of seventeenth- and eighteenth-century theories of the individual as epistemologically and morally prior to the community, so the prevailing Asian conceptions of the state are founded on the more communal and hierarchical theories of the individual in society which are drawn from Eastern religious and literary traditions. But the differences are both larger and smaller than this theoretical parting of paths would suggest.

The differences are diminished by the unavoidable and pervasive influence of Western political ideas on societies throughout the world. The ideal of liberal democracy has infected the entire world, and nearly every government pays it lip service at least. The implementation of the ideal, needless to say, varies enormously. In Taiwan a military oligarchy permits a few halting steps toward democracy while a thoroughly Westernized economy flourishes; in Thailand, a nominal democracy has been grafted onto a traditional monarchy, but effective control remains in military hands. Other countries, in Asia and elsewhere, have created other forms. Yet whatever the actual economy of political power, the rhetoric of democracy has a virtually universal appeal. In the language of political ideals, therefore, Western students and other visitors to Asia find a perhaps surprising unanimity.

Yet one is forced almost daily to adapt to the ways in which other societies fail to live up to their ideals—seeing armed soldiers posted at street corners, locking horns with autocratic customs and immigration bureaucrats, and perhaps, with a little stupidity and bad luck, being drawn into the complexities and corruptions of the criminal justice system. Because these failures are different from the failures of Western societies, they, too, both puzzle and anger Western visitors. But what is most surprising on further reflection is not the degree of corruption and abuse of power one finds in other countries but the remarkable equanimity with which citizens of those countries accept policies and practices that outrage the visitor.

In the contrast between the Western visitor's response and the native resident's assessment lies a vital lesson in political philosophy. The differences between the Western student's home and the temporary place of residence are even greater than they first appear: the idea that government must act in accord with officially stated laws and policies and that departure from these policies should be vigorously protested and quickly punished seems to the Taiwanese or Thai citizen a naive delusion of the foreigner. This is not to say that every outrage must be tolerated or that protest is never justified: Thailand's recent history is marked by several major anti-government protests, for example, which were brutally repressed. Nevertheless there is a lively Thai political press, and even in Taiwan, where journalism and political activity are kept on tight reins, there are growing demands for greater democratic control. But not every expression of petty tyranny merits a response of principled protest. It is expected that the customs official will demand something on the side, that the police officer will balance the duties of his office to his duty to friends and superiors, that the magistrate will dispense justice with a dash of tradition and a pinch of greed.

In the eyes of many Asians, it is not realistic to pretend that the language of political ideals can be applied as a universal standard to the conduct of political and economic affairs. This orientation does not make political argument useless or empty or cause ideals to be ignored or despised. (The vehemence with which Thai citizens defend their king against any criticism, while in the next breath deploring the pervasive corruption of the government, surprised us all.) But it means that all argument about the nature of justice or the proper role of the law must be tempered by the knowledge that the real world will always fall far short.

This gap is too little acknowledged in the philosophy and practice of Western politics. Everyone is aware of the imperfections of our society and its governmental structures, and yet we make too little allowance for the slippage between goals and reality in assessing either political platforms or theories of political justice.[2] The experience of studying for an extended period abroad provides a fresh perspective on the importance and the limitations of the language of political ideals.

Education

The first two topics have to do with the content of education, in philosophy or in other areas. Another potential benefit of overseas study is the shift in students' sense of their involvement in their own education as a whole. To engage in disciplined and intensive study in a completely unfamiliar setting, where books are difficult to obtain and new experiences of every kind beckon, demands self-discipline and a clear understanding of one's goals. These cannot be provided by an instructor, and previous patterns and commitments may break down. But even when a student's academic performance suffers from the competition, a clearer understanding of the responsibilities of learning is likely to result.

Difficult as it is to predict or to measure, the heightened sense of responsibility for one's own learning seems to me the most important result of studying philosophy abroad. It arises from more than merely the need to stay home from the bazaar and the student bar to study. Students whose course work demands that they sharpen the skills of critical reading and analysis of Western philosophical texts use those skills to understand more clearly the significance of the culture in which they are temporarily immersed and thereby learn something vitally important about philosophy and about themselves as learners.

To lapse into the passive role of receivers of information is a hindrance to learning of any kind, but in disciplines in which the emphasis falls heavily on the mastery of a body of information, such an attitude can be tolerated. In philosophy—as every teacher of philosophy knows and says in the opening lecture of the introductory course each semester—such an attitude is fatal to genuine learning and insight. Studying philosophy abroad may not always prevent such attitudes, which may be even more prevalent among students in the host country than in the United States. But the study of philosophy in such a setting, given the challenges of the situation and the demands of the discipline, is a powerful educative tool in bringing students to a clearer awareness of their own responsibility to take an active role in their learning.

Notes

1 Martin Heidegger, *Being and Time*, tr. John Macquarrie and Edward Robinson (New York: Harper and Row, 1962), 69–70, 83–84, *et passim.* (Page numbers from the German edition, indicated marginally in the English translation.) Elsewhere I develop somewhat more fully the reading of Heidegger, so briefly invoked here, and credit the secondary sources that have helped me arrive at this understanding. See my "Introduction" to a collaborative volume with Roger Lundin, Anthony Thiselton, and Claire Walhout, *Interpretation, Action, and Responsibility* (Grand Rapids, Mich.: William B. Eerdmans, 1985).

2 In making this assertion I have in mind particularly the institutions of punishment, where the gap is especially troublesome. In a manuscript in progress (*Captive to an Ideal: The Philosophy and the Practice of Punishment*) I try to show the roots of this divergence between ideal and reality, and I contrast contemporary Anglo-American political philosophy, exemplified by John Rawls, with Continental social theory, exemplified by Michel Foucault, and argue that each emphasizes one element too heavily and neglects the other.

A Bibliography:
International Perspectives in the
Undergraduate Curriculum

David Wiley
compiled with the assistance of Solomon Belette,
Susan Drabik, Tesema Ta'a, and Beth Woodard

This bibliography draws from a variety of literatures concerning international, global, comparative, and area studies in undergraduate education at two- and four-year institutions in the United States. While the essays in this volume concern only international perspectives in the academic disciplines at the undergraduate level, the bibliography has a wider reference and includes material concerning student knowledge of world affairs, international issues in undergraduate general studies, curricular needs in international studies, undergraduate international experience (primarily, study at foreign institutions), foreign language studies, and a variety of empirical studies and normative essays.

The bibliography is not exhaustive, but seeks to present the core of literature available in the United States in the mid-1980s concerning the need for and the programs relevant to an increased international perspective in the North American college and university. Most material prior to 1965 is excluded. Those interested to review the older literature of the field should consult: (a) "U.S. Higher Education and World Affairs: A Selected Bibliography," in Education and World Affairs, *The University Looks Abroad*, New York: Walker and Company, 1965; (b) Franklin Parker, "Governmental Policy and International Education: A Selected and Partially Annotated Bibliography," in Stewart Fraser, ed., *Governmental Policy and International Education*, New York: Wiley, 1965; (c) "Higher Education and World Affairs: A Bibliography," in Task Force on International Education, House Committee on Education and Labor, *International Education: Past, Present, Problems and Prospects*, Washington, D.C.: GPO, 1966; (d) "International Education: Bibliography," in Allan A. Michie, ed., *Diversity and Interdependence through International Education*, New

York: Education and World Affairs, 1967; and (e) Frank F. Crabbs and Frank W. Holmquist, *United Staes Higher Education and World Affairs: A Partially Annotated Bibliography*, New York: Praeger, 1967. Also useful for historical perspective on the field are David G. Scanlon, ed., *International Education: A Documentary History*, New York: Teachers College, Columbia University, 1960, and Institute of Research on Overseas Programs, *The International Programs of American Universities*, East Lansing: Michigan State UP, 1958.

We have not sought to include references concerning foreign language instruction, international students in U.S. undergraduate institutions, or study-abroad programs for North American students. A good bibliography on international students and study abroad already may be found by Y. G.-M. Lulat, "International Students and Study Abroad Programs: A Select Bibliography," *Bridges to Knowledge: Foreign Students in Comparative Perspective*, by Elinor G. Barber, Philip G. Altbach, and Robert G. Myers, ed., Chicago: U of Chicago P, 1984. Other bibliographies on educational exchange for North Americans are: *Bibliography on Study, Work and Travel Abroad*, Washington, D.C.: National Association for Foreign Student Affairs, Section on U.S. Study Abroad, 1982; Roger Paget, *International Educational Exchanges: Selected Bibliography of Recent Materials*, Washington, D.C.: USIA, 1980; and Charles S. Spencer and Vivian R. Stahl, *Bibliography of Research on International Exchanges*, USIA, 1983.

A summary of research on this topic supported by the U.S. government may be found in *International Education Resources*, A Summary of Research Projects and Reports Funded by the Office of Education, the National Institute of Education, and the Fund for the Improvement of Postsecondary Education available through ERIC. Cumulative Second Edition, 1956–77. Washington, D.C.: U.S. Department of Education, (Publication E-80-14010), 1980.

Abrams, I. "Interinstitutional Cooperation in International Studies." *Liberal Education*, 54 (1968): 20–29.

Adams, A. Hugh, and Glenda Earwood. *Internationalizing the Community College*. Los Angeles: AACJC, 1983.

Adams, H. "Rationale for International Education." *New Directions for Community Colleges*, 26 (1979): 1–10.

Adriance, Madeleine, and Dallas Blanchard. *Syllabi and Instructional Materials for Sociology of Religion*. Washington, D.C.: American Sociological Association Teaching Resources Center, 1987.

Altbach, Philip G. *Comparative Higher Education*. London: Mansell, 1979.

American Association of Colleges for Teacher Education. *No One Model American: A Statement on Multicultural Education*. Washington, D.C.: AACTE, 1972.

AACTE Commission on Multicultural Education. *Multicultural Teacher Education: Guidelines for Implementation*, 4, Washington, D.C.: AACTE, 1980.

AACTE Handbook of International Education Programs. Washington, D.C.: AACTE, 1963.

American Association of State Colleges and Universities. *A Guide: Planning and Funding International Studies*. Washington, D.C.: AASCU, 1976.

———. *1970 Census of International Programs in State Colleges and Universities*. Washington, D.C.: AASCU, 1971.

———. *To Secure the Blessings of Liberty*. Washington, D.C.: AASCU, 1986.

———. *Without a Nickel: The Challenge of Internationalizing the Curriculum and the Campus*. Washington, D.C.: AASCU, 1984.

American Council on Education. *What We Don't Know Can Hurt Us*. Washington, D.C.: ACE, 1983.

———, International Education Project. *Education for Global Interdependence*. Washington, D.C.: ACE, 1975.

ACE, Task Force on Library and Information Resources. *Library Resources for International Education*. Washington, D.C.: ACE, 1975.

American Psychological Association. *The Undergraduate Psychology Curriculum from an International Perspective: Selected Courses*. Washington, D.C.: APA, 1983.

Anderson, C.A. "Higher Education in Transition: An International Perspective." *Higher Education* 8 (1979): 3–8.

Anderson, J.S., ed. "Education for Global Communication and Understanding," (Symposium). *The Journal of the National Association for Women Deans, Administrators, and Counselors* 41 (1978): 130–68.

Anthony, D.F. "International Education: The Challenge to the Liberal Arts College." *Liberal Education* 53 (1967): 484–96.

Anthropological Curriculum Study Project (ACSP). *History as Culture Change: An Overview: Teaching Plan*. New York: Macmillan, 1968.

Arnold, D.B. *American University in World Affairs*. National Society for the Study of Education, Yearbook 68, pt. 1. Chicago: NSSE, 1969. 135–52.

Armer, J. Michael, ed. *Syllabi and Resources for Internationalizing Courses in Sociology*, for the American Sociological Association Committee on World Sociology. (paper, 194 pp.), Washington, D.C.: ASA Resource Materials for Teaching, 1983 (1722 N Street, NW, Washington, D.C. 20036).

Arnold, Don, R. Morgenroth, and W. Morgenroth. *Business and International Education*. Washington, D.C.: ACE, 1977.

Association of American Colleges. *Integrity in the College Curriculum: A Report to the Academic Community*. Washington, D.C.: AAC, 1985.

———. *Non-Western Studies in the Liberal Arts College*. Harrisburg, Pa.: Evangelical Press, 1964.

———. *Toward Education with a Global Perspective*. Washington, D.C.: AAC, 1980.

Auster, Carol J. *Syllabi and Instructional Materials for Courses in Social Stratification*. Washington, D.C.: ASA Teaching Services Program (hereafter ASA TSP), 1988.

Backman, Earl L. *Internationalizing the Campus: A Strategy for the '80s*. Charlotte: University of North Carolina at Charlotte, *International Studies Notes*, 1983.

———, ed. *Approaches to International Education*. New York: ACE-Macmillan, 1984.

Bailey, Leona G. "Teacher Education for a Changing World." In June K. Phillips, ed., *The Language Connection: From the Classroom to the World.* ACTFL Foreign Language Education Series, 9. Skokie, Ill.: National Textbook, 1977. 179–210.

Bailey, Stephen K. "International Education: An Agenda for Interdependence." *International Affairs* Fall 1975: 3–7.

———. *Higher Education in the World Community.* Washington, D.C.: ACE, 1977.

Ballentine, Jeanne, ed. *Teaching Sociology of Education: Syllabi and Instructional Materials.* Washington, D.C.: ASA TSP, 1984.

Bamford, Peter. "Original Sources in the Classroom." In Martin Ballard, ed. *New Movements in the Study and Teaching of History,* London: Temple Smith, 1970, 205–14.

Burston, W.H. *Principles of History Teaching,* 2d ed. London: Methuen, 1972.

Banks, James A. "The Implications of Multicultural Education for Teacher Education." *Pluralism and the American Teacher,* Washington, D.C.: AACTE, 1977. 1–30.

Bantock, G.H. *Dilemmas of the Curriculum.* New York: Wiley-Halstead, 1980.

Baptiste, H. Prentice, Jr. "Multicultural Education Evolvement at the University of Houston: A Case Study." In Frank H. Klassen and Donna M. Gollnick, ed. *Pluralism and the American Teacher: Issues and Case Studies.* Washington, D.C.: AACTE, 1977. 171–83.

———, Mira L. Baptiste, and Donna M. Gollnick, ed. *Multicultural Teacher Education: Preparing Educators to Provide Educational Equity.* Vol. 1. Washington D.C.: AACTE, 1980.

Barber, Elinor G., and Warren Ilchman. "International Studies Review." New York: Ford Foundation, 1979.

Barrows, Thomas S., ed. *College Students' Knowledge and Beliefs: A Survey of Global Understanding.* New Rochelle, N.Y.: Change, 1981.

———, John L.D. Clark, and Stephen F. Klein. "What Students Know about Their world." *Change,* May–June 1980, 10–17.

Barrows, Thomas S., Stephen F. Klein, and John L.D. Clark, with Nathaniel Hartshorne. *What College Students Know and Believe about Their World.* New Rochelle, N.Y.: Change, 1981; E&WV 5.

Baumann, Cecilia C. "Internationalizing the Student Body: Pomona College's Oldenborg Center." *ADFL Bulletin* 8.2 (1976): 45–59. (Association of Departments of Foreign Languages, 10 Astor Place, New York, NY 10003)

Beals, L. "Experiment in International Education." *Junior Colleges Journal* 40 (1970): 35–37.

Becker, J.M. "Education for Global Understanding: A Realistic Approach." *North Central Association Quarterly* 50 (1976): 338–43.

Bell, B.G. "Intercultural Education in Southern Collegiate General Education." *Peabody Journal of Education* 51.4 (1974): 284–87.

Bennett, W.C. *Area Studies in American Universities.* New York: Social Science Research Council (hereafter SSRC), 1951.

Bereday, George Z.F., and Joseph Lauwerys, ed. *Education and International Life.* New York: Harcourt, Brace and World, 1964.

Berger, Ronald J. *Syllabi and Instructional Materials for Sociology of Law.* Washington, D.C.: ASA TSP, 1985.

Berryman, Sue E., Paul F. Langer, John Pincus, and Richard H. Solomon, *Foreign Language and International Studies Specialists: The Marketplace and National Policy.* Santa Monica, Cal.: Rand, 1979. R-2501-NEH.

Beyer, Barry. *Project Africa.* Pittsburgh, Pa.: U of Pittsburgh, Carnegie-Mellon Institute, 1968.

Bidwell, Percy W. "Foreign Affairs in the Colleges." *Journal of Higher Education* 35 (1964): 426–33.

———. "The World Affairs Content of American Higher Education." Paper delivered at the Education and World Affairs Regional Conference of College and University Leaders, Michigan State U, October 10–11, 1963.

Bigelow, D.N., and L.H. Legters, ed. *The Non-Western World in Higher Education, The Annals of the American Academy of Political and Social Science,* 356 (1964). Special issue.

Black, Robert. "Effective Programs in International Studies: Strategies from the Council on Learning National Survey." In Anne Paolucci, ed. *Problems in National Literacy Identity and the Writer as Social Critic.* Whitestone, N.Y.: Griffin House, 1980, 59–66.

———, and George W. Bonham. "The Council on Learning Project on Undergraduate Education: Education and the World View." *The Annals of the American Academy of Political and Social Science* 449 (1980): 102–13.

———, ed. *Education for a Global Century: Handbook of Exemplary International Programs.* New Rochelle, N.Y.: Change, 1981.

Bohannan, Paul, Edith King, Irving Morrissett, and W. Williams Stevens, Jr. *A Preliminary Review of the Intercultural Dimension in International/Intercultural Education, Grades K-14.* Boulder, Colo.: Social Science Education Consortium, 1973.

Bonham, George W. "Education and the World View." *Change,* May–June 1980, 2–7.

———. "The Future Forsaken." *Change,* October 1978, 12–13.

———. "Language and Global Awareness." *ADFL Bulletin* 10.4 (1979): 5–7.

———. "The New Necessities of National Survival: Education and the World View." *ADFL Bulletin* 11.4 (1980): 34–35.

———. "What Global Knowledge is Enough?" Update 1, Council on Learning, Fall 1979.

Botkin, James W., Mahdi Elmandjra, and Mircea Malitza. *No Limits to Learning: Bridging the Human Gap.* Oxford: Pergamon, 1979.

Boulding, K.E., and Elise Boulding. *Introduction to the Global Society: Interdisciplinary Perspectives.* New York: Consortium for International Studies Education of the International Studies Association, 1974.

Bouwman, C.H. "Integrating the Intercultural Dimension in a New Liberal Arts College: The International Education Program at Eckerd." In M. Williamsen and C. Morehouse, ed., *International/Intercultural Education in the Four-Year College: A Handbook on Strategies for Change.* New York: Foreign Area Materials Center (hereafter FAMC) and Council for Intercultural Studies, 1976.

Boyd-Bowman, Peter. *Self-Instructional Language Programs: A Handbook for Faculty and Students.* Occasional Publication 20, U of the State of New York FAMC and the Council for Intercultural Studies and Programs, July 1973.

Boyer, Ernest L. *College: The Undergraduate Experience in America.* New York: Harper and Row, 1987.

————, and Martin Kaplan. *Educating for Survival.* New Rochelle, N.Y.: Change, 1977.

Boyer, Ernest L., and Fred M. Hechinger. *Higher Learning in the Nation's Service.* Washington, D.C.: Carnegie Foundation for the Advancement of Teaching, 1982.

Boyer, William. "World Order Education: What Is It?." *Phi Delta Kappan* (April 1975): 524–27.

Brademas, J. "Importance of Learning about the Rest of the World." *Chronicle of Higher Education,* April 21, 1982, 48.

Brickman, W.W. "Plan for an International University." *Intellect* 104 (1976): 405.

Brod, Richard I., ed. *Language Study for the 1980s: Reports of the MLA-ACLS Language Task Forces.* New York: Modern Language Association, 1980.

Brumberg, Stephan F. *ICED Data Bank on International Programs of Higher Educational Institutions.* New York: International Council for Educational Development (hereafter ICED), 1972.

Bruner, Karen. *International Education Resources: A Summary of OE-Funded Research Projects and Reports Available through the Educational Research Information Center.* Washington, D.C.: GPO, 1971. Institute of International Studies, U.S. Office of Education.

Bryan, M., and W. Pavord. "Lost and Not Yet Found: International Commitment for Universities." *Intellect* 101 (1973): 377–80.

Buehrig, Edward H. "Implications for the Undergraduate Curriculum of the Growing Importance of International Affairs and the Mounting Need to Understand World Cultures." *1961: Current Issues in Higher Education.* Washington, D.C.: Association for Higher Education, National Education Association (hereafter AHE, NEA), 1961, 14–20.

Buergenthal, T., and J.V. Torney. *International Human Rights and International Education.* Washington, D.C.: U.S. National Commission for UNESCO, 1976.

Burn, Barbara B., ed. *An International Perspective: Higher Education and the Current Crises.* Conference Papers 3. New York: ICED, 1975.

————. *Expanding the International Dimension of Higher Education.* San Francisco: Jossey-Bass, 1980.

————, ed. *Higher Education Reform: Implications for Foreign Students.* New York: Institute of International Education (hereafter IIE), 1978.

————. "International Education in a Troubled World." *The Annals of the American Academy of Political and Social Science* 449 (1980): 17–30.

————. "The Presidents Commission on Foreign Language and International Studies—Its Origin and Work." *Modern Language Journal* 64 (1980): 7–8.

Burns, Robin. *Development Education and Peace Education: From Conflict to Cooperation.* United Nations Development Education Paper 22. UNICEF, 1981.

Business and International Education. A Report Submitted by the Task Force on Business and International Education to the Government-Academic Interface

Committee, International Education Project, American Council on Education. Washington, D.C.: ACE, 1977. Occasional Paper 4.

Business-Higher Education Forum, Northeast-Midwest Congressional Coalition and Congressional Clearinghouse on the Future. *An Action Agenda for American Competitiveness.* September, 1986.

Byrnes, Robert F., ed. *The Non-Western Areas in Undergraduate Education in Indiana.* Indiana U Publications, Slavic and East European Series 15, 1959.

Caldwell, Oliver J. "The Need for Intercultural Education in Our Universities." *Phi Delta Kappan* 52 (1971): 544–45.

———. "Some Comments on Possible Experimental Curricula with Major Emphasis on Non-Western Cultures." In *1964: Current Issues in Higher Education.* Washington, D.C.: AHE, NEA, 1964. 172–76.

Carlson, Catherine Allen. "Foreign Languages: Can U.S. Foundations Help Bridge the Gap?" *Foundation News,* July–August 1980, 8–15, 39–40.

Carpenter, John, and Galo Plaza. *The Intercultural Imperative.* New Delhi: Mohan Makhigani at Rekha Printers (P) Ltd., 1973.

Carpenter, Peter. *History Teaching: The Era Approach.* Cambridge: Cambridge UP, 1964.

Carranza, E. "Model for Intercultural Studies." *Community and Junior Colleges Journal* 49 (1978): 30–32.

Carroll, John B. *The Teaching of French as a Foreign Language in Eight Countries.* New York: Wiley, 1975. International Studies in Evaluation 5.

Cerych, Ladislav. *A Global Approach to Higher Education.* New York: ICED, 1972. Occasional Paper 3.

Charmaz, Kathy, Nan Chico, Adele Clarke, and Sheryl Ruzek. *Syllabi Set for Medical Sociology.* Washington, D.C.: ASA TSP, 1985, 156 pp.

Cleveland, Harlan. "The Internationalization of Domestic Affairs." *The Annals of the American Academy of Political and Social Science,* 442 (1979): 125–37.

Coelho, G.V., ed. "Impact of Studying Abroad." *Journal of Social Issues,* 13 (1962): 55–67.

Cohen, Rosalie. *Teaching Social Change: Course Designs, Syllabi, and Instructional Materials.* Washington, D.C.: ASA TSP, 1988.

Coltham, Jeanette B. *The Development of Thinking and the Learning of History.* London: Historical Association, 1971.

Commager, Henry Steele. *The Nature and the Study of History.* Columbus, Ohio: Merrill, 1965.

———. *Meet the U.S.A.* New York: IIE, 1970.

Commanday, S. "Creative Alternatives in International Education." *International Educational and Cultural Exchange* 11 (1976): 5–9.

Commission on International Understanding. *Non-Western Studies in the Liberal Arts College.* Washington, D.C.: AAC, 1964.

Committee on the College and World Affairs. *The College and World Affairs.* New York: Ford Foundation, 1960.

———, John W. Nason, chairman. *The College and World Affairs.* New York: The Hazen Foundation, 1964.

Conant, James B. *Education in a Divided World.* Cambridge, Mass.: Harvard UP, 1948.

Conner, Maurice W., Madeline A. Cooke, and Constance K. Knop. *A Global Approach to Foreign Language Education.* Skokie, Ill.: National Textbook, 1981.

Coombs, Philip H. *The Fourth Dimension of Foreign Policy: Education and Cultural Affairs.* New York: Harper and Row, 1964.

Correa, J. "Intercultural Interaction and the Worldmindedness of College Students." Diss. U of Washington, 1970.

Cortes, C.E. "Multiethnic and Global Education: Partners for the Eighties?" *Phi Delta Kappan* 64 (1983): 568–17.

Council for Intercultural Studies and Programs. *Intercultural Studies Information Service,* Vol. 1, No. 2. Albany, N.Y.: New York State Education Dept, FAMC, 1972.

Council on Learning. *Education for a Global Century: Handbook of Exemplary International Programs.* New Rochelle, N.Y.: Change, 1981.

———. *Education for a Global Century: Issues and Some Solutions.* New Rochelle, N.Y.: Change, 1981.

———. *Educating for the World View: Global Understanding and the Curriculum.* New Rochelle, N.Y.: Change, 1981.

———. *Education and the World View.* New Rochelle, N.Y.: Change, 1980. E&WV 1.

———. *Recommendations of the Education and World View National Advisory Board on Undergraduate International Education.* New Rochelle, N.Y.: Council on Learning, 1981.

———. *The Role of the Scholarly Disciplines.* New Rochelle, N.Y.: Change, 1980. E&WV 4.

———. *Task Force Statement on Education and the World View.* New Rochelle, N.Y.: Change, 1981.

Cox, Gerry R., and Ronald J. Fundis. *Resources, Instructional Materials, and Syllabi for Courses on the Sociology of Death and Dying.* Washington, D.C.: ASA TSP, 1986.

Crabbs, Richard F., and Frank W. Holmquist. *United States Higher Education and World Affairs.* New York: Praeger, 1967.

Cross-Cultural Education: A Selected Bibliography, 1946–1964. Washington, D.C.: Department of State, 1965.

Davis, J.M. "U.S. Government and International Education—Doomed Program." *Phi Delta Kappan* 51.5 (1970): 235–38.

Davis, Vincent, and Arthur H. Gilbert, ed. *International Relations, An Anthology of Syllabi.* Beverly Hills, Cal.: Sage, 1968.

Deagle, Edwin A. *A Survey of United States Institutions Engaged in International Relations Research and Related Activities: A Preliminary Report.* New York: The Rockefeller Foundation International Relations Division, 1981.

DeBary, William Theodore. "Education for a World Community." *Liberal Education* 50 (1964): 437–57.

Dell, David J. "Readings for a Global Curriculum." *Change,* May–June 1980, 70–76.

Demorsek, Cheryl. "Status and Trends of Foreign Study Programs—1973." *ADFL Bulletin* 4.4 (1973): 33–37.

Deutsch, S. *International Aspects of Higher Education and Exchange: A Community Study*. Cleveland: Western Reserve U, 1965.

Dirks, J. Edward. "Strengthening Foreign Languages in Humanities and in International Studies." *ADFL Bulletin* 8.2 (1976): 26–30.

Duignan, Peter, ed. *Africa South of the Sahara: A Bibliography for Undergraduate Libraries*. 1971. (FAMC Occasional Publication 12).

Dunn, Ross. "Approaches to Teaching World History." In Joe C. Dixon and Neil D. Martin, ed., *1982 World Teaching Conference*. Colorado Springs: United States Air Force Academy, Department of History, 1983, 37–41.

DuVerlie, Claude. "The Disappearance of the Academic Foreign Language Program." *American Foreign Language Teacher* 3.3 (1973): 16–18.

Education and Global Interdependence: A Statement of Policy and Proposed Action by Regents of the University of the State of New York. Albany, N.Y.: State Education Dept, 1976.

Education and World Affairs. *The University Looks Abroad: Approaches to World Affairs at Six American Universities*. New York: Walker, 1965.

Education and the World View. New Rochelle, N.Y.: Change, 1980.

Education for Freedom and World Understanding: Report of Working Committees of Conference on Ideals of American Freedom and International Dimensions of Education, March 26–28, 1962. Washington, D.C.: GPO, 1962.

Education for a Global Century: Handbook of Examplary International Programs. New Rochelle, N.Y.: Change, 1981. E&WV 3.

Education for Global Interdependence: A Report with Recommendations to the Government-Academic Interface Committee. Washington, D.C.: ACE, 1976.

"Education for Responsible Citizenship." *The Report of the National Task Force on Citizenship Education*. N.Y.: McGraw- Hill, 1977.

Educating for the World View. New Rochelle, N.Y.: Change, 1980.

Ehrman, Edith, and Ward Morehouse. *Students, Teachers, and the Third World in the American College Curriculum*. New York: U of the State of New York-State Education Dept, Council for Intercultural Studies and Programs, 1972. FAMC Occasional Publication 19.

Elmandjra, Mahdi. "Learning Needs in a Changing World: The Role of Human Resources in a Civilization of Knowledge." *Futures* 10 (1986): 731 ff.

"Elements of a Network to Educate for World Security." New York: World Policy Institute, 1981.

Erickson, S. "Eisenhower College: Bringing the World to Seneca Falls." *College and University Business*, 52 (1972): 52–54.

Etis, Jennifer, and Don Ward. *Taking Off: An Organizatioal Handbook and Comprehensive World-Wide Resource Guide for Non-Traditional Higher Education*. East Lansing, Mich.: Center for Alternatives in/to Higher Education, 1975.

Everton, J.S. "Sources of Support for International Education." *AACTE Yearbook* 18 (1965): 162–68.

Fagel, B.R. *Design for Change: Higher Education in the Service of Developing Countries*. New York: ICED, 1977.

Falk, Richard, and Samuel S. Kim. "An Approach to World Order Studies and the World System." New York: World Policy Institute, 1982. Working Paper 22.

Farmer, R. "Global Education, Self-actualization, and World Citizenship." *College Studies Journal* 14 (1980): 209–14.

Fersh, Seymour. "Community College and the World Community." *Community College Frontiers* 9 (1981): 4–10.

———. "Worldwide Dimensions Enrich Community-Based Education." *Community and Junior Colleges Journal* 49 (1979): 14–19.

———, and Edward Fitchen, ed. *The Community College and International Education: A Report of Progress.* Cocoa, Fla.: Brevard Comm Coll, 1981.

Fiske, Edward B. "Times Test of College Freshmen Shows Knowledge of American History Limited." *New York Times*, May 2, 1976, 1.

Fitzgerald, James. "History in the Curriculum: Debate on Aims and Values." *History and Theory* 22.4 (1983): 81–100.

"Food First College Curriculum Guide." San Francisco, Cal.: Institute for Food and Development Policy, 1984.

Ford Foundation. "The University and World Affairs." New York: Ford Foundation, 1961.

Foreign Office. *Report of the Interdepartmental Commission of Enquiry on Oriental, Slavonic, East European and African Studies.* London: HMSO, 1947.

Forester, K. "Pragmatic Program in General Education; The Penn State Course in International Understanding." *The Journal of Higher Education* 34 (1963): 371–78.

Fox-Genovese, Elizabeth. "The Crisis of our Culture and the Teaching of History." *The History Teacher* 13 (1979): 89–101.

Freire, Paulo. *Education for Critical Consciousness.* New York: Seabury, 1973.

Fulbright, J. William. "International Education: Focus for Corporate Support." *Harvard Business Review* 55.3: 137–41.

Furr, Leroy A., Carla B. Howery, Corinne A. Bordieri, and Edward Kain, ed. *Marriage and the Family Courses: Print and Visual Resources.* Washington, D.C.: ASA TSP, 1986.

Friesen, J.W. "Intercultural Education Its Ground, Emphases, and Challenge." *Journal of Teacher Education* 23.2 (1972): 177–82.

Gambino, Richard. *A Guide to Ethnic Studies Programs in American Colleges, Universities and Schools.* New York: Working Papers, Rockefeller Foundation, 1975.

Gay, Geneva. "Curriculum for Multicultural Teacher Education." In Frank H. Klassen and Donna M. Gollnick, ed. *Pluralism and the American Teacher: Issues and Case Studies.* Washington, D.C.: AACTE, 1977, 31–62.

Geno, Thomas H., ed. *Foreign Language and International Studies: Toward Cooperation and Integration.* Report of the Northeast Conference on the Teaching of Foreign Languages. Middlebury, Vt.: NEC, 1981.

Gillin, Donald, ed. *East Asia: A Bibliography for Undergraduate Libraries.* FAMC Occasional Publication 10. Available from Bro-Dart, Inc., 1609 Memorial Avenue, Williamsport, Pennsylvania, 17701.

Global Perspectives in Education. *Internationalizing Undergraduate Education: Resources from the Field.* New York: GPE, 1986. (Available through American Forum, 45 John St., New York, NY 10038).

Gold, Milton J., et al., ed. *In Praise of Diversity: A Resource Book for Multicultural Education.* Washington, D.C.: Teacher Corps, 1977.

Goldsen, R.K., E.A. Schuman, and R.M. Williams. "Factors Associated with the Development of Cross-Cultural Social Interaction." *Journal of Social Issues* 12.1 (1956): 26–33.

Gollnick, Donna M., Frank H. Klassen, and Joost Yff. *Multicultural Education and Ethnic Studies in the United States: An Analysis and Annotated Bibliography of Selected ERIC Documents.* Washington, D.C.: AACTE, 1976.

Goodwin, Geoffrey L. *The University Teaching of Internaitonal Relations.* Oxford, England: Blackwell, 1951.

Gottschalk, Louis. "A Professor of History in a Quandry." *American Historical Review* 59 (1954): 273–86.

Goulet, Dennis. *World Interdependence: Verbal Smokescreen or New Ethic?* Development Paper 21. Washington, D.C.: Overseas Development Council, 1976.

Grant, S.R. "Internationalizing the College Curriculum." *New Directions for Community Colleges* 26 (1979): 19–29.

Gray, Audrey Ward. *International/Intercultural Education in Selected State Colleges and Universities: An Overview and Five Cases.* Washington, D.C.: AASCU, 1977.

Great Lakes Colleges Association. "Great Lakes Colleges Association Non-Western Program, 1964-67," Final Report to the Ford Foundation, 1967.

Greene, Maxine. *Teacher as a Stranger: Educational Philosophy for the Modern Age.* Belmont, Cal.: Wadsworth, 1983.

———. *Landscapes of Learning.* New York: Teachers CollP, 1978.

Griffin, Willis H. "International Education—American Experience." *College and University* 54.3 (1979): 252–54.

———. "International Educational Cooperation and the World's Future." *Topics in Cultural Learning.* Honolulu: East West Center, East West Cultural Learning Institute, 1975, 3.

Grimshaw, Allen D. *Syllabi and Instructional Materials for World Conflicts.* Washington, D.C.: ASA TSP, 1988.

———. *Teaching War as a Social Problem: A Report on SOC 101 at Indiana University.* Washington, D.C.: ASA TSP, 1984.

Groennings, Sven. "The American Democracy in the Global Community: Federal and University Roles in the International Education Trend." In William C. Olson and Llewellyn D. Howell, ed. *International Education: The Unfinished Agenda.* Indianapolis: White River Press, 1984. 68–88.

———. "Beachheads in International Education." *ADFL Bulletin* 14.3(1983): 1–9.

———. "The Challenge of the Successor Generation: Implications for the Atlantic Alliance and Civic Education." *Atlantic Community Quarterly* (1984): 252–58.

———. *Economic Competitiveness and International Knowledge.* Boston: New England Board of Higher Education, 1987.

———. *The Impact of Economic Globalization on Higher Education.* Boston: New England Board of Higher Education, 1987.

———. "Public Policy and National Imperatives." In Cameron Fincher, ed. *Planning Imperatives for the 1990s*. Athens, Ga.: U of Georgia, 1989, 1–14.

Gumperz, Ellen McDonald. *Internationalizing American Higher Education: Innovation and Structural Change*. Berkeley: Center for Research and Development in Higher Education, U of California, 1970.

Gunning, Dennis. *The Teaching of History*. London: Croom Helm, 1978.

Haavelsrud, Magnus. *Approaching Disarmament Education*. Woburn, Mass.: Butterworth, 1981.

Haenicke, Diether H. "Foreign Language Study in International Education." *ADFL Bulletin* 8.2 (1976): 11–15.

Hall, Robert B. *Area Studies: With Special Reference to Their Implications for Research in the Social Sciences*. New York: SSRC, 1947. Pamphlet 3.

Hamilton, D.F. "New Perspective on International Studies." *College and University* 43 (1968): 401–12.

Hancock, Charles R., et al. *Minimal List of Competencies for Foreign Language Teachers: Suggested Guidelines for Teacher Education Programs* Rev. Ed. Schenectady, N.Y.: The Language Association Bulletin, 1978.

———. "Modest Proposals for Second and Foreign Language Teacher Education in the 1980s." In June K. Phillips, ed. *Action for the '80s: A Political, Professional and Public Program for Foreign Language Education*. Skokie, Ill.: National Textbook, 1981, 179–94.

Hanke, Lewis. *Truth in History*. Cambridge, Mass.: Belknap, 1975.

Harari, Maurice. *Global Dimensions in U.S. Education: The University*. New York: Center for War-Peace Studies, New York Friends Group, 1972.

———. *Internationalizing the Curriculum and the Campus: Guidelines for AASCU Institutions*. Washington, D.C.: AASCU, 1981.

Harcleroad, Fred F., and Alfred Kilmartin. *International Education in the Developing State Colleges and Universities*. Washington, D.C.: AASCU, 1966.

Harrington, F.H., director. *International Linkages in Higher Education: A Feasibility Study*. Preliminary report. Washington, D.C.: International Linkages in Higher Education, February 1978.

Harris, Diana K., Erdman B. Palmore, and Sandra C. Stanley, ed. *Teaching Sociology of Aging*. Washington, D.C.: ASA TSP, 1986.

Hartje, Robert. "New Thoughts on Freshman History. *The History Teacher* 4 (1971): 40–47.

Hartman, Harriet, ed. *Teaching Demography: Syllabi and Instructional Materials*. Washington, D.C.: ASA TSP, 1984.

Haviland, H. Field, Jr. "Federal Programs of International Education." In Charles G. Dobbins, ed. *Higher Education and the Federal Government*. Washington, D.C.: ACE, 1963, 76–88.

Hawkins, J.N., and J.A. Takata. "Tenri University: A Religious Approach to International Education." *Peabody Journal of Education* 49 (1972): 300–06.

Hayden, Rose L. *A Rationale for International Education: Facing Facts*. Washington, D.C.: ACE, International Education Project, n.d. (mimeo.)

———. *Education for Global Interdependence*. A Report from the International Education Project. Washington, D.C.: ACE, 1975.

———. "Funding International Education Programs: An Unmet Agenda." Statement before the Senate Appropriation Subcommittee on Labor, HEW, September 21, 1977.

———. "In the National Interest: International Education and Language Policy." *ADFL Bulletin*, 6.3 (1975): 11–18.

———. "The World and Us." *AGB Reports* March–April 1979: 3–7.

———. "The World and You: Global Education Is the Answer." Washington, D.C.: Town Affiliation Association of the US, 1979. International Brief Series 6.

———. "U.S. Government Exchanges: The Quest for Coordination." *The Annals of the American Academy of Political and Social Science* 449 (1980): 114–28.

Hayden, Samuel L. "Foreign Languages, International Studies and Business (A Dubious Savior)." *The Annals of the American Academy of Political and Social Science* 449 (1980): 141–50.

———, and Leslie W. Koepplin. "International Business and International Studies: Prospects and Mutual Benefit." In Thomas M. Stauffer, ed. *Agenda for Business and Higher Education*. Washington, D.C.: ACE, 1980. 177–94.

Herbst, Jurgen. "Theoretical Work in History in American University Curricula." *History and Theory* 7.3 (1968): 336–54.

Hill, A. David. "A Survey of the Global Understanding of American College Students: A Report to Geographers." *The Professional Geographer* 33.2 (1981): 237–45.

Hill, James W. "A Series of Exchanges." *Change*, May–June 1980, 53–54.

Hill, W.M. "We Should Do More in International Education." *Junior College Journal* 38 (1967): 15–19.

———. "What One Small College Can Do." *Junior College Journal* 39 (1969): 17–18.

Hilliard, A. "Cultural Pluralism: The Domestic International Connection." Paper presented at the AACTE Conference, Fort Lauderdale, Fla., 1975.

Hodges, Luther H., Jr. "On Commerce and Language Study." *ADFL Bulletin* 11.4 (1980): 36–37.

Hodgson, Marshall. "A Non-Western Civilization Course in a Liberal Education with Special Attention to the Case of Islam." *Journal of General Education* 12 (1959): 39–49.

Hoiberg, Eric O., ed. *Teaching Rural Sociology: A Resource Manual*. Washington, D.C.: ASA TSP, 1987.

Holland, K. "Half-Century of the Institute of International Education: Only a Beginning." *School and Society* 98 (1970): 426–29.

Hood, Jane, C., and David Booth, ed. *Teaching the Sociology of Work and Occupations: Syllabi, Course Materials, and Bibliographies*. Washington, D.C.: ASA TSP, 1985.

Hoopes, David S., ed. *Readings in Intercultural Communication*. Vol. 2, Selected Course Syllabi in Intercultural Communication. Pittsburgh: Intercultural Press and Society for Education, Training and Research, 1977.

———, et al. *A Study of the Dynamics of the Interinstitutional Cooperation for International Education Development*. Pittsburgh: Regional Council for International Education, 1971.

Howard, Harry N., ed. *Middle East and North Africa: A Bibliography for Undergraduate Libraries*. New York: FAMC, 1970.

Hull, Frank W., W.H. Lemke, Jr., and R. Ting-ku Houang. *The American Undergraduate, Off-Campus and Overseas: A Study of the Educational Value of Such Programs*. Santa Barbara: U of California P, January 1977.

Hull, Frank W.; Walter H. Lemke, Jr., and Richard T. Houang, *Students in Sojourn: An Intensive Interview Study of American Undergraduates on Off-Campus Study Programs in the United States and Overseas*. Washington, D.C.: National Association for Foreign Student Affairs, 1976.

Humphrey, R.A. *Higher Education for World Realities*. National Society for the Study of Education Yearbook, Part 1, 68. Chicago: NSSE, 1969, 298–317.

Hunkins, Ralph H. *Education for International Understanding: A Critical Appraisal of the Literature*. Bloomington: Indiana U, 1968.

Hunter, William A., ed. *Multicultural Education through Competency-Based Teacher Education*. Washington, D.C.: AACTE, 1974.

Hurewitz, J.C. "Undergraduate Foreign Area Studies: The Case of the Middle East." *ACLS Newsletter* 15 (April 1964): 1–15.

Institute of Advanced Projects, East-West Center, Honolulu, Hawaii, with International Programs, Michigan State U. *The International Programs of American Universities: An Inventory and Analysis*. East Lansing: Michigan State U, 1966.

Institute of International Studies, U.S. Office of Education. *Foreign Curriculum Consultant Program for American Schools, Colleges and State Departments of Education*. Washington, D.C.: GPO, 1975.

―――. *Foreign Language, Area Studies, and Other Aspects of International Education, Completed Research and Instructional Materials Produced under the National Defense Education Act of 1958, Title VI, Section 602*. Compiled by Julia A. Petrov. Washington, D.C.: GPO, 1972.

"International Education: Cornerstone of Competition." Southern Governors' Association, 444 North Capitol Street, NW, Washington, D.C.

"International Education: An Agenda for Interdependence." *International Affairs* Fall 1975: 3–7.

"International Education and the U.S. Community College." *ERIC Junior College Resource Review*. Los Angeles: 1983.

International Education Project. *Education for Global Interdependence: A Report with Recommendations to the Government-Academic Interface Committee*. Washington, D.C.: ACE, 1975.

―――. *The International Role of the University in the 1970s*. U of Massachusetts at Amherst, May 1973.

Jacob, Louis A. ed. *South Asia: A Bibliography for Undergraduate Libraries*. New York: FAMC, 1970. Occasional Publication 11.

Jacobson, R.F. "Community Colleges Seek a Global Perspective." *Chronicle of Higher Education* November 28, 1977: 5–6.

Jain, Nemi, and Richard L. Cummings, ed. *Proceedings of the Conference on Intercultural Communication and Teacher Education*. Milwaukee: Milwaukee Urban Observatory, U of Wisconsin, Milwaukee, 1975.

Johnson, Donald Clay, ed. *Southeast Asia: A Bibliography for Undergraduate Libraries.* New York: FAMC, 1970. Occasional Publication 13.

Johnson, Dora, et al. *A Survey of Materials for the Study of the Uncommonly Taught Languages.* Arlington, Va.: Center for Applied Linguistics, 1976–77. ED 130 537, 132 883–85, 132 860.

Julianus, Sister Mary. "Humanities and the Appreciation of Cultures." *Improving College and University Teaching* 11 (1963): 164–66.

Kelleher, A.C. "A Report on the Status of International Studies Curricula in Massachusetts Community Colleges." Private study commissioned for B.B. Burn, August 1977.

Kenworthy, Leonard S. *The International Dimension of Education.* Washington, D.C.: Association for Supervision and Curriculum Development, 1970. Background Paper 2.

———. *World Horizons for Teachers.* New York: Teachers CollP, 1952.

Kerr, Clark. "Education for Global Perspectives." *The Annals of the American Academy of Political and Social Science* 442 (1979): 109–16.

———. "Introduction: Global Education Concerns of Higher Education for the 1980s and Beyond." In Barbara B. Burn, ed. *Expanding the International Dimension of Higher Education,* San Francisco: Jossey-Bass, 1980, 17–39.

King, M.C., and S.C. Hersh. "General Education through International-Intercultural Dimensions." *New Directions for Community Colleges* 40 (1982): 49–57.

Kirk, Grayson. *The Study of International Relations in American Colleges and Universities.* New York: Council on Foreign Relations, 1947.

Kirk, R. "International Education." *Journal of General Education* 28.4 (1977): 339–42.

Klassen, Frank H., and Donna M. Gollnick, ed. *Pluralism and the American Teacher.* Washington, D.C.: Ethnic Heritage Center for Teacher Education, AACTE, 1977.

Klassen, Frank H., David G. Imig, and Joost Yff. *The International Dimension of American Teacher Education: A Survey of International Education Programs of American Colleges and Universities.* Washington, D.C.: AACTE, 1972.

Klassen, Frank H., and Howard B. Leavitt, ed. *International Perspectives of Teacher Education: Innovations and Trends.* Washington, D.C.: International Council on Education for Teaching, 1976.

———. *Teacher Education and Global Perpectives.* Washington, D.C.: ERIC Clearinghouse on Teacher Education, AACTE, 1982.

Klayman, N.E. "Views on the Foreign Language Requirement in Higher Education." *Modern Language Journal* 62 (1978): 235–38.

Kleinbaum, Abby Wettan. "Women's History and the Western Civilization Survey." *The History Teacher* 12 (1979): 501–06.

Klitgaard, Robert E. "On Reviewing International Studies." *Journal of Higher Education* 52 (1975): 124–42.

———. "Why International Studies? A Prologue." *Change,* January–February 1981, 28–34.

Knudsen, R.G. "A Fault-Free Approach to an International Education Program: California State University and Colleges." Diss. abstract, U of Southern California, 1977.

Koenigsberg, Marvin David, ed. *Teaching Community and Urban Sociology: Syllabi and Materials from Undergraduate Courses.* Washington, D.C.: ASA TSP, 1981.

Koo, M. "American Students' Contact with and Attitudes toward Foreign Students." Diss., Michigan State U, 1962. *DAI,* 23/12, 4605.

Kühne, Robert J., and Gerda P. Jordan. "Integrating International Business and Language Training." *ADFL Bulletin* 2.3 (1980): 27–30.

Lambert, Richard D. *Beyond Growth: The Next Stage in Language and Area Studies.* Washington, D.C.: AAU, 1984.

———. "International Studies: An Overview and Agenda." *The Annals of the American Academy of Political and Social Science* 449 (1980): 151–64.

———. *Language and Area Studies Review,* Philadelphia: American Academy of Political and Social Sciences, 1973. Monograph 17.

———, ed. *New Directions in International Education, The Annals of the American Academy of Political and Social Science.* Special issue. 449 (1980).

———. *Points of Leverage: An Agenda for a National Foundation for International Studies.* New York: Social Science Research Council, 1986.

Lamy, S.L. "Teacher Training in Global Perspectives Education: The Center for Teaching International Relations." *Theory into Practice* 21 (1982): 206–11.

Lavizzo-Mourey, Robert J., ed. *Syllabi and Instructional Materials for Courses on Deviance and Social Control.* Washington, D.C.: ASA TSP, 1985.

Leach, Robert J. *International Schools and Their Role in the Field of International Education.* Oxford: Pergamon, 1969.

Lee, P.J. "History Teaching and the Philosophy of History." *History and Theory* 22.4 (1983): 19–49.

Leestma, Robert. "The International Role of the University in the 1970s." Address, U of Massachusetts at Amherst, May 1973.

Legters, Lyman. *Language and Area Studies: A Bibliography.* New York: FAMC, 1967.

Leinwand, Gerald. *Without a Nickel: The Challenge of Internationalizing the Curriculum and the Campus.* Washington, D.C.: AASCU, 1983.

Levine, Arthur. *Handbook on Undergraduate Curriculum.* San Francisco: Jossey-Bass, 1978.

Levine, Arthur, and John Weingart. *Reform of Undergraduate Education.* San Francisco: Jossey-Bass, 1974.

Library Resources for International Education. Washington D.C.: ACE, 1975.

Lineweber, David, ed. *Social Stratification Courses: A Set of Syllabi and Instructional Materials.* Washington, D.C.: ASA TSP, 1983.

Link, P. "College-Wide Effort in World-Wide Study." *New York State Education* 49(December 1961): 12–13.

Lockard, Craig A. "Global History, Modernization and the World-System Approach: A Critique. *The History Teacher* 14 (1981): 489–515.

Lonsdale, R.C. "Curriculum for Man in an International World, Contributions to 1970 International Education Year Conference." *Journal of Educational Administration* 10.2 (1972): 224–26.

Long, Harold, and Robert N. King. "Improving the Teaching of World Affairs: The Glen Falls Story." Washington, D.C.: National Council for the Social Studies, 1964.

Lopez, George A. *Dependence and Interdependence in the International System.* Columbus: Consortium for International Studies Education, Ohio State U, 1979.

———. "The Community College Contribution." *Change,* May–June 1980, 55–56.

Maisonrouge, Jacques. "Some Education Requirements for the Manager of the Eighties." IBM World Trade Corp., 1982.

Marquardt, William F. *Sociolinguistic Model for Selecting Literary Texts for Teaching Cross-Cultural Communication.* Mimeo. Hays, Kans.: Fort Hays State Coll, 1973.

Marshall, Robert A., ed. *Can Man Transcend His Culture? The Next Challenge in Education for Global Understanding.* Washington, D.C.: AASCU, 1973.

Martoran, S.V. "International Education, the College, and the Community—Framework for Action." *New Directions for Community Colleges* 26 (1979): 11–18.

Martorella, Rosanne. *Syllabi and Instructional Materials for Sociology of Culture.* Washington, D.C.: ASA TSP, 1988.

Marvel, William W. "The University in World Affairs: An Introduction." *The University Looks Abroad: Approaches to World Affairs at Six American Universities.* New York: Walker, 1966, xi-xx.

Massey, E.T., and J.A. Massey. *CULCON Report on Japanese Studies at Colleges and Universities in the United States in the Mid-'70s.* Study prepared for the Subcommittee on Japanese Studies, American Panel, U.S.-Japan Conference on Cultural and Educational Interchange. New York: Japan Society, 1977.

Mazon, M. Reyes. *Community, Home, Cultural Awareness and Language Training: A Design for Teacher Training in Multicultural Education.* San Diego, Cal.: Institute for Cultural Pluralism, San Diego State U, 1975.

McCaughey, Robert A. *International Studies and Academic Enterprise: A Chapter in the Enclosure of American Learning.* New York: Columbia UP, 1984.

———. "International Studies and General Education: The Alliance Yet to Be." *Liberal Education* (1984): 343–74.

———. "Current State of International Studies in American Universities: Special Consideration Reconsidered." *Journal of Higher Education* 51 (1980): 381–99.

———. "The Permanent Revolution: An Assessment of the Current State of International Studies in American Universities." A Report to the International Division of the Ford Foundation, 1979.

McClelland, Charles A. *College Teaching of International Relations.* San Francisco: San Francisco State Coll, 1962.

McGann, Mary. "International Education: It's Not Cultural Imperialism." *The Chronicle of Higher Education,* July 20, 1983. 48.

McNeil, William H. "Beyond Western Civilization: Rebuilding the Survey." *The History Teacher* 10 (1977): 509–48.

Mebrahtu, T. "Universities and the Challenge of a New International Economic Order." *International Review of Education* 28.4 (1982): 482–85.

Mehl, Bernard. "Academic Colonialism—A New Look." *Educational Leadership* 27 (1969): 243–46.

Melby, John F., ed. *The Rising Demand for International Education, The Annals of the American Academy of Political and Social Science* 335 (1961). Special issue.

Mertineit, Walter. "Strategies, Concepts and Methods of International History Textbook Revision: A German Share in Education for International Understanding". *International Journal of Political Education* 1979. 101–14.

Mestenhauser, Josef A. *Learning with Foreign Students*. Minneapolis: North Central Publishing, 1976.

———, and Dietmar Barsig. "Foreign Students as Teachers: Learning with Foreign Students." Washington, D.C.: National Association for Foreign Student Affairs, 1978. Pub. P00478.

Michie, Allan A. *Higher Education and World Affairs*. New York: EWA, 1968.

Miller, Paul A. "The Role of the University in Developing World Community." Speech delivered at the American Sociological Association, Chicago, Ill., September 2, 1965.

Mills College. *A Proposal for the Further Development of Non-Western Emphases and Perspectives in the Educational Program of Mills College*. Oakland, Cal.: The College, 1961.

Mingst, Karen. "The Political Economy of International Commodity Trade." New York: Consortium for International Studies Education, International Studies Assocation, 1976. Learning Resources in International Studies 22.

Moore, F.G. "International Education in the Seventies: Revolution or Turmoil on the Campus." *International Educational and Cultural Exchange* 6 (1970): 34–47.

Morehouse, Ward. "Adding a New Dimension to Liberal Education." *Liberal Education* 46 (1960): 380–87.

———. "Asian Studies in Undergraduate Education." *Journal of General Education* 11 (July 1958): 125-40.

———. *The International Dimensions of Education in New York State*. Albany: U of the State of New York, 1963.

———, ed. *Foreign Area Studies and the College Library*. New York: FAMC, 1964. Occasional Publication 1.

———. "What Should Be the Role of Area Programs in the '60's?" *1960: Current Issues in Higher Education*. Washington, D.C.: AHE, NEA, 1960: 190–93.

———, ed. *Asian Studies in Liberal Arts Colleges*. Washington, D.C.: AAC, 1961.

———, ed. *Asian Studies in Undergraduate and Teacher Education*. New York: Conference on Asian Affairs, 1955.

———, ed. *The Comparative Approach to Area Studies and the Disciplines: Problems of Teaching and Research on Asia*. New York: FAMC, 1967.

———, ed. *Foreign Area Studies and the College Library*. New York: FAMC, U of the State of New York, State Education Dept, Occasional Paper 1, 1965.

Morgenthau, Hans. "Area Studies and the Study of International Relations." *International Social Science Bulletin* 4 (1952): 647–55.

Morse, Richard M. "The Challenge for Foreign Area Studies." *The Educational Record* (1966): 234–43. Special supplement on the Princeton University Conference on Foreign Language and Area Studies in the United States: A Guide for High School and College Programs, December 17–18, 1965.

Müller, Kurt E. *Language Competence: Implications for National Security.* New York: Praeger, 1986. Georgetown U Center for Strategic and International Studies. The Washington Papers 119.

———. "On the Military Significance of Language Competence." *Modern Language Journal* 65.4 (1981): 361–70.

———. "A Transatlantic Perspective on Language and International Studies: Collaborators or Competitors." In Karl Koch, ed. *Area Studies and Language Teaching.* Guildford: U of Surrey and Centre for Information on Language Teaching and Research, 1988, 1–12.

Muller, Robert. *The Need for Global Education.* Philadelphia: Global Interdependence Center, 1976.

Muller, Steven. "A New American University?" *Daedalus* 107.1 (1978): 31–46.

Mundt, J.C. "Community College State Boards and International Education." *New Directions for Community Colleges* 26 (1979): 89–100.

Munski, D.C. "Geography Academic Advisors as Foreign language and Area Studies Advocates." *Professional Geographer* 36 (1984): 462–63.

Murray, Andrew M. *Peace and Conflict Studies as Applied Liberal Arts: A Theoretical Framework for Curriculum Development.* Huntington, Pa.: Juniata Coll, 1980.

Myer, Richard B. *Curriculum: U.S. Capacities, Developing Countries' Needs.* Washington, D.C.: IIE, 1979; A Report from the 1979 Conference on International Education: The Global Context, the U.S. Role.

Myers, R.G. "International Education and Exchange—Sociological Analysis." *American Journal of Sociology* 77.4 (1972): 800–04.

Nathan, J.A. "International Education and International Relations—Values and Implications of Contending Approaches." *Teaching Political Science* 3.2 (1976): 115–39.

A Nation Prepared: Teachers for the 21st Century. Report to the Task Force on Teaching as a Profession, supported by the Carnegie Forum on Education and Economy, 1986.

National Advisory Board on International Education Programs. *Critical Needs in International Education: Recommendations for Action.* Washington, D.C.: GPO, 1983.

National Association of State Universities and Land Grant Colleges. *Basic Principles for College and University Involvement in International Development Activities.* Washington, D.C.: NASULGC, 1983.

National Commission on Excellence in Education. *A Nation at Risk: The Imperative for Educational Reform.* Washington D.C.: GPO, 1983.

National Institute of Education Study Group on the Conditions of Excellence in American Higher Education. *Involvement in Learning: Realizing the Potential of American Higher Education.* Washington, D.C.: NIE, 1984.

Nehrt, Lee C., ed. *Business and International Education.* Report submitted to the Government-Academic Interface Committee, International Education Project. Occasional Paper 4. Washington, D.C.: ACE, May 1977.

———. *Case Studies of the Internationalization of the Business School Curriculum.* St. Louis: American Assembly of Collegiate Schools of Business, 1981.

Nelson, D.T. "The Impact of Foreign Undergraduate Students Upon American Undergraduate Students." Diss., Indiana U, 1966. *DAI*, 27/07, 2010.

New Jersey and the World College Learning Modules. Montclair, N.J.: Global Learning, 1987.

New York State Department of Education. *The International Dimensions of Education in New York State*. Albany, N.Y.: State Education Dept, 1963.

Newell, Barbara W. "Education with a World Perspective: A Necessity for America's Political and Economic Defense." *Annals of the American Academy of Political and Social Sciences*. 491 (1987): 134 ff.

Nostrand, Howard L. "Describing and Teaching the Sociocultural Context of a Foreign Language and Literature." In Albert Valdman, ed., *Trends in Language Teaching*. New York: McGraw-Hill, 1966, 1–25.

———, and Francis J. Brown, ed. *The Role of Colleges and Universities in International Understanding*. Washington, D.C.: ACE, 1949.

"Nuclear War Education Features." Nine articles in *Journal of College Science Teaching* (1983): 310–45.

O'Bannon, G.W. "Project Afghanistan: Undergraduates in Dynamic Cross-Cultural Experiment; University of Pittsburgh." *International Educational and Cultural Exchange* 8 (1973): 14–20.

O'Connell, Barry. "Where Does Harvard Lead Us?" *Change*, September 1978, 35–40, 61. Rpt. Bonham 1979a: 25–42.

Office of the Chancellor of the Swedish Universities. *Internationalizing Education: Summary of Reports from the Swedish Committee for Internationalizing University Education*. Stockholm: Rosenlundstryckeriet, 1974.

Owen, Wyn F., et al. *Higher Education in Economics: The International Dimensions*. Boulder, Colo.: Economics Institute, 1981.

Oxenham, J. "Internationalizing the Undergraduate Curriculum—An Initiative by the International Association of University Presidents (IAUP)." *International Education Review*. 28.4 (1982): 489.

Paine, Whiton S. *An Evaluation of Undergraduate, Problem-Oriented Interdisciplinary Courses in International Studies: Final Report*. Washington, D.C.: Institute of International Studies, U.S. Office of Education, GPO, 1974.

Palmer, Norman D. "The International Activity of the University of Pennsylvania Faculty." Philadelphia: U of Pennsylvania, 1977. Philadelphia Transnational Project.

———. "The Study of International Relations in the United States: Perspectives of Half a Century." *International Studies Quarterly* 24.3 (1980): 343–63.

Parker, Franklin. "Essay on International and Multicultural Education." *Phi Delta Kappan* 51.5 (1970): 276–81.

———. "Governmental Policy and International Education: A Selected and Partially Annotated Bibliography." In Stewart Fraser, ed., *Governmental Policy and International Education*. New York: Wiley, 1965, 295–373.

Patterson, Franklin. *Colleges in Consort*. San Francisco: Jossey-Bass, 1974.

Perkins, James A. "Report of the President's Commission on Foreign Language and International Studies." *Foreign Language Annals* 12 (1979): 457–64.

———. *International Programs of U.S. Colleges and Universities: Priorities for the Seventies*. Occasional Paper 1. New York: ICED, 1971.

Perry, Wilhelmina, ed. *Sociology of Minority Groups Courses: Syllabi and Related Materials*. Washington, D.C.: ASA TSP, 1981.

Pescosolido, Bernice, and Larry Griffin, ed. *The Welfare State: Origins, Effects, and Prospects*. Washington, D.C.: ASA TSP, 1984.

Peterson, A.D.C. *The International Baccalaureate: An Experiment in International Education*. London: Harrap, 1972.

Pfnister, Allan O. "Everyone Overseas! Goshen College Pioneers: Study-Service Trimester." *International Educational and Cultural Exchange* 8 (1972): 1–12.

———. *General Evaluation of Study Abroad Programs under the Auspices of American Colleges and Universities*. Denver: U of Denver, 1972.

———. *Impact of Study Abroad on the American College Undergraduate*. Denver: U of Denver, 1972.

Phillips, Claude S., Jr. "The Present World Challenge to Higher Education. *The Educational Record* 44 (1963): 266–74.

Phillips, June K., comp. *New Cases for Foreign Language Study*. Middlebury, Vt.: Northeast Conference, 1981.

Phillips, June K., et al. *Action for the '80s: A Political, Professional, and Public Program for Foreign Language Education*. Skokie, Ill.: National Textbook, 1981.

Pike, Lewis W., and Thomas S. Barrows. *Other Nations, Other Peoples: A Survey of Student Interests, Knowledge, Attitudes, and Perceptions*. Washington, D.C.: GPO, 1979.

Ponce, Jorge M. Perez, ed. *Intercultural Education in the Two-Year College: A Handbook on Strategies for Change*. New York: Learning Resources in International Studies, 1976. Wingspread Handbook Series on Strategies for Change in International-Intercultural Education.

Preiswerk, Roy, and Dominique Perrot. *Ethnocentrism and History: Africa, Asia and Indian America in Western Textbooks*. New York: Nok, 1978.

President's Commission on Foreign Language and International Studies. *Strength through Wisdom: A Critique of U.S. Capability*. Washington, D.C.: GPO, 1979.

———. *President's Commission on Foreign Language and International Studies: Background Papers and Studies*. Washington, D.C.: GPO, 1979.

Pusch, Margaret D., ed. *Multicultural Education: A Cross-Cultural Training Approach*. Chicago, Ill.: Intercultural Network, 1981.

Putzer, E. Rev. of *Beyond Growth—The Next Stage in Language and Area Studies*. In *Journal of Asian Studies* 44 (1985): 570–71.

Rall, Dorothy Ross. *Bridges to International Understanding*. The Office of International Students and Scholars and the Community Volunteers for International Programs, Michigan State U, 1985.

Ramsey, Clarice M. "Cultural Understanding for Global Citizenship: An Insurance Model." In Maurice W. Conner, et al. *A Global Approach to Foreign Language Education*. Skokie, Ill.: National Textbook, 1981, 17–22.

Ranwez, A.D., and J. Rodgers. "The Status of Foreign Languages and International Studies: An Assessment in Colorado." *Foreign Language Annals* 17 (1984): 97–102.

Reardon, Betty. *Militarization, Security and Peace Education: A Guide for Concerned Citizens*. New York: United Ministries in Education, 1982.

Reed, Howard A. "Intercultural or Non-Western Studies in General Education." In James G. Rice, ed., *General Education: Current Ideas and Concerns*. Washington, D.C.: AHE, NEA, 1964, 51–60.

―――. "Trends in Non-Western Studies in U.S. Liberal Arts Colleges." *1964: Current Issues in Higher Education* Washington, D.C.: AHE, NEA, 1964. 177–79.

―――. "Universalizing the Disciplines: Intercultural or Non-Western Studies in General Education." *AHE College and University Bulletin* 17 (1964): 5–6.

Reischauer, Edwin O. *Toward the 21st Century: Education for a Changing World*. New York: Knopf, 1973.

Renshaw, J.P. "Foreign-Language and Intercultural Studies in Present-Day College Curricula." *Journal of Higher Education* 43 (1972): 295–302.

Resource Book for International Education at U.S. Jesuit Colleges and Universities. 2nd ed. Washington, D.C.: Association of Jesuit Colleges and Universities, 1986.

Riggs, F.W. "On Reviewing International Studies—Some Comments." *Journal of Higher Education* 52 (1981): 143–54.

Rivers, Wilga M., et al., ed. *Changing Patterns in Foreign Language Programs*. Report of the Illinois Conference on Foreign Languages in Junior and Community Colleges. Rowley, Mass.: Newbury House, 1972.

Rivlin, Harry N. "Research and Development in Multicultural Education." In Frank H. Klassen and Donna M. Gollnick, ed. *Pluralism and the American Teacher: Issues and Case Studies*. Washington, D.C.: AACTE, 1977, 81–113.

Rogers, William C. *Global Dimensions in U.S. Education: The Community*. New York: Center for War-Peace Studies, New York Friends Group, 1972.

Rohrs, H. "Responsibilities and Problems of International Education." *Contemporary Education* 6.2 (1970): 125–35.

Romero, Mary, ed. *Syllabi and Instructional Materials for Chicano Studies in Sociology*. Washington, D.C.: ASA TSP, 1985.

Rosenau, J.N. *International Studies and the Social Sciences: Problems, Priorities and Proposals in the U.S.* Beverly Hills: Sage, 1973.

―――. "International Studies in the University: Some Problems and Issues for the 1970s." Paper prepared for ICED Conference on the Potential of U.S. International Studies in the 1970s, April 1–3, 1971. Mimeo.

Roy, William G., comp. *Comparative Historical Sociology: Teaching Materials and Bibliography*. Washington, D.C.: ASA Teaching Resources Center, 1987.

Rudolph, Frederick. *Curriculum: A History of the American Undergraduate Course of Study since 1636*. San Francisco: Jossey-Bass, 1977.

Ruffner, R.W. "Technical Cooperation in Education through the International Cooperation Administration." *Higher Education* 16 (1960): 7–12.

Sanders, Irwin T., and Jenifer C. Ward. *Bridges to Understanding: International Programs of American Colleges and Universities*. New York: McGraw-Hill, 1970. Carnegie Commission on Higher Education.

Saxon, David S. "A Role for Universities in Ending the Arms Race," *The Chronicle of Higher Education*, July 6, 1981. 48.

Sayres, William C. *The Non-Western World in New York State Higher Education.* Albany: State Education Dept, 1961.

Scanlon, David G., and James J. Shields, ed. *Problems and Prospects in International Education.* New York: Teachers CollP, 1968.

Schnabel, John F., ed. *Modules for "Internationalizing" Introductory Sociology Courses.* Morgantown: West Virginia U, n.d. Mimeo.

Schuh, G. Edward. "The Impact of Foreign Students on U.S. Economic Curricula." *Higher Education in Economics: The International Dimensions.* Boulder, Colo.: Economics Institute, 1981.

Schultz, R.E. "Two Year Colleges Move toward Global Orientation." *Community College Review* 5 (1977): 15–28.

———. "Screening Model for Community-College Program Evaluation." *New Directions for Community Colleges* 25 (1979): 11–29.

Schulz, Renate A. *Options for Undergraduate Foreign Language Programs.* New York: MLA, 1979.

Schwartz, Benjamin I. "Area Studies as a Critical Discipline." *Journal of Asian Studies* (1980): 15–25.

Scully, Malcolm G. "Canadian Studies at U.S. Colleges: Lack of Knowledge, Lack of Concern." *Chronicle of Higher Education,* August 4, 1982, 7–8.

———. "Studying the Third World on American Campuses." *Chronicle of Higher Education,* December 18, 1978, 6.

———. "Taking Language Out of the Classroom." *The Chronicle of Higher Education,* September 22, 1980, 9–10.

Seelye, H. Ned. "Performance Objectives for Teaching Cultural Concepts." *Foreign Language Annals* 3 (1970): 566–78.

———. "Teaching the Foreign Culture: A Context for Research." In Jerald R. Green, ed. *Foreign-Language Education Research: A Book of Readings.* Skokie, Ill.: Rand McNally, 1973, 74–89.

———, and Jacqueline H. Wasilewski. "Historical Development of Multicultural Education." In Margaret D. Pusch, ed. *Multicultural Education: A Cross-Cultural Training Approach.* Chicago, Ill.: Intercultural Network, 1981: 39–61.

Seff, Monica A., ed. *Environmental Sociology: A Collection of Course Syllabi.* Washington, D.C.: ASA TSP, 1985.

Shannon, William G. *A Survey of International-Intercultural Education in Two-Year Colleges—1976.* La Plata, Md.: Charles County Comm Coll, 1978.

Sharp, Paul F. "International Commitments of the American College." *Liberal Education* 50 (1964): 321–27.

Shermis, S. Samuel. "Six Myths which Delude History Teachers." *Phi Delta Kappan* 49 (1967): 9–12.

Shuster, George N. *Report to the Committee on Intercultural Studies in Colleges and Universities.* Washington, D.C.: ACE, 1963.

Simmons, Adele Smith. "Colleges Must Speak Out on War and Peace," *Chronicle of Higher Education,* June 23, 1982. 48.

Simon, Paul. *The Tongue-Tied American: Confronting the Foreign Language Crisis.* New York: Continuum; 1980.

Sims, A.G. "International Education." *Journal of Higher Education* 42.2 (1971): 151–53.

———. "International Education." *Journal of Higher Education* 42.5 (1971): 411–13.

Sinauer, Ernst M. *The Role of Communication in International Training and Education.* New York: Praeger, 1967.

Singer, Milton. "The Social Sciences in Non-Western Studies." In Donald Bigelow and Lyman Legters, ed. *Annals of the American Academy of Political and Social Science* 306 (1964): 30–44. Special issue. *The Non-Western World in Higher Education.*

———, et al. "Chicago's Non-Western Civilizations Program." *Journal of General Education* 12 (1959): 22–23.

Sjogren, C. "Partners in International Education." *College and University* 55.4 (1980): 365–66.

Slessarev, Helga. "Languages and the International Business Connection." *Change,* 1978, 48–49; Report on Teaching 5.

Sloan, Douglas, ed. *Education for Peace and Disarmament: Toward a Living World.* New York: Teachers CollP, 1984.

Smart, R. "Goals and Definitions of International Education—Agenda for Discussion." *International Studies Quarterly* 15.4 (1971): 442–64.

Snell, John L. "Teaching History in the Colleges." *Historian* 23 (1960): 405–17.

Sny, Chris. *Global Education—An Implementation Plan and Resource Guide.* Madison, Wis.: U of Wisconsin, Madison, 1980. ED 200 481.

Spencer, Richard E., and Ruth Awe. *International Educational Exchange—A Bibliography.* Urbana: Institute of International Education, U of Illinois, 1971.

Spitz, Lewis W. "Beyond Western Civilization: Rebuilding the Survey." *The History Teacher,* 10 (1976-77), 519–22.

Starkey, H. "Not Problems but Politics: Some Comments on Approaches to the Development of New Resources for World Studies." *Cambridge Journal of Education* 8.2-3 (1978): 161–64.

Stavrianos, L.S. "The Teaching of World History." *The History Teacher* 3 (1969): 19–24.

———. "What History for the Year 2000?" *The History Teacher* 15 (1981): 7–23.

Stewart, Edward C. *American Cultural Patterns: A Cross-Cultural Perspective.* Chicago, Ill.: Intercultural Press, 1971.

Study Group on the State of the Humanities in Higher Education. *To Reclaim a Legacy: A Report on the Humanities in Higher Education.* Washington D.C.: National Endowment for the Humanities, 1984.

Survey of Foreign Language Course Registrations in U.S. Colleges and Universities—Fall 1980. New York: MLA, 1982.

Sutton, Francis X., F. Champion Ward, and James A. Perkins. *Internationalizing Higher Education: A United States Approach.* New York: ICED, 1974. Occasional Paper 13.

Swift, Richard N. *World Affairs and the College Curriculum.* Washington, D.C.: ACE, 1959.

Taylor, Harold. *The World and the American Teacher: The Preparation of Teachers in the Field of World Affairs.* Washington, D.C.: AACTE, 1968. ED 022 713.

————. *The World as Teacher.* Garden City, N.Y.: Doubleday, 1969.

Tewksbury, Donald G. "American Education and the International Scene." *Teachers College Record* 60 (1959): 357–68.

Thompson, Richard T. "New Directions in Foreign Language Study." *Annals of the American Academy of Political and Social Science,* 449 (1980), 45–55.

Thorne, Barrie, Mary McCormack, Virginia Powell, and Delores Wunder, ed. *The Sociology of Sex and Gender: Syllabi and Teaching Materials.* Washington, D.C.: ASA TSP, 1985.

Tonkin, Humphrey, and Jane Edwards. *The World in the Curriculum: Curricular Strategies for the 21st Century.* New Rochelle, N.Y.: Change, 1981. E&WV 2.

"Toward Education with a Global Perspective." *Report of the National Assembly on Foreign Language and International Studies,* 30 October–1 November 1980, Association of American Colleges, Wingspread Conference Center, Racine, Wis.

The Training of, and U.S. Business' Needs for, International Specialists. Report of a conference sponsored by the U of Massachusetts, Amherst, 1985.

Tucker, J.L. "Developing a Global Dimension in Teacher Education: The Florida International University Experience (Global Awareness Program)." *Theory into Practice* 21 (1982): 212–17.

Tyrell, William G. "Developing International Understanding in the First Two Years of College." In Howard R. Anderson, ed. *Approaches to an Understanding of World Affairs,* 25th Yearbook of the National Council for the Social Studies. Washington, D.C.: NCSS, 1954, 383–95.

Tysse, Agnes N. *International Education: The American Experience—A Bibliography.* Vol. 1. Dissertations and Theses. Metuchen, N.J.: Scarecrow, 1974. Vol. 2. Periodicals, 1977.

U.S. Congress, House Committee on Education and Labor. *International Education: Past, Present, Problems and Prospects. Selected Readings to Supplement H.R. 14643.* Prepared by The Task Force on International Education, John Brademas, Chairman. 89th Congress, 2nd Session, House Document No. 527. Washington, D.C.: GPO, 1966.

Ward, Robert E., and Bryce Wood. "Foreign Area Studies and the Social Science Research Council." *Items* 28.4 (1974). (New York: SSRC). 53–58.

Watson, Paul. "Report of Survey of Post-Secondary Organizational Structures for Internatinal Studies and Programs." *International Studies Notes* 7.1 (1980): 15–16.

Watters, Pat. "The Interdisciplinary Umbrella." *Change,* May–June 1980, 61–62.

Weidner, Edward W. *The World Role of Universities.* New York: McGraw-Hill, 1962.

Weill, Frederick D., and Betty Dobratz, comps. *A Basic Bibliography in Political Sociology.* Washington, D.C.: ASA Teaching Resource Center, 1984.

Whipp, Leslie T. "Simulating World Crises." *Change,* May–June 1980, 56–58.

Whiteford, L. "Literature Education in Ten Countries—International Studies in Evaluation II." *Comparative Education Review,* 1978: 115–17.

Whit, William C., ed. *Syllabi and Instructional Materials for Courses on Sociology of Sport.* Washington, D.C.: ASA Teaching Resource Center, 1985.

Wiley, David, and David Dwyer. *African Language Instruction in the United States: Directions and Priorities.* East Lansing: African Studies Center, Michigan State U, 1980.

Wiley, David S., Robert Cancel, Diane Pflugrad, T.H. Elkiss, and Amie Campbell. *Africa on Film and Videotape 1960–1981: A Compendium of Reviews.* East Lansing, Michigan: African Studies Center, Michigan State U, 1982.

Will, W. Marvin. "American Politics in Comparative Perspective: Thoughts on Teaching the Basic Course to International Students," *Teaching Political Science* 7.4 (1980): 473–80.

Williamson, Marvin, and Cynthia T. Morehouse, ed. *International-Intercultural Education in the Four-Year College: A Handbook on Strategies for Change.* Albany, N.Y.: State Education Dept, 1977.

Wilson, James Q. "Harvard's Core Curriculum: A View From the Inside." *Change,* November 1978, 40–43. Reprinted in Bonham 1979a, 43–50.

Winkler, Fred H. "The Comparative Approach to the Survey of Western Civilization." *The History Teacher* 6 (1971): 71–76.

Wiprud, Helen R. *International Education Programs of the U.S. Government: An Inventory.* Washington, D.C.: GPO, 1980.

Wolf-Wasserman, Miriam, and Linda Hutchinson. *Teaching Human Dignity.* Minneapolis: Education Exploration Center, 1978.

Wright, Richard A., and Linda Meutschmann, ed. *Crime and Control: Syllabi and Instructional Materials for Criminology and Criminal Justice.* Washington, D.C.: ASA TSP, 1984.

Yarrington, Roger, ed. *Internationalizing Community Colleges.* Washington, D.C.: AACJC, 1978.

Young, M.C. "Political Science and Area Studies—Rivals or Partners." *American Political Science Review* 71 (1977): 567–84.

Ziff, Howard. "Sharing at the Five Colleges." *Change,* May–June 1980, 62–64.